UNION JACK

UNION JACK

A SCRAPBOOK

BRITISH FORCES' NEWSPAPERS 1939–1945

London: Her Majesty's Stationery Office

in association with

The Imperial War Museum
Department of Printed Books

Devised and compiled by Complete Editions
Designed by Craig Dodd

© Crown Copyright 1989
First published 1989
ISBN 0 11 772628 1

HMSO publications are available from:

HMSO Publications Centre
(Mail and telephone orders only)
PO Box 276, London, SW8 5DT
Telephone orders 01-873 9090
General enquiries 01-873 0011
(queuing system in operation for both numbers)

HMSO Bookshops
49 High Holborn, London, WC1Q 6HB   01-873 0011 (Counter service only)
258 Broad Street, Birmingham, B1 2HE   021-643 3740
Southey House, 33 Wine Street, Bristol, BS1 2BQ   (0272) 264306
9-21 Princess Street, Manchester, M60 8AS   061-834 7201
80 Chichester Street, Belfast, BT1 4JY   (0232) 238451
71 Lothian Road, Edinburgh, EH3 9AZ   031-228 4181

HMSO's Accredited Agents
(see Yellow Pages)

And through good booksellers

The 'Jane' Cartoons appear by kind permission of
Daily Mirror Newspapers. Artist: Norman Pett

Contents

Foreword

It is a pleasure to be asked to contribute a foreword to this selection of extracts from British service newspapers of the Second World War. When I joined the reference library of the Imperial War Museum back in 1969, I was soon made aware of the consequences of the disastrous fire which had destroyed its reading room on the night of 13/14 October, 1968. Undeniably the most tragic being the loss and damage sustained by the Museum's unique collection of newspapers and periodicals produced by British and Commonwealth forces throughout the world during the two world wars. A list of over a hundred newspapers destroyed featured titles like the *Basrah Times, Cologne Post, Eighth Army News, NZEF Times, Polar Bear News, Rhino, Springbok, Tangerine, Tripoli Times, Tunis Telegraph*, and the *White Falcon*.

Fortunately, it proved possible to rescue some badly burnt and other merely charred newspapers from the blaze. With the expert assistance of the India Office Conservation Department, my Deputy David Nash was able in the years that followed to mount a programme of laminating and binding the rarer titles that had survived. Over twenty years later in our small paper conservation workshop this restoration effort still continues on some journals which we have been unable to replace yet. To understand our difficulties in obtaining replacement copies, it is necessary to recall the circumstances in which the newspapers were produced and the way in which they found their way to the Museum.

The appetite for news in wartime was almost insatiable. This fact had been slowly appreciated by the service authorities during the First World War. During the early static period of the Second World War copies of journals like the *War Illustrated* and *Blighty* could fairly easily be distributed to the armed forces. However, when the fighting intensified and British forces found themselves operating in more remote parts of the world the need for papers to be produced locally became apparent. The Army Printing and Stationery Service established Mobile Printing Sections which undertook the duplication of what were often little more than single page newsheets. The wartime report of the P. and S.S. stresses the difficulties that they experienced in obtaining suitable machinery in places such as North Africa and the Middle East. Major Edward Budd MBE, in his excellent memoir entitled *A printer goes to war* (London: Howard Baker, 1978), recalled the traumas which he experienced in running the Tripoli Times, 'the first British newspaper in North Africa'. Having established a plant employing Italian printers and local

Arabs, he found that the daily production of the *Tripoli Times* soon exhausted his paper supplies. Since General Montgomery and Brigadier Francis de Guingand insisted that the newspaper should appear, Major Budd was obliged to drive a three ton open lorry across the desert to Benghazi and back, over 800 miles, to collect fresh paper stock. The same problem beset the Army printers during the subsequent invasion of Sicily and Italy and it accounts for the poor quality paper that was often utilised for printing purposes. Expedients tried included printing on the backs of maps, captured enemy propaganda sheets, recycling older newspapers and even toilet paper! Fifty years later this inferior paper poses a massive challenge to our conservators if we are to preserve the newspapers for generations to come. It also explains the difficulties encountered in reproducing some of the extracts included in this volume.

During the Second World War the librarian of the Imperial War Museum and his staff were most anxious to collect as many as possible of the newspapers emanating from all branches of the armed services. The Museum's correspondence files testify to their efforts which only occasionally met with a disappointing response. In November 1944, the Chief Education Officer of 21st Army Group doubted the wisdom of attempting to make a complete collection of some newsheets:

The Army Education Corps in this theatre were charged with the duty of seeing that the daily BBC news reached the troops and there are some 50 local periodicals which are repeating the daily broadcast from London to the troops. To collect them I shall have to send you 1,500 sheets a month for every month that the war continues, and should have to make extensive searches.

Happily, many of the editors of particular newsheets made tremendous efforts to ensure that their achievements were not lost to posterity. Captain D. M. Gwyn Jeffreys called at the Museum in person in January 1945 to deliver copies of *The Beachcomber.* His vivid account of the history of the paper is reproduced in its entirety because it typifies the obstacles overcome by so many other producers [Appendix A]. Lieutenant Bateson of Ceylon Command had even more unusual problems to contend with as he pointed out in a letter to the Museum [Appendix B]. Journalists in uniform always experienced the spectacle of their readers advancing well ahead of them, the inevitable response of the news-starved servicemen being to start up their own local newsheet on the battlefield [Appendices C and D]. These sheets might be handwritten and might only last a few days. 'Published daily . . . shells permitting' was an apt slogan for the newspaper press of the armed forces; it was in the words of broadcaster and journalist Colin Wills – 'a Press that is sometimes brilliantly efficient, sometimes scrappy and makeshift, but always alive, and always, in its unheroic way, heroic'.

Service newspapers remain a relatively neglected source for students of history. They are certainly worthy of study on a serious level if only because of the vexed questions of censorship and propaganda raised when journalists are obliged to be 'economical with the truth' in order to sustain morale. The War Office memorandum reproduced [Appendix E] makes absolutely clear the need to safeguard security and not to criticise official government policy. Needless to say, resourceful independently-minded journalists were not easily curbed and the correspondence columns also afforded ample scope for political opinions and grievances to be aired. Nevertheless, the papers did much to boost morale. As Captain Warwick Charlton, the editor of *Eighth Army News*, explained:

In the desert, more than in any other theatre of war, men felt cut off from the outside world. With all too few wireless sets and a camel-like mail service from home, rumour – the dry-rot of an army's fighting morale – was an enemy which had to be beaten. This was the job of *Eighth Army News*. Using the BBC for world news and intelligence sources for local battle news, it set out to kill rumour.

Besides war news they contained much humour, short stories, sport and poetry and this is reflected in the ensuing pages.

Any selection from the wealth of material published in service newspapers during the Second World War is bound to be subjective. I know that the compilers of this volume, Clive Dickinson, Virginia Hoyer-Millar and Craig Dodd, were conscious of the fact. Even the choice of which journals to feature must have been difficult when they were confronted by so many possibles. *The War Illustrated*, *Reveille* and *Blighty*, although not produced by servicemen, were drawn upon for the early 'Phoney war' period, because few service papers appeared due to official government restrictions on the use of paper. *Crusader*, *Parade*, *SEAC* and *Union Jack* were included because they contain excellent illustrations, humour, fine reporting and they also represent different theatres of the war. People stimulated by this current offering are

welcome to visit the reading room of the Imperial War Museum which is open to the public without charge as long as a prior appointment is made. There they will be able to examine other service newspapers of which the seven described below serve only as an introduction. Any help that readers can offer towards our conservation effort or by replacing missing issues would obviously be appreciated.

Blighty
A special edition of this 'budget of humour from home' was issued solely to the 'Navy and fighting forces'. *Blighty* had first appeared during the First World War as a means of saving paper by selecting 'all the best pictures and stories and jokes out of all the best papers' and reprinting them 'in one paper which would contain the cream of them all'. It was 'a paper for the boys only' sent to them 'free every week'. With the outbreak of war in September 1939 a committee of journalists was set up to imitate its Great War predecessor and the first number of the popular illustrated weekly appeared on 21st October, 1939. The magazine concentrated on cartoons, poetry and short stories, some of which were contributed by members of the armed forces and small prizes were often awarded. It also carried a limited amount of advertising. *Blighty* proudly boasted that it was 'not going to instruct you or reform your morals, or do anything but just try to amuse you'. Its title derived from the Hindustani word 'belati' meaning home. The journal survived in more civilian guise well after the war; its last issue being dated 29th November, 1958.

Crusader
This 'Eighth Army Weekly' started on 2nd May, 1942 and was edited by the 'father of desert newspapers', Captain Warwick Charlton. Charlton had also established *Eighth Army News* and *Tripoli Times* all of which traced their family tree back to *Tobruk Truth*, the first of the desert papers produced by two Australian sergeants during the siege of Tobruk and begun in February 1941. General Ritchie approved the foundation of *Crusader* after Charlton had visited Tobruk to compile an official account of the siege. As with so many service newspapers, the principal source of information was the BBC whose broadcasts were monitored round the clock. Material was usually assembled in the desert and then flown to Cairo for printing. Circulation rose to 50,000 and editorial direction passed to Sergeant D. H. Martin (*Evening News, London*). The paper subsequently moved to Tripoli and was later printed at Bari in Italy on the

presses of the former Italian journal *La Gazetta del Mezzogiorno*. Published initially by Advance Headquarters, 8th Army, it was taken over by the British Army Newspaper Unit and issued to British forces in the Mediterranean as a whole. It stopped appearing on 2nd June, 1946.

Parade

This illustrated weekly was published in Cairo beginning on 17th August, 1940. It was the first lavishly pictorial magazine assembled by members of the armed forces themselves rather than for them. *Parade* carried advertising, featuring reports from war correspondents and official war photographs as well as a staple diet of pin-ups and cartoon features. The editor was Lieutenant-Colonel Harold Ruston (formerly Cairo correspondent of the *Morning Post*) and it was printed for the publishers by Al-Hilal on their rotogravure press. Others associated with the enterprise included a New Zealand journalist Bob Gilmore and a later editor Arthur W. Parsons (subsequently New York correspondent of the *Sunday Dispatch*). *Parade* appeared in Arabic, Greek, Polish and Turkish editions and continued until 28th February, 1948 when it became, in the words of its last editor Captain M. Race, 'an economic casualty'.

Reveille

'The services' newspaper' was founded and edited by Reginald Hipwell of 180, Fleet Street, London. It was first issued on 24th May, 1940 in order to raise funds for the Church Army Associations to purchase mobile canteens. Hipwell clearly saw himself as the champion of ordinary servicemen and his columns were devoted to airing their grievances, both real and imagined. Hipwell himself stood as a candidate for Parliament in October 1941 and although defeated then, he later acted as agent for another independent candidate who won Grantham in a by-election in March 1942. Issued fortnightly, *Reveille* eventually became the official organ of the Allied Ex-Service Association.

SEAC

This was the daily newspaper of Lord Louis Mountbatten's South East Asia Command. It was published 'by courtesy of *The Statesman*' in Calcutta at a cost of one anna. The first issue, dated 10th January, 1944 had a print-run of only 7,000. From September 1945, it was printed on the presses of *The Straits Times* in Singapore. *SEAC* was edited by Frank Owen the brilliant editor of the London *Evening Standard* and later of the *Daily Mail*. Other journalists on active

service who contributed included Ian Coster (*Evening Standard*), Len Jackson (*Daily Mirror*), Tom Wilcox (*Daily Express*), H. V. Tillotson (*Lancashire Daily Post*), H. C. Stainforth (*Daily Herald*) and George Chisholm (*Daily Sketch*). Its first editorial asserted that: 'We seek to tell you as much as possible in our very short space . . . SEAC is a newspaper in battledress'. It proved so popular that a *Sunday SEAC* was issued and towards the end of the war, special souvenir issues were compiled. It finally ceased publication on 15th May, 1946.

Union Jack

'The newspaper for the British Fighting Forces' was published by the British Army Newspaper Unit in North Africa, Sicily, Italy, Greece and Austria. It had started in Algiers on 22nd March, 1943, appearing thrice weekly until eventually as the newsprint improved it became a daily. Amongst the experienced journalists who helped to produce it was its editor-in-chief Lieutenant-Colonel Hugh Cudlipp (Editor, *Sunday Pictorial*, later Lord Cudlipp of Aldinbourne), other editors included Captain Cyril James (*Daily Mirror*) and Major Ralph Thackery (*Manchester Guardian*). The well-known sports columnist Peter Wilson provided 'sports talking' with features on services competitions as well as events at home. Cartoon contributions included the famous 'Two types' by Jon, as well as 'Jane' from the *Daily Mirror*. Before our disastrous fire, the Imperial War Museum held 13 complete and 3 partially complete sets of the various editions of *Union Jack*.

The War Illustrated

Launched on 16th September, 1939, this was a sequel to the pictorial weekly of the same title which had been so successful during the First World War. It was edited by Sir John Hammerton who had also edited its Great War forerunner. In his memoir *Books and myself* [London: Macdonald, [1944]], Sir John recalled the difficulties caused by paper shortages: 'On one occasion it was necessary to curtail the circulation of *The War Illustrated* by 120,000 a week (an acceptable circulation in itself) to keep within its paper ration'. It was eventually forced to become a fortnightly magazine but still doubled the circulation of its First World War predecessor.

Dr. G. M. Bayliss
Keeper of the Department of Printed Books
Imperial War Museum

1939

German invasion of Poland begins the Second World War

British Expeditionary Force sent to France

HMS *Royal Oak* sunk in Scapa Flow

British coast mined

USSR invades Finland

Battle of the River Plate and scuttling of the *Graf Spee*

The WAR ILLUSTRATED

Vol. 1   **A Permanent Picture Record of the Second Great War**   **No. 13**

" Be Prepared " is the watchword of the armies on the Western Front, both British and French, and even in the long lull that followed the declaration of war no possible precaution against a sudden onslaught by the German army was neglected. Here in some of the underground fortifications on the sector of the front line occupied by the British troops an officer is going his rounds inspecting the sentries. Both officer and sentry are wearing gas masks—further preparation for the " real thing."

Photo, British Official : Crown Copyright

Our Diary of the War

Wednesday, August 23, 1939

German-Soviet Pact of Non-Aggression signed in Moscow by Von Ribbentrop and Molotoff, in presence of Stalin.

Sir Nevile Henderson, British Ambassador to Germany, delivered to Hitler a message from the British Government and a personal letter from the Prime Minister.

King Leopold of Belgium broadcast an appeal for peace to all nations on behalf of seven small states.

Thursday, August 24

The King arrived in London from Balmoral and held a Privy Council.

Parliament met and passed the Emergency Powers (Defence) Act.

President Roosevelt sent an appeal to King Victor Emmanuel, urging the calling of a peace conference.

The Pope broadcast an appeal for peace.

Von Ribbentrop returned from Moscow and immediately saw Hitler.

British subjects warned to leave Germany.

Herr Forster proclaimed himself Head of the State of Danzig.

Friday, August 25

Sir Nevile Henderson called on Hitler at the latter's request, as also did French, Italian and Japanese envoys.

Hitler cancelled Tannenberg celebrations.

Anglo-Polish Agreement of Mutual Assistance signed in London.

Mussolini was twice in telephonic communication with Hitler.

President Roosevelt sent messages to Hitler and Polish President urging settlement of differences by direct negotiation, arbitration or conciliation at the hands of a disinterested Power.

Germans advised by their Embassy to leave Great Britain.

German merchant ships ordered by their Government to remain in or return to German ports.

Saturday, August 26

Sir Nevile Henderson flew to London with a message from Hitler. The reply was considered at a meeting of the Cabinet at which Sir Nevile was present.

Hitler received the French Ambassador after day of consultation with his advisers.

The Nazi Party "Congress of Peace" at Nuremberg was cancelled.

Germany gave assurances of respect for the frontiers of Belgium, Holland and Switzerland.

Further messages exchanged between Hitler and Mussolini.

Roosevelt made a second appeal to Hitler for the maintenance of peace, enclosing the reply from the Polish President.

Sunday, August 27

The Cabinet met to consider the reply to Hitler's proposals.

Hitler rejected a proposal from M. Daladier that one more attempt should be made at direct negotiation between Germany and Poland. At the conclusion of the letter Hitler made the clear demand that Danzig and the Corridor must return to the Reich.

Rationing introduced in Germany.

Admiralty assumed control of British merchant shipping.

The entire German-Polish frontier was closed to railway traffic.

Stated that France now had about 3,000,000 men under arms.

Monday, August 28

British Government's reply to Hitler was delivered to him by Sir Nevile Henderson.

Defence Regulations, made under the Emergency Powers (Defence) Act, were issued by the Stationery Office.

The Mediterranean was closed to British ships on orders from the Admiralty.

Government of Holland ordered the mobilization of the Army and Navy.

Fall of Japanese Cabinet.

Tuesday, August 29

Hitler handed to Sir Nevile Henderson his reply to the British note, making at the same time verbal explanations. The reply was immediately transmitted in code to London. It was stated in Berlin that the British proposal of direct negotiation between Germany and Poland had been accepted provided that a Polish plenipotentiary arrived in Berlin within 24 hours.

At a brief sitting of both Houses of Parliament, statements on the crisis were made by Lord Halifax and the Prime Minister.

Germany occupied Slovakia as a "protection" from the Poles. Poland issued a protest.

The diplomatic representatives of Great Britain, France and Poland accepted an offer of mediation made jointly by Queen Wilhelmina and King Leopold.

Wednesday, August 30

The Poles declined to send a plenipotentiary under menace.

The Cabinet considered Hitler's last communication and sent a reply to Berlin, which was handed to Von Ribbentrop shortly after midnight by Sir Nevile Henderson.

Hitler issued a decree setting up a Council of Ministers for the Defence of the State. Field-Marshal Goering was appointed chairman and invested with very wide powers.

Thursday, August 31

The Soviet-German Pact was ratified by the Supreme Council in Moscow.

The German Government broadcast a 16-point plan for a settlement with Poland. In spite of the fact that this was the first time that the Polish Government heard of them, it was stated that the German Government had waited in vain two days for the arrival of a Polish negotiator, and therefore considered that the proposals had been rejected.

British Fleet mobilized.

French railways under military control.

The Pope made a new peace appeal, notes being handed to all envoys of foreign countries attached to the Holy See.

Friday, September 1, 1939

Poland was invaded by German forces from East Prussia, Slovakia and the main body of the Reich in the early morning. No declaration of war had been made.

Britain and France delivered final warnings to Hitler to withdraw from Poland.

General mobilization proclaimed in Britain and France.

Statements on the German invasion of Poland were made in both Houses of Parliament. In the Commons war credits totalling £500,000,000 were voted. A number of emergency measures were passed through all their stages.

President Roosevelt appealed to Great Britain, France, Italy, Poland and Germany to refrain from bombing civilians and unfortified towns, and received assurances from Britain, France and Poland. Italy replied that she was not concerned, as she was remaining neutral.

Hitler, addressing the Reichstag, gave his reasons for the invasion of Poland, and subsequently a Bill entitled " The Law for the Reunion of Danzig with the German Reich " was passed with acclamation.

The evacuation of British school children from exposed and congested areas was begun, and nearly 500,000 were moved.

The Government took over control of the railways.

Saturday, September 2

Mr. Chamberlain announced in the House of Commons that Germany's delay in replying to the British warning might be due to consideration of a proposal, put forward by Mussolini, for a Five-Power Conference.

The British and French Governments consulted on the question of a time limit for Hitler's reply.

Bill for compulsory military service between the ages of 18 and 41 passed.

Fighting in Poland increased in intensity. Warsaw was bombed six times.

Hitler sent a favourable answer to Roosevelt's appeal against bombing open towns.

British Government received pledges of support from Canada, Australia and New Zealand and from 46 Indian rulers.

Berlin officially denied that either gas or incendiary bombs had been used during raids on Polish towns.

Sunday, September 3

A final British note was presented in Berlin at 9 a.m. giving Hitler until 11 a.m. to give an undertaking to withdraw his troops from Poland.

At 11.15 Mr. Chamberlain, in a broadcast to the nation, stated that " no such undertaking had been received and that consequently this country is at war with Germany."

The French ultimatum, presented at 12.30 p.m., expired at 5 p.m.

The German reply rejected the stipulations that German troops should withdraw from Poland, and accused the British Government of forcing the war on Germany.

Fierce fighting on both Polish fronts.

A War Cabinet of nine members was created, to include Mr. Churchill as First Lord of the Admiralty.

The King broadcast a message to his peoples.

Hitler left Berlin to assume command on the Eastern front.

German submarine torpedoed and sank without warning the British liner *Athenia*, 200 miles north-west of Ireland.

Roosevelt announced that U.S.A. would remain neutral.

Mr. de Valera announced that Eire would remain neutral.

Australia and New Zealand declared war on Germany.

Pronunciation of Polish Names

The correct pronunciation of Polish names is a matter of difficulty and frequent difference of opinion. Here from time to time we shall give the best approximate equivalents in English sounds of names of persons and places of immediate interest. Note that the stress is always on the last syllable but one.

Moscicki	..	.. *mosh-tsee-ski*	Katowice	..	.. *ka-to-vee-che*
Smigly-Rydz	..	.. *shmig-li ridz*	Westerplatte	..	.. *ves-ter-pla-te*
Skladkowski	..	.. *skwad-kof-ski*	Grudziadz	..	.. *groo-jonts*
Kasprzycki	..	.. *kasp-zheet-ski*	Cracow	..	.. *kra-kof*
Jaroslaw	..	.. *ya-ros-waf*	Czestochowa	..	.. *chan-sto-ho-va*
Dzialdowo	..	.. *jal-do-vo*	Chojnice	..	.. *hoy-neet-se*

These Men Sought War

Paul Joseph Goebbels, Reich Minister of Propaganda and supreme master of German press and radio. He practises his master's doctrine, " The bigger the lie the greater its value."

Joachim von Ribbentrop, Germany's Foreign Minister, was for a time the Reich's Ambassador at the Court of St. James's.

Adolf Hitler, born an Austrian, became the apostle of Pan-Germanism. Chancellor of the Reich since 1933 he has established his power on the doctrine of the Mailed Fist. (Below) Party leader Rudolph Hess has from the early days of the Nazi movement been Hitler's most trusted adherent.

Field - Marshal Hermann Goering was recently nominated by Hitler to be his successor as Fuehrer of the German Reich.

Heinrich Himmler is the dreaded head of Hitler's secret police, the Gestapo. His system of espionage reaches into every house in Germany.

Poland Has Died Before ---To Rise Again

Flushed with victory, the Nazi warlords and their Soviet abettors in the rape of Poland have partitioned their prey, just as did the imperialist robbers of a century and a half ago.   But the pages of history give us reason to believe that the crime of 1939 will be no more successful than that of 1795.

Top left, Poland as it was before the Great War—partly German, partly Russian, and partly Austrian.   Lower left, Poland as it was after the Treaty of Versailles, with the boundaries marked by the "Curzon Line" of 1920.   Right, the new partition arranged this year by Hitler and Stalin, as announced in a joint communiqué issued on September 22, by Germany and Russia.

EASY FRENCH PHRASES FOR BRITISH SOLDIERS—6.

In this, the final section of Easy French Phrases, the Military Terms are concluded; there is a short section of Medical Terms which we hope you will have no occasion to use, and a few examples of colloquialisms and slang which you are likely to meet with.

HERE is a further selection of Military Terms, to complete those given in the previous number of THE WAR ILLUSTRATED.   It is followed by a few common Medical Terms.

MILITARY TERMS

Rifle	Le fusil (**Ler fee-zee**)
Barrel	Le canon (**Ler kanon**)
Breech	La culasse (**Lah keelass**)
Bolt	Le cylindre (**Ler see-lendr**)
Trigger	La détente ; la gachette **Lah day-tant ; gahshet**
Back sight ...	La hausse (**La ŏhs**)
Fore sight ...	Le guidon (**Ler gee-don**)
Butt	La crosse (**Lah kross**)
Sling	La bretelle (**Lah bretel**)
Bullet	La balle (**Lah bal**)
Cartridge ...	La cartouche (**Lah kar-toosh**)
Bayonet ...	La baïonnette (**Bai-ŏh-net**)
Scabbard ...	Le fourreau (**Ler foorŏh**)
Machine gun ...	La mitrailleuse **La mee-trai-yerz**
Belt	La bande (**Lah band**)
Chamber ...	La chambre (**Lah shanbr**)
Extractor ...	L'extracteur **Leks-trakt-urr**
Tripod ...	L'affût trépied **Laff-ee tray-pyay**
Trench	La tranchée (**Tran-shay**)
Communication trench ...	Le boyau (**Ler bwah-yŏh**)

FOR KEY TO PRONUNCIATION
See page iii of cover in the
issue of December 18th, 1939

SLANG AND COLLOQUIALISMS

SLANG is a dangerous medium of expression for anyone who is not well versed in a language.   Nevertheless, a knowledge of slang is useful.   Some common words and phrases are given below.

Recruit ("rookie")	Un bleu. Un Marle-Louise **Un bler Un mahree loo-eez**
Infantryman ("Footslogger")	Un biffin ; (**Un biffen**) Un pousse-cailloux **Un poos-kai-yoo**
Bully beef	Le singe (**Ler senzh**) (literally "Monkey")
Cigarette ("fag")	Une cibiche. Une sèche **Een see-beesh, Een saysh**
"Fag end" ...	...Un mégot (**Un may-gŏh**)
Heavy shell ...	Une marmite. Un macavoué **Een mahr-meet. Un mak-ah-voo-ay**
Boot	Un godillot. Une godasse **Un god-ee-yŏh. Een god-ass**
Money ("dough"; "tin")	La galette. Le fric. Le pognon. Le pèze. **Lah galet. Ler freek. ..pon-yon. ..payz.**
Casualty Clearing Station	Hôpital d'evacuation **Oh-pee-tahl day-vak-ee-ass-yon**

Penny	Un rond (**Un ron**)
To be hard up ...	N'avoir pas le rond **Nav-wahr pah ler ron**
Franc	Une balle (**Een bal**) (Not used under 10 francs.)
It's worth 20 francs	Ca vaut vingt balles **Sah vŏh ven bal**
Five-franc piece ...	Une thune (**Een teen**)
Adjutant	L'adjupète. Le juteux **Ladzh-ee-payt. Ler zhee-ter**
Colonel	Le colon (**Ler kolon**) ("Vieux colon" means "old chap; old bean")
High officers ("big wigs")	Les grosses légumes **Lay grŏhs lay-geem**
Captain	Le piston (**Ler pees-ton**)
Civilian	Un pékin (**Un pay-ken**)
In mufti	En pékin (**An pay-ken**)
Leave ; furlough ...	La perme (**Lah payrm**)
Stew	Le rata (**Ler rahtah**)
Army cook	Le cuistaud, (cuisteau, cuistot) **Ler kwees-tŏh**
To grumble ; grouse	Rouspeter (**Roos-pet-ay**)
The doctor (the M.O.)	Le toubib (**Too-beeb**)
To eat ; to feed	Bouffer (**Boo-fay**)
Food ("grub") ...	La boustifaille ; la becquetance; le frichti **Lah boo-stee-fai ; iah bek-tans ; ler freesh-tee**
Cook-house	La popote (**Lah pop-ot**)
Bed ("kip"; "downy")	Le plumard; le pieu **Ler plee-mar; ler pyer**
To go to bed ...	Se pieuter (**Ser pyer-tay**)

Britain Won't Go Hungry in this War

On land bordering a L.P.T.B. railway track an employee tends a giant cabbage.

THERE was an immediate response to the Government's appeal to farmers and gardeners to produce more food. The Women's Land Army got to work without delay in the first days of the war. Children evacuated to the country did any job on the farms for which they were suitable, from garnering potatoes in one place to helping to exterminate a plague of caterpillars in another. All the delays connected with food supplies in the early days were caused by transport difficulties and not by any food shortage; and though ration cards were announced these were only to ensure equality of distribution and the prevention of waste.

These recruits for the Women's Land Army are undergoing training in farm work at an agricultural college in Sussex.

The Government's resolve to prepare for a three years' war has necessitated modifications in food distribution as well as intensive efforts to increase production. Centre, left, is one of the temporary centres of fish supply in a country town just outside London. In the photograph below evacuated children are helping with the gathering of the potato crop. Their gas masks are handy.

1939

|||||||||||||||||||||||||||||||||||||||||||||||||||||||||||| I WAS THERE! ||||||||||||||||||||||||||||||||||||||||||||||||||||||||||||||||||

'Tommy' Lands in France Again

On September 11 it was announced that a British Expeditionary Force had been conveyed across the Channel without the loss of a single man. Here is the story of the landing of the British troops in France, as reported in the " Daily Express " by Geoffrey Cox.

IN a Channel port I have been watching columns of steel-helmeted British troops landing quietly and smoothly as if on manoeuvres, and tramping over the cobbles from the ships to their billets.

At street corners and house doors French people crowded to watch them, sometimes clapping, sometimes breaking into " Vive les Anglais."

But the landing of these Young Contemptibles was no affair of flags or flower throwing. This is ruled out by the need for secrecy in these days of air raids.

The attitude of the men seems to be : " We're here to do a job we think worth doing and we don't want any unnecessary fuss."

The French, too, share this feeling of not wishing for heroics, but the people of this port were moved by the sight of the khaki columns landing on their soil once more.

One old Frenchman who had been standing silent suddenly rushed forward to seize the hand of a great, gaunt Highlander heading a platoon.

He shook it, tears streaming from his eyes. The Highlander grinned, then carried on marching.

Out in the grey Channel I saw the dark shapes of the British and French destroyers which had escorted the latest ships to the port.

Above floated an observation balloon, scanning the port approaches for submarines. From the coastal forts great guns pointed out to sea, covering the approaches from England. Not a man was lost on this crossing.

Through the gate of their temporary barracks swung a detachment of sappers, shovels on shoulder.

Other troops, waiting for trains and lorries, crammed the bakers', the wine-shops and tobacconists'. Veterans of the last war acted as interpreters, but little interpretation was needed.

These men were taken right into French life. I saw infantrymen sitting on doorsteps like the members of any French family, with babies sitting on their knees, while hordes of little boys examined their buttons, caps and uniforms.

These men displayed the same attitude as the French towards this war—a quiet determination to see crushed once and for all this thing which has disturbed our natural life. One man told me : " A fortnight ago I was working on a building job in a remote part of Devon. I would never have believed I should find myself in France now." Two of them wore stripes from the last war.

While we were talking a whistle blew, the motor-cyclists hopped on their cycles, slung their rifles over their backs, and off went these troops, moving through villages and small towns and getting the warmest French welcome.

The troops wave back and move steadily on under the poplar trees lining the roads.

In the narrow streets of the old port town, the British troops were already completely at home. Infantrymen wearing the new battle-dress, white-belted military police, red hat-banded staff officers carrying canes, sergeants wearing the old style flat forage caps, strolled along and looked at the shop windows. Army nurses, with red-white-and-blue hatbands and with steel helmets slung over their arms, sat in their grey uniforms in the corner of a restaurant eating lunch.

The French are greatly struck by the easy air of confidence of these men, and the excellence of their bearing and equipment. An American military expert who was with me was most impressed with the calibre of this army, which he considers is probably the best fitted out in the world.

All the people of this port who remember 1914 said there was a great difference in attitude. A woman keeping a café on the port side said to me : " Then they came laughing and keen for adventure. Now they come determined to tackle the difficult job that is ahead, knowing that it is worth tackling. You tell the Old Contemptibles I've seen their sons today and they're worthy of them."

I Bombed a U-Boat from the Air

The sinking of a German submarine by a young South African pilot, laconically announced by the Ministry of Information, has stirred the imagination of the British people. Below is his own modest account of the achievement reprinted by permission from " The Daily Telegraph."

I SIGHTED the submarine on the surface and two miles away.

It was travelling pretty fast—at about 12 knots—in an easterly direction.

I took cover in a cloud to approach the submarine from astern. As I came out of the cloud, flying at 1,500 feet, I tried with my binoculars to identify the submarine. Flying closer I saw those characteristics which made me sure she was a German.

To make absolutely certain I fired some rounds of ammunition near her to give her a chance to identify herself.

She did not, so I proceeded to dive, at the same time firing my front gun at someone wearing a white hat who was standing on the conning tower.

At 500 feet the man on the conning tower disappeared and the submarine started to dive. By the time I dropped my first salvo of bombs, the nearest of which hit the water 15 or 20 yards directly ahead, the submarine was half under water.

The explosion of the bombs blew her back to the surface. That gave me time to turn round, and I then carried out an attack from the port beam.

The nearest bomb of my second salvo landed 6 feet to the side of the conning tower. It was a direct hit on the submarine's port side and there was a colossal explosion and her whole stern lifted out of the water. She dived into the sea at an angle of 30 deg.

For 20 minutes afterwards I remained over the spot watching the large whirlpools caused by escaping air coming to the surface of the water. By that time I assumed the submarine to be out of action on the bottom of the sea and returned to my base.

The U-boat seen in this photograph is just submerging in Kiel Harbour. It is approximately in the same position as was the submarine whose sinking is described by a South African airman in this page when he dropped his first salvo of bombs.

To Arms! Poland's Fair Lands are Invaded

Pho to, Keystone

IN the higher of the two towers of the old Gothic church of St. Mary in Krakow, rising 250 feet above the medieval houses, stands a sentry-box from which is sounded every hour a bugle call—a call which is suddenly interrupted. This "broken note" keeps ever fresh and green the memory of the brave Polish bugler who, in 1241, warned the inhabitants of the city of the impending approach of the Tartar hordes, and as he warned them, ere his call could be completed, fell dead with his throat pierced through by an arrow from a Tartar bow. But Krakow had heard the warning, and the invaders were repulsed with heavy loss.

In the seven hundred years which have passed since then, the bugle many a time has sounded the call to meet Poland's foes. Enemy after enemy has marched across the country's fair face, has ravaged and destroyed—and has at last been defeated and driven out.

Today the call sounds again. A new foe has swept across the frontier —this time from the west. Against tremendous odds the Polish army has fallen back, and Krakow hears once more the tread of enemy feet through her streets. But the indomitable spirit of the army, of the people, remains unsubdued.

In the past the Poles have survived invasion after invasion, internal intrigue and foreign war, partition by brute force and revolt savagely suppressed. Out of their present trials they will emerge—not alas! unscathed—but crowned with the laurels of victory.

Poland is not yet lost
While we are still living
That which foreign violence from us
*   grasped*
We shall re-take by the sword.

From the Polish
National Anthem

Warsaw Bombed & Burned to a Smoking Shambles

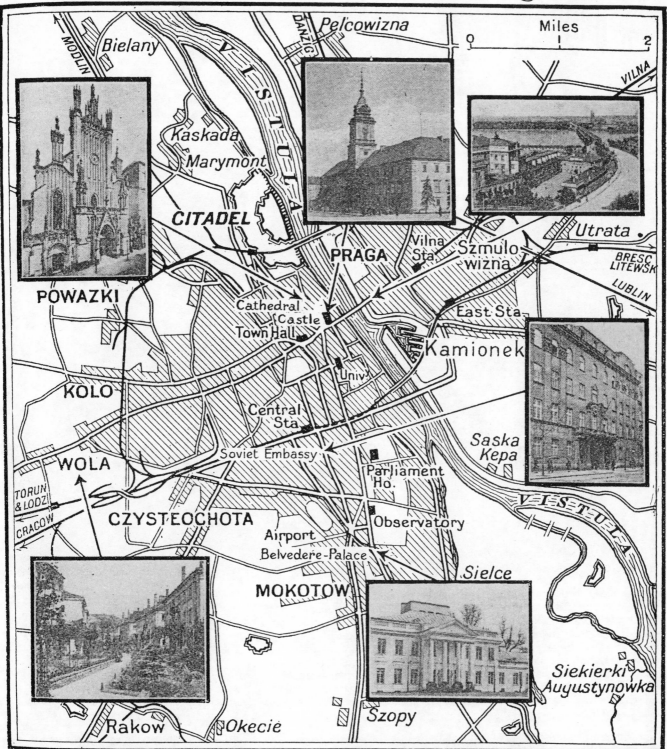

In the picture map above the principal districts and some of the finest buildings in Warsaw are shown. On the Cathedral of St. John a bomb was dropped during Mass and the roof fell on the congregation. The Zamek Palace, the home of the President, is believed to have been destroyed. In the suburb of Praga heavy fighting took place. The photograph shows the Kierbedz Bridge connecting Praga with Warsaw. The Soviet Embassy was not exempt. The Belvedere Palace, once the home of Marshal Pilsudski, was destroyed. In the suburb of Wola the Poles put up a strenuous resistance.

The German forces ringed the once proud and beautiful city, now reduced to a smoking shambles, and from time to time made desperate raids into the suburbs with their tanks and armoured cars, only to be held up by the trenches and barricades which the citizens had prepared a fortnight before. Not until September 27 could the Nazi wireless announce, so as to be believed by the world, that the collapse of long-sustained Warsaw's resistance was at hand.

While the German troops were advancing to, or retiring on, the demarcation line agreed upon with the Soviet, the Red Army was continuing its march into Poland began German and Soviet troops formally met at Brest-Litovsk—a name of ill omen in the early history of the Soviet State, for there it was that Russia signed the humiliating treaty of 1918—and the Germans formally handed over the town and fortress to the Red army. The exchange of courtesies was watched

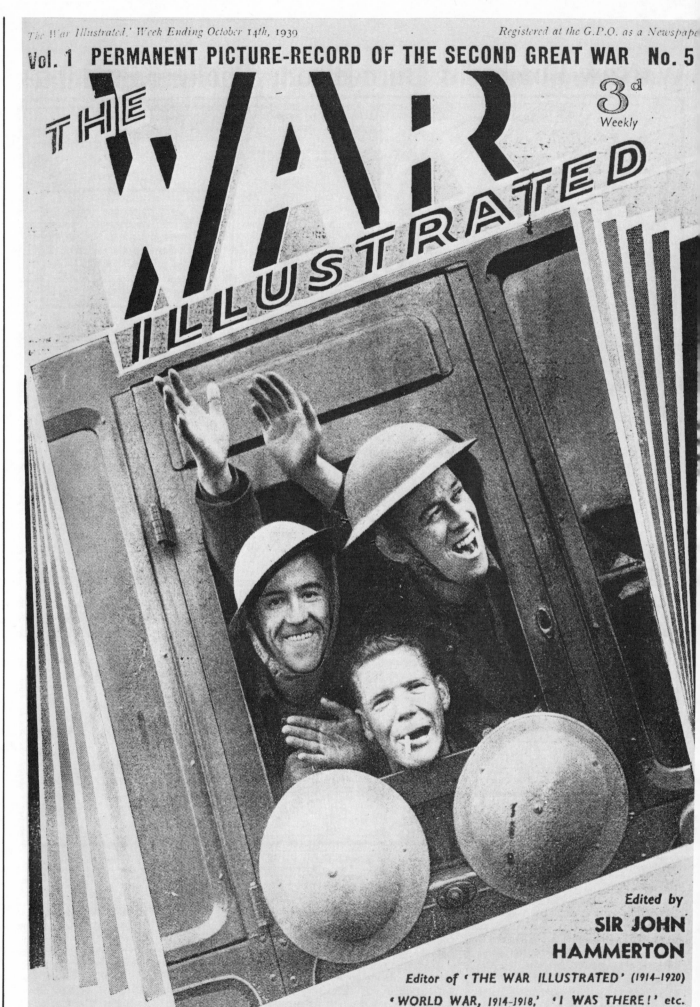

'The War Illustrated,' Week Ending October 14th, 1939

Registered at the G.P.O. as a Newspaper

Vol. 1 **PERMANENT PICTURE-RECORD OF THE SECOND GREAT WAR** No. 5

THE WAR ILLUSTRATED

3ᵈ Weekly

Edited by
SIR JOHN HAMMERTON

Editor of 'THE WAR ILLUSTRATED' (1914–1920)
'WORLD WAR, 1914–1918,' 'I WAS THERE!' etc.

Poland Fought On, 'Bloody But Unbowed'

Although the Nazi joy-bells were ringing over the end of the war with Poland, the army and people of the land so ruthlessly and treacherously invaded still here and there, and particularly in Warsaw the capital, put up an heroic resistance which evoked the admiration of the whole civilized world. But the inevitable day of surrender came.

THREE weeks after the armies of the Reich crossed the Polish frontier in their war of invasion, the German High Command was able to claim that the Polish campaign was over. "In a series of battles of extermination," read the German communiqué, "of which the greatest and most decisive was in the Vistula curve, the Polish army numbering a million men has been defeated, taken prisoner, or scattered. Not a single Polish active or reserve division, not a single independent brigade, has escaped this fate. Only fractions of single bands escaped immediate annihilation by fleeing into the marshy territory in East Poland. There they were defeated by Soviet troops." Only in Warsaw, Modlin, and on the peninsula of Hela in the extreme north of Poland near Gdynia were there still small sections of the Polish army fighting on; and these, claimed the communiqué, "are in hopeless positions."

Warsaw's Heroic Defence

While the Polish authorities in Warsaw claimed that resistance was still proceeding in some parts of the country additional to those mentioned in the German communiqué, it was obvious that the Polish front had completely disintegrated. The war, from being one of movement on a vast scale, had now degenerated into one of guerilla actions. It was at Warsaw, the capital, that the Polish resistance was finally crystallized. Scornfully refusing all demands for surrender, the Polish garrison and populace combined in presenting a firm front to the beleaguerers. Day after day the Germans bombed and shelled the city. On September 26 it was reported that the entire business centre of the city was in flames following almost continuous shelling and dive-bombing by the Nazi 'planes. On the previous Sunday, according to a communiqué issued by the Warsaw command, over a thousand civilians were reported killed, and four churches and three hospitals filled with wounded were destroyed. The communiqué went on to say that there were no longer any buildings in Warsaw remaining intact, and not a house in which there had not been a victim of the Nazi bombs or shells. Furthermore, within the previous twenty-four hours about a hundred fires had broken out following the launching upon the city of a hail of incendiary bombs. Yet, bombed and shelled without intermission, the garrison and populace kept a good heart. "The morale of the army and populace is excellent," said one communiqué.

The horror of the Nazi onslaught on the civilian population of Poland is brought home with poignant reality in these photographs. In one we see a Polish woman praying among the ruins of her home for her husband and children killed in an air raid; in the other the primitive fire brigade of a small Polish village is trying vainly to cope with the flames that incendiary bombs have started.

"One for Two"

7.30 a.m. Fell out of bed—dreamed somebody had believed some propaganda of mine.

7.45. Recovered from fit of shivering occasioned by shock. Opened secret recess in mattress, pulled out box hidden therein and counted money hoarded away. All correct, Heil Hitler! Yesterday, a mouse found my hiding-place somehow and nibbled through a couple of 50,000-mark notes.

8.20. Washed hands and ears. Gave mouth daily exercise. Find can now open mouth to extent of eight inches. Half-inch improvement. Hope to attain a foot stretch soon.

8.50. Massaged tongue, which is suffering badly from overwork. "Blitzkrieg" difficult on the mouth muscles.

9.10. Played recording of my latest speech. Too like me to be pleasant. Sound like a mezzo-soprano. Must tell recording-engineer to fake bass voice for me—make me sound like a man, not female opera-singer.

9.40. Put on my Gestapo (pronounced guess-staff-oh!) uniform, also boots with special six-inch high heels. Dressed in these ingenious boots give the appearance that I stand at least 5 feet 1 inch in my socks. Excellent.

10.00 Breakfast. Usual synthetic quaker-oats and eggs manufactured from wood compound. Never touch bacon. Can't get it, anyway. Also reminds me too much of Goering. Read English papers while eating. Disgusting! They tell the truth so shamelessly.

10.40. Adjourned to study. Checked over day's propaganda speech. Brilliant. My writer knows his job. Usual material contained in speech: "Churchill prepares to invade America"; "England attempting to surround Asia, China and the North Pole"; "British U-boats bombard Maginot Line," etc. Well up to my usual standard.

11.50. Had doctor in to give me daily treatment. Professor von Levy is my medico. He was a Jew until I found he was such a wonderful doctor. Had his pure Aryan descent traced by my own experts, then tagged "von" on to his name as proof of my discovery. Gave treatment and said I'm a pretty specimen all right.

12.40. Wrote letters to lady friends and had them delivered by hand, secretly. Because all these ladies happen to be married and people with nasty minds gossip.

1.50. Reviewed speech again. Added "Churchill plans to blow up Buckingham Palace." Puts finishing touch to speech.

ODD FACTS ABOUT THE WAR

U-Boat Commander Apologized

When a German submarine stopped the French steamer "Vermont" by shell fire, the commander, having seen the crew safely transferred to their boats, explained: "It is not my fault I have to do this, but war is war. I am sorry."

Bulgarian Beechnuts for Germany

Germany will take unlimited quantities of beechnuts, which are rich in vegetable oil. So Bulgarian schoolchildren were given a week's holiday to gather them for export.

Any Repayment?

M. Tanner, member of the Finnish delegation to Moscow, saved Stalin's life in 1905 when the latter was a young revolutionary refugee, by protecting him from the Russian secret police.

Army Pigeons

The Belgian army has at its disposal a large contingent of carrier pigeons. During the Great War the birds rendered invaluable service, and it is possible that militarized pigeons may be needed again in emergency.

The Tragedy of the 'Royal Oak'

Mr. Winston Churchill stated in the House of Commons, October 17 :

"THE battleship 'Royal Oak' was sunk at anchor by a U-boat in Scapa Flow approximately at 1.30 a.m. on Oct. 14. . . .

"When we consider that during the whole course of the last war this anchorage was found to be immune from such attacks, on account of the obstacles imposed by the currents and the net barrages, this entry by a U-boat must be considered as a remarkable exploit of professional skill and daring.

"It appears probable that the U-boat fired a salvo of torpedoes at the 'Royal Oak,' of which only one hit the bow. This muffled explosion was at the time attributed to internal causes, and what is called the inflammable store, where the kerosene and other such materials are kept, was flooded. Twenty minutes later the U-boat fired three or four torpedoes, and these, striking in quick succession, caused the ship to capsize and sink. She was lying at the extreme end of the harbour, and therefore many officers and men were drowned before rescue could be organized from other vessels.

"The lists of survivors have already been made public, and I deeply regret to inform the House that upwards of eight hundred officers and men have lost their lives."

"The Admiralty immediately announced the loss of this fine ship. Serious as this loss is, it does not affect the margin of security in heavy vessels, which remains ample."

Pathetic scenes were witnessed when the lists of survivors of the " Royal Oak " were scanned by relations hoping to find their men.

Here is the boiler-room of the "Royal Oak." In such a catastrophe the engineers and stokers are in the most dangerous position in the ship.

Four of the officers who were rescued from the " Royal Oak " are seen above. They are, left to right, Captain W. F. Benn, R.N., Commander R. F. Nichols, R.N., Lieut. Anthony H. Terry, R.N., and Lieut. Bernard B. Keen, Royal Marines.
Photos, Topical, Wide World and Fox

H.M.S. " Royal Oak " was a battleship of 29,150 tons laid down in 1914. She was in action in the Battle of Jutland, but in 1934 was withdrawn from the First Battle Squadron and reconditioned at a cost of £1,000,000. She was recommissioned in 1936. She carried eight 15-in. guns, and twelve 6-in. guns as her main armament.

Scapa Flow, the land-locked Orkneys harbour, was the Grand Fleet base in 1914-18.

How to Recognize German Raiders

Silhouettes of Nazi Offensive Machines

Here, in these pages, we have illustrations of the principal types of German bombing 'planes—and a couple of fighter models. With one exception they are all relative in size. Many of these warplanes have already appeared above the coasts of Britain, and more still may be recognized if further opportunities for the identification of enemy craft are afforded as the war proceeds.

Drawings in this and the opposite page taken by permission from "Flight"

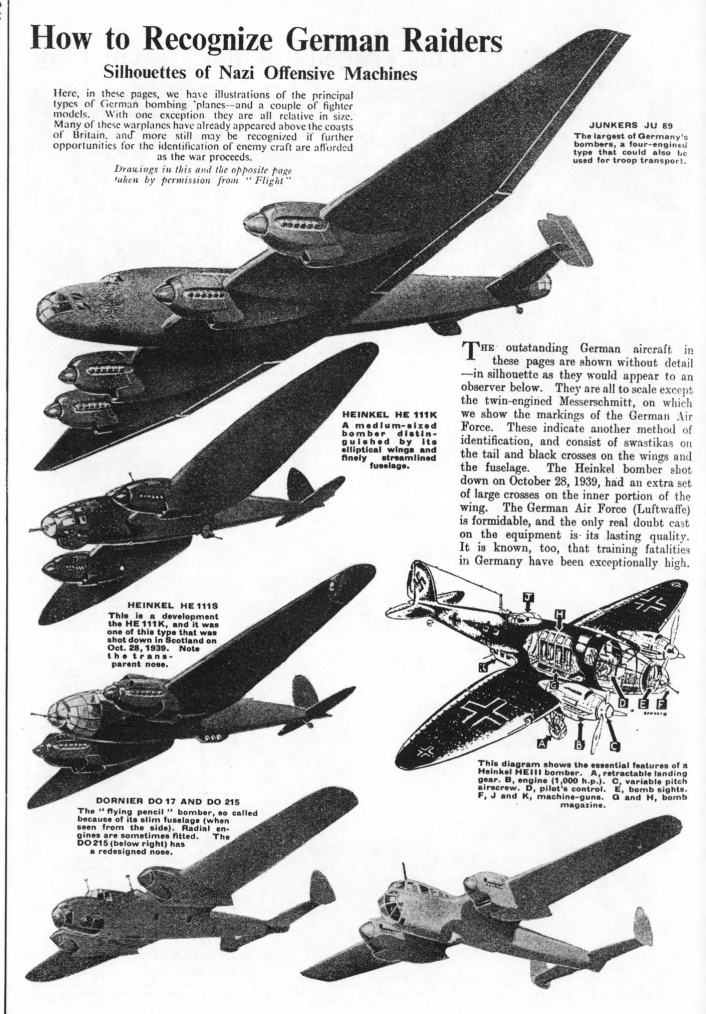

JUNKERS JU 89
The largest of Germany's bombers, a four-engined type that could also be used for troop transport.

HEINKEL HE 111K
A medium-sized bomber distinguished by its elliptical wings and finely streamlined fuselage.

HEINKEL HE 111S
This is a development the HE 111K, and it was one of this type that was shot down in Scotland on Oct. 28, 1939. Note the transparent nose.

DORNIER DO 17 AND DO 215
The "flying pencil" bomber, so called because of its slim fuselage (when seen from the side). Radial engines are sometimes fitted. The DO 215 (below right) has a redesigned nose.

THE outstanding German aircraft in these pages are shown without detail—in silhouette as they would appear to an observer below. They are all to scale except the twin-engined Messerschmitt, on which we show the markings of the German Air Force. These indicate another method of identification, and consist of swastikas on the tail and black crosses on the wings and the fuselage. The Heinkel bomber shot down on October 28, 1939, had an extra set of large crosses on the inner portion of the wing. The German Air Force (Luftwaffe) is formidable, and the only real doubt cast on the equipment is its lasting quality. It is known, too, that training fatalities in Germany have been exceptionally high.

This diagram shows the essential features of a Heinkel HE111 bomber. A, retractable landing gear. B, engine (1,000 h.p.). C, variable pitch airscrew. D, pilot's control. E, bomb sights. F, J and K, machine-guns. G and H, bomb magazine.

JUNKERS JU 88
A new bomber seen over the Forth on Oct. 16, 1939. The two engine nacelles are of unusual design.

JUNKERS JU 87
A single-engined dive-bomber much employed in the Polish campaign. It has a distinctive " cranked " wing.

JUNKERS JU 86K
Bomber version of a well-known transport aircraft. May be fitted with diesel engines (as shown) or radials.

MESSERSCHMITT ME 109
Germany's most famed fighter. A special version holds the world's speed record. The Heinkel HE 112 (not shown) is another outstanding type in this class.

HEINKEL HE 115
A twin-float seaplane for torpedo-dropping, bombing, or reconnaissance. Employed in attack on convoy, Oct. 21, 1939.

DORNIER DO 18K AND DO 24
Tandem diesel engines (one may be seen) and sponsons (" seawings ") characterize the DO 18K reconnaissance flying boat (above) already used over the North Sea. The larger DO 24 flying boat (below) has three radial engines (as shown) or liquid-cooled units.

MESSERSCHMITT ME 110
(Above) A new heavily armed fighter-bomber that could be used for escort duty. Note— This drawing is not to scale, but is included to show typical markings.

OUR DIARY OF THE WAR

Friday, November 24, 1939

Over 200 drifting mines washed up on Yorkshire coast.

Enemy aircraft made two raids over **Shetlands.** No bombs were dropped.

Admiralty announced that the cruiser " Belfast " was damaged on November 21 by torpedo or mine in Firth of Forth.

British steamer " Mangalore " sunk by mine off East Coast.

Five survivors of Dutch tanker " Sliedrecht," sunk by U-boat in Atlantic, picked up after 7½ days in open boat.

Paris announced that a small French submarine chaser had sunk a U-boat.

Belgian Government addressed a Note to Britain on subject of British reprisals against mine-laying.

Stated that two British subjects, Mr. Best and Major Stevens, kidnapped at Dutch frontier on November 21 by Gestapo for alleged complicity in Munich bomb explosion, are believed to have been authorized by British Government to inquire into genuineness of certain German peace proposals.

German liner " Watussi," thought to be a supply ship for the raider in East African waters, left Mozambique on Thursday night.

First R.A.F. man to be decorated by France for gallantry in this war died in hospital : Sergeant-Observer J. Vickers, awarded the Médaille Militaire.

Saturday, November 25

Italy, Japan, Denmark and Sweden made representations to British Foreign Office with regard to policy of reprisals.

Two bombing attacks by German aircraft made on **H.M. ships in North Sea.** No hits were obtained and there were no British casualties.

Enemy aircraft seen over Orkneys and Shetlands.

R.A.F. carried out successful flights over North-West Germany, including Wilhelmshaven and Heligoland.

British refrigerator ship " Sussex," damaged by mine in English Channel, reached port.

German liner " Adolph Woermann " scuttled by crew in South Atlantic in order to avoid capture.

Swedish tanker " Gustaf E. Reuter " struck a mine off Scottish coast and was badly damaged.

Nazi mine-layer sank after striking a mine near Danish island of Langeland.

New Rumanian Cabinet, with smaller pro-German element, formed by M. Tatarescu.

Sunday, November 26

Reported that Germans have laid mines within Swedish four-mile zone at southern entrance of the Sound, leaving a channel only 16 feet deep.

Admiralty announced that **British armed merchant cruiser " Rawalpindi "** had been **sunk.**

Polish liner " Pilsudski," under charter to British Navy, **sunk by U-boat.**

Reported that British steamer " Hookwood " was sunk by mine on Thursday.

Paris reported patrol activities during night in region of the Vosges.

Prime Minister broadcast an address on Britain's war and peace aims.

Soviet Government alleged that Finnish artillery fired on Red Army troops on Soviet-Finnish frontier, and demanded that troops should be withdrawn from frontier district on the Karelian Isthmus.

Danish steamer " Cyril," carrying coal from Britain to Stockholm, seized by Germans. This was thought to be the first capture by Nazis of a neutral ship sailing from Britain to a neutral port

Monday, November 27

Admiralty announced that the sinking of the " Rawalpindi " on November 23 off coast of Iceland was due to overwhelming attack by the " Deutschland " and another enemy warship.

Two enemy merchantmen, " Borkum " and " Konsul Hendrik Fisser," **captured.** The latter was brought into port ; the former was sighted and shelled by a U-boat, killing four Germans but none of the prize crew. The ship was abandoned.

Dutch liner " Spaarndam " mined off Thames Estuary.

Paris reported local infantry and artillery engagement east of the Moselle.

Finnish Government issued denial that shots had been fired from Finnish side of frontier, but suggested to Soviet mutual withdrawal of troops.

Reprisal Order-in-Council signed by the King.

Overwhelming response to Admiralty's appeal for drifters to assist in mine-sweeping.

Two corporations formed in United States to enable Americans to contribute towards war relief in Great Britain and France.

Tuesday, November 28

Announced that British and French reprisals on German export trade come into force on December 4.

R.A.F. fighter patrol **attacked five seaplanes** lying at mine-laying seaplane base at Borkum, one of the Friesian Islands. Attack was made at a low altitude with machine-guns. All British aircraft returned safely.

Air Ministry announced that R.A.F. machines carried out a successful flight over North-West Germany during Monday night.

Soviet Government denounced their Treaty of Non-Aggression with Finland, and alleged two more " incidents " on the Karelian Isthmus, Soviet-Finnish frontier.

Quiet day reported on the Western Front.

British steamer "Rubislaw" sunk by a mine off South-East Coast.

British steamer "Uskmouth" sunk by U-boat in Bay of Biscay.

Paris announced that two German freighters, " Trifels " and " Santa Fé," had been captured by French warships.

Eleven survivors of the " Rawalpindi " landed from merchant cruiser " Chitral."

The King opened a new Session of Parliament.

Three R.A.F. pilots were awarded the Distinguished Flying Cross.

Cargo of " City of Flint " has been bought by Norway.

Wednesday, Nov. 29

Unidentified aeroplane seen over the Shetlands.

Enemy bomber shot down by a British fighter in an air duel off the Northumbrian coast.

Two British patrol aircraft shot down Dornier seaplane over North Sea.

Russia severed diplomatic relations with Finland before receiving the Finnish reply to the Soviet Note of Tuesday.

Mr. Cordell Hull, U.S. Secretary of State, announced his Government's willingness to intervene in the dispute between Russia and Finland.

Paris reported two successful reconnaissances by French troops into territory held by the Germans in the Vosges.

British steamer " Ionian " sunk off East Coast.

Government of Eire decided to put into commission some motor torpedo boats and armed trawlers.

During week ending November 25, British Contraband Control intercepted and detained 21,500 tons of contraband goods suspected of being destined for Germany.

Thursday, November 30

Two R.A.F. fighters encountered an enemy aircraft north of Firth of Forth and chased it out to sea.

Soviet Union attacked Finland by land, sea, and air. Helsinki, Viborg, Petsamo and other towns were bombed. Soviet warships shelled Finnish coast and strategic islands were seized.

Finnish Government resigned at midnight.

Paris reported that a French torpedo boat had sunk an enemy submarine.

British steamer " Sheaf Crest " mined off South-East Coast.

Six survivors of a Greek steamer sunk west of Ireland were picked up after four days in their lifeboat.

Reported that two British destroyers, one towing a damaged submarine, had anchored off Mastrafjord, near Stavanger. The destroyers left later, and the submarine was taken to a shipyard for repair.

Admiralty announced the names of 39 officers and 226 ratings missing as result of loss of H.M.S. " Rawalpindi."

THE POETS & THE WAR
—X—
SHADOWS ON THE LAKE
By George Shelley

For long the lake had lain within those bounds,
  Unruffled and serene with quiet grace,
Unmoved, whatever challenged her command
  Or sought by means of force to shake her place.
There men had come, their hearts aflame with hope,
  With wills that seemed to brook no alien mind,
To work, and work the ways of certain peace
  That would the path to certain glory find.

" No war," they said. " The nations shall not fight
  And tear each other piecemeal yet again,
No war, and ours the watch, that they who died
  Shall not cry out that they had died in vain."
No war, the echoes rang with hollow sound—
  No war, but while those haunts were strangely still,
Across the peaceful beauty of the lake
  Moved once again that darkening cloud of ill.

With sullen force the storm from slumber rose
  Destroying all within its awful reach,
And breaking will with vain insensate rage
  Till hate and passion found the widening breach.
What means Geneva now, her life and peace ?
  For death usurps her place and by his side
Is war, red war, and men who seek to slay
  The hopes for which far nobler men have died

Is there no power to break this chain of crime
  Will not the golden dawn of peace awake
When gentle reason takes the place of hate
  And shadows cloud no more Geneva's lake ?
                    Copyright

Yet Another Sea Crime in the Nazi Score

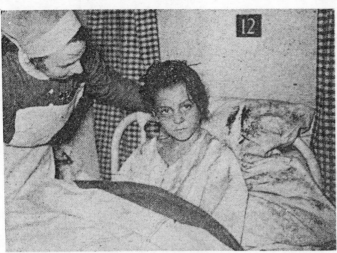

Cristina Wensvoort, left, is seen in a London hospital after her rescue. Her hair is still matted with the ship's oil. Right, one of the lifeboats that stood by all night is returning to port.

Those not needing treatment were taken to London hotels, outside one of which Joan Tresteill is standing.

THE sinking of the Dutch liner "Simon Bolivar" in the North Sea on November 18 with heavy loss of life, was described by the Admiralty as being "a further example of the total disregard of international law and the dictates of humanity shown by the present German Government." With astonishing effrontery and an almost insane belief in the credulity of neutral nations, the Nazis endeavoured to clear themselves of the guilt for this piratical crime by stating the ship must have been sunk by a British mine. That mines were strewn widely about the open seas by the Nazis is proved by the fact that by midday on November 20 it was announced that seven ships had been destroyed by mines and two others damaged.

At an East Coast port many pathetic scenes were observed. Here a survivor carries a small baby who has not been claimed.

The "Simon Bolivar," which was sunk 18 miles from the English coast by a German mine (probably laid by a submarine minelayer), was a liner of 8,309 tons. She was outward bound from Holland to the West Indies and had on board about 400 persons, of whom 140 were landed at an East Coast port. Of the eighty British subjects among the passengers a number were included in the list of over a hundred missing.

The Menace of the Hidden Mine

When what was, perhaps, Hitler's boasted " secret weapon " was revealed in a new campaign of indiscriminate sinking of merchant shipping (*see* opposite page), the whole subject of minelaying and sweeping immediately became of paramount importance.

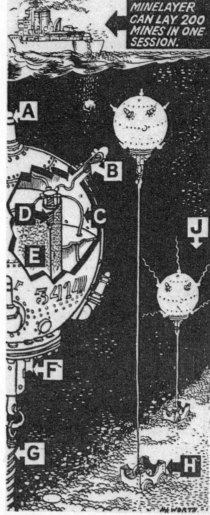

The diagram above shows constructional features of the moored contact mine. The soft lead horn (A) contains tubes of acid (B), and a ship hitting the horn breaks the tubes, the acid acts on the wire, (C) and the detonator (D) fires the explosive (E). The spring plunger (F) comes into action to render the mine harmless if it should break from its cable (G) attached to the wheeled sinker (H). Mines to trap submarines (J) are moored deeper and have feelers.

Courtesy of the " Daily Mail "

THE sailors who man the mine-sweepers—small trawlers equipped with special gear or shallow-draught sloops, but a little larger—have what is, perhaps, the most dangerous and yet least spectacular job in the Royal Navy. Just how dangerous was emphasized when, soon after the sinking of the " Simon Bolivar " and other ships in Germany's new campaign of " frightfulness," H.M. minesweeper " Mastiff " was reported lost with seven valuable lives. Yet a few days later Grimsby fishermen queued up outside the Board of Trade office in answer to the Admiralty's call for men for the minesweepers.

In the last war, when the war at sea had reached its grimmest pitch, one sweeper was lost for every two mines swept up—and each time half the crew was killed or wounded. The enemy laid altogether 43,636 mines, and of these our sweepers found and destroyed 23,873 ; over 700 fully-equipped sweeping vessels were engaged in the work.

The work of a minelayer is equally dangerous and arduous. To enable their mines to be sown effectively, the Germans are thought to be using relays of U-boats. Even the smallest of these can carry up to a dozen " eggs," and in all probability specially-built submarine mine-layers, with mine-wells in the bottom of their hulls, are now in service. A fast surface layer can put down more than 200 mines " at a sitting." Moreover, instead of the usual straight-line method of laying (which simplifies the sweepers' task), the U-boat commanders drop their mines in irregular zigzag fashion—say six here, five there, then another six farther on—forming a large area that may keep the sweepers at work for days on end before they can signal

" all clear." Unlike a U-boat, a mine cannot be detected in advance by any apparatus, and the minesweeping crews pit their wits and their lives in a warfare where chance may tip the scales against them. The principal feature of the sub-marine mine is the unpleasant-looking horns projecting from its steel casing. These are made of soft lead, and are filled with tubes of acid. Any vessel striking one of these horns causes the acid to deton-ate the deadly explosive inside the mine.

The mine, on a long mooring cable, is laid by dropping its heavy anchor or sinker to the sea-bottom after which it settles at the correct depth.

Minesweepers work in pairs, with each unit 300 to 500 yards apart. Between them, sometimes suspended from two sets of apparatus called Oropesa floats, is drawn the sweep wire, which has a series of steel cutters. Should this come into contact with a mooring cable, the mine will rise to the surface and it can then be destroyed by gunfire. The paravane (*see* page 119) is a form of mine protection hung in the sea from the bows of a warship when the presence of a minefield is suspected.

The tragic toll of the German mine-field laid off England's East Coast in November called forth much speculation as to whether the enemy were using " magnetic mines " such as are described opposite. Some at least of these may have been dropped from aircraft, with parachutes attached to reduce the shock when they hit the water. If they are laid on the sea bottom, normal mine-sweeping methods are ineffective.

The extent of the German minelaying activity is illustrated by the fact that more than 200 mines were washed up on the Yorkshire coast, quite apart from those picked up by trawlers.

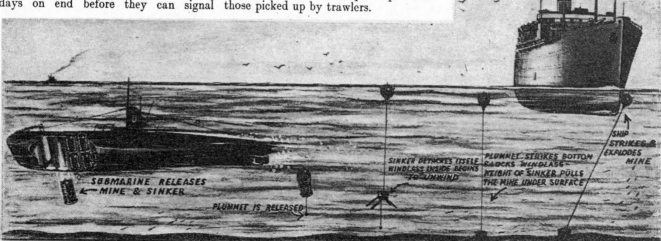

There is little doubt that, as German surface minelayers would hardly cross the North Sea unnoticed and unchallenged by the Royal Navy, recourse was had to submarines for sowing the new illegal minefields off the British coast. Above is a graphic artist's impression of the series of events leading up to the final success of the mine's evil mission with a merchant ship striking and exploding it.

The War Illustrated

Britain Hits Back at the Mine-Laying 'Planes

Here is the thrilling story of the raid by British warplanes made on November 28 on the German seaplane base at Borkum. They had been looking for the mine-layers—and they had found them.

This map shows the position of Borkum, one of the Friesian Islands, 250 miles from the English coast, on which the raid described in this page was made.

FLYING had finished for the day at the German seaplane base on the windswept island of Borkum. It was almost dark, and the seaplanes had been drawn up on the slipways ready to be put to bed in the hangars.

Perhaps these very 'planes were among those which a week before had been seen by observers on the East Coast of Britain dropping objects by parachute, and also alighting on the water and then taking off again—in other words, laying mines either of the submarine magnetic type or of the floating bubble variety, parachutes being used to lessen the shock of the mine striking the water. If such indeed they were, their nefarious activities were over, for suddenly there swooped down from among the clouds that lay low above the water a squadron of British long-range fighters.

The defence was taken completely by surprise, and the utmost confusion reigned. In what one of the British pilots described as "a few glorious moments of low strafing," five German seaplanes were machine-gunned, three out of four machine-gun posts on the Mole were probably put out of action, and several enemy patrol boats were riddled with bullets.

Flying Ten Feet Above the Guns

The 'planes flew so low—according to the German account some of them were at a height of no more than nine or ten feet—that the defenders found great difficulty in bringing their machine-guns and pom-poms into action. The raiders could see men running in all directions, and some gunners occupying a post on top of a hangar were apparently hit. After a few minutes the anti-aircraft guns and the coastal patrol boats started firing; but by this time the British 'planes had reached their objectives.

Quickly the squadron re-formed and disappeared into the mist. All the twelve returned safely to their base in England, the last 200 miles of the journey being covered in complete darkness. No enemy fighters had spotted their approach in time to come up to engage them, and no enemy aircraft were observed on the return flight. In spite of the intense barrage the British raiding party suffered no casualties, and not one of the dozen aircraft was hit. Later it was disclosed that the 'planes were twin-engined Blenheims, and of the pilots six were R.A.F. regulars and six members of the Auxiliary Air Force. Not one of the intrepid attackers had been under fire before.

Naturally enough, the Germans sought to disparage the results achieved. No serious damage was done, they claimed; but at the same time they admitted that it was "undoubtedly a daring exploit." And away back across the North Sea thirty-six airmen went in to dinner conscious of a day's work well done.

DORNIER Do.18 FLYING BOAT WITH 2 JUNKER DIESEL ENGINES

HOW MAGNETIC MINES ARE LAID FROM FLYING BOATS
A. Magnetic mines being released. B. Parachutes prevent the mines from striking the sea with damaging force. C. Mines are coupled in pairs. D. Decoy planes fly at a great height to attract the defenders while the mine-laying machines fly just above the sea. Left is a bullet hole in an East Coast pier window made by machine-gun fire from a mine-laying 'plane.

'The Glorious Battle of the River Plate'

Lord Chatfield was right when he expressed the opinion in the House of Lords that the " Graf Spee " would soon put out to sea again—for a short time. On December 17, after days of frenzied preparation, she left Montevideo, and two hours later was scuttled in the fairway by her own crew. The story of what has been well styled " Ignominy to order " is given below.

IT was late at night on Wednesday, December 13, when the German pocket battleship "Admiral Graf Spee" limped into the neutral harbour of Montevideo.

For fourteen hours she had been engaged in a running fight with three British cruisers—"Ajax," "Achilles," and "Exeter." All three were small ships of their class, and against the " Graf Spee's " six 11-inch guns and eight 6-inch guns, the " Exeter " mounted only six 8-inch guns and her two consorts eight 6-inch guns apiece. A broadside fired by

most gallantly they tackled it. They took every advantage of their superior speed, attacking the enemy from ever-changing angles. When they made their final dash, closing in at full speed from opposite directions to almost point-blank range, completing their destructive work, the spirit of their naval forefathers must indeed have cried ' Well done ! ' Here was no necessity to hoist Nelson's favourite signal 'Engage the enemy more closely ' ; it was a perfectly working team of gallant fellows each knowing what he had to do and doing it."

So it was that, sorely battered, with holes gaping in her superstructure, and riddled by shells just above the waterline, the much-vaunted pocket battleship just

managed to limp into harbour. Close on her tracks went " Ajax " and " Achilles," ready and eager to renew the battle, while the " Exeter " came up through the night ready to take part in a fresh attack. Not until the " Cumberland " arrived did the crippled ship depart to care for her wounded and injuries.

For three days the " Graf Spee " swung at anchor in Montevideo harbour ; for three days her men toiled desperately to repair the damage and plug the holes which had been torn by the British shells. Mr. E. Millington Drake, the British Minister at Montevideo, urged that the battleship should be required to put to sea at once or be interned for the duration of the war ; a battleship which could travel so fast as did the " Graf Spee " when seeking refuge must, he pointed out, be perfectly navigable. Captain Dietrich, German Naval Attaché at Buenos Aires, and a German civilian expert, also examined the battleship and, so it was believed, reported that she was navigable.

According to international law a warship that is seaworthy may be compelled to leave a neutral harbour, and the Uruguayan Cabinet decreed that the " Graf Spee " must leave Montevideo within 72 hours—by 8 p.m. on Sunday evening, December 17 (11.30 p.m. Greenwich mean time)—or be interned.

Afterwards it transpired that Captain Langsdorf protested strongly against the time limit. He wanted fifteen days in which to repair the damage that had been done, for, so he maintained, although the fighting capacity of his ship had been

the " Graf Spee " was half as much again as the total broadside of the three British cruisers, and the disparity was still further increased by the fact that early in the action the " Exeter " was hit by a German salvo which knocked out two of her four turrets, smashed three of her 8-inch guns, and inflicted nearly a hundred casualties. Though she was able to continue in the chase, the " Exeter " was forced to drop behind, and it was the two comparatively small British cruisers " Ajax " and " Achilles " which finally drove the " Graf Spee " off the seas.

Well might Captain Langsdorf talk of the " inconceivable audacity " displayed by " Achilles " and " Ajax "—of that " incredible manoeuvre " which brought the two cruisers dashing through the smoke screen to within a mile of the " Graf Spee," firing salvo after salvo into the German ship at close range.

"When the 'Exeter' dropped out of the action," wrote Admiral Sir Howard Kelly in the " Daily Telegraph," " the two small cruisers had a tremendous task in front of them, and

The superstructure of the " Admiral Graf Spee " is seen in these two photographs as it was before the action, top, and above, when she lay in Montevideo harbour. The points at which hits were scored are ringed round. The superstructure is the nerve centre of the ship from which she is navigated and her gunfire controlled.

Photos, Associated Press and Central Press

'Graf Spee' Pays the Full Price of Defeat

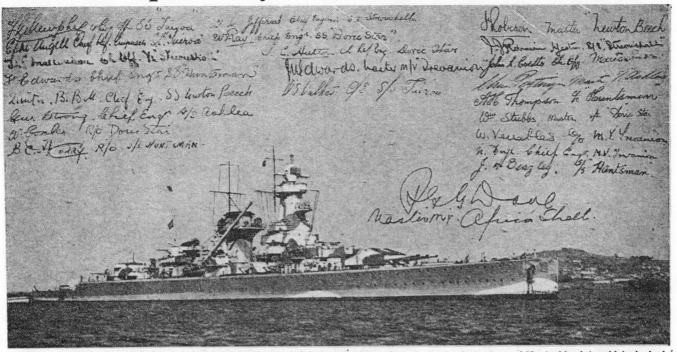

This remarkable picture of Germany's pocket battleship "Admiral Graf Spee" as she lay in the harbour of Montevideo into which she had been chased by the British cruisers was taken by Captain Henry Daniel, Special Correspondent of the "Daily Telegraph," on the morning of the day on which she sailed to her doom. The photograph bears the signatures of 23 masters and officers of British merchantmen who had been captured during the "Graf Spee's" career of depredation and were actually in the battleship during the battle of the River Plate.

War Honours Won by Sea and Air in 1939

River Plate ("Graf Spee") Action

Rear-Adm. Sir H. Harwood, in command of the squadron (Dec. 13). Awarded K.C.B.	Capt. W. E. Parry, of H.M.S. "Achilles." Awarded C.B.	Capt. C. H. Woodhouse, of H.M.S. "Ajax." Awarded C.B.	Lt.-Cmdr. (now Cmdr.) R. B. Jennings, of H.M.S. "Exeter" Promoted.	Cmdr. (now Capt.) D. H. Everett, of H.M.S. "Ajax." Promoted.

Aflame from bow to stern, the "Graf Spee" is slowly sinking into the waters of the Plate. This dramatic photograph was taken, like that above, by Captain Henry Daniel. The white funnel has collapsed in dense clouds of smoke. "Sheets of flame spread over the tranquil sea," wrote Captain Daniel, "as the oil from the bunkers of the riven ship came to the surface and caught fire. Dense clouds of smoke rose in the air, and soon the wreck was a blazing inferno from stem to stern. It was the end of the tragedy."

Vol. 1   A Permanent Picture Record of the Second Great War   No. 9

The friendliness and courtesy which the British soldiers in France showed to the French people as soon as they landed brought a quick response. It here takes material form, for a young Frenchwoman is making a lavish distribution of the last autumn flowers from her garden to the khaki quartette whose car has halted near her home. Slung across the sergeant's shoulder is one of the cases of maps which are provided for most drivers of military cars in France.

Photo, P.N.A.

THE WAR ILLUSTRATED

3d Weekly

Edited by

SIR JOHN HAMMERTON

Editor of 'THE WAR ILLUSTRATED' (1914-1920)
'WORLD WAR. 1914-1918,' 'I WAS THERE!' etc.

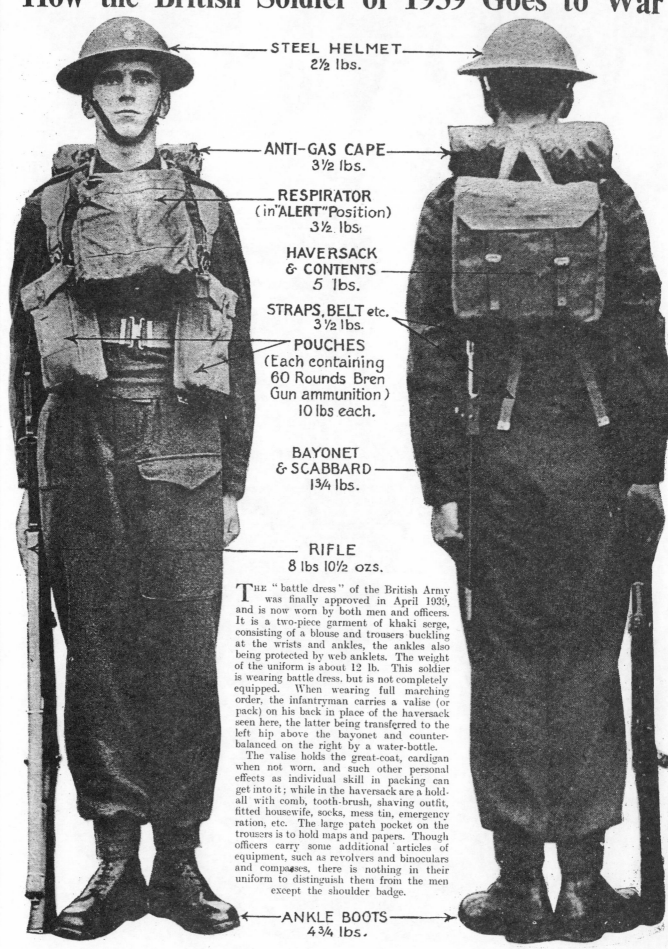

How the British Soldier of 1939 Goes to War

STEEL HELMET
2½ lbs.

ANTI-GAS CAPE
3½ lbs.

RESPIRATOR
(in "ALERT" Position)
3½ lbs.

HAVERSACK
& CONTENTS
5 lbs.

STRAPS, BELT etc.
3½ lbs.

POUCHES
(Each containing
60 Rounds Bren
Gun ammunition)
10 lbs each.

BAYONET
& SCABBARD
1¾ lbs.

RIFLE
8 lbs 10½ ozs.

ANKLE BOOTS
4¾ lbs.

THE "battle dress" of the British Army was finally approved in April 1939, and is now worn by both men and officers. It is a two-piece garment of khaki serge, consisting of a blouse and trousers buckling at the wrists and ankles, the ankles also being protected by web anklets. The weight of the uniform is about 12 lb. This soldier is wearing battle dress, but is not completely equipped. When wearing full marching order, the infantryman carries a valise (or pack) on his back in place of the haversack seen here, the latter being transferred to the left hip above the bayonet and counter-balanced on the right by a water-bottle.

The valise holds the great-coat, cardigan when not worn, and such other personal effects as individual skill in packing can get into it; while in the haversack are a hold-all with comb, tooth-brush, shaving outfit, fitted housewife, socks, mess tin, emergency ration, etc. The large patch pocket on the trousers is to hold maps and papers. Though officers carry some additional articles of equipment, such as revolvers and binoculars and compasses, there is nothing in their uniform to distinguish them from the men except the shoulder badge.

1940

British prisoners released from prison ship *Altmark*

German invasion of Denmark and Norway

German invasion of the Netherlands, Belgium and Luxembourg

Resignation of Chamberlain and formation of coalition government
by Churchill

Dunkirk evacuation

Italy enters the war

Fall of France

British attack French ships at Oran and Mers-el-Kebir

Battle of Britain

The Blitz

Italian invasion of Greece

Italian navy crippled by Fleet Air Arm attack on Taranto

First Western Desert offensive

1940

'*The War Illustrated,*' January 19th, 1940

Registered at the G.P.O. as a Newspaper

Vol. 1 ★ COMPLETING VOLUME ONE—BIND IT NOW! (See Cover iii) ★ No. 20

THE WAR ILLUSTRATED

3ᵈ Weekly

Bren Gun Section—Ready for Anything!

Disaster Overtakes the Columns of the Invader

Russian troops were driven back to the frontier and even in some places beyond it, and the Finns claimed to have killed 2,000 and to have captured 600 prisoners.

In the "waist" of Finland, in the war's central zone, the invading columns of the Red Army were similarly unsuccessful. First, the column moving on Suomussalmi was driven back, and then those troops which had moved from Salla in the direction of Kemijaervi and Rovaniemi were taken by surprise and completely routed. Here in a wilderness of forest and lake, in a world of perpetual twilight and the most bitter cold, the invaders found themselves assailed on every side by hardy fighters who knew every inch of the country and were, moreover, thoroughly acclimatized to the terrible weather conditions. After a week's struggle the Finns scored a decisive victory. The 163rd Russian division of 18,000 men, their powers of resistance sapped by the bitter cold and by shortage of food, was almost annihilated, and huge quantities of guns and war material were captured. The Finns' only complaint was over the scarcity of their ammunition. "There are more Russians in this sector," said one, "than we have cartridges."

So complete was the reversal of fortune that by the end of the year General Wallenius, Commander of the Finnish Northern Army, revealed that his troops

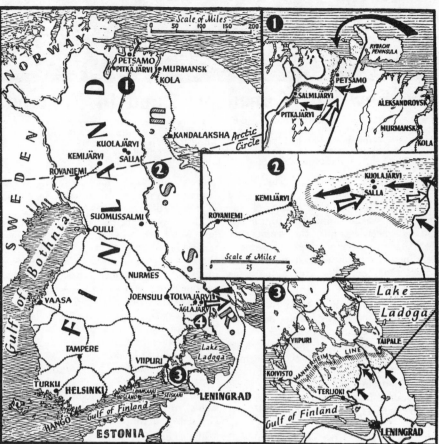

The areas in which the war in Finland is being fought are shown in these four maps. The black arrows indicate the direction of the Russian attacks, while the white arrows refer to the Finnish counter-attacks. Three of the battle areas are shown in more detail in the smaller maps inset on the right.　*By courtesy of "News Chronicle"*

Here is a scene with the Finnish Army in the southern war area. Troops are deploying to take up positions in which to meet an advance of the Red Army. The thickly wooded country, now deep in snow, is typical of that through which the Russians have attempted to advance towards the Mannerheim Line.

were now operating in enemy territory. The woods which extended across the frontier were filled with Russian dead and wounded, and there was not a spot, he declared, between the frontier and Kandalaksha, the Russian advanced base on Kandalaksk Bay, an arm of the White Sea, where the Russians were safe from attack. "We don't let them rest," he said, "we don't let them sleep. This is a war of numbers against brains. We train our men to fight individually and they can do it, whereas the Russian soldier can never rid himself of his natural gregarious instincts."

Even in the extreme north, where the Russians were able to land troops and munitions from the sea, they were so harried by the Finnish sharp-shooters moving invisibly on their skis across the snow, that they retreated on Petsamo, leaving behind them a miniature railroad and some Diesel tractors and trucks which the Finns promptly turned round and used to bring up their supplies.

None can tell what were the real losses in this campaign where the corpses of the fallen were swiftly covered by white snow and the sombre waters of the lakes. Moscow professed that the Red Army casualties were only some 1,800 killed and 7,000 wounded, but the Finns put the enemy killed, wounded, taken prisoner and incapacitated by frostbite

I WAS THERE!

Eye Witness Stories of Episodes and Adventures in the Second Great War

We Saw The Canadians Land in England

It was for most people a dramatic surprise when Mr. Churchill announced in his broadcast on December 18 that contingents of the Canadian Army had just arrived in England. Here the scene at one of the ports where they disembarked is described by a special correspondent of the " Manchester Guardian."

I T was a cold, grey day. The water, the sky and the farther shore were all cold and grey. One transport was already at anchor, and the journalists who had been let into the secret that the Canadians were coming stood on the little pier at noon and stamped their cold feet as the other grey ships came stealing into harbour.

They came in one by one, the transports looking high and heavy beside the rakish warships that escorted them. They came up the middle of the channel, so that the cheering from them seemed faint ; but we heard it, and the sound of bagpipes from one ship and shrill " Yippees " from another. That was the Westerners, the Canadian pressmen told us. On other ships some men were singing "Pack Up Your Troubles." There were not many of us to cheer back, for this was a secret till the troops and the ships were clear and safe from German bombings, and even the people of the port knew nothing.

There were the journalists, a few soldiers and the dozen or so local folk who made a daily visit to the pier, and this time had found something worth watching. Some of them, though, miraculously knew what it was all about. A tired-looking middle-aged woman went up to a young lady of fashion, all furs and lipstick, to ask her. " It's the Canadians," the younger woman told her in a bored, know-all voice, and then she thawed and grinned as though it were a lark that the Canadians were coming.

It was mid-afternoon before the Canadian G.O.C., Major-General Mc-Naughton, came ashore at another pier, with Mr. Eden and Mr. Vincent Massey. The troops had told the Dominions Secretary that the crossing had been "dandy," and the General told us the same thing. The officers had been in suites and the men in first-class cabins. When he came over in 1914 they had been cramped in hammocks for twenty-eight days. He had been a major then ; now he was in command, with many on his staff and among his N.C.O.s who had been with him twenty-five years ago.

There was more of a crowd on this pier, some naval officers and a few hundred of the local people. " The story

gets about," said a policeman. The civilians were let on to the pier and kept behind barricades.

There was nothing to do for a time but watch the warships winking their semaphore lights to the signallers on shore, and the aeroplanes manœuvring overhead. At last three machines swooped low over one of the transports, startling the gulls that had been rocking on the water. It must have been a special salute, for soon a black and white tender came puffing to the shore, overflowing with khaki. The Canadians were here, cheering wildly and waving their rifles above their heads, their bugle band blowing like mad. The sailors on the little warship at the pier cheered them as they passed.

We could see what they looked like now as they came alongside, singing : thick-set, open-faced boys in the same battle-kit that the British Army wears, but with a maple-leaf badge in their fore-and-aft caps. . . .

The men fell in on the pier, their officers hurrying them off the boat.

" Tiny " Wilson, one of the cooks of the first Canadian contingent to come ashore in Britain, carried not only his kit, but odds and ends of his kitchen utensils stuck in his belt.
Photo, " Daily Mirror "

The first contingent of Canada's Army to arrive in England was described by the Commanding Officer, Major-General McNaughton, as " a broad cross-section of the Canadian people." They had the friendliest of greetings from the spectators as they first set foot on British soil.

New Zealand Hastens to Help the Motherland

A LTHOUGH New Zealand lies at the other end of the world—so far away that her people have no need of black-outs, gas masks, or air-raid shelters—she is playing her full part in the Empire's war effort. New Zealand pilots have distinguished themselves in the air fights over the North Sea, and the "Achilles," in the glorious battle of the Plate, was manned very largely by New Zealanders. Moreover, the Dominion is raising a large force for service overseas, to be commanded by Major-General B. C. Freyberg, V.C., who played such a gallant part in the Great War, both on Gallipoli and in France.

Above, recruits for the New Zealand Expeditionary Force undergoing intensive training in their own country.

Australia's Airmen Now Comrades of the R.A.F.

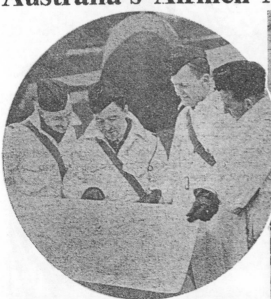

Australian airmen who have just arrived in England will have their first experience of war service with the Coastal Command. Above, pilots are studying charts before going on one of their first patrols.

I N a message to the first Australian squadron to land in Britain, Mr. J. V. Fairbairn, Australian Minister for Air, said : " A great responsibility rests upon you as members of the first Australian Air Force squadron to come on active service in this country. You will be comrades in a great and just campaign with the men of the R.A.F., and Australia is confident that you will play your part in whatever spheres you may be called upon to serve."

The first squadron of the R.A.F. came ashore on December 26, 1939. Besides pilots there were gunners, observers and ground staff.

Incendiary Bombs Illumine the Wintry Scene

Fierce fires were caused in Turku (Aabo) by the bombs dropped by Red bombers. Here A.R.P. workers are fighting the flames in the bitter cold of the Northern winter.

at some 100,000. In any case, the casualties were too great for the Soviet authorities to be able to " put over " their claim that this was not a war but an expedition of liberation. Observers in Moscow noted an increasing tension, and there were signs of increasing war fever. In Leningrad it was rumoured that all the hospitals were filled with wounded and that schools were being commandeered as hospitals. Even in distant Moscow it was understood that beds were being made available for those who had been laid low by Finnish bullets or by Finland's climate. Stories were afoot of Red Army generals being shot for their ill-success.

Everywhere outside Russia, even in Germany, there was nothing but admiration for the magnificent stand made by the Finns in the defence of their homeland. From many quarters there was forthcoming not only admiration but material help of the most valuable kind. America granted Finland credits for the purchase of munitions and 'planes, Britain and France supplied arms; some thousands of volunteers arrived from Sweden and Italy; and South Africa released aeroplanes for the Finnish front.

Many scenes of such pathos were witnessed during the bombing of Helsinki. A Finnish mother with her baby in a basket is fleeing during the air attack on Christmas Day.

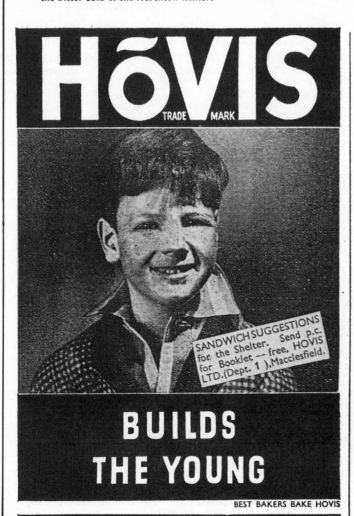

Imperial India Sends its Men—and Mules

Among the Indian troops in France are detachments of the Indian Army Service Corps, much of which is still unmechanized. Mules are largely used in this service, and here is a typical driver with his mule.

The Indian soldiers take great pride in their smartness and are as particular about being clean-shaven as the British. This barber is doing his work in the open, somewhere in France.

The man squatting on the ground in this photograph is weighing out the prescribed amount of forage for each man's animal with rather primitive scales. A non-commissioned officer stands by to see that each man gets just measure for his beast.

THE Nazi assumption that if the British Empire went to war India would rise against the British Raj and break the Empire tie has proved as completely false as all the other German estimates of the supposed weakness of the Empire. Already Indian troops are in France, for at the end of 1939 Indian contingents were joining the B.E.F. They consisted largely of transport columns with draught and pack mules, thus helping to meet the demand that mechanical transport should be supplemented ' by the more elastic animal transport.

A British officer is here inspecting a train of pack mules of the Indian contingent. The fringe of cord on the animals' bridles is a protection against which, under the conditions that have recently been experienced in France, is perhaps superfluous. Despite the mechanization of most of the Army transport, conditions with which horses and mules alone may be able to cope are by no means inconceivable.

The Nazi Slave-Ship Feels the Nelson Touch

Yet another dramatic chapter in the history of the British Navy was written when on February 16 H.M.S. " Cossack " pursued the Nazi slave-ship " Altmark " into a Norwegian fjord and rescued 299 British prisoners at the point of the bayonet. Below is a recapitulation of the episode based on Admiralty statements and eye-witness stories.

THE slave ship was almost home. Two months and more had passed since she parted company from the " Admiral Graf Spee " after receiving from the pocket battleship her last captures of British prisoners. That was on December 6, somewhere in the South Atlantic, and since then while the " Graf Spee " was resting and sinking ever deeper into the Montevidean sandbank, the " Altmark " had ploughed a zigzag course heading northward. She reached at last the cold waters of Iceland, and now turned south past the towering cliffs of Norway. On February 14 she got into Norwegian territorial waters off Trondheim Fjord and (according to the Norwegian Prime Minister) was stopped and " examined " by a Norwegian torpedo boat. She was allowed to continue her journey, but next day, 100 miles north of Bergen, was again stopped by a

Captain P. L. Vian R.N., top centre, was in command of H.M.S. " Cossack " when the "Altmark" endeavoured to escape to a German port with her load of British prisoners. In the lower photograph is his ship, a destroyer of 1,870 tons, one of the Tribal class, and, like her sister ship the "Afridi," a flotilla leader. She was completed in June, 1938.   *Photos, Wright & Logan and Topical*

Norwegian warship, and refused a request that she should be searched. The afternoon of Friday, February 16, found her approaching Norway's southernmost point; a very short distance beyond lay the Skagerrak, safety, and home.

Down below in the darkness and filth of the overcrowded " flats " the 299 British prisoners must have almost lost hope as from their single peephole they watched the cliffs of Norway sail past, and heard blocks of ice crunching against the ship's side; on the bridge Captain Dau, a hard-bitten old Nazi, was no doubt congratulating himself that he had managed to evade the Allied patrols and that very shortly he would see on the horizon the squadrons of Nazi 'planes which were to escort him to port in triumph.

But the British Admiralty decreed otherwise. Ever since that glorious day in December when they had driven the " Graf Spee " into Montevideo the Royal Navy had been maintaining a constant

watch for her auxiliary of evil repute, and now were close on her trail. It was an aircraft of Britain's coastal command that first spotted the " Altmark " as she crept past the Norwegian coast; for hours her commander had been sweeping the seas with his binoculars when he saw a smudge of smoke below him. He dived down to investigate, only to find to his intense disappointment that the ship was not the " Altmark." Just about to turn away for home he suddenly noticed that there was another ship in the near neighbourhood, the ship which—yes, it had its funnel far aft. It was the " Altmark " ! Almost at the same moment two more British 'planes sighted the ship.

Swiftly the discovery was signalled to the Fleet, and in a very short time " certain of His Majesty's ships," to quote the dry phrasing of the Admiralty statement, " which were conveniently disposed rushed up at full speed." Leading the chase was the destroyer "Cossack" which at once attempted to head off the " Altmark," but the German steamer slipped into the little Joessing Fjord. Then the " Cossack " turned and made for the entrance of the fjord into which

her quarry had disappeared. The destroyer " Ivanhoe " was already there, together with two Norwegian gunboats who apparently had been escorting the " Altmark " along the coast.

The captain of one of the gunboats came aboard the " Cossack " and Captain Vian, who, meanwhile, had received instructions from the Admiralty, offered to place a joint British and Norwegian guard upon the " Altmark," and to escort her with British and Norwegian warships to Bergen where the search for the British prisoners could be conducted and the matter properly investigated according to international law. The Norwegian captain, however, refused; he declared that the " Altmark " was unarmed, that he knew nothing about any prisoners on board, that she had been examined at Bergen the day before and had received permission to use Norwegian territorial waters on her passage to Germany.

Although far from satisfied with these assurances the British destroyers withdrew and again got in touch with the Admiralty. It was not long before further instructions were received; in effect, Captain Vian was told to go in and get the prisoners.

It was now 7.30 or 8 o'clock in the evening and quite dark when H.M.S. " Cossack " headed for the entrance to the fjord. Gliding by the two Norwegian gunboats at the entrance, the British destroyer, with her searchlights blazing, crunched her way through the ice towards where the " Altmark " was silhouetted against the thousand-foot-high cliffs. On entering Captain Vian (in command of the flotilla) went on board the Norwegian boat " Kjell " and again asked that the " Altmark " should be taken to Bergen with a joint Anglo-Norwegian guard. The commanding officer of the Norwegian warship refused the request, although he

The scene of the remarkable exploit of H.M.S. " Cossack " is shown in this map. By it can be followed the course the " Altmark " would pursue to reach Germany through neutral waters.

'It Was a Good Scrap While It Lasted'

agreed to take passage in the "Cossack" until her men boarded the "Altmark" when he declared that he had not come to look on at a fight and returned to his own ship.

Meanwhile the "Altmark" which was jammed in the ice in the inner end of the fjord began to work her engines, and in spite of an order to stop, broke free and attempted to ram the "Cossack" as the destroyer came alongside. The only result of the manoeuvre, however, was the grounding of the "Altmark" herself by the stern. The two ships were now only about 8 feet apart and grappling irons were at once thrown out from the "Cossack," and a boarding-party leaped the gap and drove the German crew before them. For a few minutes hand-to-hand fighting was going on in many parts of the ship and the Germans suffered casualties amounting to seven dead and several wounded. The only British casualty was Mr. J. J. F. Smith, gunner in charge of one of the boarding parties who was severely wounded.

Some of the Germans jumped overboard and ran across the ice and opened fire with rifles on the ship from a small eminence. The fire was returned by the British and two Germans who were scrambling across the ice were hit. Another fell into the water, whereupon two of the "Cossack's" officers plunged in and brought him aboard. It was found that he had been severely wounded and he died later in the ship's hospital.

By now the prisoners in the "Altmark" were being liberated: members of the boarding-party tried every door and hatchway, shouting "The Navy is here!"

The answer was a roar of cheering, and in a few minutes the holds had been broken open and the prisoners, many of whom had not seen the daylight for the last fortnight, ran on deck, where they were passed on to the waiting destroyers. When the boarding party were satisfied that every prisoner had been released they withdrew and shortly afterwards the "Cossack" joined the rest of the British forces waiting outside the fjord. On the afternoon of the next day 299 deliriously happy seamen were landed at Leith and

H.M.S. "Intrepid," whose captain is Commander R. C. Gordon, R.N., was the first British ship to intercept the "Altmark" as she made for Joessing Fjord. She is a destroyer of 1,370 tons. Completed in July 1937.

in a few hours most of them were on their way to their homes.

The news of the rescue was received in Britain and throughout the Empire with tremendous enthusiasm. Germany, for her part, lost no time in expressing her indignation at the boarding of "a peaceful German merchantman" in neutral waters, and the "brutal murder" of German seamen, while Norway's reactions can be summed up in the words with which the Norwegian Prime Minister greeted the British Minister in Oslo: "I have asked you to come to express the strong consternation and indignation that we feel at this gross violation of Norwegian terri-

---

Notice for prisoners.

On account of to-day's behaviour of the prisoners they will get bread and water only to-morrow instead of the regular meals.

Further I have given order that neither the prisoner-officer nor the doctor will make their regular rounds after this. Any severe case of sickness can be reported on occasion of handing down the food.

At sea, February 15th, 1940.

Commander.

This notice was torn down from the prisoners' quarters in the "Altmark," after the ship had been duly dealt with, and one of them brought it away with him. It records the brutal Nazi punishment for their attempt to break away from unendurable conditions. Thanks to the British Navy this punishment never fulfilled its brutal intent.

E.— HAMLET OF TINY STONE HOUSES SHOWING LIGHTED WINDOWS

A.— ALTMARK
B.— H.M.S. COSSACK laid Alongside.
C.— PACK ICE FLOES, SIX INCHES THICK IN FIORD.
D.— SKY STEEL BLUE— STARS OUT — NORTHERN TWILIGHT NOT ENTIRELY DARK LOFTY SNOW CAPPED MOUNTAINS DROPPING SHEER INTO FIORD.

The sketch left was drawn by Thomas Aubrey Jenkins, one of the prisoners in the "Altmark." The position of the German prison-ship and H.M.S. "Cossack" at the time of the rescue is shown. Right is Joessing Fiord where the action took place.   *Photo. L.N.A.*

From 'Down Under' Come Aussies & Anzacs with the

Australia is justly proud of her young sons who have volunteered to fight for the Empire and feels that nothing is too good for them. Each of the young "diggers," left, embarking to go overseas, carries a white linen bag containing gifts from the Australian Comforts Fund. Australian nurses, too, have volunteered for service, and below some of them are seen at the rail of a transport with the captain. Centre, men of the 2nd A.I.F., carrying full equipment, are lined up waiting to embark.

The people of New Zealand, like those of Australia, had an opportunity to give the young men who formed the first New Zealand contingent a hearty send-off. Left is their last march through Christchurch before embarking for Egypt.

The Anzac troops in this war, as in the last one, are admirably equipped. This quarter-master-sergeant at a camp in New Zealand proudly exhibits boots that are just the thing for foot-slogging in all weathers.

Photos, Keystone and Sport & General

'Bravest Message that the Nation's Power Can Give'

Mr. Anthony Eden, who flew to Egypt to welcome the troops from Australia and New Zealand on their arrival at Suez on February 12, carried messages to them from the King. He is here seen on the deck of one of the great liners that brought the troops to Egypt addressing the New Zealanders. The strategic significance of these troop movements is discussed in page 179. By their action in crossing the seas, he said, they had sent " the bravest message that the nation's power can give."

Denmark Submits to the Nazi Invader

With that suddenness which the world has come to expect from the Nazi Fuehrer, Denmark was invaded by overwhelmingly strong German forces on April 9, and in a few hours completely overrun. Here is a brief account of the course of the day's events which at one stroke placed peaceful, progressive Denmark under Nazi rule.

SHORTLY before dawn on Tuesday, April 9, strong German forces crossed the German-Danish frontier and at the same time German naval detachments were ferried across the Baltic to strategic points on the Danish islands.

With clockwork precision the invasion proceeded along lines which must have been prepared and carefully rehearsed long before. The attack was directed towards six points. In Jutland (*see* map, 1) motorized armoured troops poured across the frontier between Flensburg and Toender, and pushed rapidly northwards, and in a few hours occupied Esbjerg, Denmark's principal North Sea port, and joined hands with a second German force which had proceeded by sea up the Little Belt and had come ashore near Middlefart, where they took possession of the bridge connecting Jutland with the island of Fuenen (2). Meanwhile, another naval detachment had penetrated the Great Belt and landed troops at Nyborg, on Fuenen's further side, and at Korsoer, on Zealand (3).

The fourth wave of invasion was directed from Warnemuende on Germany's north coast. Troops and an armoured train were ferried across the Baltic to Gjedser (4), on Falster's southernmost tip, and from there moved north along the railway. At the bridge of Vordingborg (5) they made contact with the fifth wave which had already occupied this vital link between Falster and Zealand. Finally, a large body of German troops proceeded direct to Copenhagen (6) and landed on the coast of the Danish capital at dawn, while German 'planes roared overhead, dropping leaflets printed in Danish announcing the completion of the invasion—leaflets obviously printed in readiness long before. Within a short time the citadel and the broadcasting station were in German hands, and, in fact, by 8 a.m. the whole city was in the occupation of the Nazis.

The people of the city and country alike were too astounded by the suddenness of the invasion and, moreover, too overawed by the overwhelming show of military strength—to make any real resistance. Later, it transpired that the German and Danish commanders had met, and that the latter had given instructions to their troops not to fire on the invaders.

Then the blanket of censorship descended on the little kingdom. All telegraphic and telephonic communication with the world was stopped. The afternoon newspapers were able to carry only news supplied by the German agencies. Traffic on the railways was stopped and the ferry communications with Sweden were also suspended. Denmark had followed Austria, Czechoslovakia, and Poland unto the night of Nazidom.

This delightful photograph of King Christian X of Denmark shows him cracking a joke with some of his people. He was born in 1870 and succeeded his father, Frederick VIII, in 1912.

Taken from the balcony of the City Hall, this photograph gives an excellent impression of Copenhagen, Denmark's capital. With a population of under 700,000, Copenhagen is remarkable for its cleanliness and absence of slums. It has been the Danish capital since 1443, and contains many buildings closely associated with the little country's political and ecclesiastical history. For the story in brief of Denmark see pages 264-65.

The War Illustrated

How Oslo Fell to Only 1,500 Nazi Troops

In a remarkable dispatch published in the "Daily Telegraph" of April 16, a special correspondent described the strange and bewildering events of the German occupation of Oslo. Here we reprint, by courtesy of our great contemporary, those passages of the dispatch which tell of the Nazis' triumphal entry into the Norwegian capital.

HAVING described the mystifying way in which the port defences of Oslo were silent against the invader, with the fortunate exception of the "Olav Tryggvason" (*see* page 349, Vol. I) which sank a German ship, the Correspondent continues his eyewitness account:

We had spent an eerie night at Oslo's Grand Hotel, with a succession of air-raid alarms, of which the first sounded thirty-five minutes after midnight, about the time the mobilization was ordered.

I decided that the Norwegians were only rehearsing the air alarm as a precaution. So I refused to get up until seven o'clock. Then a Finnish diplomat informed me of the ultimatum and the Government's decision to leave.

At 7:45, while we still had not the slightest idea what had happened in Oslo Fjord and at Horten, five Nazi bombers suddenly came roaring over the rooftops so low that they almost touched them. We watched them come, expecting every moment that bombs would fall. For two and a half hours German 'planes dived over the city, always only three or five in number. They were intended to terrorize the populace into surrender and the authorities into inaction while the first troops were being landed by air at Fornebo, outside the city.

Thousands of Osloans gazed at them curiously and fearfully, but there was no panic. None of us dreamed that German warships were in the inner harbour and that Oslo was already doomed. We still thought that British ships and 'planes might come at any moment. It seemed utterly incredible that the Narrows could have been forced by the Germans and the powerful forts of the fjord silenced.

Norway's capital in every quarter was a scene of dazed disorganization, completely without leadership. Apparently even the men who had been called to the colours did not know where to go or simply forgot about it.

It was like this until 2.30. Then, as I walked up to the hotel desk the porter asked me, "Aren't you going out to see the Germans come in?"

"What do you mean, the Germans?"

"Yes, they're marching up Carljohan Boulevard any minute now."

We rushed outside into the strangest scene imaginable. Oslo's beautiful main boulevard was jammed with people all flocking to see the Germans come in. Strangest of all were the Norwegian policemen calmly forming lines along the pavements, clearing the streets for the Germans' triumphal entry.

Shortly before three o'clock two lorries filled with a dozen German soldiers rolled along the street. Soldiers lolled in them with rifles dangling as if they had been assured that they had not the slightest resistance to fear. From the rear of the second lorry two machine-guns poked their noses out, straight down the boulevard. Their crews lay prone, with intent, hard faces, ready to fire. This was the only show of force, and all that was needed.

At 3.3 a murmur ran through the crowd. We could see two mounted men swinging into the boulevard in front of the Palace, then six more, then the head of a marching column in field-grey.

The mounted men were Norwegian policemen actually escorting the German troops which were occupying the capital. We looked on uncomprehendingly. Later I was told that the Norwegian policemen never carry any kind of arms; this also was why they failed to fulfil the Government's orders to arrest Quisling.

A tall, broad-shouldered officer, General von Falkenhorst, and two other officers marched directly behind the mounted police. Then came the German regulars in columns of threes.

This map shows the new theatre of war resulting from Hitler's unprincipled invasion of Denmark and Norway. The Swastikas show where German troops landed. Within a few hours Denmark was completely in German hands, and many of the principal towns in Norway were occupied.

Critical Days on the Norwegian Battle Front

Although no real appreciation of a fast-changing situation is possible, this chapter gives
in summary form the position of the war in Norway at the end of April, when, for a
fortnight the Allies had been battling on Norwegian soil and the British withdrawal
from Aandalsnes had not yet been announced.

AFTER three weeks of thrust and counter-thrust, of raids and excursions and alarums, the war in Norway crystallized into a struggle for Trondheim, the history-mellowed city which, alas for its peace and security, finds its place in Scandinavia's strategical gateway.

Seized in the early hours of April 9 to fall back before they had any opportunity of destroying the bridges or blocking the railway tunnels in the one valley or the other.

The Allied Command in Norway was quick to realize the approaching danger, and British troops were rushed to the Gudbrandsdal, where they linked up with the Norwegians at Lillehammer.

swift, and after some initial resistance in the regions of Kongsvinger and Elverum, their advanced column arrived at Röros before receiving any definite check. Their advance in the direction of Stoeren was hampered owing to the tunnels on the railway line having been blocked by the Norwegian forces, but the Germans, not to be outdone, endeavoured to take the Allies in the rear by dispatching small bodies of troops across the mountains—through the deep winter snows and by tracks which were little more than goat paths. Soon the Nazis were claiming the occupation of Stoeren and to have established a connection by land between Oslo and Trondheim.

Meanwhile, to the north of Trondheim the front was stabilized in the neighbourhood of Stenkjer, where according to an American journalist, Mr. Leland Stowe, cabling from a town on the Norwegian-Swedish frontier, a British force of two battalions—according to him, undertrained and deficient in anti-aircraft guns, 'planes, and field artillery—were routed by the Germans. This sensational story was denied by the War Office, which, however, admitted that British troops in this region had withdrawn, although they were not followed up by the enemy who were now reported to be

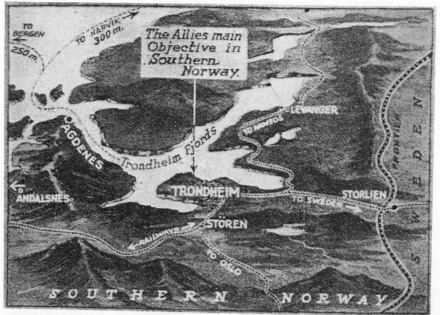

As this pictorial map shows, Trondheim is a veritable gateway to central Norway. It is situated on the shores of a deep-water fjord, and from it run several important railways. Agdenes, at the mouth of the fjord, is the site of a powerful coastal battery.

through that combination of treachery, bluff, and daring military initiative which stood the Germans in such good stead, Trondheim was garrisoned by a small but powerfully armed force under Colonel Weiss. Hardly had the Nazis established themselves in the town when they were threatened by Allied landings both to the north at Namsos and to the south at Aandalsnes. As soon as the Allied troops were brought ashore they were moved towards Trondheim by rail and were able to approach within fifty miles of the city before they encountered any serious resistance on the part of the Nazis.

With Trondheim threatened, the German commander in Oslo, General von Falkenhorst, dispatched strong forces northwards along the two almost parallel valleys, the Gudbrandsdal and the Osterdal, which act as natural highways from the comparatively low-lying country north of Oslo to the hills and dales of the Trondelag, Trondheim's fertile hinterland. Before the onward rush of the German mechanized columns the Norwegian troops, local levies hurriedly mobilized and ill-equipped, were forced

The advancing Germans were checked for a time—but only for a time, and the Allied troops were compelled to withdraw up the valley in the direction of Dombaas. Some miles to the south of this vitally important railway junction another line of defence was organized, and the Allies were reported to have received considerable reinforcements in the shape of British and French troops landed at ports on Nord Fjord and Sunndals Fjord, south-west and north-east of Aandalsnes respectively. In the Osterdal the German advance was remarkably

On this sketch map of south-central Norway are marked those towns which came into prominence in the course of the Allies' efforts to prevent the Germans in Oslo from linking up with their fellows at Trondheim. The white arrows indicate the Allied advances, while the black arrows show the approximate movements of the German troops.

Holland and Belgium, the Nazis' Latest Prey

The River Maas flows through the old town of Maastricht in Limburg, the southernmost limb of Holland. The Nazis captured a fortress of this important town on May 11 and crossed the river. Our photograph (above) shows the 13th-century bridge.

On May 12 the Allied High Command announced that the Germans had consolidated their position at Arnhem, an important railway junction on the Rhine. The town was one of the key positions in the Nazi drive towards the North Sea.

The Yssel River as it flows through low-lying ground into the Zuyder Zee is seen from the air in the photograph above. It was behind this river and the River Maas that the Dutch Army made a brave stand before the advancing German hordes.

The Moerdyk Bridge across the main estuary of the River Maas (right) is one of the most important strategic points in the Netherlands. It connects northern Holland with the south and Belgium, and carries the main railway line from Dordrecht to Antwerp. On May 14 Nazi troops crossed southward over this bridge.

The photograph, left, of a section of the Albert Canal with its steep concrete embankments shows what a formidable obstacle the Germans had to cross. Above, the Boulevard de la Sauvenière, one of the principal streets of Liége.

Picture-Diagram of the Gloster Gladiator Fighter

Main Oil Cooler

Vickers Gun

Petrol Tank

Cockpit Heater

850 H.P. Engine

Browning Gun

Ammunition Boxes

Internally Sprung Wheels

DETAIL OF PILOT'S FLYING SUIT

Jacket & Trousers Lined with Lambswool

Cockpit heated from engine

Sealed here

Cuffs and ankles sealed against cold

Zip fastened inside leg

Leather boot lined with lambswool

Planes parked round edge of frozen Lake

HAWORTH.

As the Secretary of State for Air announced in the House of Commons in the famous debate of May 8, 1940, a squadron of Gloster Gladiator fighters was dispatched to Norway in an attempt to check the German air power. These machines are not so fast as the Hurricanes and Spitfires, but are extremely manoeuvrable. In fact, the Gladiator, besides being the finest biplane ever produced, is probably one of the most useful all-round machines. Of all our machines it is the best suited to withstand the cold and rough usage on an expedition of this kind.

Engine and Performance

Powered with an 850-h.p. British Mercury IX air-cooled radial engine, the 'plane develops a maximum speed of 250 m.p.h. at 15,500 ft., with a service ceiling of 32,800 ft. The Gladiator takes less than six minutes to climb to 15,000 feet. The low landing speed of 63 m.p.h., and the brakes on the wheels, makes it comparatively easy to land the 'plane on restricted ground as shown in page 554.

Characteristics of the 'Plane

The cockpit is heated and together with the latest type of lined leather flying suits—which have often proved too hot over here—gives the pilot a chance to combat the harsh cold weather of the north. The fact that the Finnish air force used Gladiators for some time is further proof that they are capable of standing up to the job.

The Hawker Hurricane

Britain's High-Speed Single-Seater Fighter

Picture-Diagrams specially prepared by Haworth for
THE WAR ILLUSTRATED

Electric Gun Sighting-ring

Bullet-proof Wind-screen

Fuel Tank

Radio

4 Guns in Edge of Wing

Fuel Tanks in either Wing

Radiator

Rolls-Royce Merlin III Engine

4 Guns in Edge of Wing

Re-fuelling

Re-loading Guns in Wings

Re-fuelling & Re-arming of Hurricane" takes 10 Minutes

The purpose of the single-seater fighter is to intercept the enemy before he reaches his objective. And the 990 h.p. Hawker Hurricane with a top speed of 335 m.p.h., and a high rate of climb, being able to reach 19,680 feet in nine minutes, is ideal for the job. It has great endurance, a very heavy armament, and is extremely manoeuvrable, owing to the low wing-loading of 24.7 lbs. per square foot, as against the 31.4 lbs. per square foot of the German Messerschmitt 109 which has none of these advantages.

Hurricane Armament

The Hurricane is armed with eight machine-guns mounted in the wings, trained to a point about 200 yards ahead of the machine and each firing 1,200 rounds per minute. The long belts of ammunition contained in metal "tanks" in the wing are made up of armour-piercing, incendiary, and tracer bullets, which are carefully arranged to follow in the order calculated to give the best results. The effect is illustrated in page 631.

Refuelling with Special Petrol

When Hurricanes on patrol come in to refuel, special refuelling-lorries which are capable of delivering a great number of gallons per minute attend to several machines at once. The petrol used by these fighters is usually 100-octane fuel, which allows the Rolls-Royce "Merlin" III engine to develop a maximum of 1,050 h.p. Incidentally, the Germans are short of this grade of petrol and the Messerschmitts usually fly on 87-octane fuel.

IT WAS 'A COLOSSAL MILITARY DISASTER'

Superbly phrased and powerfully delivered, Mr. Churchill's statement to the House of Commons on June 4 was more, very much more—it was a clarion call to the nation to gird up its loins and out of defeat to win completest victory.

FROM the moment that the French defences at Sedan and on the Meuse were broken at the end of the second week of May, began Mr. Churchill, only a rapid retreat to Amiens and the south could have saved the British and French Armies who had entered Belgium, but this strategic fact was not immediately realized.

Moreover, he went on, a retirement of this kind would have involved almost certainly the destruction of the fine Belgian Army, of over 20 divisions, and the abandonment of the whole of Belgium. Therefore, when the force and scope of the German penetration was realized, and when the new French Generalissimo, General Weygand, assumed command in place of General Gamelin, an effort was made by the French and British Armies in Belgium to keep on holding the right hand of the Belgians and to give their own right hand to a newly created French Army, which was to have advanced across the Somme to grasp it.

However, the German eruption swept like a sharp scythe around the right and rear of the Armies of the north. Eight or nine armoured divisions, each of about 400 armoured vehicles of different kinds, cut off all communications between us and the main French Armies.

'Armoured Scythe' in Action

IT severed our own communications for food and ammunition, which ran first to Amiens and afterwards through Abbeville, and it sheared its way up the coast to Boulogne and Calais, and almost to Dunkirk. Behind this armoured and mechanized onslaught came a number of German divisions in lorries, and behind them again there plodded, comparatively slowly, the dull, brute mass of the ordinary German army and German people, always so ready to be led to the trampling down in other lands of liberties and comforts which they have never known in their own.

AFTER referring to the heroic resistance put up by Boulogne and Calais (see pages 627-8) against the "vast armoured scythe," the Premier continued :

The time gained enabled the Gravelines waterlines to be flooded and to be held by the French troops. Thus it was that the port of Dunkirk was kept open.

When it was found impossible for the Armies of the north to reopen their communications to Amiens with the main French Armies only one choice remained. It seemed, indeed, forlorn. The Belgian, British and French Armies were almost surrounded. Their sole line of retreat was to a single port and to its neighbouring beaches. They were pressed on every side by heavy attacks and far outnumbered in the air.

When a week ago today I asked the House to fix this afternoon as the occasion for a statement, I feared it would be my hard lot to announce from this box the greatest military disaster in our long history.

I thought—and some good judges agreed with me—that perhaps 20,000 or 30,000 men might be re-embarked. But it certainly seemed that the whole of the French First Army and the whole of the British Expeditionary Force north of the Amiens-Abbeville gap would be broken up in the open fields or else would have to capitulate for lack of food and ammunition.

That was the prospect a week ago; but another blow which might well have proved final was yet to fall upon us.

Treachery of King Leopold

THE King of the Belgians had called upon us to come to his aid. Had not this ruler and his Government severed themselves from the Allies who rescued their country from extinction in the late war, had they not sought refuge in what has proved to be a fatal neutrality, the French and British Armies might well at the very outset have saved not only Belgium but perhaps even Holland. Yet, at the last moment, when Belgium was already invaded, King Leopold called upon us to come to his aid, and, even at the last moment, we came. He and his brave, efficient Army, nearly half a million strong, guarded our eastern flank, and thus kept open our only line of retreat to the sea.

Suddenly, without prior consultation, with the least possible notice, without the advice of his Ministers, and upon his own personal act, he sent a plenipotentiary to the German Command, surrendered his Army, and exposed our whole flank and means of retreat.

The surrender of the Belgian Army compelled the British at the shortest notice to cover a flank to the sea of more than thirty miles in length, otherwise all would have been cut off and all would have shared the fate to which King Leopold had condemned the finest army his country had ever formed.

The enemy attacked on all sides with great strength and fierceness, and their main power, the power of their far more numerous Air Force, was thrown into the battle or else concentrated upon Dunkirk and the beaches. Pressing in upon the narrow exit, both from the east and from the west, the enemy began to fire with cannon upon the beaches by which alone the shipping could approach or depart. They sowed magnetic mines in the channels and seas, they sent repeated waves of hostile aircraft—sometimes more than 100 strong in one formation—to cast their bombs upon the single pier that remained, and upon the sand dunes on which the troops had their eyes for shelter. Their U-boats, one of which was sunk, and their motor launches took their toll of the vast traffic which now began.

For four or five days an intense struggle raged. All the armoured divisions—or what was left of them—together with great masses of German infantry and artillery, hurled themselves in vain upon the ever narrowing, ever contracting appendix within which the British and French Armies fought. Meanwhile the Royal Navy, with the willing help of countless merchant seamen, strained every nerve to embark the British and Allied troops. . . .

'A Miracle of Deliverance'

MR. CHURCHILL said that the vessels engaged were under an almost ceaseless hail of bombs and shells.

It was in conditions such as these that our men carried on with little or no rest for days and nights on end, making trip after trip across the dangerous waters, bringing with them, always, men whom they had rescued. The numbers they have brought back are the measure of their devotion and their courage.

The hospital ships which brought off many thousands of British and French wounded, being so plainly marked, were a special target for Nazi bombs, but the men and women on board them never faltered in their duty. Meanwhile the Royal Air Force, which had already been intervening in the battle so far as its range would allow from home bases, now used part of its main, metropolitan fighter strength and struck at the German bombers and the fighters which in large numbers protected them. This struggle was protracted and fierce. Suddenly the scene has cleared, the crash and thunder has for the moment—but only for the moment—died away.

A miracle of deliverance achieved by valour, by perseverance, by perfect discipline, by dauntless service, by resource, by skill, by unconquerable fidelity, is manifest to us all.

The enemy was hurled back by the retreating British and French troops. He was so roughly handled that he did not harry their departure seriously. The Royal Air Force engaged the main strength of the German Air Force and inflicted upon them losses of at least four to one, and the Navy, using nearly 1,000 ships of all kinds, carried over 335,000 men, French and British, out of the jaws of death to their native land, and to the tasks which lie immediately ahead.

We must be very careful not to assign to this deliverance the attributes of a victory. Wars are not won by evacuations.

But there was a victory inside this deliverance which should be noted. It was gained by the Air Force. Many of our soldiers coming back have not seen the Air Force at work ; they saw only the bombers which escaped its protective attack. They underrate its achievements. I have heard much talk of this, that is why I go out of my way to say this.

On Friday, May 31, 1940, Mr. Winston Churchill was present at a meeting of the Supreme War Council, it being his first attendance as Prime Minister. Mr. Churchill is seen above with M. Reynaud after the meeting. On his left is General Sir John Dill, the new Chief of the Imperial General Staff ; on the right of M. Reynaud is Mr. C. R. Attlee, Lord Privy Seal.

Wednesday, June 5, 1940

At 4 a.m. **Germans launched new offensive along Somme and Aisne** with massed infantry, tanks and aircraft. Battle became intense in regions of **Amiens, Péronne** and the **Ailette Canal.**

During night of June 4-5 Allied Air Forces carried out extensive raids into Germany, causing great damage in Ruhr and elsewhere. Oil storage tanks set ablaze at **Frankfurt** and **Mannheim.**

German raiders again attacked **Le Havre.** Six Nazi aircraft brought down by French fighters in Rouen region.

Thursday, June 6

German attack continued at all points between coast and Chemin des Dames. More than **2,000 tanks thrown against French lines.** Strong Allied resistance.

South-west of Lower Somme **German units infiltrated as far as R. Bresle,** and also near Ailette Canal. British troops holding sector on Lower Somme.

Allied Air Forces continued destruction of Rhineland railway system and factories, and made series of attacks over Somme front. French fighter units brought down 21 enemy aircraft.

German raiders crossed East and South-East Coasts at a number of points during nights of June 5-6 and 6-7. Incendiary and high explosive bombs dropped, but damage done was slight. Seven casualties.

M. Reynaud made changes in French Cabinet, five Ministers, including M. Daladier, being dropped.

Friday, June 7

Battle along Rivers **Bresle, Somme** and **Aisne** continued with great violence. Main thrust made north and east of **Soissons,** where **Germans crossed Ailette Canal** and reached heights bordering the Aisne.

French resisted vigorously, but at some points forward elements withdrew.

Enemy attacked below Péronne with 1,000 tanks, some of which infiltrated between French strong points. Big Nazi effort to cross Aisne at **Attigny** repulsed.

Allied Air Forces continued day and night to attack enemy lines of communication and numerous targets over fighting fronts.

During night of June 6-7 formations of R.A.F. heavy bombers successfully attacked oil refineries, aerodromes, etc., in South Belgium and North-West Germany. R.A.F. fighters destroyed 15 enemy aircraft.

During night **Heinkel bomber crashed in East Suffolk.** German aeroplane, flying low, machine-gunned South-East Coast town. Swedish steamer " Erik Frisell " sunk.

First V.C. of the war awarded posthumously to Capt. B. A. W. Warburton-Lee.

Concealed ammunition dumps in Ardennes bombed. Further raids made into North-West Germany.

During night of June 7-8 **French naval 'planes bombed** factories near **Berlin.**

Admiralty announced that H.M.S. "Carinthia," armed merchant cruiser, had been sunk by U-boat.

Sunday, June 9

German offensive increased in extent and violence. From Forges-les-Eaux **armoured units reached outskirts of Rouen and Pont de l'Arche,** on the Seine.

Enemy launched attack in Champagne along 25-mile front between **Château Porcien** and **Le Chesne. Parachute troops** were dropped north of **Vouziers** but were immediately surrounded.

Enemy pressure diminished in Bresle region and Aumale-Noyon sector, but was resumed south of Aisne near Soissons.

Heavy enemy raids round Paris, particularly in region of **Pontoise.**

Admiralty announced that contact had been made between British and German naval forces in northern waters on June 8.

France's Might is Humbled

On June 17, when Paris had fallen and the German mechanized columns were creating havoc in the very heart of France, Marshal Pétain appealed to Hitler for an armistice. It was not until four days later that the plenipotentiaries of France and Germany met— in the dramatic circumstances described in this chapter.

A T ten minutes past five on the morning of November 11, 1918, in a glade of the Forest of Compiègne, victorious France dictated to defeated Germany the terms of armistice. Twenty-two years later the roles were reversed. On June 21, 1940, in the same forest clearing, in the same railway coach, even seated at the same table and in the same chairs, the representatives of victorious Germany dictated the terms of surrender to the delegates of defeated France.

Beside the historic dining-car a guard of honour composed of German troops had been drawn up, and immediately in front of the Armistice memorial the Fuehrer's standard had been raised. In front of the dining-car high officers and guests of honour and distinguished members of the Nazi party awaited Hitler's arrival. At 3.15 in the afternoon he arrived, and a quarter of an hour later the French delegation, who had passed through the German lines at Tours and had spent the night in a Paris hotel, made their appearance.

Conqueror and conquered then entered the dining-car and took their places round the table. On Hitler's right sat Goering, Raeder, and von Ribbentrop, and on his left were Keitel, Brauchitsch, and Hess. On the opposite side of the table sat the French delegation—General Huntziger, General Bergeret, Admiral Leluc, and M. Noel. Then at the Fuehrer's order General Keitel read the preamble to the armistice conditions :

A T the order of the Leader and Supreme Commander of the German Defence Forces I have to make the following communication :

Trusting to the assurance given to the German Reich by the American President Wilson and confirmed by the Allied Powers, the German Defence forces in November 1918 laid down their arms. Thus ended a war which the German people and its Government did not want, and in which in spite of vastly superior forces the enemy did not succeed in defeating the German Army, the German Navy or the German Air Force.

At the moment of the arrival of the German Armistice Commission there began the breach of the promise solemnly given. On November 11, 1918, there began in this very train a period of suffering for the German people.

Whatever could be done to a nation in the way of dishonour and humiliation in human and material suffering began at this point. Broken promises and perjury were used against a nation which after over four years of heroic resistance had shown only one weakness—namely, that of believing the promises of democratic statesmen.

On September 3, 1939, twenty-five years after the outbreak of the World War Great Britain and France declared war on Germany without any reason. Now the war has been decided by arms. France is defeated. The French Government has asked the German Government to make known the German conditions for an armistice.

General de Gaulle leaving his headquarters in London, followed by an aide-de-camp. It was from this office that on June 22 he issued his call to Frenchmen in the Colonial Empire, to the French Navy, and to all his compatriots outside the jurisdiction of the Bordeaux Government, to continue to fight on for France.

TANKS ARE PART OF THE ENGLISH COUNTRYSIDE IN SUMMER NOW

People in many parts of Britain have grown accustomed to the sight and sound of tanks and other armoured fighting vehicles speeding through the village streets or lumbering along over open country during exercises. Today, however, these vehicles take on a new significance : Britain is in the battle zone, and the tanks are on active service ; light tanks like these, seen emerging from a narrow and tortuous country lane, will be in the forefront to repel the Nazi invader, should he effect a landing on our soil.

EVER A FIGHTER, THE PREMIER IS ALONGSIDE THE FIGHT

Determined as always to see for himself, the Prime Minister has visited many of Britain's coast defences. On August 28 he was at Dover when Nazi planes renewed their attack on the town and there was a fierce aerial fight overhead. Mr. Churchill, wearing a steel helmet, mounted to a vantage point and watched the progress of the battle with keen appreciation of the skill and daring of the British fighters.

TODAY in BRITAIN

London, August 13.

SEEING THE CRATER

German aeroplanes which drop their bombs on Britain's open country or suburban gardens are proving first-class collectors for the Red Cross funds.

There is a spontaneous rush, "to see the crater," the morning after and most householders who have exhibited their territory make a point of seeing to it that the Red Cross benefits. A couple of boy scouts are usually acquired to "pass the hat round" and many quite reasonable sums have been obtained by this means.

The Germans would give up their raids on Britain if they could realise that the raids tend to stiffen the British determination to fight on and win and that the areas raided carry on just as usual after the raid; except for such incidents as the sale for £18 of a machine-gunned hen (dead) not to speak of the demand for kittens born in a raid.

Many of the raiders have ended their careers in the North Sea or the English Channel. One rubber boat which the Germans carry in case of trouble has been on view in Selfridge's to help boost the campaign for the Women's Auxiliary Air Force. It has tin oars which you put together in sections and leather straps like the handles on a cabin trunk instead of rowlocks. It looked a pretty poor sort of craft for rowing in and a lot of the Nazi rubber boaters must have muttered, "Thank God for the British navy" since this war started.

⁎⁎

"TEMPORA..."

More and more Londoners seem to eat their lunch off their knees in the parks, gardens, squares and in City churchyards; wherever in fact there are flower-beds, shrubs or a bit of grass. In Millbank Gardens under the very shadow of the Houses of Parliament there is a large statue of Mrs. Pankhurst. It is within a few yards of where her fellow-workers used to chain themselves to the railings and yell "Votes for Women" till the police arrived.

The statue looks very calm as if to say, "Well, I told you so," but all around the base of it are deck-chairs full of girls who don't say a word because their mouths are full of sandwiches.

⁎⁎

FOOTBALL AGAIN

Football is in the news again with the announce- ment that the Football League Management Committee are to meet at Manchester shortly. August 31 sees the big kick-off in the London season when the 'Spurs meet West Ham at Totten- ham. West Ham, the winners of the first war cup competition, have already arranged a long list of fixtures including Clapton Orient and Southend.

Some folks are looking forward to a revival of old-fashioned football this winter for the players will have little chance to put a peace time polish on their work and the games they will play will obviously be a little slower than usual.

The boxing news is that Max Schmelling has joined the German parachute troops. He is rather over age—thirty-four—for this work but reports say that he made a special request to be allowed to join. If he meets the Home Guard with a Tommy gun when he lands, he will feel worse than when Joe Louis had done with him in New York two years back.

London, August 16.

BRITAIN CAN "TAKE IT"

There has been a good deal of talk this week about the shower of Nazi airmen which has been falling viâ parachutes over South Coast towns, the R.A.F. having made the Heinkels, Junkers and Messerschmitts too uncomfortable to sit in any longer.

The reception of these visitors has varied with their behaviour on landing. One of them who look- ed like trying to run for it, when captured by some railwaymen in a field near the line, had his boots and socks removed. The cornfield where he had come down had just been cut and the stubble is painful to bare feet.

On the other hand another Nazi fell to the lot of an old lady living in a country cottage. She asked him in for a cup of tea and, while he was drinking it, she quietly 'phoned for the police.

These German flyers say some quaint things on hitting Britain. Some of them speak good English. Many of them not so good English. One of them said to his captors, "I'm a German aviator. Will you take me to the R.A.F. please?". This must have sounded a little queer at the time considering the tremendous trouble he had just been taking to get away from the R.A.F.

In another instance all five of a bomber's crew jumped out and the pilot was the last to be pulled out of some bushes. He seemed worried about the expense of it all and grumbled, "Shell got port engine. Shell got middle engine. A million marks gone."

Of course not all the Nazi pilots have been as tactful. Some have spat at their rescuers and others have just been sillily rude and persisted in "heil hitlering."

But the ones who could speak little English were the ones who have caught popular attention. Their remarks were in keeping too with the spirit of the British people to-day. The air war is now in full blast. Serious air raids are now taking place in Bri- tain. The casualties are light so far but they are casualties none the less. And even if Nazi bombers miss their real objective they are damaging private houses and property in the area of the raid.

But the spirit of the people of Britain has not wavered a jot. News from Germany viâ neutral sources makes it clear that the areas raided by the R.A.F. empty at top speed and there will be a rush to Poland or Czechoslovakia or somewhere that might be a bit out of the way of British airmen. But in Britain no such thing. Noone can doubt to-day, that Britain can "take it."

Other flying news in London this week is Cap- tain Kelly Rogers, who piloted the *Clare*, the big British flying-boat, across the Atlantic in just over twelve hours the other day bringing a message from the Mayor of New York. It was addressed to the Lord Mayor of London at the Mansion House and read, "Keep your chin up, London."

And we shall.

⁎⁎

There are twenty-one music-halls running shows this week, including the Holborn Empire which has reopened again. You can see there such old friends as Fred Emny and Arthur Prince and Florence Desmond. And it is real old "halls" stuff, not revue or crazy gang.

"THE LONDONER"

London, August 23

The Home Front has had its most ter- rific week of the war and is still as firm as ever.

Naturally the coast towns got the worst of it but raiders did succeed in reaching Greater London, bombing su- burbs in the South West and Croydon. Not one of the machines that attacked Croydon got home again.

In the seven days since my last let- ter 570 German aircraft have been des- troyed in raids on this country and something like 1,400 of their crews kill- ed or captured. Against this we lost 111 'planes and 55 men, 56 others escaping by parachute.

Civilian casualties have not yet been published but the damage done seems to have been mostly to private proper- ty rather than to anything that could be called of military importance. The idea seems to have been to break the nerve of the folks at home. In fact it was the Nazis who were overwhelmed, many of their formations breaking up in face of our fighters and turning for home.

"IT'S STILL HOME"

The people with smashed homes have been fine. At Croydon twenty or thirty families have needed looking after because their homes have been too bad- ly damaged to live in. Neighbours, the local authorities and the Salvation Ar- my between them have seen to it that all have a roof over their head while the valuers departments have been busy with claims for compensation. Mean- while the builders men have been hard at it patching roofs and mending win- dows.

And Pa and Ma carry things out into the garden from broken sitting-rooms and battered kitchens while the repairs are being made. "It's still home," they say as the rubbish is cleared away. "And they won't bomb the same house twice." In fact, Pa's feeling fairly plea- sed with himself as he takes stock of the week.

"Headlines Tell All!"

A friend of mine who works in G.H.Q. claims that he is so hard-worked that he never has time to read the papers. At best, he says, he skims through the headlines at breakfast.

"Headlines," he claims, "tell you all that you want to know in pithy and succinct language—there is no need to wade through a long journalistic rigmarole to get at the facts."

One morning recently, having half-a-minute or so to spare at breakfast, he seized a paper, opened it and scanned the headlines according to plan. And as he read his jaw fell and a look of horror crept slowly over his features.

"H.Q., M.E. Badly Knocked About." He gulped and went on to the next headline.

"Gunners Fail in Race with Time."

That wasn't quite so bad, but the next item was staggering.

"R.A.F. Crushed at Heliopolis."

And then it went from bad to worse.

"Aussies Poor Show at Heluan."

"Base Hospital in Danger."

"H.M. Ships defeated at Alexandria."

The final headline was disastrous: "Collapse of G.H.Q., M.E."

He thought it over for a long time. Then, realising that it was too late for him to do anything about it, he put away the paper with a sigh and went to Gezira and spent the day playing golf. It would have been better if he had watched the cricket.

MR. CHURCHILL GREETS NEW ZEALANDERS: on his way to the House Mr. Winston Churchill stops and chats to New Zealanders who have recently arrived in London.

The Lighter Side

BRITISH ARMY IN EGYPT à la ROME RADIO

What do the Italians think of the British army in Egypt? Rome radio kindly provides the answer:—

"Everything has gone according to programme and, as Graziani telegraphed the Duce, the enemy has been thrown out of Sidi Barrani in confusion. 130 kms. of Egyptian territory have been taken and cleaned up by these generous Italian soldiers who have the satisfaction that only a victory can give. The General has no need of propaganda on war aims for such soldiers.

"The question now arises as to what further obstacles have to be overcome.

"It is estimated that before war was declared the British had some 60,000 men (40,000 British and 20,000 coloured). Since then a sort of potpourri has arrived—Ghurkas ceremoniously disembarked, some troops from Palestine, refugees from Shanghai and Somaliland. It is a bit difficult to calculate but we may say that Wavell has, between black and white, some 200,000 to 250,000 troops.

"These soldiers are amply provided with everything, including every comfort...

"And so British G.H.Q., don't come out tomorrow and say that the Italians had superior numbers, equipment, etc."

Well, there's Rome's opinion of us. But Graziani will find this potpourri a bit harder to digest than he thinks!

DIARY of the WAR

Sunday, September 15

The R.A.F. claims the biggest "bag" of the war when it brings down 185 German raiders over Britain. 131 are bombers. Our losses are thirty fighters but ten pilots are safe.

The Minister of Aircraft Production announces that gifts from the public in Britain and overseas have reached a total of £5,047,000.

A British fighter pilot who had baled out is captured by land girls armed with spades and pitchforks. It takes him some time to convince them that he is a British pilot. Britain is on the alert.

Monday, September 16

The official German News Agency admits that German machines raiding London have been met with an "unusual and surprising" concentration of British fighters.

Since the outbreak of war 2,143 German 'planes have been shot down in attacks on Britain of which 2,069 since June 18.

It is announced that just over 2,000 civilians have been killed in Britain as a result of aerial bombardment. 8,000 have been wounded. Casualties among the fighting services amount to 250.

Wednesday, September 18

An agreement is reached between Britain and the Spanish Government regarding the amount of imports of oil into Spain. It is officially regarded as satisfactory to both sides.

In raids on London three famous Oxford Street stores are hit and bombs are dropped on Lambeth Walk. British bombers keep up their relentless and almost continuous attacks on the invasion ports.

Thursday, September 19

The Australian Federal Government is informed that New Caledonia has broken away from the Vichy government and has joined General de Gaulle, who has appointed M. Santot as his representative in place of General Denis as Governor.

A Vichy despatch says that the Public Prosecutor at Riom has asked for an indictment against M. Daladier and General Gamelin.

Saturday, September 21

The British Ministry of Aircraft Production announces that deliveries of American 'planes now amount to five hundred monthly.

Mr. Hugh Dalton, Minister of Economic Warfare, announces that the R.A.F. have visited ninety per cent of Germany's synthetic oil factories and eighty per cent of her oil refineries.

The Royal Navy add their weight to that of the Army and the R.A.F. by shelling the advancing Italian columns from Sidi Barrani to Libya.

Revealing example of German propaganda methods

BOMBS ON BUCKINGHAM PALACE

"Bombs on Buckingham Palace: retaliation for bombs on German national monuments." (Caption under photographs of the Palace in the "Warschauer Zeitung" of Sept. 15).

*

"Some German bombers, Dornier 17 type, bombed oil-dumps near Buckingham Palace yesterday afternoon." (German Official News Agency DNB Sept. 14).

*

"The whole story about Buckingham Palace shows all the elements of a plant...so to speak—an "Athenia" case on land. The present British Prime Minister has already brought off more complicated things than

putting bombs in the Palace... never in her history has Germany attempted to kill the Sovereign of a State at war with her." (Broadcast from Deutschlandsender on Sept. 14).

*

"Above all the King of England is the supreme commander of the English army" (Dr. Otto Kreigk, "Der Montag" cabled by Transocean Sept. 17).

*

"About bombs which fell on Buckingham Palace: to German minds it seems only fair that the ruling class, and with them their symbol of power and royalty, should run the same risks as any poor family." (Broadcast in English from Bremen. Sept. 14).

Sunday, September 22

An Italian raid Haifa kills 32 civilians and injures 6

**

Attacks on Britain are on a small scale but individual raiders scatter their bombs over the countryside in the South East of England flying at great height.

Monday, September 23

The s.s. "City of Benares" (6,980 tons) taking 90 children and their escorts to Canada under the Overseas Reception Board evacuation scheme is torpedoed and sunk in mid-Atlantic. 83 children lose their lives.

**

Japanese troops invade Indo-China two hours before the expiration of the 72-hour ultimatum. The French troops offer resistance for two hours and then sign an agreement bringing hostilities to an end.

**

The Mullah of Bhutan calls for a "Jehad" (Holy War) against Italy in a sermon lasting four hours at Peshawar.

Wednesday, September 25

Senor Serrano Suner, Spanish Minister of the Interior, has a long talk with von Ribbentrop in Berlin. The subject of Africa is believed to have figured in Senor Suner's talks.

*

The Italian press takes up a virulent campaign against America and the Axis "hate" campaign against Greece is intensified.

**

It is announced from Helsinki that German troops on leave from Norway will be allowed to pass through Finland.

Thursday, September 26

An official communique from Rome admits the loss of a destroyer in the Ionian Sea.

**

His Majesty's submarine "H. 49" attacks an enemy convoy of eight supply vessels and scores direct hits on two. Another submarine, the "Tuna," destroys a large enemy supply ship.

**

The Canadian armed merchant-cruiser "Prince Robert" captures the German express cargo-boat "Weser" off the coast of Mexico.

**

A hundred French aircraft drop over three hundred bombs in an attack on Gibraltar. Many of the bombs fall in the sea but later the Lyons radio announces "The British squadron having ceased their attack on Dakar, reprisals against Gibraltar have been suspended."

Alexandria smiles !

*T*hat which Amiens was for the muddy weary troops on the Somme twenty-two years ago, so is Alexandria to-day for the sand-weary bronzed men of the Western Desert.

Though the blackout is observed with a strictness contrasting darkly with careless Cairo, Alexandria—despite frequent air raids—is a gay city, Mecca of the troops from the war zone to the west.

It is a city of a thousand reunions, for in the crowded cabarets and hotel lounges meet again old comrades who remember a younger Bill at Arras, a little less bald Bert at Suvla and the still genial Jimmy of the foretop at Jutland. The New Armies have their reunions too—the first for many since Dunkerque.

Alexandria wears a gay gown. Her beaches belie the Italian radio rot that the city is a ruin. One can drive along the four miles of sea front without seeing a bomb crater or damaged building.

One meets the Empire-at-arms where syncopation sets the feet a'tapping and makes one forget that "leave's up" in the morning.

Australians, New Zealanders, Maoris, Rhodesians, men from all the counties and green shires of England, Scotland, Wales and Ireland mingle merrily in Alexandria.

Adding a colourful note are hundreds of British nurses in red, grey, blue and white—and if there is romance to add spice to Alexandria's dish then it is in the traditions of the city.   H.S.W.L.

R.A.F. OFFENSIVE

*T*he fact that it is the R.A.F. which has so far delayed the German invasion of Britain is now generally realised.

This achievement is so important that it has overshadowed other aspects of the R.A.F.'s activities and, as a result, the extent and value of the air offensive against the Reich is apt to be overlooked and underestimated.

Even when viewed purely quantatively and without the assistance of a map and of specific information, the major R.A.F. raids over Germany and German-occupied territories provide impressive figures and give some indication of the vigour of this offensive.

Thus, between July 10 and October 1 of this year 145 important raids have been directed against German naval and military objectives and concentrations.

Between May 10 and October 1, 235 aerodromes and sea-plane bases have been bombed whilst 475 attacks have been made against road and rail communications, marshalling yards and docks. Moreover, Berlin has been severely raided fifteen times.

Crippling Effect on German Trade

These raids have not only succeeded in upsetting the Nazis' plans for the invasion of Britain but they have also served to cripple Germany by inflicting severe damage upon her vital life organs.

The destruction of barges in French Channel ports where they had been assembled for the invasion of Britain does not only represent a severe blow to Germany's military machine but also an equally, and possibly a severer one, to her home trade. Much of this is barge-borne and transported upon inland waterways.

At the KIWI CLUB

f there could be anything that would make it worth while to be ill, it is he process of getting better. In the ays before the war this meant grapes, asty morsels of food, plenty of books nd cigarettes to hand and time to indulge in that most excellent occupation —doing nothing.

In war everything is changed and ven the process of "getting better" is not quite so pleasant. But in Egypt omething is being done to make things more pleasant for the convalescent, and he Kiwi Club—for New Zealanders— s one of these things.

The Kiwi Club stands well up, with fine view miles away to the Pyramids. A house agent could write a poem about the view. Inside, the atmosphere is pleasantly homely with bright coloured upholstery and plenty of easy chairs. And the brick fireplace will make it a cosy spot for the winter. Yes, t's almost worth while being ill even n war time!

In the course of his tour of the Middle East, Mr. Eden, Secretary of State for War, found time—as only busy men can find time—to visit the convalescent men at the Kiwi—a club which like others largely owes its foundation and continued existence to the inspiration and initiative of Lady Lampson as president of the British Red Cross in Egypt.

Lady Lampson was among those present to welcome the Secretary of State for War—and the photographs in this page were taken on the occasion of Mr. Eden's visit.

A delightful study in light and shade taken during Mr. Eden's visit to the Kiwi Club

Friday, September 27

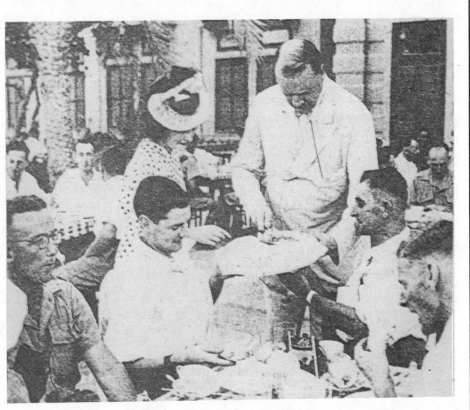

It is announced over the Berlin radio that a ten-year military, political and economic pact has been signed between Germany, Italy and Japan.

**

The Germans lose one hundred and thirty-three aircraft in their attacks on Britain to-day making a total of over a thousand for the month for the second month in succession.

**

Turkey and Roumania conclude two new trade agreements whereby Turkey will get petrol and fuel oils in exchange for raw materials for the manufacture of textiles.

**

Forty-six survivors of the "City of Benares" land in a North British port after drifting in an open boat for eight days.

**

The first flotilla of the United States destroyers which have been transferred to Great Britain arrive in a British port.

CLUB FOR CONVALESCENTS
H.E. Lady Lampson, wife of the British Ambassador to Egypt. opened the Kiwi Club at Helwan last Saturday. The club will be for the use of convalescent New Zealand soldiers. Photo shows H.E. Sir Miles Lampson helping Lady Lampson to cut the cake decorated with the New Zealand emblem, the Kiwi.

John Bull and Uncle Sam Keep Rolling Along!

The war is coming very near to America—so near that, with a speed and unanimity
which would have been altogether out of the question only a few months ago, the U.S.A.
is not only adding to her own defences but is abandoning her long-cherished and
carefully-preserved isolation.

SITTING at his desk at the White House,
President Roosevelt greeted the news-
papermen on August 16 with his customary affability. Indeed, he made it clear
that he was particularly glad to see them,
because he had three announcements to
make of very great importance, present
and future.

When the pressmen were all attention the
President announced in slow, carefully-
chosen words that the United States Government had entered into conversations with
the British Government with regard to the
acquisition of naval and air bases for the
defence of the Western Hemisphere, and
especially of the Panama Canal.

This was indeed headline news, but the
President had not finished. Mr. Roosevelt
went on to say that, in addition to conferring
with the British Government, his Government was carrying on conversations with the
Canadian Government concerning the defence of America. Finally, he announced
that, at the invitation of Mr. Churchill,
military and naval officers of the U.S.A.
were already in Britain as observers of the
great battle now raging.

It was understood that a day or two before
Mr. Roosevelt and Mr. Churchill had been
in communication—presumably by way of
the Transatlantic telephone—and had discussed the possibility of the U.S.A. leasing
naval and air bases from Great Britain.
The situation of the bases was not made
public, but it was generally believed that the
negotiations concerned Newfoundland, Bermuda, and that great chain of British islands
composed of the Bahamas, Jamaica, Leeward
and Windward Islands and Trinidad, and
British Guiana on the mainland of South
America. Bases established in any of these
territories would supplement the present

American naval and
air bases in Cuba,
Puerto Rico, and
the Panama Canal
zone, and would
obviously constitute
an immense rein-
forcement to the
defences of the
Panama Canal, per-
haps the most vital
of America's lines
of communication.

In effect, the
Caribbean Sea
would be closed
against unwelcome
intruders—and on
the subject of in-
truders Mr. Churchill
and President
Roosevelt may be
relied upon to think
alike. Only one
non-American
Power threatens
the safety of the
Canal and the in-
tegrity of some or
all of the Latin-
American republics,
and that power is Nazi Germany.

On this map America's principal naval and air
bases guarding the entrance to the Panama Canal
are shown by crosses. The white circles indicate
British possessions where the United States
hopes to lease other bases.
Courtesy of the "Daily Mail"

So much for the southern defences of the
U.S.A. Turning now to the north, we see
that vast undefended frontier—the longest
undefended frontier in the world—which for
nearly 3,000 miles separates the U.S.A. and
Canada. America has no fear of Canadian
aggression, just as Canada has no fear of
American designs on her territory. But such
is the range of modern aircraft that it is not
outside the bounds of possibility that Hitler

should attempt to
establish air bases
on the frozen shores
of America's far
north, as well as in
Greenland and Ice-
land. It was with
intense interest and
considerable relief
that Americans
learnt that Canadian
and British troops
were holding Ice-
land against Hitler;
and they greeted
with a chorus of
approval President
Roosevelt's an-
nouncement that an
arrangement was
being negotiated
with Canada where-
by the U.S.A. would
move troops to
Canada whenever it
might be necessary
to repel a threat
to the security of
the one country or
the other.

On August 17
President Roosevelt met Mr. Mackenzie
King, the Canadian Prime Minister, at
Ogdensburg on the American side of the
St. Lawrence, and the meeting resulted in
an agreement that a Permanent Joint Board
on Defence should be set up to commence
immediately studies relating to sea, land,
and air problems. In a broad sense, the
authorized statement declared, it would consider the defence of the northern half of
the Western Hemisphere.

Two years before, when making his famous
goodwill visit to Canada, President Roosevelt had made the declaration that " I give to
you the assurance that the people of the
United States will not stand idly by if
domination of Canadian soil is threatened
by any other empire"; and two days later
Premier Mackenzie King had said that
"We, too, have our obligations as a good
friendly neighbour, and one of them is to
see that at our own instance our country is
made as immune from attack or possible
invasion as we can reasonably be expected
to make it; and that, should the occasion
ever arise, enemy forces should not be able
to pursue their way by land, sea, or air to
the United States across Canadian territory."
Now the understanding and the resolve
were carried a big step further. The U.S.A.
made it as plain as could be that an attack
on Canada would be an attack on the
U.S.A., and would be resisted at once by the
great republic with all her armed might.

Closely linked in the popular mind with
the question of bases and the defence conversations with Canada—though the con-
nexion was carefully disowned by President
Roosevelt—was the suggestion that the
U.S.A. should sell a number of out-of-date
destroyers to Great Britain. In the matter
of destroyers the U.S.A. Navy is the strongest

The assurance given by Lord Lloyd, Britain's Colonial Secretary, to the Bermuda House of
Assembly in August 1940, that "there is no question of Bermuda, or any part of it, being separated
from the British Empire," followed close upon a visit of the Duke of Windsor to the island on his
way to the Bahamas. His Royal Highness is here seen inspecting a naval guard of honour on his
arrival in Bermuda on August 8.

The Destroyers Are Ready—Will Britain Get Them?

Here, in this remarkable photograph of Philadelphia Dockyard, are some 130 of the American warships which were laid up after the last war. Nearly all are destroyers, of which it is hoped that at least 50 will be transferred to the British Navy. Most of these are of the same type, of about 1,100 tons, with a speed on trials of 35 knots.
Photo, Central Press

in the world, with its 237 destroyers actually built and 60 more on the stocks ; but of the former, 167 are "obsolete," in the sense that they are more than 16 years old ; in fact, they were built towards the end of the last war. For some time before the present war most of them had been lying in the American naval yards, but when war broke out in Europe President Roosevelt ordered that they should be reconditioned so that they could be employed on the neutrality patrol in the North Atlantic—" to watch what is going on," as the President put it.

On August 4, in a broadcast to the American nation, General Pershing, who was Commander-in-Chief of the American Expeditionary Force in 1917, urged that the United States should make available to Britain at least 50 of these over-age destroyers as part of its help in defending democracy and assisting the security of the U.S.A. If the destroyers so sent helped to save the British Fleet, then America herself might be saved from another war. " We shall be failing in our duty to America," he added, " if we do not do it."

The suggestion was taken up in many quarters, and it was generally believed that President Roosevelt himself strongly favoured it. As for his opponents of the Republican Party, Mr. Wendell Wilkie, in the speech accepting his nomination as Republican candidate for the Presidency, at least gave his tacit approval when he said that "We must honestly face our relationship with Great Britain. We must admit that the loss of the British Fleet would greatly weaken our defence. This is because the British Fleet has for years controlled the Atlantic, leaving us free to concentrate on the Pacific. If the British Fleet were lost or captured, the Atlantic might be dominated by Germany, a power hostile to our way of life, controlling in that event most of the ships and ship-building facilities in Europe. This would be a calamity for us. We might be exposed to attack on the Atlantic. Our defence would be weakened until we could build a navy and air force strong enough to defend both coasts."

Before the destroyers could be sold to Britain, however, it might be necessary to repeal a law passed in 1917 forbidding the sale of vessels constructed for the U.S.A. Navy, and perhaps special legislation would be involved. It was suggested that the destroyers might be transferred to Canada instead of to Britain direct, or that they might be disposed of to private firms as "scrap" on the understanding that they should be resold to Britain. Whatever the method adopted, the American public welcomed the idea that the destroyers should be made available for Britain, more particularly in view of Mr. Churchill's declaration to the Commons on August 20 that His Majesty's Government had informed the United States Government. "spontaneously, and without being asked or offered any inducement," that they were ready to place defence facilities at their disposal by leasing sites in our Transatlantic possessions.

They welcomed it, in a word, as but one illustration of that working together which, to quote Mr. Churchill again, would cause America and Britain to become "somewhat mixed up together in some of their affairs for mutual and general advantage." With gladness in their hearts they heard him applaud the process of Anglo-American mingling. "Like the Mississippi, it just keeps rolling along. Let it roll. Let it roll on full flood, inexorable, irresistible, benignant, to broader lands and better days."

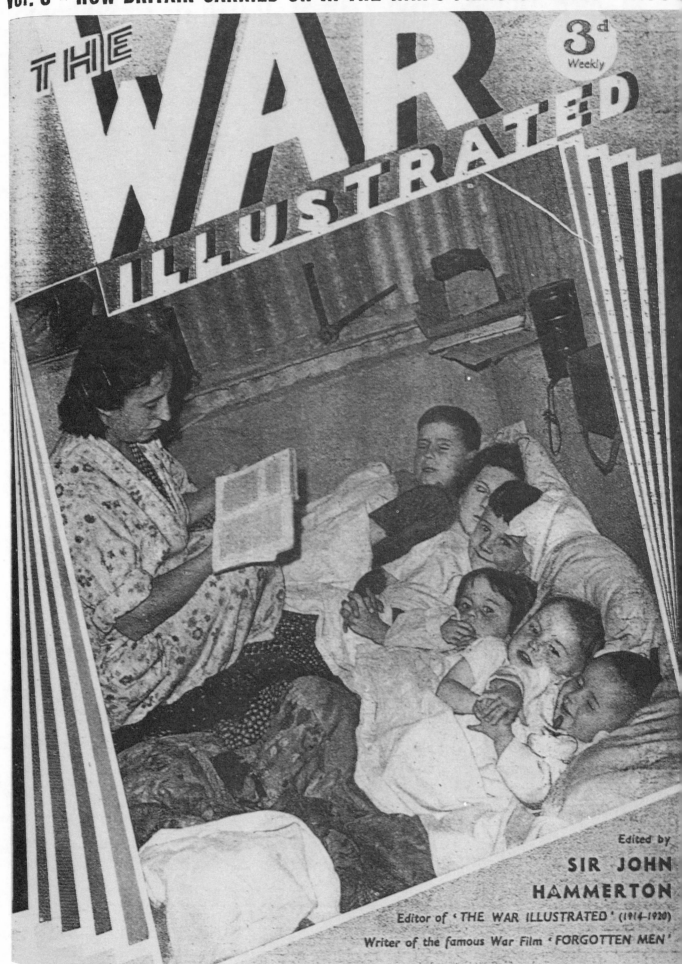

THE WAR ILLUSTRATED

3ᵈ Weekly

Edited by

SIR JOHN HAMMERTON

Editor of 'THE WAR ILLUSTRATED' (1914-1920)

Writer of the famous War Film 'FORGOTTEN MEN'

Bedtime Story in the Anderson!

Learn the Anatomy of a Barrage Balloon!

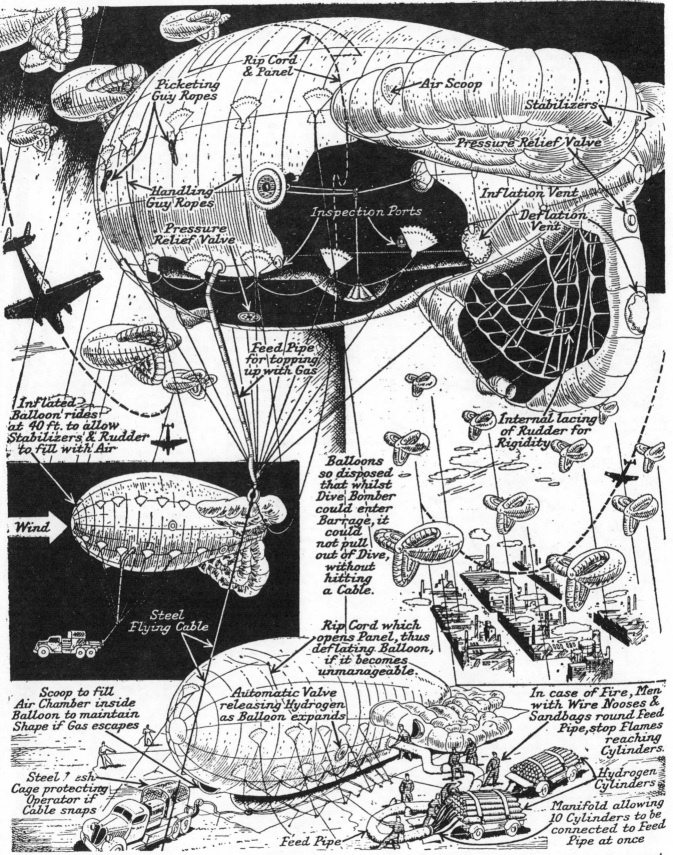

Rip Cord & Panel

Picketing Guy Ropes

Air Scoop

Stabilizers

Pressure Relief Valve

Handling Guy Ropes

Inspection Ports

Inflation Vent

Deflation Vent

Pressure Relief Valve

Feed Pipe for topping up with Gas

Inflated Balloon rides at 40 ft. to allow Stabilizers & Rudder to fill with Air

Internal lacing of Rudder for Rigidity

Balloons so disposed that whilst Dive Bomber could enter Barrage, it could not pull out of Dive, without hitting a Cable.

Wind

Steel Flying Cable

Rip Cord which opens Panel, thus deflating Balloon, if it becomes unmanageable.

Scoop to fill Air Chamber inside Balloon to maintain Shape if Gas escapes

Automatic Valve releasing Hydrogen as Balloon expands

In case of Fire, Men with Wire Nooses & Sandbags round Feed Pipe, stop Flames reaching Cylinders.

Steel Mesh Cage protecting Operator if Cable snaps

Hydrogen Cylinders

Manifold allowing 10 Cylinders to be connected to Feed Pipe at once

Feed Pipe

High up in the sky float the balloons that constitute the barrage which the Nazi dive-bombers most certainly do not like. Looked at from the ground some thousands of feet below, the balloons seem to be simple things enough; closer inspection makes it clear that in fact theirs is quite a complicated anatomy. The principal details of their construction are revealed in this page of drawings, and it will be realized that to a balloon's making there goes a wealth of ingenuity and labour. Another point brought out by the diagram is that the way in which the balloons are disposed in the sky makes it impossible for a dive-bomber who has had the temerity to enter the barrage to pull out of his dive without hitting a cable and so crashing to earth. There have even been cases of a raider meeting his end by crashing into one of the balloons themselves. Many facts about our barrage balloons have been given in earlier pages, and opposite we tell of the way in which "wounded" balloons are made fit for return to duty; here let us add that when filled with some 20,000 cubic feet of gas the balloons are 66 feet long and 30 feet high; some 600 separate pieces of fabric, amounting in all to over 1,000 yards of 42-inch material go to the making of one balloon; and the original cost of a balloon is about £500, while the gas alone costs £50.

The Grenadiers Lived Up To Their Reputation

Continuing our series of chapters describing the fighting of the B.E.F. in France in the early summer of 1940, we now give the story of the Grenadier Guards, who did magnificent work in covering the retreat to Dunkirk. It is based on information received from official sources, and makes a little epic of amazing gallantry and fortitude.

IT was into no unknown country that three battalions of the Grenadier Guards advanced on May 11, 1940, when the B.E.F. was rushed into Belgium in answer to Leopold's appeal. The Grenadiers fought their first action at Dunkirk in 1658—that Dunkirk to which nearly 300 years later they were to make a fighting retreat. On their colours are " Namur 1695 " and the names

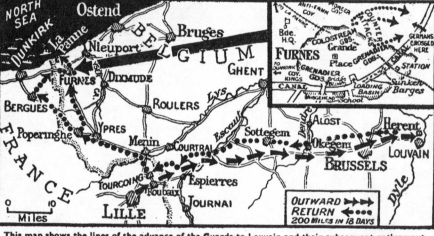

This map shows the lines of the advance of the Guards to Louvain and their subsequent retirement. The map inset, showing the counter-attack at Furnes, is from a sketch map by Brigadier J. A. C. Whitaker, who was himself at Furnes. Top, one of the Grenadier Guards lights his pipe.
Photo, British Official : Crown Copyright ; map courtesy of "The Daily Telegraph"

of Marlborough's four great victories—Blenheim, Ramillies, Oudenarde, and Malplaquet—and Waterloo. Then during the Great War the Grenadiers were continuously in action in Flanders : Mons, Ypres, Passchendaele and Lys are but a few of their battle-honours earned in the four years' campaign. Now they were in Flanders again.

Battalions which we may call " X " and " Y " advanced rapidly from the French frontier to take over part of the line of the River Dyle at Louvain. " Y " battalion was in support of " X "; " Z " battalion, belonging to a different corps, was in reserve behind the Dyle farther to the south. Actual fighting began on May 14, when strong enemy fighting patrols engaged " X " battalion in Louvain and along the railway to the north. At the same time there was considerable enemy air activity and shelling. Sniping by Fifth Columnists and parachutists added to the difficulties.

On the following day some enemy troops succeeded in infiltrating between " X " battalion and that on its right. An immediate counter-attack by a company with some Bren gun carriers drove the Germans out and restored the situation. Next, there was trouble on the left where the Germans crossed a canal

and established a machine-gun post. This was engaged and destroyed by the battalion's mortars.

Nothing of moment occurred on the next day, although both " X " and " Y " battalions were subjected to heavy shelling. But the German thrust through the French armies farther to the south had turned the line of the Dyle, and the British were ordered to withdraw to positions farther back on the River Dendre near Ninove. This was accomplished in orderly fashion despite bombing and machine-gun-attacks by enemy aircraft and the crowding of the roads by refugees and straggling Belgian soldiers.

On the Dendre, on May 18, the three battalions found themselves side by side. Presently, a German patrol of motor-cycles headed by a motor-car appeared on the opposite bank of the river, just as the commander of one company of " Y " battalion was making a reconnaissance. He himself opened fire with an anti-tank rifle and knocked out the car. A burst from a Bren gun then swept the motor-cyclists, who took refuge in

a house, and mortar fire destroyed the house. No more trouble was experienced from the enemy patrol, but in the fighting which now ensued the sniping activities of Fifth Columnists continued to be very troublesome.

By this time the German break-through to the south necessitated a new withdrawal to the line of the River Escaut (Scheldt). The Grenadier battalions took up positions on the western bank of the river, with their left on Helchin. On May 21 the enemy opened violent artillery, mortar and machine-gun fire and launched numerous determined attacks. These were repulsed, but in one place a crossing was forced and some companies of " Z " battalion had to fall back. The position was under direct enemy observation, there was no cover, and every movement drew destructive fire. The crew of a Bren gun carrier did splendid work driving across country and spotting the positions of the enemy machine-guns. A counter-attack was immediately ordered, and it was then that Lance-Corporal H. Nicholls picked up a Bren gun and, firing from the hip as he ran, silenced three machine-guns and inflicted heavy casualties on massed enemy infantry who were forced back across the Escaut. For this action Lance-Corporal Nicholls, was awarded the V.C. (*see page 139*).

" X " and " Y " battalions held the Escaut position for four days, before withdrawing to a prepared position on the Gort Line east of Roubaix, which they held for another three or four days. On the Gort Line a patrol of " Y " battalion had an interesting experience. It was reconnoitring a farm when the farmer offered the men coffee and then disappeared. Within 20 minutes the patrol was surrounded by the enemy. It put up a spirited resistance, killing many Germans, and suffered no casualties.

When the decision was taken to evacuate the B.E.F., the battalions were soon on the move again in the direction of Dunkirk. " Z " battalion had just crossed the River Lys after a long and tiring march when it was learnt that the enemy had broken through on the right, between Commines and Ypres, and that the battalion was to restore the situation. It made a counter-attack and, after a hazardous advance across open country, the battalion reached its objective and held it in spite of repeated and determined enemy efforts. Eventually it was ordered to withdraw to Messines and then it made its way to Moeres, where it was ordered to be ready to support a brigade which was being hard-pressed south of Furnes. The ground was reconnoitred but the battalion's services were not called upon.

Fierce Fighting at Furnes

Meanwhile, " X " and " Y " battalions marched on Furnes, where again there was a danger of the enemy breaking through. A reconnaissance party consisting of the Commanding Officer of " Y " and two company commanders came under fire and were all hit. A young officer found them lying in an exposed position in the main street of the town which was raked by machine-gun fire. Displaying complete disregard of his own safety, under heavy machine-gun and rifle fire, he carried the Commanding Officer who was dead and the two company commanders who were wounded into the doorway of a house. But the enemy's fire was so heavy that no stretcher-bearers could approach, and an entry had to be forced from the back.

" X " and " Y " battalions took up positions and were subjected to an intense and accurate bombardment which was obviously directed by enemy agents on the spot, and a telephone was actually found in the church tower. A reserve ammunition truck was hit and set on fire, but the mortar bombs were unloaded before they could explode and were put to good use in blowing up two German mortar positions. Many houses in the town were burning furiously, and the situation was made still more uncomfortable by the fact that little artillery support was available and no counter-battery fire could be given. Meanwhile, the enemy launched repeated and determined attacks and attempted to cross the canal on rubber boats. All these attempts were frustrated ; a section of " Y " battalion under a lance-corporal drove out and killed 20 Germans while itself suffering only one casualty.

Farther to the north two line battalions were hard pressed and a gap was opened between them. Soon after midday news reached " Y " battalion headquarters that the enemy was crossing the canal unopposed. The same young officer who had dragged the dead C.O. and the two wounded company commanders into cover was sent to learn the exact situation. He had with him the Bren carrier platoon. By resolute leadership he

They Held Up the Foe on the Road to Dunkirk

These are some of the Grenadier Guardsmen whose gallant conduct is described in this article. They are Bren gunners in a forward position before the retreat.

rallied the troops on the spot and led them back to the canal in a counter-attack. His action averted an enemy break-through between the brigade area and the sea.

During this time the transport column and other details of " Z " battalion had been ordered to the neighbourhood of Dunkirk, there to destroy all their trucks except those carrying arms, food and ammunition. All the vehicles were present and in good order, and the melancholy task of destruction was duly performed. The personnel then made their way to the sea at La Panne, where there was indescribable confusion. Trucks, wagons and cars abandoned under orders by British units were being plundered and driven away by civilians and other nondescript people. The men of the transport column armed themselves with all the Bren guns and anti-tank rifles they could collect and established a post across the road, enforcing order and putting a stop to the pilfering. Next, they contributed to the defence of the position at Furnes by holding a front of half a mile along the canal east of the town. The situation at Furnes was saved and the final withdrawal to the sea made possible.

This was not the first time that the Grenadiers had covered the withdrawal of a British army. In 1809, Sir John Moore was watching the troops coming into Corunna when he said : " Look at that body of men in the distance ; they are the Guards by the way they are marching." In 1940 a divisional staff officer, checking up the units as they were withdrawing, was heard to say as a battalion of Grenadiers marched through : " These must be the Guards."

The sea front of La Panne (once a popular Belgian seaside resort), where " Z " battalion of the Grenadiers reached the sea, is here seen as the troops found it, lined with deserted houses, and cluttered with derelict anti-aircraft guns and all the rack and ruin of war. In peacetime its sands were crowded with holiday-makers.

1940

"Strictly between you & me...."

CARELESS TALK
COSTS LIVES

Printed and published for the Committee of "Blighty" by W. Speaight & Sons, Ltd., 98, Fetter Lane, London, E.C.4.

BLIGHTY

Laughs its Way to Victory

New Series No. 57 (Not on Sale) November 16, 1940 PRODUCED SOLELY FOR OUR NAVY AND FIGHTING FORCES

GINGER GREEN, A.B.

"That's Greece, my son"
"Lumme, Ginger, it looks like snow"

NEWS FROM GREECE...

News from Greece is scarce and Mr. Churchill summed up the situation in regard to news when he said: "I hope I shall not be asked to give any definite account of such measures as we are able to take. If I were to set them high, I might raise false hopes; if I set them low, I might cause undue despondency and alarm; if I stated exactly what they were, that would be exactly what the enemy would like to know."

That of course is exactly the game the Axis is playing, the same game that it played over the Norwegian campaign. A particularly marked similarity is the use of the names of neutral countries as the source of what is really Axis news. News is falsely represented as coming from Salonika in particular whilst Cairo, Belgrade and Switzerland are also used.

Exaggerated reports of British landings were put out both with the object of making us state exactly what we had done and also with the object of disappointing the Greeks if they were found to be inaccurate. Rumours of Greek surrender were started to disturb Greek morale and the old tale was repeated that Britain had been using Greek land and waters for some time so that the Italian aggression was really a "protective" move.

Courageous Greek resistance has given the lie to this last. Against superior forces on land and in the air, the Greeks have held their own, although the main Italian attack cannot be said really to have started.

Mr. Churchill went on to say: "We will do our best. We have already established a naval and air base in Crete which will enable us sensibly to extend the activities and radius of our navy and air force.

"We have begun bombing attacks on military objectives in Italian cities and bases in the south of Italy. They will continue on an ever-growing scale.

"I should like to say that other forces are in movement with the desire and design to help Greece to the utmost of our capacity."

By striking at Italian military objectives we are giving valuable aid to Greece and what it even more important, we are deterring the Italians, by the presence of our fleet, from attempting to land troops on Greece's western seaboard, thus leaving them no alternative but a long and arduous march through the Greek mountains, mountains which are occupied by Greek troops who know the country and who have already given proof of their courage and ability to fight back.

...AND FROM TURKEY

Any doubt about Turkey's position was removed by the speeches of the Turkish President on November 1 and of Lord Halifax in the House of Lords on Tuesday. Turkey presents a very solid barrier against aggression and the Turks are united to the Allies by bonds which are unbreakable, against which German propaganda has lied in vain. The British soldiers know very well the valour of the Turks in action and will welcome them at their side if and when the time should come for Turkey to fulfil her pledges.

DIARY of the WAR

Sunday, October 27

The Air Ministry announces that Coastal Command aircraft sank an enemy supply ship off the Norwegian coast. The vessel blew up and sank within thirty seconds.

An "incident" takes place on the Greco - Albanian frontier in which the Italians allege that a Greek armed band attacked an Albanian post near Coritza. This is denied in Greece.

Monday, October 28

The Greek High Command issue the following communiqué : Italian forces attacked at half-past five this morning our sections covering the Greco-Albanian frontier. Our forces are defending the soil of the Motherland."

At 3 o'clock in the morning the Italian Minister in Athens presents an ultimatum to the Greek Government demanding the occupation of certain strategic bases by Italian forces.

Saturday, November 2

We shall honour our pledge to Greece. The Royal Navy is there. Air support is being given. British troops have landed in Greek territory. "What we can do we will do," says Mr. Alexander, the First Lord of the Admiralty.

On the northern frontier the Greek crack troops, the Evzones carry out a bayonet attack and drive the Italians back.

With the capture of Nankin, the Chinese now control the entire Kwangsi province.

American naval forces are operating in the region of the French possessions in the Eastern Caribbean.

During the twelve weeks of air attacks on Great Britain, the Germans have lost three aircraft and fourteen airmen to every one British machine and pilot. Since August 8, 2,433 German bombers and fighters have been accounted for. The loss in trained airmen is roughly 6,000 compared with British losses of 353 pilots.

"At 5.30 a.m. on Monday (October 28) Italian troops violated Greek territory and attacked the Greek sections covering the Graeco-Albanian frontier — Greece and Italy were at war."

Greetings

STOP PRESS

"The Londoner." writer of "Parade's" London Letter, telegraphs: "I want to say 'Thank you' to all the boys for giving us such a first-class Christmas present. The victory over the Italians has delighted all London and all Britain for that matter. The rout of the 'Wops' is the talk of the town.

Here's thanks from London then to all the boys from Britain and all

FROM LONDON'

parts of the Empire who are taking part in this great feat of arms. And I make so bold as to offer my congratulations to General Sir Archibald Wavell, your Commander-in-Chief, to Admiral Sir Andrew Cunningham and Air Chief Marshal Sir Arthur Longmore for having worked it all out so well.

Here's a bumper Christmas to you all !"

From **GENERAL SIR ARCHIBALD WAVELL**
K.C.B., C.M.G., M.C.
Commander-in-Chief, Middle East.

I send greetings to all ranks of the Middle East army for Xmas 1940 and the New Year of 1941 We can well close 1940 in a spirit of confidence for the future and of pride for the past and present pride for the courage and endurance of the people of the United Kingdom in face of reverses, dangers, and hardships, and pride for the manner in which the whole Empire has responded to the threat against our freedom and institutions. We have too in the Middle East representatives of our allies in the struggle against cruelty and lies and tyranny Free France and Poland and Czechoslovakia We welcome a new and gallant ally in Greece who has struck a great blow for the principles of liberty and democracy which she founded so many years ago. To all I send my best thanks for the past and wishes for the future. We will serve on together till final victory. Then will come the real struggle, to build up a world worthy of the principles we believe in and are fighting for freedom and truth and peace and goodwill.

From **ADMIRAL SIR ANDREW CUNNINGHAM**
K.C.B., D.S.O.
Commander-in-Chief, Mediterranean

Christmas 1940 finds us in a much happier situation than even the most optimistic of us could have foretold six months ago

At home the enemy has been frustrated alike by the gallantry of the R.A.F. and the indomitable courage of our own folk and we out here can feel that we also have been able to contribute in some measure on land, sea and in the air to the discomfiture of our enemies, a discomfiture which, let us hope, is the beginning of greater things.

I wish all your readers a Very Happy Christmas and may the New Year bring us a victorious peace.

From **AIR CHIEF MARSHAL SIR ARTHUR LONGMORE**, K.C.B., D.S.O.
Air Officer Commanding-in-Chief, Middle East

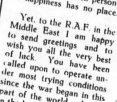

I am asked to send to the personnel of the Royal Air Force in the Middle East a Christmas message. I am glad to do so but it cannot follow customary lines. Christmas is essentially a family celebration. We are separated from our families. We are doing a job of work—a very serious job, in which personal happiness has no place.

Yet, to the R.A.F. in the Middle East I am happy to send greetings and to wish you all the very best of luck. You have been called upon to operate under most trying conditions since the war began in this part of the world, whether in the heat and dust of such places as the Sudan, the Western Desert, or the cold, icy conditions now prevailing in Greece and Albania. You have done your work magnificently. I am confident that in the New Year you will not only continue but will enhance the fine reputation you have rightly earned.

I am proud to have such a fine body of men under my command, including representative squadrons from Australia, South Africa and Rhodesia and those French airmen who have so gallantly joined us.

GREEK

ΔΙΑΓΓΕΛΜΑ
τοῦ Ἀρχιστρατήγου
Α. ΟΥΕΒΕΛ

πρὸς τὰ στρατεύματα

Πρὸς ὅλους τοὺς βαθμοφόρους καὶ τοὺς ἄνδρας τοῦ Στρατοῦ τῆς Μέσης Ἀνατολῆς ἀπευθύνω τὰς εὐχάς μου διὰ τὰ Χριστούγεννα τοῦ 1940 καὶ τὸ Νέον Ἔτος 1941.

Ἐλπίζομεν νὰ κλείσωμεν τὸ ἔτος 1940 μὲ ἐμπιστοσύνην διὰ τὸ μέλλον καὶ ὑπερηφάνειαν διὰ τὸ παρελθὸν καὶ τὸ παρόν.

Μὲ ὑπερηφάνειαν διὰ τὸ θάρρος καὶ τὴν καρτερίαν τοῦ λαοῦ τοῦ Ἡνωμένου Βασιλείου ἀπέναντι τῶν ἀτυχημάτων, τῶν κινδύνων καὶ τῶν στερήσεων καὶ μὲ ὑπερηφάνειαν διὰ τὸν τρόπον μὲ τὸν ὁποῖον ὁλόκληρος ἡ Αὐτοκρατορία ἀπήντησεν εἰς τὴν ἀπειλὴν κατὰ τῆς ἐλευθερίας μας καὶ τῶν θεσμῶν μας. Εἰς τὸν ἀγῶνα ἐναντίον τῆς ἀγριότητος τοῦ ψεύδους καὶ τῆς τυραννίας ἔχομεν ἐπίσης εἰς τὴν Μέσην Ἀνατολὴν ἀντιπροσώπους τῶν συμμάχων μας : Ἐλευθέρους Γάλλους, Πολωνοὺς καὶ Τσεχοσλοβάκους. Εὐχόμεθα καλῶς ὥρισες εἰς τὸν νέον καὶ γενναῖον Σύμμαχόν μας, τὴν Ἑλλάδα, ἡ ὁποία κατέφερεν ἰσχυρὸν κτύπημα διὰ τὰς ἀρχὰς τῆς ἐλευθερίας καὶ τῆς δημοκρατίας τὰς ὁποίας αὐτὴ ἐθεμελίωσε πρὸ τόσων ἐτῶν. Πρὸς ὅλους αὐτοὺς ἀπευθύνω τὰς θερμοτέρας εὐχαριστίας μου δι' ὅσα ἐγίνοντο εἰς τὸ παρελθὸν καὶ τὰς εὐχάς μου διὰ τὸ μέλλον ὅπως ἀγωνισθῶμεν μαζὺ μέχρι τῆς τελικῆς νίκης. Τότε θὰ ἀρχίσῃ ἡ προσπάθεια διὰ τὴν δημιουργίαν ἑνὸς κόσμου τὸν ὁποῖον θὰ κυβερνοῦν αἱ ἀρχαὶ διὰ τὰς ὁποίας πολεμοῦν οἱ λαοί μας — ἡ ἐλευθερία ἡ ἀλήθεια, ἡ εἰρήνη, ἡ καλὴ θέλησις.—

Στρατηγὸς Α. Οὐέβελ

Princess Elizabeth and Princess Margaret at the microphone during the Princess Elizabeth's recent broadcast.

London's Modest Christmas

December 23, 1940.

Fortnight Of Longest Nights

We are now on our fortnight of longest nights, and the other evening a spot of fog brought on the darkness earlier even than black-out time. One of the big stores had lit up its windows early in the afternoon to show customers what was 'going' for Christmas—gifts for soldiers, sailors, and airmen, and of course for their small sons and daughters. For the moment that big Oxford Street store looked almost like the West End in pre-war days when the 'lights were bright at night.

True, the store windows are reduced in size by anti-blast shutters, but the goods are there behind the glass just the same.

London's More Modest Christmas

London is having a much more modest Christmas than usual, but it's going to be Christmas all right.

I could tell you for instance of a London County Council Ambulance Station in the East End mostly staffed by women (all of whom are volunteers) that is busily engaged between raids in making an all-star cast for the finest puppet show ever. It will be shown to local children.

For those kiddies who will be spending Christmas night in an air raid shelter big plans are already afoot to make Santa Claus transform everything into a Christmas party. It will be a party in a cave, of course, but then caves have always been magic spots for children and old Santa is usually to be found lurking underground in some of the big London stores, even in peacetime.

210,000 Presents From American Junior Red Cross

And while air raid wardens are busy with these arrangements the American Red Cross office in London has already received a big instalment of 210,000 presents sent from the Junior Red Cross Society in America—in other words, from the kids of the U.S.A. to the kids of the U.K. So it is O.K. by both.

'The Waits' Not To Sound Like A Siren

Christmas carols as sung round the streets by London carol singers have had a tougher and tougher time of it the last few years on account of radio competition. And this year 'the waits, as some of us are still old-fashioned enough to call them, may have the barrage to beat as well. And they musn't make any noise which sounds like a siren—which will be pretty difficult for some of them. Anyhow, let's hope that on Christmas night there will be nothing worse than carollers to keep 'Christians awake.

Big Birds For The Boys

Turkeys are selling briskly at Smithfield Market and they are all home-grown birds this year, except for a biggish contingent from Ireland. The Army have bought up a good many, and the Army usually manages to have a bigger oven than the average Londoner these days, so the big birds will go to 'the Boys' this year.

London Settles Down To Shelter Life

London is settling down to shelter life now, and 80,000 three-tier bunks have been delivered, while more than thirty of the Tube Stations now used as shelters go on the admission by ticket only system. By Christmas all shelterers in the Tubes will have tickets.

All told, the London Tube now has 134 canteens on the platforms, 60 electric boilers and ovens, with half a mile of specially installed water mains to serve them, and a new staff of 1,000 They sell 12,500 gallons of tea and cocoa every night, hot pies by the hundredweight and sausages by the quarter-mile.

Helpless Husbands Club

From the northern suburbs comes news that one of them has founded a Helpless Husbands' Club for men whose wives have been evacuated. They can sleep and eat hearty for 17/6 per week all in, which includes washing their shirts and mending their socks and sewing on their buttons. The local Red Cross Society is responsible for this excellent idea. The difficulty is going to be to get the chaps to go home again after the war.

Wives And Sweethearts To Help

I was telling you something about the post office and how it plans to beat the Christmas rush this year in my last letter. Now I hear one of the plans has been to ask postmen to bring along their sweethearts and or wives to help with the extra work. There is an emergency training school which puts them through a six to twelve days course according to how quick they are in learning. Parcel sorters have some intensive geography to get into their heads. Those who are engaged on postmen's jobs will only have to carry two-thirds of the weight given to the men. But a lot of women are on this job already, quite apart from the Christmas rush, so many postmen have been called up.

From Speedway To Auxiliary Fire Service

Quite a lot of London's star riders from the motor-cycle speedways are now serving—and have been doing so since the outbreak of the war—with the London Auxiliary Fire Service.

Of the Wimbledon stars. Collins and Duggan returned to their native Australia after a spell with the Fire Service and are probably kicking up the dust around Egypt by this time. Geoff Pymar is now an air-gunner.

Play During 'Alerts'

All soccer fans welcomed the news that the ban on play during 'alerts' had been lifted at last, the attendance at Brentford on Saturday though not what you'd call big was sufficiently encouraging when the club met Reading, and the Palace and West Ham managers have both expressed the opinion that the 'gates' will begin to increase now Spurs have had to cancel their match with Portsmouth owing to the difficulty in raising eleven men who can afford the time to travel, but Portsmouth's big match with Southampton is all set for Christmas Day.

Hope for London soccer in 1941 seems to depend, at the moment, mainly on the London Counties Cup Competition. It should be launched next month if all goes well, and a big meeting of the London clubs is to be held this week to discuss this and other matters. Particularly hard hit Londoners want the comparatively prosperous Watford and Reading to be included in the ten clubs which are competing

But the latest Soccer news is that an all-star Army side may be entered for the Football League War Cup Compe

1941

Allies capture Bardia and Tobruk

US Lease-Lend Bill signed

Battle of Cape Matapan

Enemy counter-offensive in North Africa

German invasion of Greece and Yugoslavia

Revolt in Iraq

Sinking of the *Bismarck*

Allied evacuation from Crete

Allied invasion of Syria

Operation Barbarossa — German invasion of the USSR

Roosevelt and Churchill sign the Atlantic Charter

British and Soviet troops enter Iran

Second Western Desert offensive in Libya

Pearl Harbor — USA enters the war

HMS *Prince of Wales* and HMS *Repulse* sunk by Japanese aircraft

Japanese attack the Philippines

Fall of Hong Kong

The O.C. of an infantry battalion giving final orders

Buildings burning in Tobruk with the cruiser "San Georgio"

Artillery supporting the infantry attack in front of Tobruk.

Italian prisoners waiting to be escorted to a prisoners of war base.

The Command Post of a battery of artillery in action at Tobruk.

A truck load of women who were among civilian inhabitants.

AND SO

Last week another mile stone on the road to Benghasi was passed, when Tobruk fell into the hands of British Forces after only 36 hours fighting. The attack was launched on January 21st—16 days after Bardia was taken—and on January 22nd Australian troops were in the town.

The town of Tobruk is situated on the spit of land which forms the north shore of the bay and harbour of Tobruk, and was protected by two lines of defence. The inner line was some 19 and the outer some 30 miles in length, thus covering the town and bay of Tobruk from shore to shore. In the preliminary operations both the Navy and Air Force co-operated, and then the land forces launched the attack at dawn on January 21st and succeeded in penetrating the South East sector of the defences. By the evening of that day the army had succeeded in advancing to a depth of eight miles, but the Central and Western Sectors of the defences still held out. The main attack was entrusted to Australian troops, but other troops which took part included British Armoured formations and a detachment of the Free French. Before noon on January 22nd the Australians had succeeded in getting into the town itself.

An open air officer's mess with the officers having a meal.

harbour and British tanks wait to enter the burning town.

Naval prisoners leaving the harbour after the entry of British troops

A light tank of a Hussar Regiment bivouaced in a sandstorm whilst out on patrol.

Italian naval prisoners leaving Tobruk which can be seen burning.

Official War Office photographs, by Lt. L.B. Davis.

Three senior Staff Officers discussing the operations after the capture of the town.

TOBRUK

...at there was still fighting on the Western Sector. By this time the ...outh West, the South and the South East sectors were occupied ...y the British Forces. By the evening, however, the capture of the ...hole of the defended area and the town was complete.

Prisoners taken at Tobruk number over 25,000, thus making the ...rand total for the Western Desert campaign over 110,000. Mate-...al captured at Tobruk included 22 medium tanks and 28 light ...anks. At the time of writing, the enumeration of the guns is conti-...uing.

As soon as Tobruk was taken, the British Forces pushed on and ...ow Derna, "the jewel of the Mediterranean," is being invested, ...nd it is hoped that it will not be long before the British flag is ...ying there.

At Giarabub, the Italian garrison is still beseiged, but it is known that they are badly in need of water and supplies.

The country in which the campaign is now being fought is vastly different to that of the Western Desert. Arid wastes of sand are beginning to be replaced by verdant hills and valleys, and there is water available.

JACK TAR: "I'll 'ave a 'elping of Goebbels' propaganda, please"
WAITRESS: "I don't know what you mean"
JACK TAR: "You know, Missy, a plate of tripe"

The War Illustrated

Keeping Watch for the 'Deathly Glow Lamps'

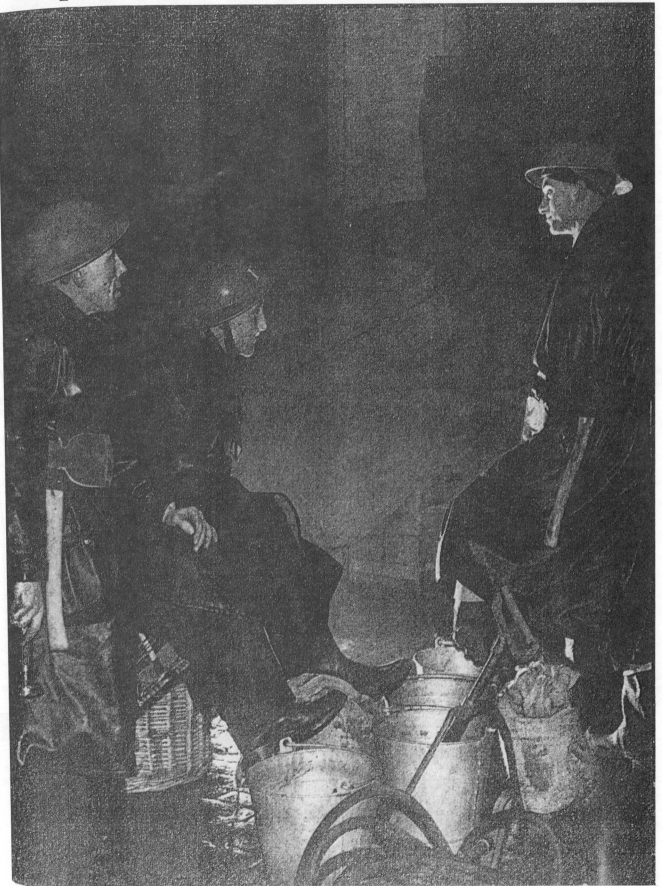

FIRE WATCHERS, whose vigilance through the dark winter nights should never be relaxed, wait at their post, ready to deal with any emergency. These three men in their steel helmets and oilskins are part of the great civilian army of Britain which is now in the "front line." On January 16, 1941, Mr. Herbert Morrison, Minister of Home Security, signed an order which made it obligatory for all persons between 16 and 60 not in Government service to register for fire-watching duty and so defeat the "deathly glow lamps"—to use his pregnant phrase. Stirrup-pump, axe, buckets and sand form the necessary equipment of the fire watcher.

A SIGNIFICANT VISIT TO THE MIDDLE EAST

As seen by "The Times"

The news of the arrival of Mr. Eden and General Dill in Cairo shows that the British Government is thinking ahead and that the weapons of diplomacy are being used as they should be, to support and reinforce the military arm, writes *The Times* in a leading article.

The initiative is once more in British hands and through British Headquarters in Cairo lies the right avenue of approach to the whole complex of problems whose present nerve-centre is somewhere in the Balkans.

The flutter caused in the Near East by the Turkish Bulgarian Declaration is scarcely justified. Turkish spokesmen scrupulously denied the various implications which Nazi propaganda has pretended to read in it. It doesn't mean that Turkey has acquiesced in any Nazi move against Bulgaria. It doesn't mean that Turkey has withdrawn from any of her undertakings to Greece. It doesn't mean that Turkey has weakened her solidarity with Great Britain and her determination to fulfil the terms of the alliance.

On the other hand, it cannot be asserted that the pact has relieved Turkey of any of the anxieties inherent in the German attitude. She is still indirectly threatened, and may soon be directly threatened, by German military activities around the Black Sea, and there has been fresh news of German preparations on the Bulgarian frontier.

Turkey has had ample opportunities for drawing the moral that timely cooperation between those who are resolved to resist is a condition of security. This cooperation has been fully maintained in the many conversations which have taken place during the past four weeks between the British and the Turkish authorities. Mr. Eden's presence in the Near East can hardly fail to stimulate it. The unflagging courage of the Greeks, their mounting successes in Albania and the close collaboration between their troops and the Royal Air Force are all a good augury for the future.

For the immediate future the role of Great Britain must be to intensify the effective assistance which she is already rendering to the gallant Greek nation, and to help make the Greek defences proof against any attack which may be launched against them. The collaboration of Turkey in this task would substantially enhance the certainty of its successful performance and the likelihood of war can even now be prevented from approaching any nearer the Turkish frontiers.

Hitler has proved himself a pastmaster in overwhelming those who temporise. But he has shown an equally marked reluctance to challenge resolute and well-prepared defences.

While, however, the vital issues now agitating the Near East are likely to be the immediate preoccupation, there are African problems which may also claim Mr. Eden's attention. When he last visited Cairo three months ago he was there in the capacity of Secretary of State for War. Events have moved so swiftly that the situation which then confronted him is now almost forgotten. The victory in North and East Africa is bringing with it problems of an administrative character, some of which are closely connected with Mr. Eden's present functions as Foreign Secretary The special status of Abyssinia has already prompted a pronouncement in the House of Commons on the future of that country. Many problems are now arising that affect the whole area which is being liberated by the armies under General Wavell's command from the Fascist yoke. It is important that these problems should not be handled piecemeal, and that it should be made clear to the world that the temporary administrations which are necessary in the liberated territories do not prejudge their future status. In none of these countries has Great Britain any territorial ambitions or designs of her own. She holds them by right of conquest until such time as they can take their place in a new order designed to promote the welfare and give the fullest satisfaction to the needs of their peoples.

"Well, boys, do we remind her there's a blackout on?"

DIARY OF THE WAR

ROOSEVELT SIGNS
LEASE and LEND BILL
...and SPEAKS
R.A.F. Batters Berlin

Tuesday, March 11

President Roosevelt signs the Lease and Lend Bill fifteen minutes after it arrives at the White House.

A heavily-laden Italian troopship is torpedoed and sunk by a British submarine.

The Italians continue to make desperate attacks on the Greek lines but they are all repulsed with considerable loss. Four hundred and fifty prisoners are taken.

The Italian column retreating towards Addis Ababa from Burye is driven out of Dambacha, 25 miles further on, by British and patriot forces advancing from the Sudan. These forces are now less than 180 miles from Addis Ababa.

Admiral Darlan makes a statement warning Great Britain that if she continues to exercise the blockade against France, French warships would escort French cargo-ships.

Mr. Matsuoka, Japanese Foreign Minister, prepares to leave Japan on a visit to Germany and Italy.

The plenipotentiaries of France and Thailand formally accept and initial terms of the mediation agreement presented by Japan. Thailand is given considerable territorial concessions affecting North and South East French Indo-China. The ceded territories are to be demilitarized and French nationals

Saturday, March 15

Mr. Roosevelt defines America's position in a broadcast to the world.

The President prefixes his speech with the pregnant phrase: "Everything I have to say is word for word on the record." He continues to say that in the last world war the Germans were informed by their representatives in the United States that the latter was in a state of disunity. "But let not the dictators of Europe and Asia doubt our unity now. Before the present war broke out I was more worried about the future than most people. The record shows that I was not worried enough. The American people are writing new history today.

"The big news this week," the President goes on, "is that the world has been told that we, as a united nation, realise the danger which confronts us, and to meet that danger our Democracy has gone into action. We know that although Prussian autocracy was bad enough. Nazism is far worse. The Nazi forces are not seeking mere modifications in colonial maps or minor European boundaries. They openly

seek the destruction of all elective systems of Government in every continent including our own. They seek to establish systems of Government on the regimentation of all human beings by a handful of individual rulers who have seized power by force. These men and their hypnotized followers call this a new order. But it is not new and it is not an order. Humanity has never permanently accepted a system imposed by conquest and based on slavery. The nations of Europe and the United States did not previously appreciate that these modern tyrants find it necessary to eliminate all the Democracies, but we do now. The process of elimination of European nations proceeded by plan through 1939 and 1940 until the schedule was shot to pieces by the unbeatable defenders of Britain. The enemies of Democracy now know that a Democracy can still remain a Democracy and reach conclusions and arm itself adequately for defence." Referring to the Lease and Lend Act, President Roosevelt declares that it was argued not only by Congress, but throughout the country and finally it was settled by the American people themselves. "It is proclaimed not with the voice of any one man, but with the voice of one hundred and thirty millions. It is binding on all of us and the world is no longer left in doubt. The decision is the end of any attempts at appeasement in our land, the end of urging us to get along with the dictators, the end of compromise with tyranny and the forces of oppression. We believe firmly that when our production outputs are at full swing the Democracies of the world will be able to prove that dictatorships cannot win. Every plane and other instrument of war, old and new, which we can spare, we will send overseas. That is commonsense strategy."

The United States was dedicated to a constantly increasing tempo of production, greater than ever known before. The light of Democracy must be kept burning. "Millions in Britain and elsewhere are bravely shielding the great flame of Democracy from the black-out of barbarism. It is not enough for us merely to trim the wick and polish the glass. We must provide in ever increasing amounts to keep the flame alight." If Democracy failed, freedom of speech and expression and the worship of freedom from want and fear would become forbidden things. That is true of England, Greece, China and the United States to-day.

"There are almost one million and a half United States citizens in the armed forces to-day," continues President Roosevelt, "and no better men ever served under Washington, Paul Jones, Grant, Lee or Pershing."

The British are stronger than ever in their magnificent morale which enabled them to endure all the dark days and shattered nights of the past ten months. They have the full support and help of Canada, the other Dominions and the rest of their Empire and of the non-British

peoples throughout the world who still think in terms of great freedoms. The British people are prepared for invasion whenever the attempt may come—to-morrow, next week or next month. In this historic crisis Britain is blessed with that brilliant great leader, Winston Churchill, but nobody knows better than Mr. Churchill himself that it is not alone his stirring words and valiant deeds that give the British their superb morale. The essence of that morale is in the masses of the plain people who completely agree on one essential fact— they would rather die free men than live as slaves. These plain people, civilians as well as soldiers, sailors and airmen, are fighting in the front line of civilization. They are holding that line with fortitude which will forever be the pride and inspiration of all free men of every continent. The British and their allies have shown magnificent will. China, through Generalissimo Chiang Kai-Shek, has asked for our help. She shall have our help. "Our country is going to be the arsenal of Democracy. It is going to play its full part. And when the dictatorships disintegrate—and pray God that it may be sooner than any of us now dares to hope—our country must continue to play its great part in world reconstruction."

President Roosevelt concludes: "We believe that the rallying cry of the dictators and their boasting about a master race will prove to be pure stuff and nonsense. There has never been and never will be any race of people fit to serve as masters over their fellowmen. The world has no use for any nation which, because of its size and military might, asserts its right to goosestep to world power over other nations and other races. We believe that any nationality, no matter how small, has an inherent right to its own nationhood. Never in all our history have Americans faced a job so well worth while. May it be said of us in the days to come that our children and our children's children rise up and call us blessed."

The President's speech is broadcast in fourteen languages including those of the countries occupied by Germany.

ALLAN FEA'S TOPICAL PARODIES—No. 9

Ode to a Dummy

And you have swanked about in all
    your glory
In Cæsar's streets not very long ago :
A time when Democrats were far less
    gorey,
And I had not begun to overthrow
Those monarchies and Empires stupen-
    dous,
Of which my gleanings really were
    tremendous.

Speak, for long enough you've acted
    Dummy,
You have a tongue, come, let me hear
    it's tune :
You gas and shriek—stick out your
    weighty tummy.
I hate your boasts and black-gloved
    features—
And now you're smashed, like all
    obnoxious creatures.

Italians used to be impulsive and im-
    passioned :
It's time you fed them up a bit, you
    know;
But don't come here for food, for we're
    blockaded;

For grub we really don't know where to
    go ?
Give up this gassy effervescence;
'Tis inconsistent quite with evanes-
    cence.

There really is no sparkle in your
    vintage;
That sort of buck-up doesn't stand a
    chance.
Referring thus to " bubbly," just re-
    minds me
Of the glorious sort of " cham " I
    sneaked from France.
To call it " Heavenly " is really no
    misnomer,
For so 'tis dubbed by that old poet
    Homer !

Tell me, for doubtless you can recollect
To what should I assign your boasted
    fame ?
Was it your bully-bluster :—vain con-
    ceit;
Or were your fighting Gladiators to
    blame ?
Why are they now so jitterbug and
    fretty ?
Go ! Stuff your paunch with garlic and
    spaghetti.

TWO BIG CONTESTS ARRANGED

News from the home "battle fronts" in-
volves title fights in the featherweight and
flyweight. divisions.

Tom Smith, of Sunderland, is to meet Nel
Tartleton, of Liverpool, the holder, for the
British 9st. championship at Liverpool Foot-
ball Ground under the promotion of Johnny
Best in a few weeks time.

Smith, however, will probably have to
take some weight off before the contest. He
has been fighting in the lightweight division for some time, and recently retained
the Northern area title with a points victory over Jackie Rankin at London Casino
Club.

Regarding the flyweight situation, news
from home is that Peter Kane, of Liverpool,
and Jackie Ryan, of Manchester, have been
matched for the British title, but this can
hardly be correct in view of the fact that
the championship is held by Jackie Pater-
son, of Dundee.

VON CRAMM LOSES BOTH FEET

Gottfried Von Cramm, the prominent German Davis Cup player, has been wounded
in action and has lost both his feet, according to Walter L. Pate, non-playing captain
of the last American Davis Cup team.

Pate said that he had received this information from a very reliable source.

Von Cramm was known on the principal
tennis courts throught the world, including
Cairo and Alexandria, where he took part
in international tournaments.

"The Stars are Cheering You!"

TALKS WITH THE STARS

By REG. MORTIMER

THIS SUNDAY OPENING idea has caught on no end—not only with the lads, but with the stars themselves. I have talked with more than a dozen stars in the theatre world, and they all have agreed that their profession has been more or less saved by "the boys" who need a show on Sundays.

Thus, boys, an ancient-old law that was created in the reign of CHARLES II. is now extinct. And a jolly good job, too!

Lets get on with the show, not with the PAST show!

* * *

FRANCES DAY, who has sung before more of you boys than I (or Frances) care to remember, is coming back into the West End.

And, if you are in town, will you boys give "Our Frances" a welcome.

Frances, after a long and tough tour of the camps, throughout the country, is coming back to town (in the security of her bombed-out flat), and will definitely appear with BUD FLANAGAN and CHESNEY ALLEN in a brand new George Black show at the Victoria Palace almost at the next moment.

So, don't forget it, lads.

* * *

MARLENE DIETRICH, whose dazzling picture you see on this page, is working in Hollywood —but her heart is in London. She is one of the few stars who have conquered both Hollywood and British studios.

Marlene was always a sensation when she appeared in public in London. I have walked beside her—and I have done all the blushing!

Actually, Marlene is a very home-loving gal—much as you might think otherwise. She has a daughter nearly as tall as herself—and does Marlene adore that daughter!

* * *

Sauciest title of the newest show in town goes to RONALD FRANKAU'S

"Nineteen Naughty One," which seems to me to be the perfect entertainment for regular patrons of the Prince of Wales Theatre.

I should think that "Nineteen Naughty One" will live up to its title until 1942.

* * *

CHARLES CHAPLIN, I see, is

MARLENE DIETRICH

tipped as being the one film artist in the United States to get the year's best acting award for his performance in "The Great Dictator."

Chaplin, I am told, is likely to refuse the honour if it does come his way.

I understand Chaplin's attitude, after his many years of service to the screen—it dates back more than twenty-five years—it seems a little late in the day that it is only now—in this year of 1941—that he should receive recognition from the industry for which he has done so much.

Chaplin has scored one big success with his "Great Dictator" film because it was timely and topical.

But to Charlie it was just another job of film work. In his own opinion, I believe, he looks upon it as being no greater than his films that have gone before.

Charlie was always original. And if he does turn down the honour of being the world's greatest comedian—who would blame him?

After all, these young Hollywood film chiefs would seem to forget that Charlie has been No. 1 comedian for the past twenty-five years.

Why should Charlie bother if they suddenly recognise his genius in 1941 — sixteen or seventeen years later!

* * *

There aren't enough British stars to go round, since so many of them have returned home in an effort to do their bit.

Still, it is nice to know that Hollywood is all "British - conscious" and wants our accent more and more.

Hollywood producers, I am told, could do with a couple of dozen RONALD COLMANS and MERLE OBERONS, which is a mighty nice compliment to us.

Maybe when the war is over, and we are celebrating victory, we will send Hollywood a few of our stars— but until then Hollywood will have to wait.

And well worth waiting for, eh?

* * *

Have just heard the story of what it really means to try and get a WEST END theatre open after it has been closed for a few months. One manager told me he could get two leading men for the price of one stage carpenter.

And, while he had the cast fixed, he had no back-stage staff!

It seems a pity, in these very unlovely times, that stage hands should quibble over Union rates—when stars are willing to work for a song just to keep the theatre open.

I LIKE SHOW PEOPLE (you have guessed that already), but I do not like to see them imposed upon as they are being done now.

THE WAR ILLUSTRATED

3d Weekly

Edited by
SIR JOHN HAMMERTON

Editor of 'THE WAR ILLUSTRATED' (1914–1920)
'WORLD WAR, 1914–1918,' 'I WAS THERE!' etc.

THE WEEK

Britons Fight Germans on Land Again: Twilight of 2nd. Roman Empire: Discussions in Far East

Greek soldiers watching for enemy patrols on the Albanian Front. There is still heavy snow on many parts of the front

This new weekly news summary replaces "Parade's" former "Diary of the War."

Germany in the Mediterranean

For the first time in nine months, British troops are at grips with the Germans. In a week which will take its place in history, Germany struck on two new fronts—Jugoslavia and Greece. As Italy was falling in line by declaring war on Jugoslavia, almost the last Italian resistance crumbled in Abyssinia and East Africa and the Greeks stood firm in Albania.

Greece's nationwide Palm Sunday broadcast from Athens Cathedral was interrupted to announce that German troops were invading Greece and Jugoslavia.

Promising both nations unqualified support, the British Government revealed that British, Australian and New Zealand troops were in Greece and that the Royal Air Force there had been strongly reinforced. General Wavell would remain in supreme command of the British troops in Greece, according to Reuters' lobby correspondent.

The presumed plan of the German offensive in the Balkans may be seen at a glance from the map on page 14.

Although Belgrade was declared an open town, it was heavily bombed by the German Air Force. German aircraft also bombed Salonika and Greek towns and villages; while the Italian Air Force bombed Split, Jugoslavia's Adriatic port, and other centres.

"Tenacious resistance" by Greek, British and Australian troops, particularly in the Struma Valley, was reported by Berlin Radio.

The same station told the German public the Balkan campaign would be "no walkover," although a later proclamation by Hitler boasted that Germany's rapid blitzkrieg successes of last year would be repeated in the Balkans.

Reuter said feeling in the British War Cabinet was "one of quiet determination."

Moscow again had the world guessing by signing with Jugoslavia, only a few hours before the German invasion, a non-aggression pact. "The efforts of Jugoslavia to preserve peace could not but arouse sympathy in the U.S.S.R.," commented the Soviet organ *Isvestia*.

"I hope Turkey will realise this is the moment for a decision—when the whole security of the Balkans is involved," the Home Secretary, Herbert Morrison, declared in London.

After a week of bad news for Berlin and Rome, the taking of Bengazi by German-Italian forces made good Axis propaganda. "But the loss of Bengazi" commented the *Daily Telegraph* (London) "is a reminder that Germany is the real enemy and is unbeaten on land. It is a refreshing thought that for the first time in this war we are fighting the Germans on enemy territory."

The *New York Herald-Tribune* referring to the British withdrawal from Bengazi wrote:

"One may read in it something of the same judgment and steadiness which at Home have enabled the British to watch the indiscriminate devastation of their cities without veering once from their course of avoiding militarily useless reprisals, of husbanding their resources, of pounding away systematically at the weakest points of their enemies' war-potential and of never being diverted from the main issue."

That German troop transports bound from Palermo to Tripoli were being allowed to use French Tunis an territorial waters was asserted by Reuters' naval correspondent. And produce from France's North African colonies definitely was going to the Axis Powers, the Ministry of Economic Warfare told London newspapers.

At the other end of the Mediterranean, widespread rioting in Syria, mandated territory still adhering to Vichy, led to political concessions by the French High Commissioner, General Dentz. Abolishing the existing "Council of Directors," the Vichy administrator gave executive authority to a new Prime Minister, Khaled El Azim Bey, and a Ministry of five. The High Commissioner retained various unrevealed rights.

In a weekend broadcast from Cairo, General Charles de Gaulle, Free French leader, declared to French colonials, particularly in North Africa: "You have only a few days left in which to choose between German domination and the fight for freedom with the Allies.".

During the Syrian disorders, a coup d'état in next-door Iraq placed Rashid Ali in power by will of the Baghdad garrison. The British Government regarded the position as "completely unconstitutional." Official circles in London, quoted by Reuter, deplored "the intervention of the Army in political affairs, as such incursions invariably react to the detriment of the people." The Regent was reported to be fleeing to Basrah.

U.S. Convoys to Middle East?

United States aid to Britain gave promise of entering a new phase with the suggestion, given prominence in all United States newspapers, that 100 American freighters might carry war materials to Egypt, termed by the B.B.C.'s American Commentator Raymond Gram Swing, "back door of the war." This question, along with that of servicing British warships in American yards, was discussed with President Roosevelt by Admiral Lamb, chairman of the U.S. Maritime Commission. In Washington on the same business was Sir Arthur Salter, Parliamentary Secretary to the Ministry of Shipping. The *New York Journal of Commerce* revealed that between 120 and 140 American vessels at present on coastal routes were being transferred to British owners.

With the collapse of Italian naval strength, President Roosevelt indicated his intention of allowing American shipping to enter the Gulf of Aden and the Red Sea and Wall Street underwriters cut by two and a-half per cent Eastern Mediterranean war risk rates.

United States aircraft production reached a new "high" in March, with 1,216 planes. Of these, 1,074 went to the United States and British Government.

Widespread strikes, which threatened to hold up war production, drew from Henry Stimson, Secretary for War, a threat of drastic Government action against the workers. Vichy Radio said 400,000 miners were "out" and that none of the night shifts at the Ford works were operating. The same source predicted an early settlement.

Unprecedented pan-American unity of action characterised the parallel action of the United States, Mexico, Cuba, Peru, Ecuador, Uruguay and Venezuela in seizing Axis shipping in their ports. "Wholesale sabotage" was taking place aboard the vessels, it was revealed by the United States Government. On the orders of the President, the immediate recall of the Italian naval attaché, Admiral Alberto Lais, was demanded, following evidence that he had ordered most of the sabotage. The Italian consul at Cristobal, Panama Canal Zone, along with the captain and two officers of the Italian liner *Conte Biancamano*, was arrested on deportation charges; the 26,000-ton liner was seized and her crew of 500 were driven aboard a U.S. Army transport for internment in the United States. In the Americas and the Philippines, something like 33 Italian, 42 Danish and five German ships were seized. Others were burned or scuttled by their crews.

Peru confiscated the hangars and three Junkers airliners of the Deutsche Lufthansa and arrested two fleeing German shipping agents. Mexico summarily closed the German College in Mexico City.

After blunt United States rejection of Axis protest, the *Deutsche Algemeine Zeitung*, quoted by Berlin Radio, complained: "This high-handed American behaviour has angered the whole world. It proves that the U.S. is suffering from hysterical hatred of Germany."

Axis Statesman Shoots Himself

Beside the dead body of Count Paul Teleki, the Hungarian Premier, was found a revolver. In his pocket was a note reading: "I do not feel able to carry on with my difficult and unhappy task." Into these words, American commentators read an inference that Germany was prodding Hungary into war against Jugoslavia. Paul Teleki had been largely responsible for the pact of friendship between Jugoslavia and Hungary. His successor was Laszlo de Bardessy, who retained his foreign portfolio. The new Prime Minister some time ago was the guest of Hitler in Berlin.

Rumania, even more under German domination than Hungary, suspended payment on her foreign debt because of "profound disturbance in international economic relations" and loss of Rumanian territory following adherence to the Axis.

Industrial unrest in conquered Norway was reflected in the arrest of trades union leaders. To compel its printing staff to work, the Oslo Quisling newspaper *Frittfolk* has 16 policemen in its office.

History's Most Expensive War

A four-hour battering of Bristol was the main work of the Luftwaffe over Britain, during a lull in which London was enjoying its 17th bomb-free night.

The shape of things to come could be discerned in the great four-day battle manœuvres in the South of England, in which Britain's new parachute army played a leading part.

And C.G. Grey, expert aviation writer, asserted in a semi-official publication: "We will have new fighters and bombers in quantities which will in due course give us such command of the enemy coasts as to give our navy and army the power to land and carry the war into enemy country."

The B.B.C. revealed that Britain's daily expenses sheet for the war had jumped in three months from £ 10,500,000 to £ 13,500,000. To finance what he termed "the most expensive war in history," the Chancellor of the Exchequer, Sir Kingsley Wood, announced in his Budget speech an increase of 1s 6d in the standard rate of income tax, bringing the tax to 10s.

In the Battle of the Atlantic, shipping losses for the week ended March 23 totalled 59,111 tons.

Matsuoka Talks with Molotov

After a winter trek across half the world to talk business with the Axis chiefs, Japan's Foreign Minister, Yosuke Matsuoka, left Berlin for Japan on April 5. In his seven and a-half days in Germany and two and a-half in Italy, he saw Hitler, von Ribbentrop, the Pope, King Victor Emmanuel, Mussolini and Count Ciano. On his return journey, the Soviet Foreign Commissar, Comrade Molotov, greeted him at Moscow Station; and Matsuoka announced he would spend four days in the Soviet capital.

Matsuoka's Rome visit was newsworthy mainly for the character and variety of his public utterances. For example:

"The Tripartite alliance is the greatest alliance ever known. It may last a century, ten centuries, or even 1,000 centuries" (Berlin Radio).

"I was very impressed with the conversations I had with the Duce and Count Ciano. As for my audience with King Victor Emmanuel, I will remember it as long as I live" (Berlin Radio).

"The Duce, Count Ciano, and Italy's other illustrious chiefs are remaking the glorious history of the great Roman Empire" (Rome Radio and B.B.C.).

While Matsuoka was in Europe, the leader of the Japanese Naval Mission met Hitler and high officials of the German Navy.

Coinciding with the Matsuoka tour, and comparable in significance, was the visit to Manila and Batavia from Singapore of Sir Robert Brooke-Popham, British Commander-in-Chief, Far East. After long talks at Manila with his American opposite number, Admiral Hart, Sir Robert made a rapid journey to the nearby British Crown Colony of Hong Kong, where Sir Archibald Clark Kerr, British Ambassador to Chungking, had flown to meet him. On his return to Manila, Sir Robert was scheduled to confer again with American Services chiefs and to meet Dr. van Kleffens, Netherlands Foreign Minister, on his way from London to Batavia by way of Washington.

The day Britain advanced to Generalissimo Chiang Kai-shek the cash needed to link the Burma Road by rail with Yungchang, Japanese police seized the cargoes of five British lighters

Skua aircraft of the Fleet Air-Arm. Adding to their great victory at Taranto, the Fleet Air-Arm put three torpedoes into the battleship "Vittorio Veneto."

Continuing

The BATTLE
of
CAPE MATAPAN

The VALIANT's captain, Charles Eric Morgan, descendant of the famed Welsh buccaneer Henry Morgan who plundered the West Indies in the seventeenth century, told me the destruction of both the FIUME and the ZARA was "a most ghastly sight."

"Great glows illuminated the sea from the FIUME as if someone had thrown a log upon a smouldering fire. The whole ship seemed to disintegrate, many of our shells exploding inside her and turning her into a raging, blazing inferno."

Captain Morgan said "there was no answering fire from either the FIUME or the ZARA. We fired some starshells to help light up our targets and the Italian cruisers apparently thought they were flares from aircraft, because they let go some of their guns in the direction the starshells were falling."

From what I learned from officers of the various warships of the Mediterranean Fleet, the whole battle of Cape Matapan was just like a shooting gallery with Italian warships operating like wooden ducks being picked off by expert gunnery.

Long after the smoke of battle had cleared, heavy gunfiring was heard,

believed to indicate, that in the pitch darkness of night the two sets of Italian warships had mistakenly opened fire upon each other. One British officer said he saw huge flames after a tremendous explosion miles away from any British warship.

Rear-Admiral Denis Boyd, at whose side I stood on the bridge when he captained the famous aircraft carrier ILLUSTRIOUS and saw forty to fifty German dive-bombers try to beat to pieces that carrier with seven direct hits of thousand pound bombs, described the attacks on the VITTORIO VENETO as "outstandingly gallant, carried out by our pilots in the broad daylight in the face of terrific fire."

Captain Manlio De Pisa of the Italian cruiser POLA, one of 258 men rescued by the British destroyer JERVIS, described the British 'planes' attacks on the VITTORIO VENETO as "the most incredible act of courage I have ever seen."

Every warship of the British Mediterranean Fleet played a vital rôle in this stirring drama of the sea.

It was the cruisers ORION, GLOUCESTER, AJAX and PERTH who "decoyed" the Italian battlefleet to within range of the British battleships'

These pictures of the action were taken by Petty Officer Keats in H.M.S. "Glo warships register a close shot on the "Gloucester." Behind, a smoke screen is be

guns and kept Admiral Sir Andrew B. Cunningham, Commander-in-Chief, constantly advised of enemy movements although these cruisers were out-ranged by enemy guns and given repeated barrages of shells from the VITTORIO VENETO and Italian cruisers.

It was the destroyer HAVOC's captain who sent the historic message when his ship pushed alongside the POLA to the Admiral saying "I am hanging onto the stern of POLA. Shall I board her or blow her stern off with depth charges ? I haven't any torpedoes left."

It was a seaman aboard the destroyer MOHAWK who taught a rescued German naval observer from the POLA his first lesson in British navy discipline.

The wise-cracking German clambered up the ladder on the destro-

yer's side and stepped upon the quarterdeck with his right arm extended crying "Heil Hitler!"

The British seaman's fist landed squarely on the German's jaw, toppling him over the deckrail into the sea.

"When you come up, take your place in line and salute properly," the Britisher advised.

The German officer, rubbing his chin, his uniform dripping, re-appeared with a smart British salute.

Blue-eyed, grey-haired, quick-thinking Admiral Cunningham obviously was delighted about taking another wave out of Mussolini's "Mare Nostrum."

He messaged every unit of the Fleet that "the operations just concluded have given us a notable success over the enemy. The skilful handling of our cruisers and the un-

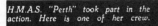

H.M.A.S. "Perth" took part in the action. Here is one of her crew.

A British destroyer of the Tribal class. "Mohawk" is of this class. Larry Allen tells how one of her seamen taught a German a lesson in good manners.

A cruiser of the Southamp The action photographs

A destroyer races across "Gloucester" laying a smoke screen. The cruisers "Orion," "Ajax," "Gloucester" and "Perth" lead the enemy within range of our battleships.

are the only pictures to be published of the victory of Matapan. Above Italian Italian gunnery was good but not quite good enough for the British Navy.

Survivors of the Italian ships sunk are rescued by the British Fleet until the action of Italy's "gallant" ally made it impossible to carry on with the rescue work.

tiring efforts of the Fleet Air Arm kept me well-informed of enemy movements and the well-pressed home attacks of torpedo aircraft on the Littorio class battleship so reduced the speed of the enemy that we were able to gain contact during the night and inflict heavy damage.

"The devastating results of the battleships' gunfire are an ample reward for months of patient training. This work was completed by the destroyers in the admirable way that we have come to expect from them.

"The contribution of the engine-room departments to this success cannot be over-emphasized. Their work, not only in keeping their ships steaming at high speed for long periods but in the work on maintenance under the most difficult conditions has been most praiseworthy.

"I am very grateful to all in the Fleet for their support on this and all other occasions. Well done!"

The Admiral told me he hopes to further speed up the job of wiping enemy warcraft out of the Mediterranean before the end of 1941.

He said he did not believe that the Italian fleet would have put to sea on this operation except under "German instigation."

But apparently they didn't "instigate" enough, for out of Mussolini's entry into war on the side of Germany he has only this naval headache:

SUNK OR OUT OF ACTION: *Twenty-five percent of his six-inch cruisers; more than fifty percent of his eight-inch cruisers; between twenty and thirty percent of his total submarine power, and sixty-six and two-thirds percent of his battleships.*

H.M.S. "Warspite," flagship of the Mediterranean Fleet travelling at speed.

which H.M.S. "Gloucester" is an example. le were taken from the "Gloucester."

H.M.S. "Formidable" from whose decks the Fleet Air-Arm left to play havoc with the "Vittorio Veneto." The "Formidable" is one of Britain's latest carriers and is engaged, among other duties, in countering the dive bombers

WHERE THE BATTLE OF BRITAIN WAS

History's First Mass Air Struggle Shown

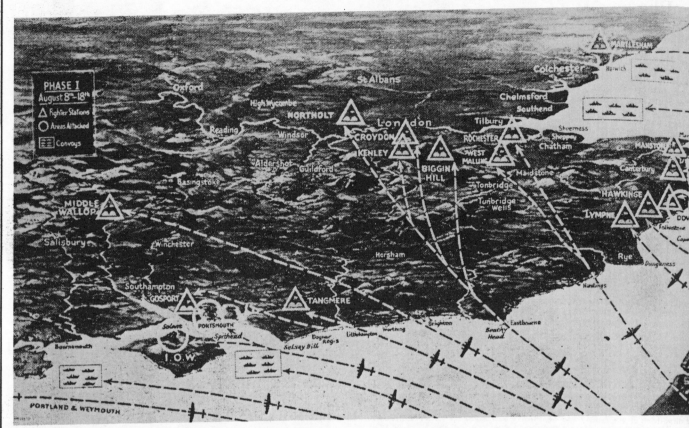

PHASE I
August 8th–18th
△ Fighter Stations
○ Areas Attacked
⊞ Convoys

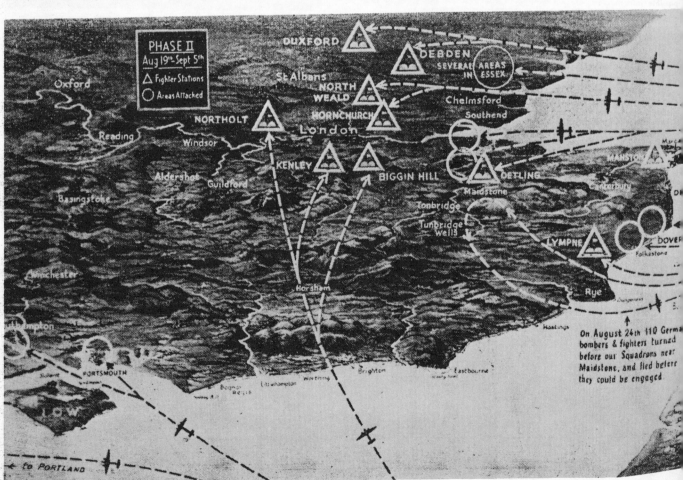

PHASE II
Aug 19th–Sept 5th
△ Fighter Stations
○ Areas Attacked

On August 24th 110 German bombers & fighters turned before our Squadrons near Maidstone, and fled before they could be engaged.

May 2nd. 1941.

UGHT AND WON
Phase

THE air Battle of Britain, in which British airmen "undaunted by odds, unwearied in their constant challenge and mortal danger," to quote Mr. Churchill, flung back the might of the German Luftwaffe, may divided into three stages.

Phase I, lasting from August 8-18, 1940, consisted of twenty-six attacks cted mainly against shipping, coastal towns and fighter aerodromes he South and South-East of England (map, left). A certain amount amage was done, but at a cost of 697 German aircraft. Our own losses e 153, but sixty pilots were saved. Phase II, from August 19-Sept. 5 was le up of some thirty-five major attacks delivered against inland fighter odromes and aircraft factories (map below, left). They cost the Nazis aircraft known to have been destroyed, while our own losses amounted 219, with a hundred and thirty-two pilots saved. The heavy task of the nce is shown in the fact that during these first two phases no fewer than 23 Fighter Patrols, of varying strength in aircraft, were flown in daylight. se III, Sept. 6-Oct. 5 was characterized by the hurling of the main strength the Luftwaffe against London and the Thames Estuary, with subsidiary d diversion attacks against the South and South-East Coasts (map below). t was on September 15 that the Germans launched their greatest attack inst Britain ; 500 aircraft, 250 in the morning and 250 in the afternoon, de a desperate attempt to smash a way through the British defences. They ied, and their attempt cost them 185 aircraft known to have been destroyed. is final phase of the Battle of Britain cost the Nazis in all 883 aircraft. e R.A.F. had gained the greatest victory in its history. Never again the Germans come in daylight in such numbers. The day raids continued a time, but on a much smaller scale; and the night raids, with less danger interception for the enemy, took their place.

The maps in this page, reproduced from the Ministry of Information booklet The Battle of Britain," show for the first time the actual targets of Goering's ftwaffe.

HE CONTROL SYSTEM of the British air defences is shown, right, in diagram form. itain's coastline is divided into Sectors, each with its own Fighter aerodromes and Q. These sectors are grouped together under a Group H.Q., which in turn comes der the control of Headquarters, Fighter Command. In the Operations Room of ch H.Q. is a large map table upon which, by means of various symbols, is shown ery available item of information which can be gleaned concerning the strength d disposition of the enemy and his direction of flight. The Controllers also have possible information before them as to the location and state of their own Squadrons, as well as meteorological reports.

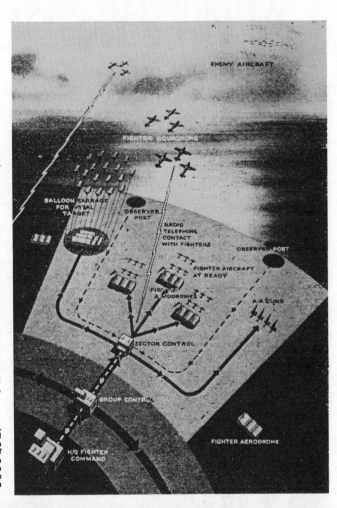

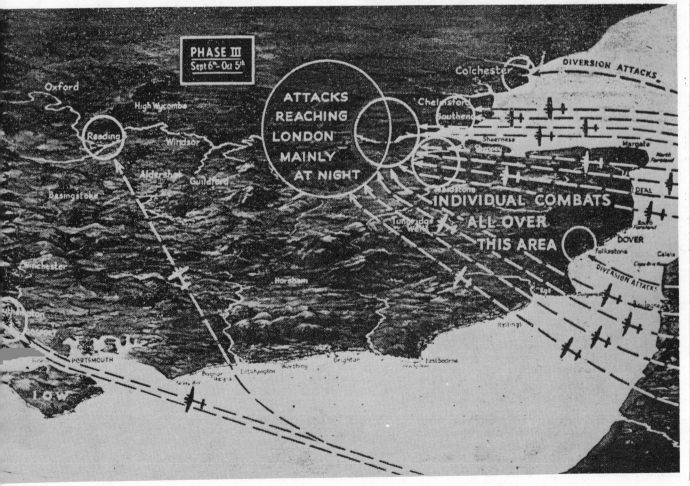

Swastika Over Acropolis :
Churchill Warns of Coming
Mediterranean Perils :
Americans Hunt U-boats

For only the second time in Greek history, alien troops occupied Athens. Half an hour after the Sunday morning entry of German motor-cyclists, the swastika was hoisted over the Acropolis. Special S. S. troops crossed the Corinth Canal after a landing by paratroops.

German seaborne troops captured the Greek islands of Samothrace and Lemnos. Lemnos is only 70 miles from the mouth of the Dardanelles.

King George of the Hellenes and his Government went to Crete.

In East Africa, Dessye fell to the South Africans, leaving only one other Italian base of any importance, Jimma.

Enemy mechanised troops, believed to be mainly Italian crossed the Egyptian frontier at several points south of Sollum.

A grave, but far from desperate, situation was outlined by Winston Churchill in a Sunday night Empire broadcast. While regretting the "damaging defeat"

in Libya and the Greek withdrawal, he stressed yet again that Britain's fate really hung on the Battle of the Atlantic. Britain had no other course but to aid Greece, who had proved a brave and worthy ally. The Dominion Governments had completely shared in this view, both before and after withdrawal started. Immense, and ever-increasing help was coming from the United States, where never before in history had we been held in such admiration. The situation was not as serious as that at the end of last summer.

WINSTON CHURCHILL

Churchill warned of fresh dangers in the Mediterranean, the possibility of the war spreading to Spain and Morocco, in the west, and to Turkey, and perhaps Russia, in the east.

General de Gaulle, in a broadcast from Brazzaville, French Equatorial Africa, warned Frenchmen of the risk of an early German coup in Algiers.

"PARADE" SCOOP: illustrating the depths of subservience into which that "whipped jackal" Mussolini has fallen—allowing his German master to appear with him on that small but sacred symbol of a country's independence—a postage stamp of the realm.

Special Order of the Day
by
General Sir Archibald P. Wavell, G.C.B., C.M.G., M.C.

5th May, 1941.

I wish to congratulate all the troops who took part in the expedition to Greece on the magnificent courage, skill and discipline which they showed in one of the most difficult and trying operations which Imperial Forces have ever experienced.

The heavy losses they have inflicted on the enemy and the fighting quality which they have shown will have a great effect on the war and enable us to face the coming struggle in the Middle East with confidence.

On behalf of the Army, I have thanked the Royal Navy and Royal Air Force for the self-sacrificing help which they gave during the operations and the re-embarkation.

AP Wavell

Commander-in-Chief,
Middle East

East Africa

News continues to come through about the capture of Dessye, the supply centre for all forces of the Italian Northern Command. Just before the final attack was to have been made on the town, a number of white-flagged cars were seen approaching. They contained military and civilian authorities, who consented to an unconditional surrender. Thus, a position which had taken three months to prepare fell into our hands in ten days—as did also the Duke of Aosta's luggage, abandoned by him in his precipitate flight.

The enemy's positions in the Tuselli Pass and around Amba Alagi are now being threatened from the North by troops advancing South along the Amara-Addis Ababa road, from the South by the advance northwards.

"Every Picture ➤
Tells a Story"

This one certainly does, for in reality these four somewhat ragged-looking individuals are usually smartly-dressed soldiers, two British, and two Greek. Their story is indeed a strange one.

When the withdrawal began the two British soldiers, part of the Headquarters Staff of the Armoured Force Headquarters, were detailed to help in bridge demolition work, under the orders of Captain "X," R.E. They were detailed to a certain bridge near Axiopolis, and on arrival on this bridge, they were met by a bullock cart, followed by an Army lorry, of British make, coming across from the opposite direction.

After the bullock cart had rumbled by, they shouted to the lorry to "get on with it," but instead it stopped dead, and out of it sprang fully-armed German soldiers, who seized them, and after cross-questioning them, despatched them eastwards with some Greek prisoners.

That evening, in company with two Greeks, they covered up their uniforms with some blankets they found, and made their escape. Soon they were able to obtain some civilian clothes from a peasant's cottage, and in this

---

The Greek campaign was not a victory for the democratic allies nor was it a complete defeat. It gained time. True, you may say, but only gained three weeks. Yet three weeks is a long time if like Hitler you have a schedule worked out well in advance. And the British Empire needs every second it can win for the United States to give munitions to us.

For the comparatively few casualties the Empire Force sustained it was a campaign worth waging. There have been various estimates of the German casualties. A figure around 125,000 is probably the most nearly accurate. That in itself is unimportant except that it shows the Empire's ability to stand up to Germany though hopelessly outnumbered and to hand out far more punishment than the enemy can give.

There is one other point before we leave Greece. Turkish journalists have made the point that our Empire force of 60,000 strong was too small ever to hope to hold the German juggernaut. That is perfectly true. Every Briton regrets that the Expeditionary Force could not have been ten times as large as it was.

But the reasons why not, perfectly understood by the Greeks, were obvious. Hitler has five years military start on Britain, we have to guard against attack at so many points with our limited forces, our shipping heavily engaged, and there were no airfield facilities in Greece to send more R.A.F. which might have been spared.

People say: "the British are masterly at withdrawals if at nothing else." That's a silly jibe.

new guise they set off via Kilkis, into Serbia, travelling west.

In the course of time, and now well into Serbia, they fell in with a German column marching south and, attaching themselves as pseudo camp followers they actually travelled with this column southwards through the mountains right down to Thermopylae.

Here they broke away, having travelled *in toto* nearly 300 miles, and approached the line held by the New Zealanders. The latter at first, naturally, were strongly suspicious of them, but things turned out all right, for by an extraordinary coincidence Captain "X" R.E. happened to be in the immediate vicinity, and so was able to recognise and vouch for them.

The story is told, but it has a moral: "You can't keep a good man down."

HOME TOWN NEWS

PLYMOUTH

Takes Three Hidings—Morale Unshaken

Although Plymouth has taken three hidings from the Nazi *Luftwaffe* recently and considerable damage has been done, public morale is unshaken. The women are keeping their chins up and are making light of the terror tactics of Goering's hordes. The children also are unafraid and the boys delight in dashing out to put out incendiary bombs. Devon, famous for its adventurers in former days, has lost none of its ardour to engage in hazardous exploits and Plymouthians particularly are only too pleased to try and emulate the feats of Drake, Raleigh and Hawkins, not to mention other natives of the city whose names have been associated with Britain's might:

Within a few days of her 101st birthday Mrs. L.R. Lillicrap of Lower Clicker Farm, Menheniot, has died.

Mr and Mrs G. Knight of H.M. Coastguard Station, Polruan, have just celebrated their silver wedding. At the time of their marriage at Exeter Mr. Knight was serving in the Submarine Service and his wife was on the staff at the G.P.O.

* * *

Plympton St. Maurice was visited by about twenty-five members of the Devon-shire Association last week-end, the leaders being Dr. E.G. Symes-Saunders, chairman, and Mr. R. Hansfordworth of the Plymouth branch. Striking features and the contents of the Guildhall and the Castle were among the ancient spots examined.

* * *

One public house in Plymouth in which windows have been broken by blast during an air raid is exhibiting a notice: 'Draughty, yes! Windy no!'

PORTSMOUTH

Portsmouth M.P. Seriously Injured

Sir Jocelyn Lucas, M.P. for Portsmouth South, who is a member of the London Volunteer Fire Service has been seriously injured in a recent raid and taken to hospital.

* * *

Five and a half million pounds have been contributed to date in War Savings by Portsmouth and Southsea.

* * *

John Pounds' old home in Highbury Street, where he used to teach and at the same time cobble shoes and which was the foundation of the Ragged School movement is to be taken to pieces, preserved and erected on a prominent site after the war.

* * *

MANCHESTER

Manchester and the rest of the cotton country is working hard to fit in with the Government's Cotton Reorganisation Plan. This scheme is in the forefront of Lancashire's mind at the moment. The cotton mills are being put in three groups. Class 1. mills are doing Government and other important work. They will remain open. Class 2. holds mills doing secondary jobs. A number of these mills will partly shut down and amalgamate with others in the same class. Others in Class 3. will shut down for the duration for else be turned over to other processes.

SOUTHAMPTON

Young Players "Never Say Die" Spirit

The chief topics of conversation are the efforts of tradesmen to get back to the sites of their *blitzed* properties, the steadiness of people in the face of war problems and—among sportsmen—the never-say-die spirit of the young players who are doing their best to keep Southampton F.C. alive in the realm of first-class football.

* * *

Mr. Tom Parker is doing his level best to keep first-class football alive in the town. Although, because of circumstances out of his control, no matches are possible at the Dell he has got together a team of very enthusiastic youngsters whose spirits are undaunted by the fact that they have to travel to their opponents grounds for every game, often after a spell of strenuous war work.

Although the youngsters haven't many points to their credit the managers of other clubs have already noted the names of the most promising and have congratulated Tom Parker on the talent he has got together. What a day when we can gather together again and let it rip with "Yi yi yi'!

SCOTLAND

Scots Just Can't Help Saving

Roxburghshire has won the thrift championship of Scotland. Its people are better savers than even those of Aberdeen. Their investments on War Savings represent an average of £61 per head of the population, first-class going for a rural county. Peebles and other towns in the county are as well-known over the border as is Aberdeen. The Scots just can't help saving. It is in their make-up.

* * *

There will be no 'old firm' Cup final. Eastern Scots will be glad to learn that Hearts beat Celtic and qualified to meet Rangers who defeated St. Mirren, in the final on May 10. Rangers have won the League and are favourites for the Cup. They have been the best team this season. A Hearts victory would be popular in Edinburgh but my 'tanner' is on the Ibrox squadron.

* * *

Sir Patrick Dollan has been asked to give more broadcasts to America and Canada. He has had a big fanmail from the United States, where those of Scots descent want to hear a Scots accent on the radio. Sir Patrick's accent is pure 'Glesca'. His last appeal to our trans-Atlantic cousins brought £20,000 for Clydesides Air Raid Fund, now nearing £100,000.

Men of the Royal Navy and the Mercantile Marine have sent £50 to the Fund as a mark of appreciation of the bravery of Clydeside civilians during enemy attacks. A H.L.I. battalion sent £10 for the same reason.

On All Fronts
WAR OVER THE MEDITERRANEAN

CRETE

After twelve days of the fiercest fighting this war has yet seen and the most murderously precise bombing, it was officially announced on Monday that our troops had evacuated Crete.

There were heavy losses on both sides. Apart from casualties, we have lost ships and equipment.

Much of the enemy's air fleet has been reduced to heaps of wreckage on the Cretan shores. Twenty-five per cent of his air-borne troops were destroyed. These were highly trained personnel, parachutists and crack German Alpine troops.

If, by the loss of Crete, we have gained experience of how to deal with air-borne invasion planned by the German to the last grim detail of destruction, we shall not have come vainly out of the inferno.

The Germans struck with bombs and Storm Troops at the air and sea ports. Because of their superiority in the air, created by numerous bases at close range, they were able to drive our 'planes from the island. It was then possible for them both to cover the landing of their parachutists and carrier-borne troops with intensive bombardments and to obstruct the operations of the Navy. At least 26,000 enemy troops were dropped or landed. At times troop-carriers were sweeping to earth every five minutes.

Together with the precision bombing that systematically reduced Canea to a heap of rubble, poison propaganda pamphlets, threatening death to Cretan civilians who resisted the invasion, were unloaded over the island.

The R.A.F., though forced to operate from 400 miles away in the desert on flights that were fraught with enormous risk, managed to deal shrewd and telling blows at the Luftwaffe, as it lay sprawled across the island's beaches, or prepared for repeated pounces on its Dodecanese and Grecian mainland bases.

IRAQ

Against the Battle of Crete, and in part because of the effect it had on the timing of Hitler's attempted drive into the Middle East, we have on the credit side last week the collapse of the rebel uprising in Iraq. Rashid Ali, his head full of half-baked ideas and his pockets full of German gold, fled to Iran, together with his Cabinet, his puppet regent, Sherif Sharaf and some German and Italian officials.

Then, on the last day of May, the Mayor of Baghdad made a request for an armistice.

Germany's failure to send any material support to the rebel army largely contributed towards the collapse of the rebellion.

Another factor was the success of the British punitive expedition, which, after the capture of Fallujah and the bridge over the Euphrates, threatened the Iraqi capital from North, East and South.

The R.A.F., which had virtually shot the rebel airforce from the sky and wrecked it on the ground, delivered the *coup de grâce* when well-directed salvoes of bombs at Cassels Post blew up over a million gallons of rebel petrol. Throughout the expedition invaluable work was done by R.A.F. Armoured Car Companies.

EAST AFRICA

During the last fourteen days our troops operating in the Lake District, S.W. Abyssinia, have cleared of enemy forces an area 10,000 miles square. There remain in this zone only 1,000 Fascist troops unaccounted for.

Through country that is in part unexplored, in part dominated by mountain peaks rising 14,000 feet above sea level, and everywhere made difficult by torrential rains, we have advanced to within 95 miles of Jimma. The decisive action in this zone was the battle that took place at Soddu. Not only did we take over 7,000 prisoners

in this engagement and the operations that led up to it, but we captured the key position in the Jimma area.

A force of Patriots is operating in the Debra Tabor area to the east of Lake Tana, while others have occupied Debarec, about 50 miles north of Gondar. The garrison in Gondar, which has been repeatedly bombed by the Free French Air Force, and is threatened by the advance of the S.D.F. from Chelga, is in a most unenviable position.

SOLLUM-TOBRUK

Another of those patrol movements described by Axis wireless commentators as "fingers in glove" operations, took place over the wire and resulted in the re-occupation of Halfaya Pass by an enemy force consisting of a number of tanks, infantry and artillery. Two other columns started simultaneously to advance over the frontier south of Capuzzo.

There is nothing to indicate that this movement is on a larger scale than the similar advance made by German columns two week ago, or that it will not end in the same way, with the enemy being forced back to his starting point and beyond.

As the enemy made his slight movement forward the Tobruk garrison twisted its spear in his side and making a sudden sortie we established positions on the perimeter.

The R.A.F. have bombed Tripoli and Benghazi and other key points in the enemy's rear and forward positions.

The total losses of the Axis in Africa up to date in prisoners, killed, wounded and deserted amount to 380,000.

While the Navy has been chiefly engaged in the Battle of Crete, units of the Fleet have bombarded the Libyan coast and sent salvoes crashing into Appolonia and Gazala. Several enemy troop-ships and oiltankers have been sunk, including the 18,000-ton Italian liner *Conte Rosso*, estimated to have been carrying at least 3,000 troops for the North African campaign.

The enemy must also have lost large numbers of ships, men and equipment in vain endeavours to slip reinforcements to Crete.

"LOVE ME, DO YOU HEAR — LOVE ME — OR I'LL KILL YOU!"
Cartoon from the London *Time and Tide*.

MESSAGE from LONDON

'Parade's' London Correspondent cables as follows: "London sends you a message of admiration. The news of the withdrawal from Crete was published today but it was clear here for some days that the island could not be held for long in view of the lack of airfields from which to combat the Nazi air force.

"No words can express the pride with which Londoners followed the details of the fighting in which troops from Britain and the Empire fought side by side with the Greeks.

"It was with infinite regret that we heard that the island had to be abandoned but the effect here has been to stiffen the country's determination to provide you in the front line with every weapon that will be needed so that victory may be assured in the end.

"Hitler may have had five years start on us but the men and women in the factories of this country—yes! and in those of the United States, too—are overtaking him.

"Carry on. Middle East! We're with you!"

Vol 4   # The War Illustrated   N° 93

Edited by Sir John Hammerton

FOURPENCE   WEEKLY

1941

"BOOTS, boots, boots, boots, moving up and down again . . ." sang Kipling à propos of the infantry of a former epoch, and this happy study of a cheery British infantryman cooling his feet after a march over scorching desert sand reminds us that, although mechanical transport has done away with a lot of unnecessary foot-slogging, in the last resort it is the infantry which decides a battle, and it does so on its feet. For this reason a good soldier bestows as much care upon his feet as upon his rifle.

Photo, British Official: Crown Copyright

BISMARCK CHASE SHOWS NAVY'S POWER

Here is the timetable of the most dramatic naval chase in history, as compiled from Admiralty communiqués.

1. — May 22. Coastal Command aircraft report Bismarck has left Bergen. Cruisers Norfolk and Suffolk ordered to Straits of Denmark.

2. — May 23, evening. Norfolk and Suffolk sight and shadow Bismarck and the cruiser Prinz Eugen, steaming fast through the Straits of Denmark.

3. — May 24, morning. Hood and Prince of Wales in company go into action with Bismarck. Hood blows up and sinks; Prince of Wales damaged; Bismarck on fire. Same afternoon. Coastal command aircraft report seeing Bismarck speeding southwest, leaving trail of oil.

4. — Same night. After action with Prince of Wales, Bismarck turns west, later swinging south. Enemy struck by torpedo from plane from aircraft carrier Victorious. Main body of Home Fleet, led by King George V, heading south-west from northern waters.

5. — Another force, led by Renown, heads north-west from Gibraltar. Rodney and Ramillies leave Atlantic convoys to join chase.

6. — Coastal Command aircraft and Royal Canadian Air Force, operating from Newfoundland, join chase.

7. — May 25. Morning. After all-night chase, Prince of Wales, Norfolk and Suffolk lose touch with Bismarck 350 miles south-east of Greenland.

8. — May 26, 10.30 a.m. Coastal command aircraft sight Bismarck 550 miles west of Land's End. Enemy attack aircraft, which lose touch, 11.15 a.m. Planes from carrier Ark Royal sight Bismarck steering easterly course. Rodney and King George V approaching, but out of range. Afternoon. Planes from Ark Royal unsuccessfully attack Bismarck with torpedoes.

9. — 5.30 p.m. Cruiser Sheffield contacts and shadows Bismarck. Planes from Ark Royal score two torpedo hits. After 11 p.m. Tribal class destroyers, led by Cossack, contact Bismarck.

10. — May 27. Between 1.20-1.50 a.m. Destroyers Zulu, Maori and Cossack attack Bismarck with torpedoes, setting her afire in forecastle.

11. — 2.50 a.m. Bismarck slows up, almost stops, 400 miles west of Brest, after 1,750-mile chase. Later reported to have made eight miles in an hour and to be still capable of heavy and accurate gunfire. Dawn. Planes from Ark Royal chase Bismarck. But owing to poor visibility no attack.

12. — After dawn. Bismarck engages British destroyers with gunfire. Norfolk attacks Bismarck. Heavy ships also join battle, but details scarce. Then, to quote Admiralty communiqué: "H.M.S. Dorsetshire (Capt. B.C.S. Martin, R.N.) was ordered to sink the Bismarck with torpedoes. The Bismarck sank at 1101 hrs."

May 22.—Coastal Command aircraft report Bismarck has left Bergen. Cruisers Norfolk and Suffolk ordered to Straits of Denmark.

"The Bismarck sank at 1101 hrs."

350 miles

550 miles

400 miles

U.S.A.

CANADA

NEWFOUNDLAND

GREENLAND

STRAITS OF DENMARK

ICELAND

ATLANTIC OCEAN

Land's End

Brest

Gibraltar

NORWAY

Bergen

ued to the *Fighting Forces in the desert*

. 22 Vol. 2 September 28, 1942

Review for the Blue

USSIA

Street by street, house by house, the Germans forced their way slowly into Stalingrad. "...The Russian army is now fighting hand-to-hand on his own doorstep, crouched behind his own domestic furniture. From windows stuffed with mattresses vicious anti-tank rifles protrude ; in cellars redolent with the acrid scent of fresh-cut birch logs sappers are laying mines," said "The Times" correspondent in Russia. Both sides brought up reserves. There was determination on both sides to win this vital battle regardless of cost. In the Caucasus the German advance was held. In the central and northern fronts the Russians held the initiative.

REAT BRITAIN

Minister of Production, Oliver Lyttleton, speaking at Leeds, said that British weapons were now better than those of the enemy, the 6 pounder better than the 5 cm., the 25 pounder and 4.5 better weapons than anything the Germans had. Defects in our tanks had been cured. On post-war conditions Lyttleton said that unemployment was not inevitable but that it rested in the people's hands whether it occurred again or not. It was essential for us to remain strong and not put pleasure before duty. "It is nonsense to talk about a "home for heroes" and "war that ends war" just by the mere fact of victory, but do not forget that these things are within your grasp. If your statesmen and ministers do not give you these things change them and get some more, because the future can be better if we use our intelligence."

ERMANY

8,000 lb bombs (more than 3 1/2 tons) continued to tear large chunks out of Germany. In the first 19 days of the month the R.A.F. has carried out 10 very heavy raids over the Reich. Aerial pictures showed that 370 acres of Dusseldorf was laid waste.

MADAGASCAR

After asking for an armistice, M. Annet, governor-general of Madagascar, refused the terms and fighting went on. A strong force landed on the east coast and occupied Tamatave, the principal port. From the north-west and the east British troops advanced on Antananarivo, the capital.

BRITAIN'S NEW TANK

Radio picture, transmitted from London just before "Crusader" went to press, of Britain's new heavy infantry tank. Known as "The Churchill," it is strongly armoured, may be used as a pill box fort and has startling speed. War Minister Sir James Grigg in speech at Cardiff referred to new tank as "Best in the world and miles better than anything provided before."

MacRoberts Fight On

Four Hurricane fighters — the gifts of Lady MacRobert — presented to an R.A.F. Squadron in the Western Desert, will carry on the work of her three sons who were killed in action with the R.A.F.

Her second son, Flight Lt. Sir Roderic MacRobert was serving with this desert squadron when he was killed in May 1941.

The ceremony was performed by Air Vice Marshall McLaughry, Air Officer Commanding in Egypt. He read to the squadron the following message from Lady MacRobert :—

"*The name of MacRobert returns to the squadron on these aircraft. My boys whose names they bear were fighters. Their spirit lives on. I shall be proud of you when you pilot these MacRobert fighters. My heart and thoughts will be with you. I am confident you will strike hard for victory. God bless and keep you all.*"

George Gumption

A young gentleman has arrived in Egypt. Perhaps you know someone just like George. Like most of us he is not much to look at — but we think George has got what it takes to win this war. His adventures begin next week.

Four New Battleships

In the last 27 months Britain has completed at least four battleships, four aircraft-carriers and 22 cruisers.

These figures can be deduced from the statement by Mr. A.V. Alexander, First Lord of the Admiralty, that Britain had replaced the capital ships, aircraft-carriers and cruisers lost in the last 2 1/2 years.

Since the war began, five capital ships — *Royal Oak, Prince of Wales, Barham, Hood* and *Repulse* — have been lost and of these *Royal Oak* was sunk before the period mentioned by Mr. Alexander.

Mr. Alexander also stated that lost destroyers have been more than replaced. Losses of destroyers totalled 80 but with the 50 handed over by the United States it is probable that new destroyers total nearly 200.

THE SYRIAN CAMPAIGN

by "STRATEGICUS"

Through military necessity, General Dentz, Commander-in-Chief of the Vichy forces in Syria, has accepted Allied terms for an armistice convention and fighting has ceased.

Summarising the campaign and its implications, "Strategicus" cables from London:

It has been a most troublesome episode for all but those who, failing to recognise their own interests, had thrown in their lot with Germany.

The wrong-headedness, which allowed the enemy to make in Syria a base of attack upon Iraq and the Middle East and would if permitted have provided a springboard for an assault on Suez from the north, has been almost more baffling than the Vichy treachery. The situation had to be cleared up but it made the task of the British command indescribably unpalatable. General Wavell had resources to mount a 'blitzkrieg' on Syria but neither he nor the

British Government could regard such a prospect with anything but horror. France had been Britain's ally and England does not lightly cast aside her loyalties.

From the first the campaign suffered from a dangerous handicap. When men take up arms and find themselves able to fight successfully there is no telling when they'll stop. In such a situation the wisest policy from a purely military viewpoint would have been to advance

with an overwhelming force from the south and east and crush resistance with a ruthless hand. That course being precluded, the British command had to face the difficulties of unfavourable terrain with manœuvres as their strongest weapon but they had firstly to give the Vichy troops a chance to make up their minds, and of course many of them came over to the British lines. Many who did not expressed their joy when taken prisoner. Nevertheless the Vichy

(Continued overleaf)

Weapon Against Luftwaffe

For Britain the most cheering domestic news of the week was the revelation by Air Chief Marshal Sir Philip Joubert de la Ferté, Commander-in-Chief, Coastal Command, that a "secret weapon" had played an important part in beating the *Luftwaffe* over Britain. A system known as "radio-location," covering the whole of Britain, detected with precision the approach of enemy aircraft and ships. The Air Chief Marshal described it as a "system whereby rays, which are unaffected by fog or darkness, are sent out far beyond the limits of our shores. Any aircraft or ship in the path of the ray immediately sends back a signal to a detecting station, where people are on watch. These ether waves keep a 24-hour watch, year in and year out; they are always on duty." The device, on which a 49-year-old Scot, Robert Alexander Watson Watt, now Scientific Adviser at the Ministry of Aircraft Production, had been working since 1935, was in operation on a small scale at the beginning of the war and had greatly aided in the routing of the *Luftwaffe* during last summer's daylight air attacks. The whole of Britain's radio industry had been at work for months on mass production of radio-locators. Britain now had more machines than operators and was calling for 10,000 technicians. Manipulation of the locator was an extremely skilled task; 2,500 Canadians who had been undergoing a special University course would proceed to Britain in September to operate locators. Simultaneously with the furnishing to the United States Government of the extremely secret designs of the radio-locator, an office had been opened in New York City, with American sanction, for the recruiting for service in Britain of American locator operators.

Services experts in the British press said it was impossible to over-estimate the importance of the radio-locator. Its use made unnecessary the maintenance of standing patrols of pursuit 'planes.

Appealing for technicians for locator work, Lord Beaverbrook said: "Radio is our golden cockerel now, warning us of the approach of the enemy."

Adoption of another secret weapon was revealed by the High Command. It is an "anti-tank device," invented by a 24-year-old Cambridge graduate serving as a lieutenant in the Royal Engineers. Described as "deadly, invisible and almost childishly simple" it is produceable quickly and in immense quantities. In a demonstration of the weapon sixty per cent of attacking tanks and armoured fighting vehicles were knocked out.

The growing strength of the R.A.F. found expression in destructive night raids on enemy territory, particularly north-west Germany and Tripolitania and in daring daylight sweeps across France. In one day, the R.A.F. brought down 30 planes over France for the loss of two and on another finished with a score of 28 to 5.

While the British press was enthusing about these weapons, the Ministry of Agriculture was warning British farmers to be on guard during the coming summer against German air attacks on crops, particularly in such form as setting fire to fields and haystacks.

U.S. Tension With the Axis

American action in ordering the closing down of German consulates and "travel agencies" in the United States was followed by prompt reprisals in Berlin, where the closing of all United States consulates in Greater Germany and the German Empire was ordered. The German press published a list of American consular officials "whose activities are not considered to be in the interests of the Reich" and enumerated various misdeeds attributed to the consuls.

"Ach! Havana! Churchill again!"

"And when you're through, Doctor, we'll just get the military censorship to run him over."

"All clear, gentlemen, please."

THE WEEK

Britain mobilises "V" Army in Europe: R.A.F. Spreads Death and Fire in Germany: Axis Shipping Losses Exceed British

"The most amazing piece of propaganda devised in this war," an American radio commentator termed Britain's dramatic "V for Victory" whispering campaign in German-occupied territories. Although the campaign started some weeks ago, it was officially inaugurated with a Saturday midnight broadcast from London by a "Colonel Britton," who said: "I have come to the studio to-night with a July 20 message for all occupied countries. It is just past midnight, July 20 and the mobilisation of the 'V' Army has begun. I have a message to you from the British Prime Minister, Mr. Winston Churchill. Here it is:

'The 'V' sign is a symbol of the unconquerable will of occupied territories and a portent of the fate awaiting Nazi tyranny. So long as the peoples of Europe continue to refuse all collaboration with the invader it is sure that his cause will perish and that Europe will be liberated.'

"That is Mr. Churchill's July 20 message to you, people of Europe. I have said that the mobilisation of the 'V' Army has begun. At this moment men and women all over Europe are dedicating themselves to the continuation of this war against Nazi Germany until the 'V' — the sign of victory and freedom — is triumphant. In a few minutes there will be millions of new 'Vs' on walls and doors and pavements all over Europe. It is dark now. If you listen you may hear distant bugles sound the 'V' rhythm or drums tapping. Perhaps you will hear a train whistle sounded by one of your comrades. Darkness is your chance too. Put your 'V' up as a member of this vast 'V' Army. Do it during daytime too. Your friends will be doing it from one end of Europe to the other and do not forget the 'V' sound. Tap it out so that your comrades of the 'V' Army will hear it and so that the Germans hear it too. They will have to pretend now that they like it. They do not.

"One word more. The 'V' Army must be a disciplined army. When the moment comes it will act in such a way that the Germans are powerless. But wait for the word. Today we sign on. Good Luck to you."

Already Norwegians in Oslo were beating out the 'V' symbol in Morse with teaspoons on glass table-tops in cafés, drawing from Quisling's Propaganda Chief, Lunde, an official complaint about "fools who spend their time knocking at tables."

Evidence of the opportunism, but also the lack of imagination, of the German Ministry of Propaganda came with a German broadcast stating that: "All over Europe, the letter 'V' representing the Nazi victory has appeared, from the North Cape to the Atlantic, from the Baltic shores to the Mediterranean, from the North Sea to the Black Sea, on the Pyrenees, on the Alps and through the Balkans, on all walls, bill-boards, newspapers, houses and tents—the capital 'V' symbolising National Socialist victory. This is like a European plebiscite, in which all Europe is testifying its trust in the German victory over Bolshevism and Capitalism." To make 'V' stand for German victory, the Germans produced the almost unknown word *Viktoria*, defined in all standard German dictionaries as a foreign word, the usual German word for victory being *sieg*. Berlin Radio said on Sunday that 'V' had appeared on walls and footpaths everywhere there were German troops. To "rub it in" and attempt to turn the British trick to their own advantage the Germans hung huge 'V' banners from the Eiffel Tower and the Amsterdam Palace. Of this ruse the *New York Herald-Tribune* commented: "For those in occupied territories, German capitulation to the 'V' must come as pure joy. Now they can chalk up the symbol, tap it out in morse code or thunder out a *Fifth Symphony* beat unmolested, with the full consciousness that the Germans have openly admitted their inability to check the swelling chorus of freedom."

R.A.F. Wipe Out Third of Town

Continual evidence from American correspondents showed that the people of France were causing the Germans as much trouble as any of the conquered races During the week, the Germans had to put up in Brest posters saying: "The German military authorities have noticed that large parts of the civil population are clearly hostile to our troops. During air raid warnings, passers-by demonstrate in the public high ways. Acts of sabotage are being carried out and injurious inscriptions are being written on walls." Then followed a list of detailed warnings. Strikes in Northern France threw more than 20 coal mines out of action and affected 100,000 workers.

Even in very unconquered Britain the 'V' idea caught on. When the King and Queen visited two munitions factories they found bold 'V's' chalked by the workers on machines of war.

Over Germany the Royal Air Force spread terror, death and destruction as never before. The *Star* (London) said: "For a month Germany has felt the full weight of an aerial *blitzkrieg* greater than anything hurled at Britain. These attacks far exceed the four weeks it has mounted to a pitch beyond Goering's power last autumn. We and he may expect that before the long nights come it will have attained a scale sufficient to lay waste every great city of the German Reich." The Royal Air Force claimed to have destroyed one-third of the German town of Aachen (Aix-la-Chapelle) and one-third of Muenster described in a Berlin broadcast as that "unhappy city." On the night of July 10 alone, 7,000 British incendiary bombs fell on Aachen. Between June 16 and July 10, it was revealed, more than 2,000 tons of bombs were dropped in the Ruhr. In the same interval, 1,000 tons were dropped on Cologne and 500 tons on Bremen.

MATSUOKA OUT: Japan's new Cabinet is notable mainly for the exclusion of Yosuke Matsuoka. He is seen above with Ribbentrop on his recent visit to Berlin.

Simultaneously, the Royal Air Force attacked with unprecedented thoroughness the German mercantile marine, both in port and at sea. It was authoritatively stated that Axis shipping losses in July were substantially greater than those of Britain. The naval correspondent of the *Yorkshire Post* commented: "For the first time in this war, the sea campaign has swung against the enemy, who cannot replace his losses at anything like the same pace as Britain and the United States." Beside attacking German ocean convoys, and scoring such successes as sinking 48,000 tons in two attacks, the British fliers made a daylight raid on Rotterdam and sank between 90,000 and 100,000 tons of shipping in one day. Following-up raids on the same port sank 10,000, 16,000 and 48,000 tons respectively.

Nine Million Men in Battle

Nine million men were stated to be in battle on the long German-Russian front. Although Leningrad, Smolensk and Kiev appeared to be threatened by the slow German advance, the Germans encountered growing rather than diminishing resistance every step they advanced into Russia. To explain away to the German public the breakdown of the *blitzkrieg* schedule the German press ran columns of graphic accounts of the stubbornness of the Red Army and the hardships of the campaign. The broadcaster Joachim Richter, speaking from the Eastern Front through the *Deutschlandsender*, said: "The Red aircraft are everywhere. We are being attacked almost continuously by the Russian Ratas (fighters)." Then Richter interviewed a German artillery commander who swore into the microphone and said: "These Russian 'planes simply won't be driven off. Such ceaseless raids we have never experienced before. The Devil knows where they all come from." A war correspondent of the *Koelnische Zeitung* said vast clouds of dust constantly enveloped the advancing German columns. "The soldiers never cease swallowing dust. The pores are blocked and the nose irritated. The eyes stream and the fingers lose any sense of touch... Waggon wheels often sink axle-deep in the sandy earth..." And the *Muenchner Neueste Nachrichten* told how the *Reichswehr* attacked five Russian forts with land troops, artillery, flame-throwers, siege guns, tanks and with *Luftwaffe* cooperation. After days of dive-bombing it was thought nobody could be alive in the forts. Yet whenever troops approached, Russians greeted them with heavy fire. Eventually the forts were smashed.

British troops marked the completion of their occupation of Syria by taking up positions along the entire length of Syria's northern frontier with Turkey. Lifting of the British blockade, inclusion of Syria and the Lebanon in the sterling bloc and the resumption of trade between the newly-conquered territory and Palestine gave promise of an early return to normality.

The *Times* air correspondent pointed out that one of the main advantages accruing to Britain from the forestalling of the Germans in Syria was the acquisition of more than 50 aerodromes, a number of them excellent, particularly those at Aleppo, Damascus, Deireszór, Palmyra, Rayak and Homs. From these fields both bombing and reconnaissance could be carried out.

The growing menace to Turkey was emphasised by the Ankara broadcaster of the National (U.S.) troops on Samos, the broadcaster asserted. Simultaneously, agencies in all non-Axis countries reported continued German and Bulgarian military preparations on the Bulgarian-Turkish frontier.

"To make room for a stronger Government and to cope with the national and international situation," the Japanese Cabinet of Prince Funimaro Konoye resigned. The new Cabinet, again headed by Konoye, had for the key post of Foreign Minister, Admiral Tejiro Toyoda and did not include the former Foreign Minister, Yosuke Matsuoka. The official Domei Agency said the new Cabinet, Prince Konoye's third, would "function as a wartime Cabinet and seek unity in military and political operations." Support of Japan's traditionally conservative commercial community for the new Cabinet was reflected in an all-round two to ten yen gain on the Tokyo stock exchange.

Foreign interpretation of the dropping of Matsuoka varied widely. Some British newspapers saw in the move the departure of a fanatically pro-Axis man, the others the departure of the man largely responsible for the Soviet-Japanese Non-Aggression Pact. Matsuoka was stated to have regarded himself as the only friend that Stalin had outside Russia. After Germany declared war on Russia, Matsuoka gave no indication where his sympathies lay. He was regarded in America as being bitterly anti-white-man, the bitterness dating from insults he was reputed to have suffered as a student at the University of Oregon.

Matsuoka Leaves Tokyo Cabinet

Most British newspapers viewed with guarded optimism the appointment of Admiral Toyoda. Like many senior officers of the Japanese Navy, he has had prolonged and cordial relations with the British. From 1922 to 1924 he was Japan's Naval Attaché in London and he attended the London Naval Conference in 1935. Even the trigger-fingering Japanese press described the new Foreign Minister as "one of the most level-headed and capable men in the Imperial Navy."

However, the Cabinet reshuffle saw no abatement of Japan's current "war of nerves" against Britain and the United States. Widely separated sources reported strong and uncompromising Japanese pressure on the Vichy Government to yield the naval base of Camranh Bay, perhaps on a "lease" basis. Definite ceding to Japan of bases in Southern Indo-China and in neighbouring Thailand would greatly increase the southward striking power of Japan's three armed services.

Air Chief Marshal Sir Robert Brooke-Popham, British Commander-in-Chief in the Far East, personally welcomed at Singapore large R.A.F. reinforcements from Britain and stressed that "we are fully prepared, come what may."

On his removal from the post of Minister of Information, Mr. Duff Cooper was appointed as Minister of State in the Far East, with headquarters at Singapore. This appointment presumably was complementary to the recent posting of Mr. Oliver Lyttelton to Cairo.

With the appointment of Brendan Bracken as Minister of Information, Britain at last had, after nearly two years of war, a man knowing something of journalism to direct its propaganda. This red-headed Irish-Australian, formerly Parliamentary Private Secretary to Winston Churchill, was credited by the press with having a live mind and a dynamic personality.

It was announced in Washington that the first shipment of farm commodities acquired by the Department.

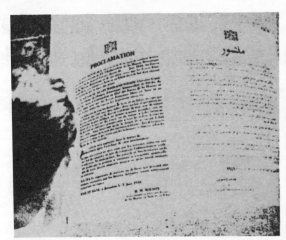

One of Beirut's citizens reads the British proclamation which has been posted up in the streets of the city in French and Arabic.

Entry into BEIRUT

ON THE AFTERNOON OF FRIDAY, JULY 18, UNITS OF THE EMPIRE'S ARMY WHICH HAD BROUGHT THE SYRIAN CAMPAIGN TO A SUCCESSFUL CONCLUSION, MADE A CEREMONIAL ENTRY INTO BEIRUT, THE SYRIAN CAPITAL. HUGE CROWDS TURNED OUT TO SEE THE TROOPS RIDE IN.

Soon after his arrival in Beirut, General Sir Henry Wilson and General Catroux held a reception at Government House for political leaders, members of the Lebanese Government and religious leaders.

French gendarmes stand opposite the crowded balcony of the Palmyra Hotel and watch the procession of trucks and all sorts of vehicles pass down the street.

General Wilson standing on the balcony of Government House after the ceremonial march into the city by the Imperial Forces under his command.

A large crowd watches Bren Gun carriers rattle through the main streets. The population now looks forward to the resumption of normal trade with other countries

The kids had a day out for a change. The arrival of the Empire's army gave them something to cheer about. They dash down the street to catch another glimpse

THE WEEK

Roosevelt and Churchill State Joint Victory Terms : U.S. And Britain Must Police Whole World : Every Aid to Soviet

When C.R. Attlee, Lord Privy Seal, revealed over the B.B.C. that Roosevelt and Churchill, each with an entourage of top-ranking defence chiefs, had just finished a three-day secret conference at sea, he gave the newspapers their greatest personal story of the war. The German Radio chose to call it "the worst joke in the world." The two leaders met alternately in *Prince of Wales*, Britain's newest battleship, still carrying scars from the Bismarck battle, and the United States cruiser *Augusta*. The President, officially on a fishing vacation, sailed to the ocean rendezvous in his motor-yacht *Potomac*.

Those present at the historic meeting included: Admiral Sir Dudley Pound, First British Sea Lord; General Sir John Dill, Chief of the British Imperial General Staff; General George Marshall, United States Chief of Staff; Admiral Harold Stark, United States Chief of Naval Operations; Mr. Harry Hopkins; Mr. Averell Harriman; Admiral Ernest King, Commander of the United States Atlantic Fleet; and Lord Beaverbrook, British Minister of Supply.

The only immediately revealed result of the three days' talking was a set of peace points. The most newsworthy of these was the last one, plainly indicating that Britain and America, as *News of the World* put it, plainly intended to make themselves policemen of the whole world until all mad dogs were rendered harmless. Other points that attracted attention were (1) the implication in clause three that no exception was taken to Communism and Fascism if these policies did not involve trampling on the national rights of others and (2) the implication in clause four that vanquished nations would be able to trade again with the whole world and have access "on equal terms" to raw materials. This suggestion that the vanquished might be treated generously contrasted sharply with the recent declaration of the authoritative *Muenchener Neueste Nachrichten* that: "Germany must tear the British Empire apart bit by bit and must not be influenced by the slightest feeling of pity. Britain must be made to bleed and every wound reopened until she bleeds to death."

Here is the joint Roosevelt-Churchill declaration :

"The President of the United States, and the Prime Minister, Mr. Winston Churchill, representing His Majesty's Government in the United Kingdom, being met together, deem it right to make known certain common principles in the national policies of their respective countries on which they base their hopes for the better future of the world.

"Firstly, their countries seek no aggrandisement, territorial or other.

"Secondly, they desire to see no territorial changes that do not accord with the freely expressed wishes of the peoples concerned.

"Thirdly, they respect the right of all peoples to choose the form of Government under which they will live, and they wish to see sovereign rights and self-Government restored to those who have been forcibly deprived of them.

Vanquished May Still Trade

" Fourthly, they will endeavour with due respect for their existing obligations, to further the enjoyment by all States, great or small, victor or vanquished, of access on equal terms to trade and to the raw materials of the world, which are needed for their economic prosperity.

"Fifthly, they desire to bring about the fullest collaboration between all nations in the economic field, with the object of securing for all improved labour standards, economic advancement and social security.

"Sixthly, after the final destruction of Nazi tyranny, they hope to see established a peace which affords to all nations the means of dwelling in safety within their own boundaries, and which will afford the assurance that all men in all lands may live out their lives in freedom from fear and want.

"Seventhly, such a peace should enable all men to traverse the high seas and oceans without hindrance.

"Eighthly, they believe that the nations of the world, for realistic as well as spiritual reasons, must come to the abandonment of the use of force. Since no future peace can be maintained if land, sea or air armaments continue to be employed by nations which threaten, or may threaten, aggression outside of their frontiers, they believe, pending the establishment of a wider system of general security, that the disarmament of such nations is essential. They will likewise aid and encourage all other practicable measures which will lighten for peace-loving peoples the crushing burden of armament."

The first press reaction in Britain after initial excitement at the sensational news was one of disappointment that the meeting's only result was a set of peace points for a war not yet won. This was followed by a

realisation that matters much more important must have come on the three-day agenda, and it was suggested further results would become apparent one by one. A question occurring to many newspapers was that of how the admirals and generals occupied themselves while the peace points were being formulated.

Results followed promptly. Lord Beaverbrook went on from the ocean meeting to Washington, where he told reporters he was "the world's biggest buyer on the hoof." And then, while the hard-fighting Red Army was being pushed out of a devastated Ukraine, a joint Roosevelt-Churchill message was delivered by an embassy courier at the Kremlin suggesting to Stalin an immediate meeting of high British, American and Russian delegates to formulate a long-term policy and discuss details of Russian requirements. This was readily agreed to by Stalin and was taken in Russia to imply Anglo-American confidence in the Red Army's prolonged resistance. Every available supply is going to Russia pending the conference and the United States tanker *St. Clair* is on her way to Vladivostock with 96,000 gallons of aviation spirit for the Red Air Force.

WRECKERS OF NAZIDOM —

— MAPPERS OF FREEDOM

Although ridiculing the meeting and the declaration —Dr. Goebbels himself spoke of "this theatrical performance" and "a scrap of paper"—the Axis press was not willing to let its readers know the full contents of the declaration. Distorted versions on the Axis radios gave the declaration the appearance of another Versailles.

On his return to the United States, President Roosevelt, "looking radiantly healthy and happy," told the press of his "complete agreement with Mr. Churchill on all aspects of the war," that America was no nearer actually entering the war following the conference, that he, the President, was confident Russian resistance would continue through the winter, and that the first positive development might be a Presidential request to

Congress for a new grant of many millions of dollars. The President made a point of his concern over "what was happening all over the world under the Nazi régime. The more this is discussed and looked into, the more and more terrible the thought becomes of having those influences at work in occupied or affiliated nations. The thing needs to be brought home more and more to the democracies."

Winston Churchill returned to England in *Prince of Wales* by way of Iceland, where he reviewed British and United States troops. Newsreels of the meeting had preceded the Prime Minister, being flown across the Atlantic by bomber. They showed Mr. Churchill meeting the President for the first time, shaking hands with him and saying: "Good morning. How are you ?"

Through another week, Germans in industrial towns continued to get a taste of their own medicine. In Britain's greatest daylight raid of the war, six squadrons of Blenheims, guarded by fighters as far as Antwerp, hedge-hopped right into the Rhineland to smash the Cologne power stations of Quadrath and Knapsack. The last-named was the largest power plant in Europe or Asia, supplying current as far north as Dortmund, and as far south as Koblenz. The Blenheims launched point-blank attacks on the great plants just before noon and left them in flames. As the bombers returned to Britain they were met again near Antwerp by fighters, which covered their withdrawal over the North Sea while another force of fighters policed the Netherlands coast as an extra precaution.

Two nights later, more than 300 British bombers blasted Hanover, Brunswick and Magdeburg; only twelve were lost. In the Middle East, the R.A.F. in two night attacks blocked the Corinth Canal by causing landslides.

France Goes Completely Fascist

From its "Venerable Marshal", Unoccupied France heard an outline of a Fascist "New Order" representing new fetters for that unfortunate land. The Marshal made few references to foreign affairs except an attack on the B.B.C., for trying to "confuse" France, a friendly remark about "the great courtesy of the Chancellor of the German Reich", and an explanation to "the great American Republic" of how French ideals would persist in the new *Etat Français*, in spite of the death of "Parliamentary democracy." Pétain opened his address by stressing that "in an atmosphere of false rumours and intrigues, a veritable uneasiness is gripping the people of France." Stressing the difficulties of governing a still prostrate France, he said the country could "only be governed from Paris" and that he hoped to return to the old capital "as soon as certain facilities are granted." Marshal Pétain announced Cabinet changes, the most important of which was the appointment of Admiral Darlan as Defence Minister. In London the *Daily Express* commented: "France went completely Nazi last night with Admiral Darlan as its Fuehrer and Marshal Pétain as its Hindenburg."

In an attempt to "remove" the 73-year-old Baron Hiranuma, a statesman known to be strongly against a Japanese-American war, a man said to be a German agent fired at the Baron in his home and wounded him. The assailant was a Japanese named Naohiko Ishiyama. Formerly Prime Minister, now Minister without Portfolio, the Baron was regarded as the "strong man" of the Cabinet and an ardent patriot violently opposed to the activities of the huge German Fifth Column in Japan. The Baron was stated to have ordered on the fall last month of the Konoye-Matsuoka Cabinet a full and open investigation into German activities.

The week in the Far East was devoid of "incidents," other than the methodical withdrawal of Japanese nationals from British and American territory, and the removal of British and American nationals from Japanese and Japanese-controlled territory. The Japanese Radio, as truculent and belligerent as in former weeks, said the Government was going to protest to the Federated Malay States against "scandalous ill treatment of Japanese citizens."

The Japanese Radio was most sceptical of any serious British or American intention to resort to arms to halt Japan. This Japanese scepticism was commented on in Singapore by the *Straits Times*, which declared: "War in the Pacific will only be avoided from the moment Britain and America make it abundantly clear to Japan that they are willing to wage war against her."

British determination at least to defend British territory was emphasised by the continued arrival of reinforcements at Singapore, mostly from Australia. After a long Australian Cabinet meeting it was announced that the Prime Minister, Mr. Menzies, probably would fly to London to discuss the Far Eastern crisis.

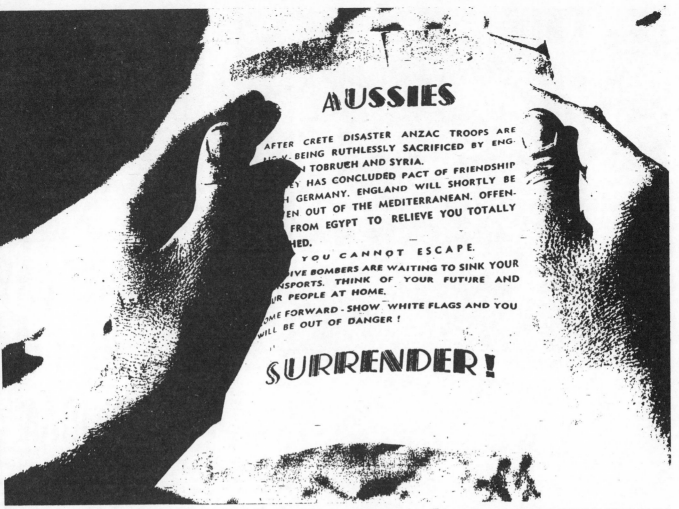

AUSSIES

AFTER CRETE DISASTER ANZAC TROOPS ARE NOW BEING RUTHLESSLY SACRIFICED BY ENG... IN TOBRUCH AND SYRIA.

...EY HAS CONCLUDED PACT OF FRIENDSHIP ...H GERMANY. ENGLAND WILL SHORTLY BE ...EN OUT OF THE MEDITERRANEAN. OFFEN... FROM EGYPT TO RELIEVE YOU TOTALLY ...HED.

...YOU CANNOT ESCAPE.

...IVE BOMBERS ARE WAITING TO SINK YOUR ...NSPORTS. THINK OF YOUR FUTURE AND ...UR PEOPLE AT HOME.

...OME FORWARD - SHOW WHITE FLAGS AND YOU WILL BE OUT OF DANGER !

SURRENDER!

PAPER BOMBARDMENT. ENEMY PLANES DROP PAMPHLETS OVER TOBRUK, WRONG MESSAGE IN WRONG PLACE. THE GARRISON HAS CONTINUED REPEATING ITS ANSWER FOR FIVE MONTHS. IN FACT IT IS THE ENEMY WHO IS ON THE DEFENSIVE: OUR RAIDS GIVE HIM THE JITTERS AS HE DIGS HIMSELF IN. AUSSIES' ANSWER IN WORDS ON PAGE 8

MEN of TOBRUK

"PARADE" WENT TO TOBRUK TO GET THESE IMPRESSIONS OF THE OR-DINARY LIFE OF THE EXTRAORDINARY GARRISON WHICH HAS LIVED FOR FIVE MONTHS IN SAND OR IN THE COLLECTION OF SHATTERED HOUSES THAT IS ALL THAT IS LEFT OF TOBRUK — IMPERISHABLE NAME WITHOUT A TOWN. THE PHOTOGRAPHS ARE BY LIEUT. NORMAN SMITH, PUBLIC RELATIONS UNIT, AND GEORGE SILK, OFFICIAL A.I.F. PHOTOGRAPHER.

TOBRUK GARRISON. Many news-paper readers far away from the scene of this epic action probably imagine a bomb and shell shattered group of buildings be-side a harbour full of foundered shipping. Actually, Tobruk Garrison con-sists mostly of an undulating, wadi-cleft desert about the same size as the Isle of Wight.

Tobruk itself—as big as a small English market town—seen from the rising ground to the south seems in an interlude of calm between bombing and shelling scarcely to have been touched. From the church tower dominating the piazza to the docks below the bright white houses terrace down in apparent-ly unbroken succession to the harbour, where the superstructure of the LADY-BIRD is the only prominent wreck that catches the eye.

Inside, the town is another matter. Splinter-scarred walls, roofless, sand-bagged. Here and there, poking from paneless window or parapet, dark against the sky, lean barrels of Lewis and Bren guns.

Driving over the segment of sand between the sea-coast and the outer defences, never for an instant is there absent the grim reminder that this is no sleepy pleasure resort on the North African littoral. True, you will find an occasional oasis with a few prickly pears, date palms and fig trees. On the sandhills by the shore there are even sparse growths of leafless white flowers, narcissus-scented, sticking out of the sand. And there are quiet-look-ing bays, fringed with fine, white sand; rocky coves by a sea that ranges through all shades of green and blue, smeared with dark, seaweed patches.

But the crevices in the rocks over-hanging the sea are sandbagged (by the Italians). Stone sangars rise like giant mole-hills all over the rocky parts of the coast. Slit-trenches alternate with bomb and shell craters everywhere in-land up to the perimeter. The whole area is hived, pocked and pitted with man-made marks of war.

And all over, it is strewn with the stark bones of General Graziani's mechanical array. The area is a ce-metery of Italian mechanical trans-port. Charred, overturned skeletons of lorries, the twisted ironwork of burnt-out Italian planes, lie bleakly over the valleys. In the frequent sandstorms that fog the clear air in some parts inside the perimeter these shapes loom up at you like spectres.

SAND, SAND, SAND

It is difficult to imagine the life of the Tobruk Garrison. It is dominated by sand. Troops live dug into the sand. A day or night is either fine or "sandy," according to the dust wea-ther. If men can be spared a few days' relief from duty, they proceed along the sand until, within some distance from the sea, desert becomes by con-vention rather than anything else "beach." There they spend their leave on the sands. And speaking of con-ventions, a few men valiantly maintain them here by wearing slips for bathing. Perhaps in this way they create an illusion of being on the beach of some far-away English or Australian bathing resort.

Sand, bombing, shelling Besides fleas and flies, these are the main pests that afflict the garrison There are two kinds of bread in Tobruk— or-dinary and "blitz." Blitzbread is fil-led with bomb splinters or shrapnel when supply lorries are caught in a raid

With the experience behind them of nearly a thousand enemy raids over Tobruk area alone—and no-one has

'Continued overleaf

TRIBUTE TO A TOBRUK HERO. AUSTRALIANS VISIT GRAVE OF A V.C. COMRADE GRAVEYARD IN TOBRUK IS TENDED BY OFFICER AND MAN, WHO KEEP IT TIDY

INDIAN TROOPS ENTER THE WORLD'S LARGEST OIL REFINERY ON THE ISLAND OF ABADAN AT THE HEAD OF THE PERSIAN GULF. ON THE RIGHT A MOVIE CAMERAMAN IS SHOWN OVER THE WORKS.

THREE-DAY BLITZ IN IRAN

rOON BRIDGE BUILT OUT OF NATIVE CRAFT OVER THE SHATT EL ARAB RIVER, WHICH SOME OF OUR COLUMNS ADVANCED DURING THE BLITZ INTO PERSIA.

THE FLAGSHIP OF THE IRANIAN NAVY, THE "BABR" WHICH WAS SUNK BY AUSTRALIAN NAVAL FORCES AT KHORRAMSHAH AT THE BEGINNING OF THE ENGAGEMENT.

The three day British Blitz in Iran to clear the country from Hitler's fifth column differed in one respect from the German variety—it was not accompanied with the slaughter and terrorization of civilians by indiscriminate bombing. Otherwise it contained all the features of this kind of war: speed, surprise, co-ordination and concentration of air and land forces, in this case, also naval forces.

Leaving the north to the Russians, our objectives were in the triangle of low lying ground on the Persian Gulf contained between the points Abadan—Dizful — Ganawah. This area includes the important oil fields at Masjid-i-Sulaiman, Haft Kel and Saran, as well as test areas and pumping stations. Abadan, port on the fifty mile long island of the same name, is the largest single refinery in the world and handles the entire oil output of Iran. Its refining production is normally one million gallons a day. Port terminus of the trans-Iranian railway, whose other end is at Bandar Shah on the Caspian, Bandar Shahpur is built on a mud flat, waterflooded at high-tide. Khorramshah, at the junction of the Karun and Shatt-el-Arab rivers, is the berthing station for the Iranian navy. There is also an oil centre at Kermanshah in central Iran which supplies all Iran's oil requirements.

SERVICES CO-OPERATE

These were the chief military objectives of General Quinan of the Indian Army, conducting operations. There were assembled at Basra for operations in the Persian Gulf area, Sikhs, Ghurkas, Baluchis, Mahrattas and other Indian troops, together with British artillery and signallers. At Kaniqin, on the western border of Iran, was a force containing the Wiltshires, the Warwick shires, Hussars, Ghurkas, Sikhs. Waiting the word go were also the R.A.F. and light units of the Australian, Indian and Royal Navies.

Though the Shah's war effective of about 125,000 men, 250, mostly superannuated, planes, and 7 small naval vessels was no doubt expecting a joint British and Russian move, the element of surprise was successfully introduced by the method and direction of our attacks. Our moves were made in the early morning hours of August 25th. Stealthy moves in the darkness. Indians, supported by British artillery and signallers, streamed out of Basra across pontoons thrown over the lower reaches of the Euphrates and the Tigris, linking the flat delta islands, and took up positions north of Khorramshah. Another force of Indians was simultaneously approaching Abadan down the Shatt-el-Arab in light craft, while a small Indian contingent made across the Persian Gulf for Bandar Shahpur Three hundred miles to the north, the small frontier town of Khosrovi was occupied by a ghost contingent of Indians operating in gym-shoes.

BATTLE AT DAWN

At dawn on the 25th, the battles began. Khorramshah wireless station, main objective of Indians advancing from the north, was taken after sharp fighting. The Persian admiral, Bayendour, attempting to defend the station, fell, riddled with Tommy-gun bullets. The battle of the docks at Abadan raged fiercely as Indians stormed the waterfront, landing in face of heavy fire from strong defences. Fighting in Abadan went on for six hours. We had to refrain from using mortar and artillery fire for fear of damaging oil installations and injuring British refinery personnel, who co-operated magnificently throughout. A landing by Indian troops was also made north of Abadan in Briam Creek, where Iranian soldiers had entrenched themselves cunningly amongst the groves of date palms on the flats.

Bandar Shahpur was occupied with comparative ease. The crews of eight Axis vessels there, which had for some days been waiting an opportunity to escape, tried frantically to scuttle the ships, but succeeded in destroying only one. The rest, together with 40 German and 60 Italian sailors, fell into our hands. The port was occupied by eight o'clock in the morning.

An engagement with the Iranian flag-ship took place north of Khorramshah, and after the barrel of one of its

APTURED IRANIAN OFFICER TALKING TO A BRITISH OFFICER THROUGH AN INTER-
TER AT A FORWARD POST. THE FIGHTING WAS FIERCE WHILST IT LASTED

INDIAN TROOPS TAKE IT EASY BEFORE THEY TAKE OVER GUARD DUTIES. INDIAN SOL-
DIERS FORMED THE MAJOR PART OF THE FORCES EMPLOYED IN THE IRAN FIGHTING.

uns had been cut clean in half by a hell from an Australian sloop, the rew jumped overboard.

The long arm of the R.A.F. had not een idle. It performed besides recon- aissance, four functions, swiftly, surely. Before operations started, it reached ut to the capital, Teheran, 400 miles rom Basra, dropping pamphlets there nd in other towns. It flew over Ahwaz n time to destroy, as they attempted to ake off, the only Persian 'planes—six f them—to leave the ground during he whole campaign. It flew troops to Iaft Kel oil field to protect employees f the A.I.O.C. and it bombed the rtillery defending the Paitak Pass, rincipal bar to the progress of our orthern columns.

PERSIAN LOSSES

After the capture of the main stra- egic positions on the Persian Gulf, two ain drives developed in the British phere of operations, north upon Ahwaz, east on Kermanshah. The Ah- vaz column captured Dorquain and a ierce battle took place at Quasr-el- heikh where some 600 Iranians were ngaged. The Persians lost 62 killed nd we took 300 prisoners. We lost a British officer of the Indian army, who vas killed after jumping into a trench y himself and accounting for four Ira- ians.

The drive east from Kaniqin was xpected to meet with some opposition n the 3,000 feet high Paitak Pass, where ,000 Iranians had taken up positions. Beyond Paitak is Karin, the Iranian base or defence of the Pass, further on still s Shahabad and the domains of the hah. A formidable mechanized array of British and Indian troops initiated a pin- er attack; besides the frontal advance n the mountain position, a column skirt- d north of Quasrishirin, cutting off the

town's communications east, afterwards joining with the main advance. Another column, proceeding south east, took Gilan and moved up against Paitak in a flanking operation. The Iranians re- treated sixty-five miles into the interior on hearing of this threat to their posi- tions, leaving a number of machine-gun nests manned to guard their rear. These were mopped up by our frontal attack- ing column, who encountered in addi- tion some road-blocks and a certain amount of artillery fire.

END OF RESISTANCE

Meanwhile, the column which had taken Gilan, bye-passing the Pass, had taken first Shahbad and then, doubling back, captured Karind, where they joined hands with the main column.

With our forces approaching Ker- manshah in the northern sector and Ah- waz in the south, and the Russians advancing in the north past Tabriz to- wards Teheran and the Caspian ports, the Shah threw in his hand. The British and Russian forces met at Kasvin to apportion spheres of occupation.

REVEILLE

The Services' Newspaper

No. 37.　　MONDAY, OCTOBER 13, 1941　　PRICE 2d.

Founded and Edited by
Reg Hipwell

THE NAVY, ARMY AND AIR FORCE INSTITUTES
is The Servant of those who Serve

Registered under the Companies Acts as an Association not trading for Profit and having no share-holders, all surpluses arising from its trading are available for the benefit of its only customers—H.M. Fighting Forces.

RANKER'S 1ᴰ. A WEEK PLAN FOR FREE LEAVE TRAVELLING

FROM a ranker in the Army REVEILLE has received a suggestion by which all men could have travel warrants on the railway for all their leaves—at a cost of one penny a week.

For months the War Office has been subjected to pressure from outside and inside Parliament on the hardship involved by the regulation which allows only two free-travel vouchers a year to men on seven days' leave.

(They have—in theory !—four periods of seven days' leave a year.)

Proposals for four warrants have been declined on account of the expense involved.

1d. Week Plan

Here is the suggestion which Ranker puts forward to give travel warrants for all leave, at no cost to the taxpayers :

Advocate, he says, that all Service men pay one penny a week from their pay, and receive for one year a free railway warrant to travel anywhere at any time.

REVEILLE has examined the finance of this interesting proposals.

What It Means

It reveals the following facts :

If there are 4,000,000 Service men (including all branches of the Armed Forces), a penny a week from each would result in £900,000 being available for railway travelling.

Actually, there are undoubtedly more than 4,000,000 in the Armed Forces to-day.

The sum should be in the neighbourhood of nearly £1,000,000, which should be enough to reimburse the railways for free Service travel.

Railways' £41,000,000

If it does not, it must be remembered that the railways are to receive from the taxpayers of this country some £40,000,000 as a free gift towards their expenses !

The effect of Ranker's proposal would be that men stationed in Scotland, whose homes are in the South of England, would be able to spend their leave at home, instead of remaining in Scotland because they cannot afford the fare to England and back.

And it would put an end to hitch-hiking, which the War Office frowns upon.

(Continued on page 8, col. 3)

BRASS NITWITS

The greatest and most popular man of our time recently visited a S.E. coast area.

For two days previously the troops were engaged painting up the railway station, and walking a mile or two along the line picking up bits of paper.

The last kind of thing this man wants soldiers to do. Must a Brass Hat *always* cover an empty head?

MISSING, FEARED KILLED

AN M.P. has made another attempt to relieve the hardships of dependants of men reported missing.

Mr. Ian Hannah asked the War Minister whether he realises

the hardship caused by the drastic cutting down of military allowances for the relatives of a soldier reported missing, thus adding financial difficulties to anxiety; and could he hold out any hope of the situation being eased?

Capt. Margesson referred Mr. Hannah to an answer given on March 25.

He added that the arrangements announced then were working satisfactorily.

The March announcement stated that when a soldier was reported missing and his fate remained in doubt family and dependants' allowances and allotments from his pay were continued for seventeen weeks. Afterwards dependants, if eligible, received a pension or continuation of allowances on pension scale.

We hardly think M.P.s will leave the matter there.

DEAFENED IN SERVICE

Since the outbreak of war 141 officers and airmen have been invalided from the R.A.F. on account of defective hearing.

Up to March 31, 287 men were similarly invalided out of the Navy, and one girl from the Wrens.

BATTALION ASKS WHY?

"M. C.," of Islington, writes to the Editor :

"Can you tell us why it is that the 8th Battalion Lincolnshire Regiment are denied forty-eight hours' leave when other battalions in the same division are receiving its regularly? "

We can't—but perhaps the W.O. will look into the matter.

A pilot tells the size of the Messerschmitt that got away !

We Get a Company Its Leave

A WEEK or two ago REVEILLE investigated complaints from a company of the Royal Engineers concerning their long period without leave.

We found that the strength of the company was about forty-six.

Of these, 50 per cent. had had no seven-day leave for more than six months, and others for longer than eight months.

Although the company was called up before the outbreak of the war, no member had had more than three periods of seven days' leave up to last month.

"Reveille" took immediate action in this case. Mr. Ian Hannah, M.P., who is always anxious to help Service men, interested himself in the case when we placed the facts before him.

The results came to hand last week, when REVEILLE received from Mr. Hannah a copy of a letter from Sir Edward Grigg, Joint Parliamentary Secretary to the W.O. It stated:

"I find that the leave position in this unit has been exceptionally difficult owing to the fact that . . . (The information given on this must be regarded by REVEILLE as confidential.)

"Circumstances have now changed, and instructions have been issued for all men who have not had two leaves since November, 1940, to be sent on leave during the next few weeks."

Glad to have been of help to you, boys; and we hope you have a pleasant holiday.

ANYONE KNOW HIM ?

Will Pte. A. V. Arnstein, of A.M.P. Coy., please write to L/Cpl. Gladys M. Hardy, of Wood Morton Hall, Guist, Norfolk. Her recent letters to him have been returned, and she cannot trace his new address.

Kind of O.C. we Do Not Want

FROM Sevenoaks, Kent, comes information revealing the kind of O.C. which the Army can well do without.

An O.C. without sympathy, without even the least human feeling.

The War Office should get rid of him.

Here is the story . . . . of a sapper.

"I was given a pass for a week-end to go home to my wife, who is very ill," he says. "On my arrival my wife was worse than I expected, and I was detained at home by the doctor in charge.

"I informed my O.C., but he did not grant me leave. I informed the police, and they said my unit would be informed by them.

"I heard no more until they came and arrested me.

"Since then I was kept under close arrest. While under arrest I have received telegrams that my wife is worse.

but our O.C. will not let me go and see her. Instead, he has given me fifteen days' field punishment.

"Is this justice? A man's wife can die, but they do not care."

A.T.S. CHIEF'S CONFERENCE

Mrs. Jean Knox (sitting), Commander of the A.T.S., in conference with some of her staff at the A.T.S. headquarters. Soon there will be 100,000 A.T.S. in the Services, working side by side with their men colleagues of the Army.

The Eyes and Teeth Do It!

By MONA MANGAN

EYES and teeth, girls! Eyes and teeth!! That was the first thing I heard when I went to learn ballet dancing. What's that to do with dancing? thought I. Next day I was enlightened: "Hey! you with the red hair," roared the ballet master, "for pity's sake use your eyes and teeth; then the poor, unsuspecting public won't notice those dreadful feet of yours, dance with your eyes, smile and show your teeth, and pray Heaven nobody will notice you are ruining my beautiful ballet steps."

Saving £'s

Well! I tried hard, but never even reached the chorus in Pavlova's company, and as I had my livelihood to earn, my teeth and eyes had to do overtime. I was young, my teeth good, and I **soon learnt the value of taking care of them. Every six months the dentist examined and brushed them up.** That saved me pounds later; and when they will no longer stand patching up, I'll part with loving memories.

* * *

Even if you use a good tooth paste daily, about once a week brush with common salt, dry on the brush, for about a minute or two, and gargle with salt and water quarter-teaspoonful in a tumbler of water every day. This cleans the mouth, hardens gums, whitens teeth and keeps away colds. This goes for whether your teeth are your own or on hire-purchase plan.

Salt and Water

Now eyes—all eyes large and small—must be liquid pools, or twin stars, or the mirror of your soul, according to the line of patter your Romeo prefers—anyway, it just means bright, clear and twinkling, and you start by keeping your tummy clean.

I told you a few weeks ago how to help that problem.

Then with a weak solution of salt and water wash out the eyes with an eye-bath or eggcupful each night. Smear lashes with a very little petroleum jelly.

During the day, if you can, shut your eyes and rest them for two minutes three times a day. That helps them. Sight is very precious, and you can't buy eyes on the H.P. plan, so take care of them.

Homely—but good

I know I'm always saying salt and water and olive oil and other very ordinary things, but anybody can look 100 per cent. if they can spend money at beauty parlours.

To-day few of us have the time or money, so I'm simply passing on the homely hints that helped me to make a modest stage success by using my eyes and teeth.

The Wrens Want a More Human Touch at the Top

WHAT IS WRONG WITH THE WRENS?

IN its last issue REVEILLE reported the prison camp conditions of a company of Wrens in the Orkneys. This week we have investigated an instance of the "Haw-Haw" attitude of a Wren recruiting office. A young married woman went to the office with the intention of joining. She wanted to be sure of certain points first.

She was interviewed in a very off-handed manner with an air of "you may join if you like. We don't care whether you do or don't."

She asked whether she would be able to have leave at the same time as her husband, an Army officer.

The brusque reply was: "You will have leave when it becomes due."

The woman is a cultured person of good position. She holds diplomas for cooking and has extensive volunteer canteen experience. An ideal woman for the Wrens. Now, disgusted, she has enlisted in the Woman's Land Army.

The same spirit seems to exist in the Wren headquarters.

REVEILLE, in sending the Orkneys complaint to headquarters, received a reply suggesting that it was not in the public interest to publish it. Our reply was that conditions under which Service girls are working are very much in the public interest.

Contrast

Again, on telephoning this week an inquiry as to the promised investigations into the complaint, REVEILLE was answered by a woman with the impertinent remark: "We don't have to tell REVEILLE anything, do we?"

It is a striking commentary that 90 per cent. of women's complaints received by "Reveille" come from Wrens.

Wren headquarters might do well to study the sympathetic consideration towards leave and Service conditions, and the personal touch of Mrs. Jean Knox, the A.T.S. commander.

A.T.S. CAN HAVE 2-WEEK HOLIDAY

Under a new War Office ruling, rankers in the A.T.S. may now take two fortnightly holidays each year if they choose.

Previously they were entitled to seven days' leave every three months, arranged to coincide with the leave of husband or sweetheart.

The order applies to privates and N.C.O.s only, and is not at present extended to commissioned officers.

WREN BOMBS COULDN'T STOP

BLOWN off her motor-cycle while carrying dispatches during a raid on Devonport, a Wren dispatch rider ran to admiralty House with her message and immediately volunteered to go out again with more.

This story of a girl's gallantry is told with the announcement that the British Empire Medal (Military Division) has been awarded to Wren Pamela Betty McGeorge.

During a heavy night raid on Devonport Wren McGeorge was carrying urgent dispatches to the Commander-in-Chief when a bomb exploded, blowing her off her motor-cycle, which was so damaged as to be useless.

Although badly shaken, Wren McGeorge climbed over a heap of debris and ran for nearly half a mile to Admiralty House with bombs falling all round and many fires blazing.

Wren McGeorge had been on duty as dispatch rider during other air raids, says the official report, when her conduct had been calm and inspiring at all times, setting a fine example to the other dispatch riders.

W.A.A.F. OFFICERS—TO GET £40 GRANT

The outfit allowance to newly-commissioned W.A.A.F. officers is to be increased from £30 to £40.

Air Ministry orders announce that the increased allowance will be payable to women commissioned on or after July 1.

NEW A.T.S. SMARTER SKIRT IS "ADORABLE"

When Mrs. Jean Knox, Commandant of the A.T.S., "passed out," the first batch of 300 officers at a S.E. Scotland O.C.T.U., she was asked by excited girls about the new, smarter skirt which she has herself designed for the Corps. She said:

I adore it myself and it will be issued as soon as existing uniforms have been exhausted.

The new issue may be sooner than many people expect.

Mrs. Knox, in an address to the new officers, said:

"You will have great responsibilities. Be kind, be understanding, and remember it is absolutely essential to see that the women you are in charge of have good food.

Mrs. Knox disapproves of the A.T.S. girls smoking in public. She says it is definitely bad for discipline and is banned.

"She is grand and so efficient," declared a party of new officers after the passing out.

NAVAL COMPLAINTS

Because (according to Mr. G. Hall, M.P.) some Naval officers appear unaware of the established machinery for the ventilation of complaints of men from the lower deck, the Admiralty has felt it desirable to issue orders calling attention to the regulation and the necessity for its strict observance.

WRENS "IN PRISON CAMP"

(To the Editor)

Sir,—I have just been reading No. 36 of your excellent publication, re Wrens "In Prison Camp." Why don't you give the name of the Chief Officer? This person should be relieved of her command immediately. You must know, as well as the rest of the British public, that girls who enlisted in the Wrens did so from patriotic motives, and they deserve the best treatment and the most encouragement possible.

J. K. RASHLEIGH (Major).
The East India and Sports Club.

"THE SPIRIT OF THE BRITISH NATION ENABLES IT TO CARRY THROUGH TO VICTORY ANY STRUGGLE THAT IT ONCE ENTERS UPON, NO MATTER HOW LONG SUCH A STRUGGLE MAY LAST OR HOWEVER GREAT THE SACRIFICE THAT MAY BE NECESSARY OR WHATEVER THE MEANS THAT HAVE TO BE EMPLOYED; AND ALL THIS THOUGH THE ACTUAL EQUIPMENT AT HAND MAY BE UTTERLY INADEQUATE WHEN COMPARED WITH THAT OF OTHER NATIONS."—ADOLF HITLER IN Mein Kampf

German radio almost subdued : Maisky appeals for materials : Bader uses his new leg : Farinacci Italian Quisling ?

THE WEEK

Reticence on the part of Germany marked the week's operations in Russia where, apart from the usual claim of the destruction of thousands of tanks, aeroplanes, tons of war material and millions of men and the vague statement that all would soon be over, concrete claims were confined to the push from Kiev on Kharkov nearly 300 miles west and the claim that Leningrad would fall by October 2.

All right! All right! Plenty o' time! That's a brace bain't it! You try & do better with only one barrel.

General Wavell, returning from a short visit to London, gave a short interview to the press. He said that he did not think it would be necessary to create a joint Anglo-Russian Caucasian or Persian command and refused to be drawn when asked whether the British Army would be sent to the Caucasus. He thought that the Germans could not push round the shores of the Black Sea till they had disposed of the Russian navy. "This fleet can only be knocked out by taking all its bases or by sending the Italian navy to the Black Sea, in which event it would have to force a passage through the Dardanelles or obtain Turkish consent to their passage, and there is certainly no sign that Turkey would consent," he said.

In Odessa, the garrison kept up its offensive spirit in the best Tobruk style and there was no sign of German progress. In fact the Russians enlarged their defences by the capture of two outlying villages. The Roumanians, who have borne the brunt of the Odessa attacks, had a bad hammering, and new divisions were sent for from Roumania. All reports pointed to the fact that the Roumanians were fighting with little spirit.

MAISKY

Help for Russia was the main British press theme of the week following M. Maisky's speech in which he appealed for greater help from Britain and America and warned against relying too much on "General Mud" and "General Winter" whom he demoted to the rank of colonel. None of the papers denied the seriousness of the situation but the Times warned against the easy victories of arm-chair strategists who suggested that we should immediately open up an offensive on the continent. "On the material side it is certainly well that every form of spur to effort should be applied. When it comes to direct military aid, criticism becomes less useful since it cannot be backed by knowledge either of the possibilities or of actual plans. In fact we have been rash rather than niggard in our exertions to help our friends and it can hardly be doubted that our present decisions are governed by a desire to do all that lies within our power. Russia's needs are urgent." The Daily Telegraph spoke of the fact that the extent of our help would stagger those not in the know if the full story could be told.

THE "BEAVER" IN MOSCOW

The arrival of the British Mission in Moscow headed by Lord Beaverbrook coincided with the "Tanks for Russia" week. Production was stepped up by 50 per cent on a month ago and it was stated that a flow of tanks for Russia had already started. There was no doubt that British workers were putting their backs into the task of helping their new allies. Welcome news was the first fall of snow in Moscow on Lord Beaverbrook's arrival.

The Prime Minister, Mr. Winston Churchill, in an opening speech to the British Association for the Advancement of Science said: "One of our objects in fighting this war is to maintain the right of free discussion and interchange of ideas. In contrast to the intellectual darkness which is descending on Germany, the freedom our scientists enjoy is a valuable weapon to us, for superiority in scientific development is a vital factor in the preparation of victory." Commented the Times, "Germany is now living on its scientific capital. Important consequences follow both for war and peace. In spite of the Nazis' intensive scientific preparations for war, this country has already surpassed Germany in many applications of science for war. The superiority of our aircraft and systems of aircraft detection are matters of public record and there are a number of other examples which for the present must remain military secrets."

Coupled with this claim was news of the performance of new Hurricane four-cannoned single-seater fighters. Some of these models carry twelve machine guns instead of the eight of the older models. In an attack with these planes on four enemy minesweepers and two "flak" ships off Dunkirk, two of the minesweepers were set on fire and both "flak" ships damaged. A sidelight on British fighter protection was shown, when in a raid on Northern France we lost 14 fighters to the enemy's 21, but all our bombers returned safely.

Berlin Correspondent of the Columbia broadcasting gave further news of the irrepressible Douglas Bader. Recently forced to bale out over Northern France breaking one of his aluminium legs, he had another delivered by the R.A.F. by parachute and this gave him the chance for an escape. The correspondent quoted a member of Richtofen's old squadron, Major Eric von Bach Banagle, as saying, "The

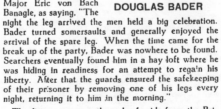

DOUGLAS BADER

night the leg arrived the men held a big celebration. Bader turned somersaults and generally enjoyed the arrival of the spare leg. When the time came for the break up of the party, Bader was nowhere to be found. Searchers eventually found him in a hay loft where he was hiding in readiness for an attempt to regain his liberty. After that the guards ensured the safekeeping of their prisoner by removing one of his legs every night, returning it to him in the morning."

The first news came through of raids from the British Isles on the continent when Canadian troops brought back twenty eight German officers from the French coast.

The last country in the Balkans not completely occupied by the Germans, Bulgaria, had another nerve wracking week with several German divisions hovering on the Roumanian frontier. Moscow radio thought that the occupation of Bulgaria was on the Nazi programme for the immediate future. In other countries occupied by Germany, the people showed no signs of lying down and taking it quietly.

General von Stulpnagel, the German military commander in occupied France pinned up the following notice, "Eugene Devigné and Mohamed Moali were condemned to death on September 26 for being in wrongful possession of firearms. They were shot today."

A stern warning was given to Frenchmen against sheltering British pilots who had landed by parachute. Execution without trial was threatened. Free French radio from London countered with a threat that the names of any Frenchmen who betrayed British airmen would be noted and that such people would be executed "without awaiting the day of victory."

VON NEURATH

In Czecho-Slovakia the appeal that German controlled newspapers should be boycotted has achieved remarkable success. According to the Times, "the circulation of the principal morning newspapers has dropped by two thirds and the evening papers have almost disappeared. So poor were the street sales that newsvendors went on holiday and in the tram-cars and coffee-houses people were seen abandoning their newspapers and reading Czech classics..." So bad were conditions that the Reich Protector of Bohemia and Moravia, von Neurath, had to take a holiday. S.S. Obengruppenfuehrer Heydrich took over.

The Italians have had an even more unpleasant time in Greece and Jugoslavia. Reuter claimed that they had had to bring no fewer than 14 divisions into Greece whilst even the Italian paper La Stampa had to admit that the Serbs were proving a tough nut to crack. "One and a half million Serbs live between Zagreb and Sarajevo, which is too many to eliminate at one blow. Although Italian troops occupy almost the whole country, the struggle against the régime continues. Serb bands fight in the Bosnian forests and on the mountain tops."

In Italy itself there were signs of a certain weariness with adherence to the Axis. Farinacci, former Secretary-General to the Fascist party, in an article in the Regime Fascista wrote, "Unfortunately, grave mistakes have been made, the consequence of which it is now necessary to face. The party has become an enormous top-heavy organisation with a rigid bureaucracy." Ravagio, prominent fascist journalist, gave his criticisms in Popolo d'Italia. "There exists an enormous mass which is trying to retard the party's progress and it is precisely among the fascists that one finds democrats, socialists, freemasons and liberals."

"Open criticism of the fascist party suggests," said the Times, "that Mussolini has planned ministerial changes and that the facts are being given publicity because he wishes to make a show of meeting the discontent wich undoubtedly exists both inside the army and inside the party."

As comfort for the Italian people it was announced that bread was to be rationed to 200 grammes per day per person. A supplement of 100 grammes will be given to workers and a further 100 grammes for those engaged in particularly arduous labour.

U.S.A. CONVOYS TO ICELAND

Admiral Stark, chief of U.S. Naval operations, made the first official statement that America was convoying as far as Iceland. Giving out that Atlantic losses had been substantially reduced in the last 60 days, Admiral Stark said: "The United States Navy is convoying plenty of ships and making no secret of it."

The next most pressing question in America once the immediate needs of Great Britain had been attended to, was whether President Roosevelt was going to repeal the Neutrality Act which would allow American ships to enter belligerent ports and combat areas. Opinion was divided on this issue but Wednesday's newspapers carried a full page advertisement issued by "The Associated Leagues for Declared War" urging an immediate declaration of war and signed by leading citizens of 223 cities in 37 states. This was backed by a message from Dr. James Conant, President of Harvard University, who also appealed for an outright declaration of war.

I Don't Want a War Baby!

★ *Here is a vital question which hundreds of young couples are considering at the present moment, and, like every question, there are two sides to it. In these articles, REVEILLE presents opposing points of view, given by two young married women in the Forces.* ★

Says Pte. Betty Hawkins (A.T.S.), wife of L/Cpl. J. Hawkins, of the Grenadier Guards

★

And, please, don't get the wrong idea about me. I'm not one of those young women who has found in the present war just an excuse for having a good time. I'm as fond of babies as anybody—and I'm quite willing to sacrifice my health, my leisure, and my money to having one—*at the right time.*

But my husband and I both agreed, when we got married eighteen months ago, that it is not fair to bring a child into the world at such a time as this.

For one thing, we have both been brave enough to face up to the possibility that my husband may not return when this war is over. Not only is it no joke for a young widow to have a child to bring up on her own, it is grossly unfair to any child to be deprived of a decent start in life because it has no father to earn the money to provide it.

Even when the war is over we shall have to fight to make a country fit for babies, as well as heroes, to live in. I prefer to wait for my child until that struggle has been gone through —until I can be sure of a fair amount of security for him.

But even if I could know now that in a year or two, with the war over, my husband could be back at his old job—I could be out of uniform once more looking after the home—I still would not have a baby now.

Consider the food problem. Milk, butter, eggs, fruit are vital in the pre-natal diet of a

mother of a healthy child—they are vital for building a fine foundation for a young baby in the first few years of his life. Every day these are getting scarcer.

And surely, in the months of waiting before the child is born it is essential that the mother should be contented and reasonably free from strain and tensions. How could this be when I am worried about my husband, stationed in far-from-ideal conditions, in a camp a hundred miles away from me, worried about the newspaper headlines, the threat of invasion, and so on.

They say a married man is only half a soldier. Is it going to help my husband to be a good soldier if he has the worry of knowing I have to shoulder this new responsibility alone?

And—lastly, but very important—the A.T.S. need every woman they can get.

Can I afford to leave the Service to which I am so proud to belong until this war is won?

But I do . . ., says Cpl. Jessie Norton (W.A.A.F.), wife of Pilot Officer J. L. Norton

Oh, I know it's a risk, but isn't it always—whether there's a war or not?

And how can I better show my faith in the future, show my defiance of the pessimists and the defeatists?

Just supposing our parents had looked on the black side in the last war—how many of our fine and gallant young men and women would be here to fight for us to-day? Not that I want my son to have to cope with another war in twenty years time— but I think that such a possibility is more remote if we can start building an A.1 nation here and now.

Oh, I know people say that conditions for having a baby aren't ideal now—the child must go without many peace-time luxuries, for instance.

But most of those luxuries we had come to look upon as essentials were unknown to our grandfathers — and they produced some healthy children!

And I believe that the adult health of the nation to-day is as fit as it ever was pre-war. Men and women in the Services are in good physical training, the slightest sign of disease is discovered and checked immediately—we don't eat more than is good for us.

War or no war, life must go on, and we women must lay the foundations now of the next generation.

And besides, I, too, have faced the unthinkable possibility that my husband, who is a pilot-officer with a daring and dangerous job, may not return.

And that's the real reason why I want a child.

"I won't have any daughter of mine dodging Military Service."
(From Daily Mail)

H₂O IS FREE AND BEAUTIFYING

It's good to know, in these days of rationed beauty products, that there's still one beautifier we can get easily, and, what's more, there's no purchase tax on it!

Have you ever stopped to ask whether you are drinking as much water as is necessary for your health and beauty? If you're ever inclined to feel slightly jealous of any sister At, Waaf, or Wren because of her bright eyes, clear complexion, and glossy hair—don't. For you can be sure she drinks plenty of water.

A liberal allowance of water is really necessary to be a healthy good-looker. So drink plain water freely—just as often as there's a tap handy. And, besides this, drink milk, lemonade, ginger ale—in fact, almost anything that will increase your intake of water.

Believe it or not, but in normal health about two-thirds of the weight of the body consists of water, and about four and a half pints are eliminated daily. The blood and lymph are largely made up of water, and when we drink less water than we should the supply of these essential fluids is lessened—and the poisonous waste products of the body are not properly eliminated.

So try, if you can, to drink six glasses of plain water daily, and when you've qualified for that you can go on to eight. Any sort of long drink is good for you, but the advantage of plain water over any other sort of beverage is that it contains no nourishment. So it cannot increase your weight but merely acts as a kind of internal bath.

A.T.S. HEROINE

Believed to be the first girl in the Services to be blinded in the war, Miss Beryl Sleigh, who was in the A.T.S. is training to be an opera-singer.

Beryl has a magnificent soprano voice, and before the war was being trained by the Royal College of Music.

She was driving an ambulance in a London blitz when she received her injury.

FIRE WOMEN FOR N.F.S.

Under new plans now being worked out by the Home Secretary, women may, in the future, drive fire engines and even operate the hoses.

The extension of the call-up may cause a drain on civil defence personnel, and many otherwise exempt women will be called upon to carry out part-time duties in the National Fire Service.

Full-time civil defence women will not be called up. Married women not yet doing full-time war work, although exempt from call-up with the Services, may be directed into civil defence on a full-time job.

AMBITIOUS W.A.A.F.

"Is it necessary to have School Certificate to be an officer," asks a W.A.A.F. in a letter to REVEILLE.

No. A certain standard of education is, of course, required. But personality and leadership are the qualities needed for a commission. Common sense is a lot more use than certificates.

HERE IS BETTY SERVICE'S CHRISTMAS PRESENT TO YOU

An A.B.C. of Beauty

These days, when every one of us has a war job to do, we've time only for the essentials of life. Luxuries must take a back place until after the war. But beauty is not a luxury, and though we've none of us the leisure of our pre-war days, it's that regular few minutes daily beauty routine that's going to carry us through to peace still looking as slick and attractive as ever.

So I've evolved a beauty schedule that won't take up too much of your precious time and, if practised regularly, will become as automatic as brushing your teeth. **Resolve to start it in the New Year, and keep it up all the year round.**

*   *   *

HAIR.—You *must* give it its 100 strokes a day, and it'll do twice as much good if you brush it in front of an open window. Spend a couple of minutes massaging the scalp to keep

BETTY SERVICE

it loose and young. Wash your hair whenever it's dirty. You'll find, with wearing a cap such a lot, it'll need more than its peace-time shampoo.

*   *   *

EYES.—You'll probably be out of doors a lot more than usual. Bathe the eyes each night to soothe them and free them from dust. If you can't manage an eye-bath and a lotion, try warm water followed by a splash of cold.

*   *   *

SKIN.—You'll have to forgo elaborate beauty treatments here. The essential is to keep your skin clear by washing away make-up and grime with a good soap and warm water each night. Just to make sure, follow up with a wipe over with complexion milk or a cleansing cream if your skin is dry.

*   *   *

HANDS.—You'll be doing a lot of dirty jobs, so before starting rub your nails over a cake of damp soap. This will prevent dirt from getting under your nails.

If you've scrubbing or washing-up to do and your hands immersed in hot water for some time, rub table-salt into them and the puffy, wrinkled appearance will vanish. And if you're wise, you'll give up all thought of those glamorous long nails till peace comes once more. Keep them just long enough to cover the finger-tip, and run round the cuticle with oil at night to keep them supple.

*   *   *

FEET.—These are most important to beauty. How can you have a smile on your face, a sparkle in your eye, if you're unhappy feet? You'll be forced to wear sensible flat-heeled shoes, and they're going to do your feet a lot of good.

Soak tired feet in strongly salted warm water to which you have added a teaspoonful of iodine. Bathe the legs, too, while resting the feet in the water. Dry, and dust the feet with talc, and then rest them as long as possible by raising them above the level of the head. This drains away the blood from them and gives them a cool, rested feeling.

"I have it in Command from the King to express to all ranks of the Army and Royal Air Force in the Western Desert, and to the Mediterranean Fleet, His Majesty's confidence that they will do their duty with exemplary devotion in the supremely important battle which lies before them. For the first time, British and Empire troops will meet the Germans with ample equipment in modern weapons of all kinds. The battle itself will affect the whole course of the war. Now is the time to strike the hardest blow yet struck for the final victory of home and freedom. The desert army may add a page to history which will rank with Blenheim and Waterloo. The eyes of all nations are upon you. All our hearts are with you, may God uphold the right." — PRIME MINISTER.

Von Kleist does a "strategic withdrawal": Japanese move: America keeps an eye on Dakar : British women sign up

THE WEEK

"Yesterday, December 7, 1941, a date which will live in infamy, the United States was suddenly and deliberately attacked by the naval and air forces of the Empire of Japan." Thus the President of the United States, leading his country into a life and death struggle with the eastern end

BROOKE-POPHAM

of the Axis. The attack had about it all the trappings of an Axis move. It came as a surprise and at a time when the Japanese representative was still talking peace in the United States. It had all the advantages of a thug attack when the unsuspecting victim has his back turned. News at first was garbled and most of it unconfirmed —

the Japs had used mustard gas bombs on Singapore, they had sunk an American battleship and captured another... they had sunk two British cruisers... they had lost an aircraft carrier, four submarines and six 'planes. Mr. Roosevelt summed up the situation as follows: "The attack yesterday on the Hawaiian Islands has caused severe damage to American naval and military forces. I regret to tell you that very many American lives have been lost. In addition, American ships have been torpedoed on the high seas between San Francisco and Honolulu. Yesterday also the Japanese Government launched an attack against Malaya. Last night Japanese forces attacked Hong Kong. Last night Japanese forces attacked Guam. Last night Japanese forces attacked the Philippine Islands. Last night Japanese forces attacked Wake Island and this morning Japanese forces attacked Midway Island." The Americans lost no time in declaring war and their Pacific Fleet steamed out.

Britain had promised that if Japan attacked America, Britain's declaration would follow within the hour. Mr. Winston Churchill revealed that he had talked over the telephone to President Roosevelt and only awaited America's declaration. As it turned out, Japan's attack on Malaya did away with the necessity of this formality. The attack on Malaya took place at one in the morning at Khota Baru, a strongly held British aerodrome. The attack was repulsed. A second landing was then attempted thirteen miles south at Sabak.

FIRST FAR EAST COMMUNIQUE

The first Far East communiqué suggested that the ships which had landed the troops and the supporting naval vessels had sheered off and that the troops were being effectively dealt with. The attack on Hong Kong was made first by bombers, and parties of three to four hundred Japanese were seen across the frontier. The communiqué stated that the garrison was confident and that the situation was developing as expected.

But whilst the news was confused as both sides got into position for the real showdown, one thing stood out like a beacon. Japan had achieved what Germany was trying to prevent, complete unity between America and Britain with her fighting allies. In one day, in one hour, the isolationists swung round. "War is forced upon the United States by an insane clique of Japanese militarists. America faces war through no violation by any American. All in the United States this day forth have but one task, that is to strike with all our might to protect and preserve American freedom and all we hold dear." Writing these words was the isolationist "Chicago Tribune." Even Lindbergh felt in fighting mood.

GREAT WORK BY RUSSIANS

With the Germans moving rapidly backwards along the north coast of the Sea of Azov, the Italians and Hungarians in close attendance, Marshal Timoshenko sprang another offensive on the enemy across the Donetz towards Kharkov. Along the 400-mile front from Kursk to Rostov, the Russians put all they knew into the fight—a million men with adequate tank and air support. Hurriedly General Brauchitsch left Hitler's Eastern Front Headquarters to try and stem the Russian advance but the Red Army by-passed Taganrog and went on towards Mariopol, leaving a large pocket of the enemy to be mopped up in their rear. Although one of the objects of the offensive was to lessen the pressure on Moscow, there were no signs that the Germans had withdrawn any troops.

One minute after midnight, Saturday, Britain was at war with Finland, Rumania and Hungary. Only Finland had replied to the British note and that reply was regarded as unsatisfactory as Mar-

BARDOSSY

shal Mannerheim made it apparent that his intention was to "liberate" Eastern Karelia, a part of the country which had never belonged to Finland. Hungary's Premier Bardossy frankly proclaimed that Hungary was in the war against the Allies as a matter of what he deemed self-interest and Rumania was too busy licking the sores

sustained at Odessa and Mariopol to say anything beyond refusing to comply with the British note. This formal declaration of war did not in any way alter anything except the tone of German propaganda which was now "Communist-controlled Britain" rather than "Pluto-democratic Britain," so that Britain now became, to the Germans, the 49th state of American capitalists and the tool of the Bolsheviks, another example of having your sauerkraut and eating it.

TAUT WIRE OFFENSIVE

With the temperature at 54 degrees below freezing point, it was felt in Russia that the German attacks must be reaching their climax where they described the Moscow offensive as being like "a taut wire at the point of breaking."

British support to Russia was acknowledged by the Soviet who published photographs of British tanks in action on the Moscow front and by the granting of the highest Soviet decoration, the Order of Lenin to Wing-Commander Isherwood, Squadron Leaders Rooke and Miller and Sgt. Howe of the R.A.F. wing for valour and courage displayed against the enemy. British submarines too were busy, the Tigris sinking five ships and seriously

MOLOTOV

damaging a sixth ; the Trident sinking three and probably sinking another four. These attacks were carried out in Arctic waters and all the ships either carried men or materials to the German front around Murmansk.

A propaganda duel was also fought between the two sides over a note sent by Comrade Molotov.

CHURCHILL ON WOMAN POWER

Points from the Prime Minister's speech on the bill for the conscription of woman power which was later passed by 326 votes to 10 were:

"Firstly, we do not propose at the present time to extend compulsion to join the services to any married women, not even childless married women. They may of course volunteer, but they will not be compelled.

"Secondly, regarding married women and industry, we have already the power to direct married women into industry. This power will continue to be used with discretion. The wife of a man serving in the Forces or in the Merchant Navy will not be called upon to work away from her home area, nor will a woman with household responsibilities be moved from her home area.

"One fifth of those who are still required will have the option to choose between the Auxiliary Forces of Civil Defence and such industrial work as may be specified by the Minister of Labour as requiring mobile workers.

"I want to make it clear that women may be compelled to join the A.T.S., but only volunteers from within the A.T.S. will be allowed to serve with the guns. I have no doubt we shall get the response which is required."

Nevertheless, it was in that great field of married women or women doing necessary household work, comprising about eleven million persons, that they saw their largest reserves for industry and home defence in future, said Mr. Churchill.

AMERICANS BUSY IN MIDDLE EAST

It was announced that America was making arrangements for the extensive construction of warehouses, docks, railways sidings and aeroplane landing facilities in the Red Sea area under the direction of Brigadier-General Maxwell, whose principal job has been the expediting of munitions to the British forces in the Near East: and that Mr. William C. Bullitt had been appointed Mr. Roosevelt's representative in the Middle East.

MAXWELL

About the latter appointment the New York Times said "The course of political events in still unconquered lands bordering on the Red Sea, the Mediterranean and the Persian Gulf, will be shaped primarily by military developments. The United States is pouring out an ever-increasing flood of war supplies to influence those developments. How our

supplies will be directed and for whose benefit they will be used it will be partly Mr. Bullitt's responsibility to determine. He has had a long ambassadorial experience and may be expected to carry out his mission with vigour. As the war moves toward a crisis his errand should assume increasing importance."

"In the opinion of this House, for the purpose of securing the maximum national effort in the conduct of the war and in production, the obligation for national service should be extended to include the resources of woman-power still available and the necessary legislation should be brought in forthwith." This motion the British House of Commons is to make a question of confidence and the proposals will include compulsion for men and women up to certain specified ages. Already a million and a quarter women have registered for national service.

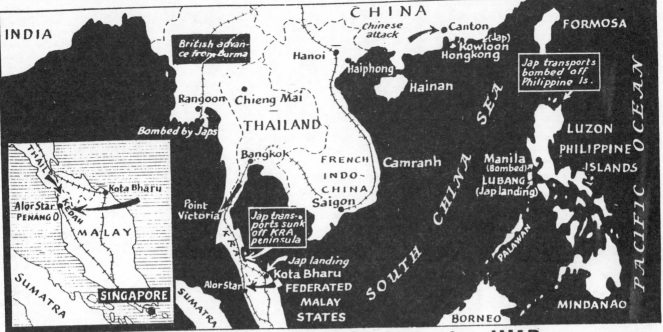

The JAPANESE ENTRY into the WAR

by "STRATEGICUS"

London, December 13.

ON SUNDAY, December 7, Japan carried out a heavy raid on the main United States naval base of Pearl Harbour (Hawaii), and an hour later presented her reply to an earlier memorandum of Mr. Cordell Hull's. Later still, the Imperial Headquarters stated that Japan would consider herself in a state of war with Great Britain and the United States, as from the following morning.

It is necessary to remember the sequence of events, since otherwise there is a danger of confusing the immediate with the remote effects of the Japanese entry into the war. From a purely military point of view, Japan is merely a group of islands with a great navy. She is in a position analogous to that of a Britain which has either great sea power or nothing at all. Japan is also, of course, a great military power, but not being joined to the mainland of Asia, her ability to carry out military operations depends entirely on her command of the sea. Her economic system is admittedly weak, her engineering industry is not highly developed, she is quite without allies or friends in her hemisphere. It follows that her strategy must be founded on the securing of decisive successes at the earliest possible moment, and her chance of doing so turns on whether she can deny to the United States those bases without which the navy of the United States cannot operate. It is clear that the sphere of action of warships depends on the use of bases, just as much as that of aircraft is a matter of the provision of aerodromes.

Japan's action in attacking without a declaration of war in spite of her signature to the Hague Convention is explained by these considerations. In 1904, she had attacked the Russian Fleet in Port Arthur by night and found it so profitable that she determined to try the expedient again. On the earlier occasion, prolonged negotiations with Russia had been broken off three days before. On the present occasion, in order to make quite certain that she could take the United States unawares, she continued the negotiations. At the very time that she sent Mr. Kurusu to act as special envoy to discuss outstanding matters with the United States, she must have determined not only on a surprise attack but also upon the actual form it took, since, as Mr. Roosevelt pointed out in his message to Congress, the distance of Hawaii from Japan is so great that the attack must have been arranged some days or weeks ago.

Japan's aim was to put out of action the United States Pacific Fleet, and she has claimed that it has been "annihilated." This, of course, is merely a characteristic way of saying that she achieved a distinct success. She proceeded to attack all the bases which lie between Hawaii and the Asiatic mainland—Guam, Wake Island, Midway Island, and the Imperial bases of Nauru and Ocean Island, and it is probable that she has either damaged or captured them. She has also attacked the Philippine Islands, Hong Kong, British North Borneo, Thailand (which promptly capitulated), North and Southern Malaya, and was reported to be moving against the Aleutian Islands and Canada.

The first point that must occur to anyone who looks at these places on the map is that they represent a distribution over literally immense distances. Japan must be very sure that she has gained a temporary immunity from interference by any other navy, since the dispersion of her naval ships on convoy duty must involve a very great challenge and risk. The second point is that, though with a population of such dimensions she must be able to raise a great army it is impossible that all these expeditions can be made in strength. The well-tried plan to "engage and then see" may, of course, have dictated her present course. She may hope to distract, to cause dispersion and confusion, and to weaken resistance at some or all of these points. But it is pretty clear that she is prepared to make her maximum effort in some particular direction, though we are at present unable to do more than make a guess as to its identity.

It may be, however, that her immediate objective is to capture North Malaya with a view to making ineffective the great naval and air base of Singapore, and securing a chance of moving on to the littoral of the Indian Ocean through Thailand. Through the capitulation of the government of Thailand she has secured the chance to concentrate her forces against the frontier of Thailand and Malaya, and though communications in the peninsula are poor, that is a great advantage. She has in addition attempted to invade the British positions also and is being fiercely challenged at the Malayan frontier. Freedom of passage across Thailand also gives access to Burma. Her attack upon Hong Kong is being resisted. The same is true of her attempted invasion of the Philippines and British North Borneo.

Japan has gained tangible advantage from her initial attack both against the American and the British fleets and, as she recognises that time is not in her favour, she is certain to do all the damage she can at once. But there is a world of difference between the first and the last blows of a campaign. The power of the United States is as notoriously strong as that of Japan is weak. Ultimately, of course no one in the world can be in doubt about the relative resources of Japan and the United States. The latter is the greatest industrial unit in the world, the richest power in the world; the biggest of the Great Powers. It is impossible to think that Japan has any chance of defeating the United States. It is equally certain that Japan will inflict more or less serious damage upon American interests and those of other nationals before she is brought to book. Whether the way be short or long, it is as certain as anything can be that the United States will sooner or later send against Japan a fleet sufficient to destroy hers, and with that this attempt to overturn the situation in Asia will pass away.

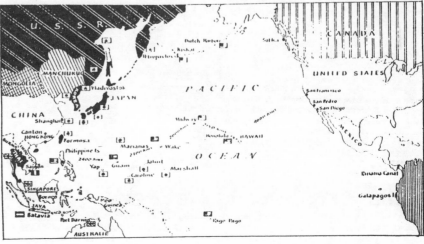

PRINCESSES and CORGI

THEIR ROYAL HIGHNESSES the Princesses Elizabeth and Margaret Rose. To quote magazine "Time," both the Princesses and their Corgi terrier, Jane (backview herewith), have gone on wartime rations; both collect tinfoil, roll bandages, knit socks for Tommy Atkins. Elizabeth contributes her savings to the Red Cross, Girl Guides, Air Ambulance Fund, buys National War Savings Certificates which are beyond the penny means of her little sister."

(Photograph by Cecil Beaton)

1942

Japanese invasion of Netherlands East Indies

Scharnhorst, *Gneisenau* and *Prinz Eugen* escape from Brest and sail

up the English Channel

Fall of Singapore

Battle of Java Sea

Evacuation of Rangoon

Raid on St Nazaire

Fall of Bataan Peninsula (Philippines)

Battle of the Coral Sea

British forces land on Madagascar

Battle of Midway island

Fall of Tobruk

US landing in Guadalcanal-Tulagi area (Solomon Islands)

First Moscow conference

Dieppe Raid

Battle of El Alamein

Operation Torch – Allied landings in North-west Africa

KNOCK HITLER OUT WITH METAL

'for Victory and Peace in 1942'

RUSSIA'S quick "turning of the tables" and the persistent drive to get back what was theirs, is due to a ready acceptance of the lesson of modern warfare—metal and yet more metal, "Pravda" writes:

THE use of masses of mortars and automatic rifles, the saturation of the fighting formations with mortar-gunners and automatic-rifle troops—this was the new feature in the first few months of the war.

At the beginning of the war we were behind in the mass use of mortars. Yet the production of mortars is simple and cheap. Mortars and shells can be manufactured with comparative ease and speed, and no great training is required to fire mortars.

The Nazis use their industry and the industries of the enslaved countries to saturate their army to the maximum with mortars and automatic rifles. Mortars have a high rate of fire. They are simple and convenient to use, and their action is faultless.

Mortar-guns defended Leningrad and Tula. Unerring fire dispersed enemy columns and lines, flinging them back. They routed the Nazis at Kalinin and Klin.

The Terror Weapon

Commanders have learned to train massed fire against the enemy, skilfully co-ordinating the operations of the mortar units with rifle, automatic rifle, and artillery units. In many cases the fire of mortars, especially large calibre mortars, can replace artillery fire.

The modern soldier must make wider use of the mortar to advance. Train more machine-gunners! Raise the skill of mortar-gunners to the level required by modern warfare.

Industry! Produce more mortars! Their manufacture is simple. It can be organised in small engineering shops. A few days ago in one of the engineering shops of a soap factory workers with initiative organised the production of excellent mortars at relatively little cost.

Mortars and mines are needed for superiority over the enemy and by the guerilla detachments operating in the enemy's rear. In the strong and reliable hands of the guerillas the mortar is a weapon that strikes terror into the invaders.

Workers! Give us more mortars and mines!

Libya G.O.C. has narrow escape

GENERAL RITCHIE and Air Vice-Marshal Coningham had a narrow escape when they visited by air one of the forward areas in Libya.

As they approached the plane to take off a solitary Ju. 88 dived from the heavy cloud cover and sent a stick of bombs hurtling to earth. One of the bombs fell 100 yards from the plane, but there was no damage or casualties.

Air Vice-Marshal Coningham was flown by a flying officer and himself acted as observer. General Ritchie sat beside the rear gunner.

FORBIDDEN TO FLY —GETS RECORD

A PILOT-OFFICER who was once advised by the medical authorities "never to fly again" has established for himself a record average of fifty hours' flying a month.

As a fighter pilot in a famous Hurricane squadron he was shot down in flames during the Dunkirk evacuation. He landed in German-occupied territory and, although in great pain, managed to reach the British lines. He was sent home, to spend a whole year in hospital.

As soon as the doctors had finished with him he asked to be put back on flying duties, and was bitterly disappointed when he was told that his medical category was too low for him to rejoin his old squadron.

He refused to give up and went on to make such recovery that he was once more allowed to fly. Now he is bent on showing the doctors that he is as good as he was before the crash.

AIR MAIL TO MALAYA

Special air mail postcard service providing a cheap and quick communication with the Forces in the Far East and China stations is in operation. Postage is 3d., and the transmission is by air all the way.

More Fire and Metal.

FREE FRENCH MEET IN SOHO PUB

Between Oxford Street in the north and Leicester Square in the south, between Charing Cross Road and Regent Street, is the liveliest, strangest, most pungent area in all London. Two years ago it was the Italian quarter. Now it is the French quarter. Following on Mussolini's declaration of war, internment and business failure have tended to push the Italians into the background. The French—Soho's second nation—have come into their own.

Soho may not be what it was, but even in wartime it is still honeycombed with cosmopolitan joints, dives and dumps. Yet the social centre, the pivot of the whole area, is a most conventional-looking English pub with a most conventional-sounding name—the *York Minster*.

Nothing else is conventional about it. Nothing else is English about it. Inside, it is a corner of France. The customers are Free French soldiers and sailors, are French Canadians, are Frenchmen in the catering trade, the cabinet-making trade, the hundred and one mysterious professions by which the French in England make a living. True there are English visitors, but they always remain foreigners. English beer is served, but rather as a sideline. Characteristic drinks of the house are the sweet aromatic aperitifs of the Continent— Cinzano, Cap Corse, Dubonnet, Pernod.

Business is always brisk. Ten minutes after opening time, there is little elbow room. The air is hazy with cigarette smoke. The walls are covered with signed photographs of French vaudeville stars, French boxers, French bike-riders—Grock, the Fratellinis, Criqui, Siki, Carpentier. It is the boast of M. Victor Berlemont, the proprietor, that no celebrity has his picture hung till he has had a drink at the *York Minster*.

Berlemont himself is one of the great figures of Soho. Though it is 41 years since he left his native St. Quentin to come to London, he has not shed an ounce of his nationality. He has been 'monsieur le Patron' at

M. Berlemont (M. le patron) presides over the Pernod machine, filtering water through sugar into an aniseed drink as near absinthe as law allows,

the *York Minster* since 1914. In between times (apart from his five years' service with the French army in the last war), he has been second to pretty well every good French fighter who has been here in the last quarter-century — Ledoux, Criqui, Thill, Carpentier. Everybody in Soho knows Victor Berlemont, for besides being the host of all Free French people, he is also the owner of probably the finest moustache in London.

Away over the other side of Soho are the tawdry pubs, haunted—and haunted is the word—by London's Bohemia. A few freaks drift into Berlemont's, but they don't seem to stay. The brisk, wartime climate does not suit them. More representative are the cheerful young sailors in the corner, who chi-ike each other in the tangy accent of Toulon, or the soldier from Oran, whom everybody calls Georges (but whose name when he is at home is Ahmed), or the girl from the Bastille district whose husband is in the navy, and who drops in to get news of him from his comrades.

To the French visitor in peacetime, the *York Minster* was always a rendezvous. To the French exile in war time, it is something more, it is a headquarters. It is France in London.

South Coast Hotel Has 6D. 'Shake-down'

It's a Question of Time

I WAS discharged as disabled on September 24, 1941, after nearly two years' service. I have received all ordinary pay due, but I am still waiting for increments of pay—about £30. Can you help me to get it?

Yours is not an individual case. In fact, there are thousands of men in a similar position to yourself.

The difficulty is that the original and official documents, having been blitzed, are not now available. The whole matter is considered of such importance that it is before the Army Council for consideration and decision.

There seems to be the question of policy involved, i.e. the payment on the basis of possibly uncorroborated statements of the men concerned. You should hear something soon.

"High-Ups" Decide

CAN anything be done to break the red tape surrounding temporary rank?

The question of temporary rank is a constant source of irritation; but it is felt in official circles that the rank itself and the pay attached to it must of necessity be regarded as temporary and, therefore, liable to be cancelled at any time. This, of course, tends to be a rough deal in certain individual cases; but it is a decision respecting which the Army Council arrived at soon after the beginning of the war, and there seems little possibility that it will be revised at the present time unless there are a sufficient number of cases to justify such revision.

Wants To Be a Padre

CAN I obtain a position as assistant to a Padre or something in a similar capacity? I am studying Theology at King's College, London, and it would help me if I could assist a chaplain in his duties.

I am obviously not in a position to say whether or not the duties of Army Chaplain could be granted to you without specific details of your personal background; but there are definite channels by which you can apply for consideration re a vacancy in one of these positions, and I recommend that you make immediate, written application.

Ask for Form 1219

AN airman writes: I got behind with my weekly maintenance order payments, and the accounts department stopped another shilling a week. Now they have stopped a further two shillings a week, leaving me with 8s. I'm rather sore about this. Another thing Before my enlistment I lived with my unmarried wife, and cannot understand why I have been refused an allowance. She is doing a light job for which she is paid 6s. I send her 8s. a week. This is all the income she has to keep herself and the two children. Can you give me any information?

Any airman against whom a Maintenance Order is in operation is placed under compulsory stoppages, the maximum in the case of your rank being three-quarters of your pay.

For what the Air Force Act refers to as "An unmarried dependant living as a wife (and no children in her care)" you can claim a special dependant's allowance at the same rate and under the same conditions as if you were actually married—provided it can be shown that "the dependant is substantially maintained by you on a domestic basis and that this was the case at least six months prior to enlistment." You should apply on Form 1219, obtainable from your Accountant Officer.

A SHILLING for a "cabin," ninepence for an "overflow bed," and sixpence for a "shake-down"—these are the prices charged to sailors, soldiers, and airmen on leave at a N.A.A.F.I. hotel on the South Coast.

Service Grants

The revision of the large number of War Service Grants in payment has been completed.

In cases where the amount has been altered an individual notification has been issued. In cases where the grant has been maintained at its existing amount no notice is given.

If in any case it is felt that the present assessment is too low owing to changes of circumstances of which the Ministry of Pensions is unaware, you can apply to the War Service Grants Department, Ministry of Pensions, Heyhouses-lane, Lytham St. Annes, for reconsideration.

"Plaster of Paris" Flying Kit

VISITORS to a Fighter Command station have been unaware that the Group Captain Station Commander carried on his duties with a broken back. But the plaster of paris in which the group captain was encased for so long did not stop his flying.

He was taking off in a Spitfire for an offensive sweep when the engine failed and he crashed outside the aerodrome. The crash broke his back. Taken to hospital, it was found that, with care, the bones would knit together. . . He was back on his job at the station within a week—in a plaster of paris coat.

In less than a month from the time he crashed he was again flying his Spitfire on local patrol "just to keep his hand in."

The group captain is thirty-five and one of the youngest in the R.A.F. He won his D.F.C. early in the war for gallantry in action.

Probing Catch-Phrases

CATCH - PHRASES — and who hasn't used them sometime or another?—"Business is business," "It's only human nature," "That's up to the Government," "It's my opinion, anyway," often confront us with challenging questions about man's behaviour, rights, duties to others, and to the community.

Beginning on Friday in the Home Service, the B.B.C. will broadcast a series of talks, "That's What 'I' Say." Many of the much-used catch-phrases will be dramatised, followed by discussion. The listener will be left to find the answer to the problem.

Servicemen who want to spend their leave near the sea—as they used to spend their holiday back in Civvy Street—can have that pleasure.

For a few shillings a day there is full board and lodging, with enough recreation to make it unnecessary to leave the building.

The White Ensign Club was started in 1907 and has been run by N.A.A.F.I. since the last war. It is the mecca of serving men off duty and on leave. Just now it is "House Full" most nights, each of the ninety-seven cabins, the fifty overflow beds, and the 150 shake-downs being booked by early evening.

The bar, the billiard-room, reading-room, and restaurant are crowded with men from all Services, including Free French, Norwegians, Poles, and Dutch. A really happy lot.

An average of 450 visit the hotel in a day and more than 200 cooked meals are served daily—so, save the shillings, boys.

Yes, we can tell you where it is, and reserve you a "shake down" if wanted—just let us know.

BUSTLING FIRST-AID TRAINING

FAR-REACHING plans for reorganising the Civil Defence first-aid services have been announced.

All wardens, whether full-time or part-time, must in future be qualified first-aid workers. All auxiliary policemen—war reserve and part-time and full-time special constables—are also concerned. Each man must attend a ten-hour course in first-aid.

Outside the L.C.C. area, where demolition work is not likely to be heavy, the former stretcher parties and rescue squads are being combined into comprehensive first-aid parties. They will undertake rescue work, first-aid, and demolition.

In the London area first-aid parties, formerly known as stretcher parties, must now extricate the injured from bombed buildings, whereas in the past they merely administered first-aid. They must be prepared also to undertake light demolition work.

OLDER MEN AS N.C.O.s

THOUSANDS of Army senior N.C.O.s may soon find themselves reduced to the rank of corporal or private if they prove unable to stand the pace of modern warfare.

Many of these men received rapid promotion because of the urgency of the position at the beginning of the war.

Now, with the higher-age call-up they must give way to the seasoned experience of the older men.

Born in ★ **It's in the Stars** ★ January

YOU will be on fire picket on Wednesday, and guard on Friday. The girl you were to meet on Wednesday outside the Red Lion will not turn up. Rather a disappointing week. However, the pass you put in on Thursday for week-end leave may possibly score a bull. To make sure about, though, corner the S.S.M. on Friday (not before, however, as he may have a liver on).

REVEILLE Jan. 5. 1942

Ideas from Big Shots

An "Ideas Committee" for British propaganda films, formed from the creative side of the industry, is to work out a scheme of constructive ideas for the Ministry of Information.

The "Ideas Committee" will act as liaison between the Ministry and the creative talent of the film industry not already in touch with the department.

TO WHAT RED HELL!

In the pocket-book of several German prisoners taken in Russia have been found the hand-written text and music of a new song which German soldiers sing—when well out of hearing of their officers.

The chorus, "Back to Germany, Russia is real hell," is sung with real warmth and feeling.

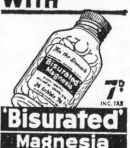

Typical of the serene beauty of Java is this view of Lake Leles in the Preanger Highlands, Middle Java. This is not far from Dutch G.H.Q. in Bandoeng.

Javanese soldiers transport a gun, split into pack loads, across a river, or kali, on horseback. In 1906 North Sumatra campaign, Javanese fought well.

Java Battlefield

Hell is about to break loose in one of the greenest and most beautiful islands in the world, where the four-hundred-year-old rule of the Hollanders is challenged by Japan.

This Batavia monument to Governor-General van Heutsz, the Clive of the Indies, often is likened to the artillery memorial opposite Hyde Park Gate.

AIR raids and the great naval battle off Bali herald the Battle of Java. In the harbours of Singapore, Palembang, Pontianak, Banjermasin, Macassar and Bali, Japan's invasion armadas have steam up. Japan wants to gobble up the United Nations' last foothold in South-East Asia—and the last big chunk of Dutch soil in the world.

Java's fate depends on the United States. Unless sufficient American troops, warships and aircraft reach there quickly to aid the Dutch, Japan must overwhelm the island by sheer weight of numbers and equipment. Both Japan and the Americans are running against time. Communiqués frequently mention American warships and aircraft operating from Java ; but so far there have been only agency reports of American troops having landed.

To a comparatively small group of white men like the Hollanders of Java the prospect of Japanese invasion must be nightmarish. But the Hollander, whose flag has flown over Java for the best part of 400 years, is undeterred. Events of the past two months in the Western Pacific have shown the Hollander to be a ruthless, tough, resourceful fighter without one streak of defeatism in his makeup. It was loss of sea power, not loss of spunk, that reduced Holland from the rank of Great Power to that of a small nation.

Weaving of batik, or sarong cloth, is an ancient Malay art.

A Dutch Colonial sailor, burly, tough and Japan-hating.

IN BRITAIN TODAY

The King is still in London

The British people have always held their Royal Family in great affection. The late King George V was deeply moved at the spontaneous reception given to him during the celebration of his jubilee. King George VI won the hearts of his people by refusing to move out of Buckingham Palace despite Nazi bombs. Britain's King and Queen stand by their people in their troubles at home.

The King and Queen stand on the actual spot in Westminster Abbey where they were crowned. Nazi bombs have laid waste the high altar and other parts of the Abbey.

H.M. is Honorary Colonel of the London Scottish. After a ride in a Bren Carrier.

A wounded airman of the R.A.F. receives a visit from the Queen whilst in hospital.

The King gets a hand from the canteen staff of a headquarters canteen of the Coastal Command during a tour.

The Duchess of Gloucester has a look at the Women's Land Army in Peterborough district. Is herself a country-woman.

Beautiful ex-mannequin and dancer, Margharita Haines, widow of a D.F.C. pilot is now working in an aircraft factory. The Duchess of Kent is interested in her story and is seen chatting with her.

This map illustrates Geopolitics, the application of strategic principles not to the artificial nation-state but to large natural geographic units and finally to the world. The final Geopolitics problem is, if the whole world is divided, land-power against sea-power, which will win? The map shows the setting for this hypothetical war. The black WORLD-ISLAND is the terrain of land-power, the seas, the minor islands, and the coastal fringe of WORLD-ISLAND of sea-power. Moving out on interior lines from HEARTLAND, your first job is to push the SEA-POWER STATES from the fringe of WORLD-ISLAND. Small squares on WORLD-ISLAND show the slow movements of armies compared with fleets. Advantage of sea-power is the swift, unexpected blow (JAPAN in this war and in RUSSO-JAPANESE war); advantage of land-power is firm consolidation (centuries-slow but permanent expansion of RUSSIA).

Hitler 18 Months Behind Schedule

New York, March 12. Hitler is already 18 months behind the war production schedule as laid down by Professor Karl Haushofer's Geopolitical Institute, declares the author Pierre van Passen in an article published in the magazine "Look." "Hitler promised that 1941 would bring to Germany the consummation of the greatest victory in our history", van Passen points out. But now Goebbels warns his countrymen they must not ask when victory is coming.

Blueprint for Conquest?

On the Russo-German Front, melting snow and ice turned the roads into rivers at some points. All along the front, the thaw uncovered the perfectly preserved bodies of German and Russian soldiers who had fallen in battle at the end of the autumn; both Tass and D.N.B. remarked on this gruesome sidelight.

Not a word came from Moscow about the talks between Molotov, Soviet Foreign Commissar, and Notake Sato, newly-arrived Japanese Ambassador. Agency messages spoke of Japanese efforts to talk the Soviet Union into a separate peace with Germany. Some sources said the Japanese were safeguarding their rear to enable complete concentration on India and perhaps Australia.

MOLOTOV

Bombs on Ruhr War Factories

While the R.A.F. was pounding at German heavy industries in the Ruhr, with Cologne as its main target, British sea, land and air forces surprised the defenders of the great German U-boat base of St. Nazaire, at the mouth of the Loire, in an after-midnight Saturday morning raid. One of the transferred American destroyers, its bows packed with delayed-action high explosives, rammed the centre of the main lock gates. Much destruction was carried out before the raiding party returned to England.

After the "David and Goliath" naval action in the Mediterranean (see pages 12 and 13), Mr. Churchill telegraphed to the C.-in-C., Mediterranean: "...That one of the most powerful and modern battleships afloat, attended by two heavy and four light cruisers and a flotilla, should have been routed and put to flight ...in broad daylight by a force of five British light cruisers and destroyers constitutes a naval episode of the highest distinction..."

Spokesman Warns Japanese

"I pledge to Australia the mighty power of my country and all the blood of my countrymen," General MacArthur announced at a dinner attended by the Commonwealth Prime Minister, John Curtin.

To the north, the R.A.A.F. and United States Army and Navy fliers continued to bomb the rapidly mustering Japanese convoys at Dilly and Koepang, in Timor, and at Rabaul and Lae, in New Guinea.

In Burma (see detailed map in page five), the Japanese claimed to have encircled the Chinese defenders of Toungoo, key railway town half-way between Rangoon and Mandalay. To maintain

something like parallel fronts, the British forces on the Irrawaddy Front withdrew toward Prome. From the Shan States two strong Chinese columns invaded Siam, crossing the frontier at two points south-east of Möngtun. Among the prisoners they took was a French officer.

Across the Bay of Bengal, the Bengal Government advised all those not engaged in essential work to leave the Calcutta area.

B.B.C. Farewells Blimp

A premature obituary notice for Colonel Blimp was delivered in an Empire-wide B.B.C. broadcast by J. B. Priestley. Describing cartoonist Low's Blimp as "a bald-headed old man with a military moustache, representing a stupid, old-fashioned, ultra-conservative viewpoint," Priestley said Blimp had created a harmful impression abroad. Blimp was dangerous. But he was on the way out. It was not so much the Blimps who stayed in the background who were the danger; it was those who refused to change and leave their jobs. Fortunately in recent weeks many Blimps had changed. The success of the Red Army and the Allied defeats in Asia had been blows for the Blimps.

BLIMPS

Twenty-Four Hours a Day in Detroit

Supplementing the figures quoted in this page last week, Donald Nelson, U.S. production chief, revealed that direct United States war expenditure now exceeds £20,000,000 a day. He said the Detroit motor-car industry was working 24 hours a day, seven days a week, turning out tanks, military vehicles and aircraft motors and parts. By midsummer, aircraft production would be so great that road and rail transport dificulties might be experienced in clearing the 'planes from the factories. American aircraft for Britain, the Middle East, China, the Soviet Union and Australia were being delivered by air through the Army Air Corps' world-wide Ferry Command. As many as 25 aircraft a day were being ferried across the Atlantic.

According to the B.B.C., the Douglas Boston 3 bomber is arriving in Britain in increasing numbers and since the beginning of the year has been replacing the Bristol Blenheim as a day bomber. The American aircraft carries twice the Blenheim's bomb load and is nearly as fast as a fighter; it carries four Browning machine-guns for forward fire and two for rear fire.

Continuing their private spring offensive, the Royal Air Force concentrated on German heavy industry and on French ports used by the German Navy. In four nights, more than 1,000 tons of bombs were dropped on the Rhineland, the Ruhr and other parts of Western Germany. It was stated in London that the R.A.F. raids on the Renault and Ford works near Paris had deprived Germany of the equipment of five armoured divisions. Ford and Renault were between them producing for the Reich 20,000 heavily-armoured trucks as well as tanks and a.f.v.'s. This achievement cost the R.A.F. four bombers and 25 men.

United Nations will Lash out at Japs from Australian Mainland Bases

(This is a digest of the week's cable news from the Dominions; most of it this week comes from bustling, threatened Australia.)

AUSTRALIA is spending more than a million Australian pounds a day on the war, according to latest Treasury figures. In March, £13,500,00 was spent from revenue and £20,250,000 from loans.

Australia's coming role was discussed by the B.B.C.'s military commentator Colonel Kennedy in a broadcast this week. "The American Chief of Staff, General Marshall," he said, "has declared that the main effort of the United States is to gather its forces for a major offensive at the earliest date. But to undertake this offensive America must have a solid base; and this probably will be Australia. I conceive a huge curving movement on the Japanese stepping-stone model, but not involving the same dispersion of forces. The first prong, based on Australia, would move from island to island toward Formosa and finally to the Japanese mainland. Another prong would make for Malaya and thence China."

The same commentator described the action of the Australian Prime Minister, John Curtin, in giving General MacArthur complete freedom of action and promising that there would be no parliamentary interference, as "establishing a precedent in Empire history." Mr. Curtin often has attacked statesmen and politicians who fancy themselves as strategists. "Military matters are for military men," is his rule.

Hustling Hank the Yank

After inspecting a United States Army camp in Australia, Army Minister Forde, said: "It is heartening and exhilarating to see the speed with which great Australian armies are coming into being." The Australian press was full of praise for the speed with which the Americans set up pre-fabricated camps, complete with electric light and hot and cold running water. According to the *Sydney Sun*, a camp is completely erected and working 24 hours after the word "go." This includes laying of metalled roads, installing of telephones, radio and sewers, and turning on of full cookhouse menu.

Australian newspapers recall that the Americans are the first "alien" troops on Australian soil in 72 years. The last were the 14th. and 18th. Regiments of the British Army, which sailed away in 1870. In continuation of the policy of doing everything possible to make "Hank the Yank" feel at home, some newspapers are running specially-cabled American domestic news sections. They contain such items as that in the *Melbourne Herald* last week from Cambridge, Massachussetts. It recorded that one Gladys Miller when seeking a divorce brought into court a box of human hair. "It belonged to me," she sobbed, "until my husband yanked it out on New Year's Eve." She got her divorce.

Following an assertion by Roman Catholic Archbishop Duhig, of Melbourne, that "American soldiers should come here to fight, not to marry," Mrs. Evatt, wife of the Australian Foreign Minister, addressed a press conference in Washington. She said she did not see why Australian girls should not marry American soldiers.

There is fresh fury in Australia at the authenticated report that in New Britain some weeks ago 60 Australian officers were bound up alive and used for Japanese bayonet practice.

From Wellington it is announced that one man in every four in New Zealand is now in military service.

While the main body of the Canadian Army trains in Britain for an invasion of Europe, a guerilla army is being formed in Canada to deal with parachutists, Colonel Ralston, Canadian Defence Minister, announced in Ottawa.

Hitler's Last Birthday ?

Monday was the 53rd. birthday of Adolf Hitler. "Because it might be his last," said the B.B.C.'s revolutionary propagandist, 'Colonel Britton,' "we ask you people of the occupied countries to celebrate it." To celebrate the Führer's birthday, his victims were urged to waste time in factories, overload public utilities and avoid deep ploughing on farms, thus conserving soil wealth until after the war.

George Cross for Malta

For the first time the George Cross has been awarded to a community. The King has bestowed it on the people of Malta. Correspondents report that already the islanders are chalking the cross on walls, alongside the "V."

U.S. Fliers' Two-Day Picnic

In the longest bombing raid of the war, 13 American bombers flew from Australia to the Philippines and back. Besides dropping 110 tons of bombs, sinking four Japanese ships, damaging four others and shooting down four enemy aircraft, the Americans attacked enemy airfields and brought back to Australia 25 Americans, mostly senior Army and Army Air Corps officers. Only one 'plane was lost. The round trip was of more than 3,000 miles. "A two-day picnic," its organiser, Brigadier Royce, called it when predicting many such raids from Burma "across China and cutting right into Japan's lines of communication."

While Japanese bombs and shells were pounding the American garrison on Corregidor Island in Manila Bay, General Wainwright in an Order of the Day told his men : "There can be no question of surrendering this mighty fortress to the enemy ; it will be defended with all the resources at our command."

They die with their boots clean

LIFE in a crack regiment like the Coldstream Guards form the background of Gerald Kersh's latest book, *They Die with their Boots Clean* (Heinemann, 8s. 6d.).

"The Raw Material," "The Foundry," "The Tempering," and "The Finished Product" are some of the chapters of the book which is a mixture of realism, military slang, toughness, and humour.

We watch the unpolished recruit till he is a fully-trained soldier.

We see the countryman, the university student, the cockney, the worker, and the miner all melted in this hard discipline.

We listen to stirring tales of Arabia, France, and Palestine where Guardsmen won fame and V.C.s, have a lecture on "spit and polish."

F. H.

Odeon Entertain H.G.

THE death of Oscar Deutsch has made no difference to the good work that Odeon does for the Forces.

Bill Thornton, manager of the Leicester Square Odeon, recently arranged a special news programme for 2,200 Home Guards.

Films shown included Home Guard and Army training shots, and uncut films of our raids on Norway, and the Battle of Libya.

Highlights of the show were captured German films of the attack on Russia.

The Odeon Evacuation Office at Cookham entertained Canadian soldiers to a dance and cabaret last week.

Major F. Stanley Bates and Mr. J. H. Davies, joint managing directors, fraternised with the boys and had as good a time as the guests.

REVEILLE

MARCH 16, 1942

Bill Evans, "Reveille" Sports Writer, Says:

MAKE PROMOTERS PLAY THE GAME

No leave for 16 weeks

By "Reveille" Reporter

WE continue to hear of Service men who go four or five months at a stretch without any leave!

This is contrary to Army Council Orders. Every man should have leave regularly every three months.

My investigations have shown me that the worst offender in this respect is the R.A.S.C.

Attached to a unit not very far from London are men who have not had their normal leave. I spoke to some of them—all at a loss to understand why their leave should be so long overdue.

Most of them have great difficulty in getting a change of kit. Some of the "battledress" I saw certainly looked "worse for wear."

"It's all very well," said one of them, "talking about looking smart, but a lot of us here haven't got a battledress that is decent to walk out in."

That a good-looking suit does "buck you up"—who will deny?

He releases the bombs

He waits for the split second when his sights cross the target . . . then down to earth fall the bombs, destined for the roof of a Paris Nazi controlled war factory.

CERTAIN sections of the sporting world have been badly jarred by the announcement that boxing and dog racing are to be considerably curtailed.

I was amazed at the reactions of the Press generally.

Let us look at the situation sanely.

Sir Stafford Cripps received practically no support, while the boxing and dog-racing fraternities were given space in which to squeal.

Where professional boxing is run as a sport, for the entertainment and relaxation of troops and war workers, it should be encouraged. More such tournaments should be run at night, or during non-working periods.

Charity boxing shows should be carefully examined for motive and result. Where they are genuine charity efforts, representing sacrifice on the part of boxers, managers, hall owners, and promoters, and they produce at least three times as much in proceeds to the charity as they cost to run, they should be encouraged.

If promoters are so keen to help charity, let them run shows for bare expenses. If civilian promoters cannot do that, they should go into a war factory and make a living that way, and leave promotions to Service sports organisers.

BOXING

There are some genuine promoters who depend solely on boxing for their livelihoods. They are the men who can be relied upon to continue to cater for the war-working public with honest, betting-free shows, and the Government ought to encourage them.

* * *

The police seem to me to have fallen down on the job of checking waste of petrol at sporting events. When owners of cars come out after a show or race meeting, they should all be interrogated; not just a few or none at all. They should be questioned where they obtained their petrol, and every suspicious character should be watched night and day by a motor-cyclist cop to see how far he can spin out a month's basic ration in attending sporting events.

We don't want the good name of sport trampled on by parasites who don't know what the word sport means.

SOCCER

Soccer football, like cricket, is a shining example of providing entertainment for war workers, except that some of the Service players might be quizzed on how much actual military duty they do in the course of a week. I think they would pass the test satisfactorily, despite the whispering campaign against them.

I want to see a Ministry of Sport to handle all the war-time problems. This may be a sort of "bee-in-my-bonnet," but it is the only solution; moreover, I can name a man who could fulfil the difficult and complex post admirably . . . Sir Noel Curtis-Bennett.

He is the only man in Britain who can do the job. I had a long chat with him on the subject last week and he showed a grasp of the many snags of war-time sport.

He is a strong man where toughs are concerned and an intensely human one when humanity is the keynote.

NEW WAYS of SERVING

CORNED ★ BEEF

WINTER HOT-POT

3 rations of corned beef
2 Oxo Cubes. (6d. worth)
2 cups shredded mixed vegetables(carrot, swede, artichoke, etc.)
1 small onion or piece of leek, finely chopped.
Small piece dripping.
8 ozs. flour.
3 ozs. chopped suet.

Melt the dripping in a medium sized saucepan or casserole and fry the vegetables lightly. Add 2 cups water and the crumbled Oxo Cubes and stir until they are dissolved. Cover and simmer 10 minutes. Prepare the suet pastry and roll to a round the size of the saucepan. Put into the pan the corned beef cut in cubes and seasoning to taste. Place the suet crust on top of the meat and vegetables, cover and cook gently for 20 minutes, or bake for 30 minutes. Serve in the casserole or on a hot dish with the crust cut in portions.

(4 servings)

Melt the fat in a small pan and lightly fry the vegetables. Stir in the flour and cook a few minutes. Add 1 cup of cold water and the crumbled Oxo cube. Stir until thickened. Draw off the heat, add cubed meat, parsley and seasoning to taste. Line a small plate with pastry and spread it with the meat mixture. Cover with pastry, seal the edges and decorate with pastry leaves. Bake in a moderate oven 30 minutes. (4 servings)

CORNED BEEF PIE

3 rations of corned beef (6d. worth)
1 cup finely shredded raw vegetables (carrot, potato, leek, swede, etc.).
1 Oxo Cube.
1 teaspoon chopped parsley.
Small piece fat.
Short crust pastry
(6 ozs. flour, 3 ozs. fat)
1 dessertspoon flour.

CORNED BEEF CAKES

8 ozs. Corned beef.
1 small cupful browned crumbs.
1 dessertspoon flour.
1 teaspoon chopped parsley.
8 ozs. mashed potato.
1 Oxo Cube.
Small piece fat.

Dissolve the Oxo in a cupful of hot water and let it cool. Flake the meat, mix it with the parsley, potato and half the crumbs. Melt the fat, blend the flour with it, cook a few minutes and then stir in the Oxo stock. Cook until it thickens stirring all the time. Bind the meat mixture with this sauce and seasoning if necessary. Form into flat cakes, roll in crumbs and press them on. Heat in a well-greased frying pan or baking tin.
(About 8 small Cakes)

All supplies of Corned Beef including FRAY BENTOS, are now distributed by the Ministry of Food.

PRODUCT OF OXO LIMITED

Yanks taught why they fight

THAT America means to *begin right*, and go *right ahead* until the brown and yellow Nazis are beaten, is further shown in a unique programme of lectures written and designed to teach the American soldier what he is fighting for.

It has attracted the interest of civilian leaders in U.S. who want to adopt it as a means of making the people at home understand and link together the military and political chain of world events.

Reports from U.S. state that several weeks ago picked troops, from generals to privates, began the compulsory attendance of twenty-six lectures—two a week for thirteen weeks.

The study includes world geography and history, democratic principles, and the current world crisis.

Soldiers are lectured once a week on military subjects outside their regular training, so as to better understand the Navy and Marines, the duties of various ranks, and the use of propaganda.

The point is, of course—Generals are included among those needing the instruction!

You can say no injections if—

Wounded soldiers, whether in hospitals or at first-aid stations, are always free to refuse antitetanus or other injections.

"But," says the War Office, "if the patient is considered by the surgeon to be incapable of rational judgment, may use his own discretion."

GRATUITIES—CABINET'S SEALED LIPS

"IS it part of the War Cabinet's scheme for general reconstruction after hostilities have ceased, that immediate consideration will be given to the question of gratuities to members of the Services?"

This is the gist of a question put to the Prime Minister in the House of Commons recently.

Mr. Churchill's deputy, Mr. C. R. Attlee (Lab.), answering Mr. Bellinger, said: "This is a question which will have to be settled by the Government of the day in the light of the circumstances then prevailing."

Asked in a rather pointed way why this should be, and if this was not part of the conditions of service just as much as the improvements in pay, and just as urgent as plans for demobilisation?, the Deputy Prime Minister curtly replied, "No, I think not!"

'NEXT OF KIN'

AN official secret is out! The greatest invasion film made in this country—"Next of Kin"—is now being shown to the Army, the Home Guard, and other defence units.

West End actors and actresses earning up to £100 a week played in the production for a few pounds, and all were pledged to secrecy.

OUR HOME GUARD notes in the last two issues were taken from Home Guard Encyclopaedia, published by Thorsons (Publishers), Ltd. We regret that we omitted to give the title and publishers—but do so now.

THE HOME GUARD

QUESTIONS have been asked as to the powers of Home Guard with regard to suspected persons.

When in uniform and on duty, the H.G. have the same rights and duties regarding the arrest and search of suspected persons, and the search of vehicles and premises, as any other officer or soldier.

A Home Guard may stop and question any persons regarding identity and the purposes for which they are in the place where found.

He may also stop and search any vehicle in any place to which the public have access, and he may seize any article found therein which he has reasonable ground for believing to be evidence of an offence against Defence Regulations.

Forces' Friend in Parliament

EX-SERVICEMEN AFTER THE WAR

The natural order of things must be:
★ Firstly, the service of human beings
★ Secondly, production to this end
★ Thirdly, money used only to this end

by W. J. BROWN, M.P.

I HAVE received the following letter from a Captain in the Army:—

I know that the views that I express in this letter are shared by many of my friends in the Army and, I am sure, by very many others of all ranks in the Services. There is amongst us a pent-up desire for a more vigorous prosecution of the war and for the elimination of those bottlenecks in production which have denied it to us before.

Above all, what perturbs us is the sense of cynicism which pervades many of us as regards our war aims. It is felt that, despite all the talk of a new and better Britain founded on a basis of social security and equality of opportunity, there is a very real chance of our passing from War to Peace without these aspirations being given positive form, with the eventual result that we shall drift back to the old conditions with all its resultant disillusionment. We know that there are very many powerful elements in political, industrial, and financial cricks whose desire is the preservation of the " status quo." Within the last week, as you will know, the Archbishop of Canterbury, in formulating his views on what basis this New Order should be formed, has been attacked by the " Daily Telegraph." These attacks are insidious and will grow, and we of the younger generation are for the most part enforcedly inarticulate.

SOMETHING DEFINITE

This tendency perturbs us, for we believe that what is lacking more than anything else in this country to-day is a clear statement or programme of how, and on what basis, we propose to lay the foundations of our new social structure.

The Nazis at least formulated a New Order. It is, we believe, an abominable Order, but its definiteness is an asset to those who believe in it. We are inclined to doubt whether we shall ever be rallied sufficiently to win both the War and the Peace unless we are given objectives as definite and as new as Hitler's New Order.

What are the men who are fighting the war going to do when it is over?

What part will they—who will have won the war—play in settling the terms of peace?

What will they do about the social order here in Britain when we turn to the business of reconstructing our shattered civilisation?

These are the things I wish to discuss in this article.

When the last war ended hundreds of thousands of ex-soldiers, ex-sailors, and ex-airmen came back to Britain. They had been profoundly dissatisfied with the pre-1914 world. They came back bent on doing something to make a better.

They failed. What we achieved after that was not a PEACE, but a TRUCE—a truce now dissolved in the fires of a new and still greater war.

And at home every vested interest which stood in the way of a new and better Britain crept out of the hole in which it had taken refuge during the war. They seized power again; they frustrated the urge to a new Britain. They re-established the power of money and privilege. The crazy anarchy of planless production was resumed. Soon there were hundreds of thousands of ex-Service men walking the streets in hopeless idleness.

To an extent the ex-Service men were responsible for this. When the war ended a host of ex-Service men's organisations came into being. But they made the fatal error of concerning themselves with effects rather than causes. They fought well on such issues as finding posts for ex-Service men in Government departments, on disability pensions, and the like. They threw up in Parliament two doughty champions in Mr. Pringle and Mr. Hogge. But in their preoccupation with limited objectives like this, they forgot the wide objective: a country organised to free men from unemployment and economic insecurity.

NON-EXISTENT

Finally, the ex-Service men's movements were combined into one body — the British Legion—from which the teeth had been drawn. It was to be " non-political "—which meant that it must say and do nothing about social conditions generally, and must confine itself to things like " pensions," and employment bureaux, and so on. The Legion was presided over by Lord Haig, which was a guarantee of its " non-politicalness " and its " respectability."

As an influence in shaping a new Britain, for ex-Service men or any other sort of men, the organisation ceased to exist. Its main function for the last ten years has been that of a club-owning institution of no political significance whatever.

Now we have learnt the lesson —have we not?—that the fate of ex-Service men cannot be divorced from that of the community as a whole. If after this war we allow ourselves to revert to the anarchy which prevailed between 1920 and 1939: if we again allow the vested interests of rent, interest, or profit to re-emerge to dominate our Parliament and our public life; if we allow the souless money values of pre-war society to again become dominant—then there is nothing to prevent ex-Service men sharing the fate which will befall the community as a whole.

And so, if they are wise, the Service men will make up their minds **now** to see that this does not happen. They will make up their minds **now** that they, who endure the burden and sacrifices of war, shall play their collective part in determining the conditions of the peace, and the post-war social arrangements of Britain.

WHAT DO THEY NEED? WHAT DO WE ALL NEED?

We need first to see that the Peace which ends the War shall be a real Peace and not another Temporary Truce.

I was a youngster of twenty when the last war came. My two sons were about the same age when this war came. One is in the Air Force, the other in the Army—their professional training interrupted, their futures wholly uncertain and insecure. They ask me: " Is this to happen all over again in another twenty years, when our sons will be growing up? " It is for us to see that it does not. They are fighting to rid the world of the foul doctrines of Nazism. Yes! But they are not fighting to make the world safe for British imperialism or for any other imperialism. They are fighting to make it safe for ordinary men and women. And they will judge the peace by that criterion only. **Will it remove from the** world the ever - recurring threat of war? If it does, it is a good Peace. If it doesn't, it will be a bad peace, whoever wins.

We need next to secure such post-war arrangements in Britain as will remove unemployment and the ever-recurring threat of economic insecurity. The world of 1939 was a bad world—a world in which no one, not even the rich, were really secure. It was a world in which men were allowed to rot in idleness with no more than would keep body and soul together. It was a world in which the natural order of things was turned upside-down.

What was the order of things in that world? It was:—
(1) Profit first.
(2) Production only if it served profit.
(3) Employment and economic security for ordinary men last.

The right and natural order of things is:—
(1) The service of human beings.
(2) Production to this end.
(3) Money—merely an instrument to this end.

HOLD STEADFAST

We must see to it that our new society is based on this order. And the ex-Service men of this war must see to it that they are not diverted from this end by any pretext or device whatever.

I don't myself care two hoots what label we apply to the New Britain. What interests me is not the label but the contents of the jar. And the real and true antithesis of Nazi society—a society where the interests of the State are paramount and the individual counts not at all—is a truly democratic order in which the State exists to serve men and to provide the environment in which the capacities of every human being may develop and express themselves to the uttermost, and where men and women may live out their lives free from the fear of war, and free from the shame of economic insecurity.

It's That Man Again

● To celebrate its 2nd Birthday, Reveille revives a popular feature of last year. Look out for Tommy Handley's "Fun Kit Bag." He will appear in every issue of Reveille.

OVERHEARD in Berlin: " Did you know, an air force is the most expensive part of the armed forces of a country? "

" Really: then I suppose we should be grateful to the R.A.F. for reducing our expenses! "

* * *

WHEN young Reggie joined the Army he was apt to lisp. They gave him the job of looking after the regimental mascot—which happened to be a panther.

The sergeant came storming in one morning. " Hurry up," he shouted, " you're late for parade."

" Pleathe, thir," said Reggie. " I can't find my panther."

" In that case," snapped the sergeant, " you'll have to go on parade without them! "

SAW a Spitfire pilot swing into a crowd of Messerschmitts t'other day.

He shot down three, then a bunch of 'em got on his tail.

He swooped, turned, rolled, dived, and looped, but finally they shot off a piece of his tail.

He pancaked down on to a nearby field, then the plane dug its nose in and turned upside down.

I rushed up and saw the pilot crawling from beneath his machine. He got up and dusted himself down.

" Ah, well," he said, " *it's cured my hiccups, anyway!* "

* * *

OVERHEARD at the bar: " Yes, he's got five brothers. Three of them are in gaol and the other two are quartermaster-sergeants."

☆

CONVERSATION with a lady of the A.T.S.:
" What's your name, beautiful? "

" My mother calls me ' Dimples.' "

" But I can't see any dimples."

" No, my good man—but you're not my mother! "

* * *

THE new recruit found himself roused up in the middle of the night.

" Turn out," snapped the sergeant. " The sirens have gone."

" I'm not surprised," said the recruit. " The people round here would pinch anything! "

(With acknowledgments to " Empire News")

You cannot 'post' him too often

IT isn't so easy to keep that man remembering you when he hasn't heard your voice or seen your face for six months.

Your only hope is the postman—but it isn't any good just addressing an envelope to Corporal Jones or Pilot Officer Green. You must make the contents of the letter—everything you feel—get across to him, too.

● Whether you're wife, sweetheart, sister, or mother, most of you can only keep in touch with that man of yours by letter these days. Remember these Do's and Don'ts next time you sit down with your pen.

You won't go wrong if you remember to write to him just as you would speak to him if he were sitting opposite you.

Tell him everything that's happening—how Betty has just got her first stripe, how well the bulbs were showing through last time you went home, how Jack has joined the Merchant Navy. It's all news to him—and he won't feel so cut off from the life you both know, the people you've both met.

* * *

Do be discreet. For instance —even if you did paint the town red with Harry on your last 48-hour leave, don't write and tell Dick about it. Keep it until you meet him—when he can see that you're still his girl.

Even if you're carrying on a violent quarrel with his sister—cut it out of the letter. It will only worry him. And by cutting out we don't mean crossing out. Quite fantastic meanings can be read into a sentence that begins, doesn't finish, and is crossed through just enough to make one really curious.

You may be his favourite sister—but stories against his wife or girl-friend won't help you. If true—better let him find out for himself. If untrue he'll never forgive you—and neither will she.

Jealousy never paid, anyway. By post it's doubly unsatisfactory. If you must tell him you'd heard about his taking that blonde W.A.A.F. to the dance last week, let it wait until you see him again.

Don't worry him with grumbles about money. Unless he's getting a field-marshal's pay, it will only make you both miserable. And he'll admire you more than anything for the cheerful way you manage on your 1s. 8d. a day.

* * *

Don't wait to hear from him before you write. Posts may be delayed—he may be busy. That's no reason why he shouldn't hear from you, but keep your letter free from reproaches for his not having written.

Read it over before you post it. Watch the punctuation and the handwriting, and remember

he may have to read it in a bad light. If he asked any questions in his last letter, make sure you refer to them. He'll know you really read and remember what he says.

* * *

Above all, be optimistic about the future and not too "patiently suffering" about the present.

Keep this in mind, and you'll find those letters of yours are going to bring you nearer and dearer with each new mail.

TO AID W.R.N.S.

The W.R.N.S. are to have a Benevolent Trust of their own to help cases of distress among W.R.N.S. and ex-W.R.N.S. of this war. All serving W.R.N.S. are being asked to subscribe, and Her Majesty the Queen has consented to become patron of the Trust. Her Royal Highness the Duchess of Kent has been elected president.

TESTING THE GUNS

These A.T.S. girls at a coastal Artillery and Experimental Station are trusted with the very important job of testing shells and guns. These two A.T.S. are seen observing a shell through an "aperture." The window is covered with centimetre square net. The shell-burst is marked in the square.

A.T.S. AT THE READY

BY switching off electrical equipment when a bomb fell on mixed heavy anti-aircraft site on the N.E. coast early last week two A.T.S. averted danger to a detachment.

The A.T.S. were Private Emily Wallcott (twenty-two), of Cardiff, and Private Elma Mills (nineteen), of Fife, Scotland. Private Wallcott was a stage dancer until about five months ago; Private Mills was a typist. They were both engaged on secret equipment during the raid. When bombs fell they were knocked to the ground by blast, but showed considerable presence of mind by remembering, as they got up, to switch off the electric current.

Lance - Bombardier Wilson, of Strathaven, Lanarkshire, who was in charge of a detachment, picked up one of the men on the site who had been slightly injured in the leg by a bomb splinter and carried him to a canteen.

The Battery Commander said the girls on the predictor and other instruments carried on although they were covered in mud from head to foot. He added: "They went on without batting an eyelid."

And throughout the raid the guns did not cease firing.

Betty Service says

Spring-clean your beauty

Your Powder Puff

How often do you wash it? If you go on using it when it gets dirty, you're not only lazy—you're heading straight for a bad complexion. What is the good of cleansing your face if you put on powder with a dirty puff. Try to have at least three in use, and wash one every two or three days.

Your Face Flannel

You should have at least three of these, and should boil them as regularly as you wash your towels. They won't get you clean if you don't.

Your Elbows

Do you remember to scrub them well when you're in the bath? This is a real beauty

hint. You'll find they won't get rough and wrinkled if you do this regularly.

Your Tooth Brushes

Are you still clinging to the nearly bald one you bought last December? Buy two at a time. Use one for night and one for morning. (This gives the bristles a chance to dry and makes them last longer.) Always buy good ones. You cannot speculate with your teeth.

Your Hair Net

Every time you shampoo your hair give your sleeping-cap a wash, too. Chiffon turbans and silk nets all accumulate creams and lotions from your face, and grease and dandruff from your scalp.

Your Rings

You'd be surprised how filmed and dirty your rings can get, especially when you're on a mucky job. They will come up fine washed in soapy water to which a drop of ammonia has been added, but if you don't like to trust them to that, any jeweller will clean them and make them sparkle afresh for a shilling or so.

Your Cream Jars

They get dirty round the rims, and that's not good for your skin either. Give them a wipe with a damp cloth once a week.

Inside Your Cap

Just take a look at the inside of your cap. You'll probably find it smeared with cream, brilliantine, and perspiration. Buy some petersham ribbon about an inch deep and tack round the band inside. You can change this as often as necessary.

Your Eyebrows

If you smooth your eyebrows with vaseline or brilliantine, you'll find they are apt to collect dust. Wash them with soap and water and see how much dirt comes off and how smooth and shiny they look afterwards.

Your Suspenders

You'll find they won't wash too well when you dip your girdle. Inspect them regularly and replace at the first sign of limpness, otherwise they will look grubby when your girdle is still as good as new.

Your Hairbrush & Comb

Make sure you wash these after every shampoo. Greasy brushes and combs collect dust and dandruff, which they will transfer to your newly washed hair if you're not careful. Use warm water and soap flakes—or water to which a dash of ammonia has been added.

SPECIAL MESSAGE TO WOMEN OF THE SERVICES

Whatever happens HAIR MUST BE KEPT CLEAN ... so find time somehow to give it its usual 'Evan Williams' — there's nothing like it for putting new life and beauty into tired hair.

W.A.A.F. WAS ISLAND QUEEN

MARGARET was the first W.A.A.F. to stay at a Coastal Command station on a lonely and remote British island. She arrived in the R.A.F. air ambulance, one of the new women medical orderlies who fly with this aircraft, and her arrival created a stir.

The W.A.A.F. girl was an A.C.W.2, and she had come to supervise the removal to the mainland of two men seriously wounded in the Vaagso raid. It was not on the programme that she should stay; but bad weather compelled the pilot to remain on the island.

Margaret was the centre of interest among the R.A.F. men. She was

royally entertained. When she asked diffidently if she could have an egg for tea she was brought enough eggs to last for a week! The island's eggs are not rationed.

Before joining the Service this airwoman was a nurse in Cheshire County Hospital. The trip to the island was her first long flight across the sea, and she enjoyed it.

"The pilot said it was very bumpy," she told the airmen, "but I didn't think so. I am going to like looking after patients in the air, particularly in long trips such as this one."

The greatest compliment paid to Margaret was when operational aircrews crossed the runway to talk to her as one of themselves. "Jolly good show!" was their comment. And that, in R.A.F. phraseology, is high praise indeed.

PARADE

Congress plays enemy's game

The showdown has come in India. The British on Sunday morning locked up Mahatma Gandhi, Jawaharlal Nehru, and the Congress President, Maulana Abul Kalam Azad. Gandhi was jailed in a private bungalow in Poona. The previous evening, in a gaudily-decorated marquee in Bombay, Congress endorsed by a huge majority the Working Committee's "British quit India" resolution. The resolution demands the immediate withdrawal of British power from India and sanctions "the starting [under Gandhi] of a mass struggle on non-violent lines on the widest possible scale." The Government of India declares it will block this struggle and "discharge its tasks in the face of the challenge now thrown down by Congress." British Official Press says the Government "had been aware for some days past of dangerous preparations by the Congress Party for unlawful and, in some cases, violent activities directed, among other things, to interruption of communications and public utility services, organisation of strikes, tampering with the loyalty of Government servants and interference with defence measures, including recruitment."

"It will throw India into a turmoil which may provide Japan with a great military opportunity," said the *Baltimore Sun*, while the *Sydney Morning Herald* commented :

"Would like to go to Japan"

"If the Congress Party were secretly allied with the Axis, it could hardly play the enemy's game better than by its present policy... of framing demands which the Indian High Commissioner in London calls 'blackmail'."

"Congress demands are fantastic," said the Moslem leader, Jinnah. "Congress appears totally to ignore India's 70,000,000 Moslems."

New Battlefield

Until five months ago, Tulagi was a South Sea backwater, a three-miles-round island in the Solomons with a deep-water anchorage. Seventy ships a year, schooners and small freighters, called there for trochus shell and copra. Events of the last fortnight will put Tulagi in tomorrow's schoolbooks. For it is in Tulagi that the Americans and Australians, eight months after Pearl Harbour, have started a real offensive against the Japanese. Backed by American and Australian fliers and sailors, the United States Marines have landed on the three Japanese-held islands of Tulagi, Florida and Guadalcanal. From all her Pacific bases, Japan is rushing reinforcements to her southern outposts. Reporting heavy hand-to-hand fighting between the Japanese and Americans, Colonel Frank Knox, Navy Secretary, said at the week-end : "I feel very good about the Solomons." But Admiral Joseph E. King, Commander-in-Chief, United States Navy, warned : "It should be understood that the operation now under way is one of the most complicated and difficult in warfare. Considerable losses, such as are inherent in any offensive operation, must be expected."

Also coinciding with the offensive in the Solomons were strong American blows at the Japanese in the Western Aleutians, probably the prelude to an offensive. As the *New York Times* commented : "The Solomons and the Aleutians represent extreme wings of a single front and Tokyo will find it significant that both were attacked simultaneously." In China, the United States Army Air Corps was hitting out further than ever before. In two weeks it has bombed the docks at Haiphong, French Indo-China and at Hong Kong, and the railway yards at Canton and Nanchang. American newspapers stressed that events in the Pacific in the past fortnight had two aims. Beside inaugurating the push against Japan they were designed to draw off some of the mounting piles of armaments along the Manchukuo - Siberia frontier. Still believed to be in Mongolia or Manchukuo is General Tomoyuki Yamashita, conqueror of Singapore.

Back-stab in Siberia ?

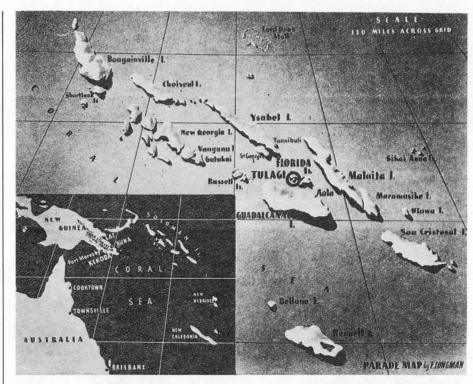

PARADE MAP by ELONGMAN

U.S. Marines go into action

Crack rifleman waits in hidden dug-out for the advance signal to be given.

U.S. Marines paratroop is the world's most heavily armed fighter.

Parachute radio operator with portable radio. Americans call it "walkie-talkie."

Marines with fixed bayonets charge up the beach after landing in pneumatic rubber boats. The first boats bring more than one hundred fully-equipped men. In the background fresh troops head for the shore in small boat to follow up the attack.

U.S. Marine Raiders are America's Commandos. Heavy artillery, borne by "crocodile" barges, whose bows unfold into ramps, follows the speed boats. "Devil dogs of war" for more than a century and a-half, they will form spearhead of attack.

Fighting equipment includes "alligator" tanks so constructed that they manœuvre with ease over such terrain as swamp lands and marshes. The technique of American marines is to wreak sudden havoc on the enemy, then stay and finish him off.

PARADE middle east weekly

"...cobwebs swept away..." THE TIMES

WINSTON SEES FOR HIMSELF...
Pages 7-9

2 PT
IN EGYPT

No. 106 Vol. 9 August 22, 1942

OUR TROOPS WAIT TO DISEMBARK AFTER BIGGEST EVER RAID ON DIEPPE. RAIDING FORCE
CARRIED AND ESCORTED BY ROYAL NAVY AIR SUPPORT AND PROTECTION PROVIDED BY RAF

Radio pictures transmitted from London to Cairo.

DIEPPE RAID - FULL STORY

This story of the Dieppe raid was told by a special correspondent with the raiding forces who saw it from a tank-landing craft.

For nine hours I watched Canadian shock troops, squadrons of British tanks, naval vessels and R.A.F. fighters battling in daylight against concentrated German opposition. It was mainly a Canadian operation, supplemented by small units of British Commandos, Fighting French and U.S. Rangers. Throughout the operation the sky was filled with British aircraft. Countless squadrons of fighters and bombers swept over the Dieppe area to carry the war into the German bases.

Only a relative handful of German bombers ever reached the waiting ships and half of those never reported back to base. Even the fighters which came over showed the utmost respect for our air umbrella. Not once did the *Luftwaffe* attempt to fight it out with the Spitfires guarding our vessels.

The craft in which I crossed carried tanks which were to be the third wave of armour to land and we were not due at Dieppe until about one hour after zero. We arrived soon after the Commandos had launched their attacks on the coastal batteries

at Berneval (about 4½ miles east of Dieppe), and at Varengeville-sur-Mer, West of Dieppe. The attack at Berneval failed, but at Varengeville the Commandos, many of whom took part in the first Boulogne raid, carried their objective triumphantly. They captured and destroyed a battery of six 6-in. naval guns with relatively light losses. 'Sneak' landings were made on the flanks of Dieppe by the South Saskatchewan Regiment at Pourville and by the Royal Regiment of Canada at Puits.

By now the whole coastline was springing into activity. In some sectors, several minutes passed before tracer bullets began to cut horizontal coloured streaks through the dwindling darkness. Simultaneously the battery at Berneval opened up. Orange red flashes streaked across the sea like a lighthouse beacon. With its opening round, the battery started a rhythm of heavy explosions which continued without ceasing during the nine hours we stayed and could be heard even when we were half-way back across the Channel. A few minutes later a great fountain of flame spurted upward from the cliffs and there was a violent explosion. The Commandos had completed their task of destroying the guns at Varengeville.

The South Saskatchewan Regiment had achieved a measure of surprise in their landing and had encountered little serious opposition. The Royal Regiment of Canada had a stiffer task in landing at Puits. Beaten back by the beach defences at the first attempt, they reformed and swept over the defences. The rising crescendo of heavy firing by the guns of the destroyers preceded the landings on Dieppe beach. As the bombardment ceased the ramps of the landing craft dropped and tanks crunched their way across the beaches. With them went Canadian engineers to clear the way for the tanks to enter the town. There was also an infantry assault on the beach by the Royal Hamilton Light Infantry and the Essex Scottish.

One tank reports by radio : "My tracks have been shot off, my turret won't work, but I am accounting for a lot of Germans." Another reports it is on the promenade near the Casino and is warned about "the pill box on the left."

It is now 7.45 and for a brief second or two all is quiet. A fresh smoke screen is being laid on the eastern side of the anchorage and the faint whirr of Spitfires is heard high overhead.

DIEPPE RAID : as seen by "STRATEGICUS"

London, August 21.

t may be some little time before the omplete story of the Commando aid on Dieppe is told, some time efore the full details of the plan and ae immediate and remote objectives re made known. The losses on the de of the Allies will soon be decla- ed, but it is the German fashion to retend they are perpetually inflict- ag tremendous losses on the Allies t the cost of quite negligible casual- es to themselves. It cannot then be xpected that we shall secure from he enemy' any truthful account of ,hat the raid cost him. But there is o doubt that this raid was an im- ressive and important undertaking nd it will be useful to remind our- elves of the standards by which it hould be measured.

There is a pretty universal ten- lency among candid friends to judge :very British initiative as if it were an attempt to end the war in one stroke — only to be estimated by its ion-success in so doing. The fact hat, for instance, Wavell didn't ad- vance to Tripoli to reduce Italy ends to make one forget what exact- y has already been accomplished in Africa. On the other hand, each move by the Germans is taken to mean all that the maximum exploi- tation of success might imply. This is only a slight exaggeration to make the point clear.

The Commando raid then was just a raid comparable with an attack on a narrow front with limited ob- jectives. It was announced at the mo- ment of its launching that it wasn't an invasion (although it was an in- vasion in the sense that we landed in country occupied by the enemy, it wasn't designed as an attempt to se- cure a permanent footing.) It must not therefore be judged as if we'd been trying to occupy French soil, but ra- ther as a concentrated attack on a very highly defended position under circumstances which very heavily fa- voured its defence. Its effects then may be greater or less, but in the case of success will include some quite concrete local objectives.

In the case of Dieppe these will probably have included batteries, ammunition dumps and various sorts of installation—possibly dock instal- lations—flak batteries, and radiclo- cation stations. The defensive orga- nisation will have been destroyed, more or less completely, possibly to some depth. It will also have includ- ed some less concrete objectives — the discovery and dislocation of the plan of defence and the disturbance of the whole elaborate organisation upon which the prevention of suc- cessful invasion depends. For of course the Germans don't and can- not know when only a raid and not an attempted invasion is in train.

They lie so vividly and pictures- quely themselves that they might think it a very suspicious circumstan- ce if we said it wasn't to be an inva- sion. It is the sort of thing they would do themselves when they had decided to invade. The raid must, therefore, have had the effect of kicking an anthill, and it is known that the German reaction on this oc- casion was very heavy. Another ef- fect it is certain to have had is the state of nerves it set up.

At first the Germans declared it was invasion just as at the time of the St. Nazaire they announced that we had been compelled to open a se- cond front. On this occasion there is no longer any doubt that a state of nerves was induced in the German command.

If this raid were an isolated thing the position would be different. But the Germans know there'll be more and more raids of different strength and intensity until at length invasion will come. They have no method of distinguishing between the feint and the main attack, hence they must meet every raid with their hearts in their mouths for fear that it is at last the real thing, which the Germans most dread, the double front attack.

The raid will also have had as one of its purposes the gaining of expe- rience in the marshalling of a consi- derable force including armoured units provided with adequate cover from the air against anything the enemy may do. On this occasion the tank-landing equipment was tested out, and that is a novel and impor- tant event.

In a mood of impatience this part of the raid — the gaining of exper- ience — may seem of little value, but either it had to be gained this way or bought in a more expensive school. Clearly the raid will have had as one of its objectives the in- fliction of losses.

THE R.A.F.'S PART

The attack on heavy gun positions at Dieppe was made by Spitfires, Hurricanes and Bostons of Fighter Command, says the Air Ministry News Service. This was carried out before the first troops reached the beaches.

An American Eagle squadron re- ported that a 4,000-ton ship had been set ablaze in the harbour. Through- out the morning fighter squadrons in relays maintained protective pat- rols while bomber squadrons, with a strong fighter escort, dealt effect- ively with troublesome gun positions.

Abbeville aerodrome, a German fighter base, some 40 miles from Dieppe, was attacked by U.S. Flying Fortresses, escorted by Spitfire squadrons. Aerodrome buildings and hangars were destroyed. A Belgian fighter squadron was involved in a general melee high above Dieppe. This squadron saw two fires west of the town and a big building in flames. Spitfire squadrons of the U.S. Army Air Force patrolling the area were continuously engaged by about 25 Focke-Wulf 190's. At the same time two R.A.F. Spitfire squadrons above were engaged in a dogfight.

Hour after hour a progression of fighters, crossing and recrossing the Channel, gave a hugh umbrella pro- tection over the retreating convoys. Other aircraft laid a formidable smoke screen.

Dorniers, Junkers, Messerschmitts, Heinkels and Focke-Wulfs fell to British pilots in combat. Time after time British fighters intercepted ene- my formations of bombers and drove them away from the coast or shot them down. The Germans used a large number of heavy bombers in a bid to hit our ships. Two Polish squadrons on an 'umbrella patrol' re- turned home with several successes. A Czech squadron claimed a long string of fighters and bombers, dam- aged or destroyed. British and Cana- dian squadrons of the Army Coope- ration Command took a notable part in the operations.

EDWARD ARDIZZONE : WAR ARTIST

Born at Haiphong, Indochina, in 1900, Edward Ardizzone moved to England when he was five and he was educated at a Public School. Until he was 26, when most men have resigned themselves to an office fate, Ardizzone tried various business jobs. He worked with a Warminster motor company and with several city firms, ending up with the Eastern Telegraph Company. He took the precaution, though, of attending evening classes at the Westminster art school. A windfall of £500 was quite enough for

Ardizzone to risk taking the plunge. It didn't last long, but long enough for the disease all his guides, philosophers and friends told him he was suffering from to have become chronic. After three years, came an order at last : a publisher gave him a book to illustrate. On the strength of this, Ardizzone got married. Followed more lean times. In his odd moments, Ardizzone wrote stories for his children, illustrated them. In desperation, he tried these on publishers. No-one rose for a long

(Continued overleaf)

Captain Edward Ardizzone in the desert. "Parade" gives readers first reproduction of his Middle East paintings.

Gunners in an

Gunners on Ruweisat Ridge.

time, until the American branch of the Oxford Press decided to try his wares out on the young Yank. They were gobbled up. Followed a trip to the U.S. where Ardizzone lectured five hundred American librarians in the New York Public Library on his next book. But things ahead looked gloomy. There seemed to be a war in the offing and less work than ever. Ardizzone rejoined the territorials as a gunner (he had served with them immediately after the last war). When war broke out he was, ironically, making more money than ever before. The Tate Gallery had bought some of his work, a show he gave had been well written up, orders were beginning to come in. He was compared to Rowlandson, and the great French cartoonist of the mid-nineteenth century, Daumier. But Ardizzone was behind an ack-ack gun in Plumstead Marshes. In March, 1940, he was given indefinite leave without pay to take up the job of official war artist in France. The job did not last long, but long enough for Ardizzone to write and illustrate one of the best war books

The commanding officer's inspection.

The colonel goes his rounds.

Scene in a troop deck.

Washing day on a troop ship.

Making the best of the blue
Desert Music Hall

By Cpl. H. G. Hudson

Imagine a wooden hut on the side of a wadi—any ordinary sort of wooden hut—a large hut. From inside comes the murmur of conversation, the occasional clink of beer bottle against glass. Now and again a shaft of light stabs the black-out as the door opens to admit another visitor.

And then we hear music — the music of a small dance band — the murmuring dies away. The show is on !

Music, and the murmurings of an audience, the sort of atmosphere surrounding a theatre where Henry Hall and his band might be giving a show. The same hum of activity, the same comings and goings, the same applause, but hardly the same surroundings. Just a dark unfriendly desert whose stillness is disturbed only by convoys moving by night.

We go inside our "theatre" and what do we see ? Not exactly the furnishings of the London Palladium, with its regal drapings. Odds bits of coloured cloth perhaps and canvas serving as stage props ; electric lights with tin reflectors, that's all. But to these men, with sand-clogged hair and sun-burned skins, they're just as good, for is not this the desert ?

> "Crusader" will be pleased to hear of how other small units entertained themselves in the desert. Write and tell us how your mob made the best of the blue.

And the attraction ? Our concert party raised among ourselves by fellows with the interest and enthusiasm. Anyone who could sing or recite, or be funny without knowing it, was dragged in. We derived as much pleasure from putting it on as our audiences did laughing at us. And we were ambitious too, for we had a band. The drums we bought from Unit funds. The saxophone, piano accordion and banjo were personal instruments, and the piano, well, we'd dragged that all over the place with us. The double-bass was born from the sweated efforts of two band-members with assistance of box-wood and telephone cable. The telephone wires certainly hummed. The canteen occupied one corner of the hut—it was a neat, compact little place, painted inside and out, and had an inviting display, the value.

of which was often £40. A weekly turn-over of £200 kept the vounteer counter-men (as distinct from the manager, who had a full-time job) very much occupied !

We did other things besides. We had small, informal bi-weekly band-nights (not that any of our affairs were ever very formal !) more in the line of smoking concerts, but invariably played to a full house.

And then there were "Tombola Nights," which, with a house valued at £10 were profitable to unit funds. From such funds we provided ourselves with chairs and other furnishings, a gramophone and large assortment of records.

Our profitmaking was brought to a sudden end when beer rationing was introduced. A mortal blow, and its effects far-reaching, indeed !

Unit's Magazine

The magazine, a product of the fertile brain of a certain Orderly Room wallah, shared, with the canteen, much popularity with the men of the Unit, for whom it was primarily intended, and of whose sayings and doings it was, as far as the heavy hand of censorship permitted, a truthful reflection.

The comings and goings of our South African visitors and troops of other Units were frequent and many.

But now we can only think of that desert home from home as merely a happy episode—a memory of things which will probably never be possible again on such a scale in such an atmosphere.

And looking back, we are given to wondering if any other Unit, semi-mobile and as small as we were, achieved as much in the way of self-entertainment, on such a scale, and in such circumstances.

Churchill and Stalin at their historic meeting in the Russian capital.

SPORT

ONLY FOUR CLUBS WITH FULL POINTS

When the Scottish matches on Satur August 15, second Saturday of the sea had been completed, only four clubs in Southern League could show full po They were Rangers, Hibernians, Fal and Morton.

Rangers were the only side who did concede a goal on the opening day, against Airdrieonians in their second m they were a goal down in 30 seconds, s ed by Flavelle. However, Rangers ral long before the end and won well.

There was considerable interest in match at Edinburgh where Queen's P opposed Celtic. Tom Gallacher, son of famous "Patsy" of Celtic face, appea for Queen's Park, and scored both goals which enabled the amateurs to dra

Newman, at outside left, played a part in Motherwell's victory over Clyde Shawfield, but a notable performance the North-Eastern League was that of bernians, who defeated Rangers by Scores were :—

SOUTHERN LEAGUE

Albion R. 1 — Falkirk 4.

Clyde 1 — Motherwell 3.

Dumbarton 4 — St. Mirren 0.

Hamilton 1 — Hibernians 3.

Hearts 3 — Third Lanark 1.

Morton 2 — Partick T. 1.

Queen's Park 2 — Celtic 2.

Rangers 4 — Airdrieonians 1.

NORTH-EASTERN

Aberdeen 5 — Dunfermline 0.

Dundee United 3 — Raith Rovers 2.

East Fife 4 — Hearts 0.

Hibernians 4 — Rangers 2.

SHORTAGE OF PLAYER HOLDS UP CLUBS

Football is due to start in England Saturday, August 29, and already clubs a sending out an S.O.S. for players. Bre ford are typical of many. At the mome they are certain of only two forwards, Ho kins, a munition worker, and Sergea Leslie Smith, R.A.F. and both are winge

The Brentford manager, Harry Curtis says he is doing his utmost to contact Chee ham, their leader of pre-war days, but far has been unable to find him. Curti has also lost touch with his inside-forward who are serving with the Forces, and unt he finds them signing-on is at a stand-stil

In addition, Brentford may be withou Jackson, the goal-keeper, who played suc an important part in the Griffin Park side success in the London Cup last seaso Brentford cannot trace Jackson either, bu Chelsea, to whom Jackson belongs, say the have no objection to their 'keeper playin for Brentford if he can be found.

At least the "Bees" are certain of thei fullbacks, Brown and Poyser, who are mu nition workers and James, their centre half, but their attack is very much in doubt

N. Ireland

re has been a lot of fuss these days t lamps in Belfast. From time imme-al it has been the custom to erect or-ental lamps outside the residences of the Mayor and High Sheriff. The lamps not lit in war-time, but why deprive of-ls of their one small honour.

* * *

War or no war, what is the Belfast man woman going to do without their dish of glass herrings when in season ? Sorry to e your mouths water, boys, but I've had dish.

* * *

he harvest is going great guns in Nor-n Ireland and everybody seems to be ious to help. I saw the minister of a l-known city church helping to gather ips and a prominent barrister collecting atoes, but those who appeared to enjoy ost were some schoolboys who had been ailed to gather apples in the countryside und Armagh. The farmers did get apples ore for the boys did not eat them all.

* * *

he Ulster film trade have made another ture to the Services. At the morning pre-w of films, men of the British and Allied vices can walk in free and bring a friend.

* * * *

On September 12, Ireland plays the Army Belfast. If the following are released by r clubs and those in the Services by their nmanding officers, the Irish team will be: en (Linfield and Manchester United) ; tler (Blackpool), Feeney (Linfield) ; lly (Millwall), Vernon (Belfast Celtic), m Jones (Blackpool) ; Cochrane (Leeds ited), Stevenson (Everton), Martin otts Forest), Doherty (Manchester Ci-, Malinden (Portsmouth).

Tyneside

r John D. Laurie, Lord Mayor of Lon-n, has visited Tyneside. Sir John told Ty-side folk that he had heard much about e splendid way in which they were help-g to speed victory, and he wanted to see m "on the job." He looked in at arma-nts factories and saw men and women rd at work producing tanks, guns and ells. He marvelled at their determination d stamina under heavy strain. Later the me day he visited a shipyard and amid e clatter of rivetters who were still carry-g on with their work in adjoining berths performed the ceremony of launching a arship.

* * *

Herbert Morrison, Minister for Home Se-irity, visited the little colliery town of ewburn-on Tyne recently. Morrison would e to see many more Newburns up and wn the country, for the little town has a cord for civil defence organisation which uld win the admiration of any Minister. 1940 this little town had inaugurated a oluntary scheme of fireguards with a per-onnel of some thousands of men and wo-en. So on Thursday Morrison acknow-dged Newburn as the birthplace of the reguards. They had called themselves fire-uards before the term became officially re-ognised by Whitehall.

Merseyside

Quite a number of innovations have been instituted on Merseysides dock estate since the war—all designed to speed-up the turn-round of shipping. Foremost among these improvements is the attention given to feed-ing facilities. Twenty-three canteens are in operation, and the benefit is reflected in output.

Now Merseyside Harbour Board are going a step further. They recently decided to frame a new bylaw to permit smoking on the docks at certain points. It merely re-mains for the approval of the Ministry of War Transport before the dockers are told whether they can smoke. It is hoped that this gesture will cut out 'surreptitious smok-ing' in dangerous areas.

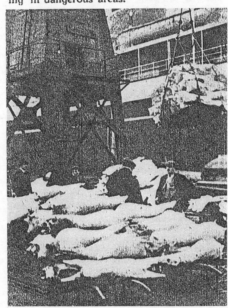

High praise for dockers.

Lord Woolton had a word or two of praise for the dockers when he opened Bootle's fifth British restaurant on August 21. "I know" he said "the food ships that come in. I know when they go out, I know because of that that the dockers have made rapid strides in getting the ships round quicker."

The provision of feeding centres like British restaurants in Bootle is providing amenities which have been wanted in the borough for a long time. Bootle's fighting sons and sailors are as tough as any any-where and its part in the war effort far greater than many would imagine.

* * *

A new trial in Liverpool at night is 'hunt the taxi.' Reaping a harvest and never idle during his working day the only re-maining horsecab in the city, owned by Mr. Arthur Seymour, is still a big attraction for visitors. Incidentally, Mr. Seymour has had a licence since 1885. Now he is driving the last horsecab in the city like he drove the last 'handsome'—which he sold to Holly-wood pictures.

* * *

Special interest was aroused by the birth of a 16 oz. baby. The proud mother was Mrs Ada Roach of Pleasant St., Liverpool. At first there were doubts of its survival, but now everything appears to be fine.

Portsmouth

Portsmouth girl prepared everything for her wedding, even to having the cake made, and awaited her fiance's arrival in a cer-tain ship. The boat struck a mine on its way home, but her fiance was rescued and intern-ed in Algeria. The wedding was postponed for the duration and the girl raffled her cake. She handed the proceeds of the raffle, which amounted to ten guineas, to the First Lord of the Admiralty and asked him to ac-cept the sum for the Royal Naval Benevo-lent Trust Fund.

* * *

H.M.S. Calliope, which was built in Portsmouth and launched from the dock-yard 58 years ago, is still in commission as a training ship.

* * *

King George's Fund for Sailors has sent £1,100 to the newly formed Wrens Benevo-lent Trust. Trust is also receiving support from canteens of H.M. ships and grants from the Royal Naval Dependents' Fund.

* * *

Film star Lieut. Douglas Fairbanks, of the U.S. navy, has been visiting Portsmouth to inspect an R.A.F. balloon barrage hospital which he has financed. Hospital has 30 beds.

* * *

Lieut. Peter Charles Dickens, great grand-son of the Portsmouth-born novelist, has been awarded the M.B.E.

* * *

Father Frederick Freeley, M.C., was giv-en the biggest funeral that has been seen locally since the war. He was Catholic chap-lain to the R.A.O.C. and during the recent season trained many winning football teams. Father Freeley was extremely well-known in the city and worked among men of all denominations. Folk of no particular belief put something in Father Freeley's hat for his work among the poor of the city.

Manchester

When the news came through that the cruiser *Manchester* had been lost in a con-voy battle the reaction in the city was swift and realistic. Within 24 hours £1,500 had been given towards replacing it, and the Lord Mayor will organise a fund. Mancu-nians were proud of their namesake, which had seen a great deal of action in the last three years.

* * *

Manchester post office girls are tough. Two who work behind a counter in the centre of the city chased and overpowered a bankbook forger last week... Manchester hospital nurses are to be barelegged in fu-ture to save clothing coupons... Bellevue is putting on free Sunday concerts for women in uniform... In an attic workshop an old Manchester man is restoring valuable docu-ments damaged during past air raids. The saving of parish and other registers will avoid legal tangles... Manchester schoolboys are building model tanks to a supplied plan. When the tanks have been exhibited the boys can keep them... Canadians and Ame-ricans spend time off in baseball work-outs in Plattfields.

* * *

(Continued overleaf)

* * *

People smacked their lips when they saw a bunch of sixty bananas in Liverpool recently. They were grown within ten miles of the store ! Anyway, they were sold for 50 shillings, the money going to the Lord Mayor's War Fund.

Scotland

The death of the Duke of Kent on active service on Scottish soil proves that war hits palace and cottage alike. Few knew the Duke was in Scotland preparing for a flight to Iceland where he expected to stay for ten days. He has been several times to Scotland during the war, touring industrial and civil defence organisations and R.A.F. stations. He was High Commissioner for the Church of Scotland in 1935, was appointed captain of the Royal and Ancient at St. Andrew's in 1937, and elected Freeman of Glasgow in 1938. In June 1939 he was in a smash at Aberdeen when his 'plane swung around the aerodrome and came to a sudden stop with one wheel buried in the turf. The ground staff and spectators thought he was injured or killed but he came out smiling and unhurt.

The crash occurred in one of the loneliest parts of Scotland miles from any village or hamlet. There are only a few shepherds and crofters homes in the area. The discovery was made by a shepherd on his rounds, while a farmer heard the engine of the 'plane stopping, followed by an explosion. The only survivor of the crash was a Grangemouth boy, F/Sgt Andrew Jack, a 21-year-old air-gunner who joined the R.A.F. three years ago. His eldest brother is a corporal in the Scots Guards. Another is an engineer in the Merchant Navy while his sister is in the A.T.S.

* * *

Clyde shipbuilders are to work two extra Sundays each month — November to February — to make up for lost time on weekdays owing to the blackout. They are also prepared to do their stuff on Saturday afternoons if it is considered necessary. This is the spirit that makes for victory.

* * *

The captain of *H.M.S. Duke of York* has sent Clydebank shipbuilders a message of goodwill on the anniversary of the sailing of the battleship. It was built and equipped at Clydebank and sailed down the Clyde a year ago. The vessel was afterwards adopted as Glasgow's battleship.

He sent shipbuilders goodwill message.

"I SAY, OLD BOY, IS THERE A BARBER IN THE CAMP ?"

The Commander 17 Area, Brigadier J.L. Chrystall, C.B.E., M.C. recently offered a prize of £20 to the writer of the best war song of 3 verses. The song was to be something stirring, redolent of King, Empire and Country, something inspiring, something which made the heart beat a little faster.

All ranks, men and women, are eligible for the competition, results to be judged by an independent committee whose decision will be final. Entries, addressed to H.Q. 17 Area must be in by November 15. The closing date has been extended because the results have not come up to standard, many of the writers not keeping to the spirit of the theme as set out above. The song must be singable, it must go with a swing, it must be a patriotic song. Music is not essential to win the prize but if you can write music so much the better.

The song published below is by Pilot Officer Nelson. Publication of his song does not mean that he wins the prize. It is just the best received to date.

"SING BRITAIN SING"

THE OUTLOOK

Rex Rasley and Reg Lever rehearse. Bonnie Downs leans on footlights.

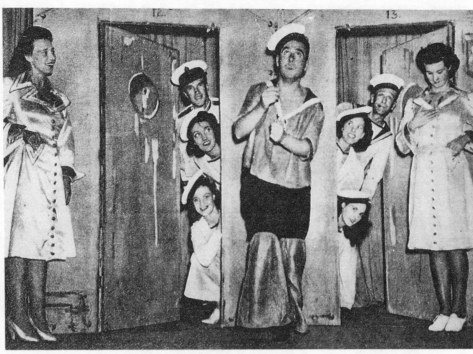

Padre Spender looks in at rehearsals and has a chat with Vera and Bette.

Elsie Winsor, Reg Lever and Carol Downs go through the ship scene as the rest of the company look on.

THE GLOBE - ALEX

You can have too much of the cinema. Not so with the music hall. Film fashions change; but the music hall show is always the same. And because it is always the same, you don't get tired of it. It is eternally sentimental and low, leggy and hilarious. The laughter at an unpretentious revue — not necessarily at the sophisticated or spectacular one — is always infectious. No Marx Brothers or Charlie Chaplin film ever won as much laughter from its audiences as any one of the two evening performances at, say, the Finsbury Park Empire.

That is why the new revue at the Globe Theatre, Alexandria — latest accretion to that great "conglobation" of services' entertainment that began as a small naval club, the Fleet Club — has proved such a roaring success, especially with troops back on leave from the desert. When *Parade* reporter went to see the new show the hall was filled one above its normal 380 seating capacity. It was in miniature — for the chorus was a quartette and the entire cast, excluding the two pianists, consisted of a dozen performers — the same show you used to see of a Saturday night in London or any provincial town.

To Naafi and Ensa who present 'Hello Happiness, and under whose auspices the show is run, to the Fleet Club which has provided the theatre, to the producer and chief comedian, Reg Lever, to Roma Clark and Leslie Romney, musical arrangers and pianists, and to the performers one and all, will go the gratitude of the Eighth Army on leave, and, for that matter, of anyone else who visits the Globe and pays his modest five or ten piastres.

REVEILLE
Service Newspaper
Nov. 9, 1942

DOUGHBOYS GET OWN DAILY PAPER

"Stars and Stripes," U.S. Services' newspaper, is the only American daily paper published in Europe, for it has now become a daily. American Forces will therefore get their own paper over here. Whilst they will get this daily, they will also get the 24-page associated paper "Yank" on Sundays.

"The Times" is printing the paper for them.

Subscribers are limited to members of the U.S. Forces in the European theatre, and the paper will not be on sale to the civilian public.

Present staff of "Stars and Stripes," which is to be enlarged, includes: editor, Major Emsley Llewellyn; associate editors, Lt. H. A. Harchar and Sec.-Lt. J. C. Wilkinson; news editor, Sgt. Ben Price; USANIF editor, Sgt. Russell Jones; marine editor, Cpl. Francis Connolly; Navy editor, Yeoman Tom Bernard; cartoonist, Sgt. Dick Wingest; additional members of the editorial board, Sgt. Robert Morra, Sgt. Hutton, Sgt. Mark Denigo, and Sgt. G. Hoderfield.

Air-letter cards issued to M.E. Forces are rationed, and it is often asked whether rationing will be applied to the air letters shortly to be provided for outgoing use. A G.P.O. official says "No," explains why below :—

Air mail for the troops

IT is comparatively simple to control the issue of air-letter cards to the troops themselves, as the potential users are readily identifiable. The rationing of civilian relatives at home is much more complicated. A scheme for the periodical issue to the next-of-kin by the Naval, Army, and Air Force authorities of a supply of special envelopes which could be given priority for air transmission is open to the following difficulties :—

(1) the next-of-kin is not necessarily the correspondent whose letters the soldier would wish to receive priority, e.g., a soldier's fiancée would not participate in the ration; and serious dissatisfaction would result

(2) even if the military authorities were able and prepared to undertake a quarterly issue of special envelopes, there would be no safeguard to ensure that the postings were evenly spread over the quarter. Without such a safeguard the posting of the special envelopes might be concentrated within a short period, and serious accumulations would result.

The possibility of combining with the rationed letter card issued to the troops in the Middle East some form of label which could be detached by the recipient and attached to an outward letter card as an indication that it was entitled to priority has been examined, but not found practicable.

☆

TERESA WRIGHT is the latest "dazzler" to join Reveille's beauty chorus.

☆

★ **Readers who would like a picture of lovely TERESA WRIGHT or any other illustrations in Reveille, should write to us, enclosing 6d. to cover postage, and marking the envelope "Stills."** ★

COFFINS—TROOPS, FOR THE USE OF?

The Air Minister is being asked by Mr. James Hollins (Soc., Silvertown) "whether he will seek the amendment of the Regimental Debts Act of 1893, under which funeral charges constitute a first charge against the estate of Service personnel, and especially the abolition of the regulation which, in effect, compels a Service man to provide his own coffin."

HARD LINES?

WE hear that schoolboy 'lines" have taken the place of "C.B." in a certain R.A.F. unit.

A party of 100 men, we are told, were ordered by the warrant officer in charge to write out their names 300 times as a punishment for neglecting to fill in a certain form.

PROXY MARRIAGES—"VITAL NECESSITY"

Says Mrs. Jennie Adamson M.P., in an interview with Vera Good

THOUSANDS of Servicemen's sweethearts are pinning their hopes on future happiness on the success of a woman M.P.'s efforts to establish marriage by proxy in this country.

Mrs. Jennie Adamson, Labour M.P., is waging this campaign chiefly that the children of those men whom duty has taken overseas at short notice may not be born without a name, and that the mother of these babies may receive the allowance, amenities and status of the married woman.

Pathetic letters reach Mrs. Adamson every day from heartbroken girls who find, after their fiancés have been home on an embarkation leave which left no time for marriage, that a baby is on the way.

They are mostly decent girls, deeply in love, who are left to face not only the shame and loneliness of such a situation, but must rely on charity to provide financially for the coming child.

The men themselves are anxious to marry their sweethearts **(this is evidenced by the fact that illegitimate births in 1940, when the majority of our Forces were stationed in this country, were 5,199 lower than in 1941, when large numbers of men were posted abroad)**, and Mrs. Adamson holds the view that if Service exigencies prevent the Government bringing them back to this country to do so, they should institute proxy marriages instead.

She cited pathetic cases of unmarried Servicemen who, out of their meagre pay, struggle to send money home to their "illegal" families, and explained the extreme urgency of introducing the necessary legislation.

But it is not only on behalf of the unmarried mother and her child that Mrs. Adamson's fight goes on unceasingly. She knows that where engaged couples have been parted for two or three years, the pain of separation would be easier if marriage were possible for them. And she believes that, in both cases, the morale of the fighting men concerned would be considerably improved.

So far, Mrs. Adamson's application to the Home Secretary has met with the usual chilly official answer—nothing can be done at the moment.

But Mrs. Adamson is convinced that something can be done if only public opinion can be brought to bear on this vital question.

She reminded me that the Government's concession to pay a marriage allowance to an "unmarried" wife who has lived with a Serviceman for six months was brought about by the insistent demands of the men in uniform themselves. She is certain that if the fighting men will demand the legislation of marriage by proxy loud enough and long enough, that, too, will come to pass.

MRS. ADAMSON WILL DO HER BIT, BUT THE SUPPORT OF EVERY SERVICEMAN IS VITAL TO HER CAMPAIGN.

A wounded Australian soldier being carried through the jungle by native bearers is handed a cigarette by his mate. Cameraman Parer says the gentleness of New Guinea natives toward Australian wounded is "touching."

Bearers carrying wounded digger start anything but a straight line causes tl

Between clashes with Japs, Australian infantrymen in Kokoda area sharpen their bayonets on an "acquired" grindstone. Japs do not like the bayonet.

WORSE THAN THE DESERT

Melbourne, November 26. Australian troops in New Guinea would gladly return to the Western Desert. The reasons may be seen in *Kokoda Front,* a film of the hard New Guinea war made by Australian official cameraman Damien Parer, stills from which accompany these notes on the campaign.

Kokoda Front essentially depicts triumph over difficulties — difficulty of supplies, communications and medical treatment. To quote from Parer's report to the Department of Information : "The jungle is not actually impenetrable ; but the difficulties of the terrain can be appreciated from the fact that 400 native carriers were required to transport 44 casualties on stretchers to a clearing station in a trek that took seven days."

Tea Leaf Cigarettes

Parer cites as an instance of supply shortage the smoking by the Aussies of dried tea leaves in place of tobacco. "Our men are fighting in appalling conditions," he told me.

"The native boys," he says, "are magnificent. They never panic, and some of the Kiwi boys (no connection with N.Z. Kiwis) carried supplies to our troops under fire. They were worked very hard. Both the Papuan and New Guinea natives were invaluable all the time. Their patience and consideration for the wounded were touching.

"When they make tracks, they always go straight. When they have to cross a mountain, they do not try to skirt it, or avoid any natural obs-

tacles. Instead, they go in a direct line. Soldiers who have been on several mountain tops say the straight native tracks are clearly visible."

Parer, who was in the Middle East with the A.I.F. (his pictures often were in *Parade*) told me why New Guinea is so different from the Middle East. "The walking is harder," he says, "and carrying is harder. There was always plenty of food in the desert and you could make tea easily. There's nothing like that in N.G. One of the shots in my film shows the boys cooking 'damper cake.' It consists of flour, egg-pulp, canned milk, raisins and sugar, all messed up together and heated on a sheet of tin over a small fire.

"Because of the terrain in New Guinea it is often impossible to give proper medical treatment on the spot, and it takes time to get to clearing stations. We had in Egypt the desert sore. But it was not as bad as an untreated New Guinea scratch. Up there the men must rub in iodine or acriflavine, and cover the scratch with adhesive tape, as quickly as possible, or else results are worse than any desert sore.

"When I was in the desert I always wanted to get away from it. But on returning to Aussie I wanted to get back to the desert. So do all the boys who came back from Egypt only to go to N.G. For one thing, you can't get Cairo leave in N.G. New Guinea would be all right if only someone would iron it out with a steam-roller."

EDNA HARWOOD

EIGHTH ARMY WEEKLY

Issued to the Fighting Forces in the desert

No. 29 Vol. 3   November 16, 1942

Review for the Blue ATTACK

The Allied nations move to the offensive. Messages from the world's battlefronts have one theme - ATTACK. Successful landings by American troops in the Mediterranean and Atlantic coasts of French North Africa with the occupation of important airfields, the rout of Rommel's remnants by the victorious Eighth Army, five large-scale attacks by the Russians, four in the Caucasus and one at Stalingrad, and the chasing of the Jap invaders half way across New Guinea by Australian infantry mark the turning of the tide of war. From London and Washington came the joint announcement : "We enter into the offensive phase of war. This is the beginning."

FRENCH NORTH AFRICA

While Eighth Army was chasing the remnants of Rommel's Army out of Egypt and across Libya, a great American army under General Dwight Eisenhower landed in force at eleven points on the two coastlines. Roosevelt announced "This expedition will develop into a major effort of the United Nations." The Royal Navy and the R.A.F. covered the landings, and an official announcement said that a considerable number of British divisions would join the Americans in the immediate future. Most southerly landing was at Safi in Morocco, most easterly at Philippeville. While Pétain called on French to fight, General Giraud who escaped from a German prison, appealed to Vichy troops not to resist and to seize the opportunity for the recovery and revival of France. Later came news of further landings at Safi, Mogador, Agadir and Fedhala. Allied Forces H.Q. communique stated that lack of resistance encountered on most beaches showed that French armed forces had no desire to oppose the entry of American troops into this territory.

NEW GUINEA

Backed by American troops flown "in force" from Darwin, some of whom had landed at Milne Bay, east of Port Moresby, Australians rounded up on beachhead every Jap remaining in British New Guinea. By painting themselves green and becoming as wily as the Japs, Australians showed they could beat them at their own pet game. Australian Army Minister Forde said A.I.F. victory was "one step in big campaign."

Continued on Back Page

"MONTY" KNIGHTED

"Monty" has been promoted to the rank of General and appointed Knight Commander of the Order of the Bath for services in the field, it was announced from London as "Crusader" went to press. General Sir Harold Alexander has been made Knight Grand Cross of the Order of the Bath.

"Monty" of Alamein

By Richard McMillan (B.U.P. War Correspondent)

A man in a black tank regiment beret stood on the turret of a tank far forward with our advancing desert forces. He was "Monty" Montgomery, victor of Alamein, watching the debacle which his genius as a commander of men had brought about.

German and Italian prisoners and our infantry walked past unaware that the man in the grey jumper, open-necked shirt and tropical khaki trousers was the British General who had beaten Rommel.

The roll of artillery and anti-tank guns drifted back in waves as our pursuit columns on coast road and desert track harrassed without rest a broken enemy.

As I watched the wiry figure with the piercing grey eyes, thin face and aggressive jaw, I thought "He is almost unknown to the British public."

"Monty of Alamein," as his victorious troops call him, is 54, the son of a bishop, and an Ulsterman. He is a front-line general, that is to say he prefers to squat in a front-line dug-out with his men, getting to

CLIMBING DOWN !

Out-generalled,' Nazi General von Thoma, climbs from tank to join thousands of his compatriots — in "Monty's" bag !

know them, sharing their ideas and ideals, and listening to their views rather than staying back in G.H.Q. He has Churchill's flair for odd headgear, and swapped hats with an Australian soldier when he first visited the "Diggers" soon after taking over command in August.

Now he's wearing a tank beret. Every hat becomes smothered in badges, as he likes to add the badge of every regiment he visits. When he visited the Greeks it tickled them immensely.

"Monty" is an "offensive" general. After taking over the leadership of Eighth Army he was driving towards the front when he found British tommies digging defence works behind Alamein. "What are you doing ?" he asked in a dry voice. "Making defences," he was told. "Then stop it," he said, "you will never need them."

He Points the Path —

You can imagine that a man of this stamp, who has given the British Army an overwhelming triumph, is worshipped by his men. They see in him his drive and dogged determination, his complete faith in his own ability, and — this is the most important part of his military dogma — absolute unshakeable belief in the fighting qualities of the British soldier.

He points the path which leads Eighth Army and the Allied Air Forces across desert tracks back to their hearths and homes in Britain, the Dominions and America. "He's the goods," a stalwart Scot told me after nine days of battle. "Our blokes would follow him anywhere."

So Eighth Army says "Hats off to a great British Commander — 'Monty' of Alamein !"

THE CRUSADER

IGHTH ARMY WEEKLY

ued to the Fighting Forces in the desert

. 30 Vol. 3   November 23, 1942

Review

for the Blue

ITAIN

Church bells pealed in England for first time since Dunkirk on Sunday. For two and a half years they were silenced so that they might ring out their warning of German invasion. Urging the nation to rejoice provided they did not relax Churchill said those who listened to peals will have thankful hearts for great British victory in Egypt.

ENCH NORTH AFRICA

To clear the way for General Anderson's advancing forces, British paratroops landed deep in Tunisia from American transport 'planes. Anglo-American forces are thrusting towards Southern Tunisia while the British Army pushes on to Bizerta and Tunis along coast. In the south the Allies are pushing on towards Gabes, 150 miles to the southeast and about 100 miles from Libyan border. General Giraud's French troops co operating with vanguard of advancing British First Army have been in fierce clashes with Axis troops near Tunis. Hitler is frantically reshuffling his forces to meet menace of encirclement. From Stockholm it is reported he is rushing troops and tanks and aircraft from South Russia to Bulgaria and Greece. An Italian naval squadron is reported to have assembled off Piraeus. (Map of North African battle area on page 7).

SOLOMONS

Two light cruisers and six destroyers were total losses suffered by U.S. Pacific Fleet which completely smashed Japanese Fleet in close range battle in Solomons area. Twenty-three Jap ships were destroyed ; seven damaged. Enemy ships sunk were one battleship, three heavy and two light cruisers, five destroyers, eight transports and four cargo transports. One battleship and six destroyers were damaged. Remnants of Jap Fleet were seen fleeing north.

RUSSIA

In five day mass assault on Stalingrad, Germans have lost 3,000 men in dead alone, as well as dozens of tanks. Soviet garrison has recaptured a number of positions in northern factory belt area. In Eastern Caucasus Soviet troops are capturing village after village. Winter has set in in Don area at Voronezh. Germans have again been taken unawares. Many are still fighting in summer uniform.

— TOBRUK —

Here is an account written for "Crusader" by an observer, of our re-entry into Tobruk. For desert rats the recapture of Tobruk has a special significance for it was here that the Germans were held for the first time in World War No 2.

No Boche, no Italian, opposed the entry of the Queen's Regt. Motor Brigade into Tobruk. It was to a deserted and indescribably dirty Tobruk they came ; and above it waved the Nazi flag. Pulling that down and hoisting the Union Jack was the first job of the incoming troops.

There was a touch almost of sadness in this purely formal occupation of the most-written about and worst-hated town in Libya. Most people thought it would have been more satisfactory to have fought for it and to have had the pleasure of ejecting the Axis at the point of the bayonet rather than to motor in without let or hindrance.

But Rommel's boys hadn't waited. No ; that isn't quite correct : three of them had. They'd hidden up while their pals pulled out and asked to be taken prisoner as soon as they were sure that we were in occupation. They said they were "browned-off." They looked it.

It has dark when our fellows settled in. The place was full of booby-traps. The road right in great stretches from the Bardia fork had been mined at the sides and a very pretty bomb had been placed under a culvert just beyond the Axis-strasse turn. Our sappers dealt with these toys at once.

Three Weeks

The harbour is worse than ever. I counted three wrecks which were not there when we left and there is a huge floating crane in ruins at the dockside. The R.A.F. bombing has been devilishly accurate ; that is clear. And not only in the harbour. Along the road there is grim evidence of their strafing. Dozens of lorries burnt-out and off the road. In what was soft mud at the time, you may see the frenzied tracks of those who dived off the tarmac for safety.

Desert fitting centre. — Troops try on clothes the enemy left behind.

Robb was Right

"DON'T WORRY MATE, WE'LL BE BACK."

Copyright "Crusader"

This prophetic cartoon by Brian Robb appeared in "Crusader" after the fall of Tobruk.

And what was left of the Ariete and Littorio armoured divisions had passed this way, also. Tanks, tanks and yet more tanks left abandoned. For them there were no conveyors ; Rommel had taken every single one for his own battered remnants of the 21st and 15th Panzer Divisions. The Italians had been left to get out under their own steam — if they could. Mostly, they couldn't.

Two Trains Smashed

Old Tobruk hands have a surprise waiting for them. The Boche have very kindly extended the railway for us. Here again the R.A.F. had been busy. There are at least two complete trains utterly smashed by their bombs. Some intensive cleaning up will have to be done before the first leave train for the Delta leaves Tobruk. But it is a nice prospect. The leave train, I mean.

The Boche left behind a good many Indian and African troops whom they'd captured months · ago. They all stated that they'd been poorly treated and been made to work extremely long hours. But now released, they were happy. They came crowding down the road saluting with enormous gusto, great, white grins splitting their faces.

The shift comes on. Soon they will be aloft on wind-swept gantrys or at work in the bowels of skeleton ships

The importance of our shipbuilding yards was fully realised at the start of the war. All labour was mobilised. Women who work in shipyards of Britain are there after careful physical and psychological tests have proved them fit.

Women are no novelty in the industry. Drawing offices always had women.

WOMEN BEHIND THE SHIPS

Today ships are being built faster than the u-boats can sink them. Britain's combined shipbuilding industry now averages more than one ship daily. Such figures speak eloquently for the magnificent effort being exerted by shipbuilding men — and women. To the yards on Tyne, Tees, Wear, Clyde and Mersey flock women workers in ever increasing numbers. Women stand on high structures and paint the sides of ships, pitch rivets with the dexterity of any fireboy. They take to electric welding like a duck to water, sometimes even put in work on marine engines. Most of the jobs on which female labour is employed demand only a short period of training. Those employed on bench work come under the supervision of a leading hand until they have mastered the job. The life is no harder than they had expected it would be. They are animated by one desire — to finish the job and Hitler. Then they can return to their domestic chores.

Fireboys are now women who feed riveters with red-hot rivets, they work amid a shattering crescendo of noise.

She has exchanged her breadknife for an oxygen and gas cutter, cleaves through steel as through a loaf.

The steam hammer operator in the blacksmith's shop is a woman. Old hands stand by until necessary confidence is acquired.

Thronging the slipways are women from every walk of life. Girl pictured here was a weaver before she built ships.

1943

Casablanca conference

8th Army enters Tripoli

German surrender at Stalingrad

Chindits cross Chindwin into Burma

Battle of the Bismarck Sea

Axis forces surrender in North Africa

Allied landings in Sicily

Mussolini falls from power

Mountbatten appointed Supreme Allied Commander in
South-east Asia

Allied conference in Quebec

Allied landings in Italy and Italian surrender

Allied conference in Moscow

Soviet forces recapture Kiev

Allied conferences in Cairo and Tehran

Pearl Harbour — USA enters the war

...trek from a forward area to a dressing station. Their reluctance to follow ...arry wounded down cliff-faces, through rivers and through thick jungle.

NEW GUINEA BOOTY

Jap beer

Pushbike

Landing barge

Bowser

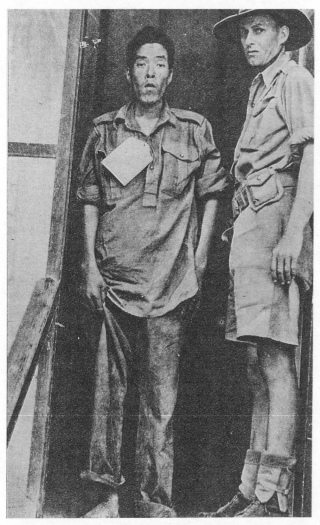

Tagged and ready for a spell behind the fence, a Japanese infantry prisoner displays for camera real Far Eastern "dead pan." Few prisoners are taken.

British representatives at Casablanca included : (front row) Sir Charles Portal, Admiral of the Fleet Sir Dudley Pound, Mr Churchill, Field Marshal Sir John Dill, General Sir Alan Brooke. (Back row) General Sir Harold Alexander, Lord Louis Mountbatten, Maj-Gen Ismay, Lord Leathers, Mr McMillan

THEY MET IN CASABLANCA

For ten days Winston Churchill and Franklin D. Roosevelt and their military and political lieutenants talked at Casablanca. Item one on their agenda was the means by which they could immediately aid Russia to the greatest extent. With their combined general staffs they surveyed the entire field of the war and reached complete agreement on the pattern of Anglo-American of-fensives in 1943. They emphasised in official statements that the United Nations would accept nothing but the unconditional surrender of Ger-many, Japan and Italy. Josef Stalin was "cordially invited" to attend, in which case the talks would have been held much further east. But personal direction of the Red Army's successful winter offensive tied Stalin to his desk in the Kremlin

Grand strategy conference at Anfa Hotel, Casablanca. Left of table, Admiral King, C-in-C U.S. Navy, General Marshall, Chief of Staff U.S. Army, Lieutenant-General Arnold, U.S. Army Air Force. Right, Field Marshal Sir John Dill, Sir Charles Portal, General Sir Alan Brooke, Admiral of the Fleet Sir Dudley Pound and Lord Louis Mounbatten.

General Henri Giraud (High Commissioner for French North Africa) shakes hands with the leader of the Fight-ing French, General Charles de Gaulle, at historic meeting of the two Frenchmen on French Imperial soil.

President Roosevelt and Prime Minister Winston Churchill talk to the Press during the 10-days conference at Casablanca.

President Roosevelt dines in the open air on soldier's rations after inspecting U.S. Forces. On left is Mr Harry Hopkins who accompanied the President on his trip.

Awaiting transport by hospital ship to Nile Delta. Eighth Army wounded lie on dockside in tepid winter sunshine. Although enemy usually respects Red Cross, there have been several daylight attacks on hospital ships.

bandaged, with slits for eyes, nose and mouth Next to him, snoring heavily, is the man who has had a head operation His eyes are bandaged. The Kiwi sister in her blue-grey dress and red blazer is kneeling down by a stretcher feeding the officer who was too near to a bomb when the Stukas attacked a wadi near Beni Ulid The food is not much, for we are a long way from a D.I.D and lines of supply are stretched, anyway bully, tinned potatoes, biscuit, pudding, brackish tea

Most of the patients are not seriously injured, though. At least, not badly enough to forget Tripoli and their units struggling on against the 88 mm's and through the mines. These mines are one of the chief topics of conversation One and a-quarter million of them are said to have been sown by the enemy between El Alamein and Buerat -- 100,000 on the so-called 'Buerat Line' alone : after that he seems to have started running out of mines Many of the casualties here are from the Italian S mine — drive over or step on its hidden prongs and it springs up, bursts in mid-air in a shower of ball-bearings. The German Teller has taken its toll too. A Sapper officer has just come in whose last 'recce' cost him two broken legs as he drove over a cluster of them — but his job took several hours off Eighth Army's advance.

Jig-Saw Of News

Conversation sweeps over the ward in gusts, stimulated now by an M.O. who comes in and tells us Tripoli has fallen, now by an orderly who enters the minute after and quotes the B.B.C. "70 miles east and 40 miles south."

"Damned place seems to be retreating from us" someone mutters. Has it, hasn't it ? — the thing becomes an obsession.

Fragments of the advance are furnished by each casualty as he confides half inaudibly to his next door neighbour. You try and fit them into a picture, sorting a jig-saw.

"We lost (such and such a number) of tanks."

"Lovely country for anti-tank guns —holes hidden by long grasses and damned flowers."

"War getting a bit sticky when I left — they started bombing The M.D.S."

"Funny things, mines — one spot — major in jeep ran over one — hat blown off, that's all — colonel in

"TRIPOLI HAS FALLEN..."

by PAUL CHADBURN

"Parade" Army Observer

Tripoli has fallen. The Eighth Army marches with phlegmatic curiosity through the streets of the one-time capital of Mussolini's North African Empire. What is left of the Italian colonial army meanwhile withdraws to the German bridgehead in Tunisia, to the doorway of a country it was once Il Duce's intention victoriously to invade.

Tripoli has fallen : and so, during the long advance against guns and through mines, have many men of the Eighth Army. Many, killed, many wounded.

You watch them come into this casualty clearing station after the terrible jolting ride in the ambulance from the Regimental Aid Posts or Advance Dressing Stations. — Rough places, these C.C.S.'s, with many a makeshift device -- extensions for a leg fracture have to be made here by filling the foot of a sock with sand and hanging it off the ankle — but all of them have the two essentials : an expert staff, up-to-date surgical equipment.

Here is the scene in the officers' ward of a forward C.C.S. during the final advance from Buerat to Trip-

oli. The ward is two E.P.I. tents. The inside of a three-tonner at one end makes more space, provides a sort of pantry-cum-store room. Lucky casualties lie on iron bedsteads, later arrivals on stretchers ranged down the middle.

A convoy comes in of more of the men who did not reach Tripoli. Some arrive from the operating theatre, reeking of anaesthetics. Their bandages are clean. They are not a spruce lot these men who return by stages through these grim coaching-houses of the desert. One opposite, burned in a tank, has hands and face

Sister and medical officer on daily round of personal questions, sister records ans

tank over another — track off — decided to brew up then — driver digs for a spadeful of sand fuel. spade disappears in smoke — another chap decides to loot lorry. finds booby and lorry goes — chap all right — a bloody fool sets off S mine 40 yards away — here I am."

Each arrival is examined for news. But they know only of the happenings on the small sectors covered by their own units.

The orderly at intervals stolidly repeats the B.B.C. news as he goes round with thermometer or bottle.

"Temperature on the cold side. sir. B.B.C. says we've reached Tarhuna. Came through at lunch-time — had to stop eating ration biscuits to hear it."

From time to time the orderly gets out a broom and immediately a dust storm fills the ward.

"Got a job there for life" someone tells him "sweeping the desert."

Breathing Chloroform

Night is bright in the ward. beaming down on the casualties from strong bulbs. Every so often the night orderly comes out of his screened-off cubby hole. brings the bottle. injects morphia, distributes periodic pills.

The air is sickly with anaesthetic, vibrant with snores of drugged men. Patients gradually coming, to mutter and moan : 'It's dark this morning" then, with sudden anxiety, "is it dark ?"

"Orderly, please put my feet together ; I can't move my foot."

Six o'clock. While it's still dark outside, the men come in with the stretchers. carry the casualties out of the ward, slip them into the waiting ambulances to catch the 'planes going eastward.

Eight o'clock. The B.B.C.

"The Eighth Army is moving steadily westward from Homs and north from Tarhuna toward Tripoli. It is reported that advance elements are now...".

Falling by the wayside. "Parade's" desert reporter. Paul Chadburn, had to write his Tripoli piece from a stretcher in a casualty clearing station. He draws attention to the many men of the Eighth Army and the R.A.F. who through misfortune did not reach Tripoli.

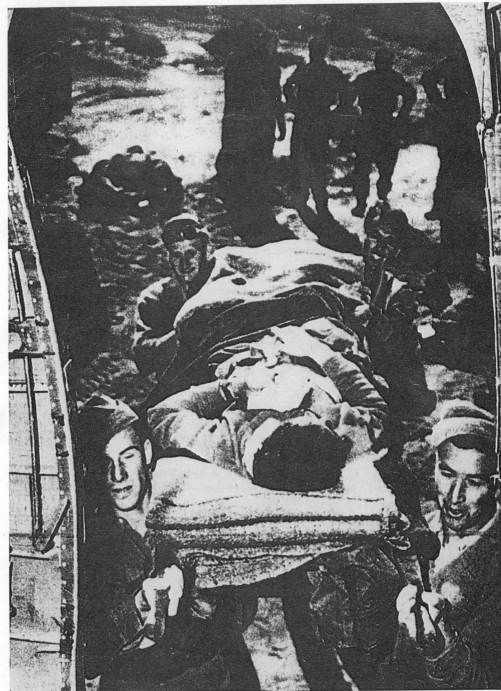

U.S. Ninth Army Air Force picture shows Eighth Army wounded being loaded in American DC3 for joltless transport to base hospital. In morning 'plane carted munitions. mail and supplies to advanced landing ground.

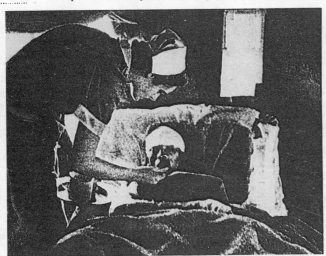

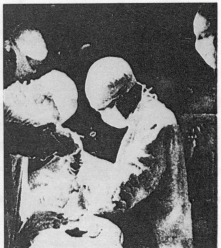

d ward ask patient no end r neat daily report book.

New Zealander. Sister Murray. gives medicine to South African native soldier. In desert between Cairo and Tripoli serve nurses of nearly all Allied nations.

Airman has appendix out in night operation. Appendix trouble can come with little warning.

UNDERGROUND CITY

Tuesday February 23 was the 25th birthday of the Red Army. In the defence of Stalingrad the Red Army fought one of the greatest defensive battles in history. In a despatch to the "Sunday Times" Alexander Werth describes how he found the city after the German Sixth Army had been wiped out

I am writing this message from a dug-out on the side of a steep cliff overlooking the Volga two miles from Stalingrad. Everybody in Stalingrad lives in dug-outs because no houses are left. Mine is a small dug-out which I am sharing with a Russian friend and an elderly soldier who both went through the whole of the Stalingrad battle and who frequently comment on the uncanniness of the silence round the place now. Until the encircled Germans in the factory district of Stalingrad surrendered the fighting had continued night and day for nearly six months.

Gen. Zhukov told me of the defence when he received me in his dugout. Describing the ferocity of the German offensive on October 13 after Hitler had formally announced that Stalingrad would be taken, he said : "It began with a terrible barrage of gun and mortar fire and during that day there were 2,000 *Luftwaffe* sorties over Stalingrad. Separate explosions could not be heard because there was one continual roar of explosions. This went on for four or five hours. Inside the dug-outs the vibration broke everything into thousands of pieces. That day the Germans advanced one mile but their losses were so heavy that they could not keep it up the next day ; and so their most massive attempt to break through our defences failed. This was what probably baulked the German offensive against Stalingrad. But there were many other factors and I should like to tell you just what one of our gallant soldiers said to me when the battle was at its height. He said to me 'I think I would rather put a bullet through my head than endure this but we know that we must stick it out because the whole Russian people and the whole world expect it of us'."

And so, with the fall of Stalingrad, 330,000 Germans have been lost to Hitler. Thousands have been buried and many more thousands of dark-skinned, frozen, wax-like corpses litter the countryside round Stalingrad. Inside Stalingrad itself 90,000 were lucky enough to have been taken prisoner by the Russians, including 23 generals and 2,500 officers.

I have just been outside my dugout. From the slippery path on the slope of the ravine which separates the two cliffs I saw the vast white snow-covered expanse of the majestic Volga. On the frosty cliff some soldiers were sitting round a bonfire. They were burning something which is familiar to us in England—bomb wreckage. The scene was perfectly peaceful and I could see the the road across the Volga ice-flows to the island nearly a mile away, the island of fruit trees, oak and poplar, the island several miles long which played so great a part in the defence of Stalingrad. It was this island which the Russians used to hold the road against the German tanks and from which they pounded the Ger-

Outside Stalingrad a family forced underground awaits deliverance by the victorious Red Army.

man positions and kept the Germans away from the Volga. Today armoured cars as well as horse-drawn sledges are driving across the Volga and there is so much motor traffic along the ice road that it looks like a promenade. Except for the occasional explosion of mines, as the minefields are cleared, and the bright flares of the rockets which are being sent up, everything is extremely still. The rockets were captured along with vast quantities of other German war material and, since these rockets are no longer used, the Russian soldiers amuse themselves with these fireworks.

Wrecks In Frozen River

But what a story everything tells here ! For example, this pleasant road across the Volga with its leisurely scene. Look closely at the Volga River and you see on either side of the ice road, frozen into the ice, wrecks of ships and boats hit by the fearful bombing under which thousands of men and women lived while engaged in the task of supplying Stalingrad across the Volga.

From the top of the Mamaev hill, a famous landmark, I looked down and saw the centre of Stalingrad. It looked like a huge block of modern flats. But these buildings are mere shells. From this hill I could see stretching in the same circle the great industrial area, the tractor plant and the steel works of the Red October factory. Thousands of shells had been fired into this factory area by the Russians and the Germans. Amid the twisted metal skeletons of these enormous steel structures was the tangle of Russian and German trenches and dug-outs.

Through the wreckage of masonry and steel girders today a frozen hand or leg or boot protrudes, grotesque rather than frightening. Can you imagine the scene of Coventry multiplied hundreds of times, or the most blitzed parts of London multiplied five times ? Then you might have a remote idea of Stalingrad but with this difference — that there is not a single house left standing. That is not quite true. Driving through Stalingrad for ten miles, along boulevards littered with burned-out wrecks of tramcars, I noticed one little wooden house. That's all I could find of normal human habitation. With its lace curtains in its windows and a little puff of smoke rising from its chimney — one little wooden house.

Some of the heaviest fighting in Stalingrad was mostly house-to-house fighting. The fighting inside the houses was carried on by small units of men armed with Tommy-guns and hand grenades and supported by bands of sappers who bored their way through cellars or ceilings. Some of this fighting occurred in the central part of Stalingrad and it was here also that the final act in the great drama was staged. Here the Germans with Field-Marshal Paulus were trapped, held down by the fierce Russian artillery and mortar fire, and forced to surrender. In the basement of the burned-out shell of a famous Russian department store where Field-Marshal Paulus had his headquarters, which was terribly shelled by the Russians, it was decided to ask the Russians for terms of surrender.

The German envoy informed the Russians that their Commander-in-Chief wished to see the Russian Commander-in-Chief. So it happen-

Continued overleaf

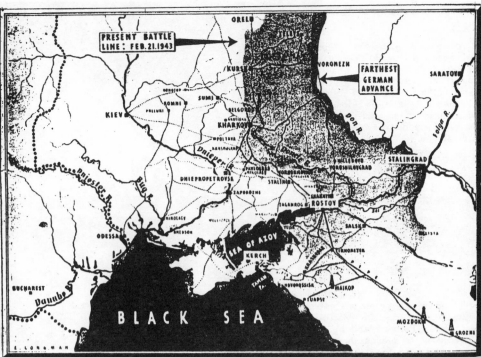

Stalingrad's Revenge

Announcing the lifting of the siege of Leningrad, a Soviet communiqué announced the capture of Schlusselburg by Russian troops, the crossing of the southern Donetz and Manych rivers, and the capture of Divnoe and Cherkessk, two large towns near Kamensk.

Stalingrad which stood out for three months against the fury of the Nazis is now having the starkest revenge of the war. The 220,000 attackers are reduced to a tattered remnant of 70,000.

Germany's Göbbels and Italy's Ansaldo both tried to scare their countrymen over Russia. Said Göbbels : We are fighting an enemy which has brought total war to the point of inhumanity and barbarism." And this was Ansaldo's line : "It is a conflict which gives us an idea of how the Mongol invasions appeared to our distant forbears as terrifying."

OUT-CLASSED

General Sir Thomas Blamey, commanding land forces in the South Pacific, has announced after his tour of New Guinea, that the Japs have been out-classed, out-marched and out-fought by the Allied troops. He warned Australia that Japan would do all she could to destroy Australia before Australia became a base for Japan's destruction.

SOUTHWEST PACIFIC

The two outstanding developments during the week in the South West Pacific were a heavy and successful attack by Allied bombers on Rabaul, and the meeting of Australian and American forces in New Guinea, following the capture of Sanandar. Five more Japanese ships were sunk or badly damaged in the raid on Rabaul.

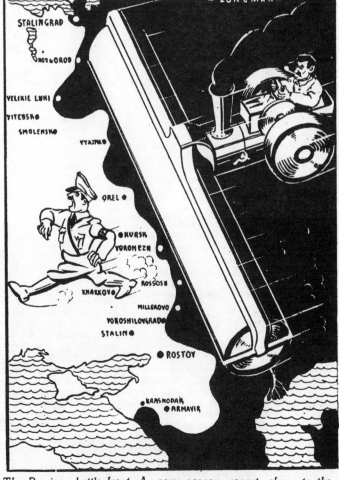

The Russian battle front. A news agency report refers to the "relentless Red Army steam-roller."

London

February 22.

Even seasoned Londoners got excited over last week's debate in Parliament on the Beveridge Plan for social security after the war. It recalled the days of peace when we loved nothing better than to watch a Parliamentary fight in the House, with party whips sending out telegrams summoning wayward supporters to the voting lobbies on a great day.

Looked ahead...

Mr Morrison told the House that the basic thing about the Beveridge Plan was how best the community might get its living and a reasonable standard of life in the years ahead. They were not (he added) to have any repetition of soldiers coming back and being promised a Paradise and not getting it. But, said Mr Morrison, we will work for a Paradise and by the way the Government is moving there will be far more preparation for stability after this war than there was last time.

* * *

To turn our thoughts immediately back to the war there was one of those grand ceremonies which the London public so dearly loves at the Albert Hall in celebration — in common with the rest of the country — of the 25th anniversary of the Red Army. We may make mistakes elsewhere but in a demonstration of this sort we take a lot of beating. There were massed bands, rows and rows of Civil Defence workers, war police, firemen and factory hands. Mr Anthony Eden represented the Government and behind him was an enormous Soviet flag and a Russian soldier standing on a high plinth. The Russian Ambassador and Mrs Maisky were in the Royal Box beside Mrs Churchill and other boxes were filled with heads of the Services and representatives of all the United Nations. It was a grand moment as all rose at the request of Mr Eden and stood in silence as a tribute

With Mrs Churchill

to the dead of the Red Army. Stalin sent a message and in a pungent speech Mr Eden said : "Let Hitler lead this monstrous machine which he created to utter destruction and let him become for his own Germany and for the world such an awful monument to evil doing and evil thinking that men will be for ever warned to combine in time to prevent the rise of such another."

* * *

So much do we owe to the womenfolk of the country today that it was particularly fitting that the Lady Mayoress of London should have conceived the idea of honouring every branch of the Allied war effort by inviting to lunch to the Mansion House 264 women leaders, led by the Princess Royal, controller and commandant of the A.T.S. The City gold plate was brought out and there were only five men present besides the Lord Mayor. Many of the women present were in uniform but among those in mufti were three representing British housewives — Mrs Ethel Hore of Reigate who

has had 28 evacuees in her care since war began ; Mrs Linwood who has lived and worked in the City all through the bombing ; and Mrs Searle, wife of Sergt.-Major Searle who won the B.E.M. and was missing at Tobruk. She has three war workers billeted in her home at Hayes.

* * *

When 'Plum' Warner was reelected president of Middlesex County Cricket Club in the pavilion at Lords last week he naturally referred to post war cricket and the difficulties that would have to be overcome. Sir Pelham said he could see nothing wrong with modern cricket except that there were too many counties and that some wickets were over-prepared and over-doped. He mentioned the Findlay Commission of 1937 which recommended reduction of the counties from 17 to 15. "This is a splendid report" he said. "By reducing numbers each could play all the others and it would then be possible to do away with averages in calculating results." Bearing in mind the influential position held by 'Plum' Warner in the world of cricket, this expression of opinion may give one clue to what is likely to happen when cricket is in everyone's thoughts again.

* * *

It is on the cards that the Services rugby XV will be able to do to Scotland what the Services soccer team achieved when on Saturday it put seven goals into the nets at Hampden Park without reply from the Scots. Jack Robinson (Sheffield Wednesday) got four, Westcott (Wolves) three. At all events it is about time we had a resounding English rugger win for since the spring of 1940 the Sassenachs have lost games in a row. This may account for the drastic changes the Service selectors have made in the side that lost to Wales last November. Only two players remain, R.T. Campbell (St Mary's) at full back and L/Corpl Ward, a Bradford Rugby League player, at centre three.

* * *

Closed, as a result of the blitz, for more than two years, the Tivoli in the Strand has reopened with an English film featuring

radio's most popular actor Tommy Handley in a screen version of *Itma* (*It's That Man Again*). Relying on the fact that what one has enjoyed over the air one can enjoy again on the screen, Walter Forde, who made the film, has stuck faithfully to the pace of the non-stop humour of Tommy Handley and his 'wisecrackers.' It is a screamingly funny picture and a credit to British studios, besides adding another theatre to London's already crowded houses.

Now he's Schubert

Old Chelsea is the the title of a new Richard Tauber musical built round Schubert and with the famous tenor singing to his heart's (and the audience's) delight. It has opened at the Prince's and looks like staying. Carole Lynne, niece of Debroy Somers, sings enchantingly along with Nancy Brown ; and eighteenth century dresses and comedy touches make up an altogether worthwhile evening.

* * *

At a meeting of the Zoological Society in London it was reported that the Prime Minister had accepted the gift of an African lion in commemoration of his trip to North Africa, but Mr Churchill had made it a condition that he should not be expected to keep the lion in Downing Street or Chequers. It will remain at the zoo.

Cardiff

By the death of Mr A.G. Bradley at 93 Wales loses one of its most distinguished writers. His work from 1898 when he published *Highways and Byways of North Wales* to 1929 when he wrote *The Romance of Wales* was always dependable for its historical and topographical accuracy.

Flying Officer Rex Harrison, the stage and screen star, leaves Caxton Hall after his wedding to Miss Lilli Palmer, 28-years-old Viennese actress. Flying Officer Harrison is 34.

Container keeps pictures at the correct temperature on their quarter-mile trip from underground store to the restoring studio.

TREASURE CAVE

Britain's greatest art treasures, in peace-time housed in the National Gallery, Trafalgar Square, are in caves beneath a mountain now. But they receive the same expert care, even to the regulation of the temperature of the chambers in which they are stored, as they did in pre-war London

On its way to be loaded with pictures which require restoration, container passes over points in a tunnel.

Guards — all picked men — come on duty, are handed the keys by Mr E.B. Harrison, the chief attendant.

Pictures are placed in hall, hewn out of the mountain, for inspection. Landscapes are on end to save space

A Canaletto is carried past Sir Joshua Reynold's "The Three Graces" to be given a periodic examination.

Old and valuable frames which contain famous pictures are repaired in subterranean workshop in the mountain.

Mr W.A. Holder, an expert at restoring old masters, works with a magnifying glass in the restoring studio.

THE WIT TO WIN

The nose is a little more pointed, and frequently in need of a handkerchief; but the same preposterous moustache juts from beneath it, and the thought directing the pencil of the Russian artist was the same as that guiding British cartoonists who draw Hitler.

The Russian artist, like the British, turns his wit on the inflated figure of Siegfried-Hitler and shows us that the chief of Nordic supermen is a horrid little fellow after all, with beastliness and weaknesses and feeble excuses as his stock in trade. Russian and British alike rip the veil of pomp and circumstance and lies and brute force by which the Teuton has tried to justify his crimes and terrify the victims into submission. The pencil becomes a weapon, with wit for ammunition—the wit to win. It is a wit which reflects and stimulates the spirit of the Soviet and British peoples and has done so through the most evil days of the war.

In this they continue the work of those British and Russian cartoonists who inspired and amused, even if grimly, their countrymen when they were allies fighting for freedom against Bonaparte. British artists turned the terrible Napoleon into "Little Boney" and helped his opponents everywhere to feel that he really could be beaten if they stuck to the task.

And as the *Grande Armée* marched toward Moscow and then turned homeward through the snow Russian caricaturists poured out works telling of the courage of the Russian people, the criminal ambition of the invader and his wretchedness in retreat. Many of these pictures were brought to England and adapted for the British public by Cruikshank. Examples of them in these pages, with the work of British and Russian cartoonists of today, are taken from *Russia, Britain's Ally* by F.D. Klingender (Harrap).

Cruikshank was joining hands with Russian artists to give a message to the Russian and British peoples—the bear and the bulldog—in their fight against a man bent on world domination.

It is a pity Hitler confined his youthful studies to architectural drawings. He would have found old prints more instructive.

NON-STOP HAMMER
AND SICKLE
Cartoon by Zec

A PROMISE KEPT (Efimof)
"*Each one of you will receive Lebensraum in the east.*" And they received six feet of earth each.

AN EVENING STROLL
Cartoon by Efimof

AT THE HISTORY LESSON
Cartoon by Efimof

"*It's nothing, Tovarishi, you should have seen the one that got away*" — Cartoon by Giles.

STEPS TO TUNIS

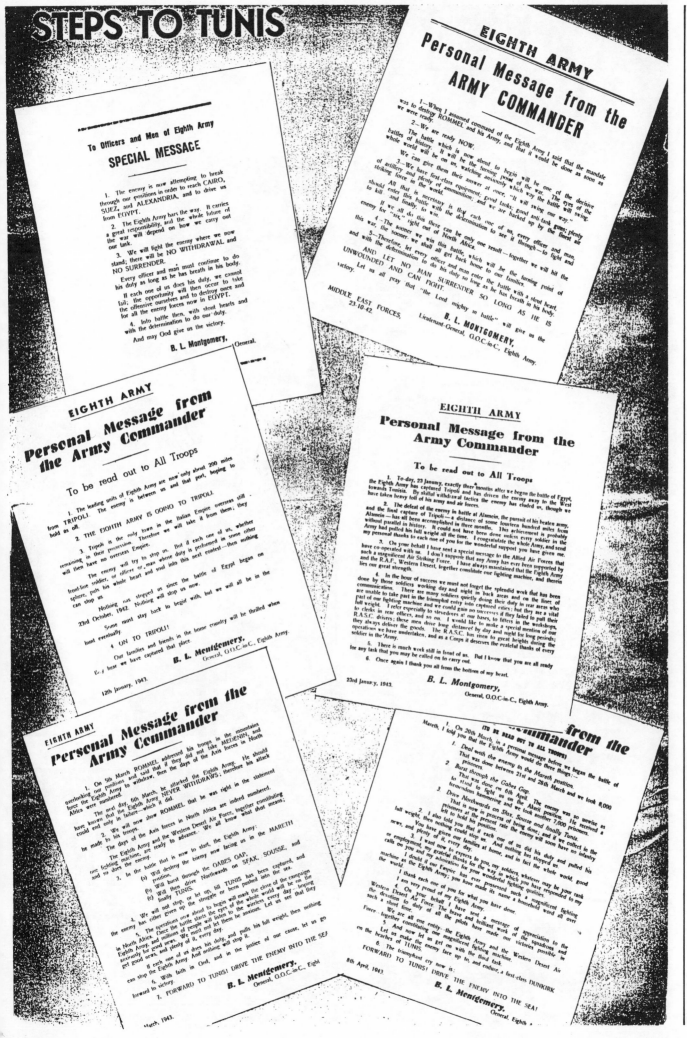

PARADE

No. 143   Vol. 11   May 8, 1943

MASTER RACE

FRANCE IN MINIATURE

Pages 7-9

EGYPT P.T. 2   CYRENAICA P.T. 2   CYPRUS 4 1/2 C. Prs   ERITREA 55 Cents   IRAQ 30 Fils   IRAN 3 1/2 Rials   KENYA 6d   LEBANON 20 S. Prs

MALTA 4d   PALESTINE 25 Mils   SOUTH AFRICA 6d   SUDAN 20 Mills   SYRIA 30 S. Prs   TRANSJORDAN 25 Mils   TRIPOLITANIA 6d   TURKEY 10 Krs

BULLY FOR BLIGHTY

No hope of improvement of rationing during the war was held out by Lord Woolton, in a speech at Battersea, after the Government's Chief Officer had ascribed the nation's continued good wartime health to the simpler diet to which all had been subjected.

Lord Woolton said that only by drawing on reserves of bully beef had it been possible to maintain the 1/2d. weekly meat ration, which he described as «pretty bare going». But he believed this meat allowance would continue till the end of the war.

Powdered Mash

Lord Woolton has announced that it is now possible for troops in the desert to have sausages and mash at a few minutes notice.

He told an audience at an East Anglian «mash» factory that sausages are a regular feature of the food pack for troops, but the problem was to supply the mash.

Long experience in dehydration at last produced a perfect potato powder

IT'S AMAZING   HOW A SAILOR'S CAP   LOOKS, QUITE O.K.

WHEN WORN IN   ANY BUT THE   CORRECT MANNER !!

FLUX

WHO'S WHO OF THE WAR

E

Eden, ANTHONY ; Secretary of State for the Dominions : entitled to attend all meetings of War Cabinet.
Elizabeth, QUEEN OF GREAT BRITAIN.
Ellington, SIR EDWARD ; Marshal of Royal Air Force ; responsible for expansion scheme as Chief of Air Staff ; now Inspector-General.
Elliot, WALTER ; Minister of Health.
Elliot, MRS. WALTER ; Women's Volunteer Services for Civil Defence (with Stella, Lady Reading).
Evans, ADMIRAL SIR EDWARD ; Regional Commissioner, London Area, representing Government departments in event of breakdown of communications.

H

Halifax, Lord, British Foreign Minister.
Hankey, LORD ; Minister without Portfolio, British War Cabinet.
Hertzog, GENERAL ; ex-Prime Minister of South African Union ; favoured neutrality in present war.
Herzog, DR. I. ; Chief Rabbi, Palestine.
Hess, RUDOLF ; was Hitler's private secretary, been nominated Hitler's successor, after Goering.
Hicks, SIR SEYMOUR ; Controller of the Entertainments National Service Association (Drury Lane).
Himmler, HEINRICH ; Chief, Secret Police, Germany, and leader of Storm Troops.
Hitler, ADOLF ; Fuehrer of German Reich.

«But surely Paul, there MUST be times when you're tired of simply TALKING sport!

On The Burma Border, Thanks To Manipuri Fisherwomen, British Troops Have —

FISH AND CHIPS FOR SUPPER

ALTHOUGH they are hundred of miles away from the sea, British troops on the Burma borders often have fish-and-chip suppers.

Fishing in some parts of Assam is a major industry, especially in the small state of Manipur, where many troops are stationed.

Troops used to the ordinary methods of fishing with net or rod and line, are fascinated by the curious ways in which the Assamese and Manipuris catch fish.

Most of the fishing is done by women in flooded paddy fields. Often along the roads, troops watch women fishing by dragging bamboo baskets tied to a piece of string through flooded fields. The baskets come up full of mud—and tiny fish like whitebait.

SOLD IN MARKETS

The fish are sold in the local markets, lying squirming and still alive on large banana leaves from the jungle. Often they are only small fish like sprats, but they are eagerly bought for the messes.

And that night the corned beef is laid aside in the cookhouse, and the troops have fried fish, just as they did back home in the Old Kent Road.

EIGHTH ARMY WEEKLY

Issued Free to the Fighting Forces

No. 55 Vol. 4. - May 17, 1943

WE'VE DONE IT!

We have avenged Dunkirk !

As "Crusader" went to press Axis troops herded in the Cap Bon peninsula were making desperate efforts to escape from the Tunisian tip, while non-stop bombing and machine gun attacks from Allied Air Forces caused a havoc the Luftwaffe tried in vain to create on the beaches of Dunkirk,

Enemy troops unable to stand the strain were giving themselves up at the rate of one thousand an hour.

- Farewell To The Blue -

FIRST AGAIN !

First into Tripoli city when it was captured by General Montgomery, the 11th Hussars were among the very first to enter Tunis.

They have a record of battle service in North Africa from the Valley of the Nile to the tip of Tunisia unexcelled by any regiment. They were in the Western Desert in May 1940, before Italy came into the war. Exactly three years later they were in at the death two thousand miles away.

The Derbyshire Yeomanry, one of the first two units to enter Tunis, arrived in North Africa in November 1942, and was immediately involved in hard fighting.

The collapse of Tunis and Bizerta came with spectacular suddenness. Their surrender spelled the final farewell to the blue for men who in many cases had endured the hell of desert warfare for long months — even years.

History will record that the seal of the Allies' great victory in North Africa was set in the smoke, dust and din of desert battle; in the reverses and successes of the old Western Desert Force and the Eighth Army.

The spring of 1943 has seen the end of the beginning of our assault on the citadel of Nazi-stricken Europe. The stage is now set for the final blow at the crumbling castles of the Nazi and Fascist fanatics.

The beginning of the end is at hand.

What Eighth Army's role will be in the future we do not know. What we do know is that the comradeship among the men born in the dust of the Libyan desert and our unshakable confidence in our leadership, will keep the name of the Eighth Army on the lips of the peoples of the world.

We have no regrets in bidding our final farewell to the blue Like Alexander of old we look for fresh worlds to conquer, secure in the knowledge that our toil, sweat and determination in the Western Desert and Libya have made the end immeasurably nearer.

CHURCHILL IN WASHINGTON

Churchill's on the move again. On Tuesday, news from London brought Churchill's congratulatory messages to Allied Chiefs. Wednesday's cables announced that early in the morning he had met F.D.R. in Washington.

Привет 8-мой Армии

Hello — Eighth Army

Issued Free to the Fighting Forces

No. 54 Vol. 4. - May 10, 1943

Metro-Goldwyn-Monty!

During a radio quizz session at Auckland, New Zealand, one of the questions was «Who is the commander of the Eighth Army?» The lady to whom the question was directed promptly replied «Robert Montgomery.»

Yank Hits £129 Malta Jackpot

Malta—A 25-year-old American Squadron John Lynch, of Alhambra, California, won a sweepstake prize of £129 by being the pilot of the R.A.F. based at Malta to shoot down the 100th Axis plane. Lynch, who joined the R.A.F. in July 1941, shot down a Ju-52 transport near the Sicilian coast.

Virtually all the members of the Royal Air Force at Malta contributed to the sweepstakes.

Being Prepared !

Scout «Commandos.» British Boy Scouts prepare for the future and carry out exercises on Commando lines.

Here an Allied correspondent who has seen much fighting on the Russian front tells «Crusader» some of the things that have impressed him here in North Africa.

«ONE of the first things that strikes me coming from Russia,» he says, «is that the British soldiers seem to sing so little. The Russians sing on all possible occasions, on the march or in bivouacs. In fact, they've been famous for it for generations. And the quality of thir singing is often first class — most Russian «squaddies» could step right on the professional stage in London or New York and get away with it.»

We suggested that perhaps the average Eighth Army man's throat was too dry with dust to make him feel like opening up very often.

«Well, maybe there's something in that,» said the correspondent. «Another thing that struck me when I first met the Eighth Army was the amount of bedding people carted around. Every man seemed to have at least four blankets. Of course, it does get chilly in the desert on a winter's night; but even in winter the Russian soldier only has a couple of blankets. True, he has very much thicker clothing than the British battledress, which partly makes up the difference when he sleeps fully dressed. And there is usually plenty of wood around to make fires in the dugouts.»

«What do you think of Eighth Army's rations?» we asked next.

«Well, they seem pretty good to me, considering the difficulties of bringing them up.

STAFF WORK EXCELLENT

With regard to Eighth Army's equipment, the correspondent said that our Sherman tanks appeared to be as good as the famous Russian T.34 which has cost the Germans such a lot of heart-burning in the past few months. Our staff work, too, struck him as excellent.

We then remarked on the important part played in both the Russian and Eighth Army offensives by the artillery in clearing a way for the infantry and tanks. «Yes, the Red Army artillery is certainly first class,» he said. «In fact, the Germans have often complained that the Russian artillery officers seem to be walking calculating-machines, who can switch the fire of their guns with almost inhuman precision.

Maybe the well-known Russian ability at mathematics has something to do with it. The Eighth Army gunners are excellent, too, I have noticed, however. that they seem to go in for pure barrage shots more than do the Russians. The latter consider a barrage most effective when combined with shoots by individual batteries, or even single guns. on individual enemy pillboxes and strongpoints.»

«Of course, any true comparison between the fighting here and in Russia is very difficult to make. Here everything is on such a small scale — where you think in battalions the Russians think in divisions. And the North African front is about 130 miles long, while the Russian is more than ten times that distance.

"Of course, the almost ferocious hatred of the average Russian soldier for the enemy make this easier. Partly this is due to the Russian temperament, which is much more violent than that of the average Britisher. I have often seen a dying Russian tear his shirt open and bear his breast as a last act of defiance to the foe.

The Russian soldier is fighting in his own country — very often in his own neighborhood. He sees with his own eyes what the Germans have done to his kith and kin and that is a constant spur to the «do or die» spirit typified by the defenders of Stalingrad.

«But considering that your boys are fighting far from their homes in a strange country I think the offensive spirit shown by the men of the Eighth Army is fine».

«And that, gentlemen, is the only damage the R.A.F. have inflicted on Italy.»

Powdered Mash

Lord Wootton has announced that it is now possible for troops in the desert to have sausages and mash at a few minutes notice.

He told an audience at an East Anglian «mash» factory that sausages are a regular feature of the food pack for troops, but the problem was to supply the mash.

Long experience in dehydration at last produced a perfect potato powder

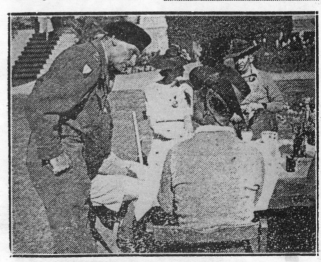

The Army Commander who paid a surprise flying visit to Cairo chats to a wounded Aussie, about to be repatriated

'DESERT VICTORY' HAILED FILM OF WAR

The London newspapers are unanimous in declaring "Desert Victory," the feature-length film of Eighth Army's advance to Tripoli as the greatest film of the war.

Seton Margrave of the "Daily Mail" says : "This is the most real, most moving and most important film ever made. It is impossible to take your eyes from the screen for a single second."

Full of Highlights

The "Daily Express" says "Desert Victory" will make the blood of millions tingle. Ernest Betts tells the story of the thirty odd sergeant-photographers of the Army Film and Photo Unit who were given a camera instead of a rifle. Some of them were killed, a number wounded or taken prisoner.

"The result of their work," he says, "is a drama so full of highlights that it is hard to pick out a transcendent' scene."

Most of the national newspapers, on the day following the film's London premiere, published a shot of three begrimed, gunners lighting cigarettes during a lull.

The "Daily Mail" captions this picture : "These men are only three of the many stars of this great film who not long ago were bank clerks, shopkeepers and engineers, but are now the world's finest fighting material.

Flown to Cairo

Copies of the film are being flown to Cairo, Palestine and other Middle East countries and arrangements are being made for the early release of the film in America.

Here "Crusader" presents some of the men, who to paraphrase E. V. Emmett, the popular Gaumont-British news commentator, were responsible for presenting Eighth Army to the world.

The Men Who Made It

The men with the red and blue flashes bearing the letters A.F. P.U. were a familiar sight to desert rats from the start of the battle that ended in the first great victory of the war for an Allied army. The pictures they took of the battle were praised highly by the British and American newspapers and by the public who were given an insight of the magnitude of the task of Eighth Army through the medium of the newspapers and the screen. The Army Film and Photo Unit was formed just over a year ago. The cameramen were in the thick of the battle from the start. The great reception accorded "Desert Victory" is the culminating tribute to the work of these desert rats with cameras.

"Illustrated London News" describes this battle picture, which provides a background for the heads of some of the desert rat cameramen, as one of the finest of the war.

CRUSADER

EIGHTH ARMY WEEKLY

Issued Free to the Fighting Forces

No. 58 Vol. 4. - June 7, 1943

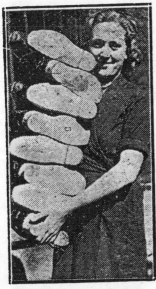

A.T.S. girls in England are now issued with wooden clogs for work in garages. A pile of finished clogs ready for despatch.

War Worker

Mr. B——is 77 and a tool turner in a Midlands aircraft factory. His name has been sent to the Ministry of Labour in London as an example of a «marvellous war worker.»

He rises at 6 and makes breakfast for himself and his wife, who is crippled. From 8 a.m. till 6 pm. he stands at a machine, tool turning for aircraft.

When he gets home he does the shopping and helps with the housework.

He has been with the same firm for 53 years.

Four sons are in war work, one of his daughters billets war workers, and three of his grandsons were at Dunkirk. Two came back.

He is the father of 11.

❖ ❖ ❖

U.S. HAS SEVEN FLEETS

The United States Navy Secretary Colonel Frank Knox has declared that the United States now has seven fleets in existence. They are in Australian waters, the South Pacific, North Atlantic, South Atlantic, the European area, the North Pacific and North-West Pacific.

What Germany Is Doing In The West

by
George Slocombe
of the «SUNDAY EXPRESS»

THE clue to Hitler's strategy this summer may be found in France.

Intensive German military preparations are known to be proceeding on French territory in anticipation of Allied operations both from the north and north-west, the Channel and the Atlantic coasts of France, and from the Mediterranean.

At the same time large movements of men and material have taken place from Northern France to the Pyrenees frontier of Spain and the frontier zone has been declared a prohibited area to a depth of 50 or 60 miles. Such measures may be interpreted as indicating the imminence of war operations across the Iberian Peninsula, against Gibraltar and the Western gate of the Mediterranean.

THIRTEEN POINTERS

However much truth there may be in reports of a possible Hitler offensive in the West to counteract the great German defeats in the East, the following facts in the military and political situation in France are of interest :

1 Since German reconnaissance pilots have reported mysterious preparations in British ports, whether or not such preparations are related to Allied plans for an invasion of Europe this year, tension among the German garrisons on the Channel and Atlantic coasts of France has redoubled.

2 German defensive works on the Atlantic and Mediterranean coasts have been speeded up.

3 Large sections of coastal towns like Lorient, Marseilles and St. Nazaire — when they have not already been blitzed by the RAF have been dynamited by the Germans to provide not only clear zones of fire but also rubble and building stone for use in concrete gun positions blast walls, etc.

4 The Germans are salvaging by force without compensation, every kind of metal from occupied France.

THE SIEGFRIED LINE

5 The Siegfried Line, which was abandoned when the Germans were certain of victory and which was only employed here and there as an extended A.A. shelter during the R.A.F. raids the Ruhr and Rhineland is now being reconstructed and refortified as Germany's final line of defence against attack from the west.

6 The Maginot Line, which was equally disregarded by the Germans during their victorious phase, except that its heavy guns were transferred to the Channel coast for artillery operations against the British is now being rapidly dismantled. All salvageable metal is being sent to Germany. When this has been done, the fortresses are blown up.

7 Ostensibly to encourage Laval in his role as champion of the New Order and archenemy of Bolshevism, the demarcation line between the old occupied and unoccupied zones of France has been abolished. Postal and railway communications will shortly be resumed between the two zones but always subject to permits from the French police (under the surveillance of the Gestapo) and the limitations of the French railways, now two-thirds denuded of their rolling stock by the German military authorities.

LAVAL'S REPLY

8 Laval is now German Gauleiter No. 1 in France. To the Mexican Minister who told him bluntly in Vichy some weeks ago that his pro-German proclivities were utterly incomprehensible, Laval replied coldly that he was determined to do everything for a German victory.

9 Nevertheless, Frenchmen who have long known Laval intimately believe that he is playing not so much for a German victory as for a compromise peace, in which he would act as negotiator.

10 Laval's implacable enemies in France are the Communists and the de Gaullists Laval has formed a militia in the old unoccupied zone to crush any attempt at insurrection before or synchronised with an Allied landing.

FRENCH THREAT

In the old occupied zone a similar anti-revolutionary militia has been formed by Marcel Deat ex-Socialist like Laval and one of the political stooges used by the Nazis since 1940 to keep Laval in check.

11 Notwithstanding these counter-preparations, both Laval and the German High Command realise that France is on the edge of serious internal disorder. A German-controlled newspaper in Paris, Le Progrès, admits that «Communism in France has installed itself on a dangerous scale. It has passed from the merely revolutionary to the patriotic stage. Social classes which were not contaminated in 1936 are rallying to it. «Industrialists warn us of troubling changes which they observe in the mentality of their workers and employees.

FISHING BAN

«If by misfortune the French people were left to themselves France would be put to fire and sword within 15 days.»

12 Sabotage, industrial accidents and attacks on Germans are on the increase. Eleven men and women in the Lille industrial district have just been shot after military court-martial

(Continued on Page 7)

PARADE

No. 148   Vol. 12   June 12, 1943

ALGIERS MEETING

THE GRANDEST GRAND ALLIANCE

Page 5

Troops on sand outside beach pavilion of a N. African convalescent home sing National Anthem as King George VI appears on balcony, takes salute.

The King drove away from the airfield in a jeep flying the royal standard when he arrived in North Africa to visit British, U.S. and French forces.

THE KING IN NORTH AFRICA

Gen. Eisenhower, Commander-in-Chief of the Allied Forces in North Africa, greets the King.

In an African vineyard the King watches display of modern street fighting tactics by United States troops. Brig.-Gen. of U.S. Army explains the demonstration. Afterwards H.M. took the salute at a parade.

At airfield. The King talks to Gen. Anderson, G.O.C. British First Army, and to a Brigadier.

The King's tour of American forces included a visit to a large body under Gen. Clark. Here, with Gen. Clark, he inspects American guard of honour.

The King shakes hands with a South African pilot. On the airfield he met pilots from Britain, the Dominions, the United States and the French forces.

EIGHTH ARMY WEEKLY

Issued Free to the Fighting Forces

No. 60 Vol. 4. - June 21, 1943

THANKS EIGHTH ARMY!
Cables Of Congratulation
From East And West

"You not only got them on the run but you chased Hell out of them. A grand job!"

THIS cable from the women workers at Armstrongs Ltd., Hull, is one of the many hundreds received by General Montgomery since the surrender of the Axis forces in North Africa.

Scots factory girls, English munition workers, Canadian trainees South Africans ,Indians and Arabs have united in showing their appreciation by cable and letter of «the good news and plenty of it» which we have given them.

Mary Cameron shop steward, Scottish Bolt Works, cables to General Eisenhower:

«We, the girls of the Scottish Bolt Works, wish to congratulate you on your brilliant victory in the recent campaign. Also Generals Alexander, Montgomery and Giraud with the officers and men of the combined Allied Forces. We are glad to think that we helped supply them with the tools to beat the Fascist horde. We wish you the best of luck and many further successes.»

Standard Telephones, London, sends heartiest congratulations «to our Eighth Army» and pledges full support on the factory front in the next and final offensive in Europe.

«On to Berlin for victory in 1943» cable the workers in Building 3 of the same factory to General Montgomery. *«We congratulate you and the boys for the great victory. We stand solidly behind you.»*

The men and women of the Tarran Joinery Works, Hull, express what is perhaps the most deep-felt of all sentiments on the Home Front when they cable:

«We are watching and praying for your safe return. Keep them running straight through to Berlin. May God Bless you all.»

«WE'LL GIVE YOU THE TOOLS»

Most of the messages express the hope that our North African victory may herald the begin-

ning of a quick end to the war and pledge the munition workers to do their share. The workers of Fairey Aviation, for instance, cable the Army Commander:

«We extend to you and all ranks our warm congratulations and appreciation on the fight and successful issue of your noble efforts in clearing Africa of all Axis contamination. May this wonderful result be the prelude to the successful conclusion of the war. We would ask that this message be conveyed to all ranks; and finally we pledge ourselves to do all in our power to see that your Armies are supplied with all the necessary arms.»

Similar promises of all-out war production are given by the workers of the Baldwin Instrument Company, «so that the final blow against Hitlerism in the near future will be struck», and by the workers of F. Austin Ltd, who pledge themselves «to work unstintingly and give of their best in support of such fine achievements until the day of victory dawns »

THANKS GRUB !

A very practical note is struck by the Victoria League of Durban which, after congratulations to General Montgomery, adds: «In response to your appeal for comforts we have sent you 2,000,000 cigarettes 2,500 filled Glory Bags, 1,565 hand-knitted socks and 248 hand-knitted pullovers from ourselves and the people of Durban.»

From farther afield comes a message from His Highness the Maharaja of Nepal, homeland of the Ghurkas; while Sheik Hussein Suhail sends from Baghdad his own congratulations and those of the tribes of 'Beni Tameen for a victory «which sounds the doom of Axis hopes in the East.»

Here are a few of the many others who have sent messages of congratulation to the Army Commander and the Eighth Army :

Shop stewards, B and K department, Napier Aero Engines
Morris Radiators
Employees of Curtiss Ltd; Leeds.
Workers of Northgate Wire Mills, Darlington.
Waddington war workers, Hull.
Austin Aero Tool Room.
S,S, Cars, Coventry.
Naval Lodge workmen, South Wales Miners Federation.
Shops stewards, Royal Ordnance Factory, Scotland.
Short Seaplane Works Committee.
Gunnery School, Lethbridge, Alberta, Canada.

Finally, the British Legion of Scotland not only, congratulates Eighth Army but asks that all Scotsmen in it be informed «that the Legion is carefully watching their future interest and actively assisting in the welfare of their parents.»

Mrs. E. Phelps was formerly a mineral factory employee. Now she's a sprayer in a large government factory.

OODUNIT?

A variation of the once-famous jazz pioneer song "Yes, We Have No Bananas" arose when a British film company became determined to have one real banana in a scene lasting only a few seconds in a war film.

The production manager turned in sanguine hope to the Brazilian Embassy, but their fruit-stand was bare. The Embassy Secretary, however, had heard of a Chilean friend who had just landed from Algiers bringing with him two bananas.

There was joy in the studio when the loan of one of them was promised and a full-sized motorvan arrived to take delivery of the one piece of precious fruit, carefully packed in a wooden box and guarded by a special attendant.

The scene was shot in the studio and after a quick run through of the negative to make sure everything was all right, an order was given for the banana to be returned to the Chilean with the same care as it had been brought. But it was nowhere to be found.

Eventually a full confession was made by the studio's most juvenile messenger boy. He had been unable to resist the temptation.

She used to be a Lyons nippy. Now she's getting her own back after being bombed out, by working in a Midlands war factory.

Mrs. Rose Lynch was a waitress before the war. Now she's in a steel works cutting large plates for munitions.

What next?

INVASION DIARY

In these pages begins the undying story of British soldiers who have gone to the assault of Axis-held Europe. It is written by R. J. GILMORE, "Parade" reporter, illustrated by BELA ZOLA, "Parade" cameraman, both of whom landed on Sicily with the British vanguard

BEFORE EMBARKATION. Army Commander inspects division. His greeting to the G.O.C.: "Good morning. How are the soldiers?" Every hundred yards Gen. Montgomery stops to talk from his open staff car to groups of sweaty, grinning men. Mostly small men with hard faces, thick wrists and nobbly knees. No excessive spit and polish in this div. "It wouldn't cut any ice with Monty" they say. Monty clicks easily with the men, but not as man-to-man. It is more like a favourite uncle being greeted by smiling children. His cheerful banter dispels shyness and puts them at their ease. Skipping shop he questions them mainly about home towns. With officers his smile is briefer, his words fewer.

* * *

At voluntary C. of E. service in a sweltering tented Naafi the padre comments on the growth in church attendance as zero hour approaches. He chides backsliders for "using God as a spiritual slit trench" and cites an American padre in the Solomons: "There are no atheists in a slit trench." Troops sing with unaccustomed gusto *Eternal Father strong to save.*

* * *

This part of Div. embarks in transport, in peacetime a Union Castle liner on the Cape run. After stinking flyblown Africa this is a new Anglo-Saxon world smelling of soap, seawater, floor polish and starch. Snow-white table linen, heavy silver plate, glasses with smooth edges, carafes of ice-water, soft sheets, cushy mattresses and pillows. First class to the second front. Brief new world.

After dinner white-starched stewards serve from bottles beaded with frigidaire-dew mellow English beer. Brown clinking pennies come as change from paper money. With its shoddy roadhouse luxury the lounge is a waiting room for the second front. The palms and aspidistras have died and been cast overboard. The lift has been locked up for the duration: the lift-boy is in the R.A.F. The "nurses and children not allowed" brass plate has tarnished green.

At the bedsides are still bell-pushes marked "stewardess"; but the only bells in this ship warn of peril.

* * *

From a wharfside canteen troop jeer at the ship. They think the boy are going home on leave. Two-wor retort, first word of four letters, second of three, combination unprint able. Binoculars train on nurses sun basking at a Y.W.C.A. Before sun

HOME NEWS

Birmingham

Seventy-one-years-old Mrs Sarah Bell, who had not worked for 18 years, decided she would like a job, so she applied direct to a factory in the area. For the past two years she has only been absent one day — and that was when she had new windows put into her house after it had been damaged by air raids. Mrs Bell leaves her home at 6.45 each morning and arrives at the factory half an hour before she is due in, at eight, and has a cup of tea. She can sit down to her job and says she is not tired although she works until 6.30 in the evening. During the last war Mrs Bell worked at a station canteen.

* * *

A team of Birmingham allotment holders did some deep mental digging last week with a team of diggers for victory from Manchester in a gardening "Bee." The match was the outcome of a challenge to Manchester by the Lord Mayor of Birmingham, Councillor W. S. Lewis, and was organised as one of the attractions of the National Food Exhibition now running in Birmingham. After a two-hours session the Birmingham team bowed its head in defeat — but only by one point.

* * *

The "Hullo girls" from the Birmingham Telephone Exchange were praised by their Lord Mayor at the annual conference of the National Guild of Telephonists. "I have come" he said "to pay tribute to your magnificent work while we were being attacked in this city. I think the telephone service was really magnificent. We who know what you had to go through don't know how you did it."

Norwich

King Peter of Jugoslavia spent Whitsun weekend in Norfolk as the guest of Sir Thomas Cook, M.P., at Sennowe. He went to a reception by the Lord Mayor at Norwich City Hall, visited several factories and Norwich Services Club. At Castle Museum King Peter opened a collection of pictures and national costumes, presented by the Jugoslav Government, illustrating the art and history of Jugoslavia. On Sunday His Majesty was at Cromer taking part in functions connected with the opening of the local Wings week.

* * *

The restrictions on the use of the Norfolk Broads which have been in force for the past two years are to be relaxed, though the navigation of boats on tidal waters will still be subject to Admiralty instructions. While relaxation of the restrictions is welcomed this does not mean there will be any immediate resumption of yatching on the Broads. Cruisers, yachts, sailing and rowing boats that used to be seen on Norfolk's waterways have long been laid up and the shortage of labour and materials for refurbishing will not permit large-scale return to pre-war activity for some considerable time. It is suggested that some of the houseboats may be used for the accommodation of people coming to assist in fruit picking.

Portsmouth

The Wings for Victory target — £1,000,000 —was passed by nearly £200,000... Dr T. Beaton O.B.E., Medical Superintendent of St James Hospital, has affirmed that the mental health of the city has never been better in spite of many raids. There isn't a single case of "mental disease" from blitzes registered in the city.

* * *

Surgeon Commander L.S. Coulter R.N., well known in Southsea social and sporting circles, has been awarded the D.S.C.... The new president of the Rotary Club is Canon H. C. Robins, vicar of Portsea... Ensa has done it again. The most ambitious programme of music ever planned for the Royal Navy has achieved truly remarkable success. The week's music festival at the Royal Naval Barracks was a triumph of organisation and of brilliant performance. B.B.C. Symphony Orchestra and Royal Marine Band, Eastney, shared the honours and artists were drawn from all over the country. The audiences were all from the Services.

* * *

Scotland

All war fund campaigns in Scotland were beaten by Glasgow's £16,500,000 for Wings week. Works, schools, offices and other small savings organisations surpassed all previous achievements. Small savings averaged about £1 12s per head... A £6,000 memorial fund to the most famous of all Scottish fiddlers, Neil Gow, is to be raised at Dunkeld where he lived, to provide violin scholarships at the Scottish Academy of Music. Carnegie Trust is interested in the plan and has already made a contribution.

* * *

Dr Wellington Koo, Chinese Ambassador, has visited the cottage of Robert Burns at Alloway and his immortal memory was celebrated in the Chinese Embassy on January 25. There are Burns clubs in China.

* * *

An Angus landlord has planted trees on his estate but has been told that as they do not comply with the new road planning regulations which requires trees to be 25 ft. from the centre of the road they must be removed.

THE SPLINTERING DOOR

"A fighting man in the most realistic sense of the word." Lord Louis Mountbatten shakes hands with men who have distinguished themselves in action.

THE MOUNTBATTEN TOUCH

Offensive against the Japanese is foreshadowed by the appointment as Supreme Allied Commander in South-east Asia of Vice-Admiral Lord Louis Mountbatten, former Chief of Combined Operations. This Canadian article was written before his new appointment

Lord Louis Mountbatten holds one of the war's most important jobs. As head of Britain's department of Combined Operations, he works at the nerve centre of Allied strategy and, as commander of the commandos, he operates the shifting spearhead of men and machines which pave the way for execution of the military plans entrusted to him.

Most observers agree that Lord Louis is the ideal man for the job. He possesses most of the virtues Tommy Atkins admires in a fighting man. At 43, he is the youngest Service chief. His position as a member of the Royal House makes him immune to the virus of social ambition. As a sailor whose active life has been spent at sea, he neither understands nor cares a hoot for bureaucratic niceties. And what England's fighting men like most about him is his boyish enthusiasm for ideas and gadgets.

The Mountbatten touch is apparent throughout the Combined Operations setup. For instance, Lord Louis saves months, if not years, of interdepartmental

consideration by his system of dealing with admirals and generals. "What would you do" he asks, bursting in upon a typical conference, "if Jerry turned up with a trench mortar shell that had 50 per cent more range and 25 per cent more explosive power than ours?"

The generals and admirals begin to look worried. "Well, he hasn't got it" Lord Louis snaps "but we have." He slaps down specifications and test reports and usually gets an on-the-spot decision.

Combined Operations headquarters (COHQ) gives off an atmosphere of industry and efficiency, like a boy scout camp. The walls are lined with cautious posters—"These Walls Are Not Soundproof"—and with photographs from commando raids captioned "A Grand Job Because No One Talked." Young officers with their coats off and sleeves rolled up rush in and out of each other's rooms and form earnest, enthusiastic groups in the corridors. They appear to be in their 30s, following the Mountbatten axiom: "Under 30 they wouldn't be experienced enough and much over 40 they wouldn't be young enough."

Officers give the impression of being a little aghast at their own audacity in "mucking together" in defiance of traditional inter-Service

barriers and rank insignia. Lord Louis himself sets an example of hard work for his men by arriving at 9 a.m. in the small car he drives himself, and never leaving his desk until around midnight. His staff, which includes a rear-admiral, major-general, air vice-marshal and a major-general in the United States army, keeps the same hours.

The stories of Mountbatten inventiveness and general ability to get things done are innumerable. Simply to convince himself that any natural inaptitude can be overcome through diligent application, he learned to play polo by studying slow-motion films of international players in action, then practised until he had mastered each stroke. He formed a sailors' team, the Bluejackets, which learned its tactics by moving balls on a billiard table. This outfit trounced the crack Army team of the Royal Horse Guards and galloped off with the Hurlingham championship.

While in transit through the polo world, Lord Louis invented a new

"His flagship, 'Kelly', ran through a series of exploits which constitute one of the war's great stories." Here, decks awash, she staggers home across the North Sea. 'Kelly' was rebuilt but was sunk by bombing off Crete.

Continued overleaf

No. 159   Vol. 13   August 28, 1943

MESSINA PARTY
EN ROUTE

STAGE BOX FOR ITALY

Pages 3-5

As comparatively few of the Navy's landing craft could run their bows ashore on gently shelving beaches off Avola troops had to carry themselves and kit on foot through waist-deep warm sea. Sensible ones wrapped wrist-watches and valuables in Army-issued rubber containers before jumping.

INTO SICILY

Sicilian scenes as the Allies landed, conquered and organised a military government are given as an Invasion Diary in words and pictures by R.J. Gilmore, "Parade" reporter, and Bela Zola, "Parade" cameraman

July 10, 0530 hrs. Am going ashore. In the grey dawn the smoke of shellbursts fogs the beaches. A big L.C.I. (landing craft, infantry) has been knocked out on the main beach, otherwise no L.C. casualties visible. Very lights still being fired. Monitor, with a 15-inch gun, and destroyers aid Army by shelling remaining enemy strongpoints behind little town of Avola. Otherwise coastal plain and high country appear largely clear of enemy. Ops room on navigation deck, linked with battalions through crackling radio earphones, says that in spite of very late landings on wrong beaches battalions are doing well.

0800 hrs. But for demolitions by sappers all quiet ashore. Shellfire inland.

0900 hrs. Ashore in an L.C.A. (landing craft, assault) passing three different types of amphibious vehicles "driving" ashore under own steam. L.C.A.'s land you in three feet of water. Even the general and an elegantly rigged out liaison officer have to jump into the drink. Beach as busy as a country fair. From dozens of landing craft with their fronts let down trucks, carriers, quads and jeeps, previously waterproofed, bounce into four and five feet of water. With seawater gushing from driving cabs and toolboxes they roar up on to the beach in first gear. Wiremesh track leads across the soft sand and up a wadi to the "dewater-

proofing park," where slick and expert R.E.M.E. (called reemy) specialists strip adhesive tape and grease and waterproof cloth from ignition and induction systems.

Down on the beach clanking belching bulldozers splash into the sea to extract the one vehicle in 20 that stalls in the big splash. Without the bulldozers and their drivers — R.E. and R.E.M.E. — there would be chaos.

Through a loudspeaker the Navy's beachmaster harangues the tardy, abuses the odd fool and stage-manages the whole incredibly efficient show. "L.C.T. (landing craft, tank) 313, come in now. Come on. Hurry. There's ample depth. What are you waiting for ? Come on that Dodge truck in L.C.T. 198. Give her everything you've got. L.C.A. 190, get the hell out of here. Get to your proper place along the beach. Party loafing near the wire track get in the water and push that jeep. Party landing from L.C.I. 786 double off the beach and get inland. Enemy aircraft approaching from the west. Come on, double. At any moment you are liable to be dive-bombed and machine-gunned."

Stukas, the first ones, go for the ships. But the ship's balloons and flak from both sea and land keep them high. Much splash and bang but no hits... On approach of Stukas, Italian P.O.W.'s in beach cage panic. Three captive *Luftwaffe* linesmen look on with icy contempt.

Mile march in soaking boots and with leaden kit through almond, citrus and olive groves in Avola, an almost undamaged little town, poor and shabby but with some character. Cypress trees, "like black candle flames against the sun," and last century wrought iron balcony rails. Few dead in the gutters. Townspeople

simple folk, friendly and welcoming. Red-eyed British infantry comparing notes with soot-faced American paratroops dropped in error outside Avola instead of at Syracuse, 23 kilometres north (some British paratroops were dropped in the sea).

Continued overleaf

Italian woman on seeing Marines commandos commented on strapping fitness and suggested they could "take the world." Many dress like pirates.

It is soon after dawn. One of the great tank-landing ships is disgorging transport on to awkward patch of beach. Depth of water along shore varies and vehicles are having rough time as they bump from ramp into bogged sand. But R.E.'s will soon reinforce beach, and later arrivals have easier passage

LANDING AT SALERNO

To nobody did the news of the Italian surrender give greater surprise than to the troops aboard tank-landing ships in the great invasion fleet approaching the Italian coast during the moonlit night of September 8. Described by "Parade" Navy Editor, LAMBTON BURN

Wednesday evening, September 8. The main invasion of the Italian mainland was timed for 03.30 next morning, and was directed at the marram-bound beaches near the mouth of the river Tusciano, some 30 miles south of Naples.

It is a good old practice to change into clean clothing before going into action. Aboard our tank-landing ship, we were having a final shower-bath—when the unexpected news came through.

The door opened, and a steward poked his head in.

"Captain's compliments, sir, and would you go to the Bridge at once and bring your camera."

I spluttered a moment. "Tell him I'll be right up... just as soon as I can get my gear on."

Quickly as possible, I dried myself and rushed on a singlet and a pair of shorts. Then the Captain himself appeared.

"You'd better come up at once if you want a photograph of the signal" he said. "Italy has surrendered... We can't keep the signal hoisted much longer. The others have taken theirs down."

Incredulous, I rushed up on deck. Out came camera, and I photographed the hoist a dozen times and with a dozen different exposures.

Then I climbed to the Bridge to find out the details.

"International code" commented Number One. "Sensible thing to do seeing that there are merchant ships in the convoy."

Historic signal "Italy Surrenders" astonished crews of invasion craft as it was passed down the line at 7 p.m. on eve of Salerno landing.

I glanced once more at the signal before the order was given for it to be hauled down. Four flags in one hoist: three in the other. "Let's see," I said, trying to be wise: "Four flags... that's—"

"Italy" said the Captain.

"And the other three?"

"That took some time finding" he replied. "Number One didn't know where to look for the word 'surrenders'."

*

The next hours were full of speculation. The Army types aboard studied their maps and wondered just what modifications might be made to the original plan.

At eight o'clock, the news bulletin came through and we crowded round the loudspeaker to if the news of an armistice was confirmed. A in dulcet, well-fed tones, the announcer did confirm the news. We looked at one another as though we had made an even more recent discovery. And then we waved our hands and left the matter of high strategy to the generals.

Those of us who were to land in the morning went to our bunks. The others who were to take watch later stayed in their seats, reading.

But we were not long left in peace. A succession of short rings on the alarm bell brought us out on deck. Parachute-flares hung over the water some distance ahead of the convoy. There were gunflashes from ahead and from the horizon. to the north-west.

Continued overleaf

Although beribboned and magnificently attired, tactical staff of Napoli Division, captured by one British sergeant near Solarino, was scruffy and unshaven. Below is their G.O.C., Maj.-Gen. Julius Caesar Gotti-Porcinari.

taking prisoner of his soldier son "He didn't fire a shot. He was just home on leave for a few days. You have no right at all to make him a P.O.W."

No transport yet for the Press and it is impossible to trail along with the battalions. They are doing well. In spite of sticky landings casualties were low. *Luftwaffe* active over the beach. Italian P.O.W. harmlessly shot in the tail by German straffers. First night in Axis Europe spent on bank of small stream in cool lemon grove. No mosquitoes. Army's new 48-hours' invasion rations issued to each man are excellent. Biscuits, first quality chocolate and barley sugar. Cheese. Dripping. Tea, sugar and milk powder all in one container. And, the highlight, chemical cookers containing some phosphorus compound, good for cooking two mess-tins of tea. Also some bully.

July 11. Fleeting visit to Syracuse, hometown of Archimedes, taken yesterday by another Div. Ancient city, mixture of baroque and modern Fascist design, the latter disappointing. In every street large-scale destruction. Italian dead still unburied in suburban streets. Citizens say Friday night was hell.

Another Div. take Noto, south of Avola. Italian military said to have fled, significantly day before invasion after looting shops. Police galloped off on horseback.

Inscription written in blood on a wall in Florida above two dead Italian soldiers : "Here are the remains of two— —." Probably they had been up to white flag or red cross trickery. An older, neater inscription: "Great Britain has finally felt the fangs of the Roman wolf."

July 13. An R.T.R. sergeant captured near Solarino this morning the tac staff of Napoli Div., believed to be the Italians' only proper field div in Sicily. Circumstances not yet known. But Maj.-Gen. Julius Caesar Gotti-Porcinari, his Chief of Staff, and his C.R.A. are sitting beneath a nearby olive tree. All red-eyed and with a day's growth. Beribboned, overdressed and paunchy. While waiting there a small man in a beret enters the olive grove from the road. He pauses a moment while he studies the scruffy group and then walks up to an interpreter. It is Gen. Montgomery. "Ask them what Germans

Americans, husky, amiable, game-looking, say that on the way down they realised they had been dropped at the wrong place. But they immediately set out to shoot-up and terrorise Avola. They were immensely relieved to be met in town later by seaborne British infantry. Doubtful who really took Avola.

Told The Charwoman

Italian-speaking civil affairs officer working for new AMGOT (Allied Military Government of Occupied Territories) hikes from beach to town with bundle of proclamations, goes to frugally furnished office of *podesta* and announces to the charwoman that he is the new town boss. The proper *podesta* has fled to the hills. First enemy caller is a middle-aged man who protests against the

Roman Catholic priests at Syracuse waterfront seek contact with Italian prisoners of war. Throughout Sicilian countryside priest and nun are much in evidence. They comfort wounded, aid the sick.

Ratings are British: steel helmets, lease-lend.

R.A. men in vineyard opposite tobacco factory—a heavily defended German strongpoint near Battipaglia—pick, and eat, grapes during off duty period

German prisoner said he was 19, looked more like 15.

BETWEEN TWO ARMIES

Parade photographer Bela Zola took pictures of the Army and R.A.F. fighting in the Salerno area, then—with an A.F.P.U. captain—decided to go southward on a visit to the Eighth Army. They covered nearly 200 miles, of which about half was absolutely free of any troops. The trip, partly along the coast and partly inland, took them through beautiful country where vineyards, fruit trees and pastures made sharp contrast with memories of last year's deserts. Everywhere the Italians had welcoming smiles; once a little girl came forward with a bunch of flowers for them.

From a starting point near Battipaglia they drove to the coast at Paestum, found an American field unit having lunch in the ruins of the doric Temple of Neptune; through Antico, stopping to ask an Italian soldier if the way to the next village were clear of Germans, and on to Agropoli where an Italian major pointed out on the map detours they would have to make to avoid blown up bridges. At

the little seaside town of S. Maria di Castellabate children ran toward their jeep, which had a "new toy" interest as it was apparently the first they had seen; but when they sat down to lunch at a restaurant a good portion of the adult population gathered to watch them. "I was glad of my previous training in eating spaghetti, so I didn't cut too bad a figure in front of 'professionals'" Zola records. Beyond Castellabate they turned inland, to Vallo di Lucania, passing a 5,600-foot peak and meeting an advanced Eighth Army recce party; and so came to Nicastro, not long in Allied hands but with life already returned to normal, civilians in their Sunday best, women going to market, soldiers playing with Italian children.

On the way back, they stayed the night in Torre Orsaia, a little village near Sapri. The barber who shaved Zola next morning has a son, a prisoner of war in America, from whom he receives enthusiastic letters. "I wish you were here with me" one letter said.

Covering road to tobacco factory. Hole in the shield was made by German tank before it was knocked out.

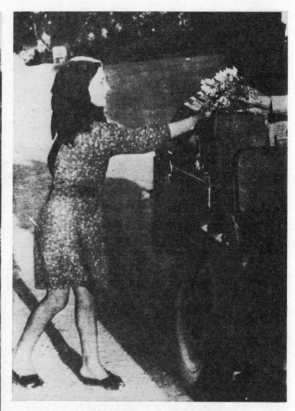

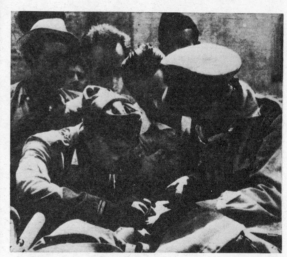

Early in their journey along the coast Zola and his companion reached Paestum, found men of an American medical field unit lunching, reading papers in Temple of Neptune.

An Italian major at Agropoli pointed out, with the aid of a map, route to be followed to avoid bridges which had been blown up.

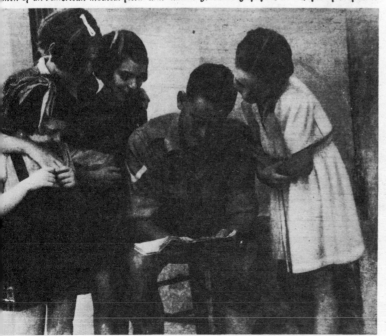

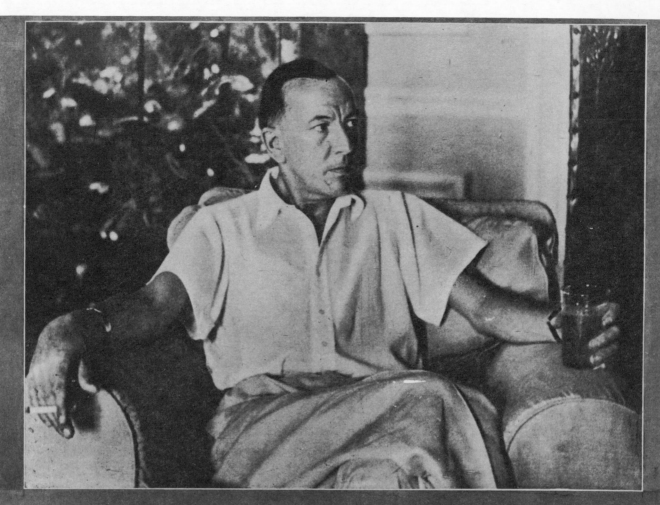

I'VE JUST COME OUT FROM ENGLAND

By NOEL COWARD

I've just come out from England, and I feel
Foolishly empty-handed, for I bring
Nothing to you but words. But even so,
Even mere words can now and then reveal
A little truth. I know, or think I know,
If only I had had the chance to go
To all your homes and talk to all your mothers,
Wives and sweethearts, sisters, fathers, brothers,
What they'd have said and wanted me to say.
Those messages, unspoken, wouldn't ring
With sentimental pride, they'd be restrained.
We British hate to give ourselves away,
All our traditions having firmly trained
Our minds to shun emotional display.
Our people always under-state with such
Determined nonchalance, whether it's praise
Or blame, anger or joy or woe,
However moved they are, or may have been,
They'll very very seldom tell you so.
But still, beneath the crust we feel as much,
If not a great deal more than those who sob
And weep and laugh too easily. My job,
Being a writer, is to read between
The lines that others write; to look behind
The words they string together and to find
The right translation, the right paraphrase
Of what they feel rather than what they say.
What they would say, those patient people who
So very lovingly belong to you,
Would be extremely simple, almost off-hand:
'Give Jack my love' 'Tell Bert to come home soon'
'Tell Fred Aunt Nora's gone, he'll understand'
'Tell Jimmy everybody's doing fine'.
'Give George our love and tell him Stan's had leave

And Elsie's doing war-work. nine till nine'
'Tell Billy that last Sunday afternoon
We saw a newsreel and we recognised
Him on a tank—we weren't half surprised!'
It wouldn't take a genius to perceive
What lies behind those ordinary phrases
But on my own responsibility
I'd like to tell you what I know to be
Deep in the hearts of all of us in Britain.
The war's been long, it's had its tragic phases,
Its black defeats, its violent ups and downs,
But now, in all the villages and towns
That lie between Land's End and John o'Groats,
Hope is restored, new faith in victory,
New faith in more than victory, new pride
In something that deep down we always knew,
Thus, at long last, through you and all you've done,
We have been proved again. Much will be written
In future years. Historians will spew
Long treatises on your triumphant story,
They'll rightly praise your gallantry and glory
And probably embarrass you a lot.
They'll make exhaustive military notes,
Argue each battle fought, from every side,
But maybe they'll forget to say the one
Important thing. Four simple words are not
Unlikely, midst so much, to get mislaid.
For once I feel I need not be afraid
Of being sentimental. I can say
What those at home, who miss you and have such
Deep pride in you, would wish me to convey,
In four short words—note the true English touch—
The words are simply: 'Thank you very much.'

Mr Noel Coward is now visiting the Middle East to collect material for broadcasts.

R.A.F. ARTIST

"HE HAS A PLAN TO SINK SHIPPING AT TOBRUK SIR"

Artist who did these pictures is Flight-Lieut. A. B. Read, R.A.F. Intelligence Officer. His murals brighten R.A.F. desert messes. His caricatures frighten R.A.F. desert heroes. Read was Guards officer in last war, spent five years at Royal College of Art under Rothenstein, then started a commercial art studio in the Strand doing interior decoration and industrial design. He hopes to start organisation for decorating all messes in the Middle East.

At end of his stay in Cairo on way to Moscow, Mr Anthony Eden (Britain's Foreign Secretary) chats at aerodrome to Mr R.G. Casey (Minister of State Resident in the Middle East) and Gen. Sir Hastings Ismay (Chief of Staff to the Minister of Defence). Gen. Ismay went to Russia with Mr Eden.

EN ROUTE TO MOSCOW

The morning Mr Eden left Cairo, Mr Cordell Hull, 72-years-old U.S. Secretary of State — also bound for Moscow conference of Foreign Ministers—landed at an airport near Cairo, stayed one day.

On their way to Moscow for the three-power conference, Mr Anthony Eden, Britain's Secretary of State for Foreign Affairs, and Mr Cordell Hull, U.S. Secretary of State, stopped for a short time in Cairo. Mr Eden remained four days, Mr Cordell Hull only one. They did not meet, as Mr Hull's plane arrived when Mr Eden was about to take off.

Mr Eden was received in audience by King Farouk at Abdine Palace and lunched with Mustapha Nahas Pasha, the Egyptian Premier, at the house of Mr Terence Shone, the British Minister; he was the guest of Mr R.G. Casey, Minister of State Resident in the Middle East, during his stay in Cairo.

Between his official engagements Mr Eden worked with members of his staff at the British Embassy, Cairo. He met many of the leading American civil and military officials in the Cairo area and was the guest of Mr Alexander Kirk, American Minister to Egypt, at dinner one evening.

King George of Greece and King Peter of Jugoslavia received Mr Eden and he had talks with the Greek and Jugoslav Prime Ministers. A whole day was spent visiting British Forces in the Cairo area with Gen. Sir Henry Maitland Wilson, Commander-in-Chief, Middle East.

During the afternoon of his one-day visit, Mr Cordell Hull signed the visitors' book at Abdine Palace and went to the Pyramids. He dined informally at the house of the American Minister to Egypt with whom he stayed in Cairo.

See overleaf

Mr Eden, visiting British Forces in the Cairo area, hears Gen. Sir Henry Maitland Wilson, C.-in-C. Middle East, explain a point of interest. Mr Eden's brief tour included both Army and R.A.F. units.

Mr Eden squashes his hat under his arm, holds position with his elbow and so frees both hand

DIPLOMATIC EVENT NO. 1

Problems before the Foreign Ministers of Great Britain, the United States and the U.S.S.R. at their Moscow conference, and the significance of the meeting are explained in a leading article in "The Times" from which these extracts are taken

The third member of the conference—M. Molotov, Soviet Commissar for Foreign Affairs—met Mr Hull and Mr Eden at the Kremlin on Tuesday.

"The three-power conference of Foreign Ministers which assembles this week in Moscow is the most significant diplomatic event in the history of the war. That no such meeting should have taken place until Russia had been for more than two years, and the United States for nearly two years, in the war, suggests the extent of the delay in establishing adequate inter-Allied machinery of consultation. That the meeting has at length been arranged, is a matter for the warmest congratulation and a promise of better things to come.

"Of the three great powers who provide the major part of the striking force of the United Nations, Russia alone has seen, and still sees, vast expanses of her home territory exposed to all the horrors of battle, pillage and ruthless and deliberate devastation. It was therefore appropriate that Moscow should be the meeting-place of the first regular three-power conference, and it is auspicious that it should meet at a moment when Russia's liberating offensive is moving toward fresh triumphs.

"Mr Eden, who will be meeting M. Molotov for the first time since the signature of the Anglo-Soviet treaty in London, has laboured patiently to overcome every practical obstacle to the conference, and no one is entitled to feel greater satisfaction that these efforts have been rewarded with success. But a special tribute should be paid to the indomitable energy and devotion of Mr Cordell Hull, who in spite of his 72 years and long-standing disinclination for foreign travel—only twice before, during his long tenure of office, had he left the shores of North America on an official mission—has made the long and exacting journey by air in order to attend the conference with Mr Eden and M. Molotov. No clearer proof could have been furnished of the exceptional importance attached to the occasion by the American Government and by its Secretary of State, or of their determination to establish the future of Russian-American cooperation on the friendliest and most secure foundations.

"The primary object of any conference, as the Russian semi-official Press has been quick to point out, must be to hasten by every possible means the downfall of the principal enemy of the United Nations, and to make their victory prompt and complete; and Marshal Stalin and M. Molotov will doubtless impress once more on their visitors the urgent need for intensifying the force and extending the scope of the Allied offensives in Europe. These issues are beyond doubt under the constant attention of the military authorities of the three powers. But even if the decisions of a conference of Foreign Ministers are likely to be taken in the sphere of politics rather than of strategy, this does not

With Germans driven out or captured, Ajaccio citizens relax at pavement cafés. Atmosphere of town has instant appeal for sight-seeing Service men.

CORSICA COMES BACK

In this famous French island, liberated after more than two years, 'Parade' Observer J. MURRAY SMITH found that "necessity is the mother of many evils"

Ajaccio, Corsica.

As an example of the triple entente in North Africa, present edition, it could scarcely have been bettered. We were to have been flown by an American general, no less; but at the last moment he was detained and very kindly sent his Lieutenant, "Mac," instead. We took off in the comfortable little Cessna (UC 78), which is used by the U.S.A.A.F., incidentally, as an advanced trainer for bomber pilots, in company with a Harvard flown by a French *commandant* whose passenger was an engineer Wing Commander.

It was fun flying through the mountains until our electrical system went unserviceable. Then some of the important needles on the instrument panel stopped quivering and died, and we spent some little time in inspecting fuses and optimistically tweaking wires. Such inexpert efforts clearly unavailing we wound down the undercarriage laboriously by hand for Mac to put the Cessna on the deck at our refuelling point

without flaps at a speed that used up a runway built for bombers.

The R.A.F. ground crew promptly traced the trouble, changed the batteries and sent us off after lunch on a course from Africa that brought us over the coast of Sardinia in less than an hour. The island was covered in cloud, most of it full of mountain, so we followed the Harvard in a game of hide-and-seek until we came out into bright sunshine over Corsica.

Truth to tell, one had expected a rocky coastline and a barren interior. At least that is what the guide books lead one to expect, though guide books are notoriously uninspired. With some drab experience of Sicily we were unprepared for the warm colours of this other island, for the gay patchwork of fields and orchards in the foothills and the paintbox farmhouses contrasting with the majestic mountains beyond.

It had been raining before we passed over Ajaccio Bay but the sky was repentant in raiment of old lace

and mother of pearl. Breath-taking were the colours of the rainbow which hung from the still sullen mountains and threw its myriad reflections into the sea. Livid as a scar was the pure white beach, and gleaming, too, embracing the ocean in its perfect curve.

There is no runway at our destination but we land on a field as smooth as a lawn to find ourselves the centre of interest for the strangest possible crowd. At first there appears to be a bunch of American pilots but these, in fact, are members of French fighter squadrons based here who wear American drill with their own brevets and badges of rank. They fly Spitfires in place of their old Dewoitine 520's, and to such good effect—as we shall

relate—that while we were there an American colonel brought them the congratulations of Gen. Spaatz and Air Marshal Sir Hugh Pugh Lloyd.

Also in the crowd we observe some quite villainous-looking characters armed with sub-machine-guns. These, we learn, are some of the patriots who helped to drive the Germans out and have now taken on the duties of aerodrome guards.

From the aerodrome to Ajaccio we drove between hedgerows gay with autumn flowers and through village streets where pretty girls smile shyly and then decide to wave. Ajaccio itself is any French provincial town with its *Grande Place*—in this case, inevitably, *Place Napoléon*—its municipal casino, its sidewalk

Peasants who took up arms to help drive out the Germans, these patriots led regular troops through mountains, fought with ferocity. Sten and other guns were supplied by the British from submarines.

More friendly Anglo-French cooperation; R.A.F. corps craft unit. On this camp site some guards were Italian;

"V" sign, with Cross of Lorraine — badge of Fighting French — is seen everywhere.

War or peace, French women are always interested in personal attractiveness. Perfume seller does brisk trade in scents distilled from island's flowers.

cafés, its flat-faced yet rambling buildings and roofs of red tiles.

At this point a word of advice to Britishers visiting Corsica might not be out of place. Let us warn you then, if you would avoid embarrassment, to establish your identity quickly. On one or two occasions we were taken aback, when entering shops and other establishments, to find ourselves confronted by a stout matron with arms akimbo roaring "*Finito! Finito!*" in the sternest style. Indeed, we were actually fortunate to escape injury when about to cross a threshold, for *la patronne* reached the door before us and slammed it in our faces.

Then again, we entered the *Banque de France* with the simple object of exchanging a few pounds sterling into francs; but when our turn came the cashier lost all apparent interest in his occupation and actually strolled away from the little window to light a cigarette.

Only after such unhappy incidents did it become apparent that the good Corsicans were confusing our uniform with that of the Italians. Therefore, we advise, announce your arrival in a rapid sentence of execrable French, when faces will light up and voices will cry, "*Voilà, des Anglais!*"

It would not be true to say that the Italians are entirely unpopular, especially in the rural districts. Good farm workers, they have helped to get in the harvest and have made themselves useful in other ways. Unfortunately from the Corsican point of view they have been much too successful with some of the young girls and this has led to drastic action. No blood has been shed, but young women known to be partial to the company of Italians have had their hair cut off by patriots, in some cases even by their own brothers.

For the most part, though, the Italians here are inoffensive and anxious to be as helpful as possible to the Allies. Thus, one R.A.F. unit we visited actually had an Italian guard on duty; and Italians are digging air raid shelters in some towns. Others are driving their own trucks carrying supplies about the island.

One hateful legacy from the enemy occupation of Corsica is the black market which affects every commodity. The peasants will not part with their produce in the open market since everything they require from the towns is marked up to ruinous figures. And the swarms of young men who have been rendered idle by the war have existed largely by illicit trading.

The consequence is that an ordinary meal in a restaurant costs anything between one pound and two pounds sterling. We were present in a café-dancing one evening—in which the music was provided by a wheezy accordion and an off-tune piano—when a British naval officer entered and walked to the bar. He was greeted by some Frenchmen who evidently knew him by sight and after a few moments conversation he ordered a round of drinks. We know about all this because we were included in the party.

The "drinks" were set before us, thimble-sized glasses of some light-coloured fluid which our outraged palates instantly recognised as raw *eau-de-vie*. This vile stuff, called cognac, cost our naval friend 740 francs, with the franc at 200 to the pound sterling.

Still, these are troubles which may quickly pass. Necessity is the mother of many evils. Control of prices and the mobilisation of the young men—who are anxious enough to be mobilised—will have their effect.

One heartening aspect of this investigation is the knowledge that the French fighter squadrons based on the island have done magnificent work. Of ten Me 323's which they encountered eight were shot down; and the score was exactly the same, for the loss of one Spitfire, when Ju 88's came over to attack shipping. Only yesterday two French fighters met a Ju 88 some 60 miles off the east and shot it into the sea, each using only 50 rounds of ammunition. Two members of the German crew baled out and the bomber exploded when it hit the sea. For the rest of the day Italian float-'planes were out in an endeavour to locate the Germans in the sea. They went out again before dawn today. As Captain Lamaison said in the mess. "They are the enemy, you know, but we are fliers, too. I hope we find them."

Next week: "Signpost to France."

At the Teheran conference. Marshal Stalin, President Roosevelt and Mr Churchill with some of the other delegates and advisers. Behind Marshal Stalin is M. Molotov; behind President Roosevelt is Section Officer Oliver, Mr Churchill's daughter. Beside her is Anthony Eden, the Foreign Secretary.

SHAPING A NEW WORLD

Three men who between them control the greatest concentration of military power in world history met at Teheran to plan the final three-way assault on Germany and to shape a post-war world in which peace will endure for many generations. Here Robert Stephens describes the work of the Conference

The meeting the world has been waiting for took place on a fresh autumn afternoon in a modest brick building surrounded by a tranquil walled garden with an ornamental pool, weeping willows and rose-gardens such as the painters of Persia's miniatures have made famous.

In this peaceful setting, three men who between them control the greatest concentration of military power in world history met for the first time to perfect plans for the coordinated use of some 25,000,000 troops, scores of thousands of aircraft and thousands of ships of war. They were planning the final three-way assault on Germany and the establishment of an unshakeable basis for a just and prosperous world peace.

The first meeting between Marshal Stalin, President Roosevelt and Mr Churchill took place at 4.30 on Sunday afternoon, November 28, in the Soviet embassy at the Persian

capital of Teheran. Marshal Stalin had previously had a private talk lasting more than an hour with President Roosevelt and the famous trio was then completed by the arrival of Mr Churchill. Accompanied by their diplomatic and military advisers, the three statesmen conferred for three hours that afternoon and on the two following afternoons. By the end of the third meeting complete agreement had been reached on questions of military strategy.

The conference reached a climax on the fourth day when the big three accompanied by their diplomatic advisers, Mr Eden, Mr Molotov, Mr Harry Hopkins, Mr Harriman and Mr Winant, met for a marathon session to hammer out post-war problems. This meeting began after lunch, continued right through the afternoon and through dinner until ten thirty in the evening. Those eight hours during which the terms

of the communique were fixed can be counted as one of the most momentous periods in modern history.

The Teheran meeting was a direct continuation of the Moscow conference and also of the Pacific conference in Cairo. In Moscow, detailed examination of European problems and of points of difference between the western democracies and the Soviet Union cleared the way for the political thinking on a world scale which was the pre-occupation of the three great powers at Teheran. The ground was further cleared by the results of the Cairo conference which established the basis of a definite post-war policy in the Far East.

In Teheran, the threads were drawn together and the pattern of the post-war world, as designed by the three nations which will be left as the most important military powers, emerged in more complete form.

What sort of post-war world did the Big Three plan? In the terms of their joint communiqué, it will be a world in which peace will endure for many generations. The determination of Britain, the United States and Russia to work together will ensure that. The peace is to be a peace which "will command the goodwill of the overwhelming mass of the peoples of the world." There will be a "world family of democratic nations," freed from tyranny and slavery, oppression and intolerance. It will not be a Tri-Partite Empire in which smaller nations will be helpless appendages, for, say Roosevelt, Stalin and Churchill, "We shall seek the cooperation and the active participation of all nations, large and small, whose peoples in heart and mind are dedicated, as are our own peoples, to the elimination of tyranny and slavery, oppression and intolerance."

Continued overleaf

1944

Allied landings at Anzio

Soviet forces recapture Leningrad

British forces halt Japanese offensive in Arakan (Burma)

Soviet forces recapture Odessa

Capture of Rome

D-Day

First flying bomb lands in Southern England

Soviet forces recapture Minsk

Assassination attempt on Hitler

Allied landings on South coast of France

Liberation of Paris

Arnhem

Allied landings in Greece

Second Battle of the Philippines

RAF sink the *Tirpitz* in Tromso Fjord

Battle of the Bulge

Crimea Landing

LONDON, Tues.—The German news agency states that Russians landed troops yesterday on the northern part of the Kerch Peninsula in the Crimea. No confirmation of this report has been received as yet from Moscow.

where Rovno and Sarny—35 miles across the frontier—now face a double threat through the fall of Brezno and Lyudvipol.

German units west of the Dnieper are now in a still more perilous position. Soviet troops are only 10 miles south-east of the key town of Vinnitsa, which is threatened from the flank.

New gains on this front have also narrowed still further the 30-mile "funnel" of German-held territory stretching to the bank of the Dnieper. This "funnel" is their only hope of escape.—Reuter.

5th ARMY TIGHTEN GRIP ON CASSINO

Allied HQ, North Africa, Tuesday.—The Fifth Army, by capturing three more heights, are within four miles of Cassino, 75 miles SE of Rome. Prisoners say the German High Command is preparing for its fall, but they have been instructed to hold on until all hope has gone.

Flying Fortresses by day followed by night bombers attacked Sofia, the Bulgarian capital. Rail yards there are the hub of German supply system in SE Europe. They were heavily damaged in previous raids.

Allied naval forces have sunk three schooners in the Adriatic.

DOVER GUNS IN FIERCE DUEL

LONDON, Tues.—Big guns were in action over the Straits of Dover again last night from 9-57 until 11.13 guns on the south coast opened fire on German shipping in the straits.

Bombardment was one of the fiercest for some time with many guns on both sides of the channel engaged.

TITO STRIKES

LONDON, Tues.—Yugoslav partisans have inflicted heavy defeat on German forces along the Serbo-Bosnian border, according to today's communique from Tito's HQ.

In Croatia a German attempt to thrust forward into liberated territory was frustrated in fighting at Ogulin on the Fiume-Zagreb railway. Two hundred and fifty Germans were killed or wounded in this action.

PIPES FOR BLIGHTY

Another 300,000 pipes from Malta and North Africa are being sent to Britain to relieve the great shortage.

ALICE DELYSIA at the height of her fame.

DELYSIA WEDS

LONDON, Tues.—Alice Delysia, stage favourite of the mud-stained warriors of Flanders in the last war who has just returned after two-and-a-half years singing to their sons in the Middle East, was married at Caxton Hall Register Office today to Commander Rene Bernard, of the Fighting French Navy.

Delysia, who is 53, wore the navy blue Fighting French uniform of E.N.S.A. Only a few friends and relatives attended the wedding, time and place of which were secret.

NAVY HITS HARD AT JAPS

ALLIED HEADQUARTERS, SOUTH-WEST PACIFIC, Tues.—Allied naval units have hit hard at the Japanese in the past 24 hours.

Racing among the Jap barges in the Saidor area of New Guinea, light naval forces have sent seven crowded with troops and supplies to the bottom.

At Gali, 11 miles to the southeast of Saidor, destroyers opened up at night on the Japanese barge base and bivouac area. Other warships bombarded targets in the Solomons.

Liberators made a round trip of 2 000 miles to bomb Endari in the Celebes. Six Japanese fighters were destroyed and 4 probably destroyed for the loss of one Allied bomber.—Reuter.

MARINES TAKE ANOTHER JAP BASE

ALLIED HQ, New Guinea, Fri.—U.S. Marines supported by Allied planes have captured Natamo, former Japanese barge base in north-western New Britain, says the official report today.

Since the beginning of this month, Allied air forces in the S. W. Pacific have shot down 463 Jap aircraft, probably destroyed 109, and sunk 23 ocean-going Japanese ships.

WHAT TO PAY FOR DRINKS
—Official

NEW DELHI, Fri.—Maximum prices for wines and spirits, both imported and locally manufactured, were fixed today under the Profiteering Prevention Ordinance

Prices of foreign gins, brandies, wines and vermouths per quart bottle are: Gin (Cyprus) Rs. 19-8, all others Rs. 17-8; brandies (Cyprus) Rs. 19-8, others Rs. 18-8; wines (Cyprus) Rs. 11, others Rs. 10; vermouth (Cyprus) Rs. 11, others Rs. 9.

Australian beers are to be charged Rs. 2, South American Rs. 3 and American Rs. 3-12 per quart bottle.

BERLIN HIT AGAIN

LONDON, Tues.—Mosquitos bombed Berlin and Western Germany last night. Military objectives in Northern France were attacked by small formations of Typhoon bombers and Mosquitos escorted by Spitfires. Good results were observed. One Junkers 88 was shot down. Four Allied fighter-bombers are missing.

STILL MORE GERMANS

There were 42,000 more births in Germany in the first three-quarters of 1943 than in the corresponding period of 1942, says the German news agency.

This is striking contrast to first four years of war when 223,000 fewer children were born each year than in 1939.

DOCTORS SEE MUSSO

GENEVA, Fri.—An unconfirmed report from the Chiasso correspondent of La Suisse says that Mussolini's health is worse. He is said to have moved from his Lake Garda villa to Villa D'este near Como, where he has been visited by several specialists.

They have advised against an operation owing to his general condition.

NOW'S THE TIME

French people living in the coastal regions of the Mediterranean were advised yesterday by Vichy radio to leave for "safer areas." Warning added: "Now is the time, when conditions are comparatively peaceful."

Arakan Epic: The first full story

LAND-AIR TEAM SMASHED JAP OFFENSIVE

d Morning . . .

Supreme Allied Commander ks:

DER OF THE DAY

e Fourteenth Army, the tern Air Command, and the akan Naval coastal forces.

have come victoriously ough your first battle since formation of the Fourteenth my and the 'Eastern Air mmand.

have given the Japanese a ck they will remember.

are learning that, just as rs cannot be won by sudden acherous assaults, so too ttles are not decided by sur- se attacks.

e weeks ago the enemy sent large and formidable force rough the jungles to cut your es of communication and ack you in the rear.

launched a major offensive the Arakan in the hope of feating you and sweeping on to India.

have met the onslaught with urage, confidence and resolu- on.

y of you were cut off and circled, dependent on supplies opped from aeroplanes. But ery one stood firm, inspired d strengthened by the know- dge that powerful support was hand from land, sea and air.

, after bitter fighting in the ngles and in the skies, the apanese attack has been mashed.

enemy forces which infil- ated into your rear have been estroyed or scattered. The reatened passes are clear, the oads are open.

u have gained a complete vic- ory.

ir splendid spirit was clear to ne when I visited you recently.

w that spirit, that tenacity, hat courage, have been dem on- strated to the enemy and to the world.

alute you.

Lord Louis Mountbatten, Supreme Allied commander.

The story of the Battle of the Arakan, told in the world's press today, reveals that the Japs threw in a major land force, and virtually their entire air strength in this theatre, in an effort to destroy the Fourteenth Army.

It tells, too, a story of brilliant supply equal to that of the Russians or Germans at their most effective. For three weeks, the 7th Indian Division, all their lines of communication by land severed by the infiltrating Japs, were fed, munitioned, and had their tanks fuelled, by Dakotas of the Troops' Carrier Command despite the all-out effort of the enemy's air force.

In three weeks the Dakotas dropped 1,500 tons of supplies. Flying in daylight with escorts of Spitfires, Hurricanes and Beau- fighters, they came in at zero height to ensure that the supplies did not miss the trapped forces.

On land, the men of the Four- teenth reached heights of endur- ance, gallantry and fighting craft hardly matched in British fight- ing history.

The Jap High Command com- missioned Colonel Tanabashi, with a force of between 7,000 and 8,000 men, to seize the Ngakye- dauk Pass, through which all our forces east of the Mayu Range were supplied, and then, in a series of co-ordinated attacks, to "destroy the enemy."

Grimly Held

In the opening stages of the battle, the Japs, following their plan with accustomed boldness and ruthlessness, met a large measure of success.

They took the Pass, isolating the 7th Div., and cut the Bawli Bazar-Maungdaw road. They launched their fiercest assaults on the front and rear of the 7th. But everywhere our men held grimly to their positions. In front the enemy bore down time after time to be hurled back with ever- mounting casualties.

His attacks on the rear met, not "soft" administrative de- tails, but grimly-held defensive boxes. Here and there he broke in. Everywhere he was counter- attacked by gunners, clerks, signallers and cooks—and driven off with bayonet and grenade. Four Jap battalions took part in these attacks on the rear. In this sector alone several hundred of them died.

1,000 Japs Died

Total Jap casualties are esti- mated at 1,000 dead, 2,000 wound- ed. Our own are said to be "immeasurably lighter." Our dead are reported at about a third of the Japs'—something over 300.

The Japs never succeeded in stopping the flow of our traffic along the Chittagong highway, al- though raiding parties again and again brought the road under fire and managed to demolish one bridge. This was quickly repair- ed.

The headquarters of the Divi- sion were overrun. Staff officers and clerks joined with the infan- try in confused hand-to-hand fighting.

General Messervy and his staff fought their way out and slipped through the Japanese screen by wading shoulder deep down river bed.

Hour after hour this desperate game of hide-and-seek went on until the party reached safety inside another British perimeter. Here, General Messervy re- organized his headquarters.

While fighting for divisional HQ was going on, the third Jap group crossed the Mayu range and attacked supply dumps and bridges on the Chittagong- Maungdaw road. This had little more than nuisance value.

Far more serious was the infil- tration into the eastern end of the Ngakyedauk. With Jap sni- pers, machine-gun and mortar crews looking down on the track, both from north and south, it meant that the only supply route for our forces on the east side of the range was closed.

So far, Jap plans had prosper- ed. By smashing the division headquarters administration and supply lines, Col. Tanabashi evi- dently reckoned on a disorganiz- ed mob squeezing their way as best they could to the sea through the enfiladed Ngak- kyedauk Pass, while the other section of his forces, having cut the supply lines of our troops on the west side of the range, would have helped him to hem in the whole of our Arakan forces.

Hedgehog Defence

Our trapped army, by Jap reckoning, would then have only two alternatives—surrender or evacuation by sea.

This plan was frustrated by the refusal of the Fourteenth Army to yield ground. The Japanese faced not a retreating and vulnerable rabble, but a hedgehog of tanks and infantry against which they battered themselves to a stand- still.

In the meantime, while our "box" positions remained firm, fresh British troops drove down from the north and the tables began to be turned on the Japa- nese.

Split up into groups, they found themselves in the predicament in which they had tried to place the 7th Indian Division—cut off from their lines of communication.

But not for them was the ad- vantage of a continuous flow of airborne supplies. Steel rings of British and Indian troops were forged around their pockets of resistance and the Japanese within them were exterminated, me- thodically and ruthlessly.

All this time a passage was being slowly forced through the Ngakyedauk Pass. Point 1070, a height overlooking the eastern exit, proved the greatest obstacle. Surrounded as they were, the badly-shaken Japs held on grimly until they were finally dislodged after severe fighting on 21 Feb. There remained one command- ing feature, Point 1010, and when this was captured the next day it was possible for traffic to pass for

Continued in Back Page, col. 1

Maj.-Gen. Messervy, Com- mander 7th Indian Div.

Maj.-Gen. H. R. Briggs, Com- mander 5th Indian Div.

ARAKAN JAPS' HEAVY LOSSES

NEW DELHI, Mon.—The Japs made local counter-attacks on both sides of the Mayu range yesterday. These were unsuccess- ful and the cost to the enemy was considerable, says to-day's SEAC communique.

West Africans inflicted heavy casualties in a clash east of Kaladan village.

South of the Imphal plain enemy pressure increased along the road from Tiddim. In the foothills north-east of the plain, they suffered further losses.

Small parties of the enemy have been contacted by our troops south of the track leading west from Bishenpore on the Imphal- Tiddim road. Casualties were inflicted.

Jap pressure in the Kohima area was maintained yesterday, but all parties which penetrated our defences were eliminated. Fifty dead were counted and pri- soners captured.

Long-range fighters, in daylight on Saturday struck at commu- nications in Siam. Chengmai railway station was one of the targets. One enemy aircraft was destroyed in the air.

Medium bombers last night at- tacked Rangoon docks. Fires and explosions in the target area were seen 60 miles away. From all operations 2 Allied aircraft are missing.—API.

SEAC

THE DAILY NEWSPAPER OF
SOUTH EAST ASIA COMMAND

No. 48   One Anna
SATURDAY, 26 FEBRUARY, 1944
Printed by Courtesy of
THE STATESMAN in Calcutta

RAF FOLLOW FIRES LIT BY U.S. PLANES

LONDON, Fri.—Schweinfurt in north-west Germany and Steyr in Austria, already blazing as the result of heavy Allied daylight attacks yesterday, were again pounded last night—this time by the RAF.

Bomber Command made over 1,000 sorties during the night, and Schweinfurt, was hit by two waves of attackers. The first bomber force went out from Britain's east coast and took three-quarters of an hour to pass. The second swept out over south-east England in a stream lasting 40 minutes.

GERMANS QUIT VITEBSK

LONDON, Fri.—The German News Agency today reported that the Germans have withdrawn from Vitebsk, bastion of the northern sector of their White Russia defence line. The Russians have not yet announced the fall of Vitebsk.

Zhlobin, German base at the southern end of this sector, is gravely threatened.

A month ago Hugo Morero, who reported the Tunisian, Sicilian and southern Italian campaigns for the German radio, told Germany:

"Vitebsk is one of the vital keypoints which hold the German eastern front together. If the enemy succeeds in breaking through at Vitebsk, he will be in a position to roll up the whole of the German front in the north.

"Then the entire hinterland of northern Poland, Lithuania and Latvia up to Riga would be at the enemy's mercy."

Drive On Bobruisk

General Rokossovsky's armies, having stormed Rogachev, are pushing rapidly along the great motor highway to Bobruisk, less than 25 miles ahead of the advanced Russian columns. One unit alone claims to have killed 4,000 Germans in the battle.

Bobruisk, the scene of the first great armoured battle of the Russo-German war, in August 1941, is the Germans' last stop before Minsk, capital of White Russia.

To the north, the enemy is struggling hard but unsuccessfully to check General Govorov's massive drive on Pskov, gateway to the Baltic Republics.

On other sectors of the front, today's Moscow communique records only reconnaissance activity and artillery duels. Eighteen German planes and 29 tanks were destroyed yesterday.

Finns Ready For Peace

LONDON, Fri.—Finnish radio today quoted a statement by Finance Minister Vaino Tanner denying that he had opposed talk of peace with Russia.

"If anyone wants peace," he said, "I am that man. But Finland cannot accept any conditions. If terms are unacceptable, we will fight on with clenched teeth. If terms are acceptable, we will accept them immediately."—Reuter.

"ALEXANDER KNOWS"

WESTMINSTER, Fri.—Viscount Cranborne, Government spokesman in the Lords, said yesterday that Allied commanders on the spot in Anzio never took a lighthearted view of the prospects ahead. They were clearly satisfied that a reckless rush forward to cut the enemy communication line—or even to Rome.

Wellington bombers crossed the Alps from southern Italy to bomb the ball-bearing plants at Steyr.

Other targets in north-west Germany were bombed and mine-laying was extensive. We lost 35 aircraft.

Schweinfurt's ball-bearing and roller-bearing factories, paralysed by our heavy raids last autumn, had been partly rebuilt by hundreds of workmen drafted in specially for this job.

156 Enemy Planes Down

The U.S. strategic air forces in Europe announced today that 156 German aircraft were destroyed by the 8th, 9th and 15th USAAF in the Schweinfurt and Steyr battles over Germany and Austria in daylight yesterday.

Forty-nine Fortresses and Liberators of the USAAF are missing as well as 10 British and American escorting fighters.

Medium bombers maintained a non-stop attack on the "secret weapon coast" of Northern France, where military objectives were officially stated to have received "appreciable damage."

More than 250 Marauders attacked airfields in Holland and the attacks were timed so that "a record bomb load was falling on 3 German air bases in a 3-minute period."

One formation made the deepest Marauder penetration into Europe so far—it went within 10 miles of the German frontier to attack Deelen, fighter base near Arnhem. Not one plane was lost in these raids, which left runways shattered and ammunition and fuel dumps blazing. Luftwaffe opposition to all these Allied sorties was negligible.

LONDON DANCE HALL HIT

LONDON, Fri.—Ten German aircraft were destroyed in raids on southern England last night bringing the total to 31 in 7 days.

In some London districts the bombers dropped HEs first, then incendiaries. A dance hall was hit while dancing was going on. A number of people were killed.

Churchill last night visited a big London fire and watched NFS men at work.

The King and Queen this afternoon toured bombed areas in London.

Three giant cranes are still lifting tons of rubble from the wreckage of the estate of working-class flats straddled by 4 HEs in Wednesday night's raid. Casualties there are heavy, and it is feared a high proportion will be children.

ANZIO NAZIS THROW

ANZIO, Fri.—The Germans on the Anzio front have been reinforced by another division—the 362nd Infantry Division—which has come from the North. This means that the enemy now have 10 divisions ranged opposite the beachhead.

SCOTS OPEN VITAL ARAKAN PASS

Ngakyeduk Pass, Arakan, vital highway on the South Burma front, has been cleared of all Japanese and the encircled 7th Indian Division has been relieved. Here are two despatches from British war correspondents on the front:—

JAPS LOSE 3,000

By Philip Wynter, Evening Standard.

HQ 14th Army, Feb 25.—The tangled situation on the Arakan front, which followed a strong Jap outflanking move nearly three weeks ago is now being finally stabilised.

Ground communications with the 7th Indian Division, which has been cut off since February 6, reopened yesterday Mopping-up operations are going on against what still remains of the Jap task force, which striking from the left flank on Feb. 6, penetrated between 10 and 15 miles behind what had been the British formal front in Arakan.

This task force is now officially estimated as having a strength of 7,000. Previous official estimates were 2,000, then 4,000, then 6,000.

Some Escaped

It is officially estimated that this force has thus far lost more than 1,000 killed and about 2,000 wounded It is believed that some of the remaining Japs have escaped from British-controlled territory.

Although there are a few Jap snipers still in the hills, the first convoy since Feb 5 yesterday rolled through Ngakyedauk Pass, across the Mayu range and reached the 7th Indian Division. Tanks, guns, infantry and dive-bombers have been used to smash the Jap groups which have been blocking the division's ground supply route through this pass.

Convoys immediately began bringing out the wounded who had been held in the divisional box defences since the pass was closed.

WOUNDED OFFICER SAVED BY TANK

ARAKAN FRONT, Feb. 25.—Tanks went into action in the Ngakyedauk Pass on Monday to rescue a wounded officer who was lying beside a carrier within 30 yards of a heavily armed Jap bunker, writes an Indian Army observer.

The mortar officer of an Indian battalion attacking Hill 1070 had gone forward in a carrier leading a supply party, when he was severely wounded in the right leg. It was impossible for infantry to get him back to safety.

Lt. E. Boxwell of London, whose tanks had just finished their daily task of blasting enemy strong points, again took his troops down the Pass.

While 2 tanks pounded the position, a third placed itself close in between the wounded officer and the enemy. The crew lifted the officer into their tank, and within 10 minutes he was in an ambulance ready for evacuation.—API.

ATTACKS BROKEN UP

NEW DELHI, Fri.—To-night's SEAC communiqué says.

Throughout Wednesday and yesterday there was an increase of activity on the main front, where the enemy made small-scale attacks on the centre of our position and immediately to the east among hill features north of the Maungdaw-Buthidaung road.

These efforts were all broken up without our losing ground except at one place, where some enemy infiltration occurred and is being dealt with by our troops.

IN NEW DIVISION

Anzio and Albano have been relieved after spending 2 days in caves, ditches, and trenches, under heavy fire from German tanks only 300 yards away. They were without food or medical supplies. Radio was their only means of communication to our main forces.

18 DAYS' FIGHTING

By Stanley Wills. Daily Herald

NGAKYEDAUK PASS, Arakan, Feb. 23.—For fully 10 minutes this morning Capt. Gordon Howe, adjutant of Punjab infantry lay at full length in the scrub of Arakan's Sugarloaf Hill.

His glasses never wavered from the party of men moving up the winding Ngakyedauk Pass road a few hundred feet below. Then, as tanks lumbered round a bend he shouted "It's the Scotties coming through from the other side!"

A quarter of an hour later he came out of the jungle on to the road, seized an officer of a Scottish Lowland regiment by the hand and shouted "Greetings" above the throb of tank engines.

The 7th Indian Division was no longer encircled beyond the Mayu Ridge. At dawn these Scots had marched out of their administrative "box" and, after 18 days, made contact with the men fighting through the pass to relieve them.

2-Day Jungle March

To-night with a small party of Japs dug in on Ostrich Hill as the last real obstacle, it is clear that the reopening of the pass to supply columns can only be a matter of hours.

Bombs Miss Queen Wilhelmina

LONDON, Fri.—Queen Wilhelmina of the Netherlands, it was revealed today, had a narrow escape when a bomb fell close to the house in London in which she is staying, and killed 3 of her household.

The Queen, who is 63, was uninjured.

JAP AIR BASES NEUTRALISED

ALLIED HQ, Southwest Pacific, Fri.—Allied destroyers shelled the aerodrome and docks at Kavieng, says today's official communique. More than 164 tons of explosives were dropped at Kavieng scoring hits on 8 vessels and numerous barges. Two vessels were left in flames. Large explosions and fires were seen on the aerodrome.

All Jap airbases in Bismarck islands including one at Rabaul have been temporarily neutralised and sea lanes are dominated by Allied craft at sea and in the air

A Japanese warship and two cargo ships—one of them of 3,500 tons and loaded with troops—were sunk fleeing from the Bismarck islands.

THE KING VISITS INVASION TROOPS

LONDON, Fri.—The King last night completed a 2-day visit to invasion troops "somewhere in England."

During his tour the King watched men practising beach assaults and night raids. At many points during the first day he stood with live shells whistling over his head.

RAMIREZ QUITS

BUENOS AIRES, Fri.—President Ramirez resigned last night, and the presidency has been taken over by Vice-President Gen. Edelmiro Farrel. Practically the entire Argentine cabinet is stated to have resigned with Ramirez.

Polish Army's 36-year-old sturdy, cherubic, brown-eyed 2nd Lieut FELIKS TOPOLSKI, Polish and British Official War Artist, drew these rough sketches. Topolski draws it rough, leaves it, works in detail on it long afterwards. He does not flatter his subjects.

Born Poland, left for rest of Europe 1935, wounded in blitz on London, in Russia 1943, has just visited Burma Front. Topolski has several books of drawings to his credit, including "British in Peace and War" and "Russia in War." Next will be "India in War."

TOP LEFT.—Soldiers on the Burma front. TOP RIGHT.—Outside the Continental Services Club, Calcutta. BOTTOM.—Tunnel, Arakan.

Repat: MP wants an Explanation

LONDON, Thurs.—John Dugdale (Lab. W. Bromwich) has put down this question to the Prime Minister:

Is the Prime Minister aware of the dissatisfaction existing among troops who have had long service abroad owing to the fact that RAF personnel are sent home after a much shorter period? Will he, to allay this dissatisfaction, make a statement explaining the reason for this differentiation?

SERVICE PAY: DECISION 'SOON'

LONDON, Thurs. — Discussion between the All-Party Committee of MPs and the Government on Service pay and allowances have been concluded, and the Government will announce their decision shortly, said Deputy Premier Attlee in the Commons today.

Major Lyons (Con., Leicester, East): May I ask whether the Government is aware of the great tide of public anger at the smallness of service pay and allowances, and will he take steps to bring the matter to an early decision and give some satisfaction.

Emmanuel Shinwell (Lab., Seaham): Is it the Government's intention to make a statement on this matter before the budget?

Attlee: I cannot say within a day or so. I can only say as soon as possible.

DEMOB BONUS: NO PLANS YET

LONDON, Thurs.—Sir John Wardlaw Milne (Con, Kidderminster) asked War Secretary Grigg in the House yesterday whether he would make a statement on the Government's attitude towards payment of bonuses to servicemen on demobilisation.

Grigg referred him to the Premier's recent broadcast in which he said he was unwilling to disclose demobilisation plans yet.

SALES TAX PUTS UP NIGHT CLUB BILLS

NEW YORK Thurs.—American night-club patrons now have a 30 per cent sales tax added to bills. It used to be 5 per cent—USOWI.

COMMONS LIFT BAN

LONDON, Thurs —Anthony Eden, Leader of the House, announced in the Commons today that dates of future Parliamentary sittings will be announced. Hitherto they have been secret.

EMPTY CELLAR

Complete ban on the sale of coal has been imposed in Eire because of dwindling stocks.

TANK SLID TO EDGE OF IMPHAL RAVINE

When they attacked Jap bunkers on the top of a 3,600-ft hill near Imphal, 3 tank NCO's found their tanks sliding away out of control, writes a 14th Army observer.

Cpl. L. Moore, of Bolton-Rd., Bury, Lancs., who took command when his officer was killed at the turret by a sniper, said:

"Every time I tried to shut the turret Jap snipers loosed off and we had to drive 'blind'

V's DRESSED UP AS WOODBINES

SEAC Staff Reporter

V-cigarettes have sneaked back into the news—disguised as Woodbines.

Into SEAC's office yesterday came Sergeant R. H. Saggers, now at a camp near Calcutta awaiting repatriation after a long term in the Arakan

He produced three Woodbine packets. Two had been opened. Each contained ten of the too-familiar V's. The third, still in its sealed cellophane wrapping, was opened in this office. That too contained ten V's

Sergeant Saggers said, " I received these in my weekly free issue. This is the second time that V-cigarettes, in Woodbine packets, have been distributed at the camp.

Investigation

" I came recently from the Arakan, where the cigarette position was good. The lads are getting De Reszkes and are pretty well satisfied. But if anything like these get to the front the lads may feel as the Eighth and Fifth have.

It is understood that the authorities at Saggers's camp have lodged a complaint with the supplying depot, and an investigation is being put in hand

SEAC will send one of the packets to the head office in Britain of W D. & H. O. Wills, whose trade-marked packets were used, for their comments.

VERA WILL BE AT THE FRONT

SEAC Staff Reporter

Vera Lynn, Forces' Sweetheart, trim in ENSA khaki, arrived in Calcutta yesterday, confounding the Reuter report (SEAC 6 April) that she had already been and gone

In her hotel bedroom, she said that until she started on this tour she had never been farther from her home town, London, than Holland, had never been in a 'plane had never been to a race meeting.

"I was a bit scared of flying at first" said Vera, "but now I'm getting a bit bored with it."

Her first race meeting was at Cairo. "I backed four winners in five races," she said, "And I made 30 shillings. I had my first banana for five years in Gibraltar. I saw a barrel of them, grabbed one and ate it in the street."

She was recognised the moment she set foot in Calcutta. At Bombay she went swimming in a scanty swimming suit, one of those panties and brassiere jobs, (she showed 'em to the Press).

She Has New Songs

RAF types about saw her and shouted, "Sing us a song, Vera." At a Basra mess she gave a concert with no piano and no microphone, which gave her pianist, Len Edwards a rest.

Says Edwards, "There were 50 piano-players who wanted to make this trip."

Her latest songs are "Besa Ma Mucho," which is South American for "Kiss Me," and "With All My Heart" But the boys still insist on "We'll Meet Again."

"I came to India because I heard the boys wanted entertainment," she says She'll be in Calcutta, singing at hospitals mostly, for a fortnight before she goes on a tour of the front.

She's a bit nervous of the title "Forces Sweetheart," voted her by the BEF in France. But she can't think of another. She's just made her fourth film "One Exciting Night" and she has to be back in London by June to start another picture and do a

What will W D and H O say?

MONTAGU NORMAN LEAVES THE BANK

LONDON, Thurs.—Montagu Norman, 72 years old, 25 years Governor of the Bank of England resigned today on the advice of his doctors.

Lord Catto, who began his working life as an office boy in Scotland succeeds him.

Norman, arch-priest of orthodoxy had a powerful influence at one time, not merely on domestic policy, but on foreign policy.

JAPS AMBUSHED AROUND IMPHAL

NEW, DELHI, Thurs.—North of Buthidaung an enemy counter-attack on one of our positions was repulsed yesterday, says tonight's SEAC communique. South of the village the enemy still offers resistance to our advance.

On the Assam front the Japanese continue to exert pressure north of Imphal. Successful ambushes in which casualties were inflicted on the enemy were laid on roads north and south of Imphal

A small attack against one of our positions on the Palel-Tamu road as repulsed with loss to the enemy. Among equipment captured on the Tiddim-Imphal road were the sword and medals of the commander of the Japanese attacking force.

Kachins Advance

Chinese troops in the Upper Mogaung Valley have captured Marangah Tawng and Mahloigar Tawng. They are in contact with the enemy and are advancing on Wakawng.

A strong Jap position is being eliminated near the confluence of Hpalu Hka and Kathan Hka.

On the Sumprabum-Myitkyina road, Kachin levies advancing southward have reached the Tiang Hka

In a strike against Aungban airfield in Central Burma on Tuesday, the Air Commando force of the Tactical Air Force in six minutes destroyed 24 enemy aircraft on the ground, probably destroyed two and damaged eight others.

The Commando force also shot up AA positions and buildings north-west of the airfield One enemy bomber was also destroyed at Anisakan airfield.

JANE GOES ON A COMMANDO RAID

ACH! HERMAN, HOW'S THIS FOR PRETTY SHOOTING?

I ALWAYS GET WILLING HANDS TO HELP ME!

I'VE GOT THE TOOLS TO FINISH THE JOB!

I'LL TEACH YOU TO TAKE LIBERTIES WITH ME!

5,000 Flee Vesuvius By Night

NAPLES, Tues. Five thousand villagers from San Sebastiano and Masso carrying what clothes and household goods they could grab in time, were tramping into Naples early today fleeing from great lava streams from fiercely-erupting Vesuvius.

The lava is flowing down the shallow valley at 12 feet a minute. It shows no signs of slowing up.

People fled panic-stricken through the night to Allied help in Naples, where Lt-Col Kincaid, Allied Commissioner, is preparing for the villages being laid waste.

NAZI CHUTISTS KEEP CASSINO

LONDON, Tues.—A German parachute battalion has now joined the Panzer Grenadiers who are fighting savagely to hold the western outskirts of Cassino, it is reported today.

Our troops have reduced more enemy strongpoints and taken some prisoners, but they are facing a grim situation, since every Allied move is under direct observation from German positions on the surrounding hills.

Our men are closely packed in a triangle bounded by the Rapido, the Garigliano and Monastery Hill, and there is little scope for manoeuvre. Despite our gains on the hills, we cannot outflank the Germans, and every point must be carried by frontal assault. This is proving costly.

Another complication is that the ruins of the town hamper rapid movement.

Some of our units on the lower slopes of the hills are not only subject to sudden counter-attacks, but are virtually cut off from their comrades in the town. They are depending on airborne supplies. One unit yesterday got its first supplies for 48 hours.

At Anzio British troops made two successful raids, inflicting heavy casualties. We shot down 6 aircraft for the loss of 3.

GOT THE BULLET

Because diners at Ipswich British restaurants complained that canned peas were as hard as bullets the cooks now put them through a mincing machine.

GERMANS DRIVEN OUT OF ODESSA

LONDON, Mon.—The German News Agency announced today the evacuation of the Black Sea port of Odessa. "In the course of large-scale withdrawal movements on the extreme flank of the southern sector of the eastern front," says the announcement, "the town of Odessa was evacuated last night."

With the fall of Odessa the Red Army is now only 80 miles from the mouth of the Danube. Largest port on the Black Sea and third largest city in the Ukraine, after Kharkov and Kiev, Odessa had a pre-war population of more than 400,000.

It has been recaptured after 2½ years in German hands. Soviet troops held out there for 2 months in 1941 before evacuating by sea on 17 October.

No announcement has yet come from Moscow regarding the fall of the city.

He WANTS "Vs"!

If repeat, if you have a packet of "Vs" in the bottom of your kitbag, send it to the Imperial War Museum, Lambeth-road, London, S.E.1. where it will be preserved for posterity as a relic of World War II.

In Britain "Vs" are regarded as a "find" by souvenir hunters.

"So much has been said and written about them that we want a packet for exhibition," L. R. Bradley, Director of the Imperial War Museum, says.

DRINK BAN ON CAFE GIRLS

CAIRO, Mon.—Cairo cabarets catering chiefly for NCOs and other ranks in the British Army in Egypt have closed their doors in protest against the law forbidding "artists" to drink with patrons.

A few days ago the Minister of the Interior reminded the Morals Bureau officials of the need to enforce this regulation.

Chief of the Morals Bureau told a meeting of cabaret proprietors that waiter, dancer and proprietor would all be prosecuted in cases where "artists" were found drinking at tables.

This action by the Egyptian Government is part of a vigorous drive, in collaboration with the British authorities, to protect British soldiers.

The "artists" practise a dubious "art," and their main job is to wheedle piastres from the pockets of troops on leave.

Cabarets charge a soldier 10 piastres (half-a-crown) for a bottle of beer or a single whisky. If he buys one for the so-called "artist" or hostess, he has to pay 15 or 20 piastres for her drink (3s. to 4s 6d.).

And though it looks like creme-de-menthe it is only coloured water.

CHURCHILL'S CRITIC

LONDON, Mon.—The Common Wealth Party, at a conference today, voted its opposition to Prime Minister Churchill, saying that he was "hostile towards the forward march of the common people."

CHESTNUTS

"DARLING, your clutch needs tightening," complained the A.T. to the R.A.S.C. driver.
CPL. J. SADLER, R.A.O.C.

*　*　*

"AND to think I reach twenty-five years of age before knowing my father and mother aren't married," exclaimed the soldier.
"When did you find out?"
"The Sergeant-Major just told me."
GUNNER GEO. PRENTICE, R.A., OXON.

*　*　*

"GOOD-BYE, Mother. I'm off to a party with Jim."
"Bye, bye, dear. Have a good time and be a good girl!"
"Well, mother — make up your mind."
FIREMAN D., MORDEN.

GERMAN (to French prisoner): "What is your favourite sport?"
"Football."
"Why football?"
"I like shooting for de Gaulle!"
GUNNER GEO. PRENTICE, R.A., OXON.

*　*　*

"WHAT you need is a good sea voyage," as the doctor said to the Italian Admiral.
A.B. L. GREENSMITH, H.M.S. NELSON.

*　*　*

"I'D like to take you somewhere where we could be alone together," he told her passionately.
"For good?"
"Don't be so old-fashioned."
MISS J. ARDLEY, CHEAM, SURREY.

"IS that new A.T.S. secretary satisfactory, Major?"
"No. As a matter of fact I'm thinking of having her transferred to the Quartermaster's Stores."
"You are? Why?"
"Well, she does nothing but make slips and bloomers."
E. H. D. (R.A.F.), SURREY.

CASSINO ATTACKS BROKEN UP

ALLIED ADVANCED HQ, ITALY, Mon.—Mediterranean aircraft attacked a German airfield near the Spanish frontier yesterday, destroying 3 planes on the ground.

New Zealanders inflicted casualties on Germans attacking 2 strongpoints south of Cassino.

Several tanks were knocked out near the coast on the British sector along the Garigliano River.

LETTER FROM HOME—3.

Dear Son:—I just received your letter telling how cold it was at night and I've sent you two comforters, the pink ones that used to be in the Guest Room. I thought it would be nice if you gave one to the General—sort of a peace-offering in case you're still angry with each other. The Post Office didn't want to send them, at first, but I told Mr. Petty, the Postmaster, that if he refused to send fighting men a comforter, I would report him to the Governor through Mr Hawkins, whose daughter knows a sister of one of the downstairs maids who used to work for the Governor's aunt. I guess that scared Mr Petty, because all he said after that was "Humph."

Poor Aunt Hilda had to go back to Elk's Gap again as she forgot her travelling bag in the hotel. I do hope she gets a seat on the train this time since her feet are killing her.

Well, darling, I must get back to work. I'm crocheting a heavy sweater for you which should be finished and in India in time for summer.

All my love, Mother.

JANE

BOTHER THAT PHONE!— IT'S ONLY SOME BORE!— I'LL DISCONNECT IT!

JANE! JANE!

JANE!— DARLING!— ARE YOU THERE?—
HI, MISS, I CAN'T GET AN ANSWER!—
OH, THERE YOU ARE, SWEETHEART!— NO— NOT YOU, MISS!— GET OFF THE LINE!— NO, NOT YOU, JANE!— LISTEN....

PARADE
No. 193   Vol. 15   April 22, 1944

READY FOR THE DAY
Pages 10-12

Men who lived in old farmhouse saw earlier conquerors destroyed. Through the quaint porch walked some bygone occupant with the news of Waterloo; and another with tidings that the Kaiser was in flight. Now beside the stone wall are parked 90 mm. anti-aircraft guns which will help to destroy Hitler's power.

READY FOR THE DAY

Under the branches of trees now turning green, in fields, around the farmyard—everywhere in the English countryside, camouflaged as far as possible, are piled up unbelievable quantities of stores for the Second Front. There are guns, tanks, landing barges, bulldozers, cranes, pontoons and gliders, everything that is necessary to crack open the fortress of Hitler's Europe. The joint production of the factories of Brit-

ain and the United States has gone into the accumulation of stores of war material. At many British ports and at a number of American air bases in Britain thousands of men are busy handling aircraft and other equipment pouring in. So vast is the amount of equipment coming from the United States for the Second Front armies that one correspondent cabled: "The island is sinking under the weight of it."

American-built locomotives which will haul Allied trains on the Continent do a 600-miles test run.

Diesel locomotives will be employed on the railways of Continent in places where it is difficult to obtain coal.

Quayside and surrounding dock area a like material in a never-ceasing flow. W

COMING OF AGE

Princess Elizabeth comes of age on April 21. her eighteenth birthday, not in the full legal sense but in accordance with royal procedure. The significance of this coming of age lies principally in the fact that after her eighteenth birthday she would ascend the throne. if called to, as Queen regnant; there would be no necessity for a regency. In February, after the Welsh Parliamentary Party had sponsored a movement to have the title of Princess of Wales conferred upon Princess Elizabeth, it was announced that the King did not contemplate making any change in the style and title of the Princess. The King has asked Parliament to decree that the Princess shall be a member of the Council of State which rules in the event of his absence. Photographs by Cecil Beaton show the Princess at home with the King. the Queen and her younger sister. Princess Margaret Rose.

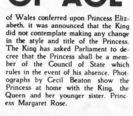

TOBACCO SMELL COST HIM RANK

LONDON, Sat.—For attempting to exchange two ounces of tobacco for a pair of shoes belonging to a soldier under sentence at the Aldershot detention barracks, Sgt George James Vango, aged 30, of the Military Provost Staff Corps, has been sentenced by court martial to be reduced to the ranks and six months' imprisonment.

Aircraftman McIntyre, who was said to have acted as an intermediary, told the court that he carried the shoes, hidden in a bucket, to the barber's shop, where he found the tobacco in the pocket of an overcoat which was afterwards identified as Vango's.

Vango denied that there was any arrangement to make an exchange.

It was stated that McIntyre produced the tobacco after a sergeant had smelt stale tobacco smoke in a cell and began to search the occupant.

GERMANS REPORT EVENING AIR BATTLE

LONDON, Fri.—Berlin Radio reported this evening that air battles were taking place over south west Germany.

Since dawn today aircraft have flown out from Britain to bomb railways and airfields and other objectives in Northern France and Belgium.

Last night Lancasters and Halifaxes were out in strength for the sixth night running. They went to France and Belgium, Boulogne being one of the main targets. There was also mine-laying. Sixteen aircraft are missing.

NAZI ARTILLERY BUSY AT ANZIO

ADVANCED ALLIED HQ, Italy, Wed.—The German withdrawal on the Adriatic front, which has given the Eighth Army a 10-mile advance, is due to relentless pressure by Allied fighting patrols and the battering of supply lines by artillery and aircraft, says a front-line reporter.

It has enabled the Eighth Army to straighten their line at many points.

In the Cassino area German artillery again shelled the railway station area held by Allied troops since their last offensive through the town.

The Germans have been pouring a larger number of shells into the rear areas on the Anzio beachhead, evidently in an attempt to destroy Allied supply dumps.

Last night RAF bombers attacked the harbours at Genoa and Leghorn, and also attacked Civita Vecchia and the Rome area. The MAAF yesterday lost six aircraft from 1,100 sorties.

HEAVY JAP LOSSES IN CENTRAL BURMA

KANDY, Wed.—In Central Burma our troops have inflicted heavy casualties on enemy parties south of Mogaung, and near Mawlu, north-west of Katha, says today's SEAC communique.

In the Mogaung Valley, east of the main road and south of the Hwelow River, Chinese troops, supported by tanks and artillery, have attacked strong Jap positions. The fighting continues.

Our levies have repulsed the Jap attacks in the Fort Hertz valley inflicting considerable casualties on the enemy.

Troops in the Kohima area have continued their operations against Japanese posts in the outskirts of the town.

RAF medium bombers of the Strategic Air Force yesterday attacked enemy positions near Moirang. RAF and IAF planes continued their intensive offensive against enemy positions, rivercraft, tanks and a Jap HQ.

From all operations two Allied aircraft are missing.—API.

'ZIP YOUR LIP' ORDER TO GIRLS

LONDON, Wed.—"Zip your lip" is the security warning issued to NAAFI girls who will go up the line with their mobile canteens when the second front beachheads are established.

They will wear siren suits and tin hats.

Security officers at all NAAFI HQs are impressing on staffs that there must be no careless talk.

Canteen service for troops will be staffed by men and girls drawn from 2,000 who have volunteered for overseas service.

Small mobile canteens carrying tea, beer, chocolate and cigarettes will do "close support" almost up to the firing line.

A team of tent pitchers will build camps equipped to feed thousands of troops at each sitting.

JAPS DRIVEN BACK

CHUNGKING, Wed.—Japanese forces striking for Loyang, in the province of Honan and six times the capital of China, have been driven back across the Yiyi River south of the town.—Reuter.

EFM Suspended

LONDON, Wed.—The use of short expeditionary force telegram messages by code numbers has been suspended. No explanation was given, but it is known the messages imposed a heavy load on communications already overloaded. These telegrams numbered 100,000 weekly. Concession telegrams sent by next of kin through Service channels on urgent family business will continue for the present.

Hell Hits Bishenpur Japs

FIERCEST BOMB DISPLAY EVER

IMPHAL FRONT, Mon. (delayed).—For above an hour this afternoon the Jap held Manipur village of Ningthoukhong, just south of Bishenpur on the Imphal-Tiddim road, became an inferno of steel and flame, writes a 14th Army observer.

The Strategic Air Force was giving the biggest bombing display ever seen on the Imphal front.

As the first bombers flew up with their fighter escort storm clouds broke on the mountains west of Bishenpur. For a time the rain was torrential and it seemed doubtful whether the planes would see the heavily-wooded, 1,000-yards square village, which looks like any other village of the plain.

Zero Hour

Just before zero hour for the air strike the storm cleared and, from a hill about 1,500 yards from the village, I saw the first Liberators drop their bombs.

Then came wave after wave of Mitchells, straddling the target area from east to west and north to south.

Gurkhas, Punjabis and British troops left their holes in the ground, their cover and their tanks and walked across the open to see the village become momentarily shrouded by the rising pall of smoke.

Then the fighters, like kite-hawks round a cookhouse, circled and dived to take whatever was left.

Earlier in the day I watched Punjabis and tanks attack the Jap-held village of Potsangbam, near the bombers' target.

LABOUR 'REPRIEVES' ANEURIN BEVAN

WESTMINSTER, Wed.—The Parliamentary Labour Party has defeated the motion by the administrative committee to expel Aneurin Bevan.

A compromise solution put forward by Emanuel Shinwell to refer the matter to the joint consideration of the national executive committee of the Labour Party and administrative committee was carried by 71 votes to 60.

It is understood that the leader of the Parliamentary Labour Party, Arthur Greenwood, subsequently offered his resignation.—Reuter.

DSC BEFORE 20

Midshipman Norman Earnest Draper of Leyton, who is under 20, has been mentioned in despatches and awarded the DSC. He has been on Mediterranean Commando raids.

Newcastle's Police Chief
QUITS, BUT GETS £800 A YEAR

LONDON, Wed.—At a special meeting of the Newcastle City Council, called to consider the report of the official inquiry into allegations of mismanagement of the city's ARP services, a letter was read from Coun R. Embleton, former Deputy ARP Controller and Chairman of the Watch Committee.

In it he said, "I feel it is in the best interests of all concerned that I should now retire from public life."

A second letter, from Home Secretary Herbert Morrison, said the Watch Committee should consider, as a matter of urgency, the question of F. J. Crawley's fitness for retention as Chief Constable in view of the report.

Roland Burrows, KC, conducted the inquiry and criticised Crawley for grave indiscretions—among them one of approaching the Recorder of Newcastle to try to get the inquiry hushed up. Embleton he found guilty of concealing material facts in the matter of fire engine BB999, which was taken from the Council's station to a company of which Embleton was a director, without authority (SEAC 21 May).

'Tried For Hush-up'

At the meeting, a member urged that Crawley too be called on to resign, but was pointed out that his appointment was vested in the Watch Committee.

Next day, however, the Chairman of the Watch Committee received a letter from Crawley giving notice of his resignation. The Committee voted him leave of absence until 10 Aug, when the resignation becomes effective.

His pension, secured at £800 a year a few years ago, when he resigned but was asked to continue, is not affected by the inquiry or the circumstances of his resignation.

He had already abandoned the offices of Civil Defence Controller, Chief Warden and Fire Guard Officer in March, when the inquiry was looming.

CHINESE REACH THE BURMA ROAD

CHUNGKING, Wed.—Chinese forces driving towards the Burma border from Yunnan have captured Chefang on the Burma Road, west of the Salween River, the Chinese High Command announced last night.

The capture of this town outflanks and cuts the road of retreat for the Jap garrison at Lungling, main advanced base on the west bank of the Salween River, and brings the Chinese to within 100 miles of Lashio on the Burma Road to the south.

Chefang is 70 miles east of Bhamo on the Irrawady, near which the Chindit forces are operating.—Reuter.

TITO'S MEN TAKE ANOTHER TOWN

LONDON, Wed.—A communique from Tito's HQ says that on Sandjak, Serbian frontier units of our 37th Division have taken Ljubis on the Varesganova road, capturing a quantity of war material.—Reuter.

INDIAN OIL · STRIKE

NEW DELHI, Wed.—The Attock Oil Co. are reported to have struck oil in quantity at one of their drilling sites outside their present main producing fields at Dhulian.—API.

BERLIN GETS IT NIGHT AND DAY

LONDON, Wed.—Berlin, after a night punctuated with 4,000-pounders dropped by Bomber Command Mosquitos, was today attacked by USAAF heavy bombers "in very great strength."

A force of 1,500 Fortresses, Liberators and escorting fighters was out. Most went to Berlin, the others attacked airfields near Paris.

Mosquitos last night also attacked Dortmund, great Rhineland rail centre which was battered in Monday night's big raid. None is missing.

The Germans today also reported heavy air battles and presumably with American day bombers—over Schleswig-Holstein, most north-westerly province of Germany, and Luebeck, the great Baltic port.

Yesterday's American daylight raids over France and Western Germany were accompanied by the greatest fighter force ever sent on a single mission, it is reported today. Flak was meagre, and the few German fighters encountered were unwilling to give battle.—Reuter.

SHOT AIRMEN : NO RIOT, SAYS AIR MIN.

LONDON, Wed.—The Air Ministry today announced: "With regard to the report on events at Stalag Luft III which appeared in the Press yesterday, while insufficient information is at present available to issue a further statement on the circumstances in which 47 Air Force officers were killed, the suggestion that guards ran riot and shot the prisoners is without foundation.

"The Government will make a full statement as soon as the report is received from the protecting power."—Reuter.

RUSSIANS SEIZE STRATEGIC HILL

MOSCOW, Wed.—Hand-to-hand fighting north-west of Tiraspol in a Soviet reconnaissance raid is reported in a supplement to the communique. Prisoners and booty were seized.

South-east of Stanislavov, a Russian unit occupied a dominating height against strong opposition.

The communique says there are no material changes at the front.—Reuter.

TRUK HIT AGAIN

ALLIED ADVANCE HQ (New Guinea), Wed.—Today's communique reports an attack before dawn on Truk, a 150-ton raid on Biak Island (Schouten group) and an 80-ton attack on Wewak.

In the Bougainville sector, the Mibo river area was bombarded by light naval forces co-operating with air units.—Reuter.

Battle of Italy: Phase II Opens
FIFTH ARMY LAND BEHIND GERMANS

German communiqué last night reported : " The enemy continued his major attack from Nettuno beachhead with increased violence. Throwing in strong artillery and tank forces and supported by numerous planes, he succeeded in driving deep penetrations into our front on a number of sectors." German Transocean Newsagency says General Mark Clark's beachhead forces attempted a new " Leapfrog " landing to take the German defences in the rear.—Reuter.

ALLIED HQ, ANZIO BEACHHEAD, Wed.—Striking in great force from the Anzio beachhead, the Fifth Army has begun the second phase of the Battle of Italy. British tanks have crossed the Moletta River while American troops have occupied a 2,000-yard sector of the Appian Way within half a mile of Cisterna.

The attack from the beachhead synchronised with a powerful assault by the Eighth Army against the Hitler Line in the Liri Valley.

From all points of the front come reports of successes. French troops have taken Pico, strongpoint of the northern sector.

Churchill Reviews the Great Alliance, Says:
TURKS TOO TIMID

LONDON, Wed.—Premier Churchill gave a broad review of the war in its political perspective when he opened today the two-days' debate on Foreign Affairs in the Commons. Here are the main points of his speech :

Meeting of Dominion Prime Ministers : I should not pretend that we have arrived at hard and fast decisions upon all questions that torment this afflicted globe. But it can fairly be said that there was revealed a core of agreement which will enable the British Empire to meet in discussion with other great organisms in the world in a firmly-knit array.

MYITKYINA: JAP ATTACK BROKEN

KANDY, Wed.—After beating off a Jap counter-attack, Gen. Stilwell's Chinese troops on the western outskirts of Myitkyina have advanced to the junction of the railway and the road leading from the landing strip, says today's SE Asia Command communiqué.

Other elements have effectively blocked the road between the airport and Myitkyina proper. South of the town other Chinese troops repulsed enemy attacks near Zigyun Ferry.

Chindits continued to exert pressure south of the Mogaung, and during the past 48 hours have killed more than 100 Japs.

East of the Mogaung Valley, the Chinese 38th Div. made headway in the Sharaw (12 miles north of Kamaing) area and south of West Valaw. West of the Mogaung River the Chinese 22nd Div. took six enemy positions along the Hwelon River and further to the west.

Kohima Advance

South and south-west of Kohima yesterday our troops improved their positions on the ridges overlocking the town by occupying further enemy strongpoints.

CRUSADER

BRITISH FORCES' WEEKLY

No. 106, Vol. 18   Two Lire
Sunday, June 11, 1944

FOUNDED BY EIGHTH ARMY

In one historic week

ROME FELL –

– AND THE GREAT INVASION BEGAN

WE ENTER ROME

PHILLIP JORDAN, well-known correspondent of the "NEWS CHRONICLE," was amongst the first of the Allied troops to enter Rome, on the morning of the 5th of June. In this front-line dispatch, sent the same day, he tells of the joy and excitement of the civilian population—of the welcome they gave their liberators—of the calm serenity of the Vatican City.

THANKS to the valour of the Eighth Army, the Fifth Army was able to stream into Rome this morning, after patrols had penetrated the city limits late last night. The last Germans withdrew at about two o'clock this morning, and at first light we drove in past the city limits, which yesterday were all that any Allied personnel had been able to reach.

The spirits of the crowd were high, and one of the first things we saw when we entered the great square, where from one of the balconies Mussolini used to address the crowd, was a soldier posturing from that demented balcony just as the Duce used to do before him. I could not but recall the prophesy made twenty years ago by a Fascist: Fascism will live until Charlie Chaplin marches into the palace and addresses the people of Rome.

Other writers will tell the story of this delirious day. How suddenly, out of nowhere, red flags flying the five-pointed star and hammer and sickle appeared on balconies and even on one occasion flew from the windows of a bank. How roses seemed to grow in the streets and the Italian flag flew at half-mast from the high and beautiful tower of the golden Capitol. How the Allied planes flew contentedly overhead all day.

They will tell how "Il Risorgimento Liberale" saw the light of day for the first time in its continuous publication of over two years, when it appeared on the streets at mid-day. For to-day it is no longer clandestine and is selling faster than hot cakes ever sold on a cold Good Friday. Its main heading reads "Nazi and Fascist terror is ended"—with the words "Rome is returned to the Italians" beneath in huge letters that crowd more than a quarter of the page.

The Germans must have been moved in some way here by world opinion for they have left the capital more or less intact. The water supply is still running, although light is off. And as far as can be ascertained only two telephone exchanges out of twenty have been destroyed. That at least is what the preliminary report submitted to General Hughes, head A.M.G. official, stated.

As for the buildings in the city, none have blown-up since we arrived. Touch wood, for this is being written in "Stampa Estera," a building Mussolini erected to flatter the foreign Press and gain their esteem. It is highly useful to-day, and for the first time in its strange career men in it can write with comparative freedom.

No personnel in uniform are allowed in the Vatican City, at whose doors Swiss guards in their wartime "battle dress" of plain blue tunics. and breeches and black wool stockings, stand armed with bayonets fixed to their modern rifles.

So I knocked up a clothing store and fitted myself out in a strange mixture of civilian clothes so as to be able to pay a visit to the Papal Secretariat of State.

Looking something like a cross between a Blackpool Bank Holiday tourist and an ill-fitted deserter from the Army, I presented myself with a colleague at the door of the Vatican City and, after a good deal of fuss due to the somewhat unorthodox circumstances of our call, was shown up to the Papal Secretariat.

Henri Bérard, French Minister to the Holy See, in full dress and accompanied by his exceptionally beautiful daughter, was leaving the Papal audience when we arrived. The corridors were alive with his colleagues.

Only the German Minister to the Vatican was missing.

He left this neutral territory last night and has not yet returned. No one knows where he has gone. The Pope had also received Monsignor MacHugh, American priest attached to his foreign secretariat, with whom he spent some time.

According to the Vatican authorities, most of the major treasures of both northern and southern Italy are already housed in the Vatican for safe-keeping, none of whose extra-territorial properties have been in any way harmed by Allied bombing.

For instance, the library from Monte Cassino is now safely stowed away in the Vatican library. And the greatest part of whatever other treasures it possessed are now at Spoleto.

Contrary to some reports which have been made, the Pope did not appear on the balcony of Saint Peter's this morning and bless the crowd that was waiting. He was too busy with his appointed audiences.

From high Vatican sources I have it confirmed that the Germans did massacre three hundred and twenty leading Italians, including three generals, on March 24 in retaliation for some slight act of resistance. Their bodies were seen by a pastor of San Sebastiano on the Appian Way before the cave in which they had been placed and had been blown up.

MUSTANGS GET 13 JAPS FOR 0

ARAKAN FRONT, Thurs (delayed).—Thirteen of a formation of 25 Jap fighters were destroyed today by an American squadron of P-51's (Mustangs). Two were probably destroyed and six were damaged. The Americans did not lose one aircraft.

This long-range fighter-bomber squadron of the USAAF already had 26 enemy aircraft to its credit. Its total is now 39 destroyed, with several probables and a large number damaged, since its arrival on this front.

The squadron was led by 24-year-old Major S. M. Newcombe, from Green Village, New Jersey.

Japs out in Force

"We reached the Irrawaddy River," he said, "and went on to Meiktila airfield. We gradually reduced height to 16 000 feet. No Jap planes were visible, so we went on to Aungban, where I saw two enemy planes in the air.

"I delegated a section to drop their long-range tanks and attack, but quickly realised that the Japs were there in force.

"There were about 29 of them. They were all flying close together. The whole squadron then went in to attack them. I noticed that the Japs showed a tendency to fly in formations of two and four, presumably for protection. I dived out of the sun on to the tail of two of them, and gave one of them a short burst at 200 yards.

"The enemy plane seemed to belch flame out of its engine and cockpit, and explosions shook its wing roots. It seemed to me that either the Jap pilots were poor or they were out of ammunition. Not one of my boys got a scratch."

Another pilot, who shot down two Japanese, was Lt. K. Granger, age 25, of Poland Manor, Poland, Ohio. He was in the steel business before the war.

"On my first attack I gave a Jap fighter a two-second burst and saw white smoke pour out," he said. "As he dived away I was making a steep turn to the right to join my leader when a Jap came across in front of me and started to climb vertically towards our formation above. As I fired two long bursts I saw the canopy of his plane break up and black smoke come out of his engine cowling. He went down.

At 200ft Range

"Later, I saw another Jap straight in front of me at 200 feet range. I made my attack from a five degree angle and started a petrol fire at the wing root.

Lieutenant R. F. Mulhollem, a 23-year-old graduate of Pennsylvania State University who comes from 2522 Wilson Avenue, Chicago, Illinois, and Capt. J. J. England, 29-year-old ex-credit manager, of 114B Westwood Gardens, Jackson, Tennessee, each got two of the Japs.

" And if we got held up at the crossroads, your section will carry out a flanking movement, thus turning what might have been defeat into a glorious and complete victory unequalled in the annals of the British Army."

Strange Men

" Why didn't you tell the ticket collector at the station that you had lost your ticket?" asked an inspector for the L.P.T.B. during an investigation.

" I never speak to strange men," was the alleged reply by Miss Bluma Zadel, of Lynford-gardens, Edgware, who appeared at Hendon accused of travelling on the railway with intent to avoid payment.

She was fined £2 with £2 costs.

Italia sunk in a minute

ROCKET-FIRING Hurricanes of the Coastal Air Force in a daring and spirited attack lasting little more than a minute recently destroyed an enemy motor vessel of 5,800 tons in the northern Adriatic.

The vessel, the Italia, was at one time a first-class passenger liner, but she was converted into a cargo ship and was employed in running supplies from Trieste to ports along the Dalmatian coast.

The Hurricanes, covered by Spitfires, attacked in the early evening, coming in low over the land seeking every atom of cover, then descending one by one on the unsuspecting Italia.

F/Lt. Arnold E. Walker, of West Borough Drive, Halifax, Yorkshire, noted three black German crosses on the hull of the Italia, and aimed at the centre one. His salvo scored and almost at once the escorting Spitfires reported a dull red explosion and much oil on the water.

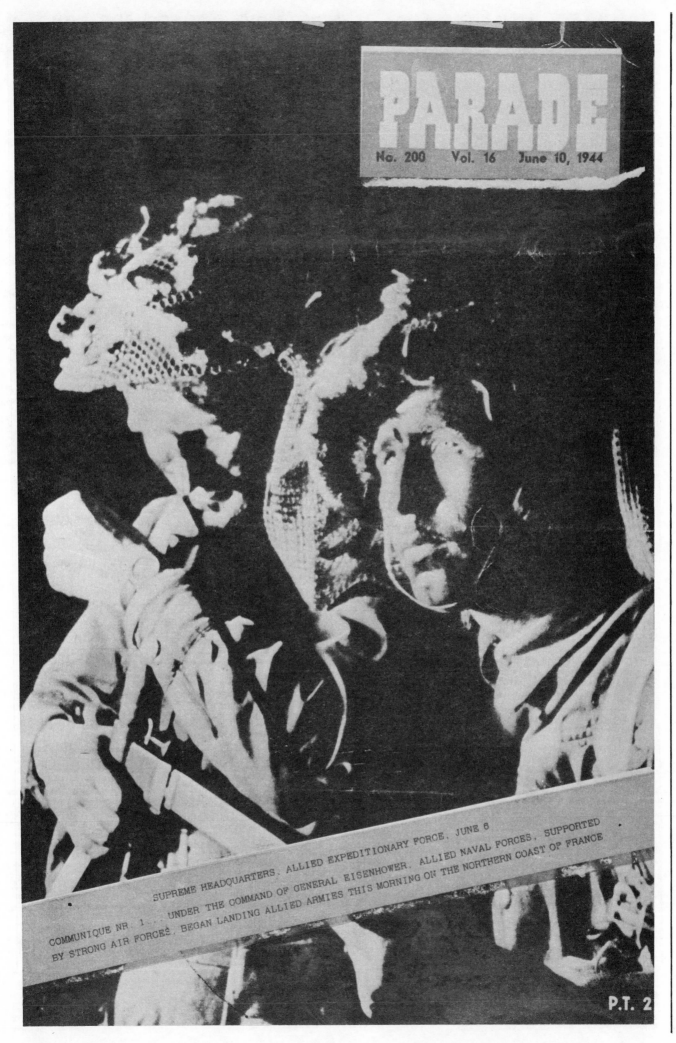

PARADE

No. 200   Vol. 16   June 10, 1944

COMMUNIQUE NR. 1 . . . UNDER THE COMMAND OF GENERAL EISENHOWER, ALLIED NAVAL FORCES, SUPPORTED BY STRONG AIR FORCES, BEGAN LANDING ALLIED ARMIES THIS MORNING ON THE NORTHERN COAST OF FRANCE

SUPREME HEADQUARTERS, ALLIED EXPEDITIONARY FORCE, JUNE 6

P.T. 2

Scene on coast of Normandy after the first troops ashore had pushed inland and vast quantities of equipment and material were quickly landed on beaches strewn with wreckage of defences. Tanks, motor transport, bulldozers, amphibious "ducks" formed untidy, purposeful pattern (picture by radio).

SPEARHEAD INTO FRANCE

How tank landing craft of a flotilla carrying men of the Royal Engineers were first to touch down on the shore of France at the opening of the western front is told by "Parade" Navy Editor LAMBTON BURN who was aboard the leading craft

Dawn, June 6, 1944. Tiny sampan-hulled tank landers in the midst of the mightiest invasion fleet in history. Heavy clouds overhead. Sea still rough. We stand on the bridge and ponder on the responsibilities of the meteorologists and those who base their plans on their forecasts.

Our battle ensign has been hoisted. It is a large white ensign and still shows the creases of its virgin folds. Before the day grows much older it will no longer be immaculate and we shall hold our heads the higher for its many holes. But at the moment we know nothing about that. We are as babes heading into something unknown, maybe exciting. Or rather, most have crews like that. They have trained for long months landing and re-landing the same troopers or brown jobs until both they and their season ticketers know the job they have to do and the capabilities of one another. There is friendship and mutual confidence.

We can handle our unwieldy craft well and we know it. We can fire our Oerlikons and our machine-guns—and the enemy know it.

It has been a quiet night. Minesweepers went on ahead some hours ago and left channels well marked. There is something very systematic about the way we sheer steadily onward through the enemy minefields. We almost expect to find a traffic policeman at the points where we alter course. But we are one-way traffic at the moment. We extend from one horizon into the other. Far distant we can see other parties. Beyond them another large party.

Candelabra in the sky show us that the R.A.F. are busy tuning in to the enemy defences. Well over on the starboard bow a great fire blooms gold then red. We look at our charts—that must be somewhere in the direction of Cherbourg. Our own destination lies farther east. We are bound for the shelving limestone-ridged beaches at Lion-sur-Mer, opposite the little town of Ouistreham, the ancient port of Caen. We know the landmarks well. There is the pointed spire of Ouistreham church for example; then there is the mediæval-looking manor at the westward end of a small wood and an isolated modern flat-roofed villa marking the eastern limit of one of our assault beaches. Lion church has a square tower and we know it by heart. But there is a comforting footnote in our navigation aids "It must be stressed that whilst landmarks were very prominent at the beginning of May, 1944, they may well have been destroyed before the assault, either by our own or enemy action."

We open our eyes wide as the light grows stronger and reveals the invading fleet in all its beauty, its majesty of purpose. "Was there such shipping as this at Salerno?" our Captain enquires. There is a hint of local pride in his voice. I grin at him, shake my head. He is an R.N.V.R. lieutenant from Sutton, Surrey and our tank landing craft has been adopted by Sutton and Cheam;

...bound for the shelving limestone-ridged beaches at Lion-sur-Mer, opposite the little town of Ouistreham.

presents of tobacco and chocolate in the stores below are to him like gifts from home.

We move on through lines of destroyers and transports heading for our deployment area, for we are destined to go in first. We are carrying a handpicked troop of Royal Engineers charged with the task of clearing the beaches of mines and obstacles. They have bulldozers with them together with a variety of other gadgets which represent Britain's latest contribution of secret weapons to the Allied cause.

Now in this story there will be many gaps for it is one of the minor tragedies of the naval side of a landing operation that so much that is done by the men cannot be reported because of new types of vessels, new weapons, new tactics. When in due course the full story can be revealed it is told to a public by then interested in other novelties; so the full effort of risks and sacrifices of the sailor can never be appreciated at their real worth at the only time when they command attention—the moment after their performance.

But the soldier who lands on an enemy shore knows the full story. The Royal Engineers with us understood, indeed, they were working under the same handicap. When the time came they would go forward with their secret devices, ready to give their lives doing something of which nothing can be said.

The men who came aboard with us are tanned of face, strong in wind and limb and possessed of the spirit of patient determination of which we saw so much in the Eighth Army. There is Donald Robertson—just by the landing craft door. His tank is a Sherman—he is mighty proud of it, has painted over its visor the name "Stornaway." Bob Brotherton has a Sherman too. Don

Continued overleaf

SECRETS OF D-DAY

Here are facts the Germans desperately wanted to know before the invasion of France started. The success of the operation was in direct ratio to the degree that 'nobody talked'. And nobody did talk — the enemy was completely surprised

Ten thousand officers and men manning more than 200 fleet sweepers, trawlers, drifters, motor-mine-sweepers and motor-launches had taken a direct part in the Second Front before the first soldier set foot ashore. Working quietly, grimly, unadvertised in the grey depths of the North Sea and the Channel they risked their lives nightly clearing all the channels leading to the operational areas. Two thousand eight hundred tons of minesweeping gear were used during preliminary operations and the length of the sweep wire embarked for the final sweeps would reach from London to Southampton. This work had to be masked in such a way that the enemy would be kept in ignorance of the actual areas swept and would continue to live in a fool's paradise. Diversionary manœuvres both by aircraft and motor-torpedo boats kept the bulk of the German scouting units too busy to observe all that was going on. To many of the minesweepers the work of "sweeping in" an invasion fleet was not new for they had already acquitted themselves with honour in North Africa and the Sicilian and Salerno landings. The minesweeping fleet included even Smokey Joes—veterans of the last war—craft which played a great part during Wavell's advance and whose achievements in other waters have earned from My Lords of the Admiralty the comment "They were minded of the old adage that many a good tune was played upon an old fiddle." Some came from Russian waters where they had helped in clearing the White Sea channels after sweeping convoys through the Murmansk run; others came from the Atlantic. At least one ship could claim to have taken a convoy to both Russia and Malta.

As at Sicily and again at Salerno a terrific naval bombardment preceded the landing. A nightlong sustained fire by cruisers and destroyers aiming at specific targets culminated in a tremendous climax when the Royal Navy's hush-hush rocket-ships opened fiery lanes through the sky with the atmosphere snapping back into place as though opened and closed by flaming zip-fasteners. This final bombardment had the object of "softening" the beaches, exploding land mines, eliminating strong-points and dispersing barbed-wire. From each rocket-ship projectiles seared the heavens, their explosions sounding like thunder in a cullender when they splayed their concentrated hell on the beaches. In face of such a bombardment nothing could stand, nothing could live.

Wavy Navy lieutenants commanded by a bearded R.N. flotilla officer stood on their bridges with midshipmen at elbows intoning range and bearing as they ran in. The most accurate navigation is essential on the part of these "rocketeers" as an error in position might result in tank landing ships and infantry assault craft which are already close inshore being blown skyhigh.

Lessons From Anzio

Lessons learned at Anzio governed the deployment of craft engaged in the initial assault. The greatest problem at Anzio had been to bring up sufficient guns and armour early enough to reinforce the lightly armed Rangers and other assault troops and this was complicated by the fact that the unfavourable slope of the "Peter and X-Ray" beaches on either side of Anzio made the rapid discharge of armour from tank landing ships most difficult. "Ducks" performed sterling work at Anzio bringing up small field guns but were an incomplete answer to the problem of providing early powerful support.

Assault craft loaded with infantry and engineers brought up the rear of the first wave. Farther from the shore large "infantry landing ships" filled and refilled the assault craft which were lowered rapidly from the davits and headed for the shore, returning and loading from the doors in the ships' sides, establishing a fast, regular ferry service to the beaches. At the same time other tank landing craft with bulldozers and cranes reached the beaches.

Meanwhile small, lively Hunt-class destroyers were weaving in and weaving out, pouring shot and shell into the defensive areas to rear and flank; and under the protection of a fleet of destroyers, the main fleet of sauceboat hyphen-shaped tank landing craft approached with the weightier armour and mobile guns. For the first time the problem of tides was of paramount importance, contrasting with previous landings which were mainly in the Mediterranean or Pacific. "Rhino" ferries made their debut to solve the questions of how armour could be landed on shelving beaches without delay and how to prevent the ebbing tide stranding the tank landing craft and presenting a pretty target to enemy fighter-bombers, in addition to immobilising such stranded ships.

Rhinos are American self-propelled rafts constructed on the unit principle with watertight rectangular steel tanks clamped in rows, like railway sleepers, two or three abreast, and with detachable motor-units in the port and starboard bows for propelling. They are manned by an Army sergeant and men drawn from inland waters patrols. Separate "tug" units built on the same principle manœuvred in the vicinity for assisting the unwieldy rafts where the tide was most difficult. Heading their bows toward the tank landing ships the Rhinos quickly made fast; extra portable ramps were placed in position and tanks, lorries, mobile guns clanked out of the tank landing ships and took up positions abreast aboard the Rhinos which carried on to the shore without delay, returning for more loads as soon as possible. The tank landing craft's job was not finished when they were empty— many of their holds are fitted up with "stretcher racks" and complete surgical units aboard for tending and carrying back the wounded.

Tidal Peculiarities

The problem of the tides dictated not only the necessity for Rhinos but governed in the main the most imaginative part of the operation.

A phrase often used in the past— "We learned many valuable lessons from the operation" — and Dieppe demonstrated in the clearest manner the hazards of a frontal attack against defended ports. It was argued—and the argument was supplemented by reports brought back by daring parties and individuals landing at night in Europe—that the enemy, knowing the tidal peculiarities of that section of the coast, thought it safe to assume that even the "mad English" would not attempt a landing on open beaches with the danger of landing craft broaching and landing ships becoming helplessly stranded on the shelving beaches.

A European landing obviously required the most speedy reinforcing of troops ashore and the previous technique which relied entirely on assault craft unloading from infantry ships would not prove able to cope with the situation. Clearly the problem was firstly the manœuvring of a mighty fleet. The ungainly landing craft, which are most difficult for station keeping, required certain conditions of moon and tide and since knowledge of the composition and tactics of the attacking fleet would have told the enemy all he wished to know, it can be underlined now that the success of the operation was in direct ratio to the degree that "nobody talked."

Petrol Barge Fleet

Hardly less imaginative and thrilling than the main clash of steel with steel was the manner in which the petrol supplies for the Army's armour were brought to Europe's shores. There was placed in commission as recently as November, 1943, a whole fleet of former Thames barges powered by Chrysler 95 h.p. marine engines and each manned by seven ratings with three officers per flotilla of 12 barges. Each barge is fitted in the stern with ramps for vehicles and a proportion are fitted up with tanks for fuel. Most of the coxswains and senior deckhands are former Thames or Humber lightermen and know their stuff.

In this way these gallant barge flotillas sailed to the fray and the phrase "concentrations of barges in the enemy's ports" was once more true, but this time under the White Ensign.

To the rear of the assault forces lay bigger ships. Covering forces of capital ships hovered protectively beyond the horizon. But it was the mighty fleet of "imponderables and expendables"—the little ships of the proverbial little men of England who this day flung the gauntlet for the final challenge on the doorstep of Mr Hitler.

LAMBTON BURN

Covered by naval guns, which provided screen for first landing parties, infantrymen wade to shore of France. Assault went according to carefully worked out plan

UNION JACK

Wednesday, June 14, 1944
No. 2   **Two Lire.**

FOR THE BRITISH FIGHTING FORCES

STOP PRESS

STATED AT SUPREME HEADQUARTERS LAST NIGHT THAT GERMANS HAVE COUNTER-ATTACKED AT MONTEBOURG AND CARENTAN. SITUATION FLUID. STATIC FIGHTING ON WHOLE FRONT.

ALLIES PUSHING ON IN GRIM FIGHTING

FURTHER important gains have been made in the Cherbourg peninsula, and the general situation was described at Supreme Allied Headquarters yesterday as "very gratifying."

Shortly after the capture of Carentan came news that Montebourg had fallen to an attack by the Fourth U.S. Infantry Division and that on the extreme left flank British forces had pushed forward five miles to take Torvam.

The Forest of Cerisy, which the Germans turned into an important supply dump, has now been cleared, and although the enemy still hold Caen the town is being threatened by a pincer movement.

Montebourg is 15 miles from the port of Cherbourg. It is on the peninsula's main highway at the junction of a number of secondary roads.

A correspondent with the U.S. forces said the conquest was the result of the stiffest action that the American forces have so far fought in France.

The Germans were so bent on holding it that they threw in reinforcements brought from Cherbourg itself.

A small force of German tanks counter-attacked repeatedly before Montebourg fell, and one correspondent reports that the mopping up was still going on in the streets at dawn yesterday.

Earlier, the Allied communique stresses the importance of the fall of Carentan, at the eastern base of the peninsula. Thanks to it the link up between our forces, that is to say, between those in the peninsula and those to the east, has been materially strengthened.

Besides this, the fall of Carentan, considerably narrows the bottleneck through which the Germans defending Cherbourg can get reinforcements.

A correspondent at Supreme Allied Headquarters adds that there are signs of some enemy traffic still going on along the road from the west. There is no news of a planned counter-attack against our forces in the peninsula.

During the assault on Carentan the U.S. paratroops who took the town could only attack in single file along one highway, often wading chest deep through swamps and mire in the face of withering machine - gun and 88mm gun fire.

On Sunday they called a two-hour truce to give the Germans in the town an opportunity to surrender, but the offer was refused. The young German Captain in command declined to accept the responsibility for such a decision in the absence of a senior officer. An American officer accompanied by captured German soldiers carried the rejected terms to the enemy headquarters under a white flag.

All day wave after wave of Allied aircraft swept over the Channel to smash at German defences and communications and, although the Luftwaffe is making a more spirited reply, it is obvious that the Germans are seriously perturbed by the Allied air supremacy.

Ian Munro, Reuter's Special Correspondent at S.H.A.E.F., said that German air reconnaissance activity before the invasion was so

TURN TO PAGE 4.

CHURCHILL IN FRANCE

See Page Three

Leopold in Germany

THE Belgium Government in London announced yesterday they had received confirmation that King Leopold was sent to Germany on June 7.

On news of the Allied landings the Germans moved King Leopold from Belgium as a security measure, an understandable move in that he is technically Commander-in-Chief of the Belgium Army and, therefore, a potential rallying point for Belgium resistance, states the Associated Press.

King Leopold assumed supreme command of the Belgium army in September, 1939.

While he did not follow his government into exile, he refused to reign under German rule, preferring to remain, as he termed it, "a prisoner of the Germans," in a castle near Brusels.

Greeks fight soon

The new Greek Government of National Unity held its first meeting in Cairo, with the only Ministers absent those still to be nominated by the Left Wing organisations inside Greece, the B.B.C. said on Tuesday.

Prime Minister Papandreu announced that all Greek naval units were again in action and that the Army was being reorganised and might be in the field next month.

According to the B.B.C. declaration by the Ministers of the Greek Government made it clear that the King of Greece would not return until he was invited to do so by the free vote of the people and that the King had completely accepted his position.

Air help for Tito

YESTERDAY'S Italy air communique stated that fighter-bombers struck at shipping and communications in the Korcula harbour area in Yugoslavia and also bombed Hungary.

This followed an earlier statement from Marshal Tito's Headquarters that Allied aircraft have in the past few days destroyed more than 70 wagons in various parts of Yugoslavia carrying ammunition and fuel.

Enemy ships in the Adriatic had also been sunk, said the communique, which was quoted by Reuter from London.

Offensive operations were reported in the Sandjak, Herzegovina and western Bosnia, where Sicevo was recaptured. Allied warships were in action off the Dalmatian coast, said Reuter, and sent several German ships to the bottom.

Yugoslavs freed by the fall of Rome expressed an immediate desire to join Marshal Tito.

Air-Marshal Tedder, Deputy Commander of the invasion force, must be feeling happy and confident at the initial success of the landings. This picture, taken before he left the Mediterranean, shows just how happy he can be.

Russians capture Finn key town of Viborg

"UNION JACK" Central Italy Edition

The Central Italy Edition of "Union Jack" will serve areas farther forward than those formerly supplied by the Western Italy Edition.

Units interested should write, stating their requirements, to Administration Officer, "Union Jack," Central Italy Edition, "B" British Army Newspaper Unit, C.M.F.

Six subs sunk

The sinking of six enemy submarines in an action extending over 10 days is announced by the Royal Canadian Navy. No details were given.

The announcement came with the award of a decoration to Lieutenant W. J. Chipman, who served in one of the ships during the action.

YESTERDAY, three days after the opening of their offensive against the Finns, the Russians occupied the key town of Viborg as well as 30 other minor places. The Finns are reported to be bringing up reserves and putting up a stubborn resistance to the Soviet advance.

The Soviet army has already broken through the first defences of the Karelian Wall, built to the plans of the German Todt organisation, responsible for the Gustav Line and the Atlantic Wall, and is battering against the old Mannerheim Line of the 1940 war.

A report from Stockholm says that officials there are reported as reckoning on a complete Russian breakthrough.

Duncan Hooper, Reuter's correspondent in Moscow, says that Soviet tanks and mobile artillery screened by fighter-bombers and backed by infantrymen have been moving through a swiftly-broadening gap. On Monday night they were driving back defeated Finnish garrisons in the direction of the old Mannerheim Line zone.

After the original break-through the Russians are pushing one spearhead north and west, while another strikes eastward. Fighting so far has been very savage, with heavy Finnish losses under intense Soviet bombing and shelling.

Russian Army men and Finns have come to grips in the shattered trenches—the Russians wielding bayonets and grenades, the Finns fighting back with the deadly "Finka," as the long, razor-sharp Finnish knife is known.

The Russians have massed air and artillery support on a vast scale, Hooper reports. They appear to be using at least as much material as was used to smash the German arc around Leningrad earlier this year.

This is regarded as evidence of the Soviet's determination to settle with Finland in the shortest possible time, following

the rejection of her proffered terms and warning to Finland to get out of the war or court national disaster.

Tanks, guns, planes and infantry are all co-operating in the Soviet advance. In many respects the initial Soviet onslaught, with the big guns of the navy hurling in shells from the sea, resembled the tactics of the Allied landings in France.

Dispatches from Moscow emphasised the complete surprise which the offensive was able to achieve and the devastating effectiveness of its opening blows.

The planning of this offensive began two years ago, a few months after the Finnish-German drive on Leningrad was stopped. An indispensable preliminary was the lifting of the siege of Leningrad and the rout of the German northern army group—an operation successfully completed last winter.

Questions on Service vote

NUMEROUS questions will be put to the Secretary for War, Sir James Grigg, in the House of Commons this week regarding Army Form B3526. Only by filling in this form will Servicemen be able to vote at the next General Election.

Grigg was questioned on this subject last week and said he presumed the military authorities were carrying out their instructions, but it is clear that members of all parties are not so sure.

The "Daily Mail" reported yesterday that it took 100 Servicemen at random in the street and railway station, asking, "Have you filled in your voting declaration card?" Sixty men said "Yes" and 40 "No."

This means two out of every five men still in the Army will probably find themselves disfranchised

RESISTANCE IN ITALY GROWS

FIFTH Army troops are now 70 miles north of Rome—"chasing the enemy"—General Clark told more than 2,000 combat troops when he opened a Fifth Army Rest Centre on the outskirts of Rome.

Yesterday's official communique reported progress against increasing enemy resistance east and west of Lake Bolsena, and fierce fighting around Bagnoregio.

On the coastal sector, the enemy continues to resist south-east of Orbetello. In the central sector heavy fighting is still going on south of the important town of Terni.

The advance toward the Saline River, on the Adriatic Sector, continued unchecked.

Michael Reynolds, B.B.C. correspondent at General Alexander's Headquarters, says that no real progress has been made east of the Tiber in the past day or two, but west of the river resistance is increasing around Lake Bolsena. Particularly fierce fighting is now taking place near Bagnoregio.

South-east of Orbetello, American troops have cut the main road and seized some high ground overlooking the town.

Rome radio reported last night that German rearguards and Allied units are locked in very fierce fighting on the shores of Lake Bolsena, while on the western side of the lake the Germans have been forced to fall back on new positions.

From these operations four of our aircraft are missing. No enemy aircraft were encountered over the battle area during daylight.

When General Clark opened the Fifth Army Rest Centre, he said : "It is a great tribute to the Fifth Army that French, British and American troops accomplished this outstanding job."

He told front-line infantrymen : "You are the men who hoof it, who slug it out with the enemy. I do not mean to minimise the importance of other branches-air, armour, artillery and all the others, for this is a combat team —but you are the men who carry the biggest load."

General Absolution

Civilians in imminent danger of death from air raids as well as soldiers in mortal peril because a battle has begun, or is about to begin, may now be given collectively a General Sacramental Absolution, even though they have made no previous confession, it was announced yesterday

CHURCHILL IN FRANCE

Seven-hour tour of allied beach-head

By DESMOND TIGHE, Reuter's Correspondent Aboard British destroyer, Kelvin.

NORMANDY BEACH-HEAD, Tuesday.

MR. CHURCHILL, Field-Marshal Smuts and Field-Marshal Sir Alan Brooke visited the Normandy beaches yesterday. They spent several hours ashore, lunched with General Montgomery, visited Army Headquarters and watched troops and supplies landed.

The Kelvin—carrying the Prime Minister and other distinguished people—herself bombarded a German position on north-eastern flank.

Mr. Churchill saw bombs falling on the anchorage, watched a dog-fight and saw a German daylight intruder shot down.

The Prime Minister arrived on the beaches at eleven o'clock in the morning and left after six in the evening.

General Montgomery was there on the beach to meet the Prime Minister.

General Smuts smiled cheerfully and swung round his cine-camera as the party clambered into wait-

MR. CHURCHILL.

ing jeeps and drove off to General Montgomery's headquarters.

The sun is now setting and the Kelvin is racing at full speed ahead for a British port. The Prime Minister, resting in the captain's cabin, has had one of the most exciting days any Prime Minister has ever had in the whole course of his career.

Six days after the invasion of Western Europe was put in action Churchill landed and spent nearly seven hours with his troops.

Some recognised him, others were too busy at work to look up, but those who did gave him a grand welcome.

— Troops marching towards the front cheered him as his jeep drove past. French people gazed rather bewildered, unable to believe it was Churchill.

It was just after dawn when the Kelvin slipped quietly from

FIELD-MARSHAL SMUTS

her moorings in a British port and steamed out into the English Channel.

Churchill, Smuts and Brooke stood on the bridge wearing "Mae West" life-jackets.

General Eisenhower, Supreme Commander of the Allied Forces, also led a party of top United States Military and Naval Commanders on a tour of the American-held section of the Normandy battlefront.

HOME POSTINGS ASSURANCE

AN assurance that the arrangement under which soldiers serve five years overseas to qualify for home posting will not be "continued automatically" has been given to Mr. Henderson Stewart, Liberal M.P. for East Fife, in correspondence with the War Minister.

Sir James Grigg's secretary replied to his questions: "It is correct under existing arrangements that Army personnel must serve five years continuously overseas to qualify for reversion to home establishment. But it would be a mistake to assume that this arrangement will continue automatically.

"If at any time it is possible to reduce the five year qualifying period the opportunity will not be lost."

Banks re-open in record time

ROME banks are reopening on the orders of the Allied Military Government. Restoration of these vital financial services only a week after the occupation makes a new record. It took six weeks in Sicily and a month in Naples.

Rome post offices are also to resume their banking operations, and the order lifts the moratorium which was applied when the Allies entered the city.

Removal of Vincenzo Azzolini as head of the Bank of Italy continues to arouse widespread interest.

Azzolini, who is being held in custody in his own home, was arrested on a charge of having given up all the gold in the bank to the Germans. Azzolini says he was forced to do this on a German threat of death for refusing to obey this demand.

Another Regiment For Palatine Guard

VATICAN CITY, Tuesday.

The Palatine Guard of Pope Pius XII, will be further enlarged by the addition of another regiment, it was announced to-day. The existing regiment includes 2,500 officers and men.

Before the German occupation of Rome the Palatine Guard consisted of only 500 men. It was increased to help guard the Basilicas and pontifical buildings scattered throughout the city of Rome, all of which enjoy extra-territorial rights.

The Palatine Guards wear grey-green uniform, red berets and are armed with Italian Army rifles. They are independent of the Swiss Guards who serve the Pope personally within Vatican City.

Eighth Army Holds An Exhibition

Troops examining the 7.5 cm assault gun on a Mark IV chassis and a Mark III chasis (background) at an exhibition of enemy equipment captured by Eighth Army

They Even Destroyed The Kitchen Garden

ROME, Tuesday.

FRESH evidence of Nazi destruction was found at Genzano, where St. Patrick's Irish Augustinian College was used as a transmitting station by Hitler's troops during the battle for Valmontone, some 25 miles south of Rome.

"German troops tore down and burnt the Irish flag and diplomatic documents posted outside the church and threw out the caretaker and his family," said Father Thomas Toomey, of Tralee, County Kerry. "They then brought in a radio transmitter and took control of the premises.

"No damage was done to the buildings by Allied shelling, but the German troops before leaving practically destroyed all the furniture," added Father Toomey.

The interior of the building, which was built by the late Doctor Maurice Magrath, of Dungarvan, County Waterford, was completely wrecked.

Furniture was smashed, doors burst open and rooms were littered with wool from mattresses wantonly ripped open. In the cellars, the Nazis shot holes into barrels of wine after helping themselves to their fill.

In the kitchen garden, every potato, bean or pea which the Germans couldn't eat they destroyed.—*U.N.N.*

United nations day

To-day is being observed in Britain as United Nations Day.

In a special message commemorating the celebration, Mr. Churchill said yesterday: "As we draw towards the final victory for which we long it is fitting that we should emphasise the unity which alone can make it possible."

Army Paper In France

A liberation issue of "Stars and Stripes," United States Army newspaper, was delivered on Monday to the soldiers in France.

The newspaper contains eight pages instead of the usual four. The extra space is used for a complete review of news and pictures to bring front line soldiers up to date on what has happened since they crossed the Channel last week.

"Stars and Stripes" regular edition will be delivered to its readers in France daily.

Welsh Floods

Couple Cling To Clothes Line

RESCUE of an aged couple from a flooded cottage when they were already up to their necks in water was one of the most dramatic incidents in Whitsuntide storms which were more violent and prolonged than any in living memory.

The couple, Leonard George Webb, aged 73, and his bed-ridden wife, were alone in a one-story cottage at Cilycwm, near Llandovery, when the cottage was surrounded by flood waters from the River Dynant.

Recognising their danger, Constable Glyin Hopkin and Roadman Thomas fought their way to the cottage and through a window saw that the flood waters had reached to within eighteen inches of the roof.

Webb and his wife in a state of exhaustion, were hanging on to a clothes-line with their heads just above water.

Thomas and Hopkin managed to get them out with only a few minutes to spare.

CHILDREN PLAY IN ORTONA AGAIN

A few days ago I drove through the streets of deserted Ortona, writes Capt. T. H. Muschamp, official observer, its walls pitted with shell fragments, houses demolished and signs of life were rare, as the Germans shelled the town causing remaining inhabitants to seek refuge in cellars.

But to-day it was different, with tanks and self-propelled guns driving through Ortona again.

From the balconies of ruined houses, from shell-pitted pavements, women, children and men that remain stood silent at first, not understanding, then the full realisation of what this influx of vehicles, tracked and wheeled, meant swept through the crowd that came pouring from side streets, with names like Edmonton Avenue, Manitoba Way, reminders of when the Canadians fought from house to house and street by street.

Suddenly these people standing in streets smiled again, where for past winter months smiles and laughter were unknown. From being a front line town, shelled nightly and sometimes by day, the people realised the significance of the vehicles passing through, the Germans had gone. In the ruins of their once beautiful town children are beginning to laugh and play in the streets again.

World's biggest airport

LONDON, Tuesday.

LONDON is to have the largest airport in the world after the war.

It is to be constructed at Staines and will cover 2,800 acres, 300 acres more than New York airport. The site lies between the Great West road and the Great Western line.

In addition to the existing easy comunication with the centre of London, the underground line is to be extended from Hounslow.

The Air Ministry have secured land options to prevent the aerodrome being surrounded by new housing estates as at Croydon and Hendon.

Former Minister Died In Concentration Camp

Reuter dispatch reports that Doctor Markovic, a former Czechoslovak Minister of Education, died in a German concentration camp.

Markovic, a Slovak by birth, was a leading member of the Czechoslovak Social Democrats. **P.W.B.-Reuter.**

General Montgomery:

"We have won battle of the beaches"

From DOON CAMPBELL, Reuter's Special Correspondent.

"WE have won the battle of the Beaches," General Montgomery told nearly 50 bridgehead correspondents at Tactical Headquarters in Normandy on Sunday night.

General Montgomery declared: "I am very happy and very pleased indeed with the situation so far, but there is a good deal to be done yet.

"There are no longer any gaps between British and Americans—that is good, very good.

"The width of our lodgement area is over 60 miles from east of River Orne to the American troops, who are only 18 miles from Cherbourg.

"The depth varies. In some places it is 10 miles, in other places not so much. It is a good firm lodgement area which we can use as a firm base for developing operations."

General Montgomery went on, "As you know—and the Germans know, too—we landed at certain places—here and there— and there were gaps between landing places.

"The violence, power and speed of our own initial assault carried us right over the beaches and some miles inland very quickly.

"With violence and power we left the beaches behind us except in one special case.

"On these beaches there were concrete defences, and in a great many cases they were passed with the German garrison still remaining in them. Of course, in places we did not take—places between landings—the Germans were still left.

"But our soldiers penetrated inland. I said beforehand that every man must be imbued with one idea, and that was to penetrate quickly and deeply into enemy country and peg out claims inland. That was my initial instruction to senior officers.

"That had curious repercussions in that there were defended localities which still held out when we were three miles inland.

"They had to be dealt with and reduced later. In that process we had losses because they were held by stout-hearted Germans who fought very well indeed in their concrete-built boxes.

"They were a great nuisance in that for some days there were wandering about inside our area a considerable number of loose Germans and snipers.

"AMONG THESE SNIPERS ARE SOME VERY STOUT-HEARTED WOMEN. WOMEN SNIPERS HAVE BEEN KILLED DEFINITELY WHILE DOING THEIR STUFF.

"I made one exception when I spoke about the beaches, and that was the beach where the landing of American troops took place east of Carentan Estuary.

"They found that sector of the beach being defended by a German division which was not a coastal division. This was a field division which had been brought in to that sector. It was a very good division and fought very well.

"There is no doubt about it that those American troops did absolutely magnificently, because they recovered from a very unpleasant situation, and to-day these same troops are about 10 miles inland.

"That situation was retrieved by three things: First, the gallantry of American soldiers who are very brave men; second, very fine supporting fire given from the sea by the Allied Navy; and third, very good support given from the air by fighter-bombers who came down low to shoot up the Germans at close range.

"The situation to-day is that these landings we have made on the coast of Normandy have all been joined up into a solid line—a continuous lodgement area.

"A great many enemy troops have been killed. Among prisoners are some Japanese and Poles forced to serve in the German Army.

"Our own soldiers—American and British—are in tremendous form.

"The troops have their tails very high up in the air. They are in tremendous form, full of beans.

"They are very confident and have already got the measure of the enemy."

UNION JACK

Friday, June 16, 1944
No. 4   Two Lire

FOR THE BRITISH FIGHTING FORCES

STOP PRESS

WOMEN SNIPERS TAKEN IN NORMANDY ARE TO BE TREATED AS PRISONERS OF WAR, SAYS S.H.A.E.F. SPOKESMAN. WILL BE GUARDED BY A.T.S. ATTACHED TO C.M.P., BUT UNARMED.

"UNION JACK"
Central Italy Edition

The Central Italy Edition of "Union Jack" will serve areas farther forward than those formerly supplied by the Western Italy Edition.

Units interested should write, stating their requirements, to Administration Officer, "Union Jack," Central Italy Edition, "B" British Army Newspaper Unit, C.M.F.

9-mile drive by Russians

MAINTAINING unremitting pressure, the Russian forces have advanced nine miles on the central sector of the Karelian Isthmus and captured an important town.

The strength of the Russian drive is forcing the Finns to throw in still more reserves, says Duncan Hooper, Reuter's correspondent in Moscow. In the past two days, he says, more and more infantry have come to grips in bitter fighting under strong Soviet air support.

Supporting the land operations, the Soviet battleship October Revolution and the heavy cruiser Kirov have pounded Finnish positions in the Isthmus. All the fire power of warships based on Kronstadt, the Soviet naval base off Leningrad, is supporting the army.

While other sectors of the eastern front remain "quiet," the Russian Air Force was out in strength on Tuesday night attacking a string of aerodromes behind the central front.

The bases of Brest Litovsk, Bialystok, Barenovichi, Pinsk, Minsk, Bobruisk and Orsha were hit. Fires were started in hangars, dumps and dispersal areas and a number of enemy planes were destroyed on the ground.

ALLIES HOLD OFF 800 TANKS

A FURIOUS armoured battle is raging along the line from Tilly-sur-Seulles to Caen, where Rommel is reported to have thrown in a large force, including 800 tanks, in an effort to stem the Allied advance in the eastern sector of the Normandy front, says a Reuter report.

The Allied line is holding firm and all the counter-attacks have so far been beaten off with heavy losses, having failed to dislodge our troops from any position.

The defence is vigorous, and yesterday's communique from Supreme Allied Headquarters said: "Allied forces continue to carry the fight to the enemy."

Heaviest fighting has taken place in the Carentan, Montebourg and Caen areas. Airborne troops have successfully beaten off German attempts to retake Carentan and are once more pushing southward from the town. They have also advanced farther to the west in the vicinity of Les Sablons-Bospte.

Strength Built Up

Meanwhile, Allied armoured strength is being built up, and the arrival of reinforcements has been facilitated in the past few days by good weather in the Channel.

The Germans appear at the moment to be concentrating their main effort around Balleroy and Tilly, with the aim of hampering General Montgomery's drive around Tilly to the south-east to Caen. Allied armour has already found the German flank west of Tilly.

The enemy is reported to have mustered four panzer divisions in the Caen area.

It has been revealed in London that the four divisions are equipped to some extent with French, Czech and Russian tanks. This variety of types makes the problem of replacement and supply even more difficult than normal. It is pointed out that this reliance on foreign-built and captured tanks is a direct result of Allied bombing, which has severely damaged the Reich tank industry.

The outstanding fact of the nine-day battle is that the Allied armies still hold the initiative, a B.B.C. commentator said: "There have been local fluctuations, of course, but it is General Montgomery, not the Germans, who is dictating the shape of the battle.

"Plugging up holes is a wasteful business, and that is what the Germans have so far been compelled to do," he continued. "We have always been at least one jump ahead of the guns of our warships. That can only mean we are satisfied with the power of our field artillery."

William Steen, Reuter's Special Correspondent at S.H.A.E.F. (Supreme Allied Headquarters) says that the latest advances by American troops thrusting westward in the Cherbourg peninsula threaten to isolate the great port. Seven miles now separate them from high ground dominating the only main road and railway left through Le Haye du Poits.

Momentous

"An advance to these positions would be momentous," an official at S.H.A.E.F. told Steen "but at our present rate of progress it will take some time." The isolation threat is developing on a nine-mile front as American airborne troops thrust south and south-west from Carentan.

Describing the heavy fighting in the Caumont, Villiers and Bocage sectors, Steen says the situation is thought to be "satisfactory" at S.H.A.E.F., though there is no doubt that the enemy is using very considerable forces. The Allies hold high ground to the west of Villiers, and the Germans on the other side of the river are in the town and on high ground to the east.

Some two or three miles separate the highest points of ground held by the opposing forces, and between them is a steep valley about a quarter of a mile wide. Artillery is being brought up to support the Allied thrust.

It is not yet clear how much of the tank strength of the four armoured divisions has actually been committed to battle, but they have been used in such concentrated masses in some cases that our own tanks and guns have created havoc.

The German commanders, apparently realising the mass onslaughts can be smashed in this way, are now employing their tanks in smaller groups and with more skill.

The Germans are leaving behind a trail of broken wreckage like that scattered by the Allies during the great retreat of 1940, says a Reuter's corespondent. "The stretch between the beaches and the advanced US. lines looks like a gigantic wrecking yard," he said.

He added that scores of vehicles and armoured material, from bicycles to truck-mounted anti-aircraft batteries, litter the roadside and ditches. Occasionally.

(TURN TO PAGE FOUR.)

During a visit to invasion troops in Britain, the King inspected General Montgomery's caravan on which is marked the names of the campaigns in Egypt, Tripolitania, Tunis, Sicily and Italy.

Places in the battle

LA POISSONIERE, where fighter-bombers struck at a railway bridge, is on the Loire River, 50 miles north-east of Nantes.

The ETAMPES - ORLEANS railway, sections of which are being constantly attacked from the air, is a 50-mile stretch running north of Orleans in central France.

DOMFRONT, where medium and light bombers set a fuel dump aflame, is on the Varenne River, 55 miles south of Caen.

BEAUVAIS, a target for heavy bombers, is 30 miles north of Paris on a main railway line to Paris.

BEAUMONT, another town hit by heavy bombers, is on the river Oise, 20 miles north of Paris and on the Paris-Beauvais railway.

CAUMONT, scene of heavy land fighting, is 18 miles south-west of Bayeux, 26 miles west of Caen and 16 miles south of the Normandy coast.

'..To the end.'

GENERAL MONTGOMERY has sent the following personal message to troops of the 21st Army Group: "After four days of fighting Allied armies have secured a good and firm lodgement area on the mainland of France.

"First, we must thank Almighty God for the success we have achieved and for giving us such a good beginning towards the full completion of our task. Second, we must pay tribute to the Allied navies and air forces for their magnificent co-operation and support. Without it we soldiers could have achieved nothing.

"Third, I want personally to congratulate every officer and man in the Allied Army on the splendid results of the last four days. British, Canadian and American soldiers fighting gallantly side by side have achieved great success and have placed themselves in a good position from which to exploit this success.

"To every officer and man, whatever may be his rank or employment, I send my grateful thanks and my best wishes for the future.

"Much still remains to be done but together, you and I, we will do it, and we will see the thing through to the end. Good luck to you all." Signed, B. L. Montgomery, Commander-in-Chief, 21st Army Group, France.

In a special message to the Commander, 50 (Northumbrian) Division, General Montgomery expressed his "heartfelt congratulations on the achievement of 50 Division, to yourself and all ranks."

The Corps Commander adds his congratulations. His message said: "All our objectives have been gained and vigorous reconnaissance thrusts are now proceeding towards vital spots. Well done indeed. Grandly lads!! champion!!!"

Eighth Army take Orvieto, push on to North

IMPORTANT gains have been made all along the front in Italy. Eighth Army troops have captured the important road centre of Orvieto. Other troops have reached the outskirts of Terni, the big industrial and communications centre.

In addition to reporting these gains, yesterday's official communique reports that the stiffening enemy resistance which the Allied armies in Italy have encountered during the past three days has at least temporarily been overcome.

Highway 74 has now been cleared of the enemy throughout its length, and further advances have been made in the coastal sector.

The capture of Orvieto followed the advance of the Eighth Army up the Tiber Valley. Forward elements then continued to push farther north. East of the Tiber progress is slower through the mountain country, but further advances were made.

Fifth Army troops in the coastal sector overcame determined resistance on the road to Magliano before capturing the town on Wednesday. German horse cavalry took part in the action.

French troops in the vicinity of Lake Bolsena continued their advance against lessening resistance.

Mannerheim line gone

SOVIET troops have broken the Mannerheim Line and captured more than 120 Finnish towns and settlements, says the Soviet communique.

In one battle a Russian formation put out of action 2,000 Finnish officers and men and took many prisoners. Seventeen guns, 20 mortars and 67 machine-guns were captured.

Active support was given the ground forces by Russian aircraft, which attacked Finnish reserves advancing to the front and accounted for approximately 60 motor vehicles carrying enemy infantry and munitions. Fifteen Finnish aircraft were brought down in air combats.

Pay concession for paratroops

Paratroops and airborne troops who are wounded on active service will continue to receive their extra allowance for 91 days, the War Office has announced.

If they remain in hospital longer than that they will lose their extra pay, which will be restored as soon as they return to their units, it was stated.—Reuter.

Prisoners hid in Vatican

DURING the German occupation of Rome, nineteen Allied escaped prisoners-of-war sought refuge in the Vatican, says a Reuter message from London.

They comprised 11 Englishmen, two Americans, two Canadians, one New Zealander, two Poles, one Australian and one Austrian, the last a deserter from the German army, according to Archbishop Gustave, the former Apostolic Delegate in Egypt.

de Gaulle may visit F.D.R.

General de Gaulle has welcomed President Roosevelt's invitation to visit Washington, says Reuter's Diplomatic correspondent, but well-informed quarters believe he considers it necessary to consult the French Committee of Liberation and secure their collective support.

REPUBLIC OF ICELAND

The Republic of Iceland was inaugurated on Saturday at Thingvellir, where for centuries the Icelandic Parliament, the oldest parliament in the world, used to meet every summer in the open air.

War newsreels pack the home cinemas

FROM "UNION JACK" LONDON REPORTER, CYRIL JAMES (by Radio, Monday)

THE longest queues in Britain to-day are lined up in front of the fishmongers, and the newsreel cinemas. The fishmongers reputedly have an unexpectedly large supply of fresh herrings and the newsreel cinemas are showing two films which have knocked Hollywood's efforts clean out of the screen.

The first film is a day-by-day record of the invasion and the second is the fall of Rome. People who have regularly visited the hour-long news film shows since the war began tell me that they have never known such an exciting programme.

But the real reason why at a quarter past three on Saturday the queue outside an Oxford Street, London, newsreel cinema stretched for more than 100 yards is that people are hoping to glimpse on the crowded screen just a flash of someone dear to them in the great adventure in Normandy and Rome.

There's our George !

Many of them have been lucky. Cries of "Look, is that Harry?" break the tense silence in which audiences watch the landings on the beaches or the parades through Rome.

For instance, Mrs. Paltridge, of Waterloo Road, South Shore, Blackpool, has written to her Commando son, George Paltridge, as follows: "We had a nice surprise, George, seeing you in the invasion film. I was with Mrs. Sharpe and at once exclaimed, 'Oh, there is our George.' She also recognised you at once. The next day 'Pop' and I went and both recognised you without doubt."

This homely little letter, which was printed in the "News Chronicle," tells more vividly than any elaborate message the intense interest with which your people at home are following the screen record of the war in Normandy and in Italy.

The news reel shots of the invasion are magnificent stuff. I had something to do with the making of "Desert Victory" in Libya and know the "real stuff" when I see it on the screen.

The sticky fighting on certain sections of the beach has been placed on the screen without mincing or cutting. You see our troops falling before withering cross-fire. You see their determined advance in the face of bitter opposition.

Some early reports of the invasion suggested that its early phases had been a "walk-over." Quite rightly the troops protested against this facile verdict and later reports put the matter right. Newsreel shots clinch the matter, and ensure that the scale of our troops' first efforts on the Continent will not be minimised for posterity.

Rome triumph

If the note of stern realism and stubborn effort dominates the news reels of the invasion, the pictures of the occupation of Rome by way of contrast provide an almost lyrical note of triumph. The delirious delight of the Rome populace, the evident bounding spirits of the occupying troops, live more vividly on the thousands of screens now reflecting the pictures than in the cleverest dispatch.

It is interesting to listen to the audience reacting to the appearance of Allied leaders on the screen. General Montgomery receives a tremendous round of applause whenever his figure appears. General Eisenhower and Air Chief Marshal Tedder also cause a storm of hand-clapping. And shots of General Alexander in Italy call forth a deep note of admiration and delight.

Fighting P.M.

I have not yet seen news reels of Mr. Churchill's visit to France but I can prophesy that audiences will react enthusiastically because, whatever a few members of Parliament may think of the Prime Minister's action in visiting the beaches, most of your people have thoroughly endorsed his action in their hearts and minds.

They realise what a stimulant it must have been to the "boys" to see their fighting Prime Minister so quickly among them.

One London newspaper summarised the feeling admirably by publishing to-day a cartoon showing a platoon of riflemen busily firing at the enemy. Mr. Churchill is shown with them lying prone and blazing away with a rifle.

The King goes to Normandy

KING GEORGE VI. visited the Allied battle area in Normandy on Friday and lunched with General Montgomery at his advanced headquarters after holding an open-air investiture less than six miles from the front lines.

The King made the crossing on the British cruiser H.M.S. Arethusa, which was escorted by the destroyers Scourge and Urania. A few miles off the French coast he transferred to a motor-launch, and thence to a "duck" just off the beach from which he started his tour of the battle area.

After his visit the King sent a message to General Eisenhower which said: "To-day I have visited the beaches of Normandy.

"I have come home feeling intense admiration for all those who planned and organised so vast a project, and the gallant and successful execution of it in all its varied phases by everyone now engaged in this great battle."

U.S. casualties total 15,883

U.S. casualties in the invasion of France totalled 15,883 up to midnight on Friday. Of these, 3,283 were killed and 12,600 wounded.

Giving these figures, General Omar Bradley, Commander of the American forces in France, said that casualties were higher than expected on the mainland beaches but those in the peninsula landings were lower than expected.

He also announced that the total number of prisoners evacuated from the American area numbered 8,500.

Czech oil plant hit

STRONG forces of escorted 15th A.A.F. heavy bombers attacked five oil refineries in the Vienna area and a sixth by Bratislava, Czechoslovakia, on Friday. Results were reported good at all targets. It was stated at Allied Force Headquarters.

Lana Turner has forsaken her slinky gowns in this picture. The man from Hollywood who sent it to us says this is how she looks when she is at home.

— AND WAR ARTISTS STAND BY TO MOVE TO FRANCE

MANY people are attending another kind of picture show in London. But these pictures are not flashed on a screen. They are hanging on the walls of the National Gallery and look like staying there a long while, judging by the interest taken in this exhibition of paintings and drawings by official war artists.

These are the works which unborn generations will study when they want to know the inner feeling of these stern and terrible times, because finally the eye of the artist will return a truer verdict than the lens of the camera. There are paintings of war in the desert, in the Burmese jungle, on the high seas, in the air.

There are pictures of war workers in the factories and the coal mines. There are portraits of generals, admirals, sergeants, and Wrens and police constables, who have distinguished themselves in the five years of struggle.

Three purposes

Perhaps you may be interested to know how the war artists' scheme works so let me quote what the National Gallery trustees have to say about it.

"The war artists' scheme dates from the beginning of the war," they say, "when a committee was appointed to choose artists who could make what was described as 'an artistic record of the war in all its aspects.'

Three purposes were served by this scheme. First, that posterity should have some notion of what these extraordinary times looked like to the sensitive eye of the artist; secondly, to show contemporaries at home and overseas something of our war efforts, and thirdly, to provide employment for a section of our best artists during what would inevitably be a difficult period for the arts."

Accordingly the committee picked its "runners so that at the end of the war Britain would have not only an accurate record of the fighting and other war effort but also a representative collection of modern English paintings.

They commissioned six artists and attached them to the Army with the rank of captain. Two were attached to the Navy, two to the missions by the Ministry of Information. Still others are asked to do a single piece of work.

The report continues: "The war artists have not been confined to their studios. Edward Ardizzone and Edward Bawden were at Dunkirk. Bawden then went to the Middle East and painted the Ethiopian campaign, following Wavell's armies as far as Benghazi. He then turned eastward to Syria and after several months of life among the Arabs when his ship was sunk and his drawings, the best, in his opinion, he had done, were lost.

"After seven days in an open boat and some months in an internment camp at Casablanca he reappeared in England, but at his urgent request was soon sent back to work and thence to China.

"Ardizzone has followed the fortunes of the Eighth Army in the front line from Alamein to the Sangro River, retaining his natural good humour but also responding to the tragedy of death and devastation in southern Italy and Naples.

"But perhaps the artist who has been closest of all to the enemy is Anthony Gross, who was sent to record the war in Burma and some of whose drawings were done in a trench within 25 yards of the Japanese.

One artist was killed, Eric Ravilious, whose plane was lost near Iceland. Another, John Worsley, is missing.

Other artists are standing by to move into France as the armies advance.

Their pictures are not solely at the National Gallery. Many have been sent overseas to the Dominions and Colonies. Some are touring Great Britain. Five hundred were sent to British Restaurants and many others to canteens and special exhibitions in Service stations.

After the war these works of art will go to appropriate Service collections. The finest may be included in the national art collections and it is hoped a quantity of pictures and drawings will be sent to provincial galleries, especially where the subject has some connection with the locality.

So you see both on the cinema screen and the walls of the art galleries the pictorial record of this world struggle, so varied in background and terrain, is already steadily taking shape.

Sir Aubrey

C. Aubrey Smith, the "Great Englishman" of Hollywood, has been knighted.

He has done much to bring understanding of the British to America, and has broken down Hollywood's prejudice against cricket to such an extent that San Francisco has a cricket ground named after him. He is 80 years of age.

Div parade in Rome

BRITISH troops and Romans lined the street between All Saints (Church of England) and the Piazza del Popolo yesterday morning to watch a march past led by the Massed Pipe Band.

The march past, at which the salute was taken by the Commander of a British Division, supported by several senior British Naval, Army and Air Force officers, concluded a dual ceremony.

The morning service at All Saints, which had been closed since June 10, 1940—the day on which Mussolini declared war on the side of the Axis—was one of thanksgiving for the preservation of Rome and of the church, of which it marked the reopening. Sunday was also the 129th anni-

played a conspicuous part in the advance of the beach-head forces from Anzio celebrated the occasion with a march through Rome.

Some 200 men of the battalion were among the 500 British troops who attended the service at All Saints.

Despite drizzle, a crowd gathered round the saluting base in the Piazza del Popolo some time before the march past.

As the kilted pipers swung down the road from the church, the rain stopped and the sun broke through the clouds.

Besides detachments of the First Battalion, Duke of Wellington's, other units in the march past represented the Cheshire Regiment, R.E., R.A.S.C., R.A.O.C., R.A.M.C., C.M.P. and R.A.F. Regiment.

D-day joy in Moscow

MOSCOW'S streets were crowded till curfew time on the night of D-day, and everywhere the talk was dominated by the "blow in the west."

There were no special celebrations, but the air was vibrant with hope and gaiety, suppressed so long in expectation of invasion day, says Alaric Jacob, of the "Daily Express."

"Not since the victory at Orel nearly a year ago have I seen so many smiling Russian faces," he writes. "On them you could read the gratitude of faithful Allies and gladness that the pledged word was being carried out.

"For well nigh 200,000,000 people June 6, 1944, was a day that will never be forgotten.

"I met the Soviet author, Boris Voytechov, who wrote 'The Last Days of Sebastopol.' He was delighted with the news and accompanied me to the Hotel Moskva, where British and American officers had assembled to drink a toast to victory in the Russian style with Russian friends.

"Earlier in the day, Moscow's telephone system had been overwhelmed with calls by friends ringing up each other to offer congratulations.

"One old lady I know has been keeping a bottle of wine for two years against Second Front day, and asked all her friends in for a sip.

"In streets and hotels British and Americans were embraced by strangers and everywhere there were handshakes among people working for the Western Allies.

None of the papers calls the invasion the Second Front, but "the blow in the west" or "Allied landings."

"Entire back pages of four-page papers are filled with stories from London. Inside pages have articles by military commentators, with photographs of Eisenhower and British troops disembarking from landing craft."

CRUSADER

FOUNDED BY EIGHTH ARMY

THE BRITISH FORCES' WEEKLY   No. 108, Vol. 11   Two Lire   Sunday, June 25, 1944

Behind the enemy lines in Normandy

PARATROOP REPORTER No. 1 TYPES HIS DISPATCH IN BATTLE

By LEONARD MOSLEY

who was dropped in France before dawn on D day.

THIS IS ONE OF THOSE STORIES THAT WILL HAVE TO WRITE ITSELF BECAUSE I AM TOO EXHAUSTED EXCITED AND EXHILARATED TO HAVE ANY CONTROL OVER WHAT GOES DOWN ON THIS TYPE-WRITER.

I parachuted into Europe at two minutes past 1 a.m. this morning (D-Day), six-and-a-half hours before our seaborne forces began the full-blown invasion of Festung Europa.—And I have seen, done and experienced a lot since then.

I have seen a few thousand paratroops and glider-borne troops, whom I nominate now as the bravest, most tenacious men I have ever known, hold the bridgehead against Hitler's Armies for over sixteen hours despite overwhelming odds.

There is a saga to be written about what our airborne troops have done and I only wish I could catch up with myself enough to tell it cogently.

One of the reasons I can't is that there's a helluva battle going on here as I write, and bullets, mortar bombs, shells—not to mention a couple of snipers—are producing conditions which are hardly conducive to consecutive thinking.

And my job is not made any easier by the state of my type-writer.

I parachuted into France with it strapped to my chest under my equipment, and it got a bad basing when I rolled over on it after a hard landing. So please accept the story as it comes.

OUR BRIDGE JOB

OUR job as an airborne force was to silence a vital coastal battery, which, if still in operation, might have blown our ships to bits as they came to the shore. We silenced it.

And our other just as vital job was to secure two important bridges over the canal and river north of Caen, to prevent them from being blown up, and to hold them against all comers until the main armies arrived.

We are still holding them. They are still intact.

So let's begin this story as I emplaned in "C for Charlie," a great black bomber, at 11.20 p.m. last night, and we took our place in the taxi-ing line of planes that stretched from one end to the other of one of the biggest airfields in Britain.

There were Lancashire men, Yorkshiremen and Northumbrians mostly among the paratroopers.

Preceding them by half an hour

were the gliders and planes of paratroopers who were going to make a do-or-die attempt to take vital bridges before they could be blown up.

Those gliders were going to crash themselves on the buttresses of the bridges themselves, and then, aided by paratroopers, were to capture the bridges and all surrounding land.

It was our job to bring them aid within 30 minutes of their surprise attack, and to "infest" the whole area for a hundred square miles around to prevent the Nazis from counter-attacking.

"HOOK UP!"

AS our plane, the third in the formation, took the air and pointed for France, little Robson, next to me, was singing softly

Young Rowbottham was repeatedly clipping and unclipping his Sten gun. All of us were doodling in one way or another. We doodled for an hour and then down the plane from the pilot came the signal, "Hook up your 'chutes."

It was five minutes to one when the light snapped off and a hole in the plane was opened. Under it we could see the coast of France below—and a garish sight it was. For flak from the coast defences was spouting flame everywhere.

And we scared by it—until the red light flashed before our eyes and then swiftly changed to green, and we were all madly shuffling down the hole and jumping into space.

I looked, as I twisted down, for the church I had been told to spy for a landmark, and for the wood where we were later going to rendezvous as a fighting force. But the wind had caught me and was whisking me east.

IN OUR THEATRE

PERUGIA

(See page six)

Faster and faster I twisted, and I had to wrestle with my straps to get myself straight. And by that time I had come down in an orchard outside a farmhouse.

HOPELESSLY LOST

AND as I stood up with my harness off and wiped the sweat off my brown-painted face, I knew I was hopelessly lost. Dare I go to the farmhouse and ask for directions? This was the question I turned over in my mind as I crawled forward through the trees.

What the answer was I shall never know, because suddenly there was a rip and tear in my flapping jumping-smock, and I flung myself to the ground as machine-guns rattled.

There was a sudden silence, and then two more smashing explosions.

Hand-grenades this time. What do you do in those circumstances, when you are not allowed to carry arms?

I could now see figures manoeuvring in the moonlight, and I decided to try to get away. I dived through a bunch of nettles and fought my way through a tangle of barbed-wire into the next field, and began to run at the crouch.

Suddenly, at the farther edge, there were two more figures, and they were coming towards me and I could see that they were carrying guns.

What might have happened is one of those "ifs" of my private history—only there was a crash of Sten gun fire instead and both men crumpled up not fifteen yards from me. Into the field stealthily came five men to challenge me—and I was with our own paratroopers again.

This is no moment, with a fierce counter-attack developing against this headquarters to write too long about what followed. All I know is that for two long, weary hours we wandered the country. We hid from German patrols in French barns. We shot up a Nazi car speeding down a lane.

GLIDERS ARRIVE

AND just after 3 a.m. we made our rendezvous.

And then, at 3.20, every Allied paratrooper behind the Atlantic Wall breathed a sigh of relief as he heard the roar of bombers. Bombers coming in slow. Bombers towing gliders towards the dropping ground.

We watched them, in the pale moonlight and glare of flak, un-hooking and then diving steeply for earth. We saw one, caught by ack-ack, catch fire and fly around for three or four minutes, a ball of flame. We heard the crunch of breaking matchwood as gliders bounced on rocks and careered into still-undestroyed poles.

But it was hard to restrain the impulse to cheer, for, out of every glider men were pouring, and jeeps, and anti-tank guns and field-guns—and we knew that even if Nazi tanks did come we could hold them.

And now, as a faint glow began to appear in the eastern sky, our eyes turned upwards and west-wards. For there was a roaring that rapidly grew to a thunderous roll that never stopped.

Here were bombers, swarming like bees to give the Nazi coast defences their last softening before our seaborne forces landed. And what a sight it was to see.

As dawn came I moved across country through Nazi patrols to get nearer to the coast. Wherever we moved there were traces of our airborne invasion. Emptied containers, still burning their signal lights, were scattered in fields and orchards. Wrecked gliders littered the ground, some of them splintered to matchwood. There were parachutes lying everywhere.

It was hazardous going, because Nazi patrols were numerous in the area, and once were within a few yards of us, but we hid in a quarry and dodged them. Eventually we reached high ground overlooking the coast and wait until our watches showed 7.15.

A few minutes before it there was an earth-shaking holocaust of noise. The invasion barges were coming in, and coming in firing. It was a terrific barrage that must have paralysed the de—

(Continued on Page 6)

—Later, on the beaches, the traffic of invasion is carefully marshalled and deployed

Here the fighting is over. The beach-heads are won. Our leading troops are well inland and the following waves can come ashore almost without interference. The barrage-balloons cover hosts of Allied craft. The orderly prevails. field. confusion of the scene is the measure of the confidence that But only a few hours before, this snowy beach was a battle-field. Men died by the hundred to make this scene possible.

THE CRACKS THEY MADE ABOUT INVASION

"If wet, it will be in the Albert Hall!"

SOME of these stories were told with a grin back home. Others were purveyed with an air of almost comical seriousness, but all reflected the mood of the people, dealt with the one pervading topic of national conversation. Samples:

WEEK - END

REPORTING IN LONDON IS HIDE - AND - SEEK

CHARLES DICKENS'S Circumlocution Office had nothing on Whitehall in wartime. Claiming that reporting in London nowadays is "just hide-and-seek," Staff Correspondent J. S. B. of the Christian Science Monitor (Boston, U.S.A.) wrote in an issue which reached Britain last week:

"The inquirer sallies forth hopefully, believing that all he wants from the 'Wartime Department' is a simple answer to a simple question"

He makes an appointment believing that all will be over in a few minutes. Not so:

The official lifts one out of his battery of telephones and asks for Extension 439.

"Is Colonel So-and-so there? Can you tell me who is the right man to answer a question regarding . . ."

The Colonel is not the right man. He suggests Major Thomas, Extension 3492. But the Major replies that he is not doing that work now. In turn he suggests Extension 738, and ask for Captain Dixon.

Naturally enough, it turns out that the Captain is away for a week, but his helpful secretary suggests trying Extension 359, and asking for Colonel Harris.

Unfortunately, there has been a new order since the Colonel took over, so he suggests Mr. Dash of Extension 110, R.S.V. Department.

Mr. Dash is tracked to earth, and actually believes he can put the correspondent on the right track. Accordingly, an appointment is made for next week.

But Mr. Dash's first words are: "This is something I don't really deal with, but I will call up Colonel Blank at Extension 478."

The Colonel suggests Captain East of Extension 990. But at this point the inquirer feels he is the only one who is going to lose this marvellous game.

No Department has attempted an answer to the inquiry. Perhaps, after all, it does not really matter whether he knows the answer or not. Anyway, it is now about lunchtime.

"Exaggerated?" harassed, J. S. B. asked in his article. "I assure you, it's not."

"I'm told the Second Front is opening on Friday afternoon. If wet, it will take place in the Albert Hall."

* * *

"There won't be a Second Front until the Autumn. After all, with half Europe starving, we're not fools enough to do anything until the harvest has been gathered in."

* * *

"There's not going to be a Second Front at all. It's all bluff. Hitler's dead; died of cancer several months ago. We're only waiting for the German people to find out about it. When they do, Germany will collapse."

* * *

A German soldier, standing all alone on the beach near Calais, was asked what he was waiting for.

"Why, I'm waiting for the Second Front," he said.

"But aren't you fed up?"

"Oh, no," he answered. "It's a permanent job, and there's a pension to it."

* * *

"Eisenhower is waiting for a long spell of good, dry weather, but not too hot . . ."

* * *

"Eisenhower is waiting for a spell of wet weather, but not too cold . . ."

DIGEST

Prefabricated houses

What's wrong with them?

LONDON'S first prefabricated house, promoted by Lord Portal and erected last April on a site near the Tate Gallery, has had a good Press during the first few weeks of its existence. But last week some big guns were trained on the Works Minister's project.

Estate agent W. H. Slater-Eiggert of Finchley Road, N.W., condemned the planning of the rooms. The living-room must be entered through the kitchen, which means that not only the family "but all visitors must pass through the kitchen at all times of the day when the housewife is busy cooking and cleaning and wants it to herself."

To reach the lavatory from the bedrooms, occupants must pass through the living-room and kitchen, a very undesirable thing.

A still more scathing criticism came from another *Times* reader. Sardonically remarking that the geraniums blooming outside the "Portal house" do not compensate fo the extremely bad planning of the interior, she endorsed every word of Slater-Eiggert's criticism.

These kicks were too much for architect Alfred Charles Bossom (63), Conservative M.P. for Maidstone, who last year spent three months in the United States with the Building Mission appointed by Lord Portal.

DIRECT ENTRANCE

Counter-claimed he: There is to be direct entrance from hall to living-room, so that visitors do not pass through the kitchen.

There is to be a separate shed for bicycles, etc., allowing for a square hall approximately 8 ft. by 6 ft., large enough to take a pram comfortably.

These and other improvements are to be incorporated in another prototype.

Writing in America's *Technology Review*, engineer William W. Rausch meanwhile predicted that prefabrication will never become "another Detroit" (big centre of the American motor-car industry), because the bulk and weight of the average house, is 12 tons as compared with the ton and half of the average car.

Consequently, prefabrication will be regionalised in the United States. Factories will be strategically situated, with a maximum delivery radius of 250 miles, trailer trucks hauling all the sections of each house in one load.

Whole communities will live in prefabricated houses, yet monotonous outward uniformity will be avoided. Additions of various designs of porches and garages need not interfere with the standardisation of panel sections.

Troops took ten bob

NO British soldier in the invasion forces has been allowed to take with him more than 10s.

This low maximum has been fixed to prevent a "run" on commodities in France as territory is liberated.

One question which General de Gaulle has come to London to discuss is that of the rate of exchange to be established between the pound and the franc for the period of the liberation operations.

RUINOUS RATE

At one time it was suggested that the rate should be 300 francs to the pound, but it was realised that this would be almost ruinous for the French

At General de Gaulle's headquarters in London, it was stated: "In North Africa the rate is 200 francs to the pound. It is possible the same rate may operate in liberated French territory."

Quad - Problem

FIVE SETS of quadruplets have been born in England in the last 12 months.

The second set within a fortnight, three girls and a boy, were born to Mrs. Edith Knee-Robinson, 32-years-old wife of a leading aircraftman, of Baring Road, Lee, S.E., in Lewisham Hospital, on Saturday.

Medical statistics collected over the last 100 years place the incidence of quads at one in every 375,000 births. Births in 1943, in England and Wales totalled 682,000, so that the incidence of quads has more than doubled.

Doctors are seeking an explanation of the marked increase in multiple births. Normally, triplets are born once in every 8,000 confinements: yet this rate has been greatly exceeded in the last two years.

Heat at Dover Snow in London!

BRITONS went around in their lightest summer clothes, drank public-houses dry, dreamed of peacetime's ice-cream sundaes, flocked to swimming pools.

The reason: a heatwave in the Straits of Dover.

From a million news clues and official announcements, from innocuous photographs passed for publication by M o I censors, the wideawake Nazis knew last week that Britain was sweltering.

Obstinate as ever, the Air Ministry stuck to its ten-day ban on weather reports, said it was "still necessary for security reasons."

Neatly, pungently, *Daily Mail* cartoonist "Neb" summed up the longstanding weather censorship farce, showed a newspaper Art Editor telling one of his minions: "That picture of a man frying an egg on a London pavement should be O.K. if we omit the egg, and don't say what's trying it."

Imposed at a time when the United Kingdom was under constant threat of daylight bombing, the weather gag is quite unnecessary, in the opinion of meteorological experts. If it's worm and sunny in the Straits, there is little chance of snow in London.

If fruit farmers had been officially warned about last month's frosts, hundreds of acres of fruit countless boxes of tomato plants could have been saved.

At week's end Service chiefs were said to be reconsidering the whole matter.

"Got any pink dye? I want to play a joke on a character!"

In liberated Perugia

I meet a Boer war veteran

By SYD FOXCROFT

WHEN THREE JEEP LOADS OF GRENADIER GUARDS ENTERED AND OCCUPIED THE IMPORTANT ROAD AND RAIL JUNCTION OF PERUGIA, THEY WERE GREETED BY A FLOWER - THROWING CROWD OF PEOPLE OF ALL NATIONS OF EUROPE, INCLUDING MANY WHO, IN THE CLOSING DAYS OF GERMAN OCCUPATION, HAD ESCAPED OR BEEN RELEASED FROM PRISON CAMPS.

Confetti and flowers rained down from balconies draped with the Italian national colours; women leapt into the slow-moving Jeeps to embrace the liberating troops. Only a solitary German remained to be made prisoner.

Little damage was apparent as I drove up to the main hotel in the town, headquarters of the Town Major, Major Freeman, who with Driver F. J. Kyte, of Senghenydd, was among the first troops to enter the town. The Grande Albergo Brufani, where only two days previously, the German troops had staged, entertainments now resounded to the piano-accompanied singing of British Tommies.

An elderly colonel, his age betrayed by the South African ribbon on his breast, greeted me at the entrance. His face beamed as he extended a welcoming hand.

"I am certainly glad to see you," he told me, "I have awaited this day impatiently for four years, since the day the Fascists placed me under armed guard."

This was Colonel Cyril Rocke, who was Military Attache in Rome for three years. He commanded a Battalion in which General Alexander served as second in command in France in the last war. He had been in various Fascist prison and hospital camps up to the time of his escape on the 12th of June.

"I was in hospital at the time, having evaded transfer to Germany by feigning illness, but on Monday my wife and myself were to be sent to a Nazi prison camp.

"We determined to escape and carried out our plan last Monday. In dark glasses, simple clothes and with bandages round my head, I made my way with my wife guided by the hotel housemaid to her mother's house on the outskirts of the town. Here we remained until we learned that the Germans were preparing to evacuate the town.

"We made our way, in disguise back to the hotel, where we established ourselves in the cellar.

"Eventually, news came of the Germans' withdrawal and I climbed on the balcony of my room to watch the battle.

"This morning I saw trucks approaching and hurriedly dressed in my uniform, which I'd managed to secret in the hotel. Then I wandered down the road to greet the troops. First man I met was Captain Aubrey Ponsonby, son of a great Service friend of mine."

fanatical local Fascist chief a few days before the arrival of the British troops. Many, however, were carried off to Germany.

Surrounded by a crowd of admiring fellow-countrymen in the town square were the bunch of Italian partisans who, prior to and during the battle for the town, had worked night and day destroying communications and assisting with the dislocation of the retreat.

Unshaven and tired after two sleepless nights—they had anticipated the British force the previous evening—they told me how, after equipping themselves with rifles and ammunition taken by force from Fascist headquarters they had killed at least nine Germans.

PARATROOP REPORTER

(Continued from Front Page)

fences. We shook each other's hands in the knowledge that the invasion at long last had begun.

JUST IN TIME

SINCE that time we have heard little of how that invasion has been going, for ours has largely continued as a private war. It was a morning of tense excitement for us, for the immediate reply of the Nazis to our arrival was an infiltration into our positions by armoured cars, mobile guns and hordes of snipers.

By 10 a.m. the area of ground where we had established headquarters was getting a roasting from shells and mortar bombs.

I went into the village to drink a glass of cider with the mayor.

"Thank God you've come now, monsieur," he said. "You were just in time. Next week all the men in the area were to be conscripted to drape barbed-wire across the poles in the area where you dropped."

He arranged to give us a regular supply of milk and eggs from his farm and would not take payment.

There were children playing in the streets, unmindful of the war only a few yards away.

We could not expect substantial help from seaborne forces that day, but relief from the sky.

They didn't let us down. It was just on nine p.m. when the sky was suddenly filled with twisting and turning fighter planes. And under them a great fleet of bombers and gliders sailed slowly over our heads.

We could see splinters flying off them as Nazi machine-gun bullets flayed them as they dived. P

Seventy-eight year old Lady Montgomery is sturdy and active. Here she is driving her pony trap at the family home, New Park, County Donegal.

LADY MONTGOMERY

Lady Montgomery, mother of Gen. Montgomery, lives alone at the family home New Park, Moville, County Donegal, Eire. Her husband, who was Bishop of Tasmania, died 11 years ago. She is proud of the achievements of the Eighth Army but its commander is no more important to her than any of his four brothers and two sisters. All five of her sons are abroad in the service of the British Empire.

Lady Montgomery, at 78, is exceedingly active and spends most of her time doing war work. She has raised more than £2,500 for the comforts fund of the Eighth Army. Gen. Montgomery's mother is outspoken and like her famous son deeply religious. One of her many efforts on behalf of soldiers has been the despatch of more than 2,000,000 razor blades to men in the Middle East. The General's fame has broken in on the peace of quiet New Park and the postman brings his mother a heavy mail bag most days. It contains letters of congratulation, requests for autographs and, most welcome to Lady Montgomery, gifts to pass on to Eighth Army.

POW TOOK A NEW COURSE

LONDON, Sat.—A prisoner of war in a German camp who was taking an honours course in English literature with the aid of books sent by the Red Cross had to interrupt his studies.

In a letter to the Red Cross and St. John he tells why.

"The course was most enjoyable," he wrote. "It is regrettable that my determination to escape prevented my going through with it."

The letter was written in England.

R.A.F. RESCUE PARTISANS

Evacuation to hospitals in Italy of Partisan wounded and civilians, including children, carried out by the R.A.F. with Dakota aircraft. About 10,000 have now been evacuated; during single operation Dakotas escorted by fighters brought out 900 in daylight without losing a man a 'plane. In Jugoslavia medical arrangements in action can scarcely be said to exist. There is no Geneva Convention, as the Partisans are regarded as rebels so local girls form the Red Cross almost entirely and their medical work is secondary to their combatant duties. As the Germans kill all wounded an there is little transport for initial evacuation the girls hide the wounded, often on hillsides, and there they remain without dressing or treatment until they can be rescued and taken away.

THE DOCTOR

In the space of ten days, during which the Russian forces launched what front-line reports described as "the greatest Red Army offensive of the war," the face of Hitler's European battlefields was drastically changed. The first assault on the German defences in the western Ukraine was followed in rapid succession throughout the Dnieper Bend, until three Russian armies were sweeping forward over a 500-mile front.

A front-line report described the battlefield as a sea of mud, "mud that is littered with the bodies of German dead and the carcasses of their horses, shell-shattered dugouts and their bogged-down tanks and lorries." German prisoners confessed that adverse weather conditions had seemed to rule out an offensive; they were caught napping. The Russians, for their part, overcame ground handicaps by concentrating their artillery at certain points and smashing breaches in the enemy lines, through which tanks and infantry surged forward. Captured enemy tanks were used to tow light guns.

MAJOR SLIPS, SHOOTS WIFE

LONDON, Tues.—Major William Robert Hope Mackay of Latheronwheel, Caithness is a man whom Tragedy has marked out for her own.

Two years ago his 3-year-old son was drowned in a pool close by his father's home.

Last Saturday, home on leave from the RAMC, Major Mackay went down to the shore to practice shooting with a .22 rifle. Clambering down a gulley his foot became entangled in his dog's lead. He stumbled and his rifle went off.

His wife, walking in front of him, fell dead.

750 U.S. BOMBERS HIT GERMANY

LONDON, Tues.—More than 750 Fortresses and Liberators, escorted by an almost equal number of fighters, went deep into Germany today. German news agency reported heavy air battles over Hanover and Brinswick.

Marauders, escorted by Thunderbolts, were at the same time smashing railway targets in Belgium.

Last night 900 RAF inflicted new devastation on railway targets in France and Belgium. Watchers on the English coast say that the night was one of ceaseless activity. Chief objectives were at Ghent, Tours, Haulnoye and Laon and to the North-east of Paris. Mosquitoes attacked Hanover and targets in the Ruhr. 22 RAF aircraft are missing.

Monday's US raids on Belgium and France was its heaviest yet. More than 1,000 tons of bombs were dropped. Of the 600 Marauders which took place only two are missing.

SHOT AT MEXICAN PRESIDENT

MEXICO CITY, Tues.—An unsuccessful attempt to assassinate Pres. Avila Camacho was made by Antonio Lama Rojos, an Artillery officer of the Mexican Army.

Rojos entered the National Palace and fired point blank at the President. The shot missed and Camacho grappled with his assailant, holding both his arms while members of the Presidential party seized his gun. Rojos who was shot in the stomach while trying to escape was found to have Nazi documents in his possession.

KNOX CONFIDENT

WASHINGTON, Tues.—Col Knox, US Navy Secretary said to-day that he was confident that the British forces in India would be able to halt the Japanese drive near Imphal.

He said he did not regard the Japanese thrust as serious, since it involved only a small number of men, and added "the British are out to beat it and no doubt will."—Reuter.

GREEK GOVT. CRISIS

LONDON, Tues.—The King of the Hellenes has left for Cairo to deal at first hand with the Greek Ministerial crisis (SEAC, 7 April).

Premier Emmanuel Tsouderous declared today, "The Government stands by its resignation, but pending a settlement of the crisis by the King, Ministers will remain at their posts to carry on with current service matters."

IMPHAL CLASH IN FOOTHILLS

NEW DELHI, Tues.—Offensive patrols from the Imphal Plain inflicted casualties on the Japs in clashes in the foothills and near the Tiddim road, where our troops laid a successful ambush says today's SEAC communique.

An attack on one of our positions in the Palel area was driven off.

In the Kohima area Jap pressure against the defended locality and in the hill country both north and south of the road has been maintained. No important change is reported.

There has been increasing fighting in Central Burma, where our troops continue to inflict heavy casualties.

Hill Feature Captured

On the Arakan front, enemy resistance stiffened yesterday, particularly near the main Mayu Range, south of the Maungdaw-Buthidaung road. In the foothills south-east of Maungdaw a feature overlooking the plain was occupied by our troops.

Chinese troops have captured Wakawng in the Mogaung valley area, 6 miles south of Shaduzup. 54 Japs were found dead. Our troops are in contact with the enemy west of Warazup.

U.S. medium bombers attacked Sinthe and Thiyabin bridges yesterday, heavily damaging both. The previous night, RAF heavy bombers attacked Moulmein, starting fires in the station and jetty areas.—API.

17 DIV THANKS RAF

IMPHAL FRONT, 8 April (delayed).—Maj-Gen Tennant Cowan, commanding the 17th Division which recently fought its way through the Chin hills for 3 weeks, visited a RAF mess personally to thank the men who had helped him in his movement of the division from Tiddim.

Aircrews from Hurricane and Hurribomber squadrons were gathered together with the A-O-C the group and all his officers to hear the General tell of the fierce battles in which his troops defeated the Jap attempt to wipe out the division.

"It is the opinion of all ranks that you—the RAF—did a grand job," Gen Cowan concluded. "Your support was given at very short notice but with extreme accuracy and you got right on top of them. On more than one occasion you alone were responsible for enabling our forces to counter-attack in the face of heavy opposition.—API.

SOVIET SMASH THROUGH CRIMEA DEFENCE LINE

MOSCOW, Tues.—Following hard on the news of Odessa's fall, the Soviet communiqué announced last night the start of a new drive against the Crimea.

Gen Tolbukhin's Fourth Ukrainian Army, of which little has been heard since it took Perekop at the northern gateway to the Crimea last November, went over to the Crimea offensive several days ago, the communiqué disclosed.

They have broken through the powerful defences of the land gateway to the Crimea and captured the town of Armyansk, 5 miles south of Perekop, and a number of other places along the Isthmus.

At the same time they have forced the Sivash—a shallow ragged channel that separates the Crimea from the mainland—east of the Isthmus, and captured a number of places in the Crimea itself.

In 2 days more than 5,500 Germans have been killed and another 1,000 taken prisoner.

Sebastopol Threatened

With Nikolaev and Odessa both back in the hands of the Red Fleet the great naval base of Sebastopol in the Crimea now faces a sharply increased threat.

In Rumania the Red Army is across the Sereth at a new point and has forced another river, the Succava, south-west of Botosani. Another thirty places have been captured further south in the Jassy sector including one 5 miles north-west of Jassy.

Soviet troops are now 60 miles into Upper Rumania.

In the final battle for Odessa fierce street fighting raged all night and resulted in Soviet troops capturing the whole of the town. Enormous booty was taken including many tanks, hundreds of guns and mortars, a great number of locomotives, several thousand railway carriages and trucks loaded with war material.—Reuter.

'PERFECT CRIME'

Twice tried for the murder of an old woman in her beerhouse at Portsmouth, 47-year-old Harold Loughans was found Not Guilty by an Old Bailey jury after a 6-days' trial. At Winchester Assizes the jury had disagreed.

J. D. Casswell, KC, for the Crown, called the murder of Mrs. Rose Ada Robinson, licensee of the John Barleycorn Inn, the perfect crime.

The woman died from strangulation at a time when Loughans was able to prove he was in Warren-street station tube shelter.

Loughans lost 2 fingers of a boy, and Sir Bernard Spilsbury said his hand could never have strangled the woman.

BITTER FIGHTING IN HEART OF BURMA

SPECIAL FORCE HQ, 10 April.—First detailed story of the grim hand-to-hand fighting which led to the capture of a village, 150 miles in the enemy's "guts" in Burma, has reached this HQ. The official Army Observer who was present at the capture was killed in the same area a few days later.

20 MARCH: the attack by our infantry was the climax of two days' fighting during which the Japs, after infiltration, had wounded a number of our men and subjected isolated platoons to intense mortar and machine-gun fire.

Air support was immediately given and the officer commanding our troops himself led the counter-attack on the blazing village. Surprised by our determination and ruthlessness, the enemy broke and fled in confusion down the railway line, pursued by accurately-aimed bursts of LMG fire.

It is estimated that over 50 p.c. of the Jap troops in this area were either killed or wounded. Jap communications by rail to the north have been severed but the enemy are bringing up reinforcements, including artillery.

KEY
- Railroads
- Main Roads
- Swamps & Marshes

Scale in Miles
0 10 20 30 40 50

Section of the priceless Bayeux Tapestry, showing part of William the Conqueror's invasion armada.

HIMMLER STOLE THIS TAPESTRY

THE unique 11th-century Bayeux Tapestry, longest in the world, has been stolen from Bayeux by the Germans.

News of this last Nazi vandalism is now published by the American Commission for Protection and Salvage of Artistic and Historic Monuments.

The priceless tapestry, according to information obtained by the commission, was seized by order of Heinrich Himmler in 1940, at the time the Nazis were looting the palaces, museums and galleries of Europe for their personal collections.

Twenty feet wide and 230 feet long the tapestry depicts the Norman conquest of England and was long kept in the Bishop's Palace. It is one of the most important relics of the period and was invaluable to historians as first-hand evidence on social history, costumes, weapons and instruments.

Looting

Tradition said that it was embroidered by Queen Matilda, wife of William the Conqueror, and her maids, but it is now universally thought to be of somewhat later origin.

The commission is amassing a careful record of the gigantic Nazi looting of art Francis H. Taylor, director of the US Metropolitan commission, said the looting was the "greatest art steal in history."

The commission's files are fed by underground contacts, official reports and information from refugee scholars. They show a clear-cut pattern of systematic looting, especially in Belgium and Holland. It is feared that most of the Netherlands' art has gone to Germany. Where the Nazis didn't requisition outright, they imposed "fines" and exacted "gifts" to move masterpieces to Germany.

Postwar Task

The Allied governments are prepared to examine very closely all art "auctions" which have been held in occupied countries and which are suspected of being merely a legal disguise for what in fact was theft. Unshuffling Europe's art will be a big postwar task.

The commission's art experts, previous to the invasion of France, prepared 700 maps of cultural objects in Europe. The Allied commanders were informed in advance that the Bayeux Tapestry was not in their path from the Channel beachheads.

The Allied attitude towards art treasures on the Continent was expressed by Gen Dwight G. landings in Italy, when he enjoined all commanding officers to avoid culturally important places within the limits of military necessity.

GOC spinsters. Mild but resourceful **Florence White**, middle-aged secretary of National Spinsters' Pension Association, is mobilising her forces against Government's latest plan for social insurance. "The White Paper," says Florence, "is an excellent thing, but in return for our contribution we spinsters want 10s. a week at 55." With 100,000 spinsters at her back and more than 3,000 subscription-paying recruits enlisting every month, Florence looks like getting her way. HQ of the spinsters' campaign is bedroom over the Bradford baker's shop where Florence sold buns before she founded the spinsters' army. She has no time for buns now.

FAITH and Reason. For four Sundays at 16.45 to 17.00 beginning tomorrow, Nagpur's Bishop, the **Rt. Rev. A. O. Hardy**, will broadcast from Calcutta in the series "Faith and Reason: The Padre Replies," taking the place of the usual Service chaplains. Servicemen whose interest in religion has been aroused are invited to ask questions to be answered in the broadcasts. Address to: "The Padre Replies, AIR, 1 Garstin Place, Calcutta.

'PM MUST TAKE RISKS IN DUTY'

LONDON, Fri—Replying to criticism of Premier Churchill for risking his life in his visit to Normandy on Monday, Brendan Bracken, Minister of Information said in the Commons yesterday:

"The Prime Minister is also the Minister of Defence, and it is his duty to see things for himself. As a consequence of one of his visits to the Middle East, Gen. Montgomery was introduced to that theatre.

"In war no one can avoid risks. For that reason the Prime Minister's colleagues are always pleased when he gets out into the fresh air and gladdens his heart by contact with fighting men."

ALL-FRONT ADVANCE IN ITALY

ALLIED ADVANCE HQ, ITALY, Fri.—Today's Allied communique says: Allied armies in Italy have again advanced all along the front. In the Adriatic sector the enemy has withdrawn and only slender contact has been maintained.

Troops of the Eighth Army captured Narni and Terni, advanced rapidly 25 miles and took Todi yesterday.

German Losses 750,000

SHAEF, Sun.—Latest estimate at Allied HQ of the campaign in Western Europe is " nearly 750,000 men."

It is pointed out that the forces under General Bradley have taken 250,000 prisoners, General Devers' Sixth Army Group has taken 82,000, Field Marshal Montgomery's troops have taken more than 70,000.

Quiz

1. A sicca is a small knife, dry wine, new coin, insect, gum-tree?

2. What is the proper name of the bird sometimes called the shuflewing?

3. If you scored a "sice" in a game, with what would you be playing?

4. How many grooves would you say there were in the milling round the edge of a sixpence?

5. Where is the Kalahari Desert?

6. Which of the following are mis-spelt? Porridge, Borridge, Tonnidge, Midge, Collidge.

Answers in Col.

"Are there any ships due in from a specially long spell at sea?"

PILOTLESS BOMBERS

By TOM WILCOX

WHAT is this new weapon that Nazidom has sprung upon Britain in the last few days —the pilotless bomber? Already in news from Home there is evidence on which we can build a case that this is no new weapon in fact, but a development of a known and already-defeated effort by Germany's scientists.

By those who have seen the new sky terror it is described as a black streak by day, a fire-spitting, comet-like trail at night. From that the logical inference is that the craft is jet-propelled. There is nothing new in that. It began in the 1920's when Fritz Opel built a jet-propelled car, then a plane in which he was killed.

Well-tried Principle

In 1941 the Italians were using, without much success, a jet-propelled fighter.

Then it is said that at the tail of the fuselage of the new bomber is a square "box." Deduction is that here is located the oversize radio equipment which converts radio signals into physical impulses operating the aircraft's controls.

Again a well-tried principle, for it was soon after the last war that Britain produced the first pilotless plane, the Queen Bee, as an AA target.

What are the problems in dealing with this weapon? Less, in fact than those that face the defences in the case of a resolutely-flown Dornier or Junkers. The machine is catapult-launched, then directed on a level course plotted on a map and kept in flight until the operator calculates it is over the "objective." So that to attack a chosen target, the enemy would have to have the most minutely-detailed meteorological information covering the whole course.

That is so clearly impossible for the Germans that the weapon is immediately seen as wholly indiscriminate. For that reason, in fact, the Air Ministry some years ago turned down an almost identical machine. We have that on the authority of F. G. Miles, one of the world's dozen best aircraft designers.

Ready Target

There is, too, the radio approach. At sea the "Chase-me-Charlie" bomb was mastered by the dexterity of our operators of the Radio Direction Finders, who very quickly find the frequency on which the aircraft's controls are being manipulated, and, by jamming the enemy signals, convert the machine into an uncontrolled runaway—flying on the course set at the moment of jamming—a ready target for the guns.

We can rest assured that this method of combating the "ghost-plane" is already highly developed.

It would be difficult to deny that, had this weapon appeared three years ago, its effect would have been devastating. It didn't. Not because, as Goebbels would have us believe, the enemy was reluctant to use it, but because the Germans had not thought it up.

Flying Bomb: Official Picture

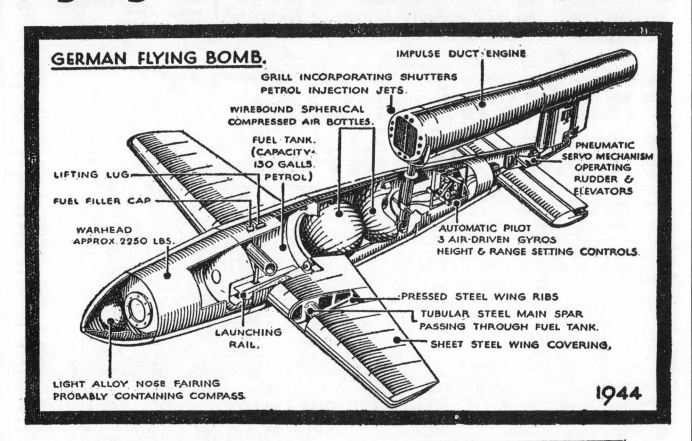

GERMAN FLYING BOMB.

IMPULSE DUCT ENGINE

GRILL INCORPORATING SHUTTERS
PETROL INJECTION JETS.

WIREBOUND SPHERICAL
COMPRESSED AIR BOTTLES.

FUEL TANK.
(CAPACITY·
130 GALLS.
PETROL)

LIFTING LUG

FUEL FILLER CAP

WARHEAD
APPROX. 2250 LBS.

PNEUMATIC
SERVO MECHANISM
OPERATING
RUDDER &
ELEVATORS

AUTOMATIC PILOT
3 AIR-DRIVEN GYROS
HEIGHT & RANGE SETTING CONTROLS.

PRESSED STEEL WING RIBS

TUBULAR STEEL MAIN SPAR
PASSING THROUGH FUEL TANK.

SHEET STEEL WING COVERING.

LAUNCHING
RAIL.

LIGHT ALLOY NOSE FAIRING
PROBABLY CONTAINING COMPASS.

1944

What Britain Thinks

It Worries the Old :

How the people of Southern England are reacting to the German flying bomb attacks and how these attacks compare with normal raids is revealed in this despatch just received from a CRUSADER reporter at home in England:

"Give me these flying bombs every time," was the remark of one girl who has been through all the blitzes and who, the other day, had her windows blown out for the sixth time since 1940.

"For one thing you know much better what is going on. Long before they arrive you can hear them, and see them too. If they seem to be coming too close for comfort you usually have plenty of time to take cover. When the buzzing stops, there is a bang within a few seconds and then nothing more until the next comes along. That may be in 5 minutes or 5 hours, but in either case, you can relax in between.

"These robots rely entirely on blast, without penetration, so you feel quite safe in the shelter. One of my friends had one drop right beside their shelter the other night and nobody was hurt at all. There is nothing like the strain of the old-time raids."

This is the general opinion of the younger folk, but the older ones think somewhat differently.

One old lady said that she definitely preferred "proper" bombs. These robot things were not quite natural. Even if this did kill less people than bombs, she felt they were uncanny. She disapproved of them strongly.

"It fair gives me the creeps to see these things flying along and nobody inside them," said another elderly person who had just been blasted out of her home. "It don't seem right, do it? Bombs felt more human-like. Give me bombs every time, if we've got to have one or the other."

Men are generally agreed that these "secret weapons" are less formidable than ordinary bombing. Last war veterans compare the robots to long-range harrassing fire.

"They remind me of those whizzbangs Jerry used to send over in France," said one middle-aged Home Guard. "A lot of noise but their bark is worse than their bite.

"Naturally it isn't so funny if you happen to be in the line of fire, but you can usually see these things coming if you watch out and get ready to duck if the buzzing stops. You can sleep much better than during the old raids. There isn't that continual banging and crashing all around. Robots come fewer and further between than bombs did, and its only a near one that is likely to wake a sound sleeper like me."

Public opinion varies slightly about this latest brand of German air frightfulness, but one thing is clear. Those in the danger areas are following the Minister of Home Security's injunction to "carry on" with their own particular job, sensibly and with a minimum of risk. Germany is striking, not at Britain's industrial and military might, but at Britain's morale. The attack is failing.

What Germany Says

Reprisal Weapon No. 1

Germany is gloating. Her rulers hail the flying bomb as the greatest weapon yet produced in this war. Their official name for it is VERGELTUNGSWAFFE 1, which means REPRISAL WEAPON Number one.

They say that the V 1 is merely the forerunner of a series of reprisal weapons, and they hasten to assure us that larger and better flying bombs are ready and waiting for the word "Go" from the Fuehrer.

They insist that bad weather is an advantage and that even if a large percentage are shot down, the fact that they carry no pilot will enable them to sustain huge losses which will be the result of costly and expensive fighter patrols and A.A. barrages, which the English cannot afford.

BERLIN'S COMMENTS

Here is what Berlin is saying:
"It may be taken for granted that the actual range of the new German Weapon is far beyond its present range. The effect of one single V 1 machine is enormous. It can neither be compared with that of shells from big long-range guns, nor with the effect of the heaviest calibre bombs dropped by any plane. The flying altitude of the new German weapon can be changed according to the desired effect. Sometimes it is necessary that the machine crash from a high altitude on to its target, while other targets make an approach at low altitude if necessary. The shelling of South England is carried out according to a carefully prepared plan."

A recent broadcast by Martin Hallansleben claims:

"The harrassing fire from the new German Weapon against London which has been going on unceasingly for 160 hours, has been intensified by the introduction of "fire sheaves"—simultaneous salvos from a maximum number of batteries."

Lord Haw-Haw jeered that "British soldiers in Normandy, would be very greatly dismayed if they really knew what happened in the last few days in Southern England."

CALAIS REPORT

Radio Calais reported that great fires burning in London could be seen from France and said that the greatest mass exodus in history was occuring from the capital.

As is usual in propaganda issued by Dr. Goebbels' department, truth in small doses is mixed with downright falsehoods and a great deal of mystery. For instance, the Flying Bomb is reported to be only a small part of a great new arsenal of secret weapons prepared by the scientists of the Armaments Ministry, who have had every technical facility available in the Reich put at their disposal for four years.

It is noteworthy that Goebbels finds it necessary to exaggerate all the time about the V 1.

Arthur Cummings, the commentator of the "News Chronicle," gave perhaps the best concise summing up of the Flying Bomb. He called it "a lethal nuisance."

UNION JACK

FOR THE BRITISH FIGHTING FORCES

Tuesday, July 4, 1944
No. 19   Two Lire

STOP PRESS

INDEPENDENT BELGIAN NEWS AGENCY REPORTS GERMANS HAVE CLOSED BELGIAN-GERMAN FRONTIER. PORTUGUESE RADIO BROADCAST SAME REPORT.

Eighth Army dislodge enemy in rapid advance

FRENCH FORCES TAKE SIENA

FRENCH troops of the Fifth Army occupied the ancient town of Siena early yesterday morning. Siena, capital town of the province of the same name, is famous for its Gothic cathedral and medieval walls and gateways. It manufactures machinery and ironwork and had a pre-war population of 48,000.

Eighth Army troops in the most rapid of recent advances have dislodged the enemy from the positions which he had occupied east and west of Lake Trasimene.

After days of heavy fighting and slow progress troops of the Eighth Army have surged forward into the Chiana Valley taking a number of towns. North-west of the lake Fojano was captured and Sinalunga was passed.

Farther to the east a column pushed forward along Highway 71 to within four miles of Cortona. The important road junction village of Gabbiano was also taken.

Between Trequanda and Sinalunga the enemy opposed the advance with Tiger tanks.

Although the Fojano canal bridge was blown our armour crossed and advanced towards Bettolle after the capture of Torrita.

Fighter-bombers attacked six enemy batteries in the Cortona area and also the road used for the withdrawal of the Herman Goering Division.

East of Lake Trasimeno Eighth Army troops pushed forward as far as the north-east corner of the lake, and Mantignana was cleared. Demolitions impeded progress towards Fojano, and the enemy's initial intention to withdraw was heralded by sounds of many explosions in his rear.

Petrignano was taken after heavy fighting all day on Saturday. As the enemy pulled back, the tanks advanced followed by infantry which was almost immediately pinned down by machine-gun and mortar fire and forced to dig in for the night.

North-west of Perugia, Nocera and Monte Castellacco were taken in spite of severe enemy artillery opposition.

Roads shelled

The roads in the Valfabbrica area were observed from enemy O.Ps. in the Apennine foothills and were shelled throughout Saturday—points on the roads likely to be used by us being carefully registered.

In their eagerness to knock out our leading tanks, the enemy used 88 mm. dual purpose guns in an anti-tank role well forward, and large numbers of them were captured.

Forward elements of our troops in the Adriatic sector are now within ten miles of Ancona and have pushed on several miles beyond the Musone river where the enemy had been expected to make a stand. Osimo, Castelfidardo, and Monte Fano were occupied.

Fifth Army forces in the coastal area have been involved in the heaviest fighting since Rome, but Riparbella, Casale d'Elsa, Monteroni and Asciano have been taken.

Heavy losses

It is estimated that the Fifth Army is facing elements of some ten divisions across its front, but many have suffered devastating losses in manpower and material.

It is now known that the capture of Cecina on Saturday night was the most difficult of recent Fifth Army operations and the most vicious opposition was encountered. Exceptionally heavy street fighting occurred and prisoners state that they had been ordered to hold Cecina at all costs.

fuehrer Division and the 19th German Air Force Division.

Italy - based Allied heavy bombers, numbering about 750, dealt stunning blows on Sunday to oil refineries, railroad yards, airfields and industrial installations near Budapest, and at other places in Hungary and Yugoslavia.

A Greek bomber squadron, operating as an independent unit of the coastal air force of the Middle East Command, is playing an important part in the attacks on German communications in Italy. The Hellenic squadron, equipped with Baltimores, is part of a South African light bomber wing. Most of the crews have been trained in South Africa.

Mackensen removed

FROM an enemy document recently captured by French troops, it appears that Colonel General Von Mackensen has been removed from the command of the German Fourteenth Army. General Lemensen is now G.O.C. Fourteenth Army.

General Von Mackensen's removal seems not unreasonable in view of the fact that his army was practically destroyed in the heavy defeat inflicted on it, and another document also taken by the French contained an order that he has achieved the impossible—it has retreated 130 miles and is still going strong.

Balkan oil plants hit

RUMANIAN, Hungarian and Yugoslav oil refineries and storage and transport facilities were hit again yesterday by strong American heavy bomber formations based in Italy.

R.A.F. night bombers on Sunday dropped blockbusters on the important Prahova refinery on the outskirts of Bucharest which had been a recent daylight target.

The Germans sent up night fighters as well as heavy flak.

Sunday's day bombers ran into a series of running battles with aggressive German fighters numbering 135 near Budapest. The bombers shot down 23, the escort 25, and Mustangs sweeping over Budapest shot down nine.—Reuter.

When Bayeux, in Normandy, was freed the townspeople gathered to welcome the Allies. A French war correspondent is shown here addressing his fellow countrymen during the celebrations.

Russian army capture Minsk, trap 200,000 Nazis

SOVIET forces have captured Minsk, capital of White Russia, after a wide encircling movement in which they overran the German positions round the city cutting the main railways and roads to the west, and trapping the German garrison of 200,000 men.

The main railways cut are the Vilna line to the north-west and the Brest-Litovsk line to the south-west. The following towns were captured: Wilejka, 44 miles north-west of Minsk, and Krasnoye, south-east of Wilejka, about 80 miles north-west of Minsk, on the railway to Vilna; Stolpce, 44 miles south-west; and Nieswiez, 50 miles south-southwest, on the railway to Brest-Litovsk.

Correspondents say that the 200,000 German troops defending the capital of White Russia fought desperately to hold off the frontal attack.

A Soviet front-line report says that this offensive is the biggest in scope and results that the Russian Army has ever undertaken, and following one encircling movement after another the German army is rapidly disintegrating.

The southern arm of the encirclement drive was led by Marshal Rokossovsky, whose troops of the First White Russian Front advanced

of Stolptsy, 45 miles south-west of Minsk on the main railway from Germany and Poland.

The garrison was taken completely by surprise and 2,700 Germans were killed in the town and 1,500 taken prisoner.

Marshal Rokossovsky's men went on to break German resistance at the approaches to Baranovichi, while sending tanks and mobile guns forward to cut the Germans south-westerly escape route, the Minsk-Warsaw railway.

North of Minsk, General Chernakhovsky's troops of the Third White Russian Front advanced up to 35 miles during the day, took Wilejka, 50 miles north-west of Minsk.

Krasnoye, 125 miles along the railway to Vilna, was also captured, cutting the last dependable line of communication between Minsk and the German

TURN TO PAGE 4

ROMMEL'S 11 DIVS REGROUP

GERMAN counter-attacks against the Odon bridgehead were on a reduced scale on Sunday, "owing probably to the severe mauling the enemy received on Saturday," yesterday's S.H.A.E.F. communique stated.

Front-line correspondents report indications that Rommel is withdrawing his armour, which up to now has been used piecemeal in small groups, so that he can wield it as cohesive divisions.

The anxiety with which the German command views the British wedge is shown by the fact that eleven divisions are now known to be in the area. There are five panzer S.S. divisions, two normal panzer divisions, and four infantry divisions.

A complete panzer corps, which may include from two to four divisions, has been brought from the Russian front, it is officially stated at S.H.A.E.F.

To meet the expected attack, which a British staff officer told a Reuter correspondent would probably be "the biggest test of strength since the landings, the salient has been further strengthened. A great weight of artillery, including our most powerful anti-tank guns, is in position. "For sheer concentrated weight of weapons this salient has never been matched in military history," says Reuter.

These guns destroyed a further 40 tanks. Sunday night's S.H.A.E.F. communique revealed. All the counter-attacks, by virtue of their limited strength, have suffered heavy losses. Only one has so far succeeded in penetrating the outer defence fringe. It was encircled and destroyed, and our lines restored, within two hours.

A S.H.A.E.F. spokesman, saying that the position was "extremely satisfactory," pointed out that Rommel has now been forced to commit strategic reserves, and still does not know where the next Allied blow will fall.

Major-General de Guingand, Chief of Staff of the 21st Army Group, has been created a Knight Commander of the British Empire for his work in Normandy, it was announced yesterday.

YANKS LAND ON SAIPAN
—and Bomb Tokyo

WASHINGTON, Fri.—Under cover of a smashing bombardment from a naval task force including battleships and aircraft carriers, American ground forces have landed on Saipan Island, Jap fortress isle in the Marianas.

Reporting this last night, Admiral Nimitz, C-in-C Pacific, said that US losses were moderate despite fierce Jap resistance.

Other isles in the group, including Guam, Pagan, Rota and Tician, were also beaten up in the preparatory bombardment.

Saipan the largest of the Mariana group, has been in Jap hands under mandate since 1919. Admiral Nimitz regards it as an essential base for operations aimed deeper at the heart of the enemy's defences.

Tokyo's Second Raid

From its airfields, Fortresses, operating at just about their extreme effective range, could bomb Tokyo, 1450 miles to the North.

News of these operations reached Washington a few hours after the sensational announcement that Tokyo had been bombed for the second time—this from land bases in China.

This raid was carried out by Super-Fortresses, the new B 29's and a number of the B24's with which Jap and German are now familiar.

Rep Starnes, of Alabama, announcing the raid to the House of Representatives, said that great destruction was caused in Tokyo. Later he told the Press that losses were "negligible since the Super-Forts flew above the ceiling of the Jap AA and the Zeros."

Try-Out Over Burma

The Japs admitted only that Moji, Yawata and Kokura, industrial centres on the isle of Kyushu, southernmost of the main Jap isles had been attacked. They admitted that a railway had been damaged.

A Columbia Broadcasting reporter who accompanied the super-fortresses which attacked Yawata said that many tons of bombs were dropped on coke ovens and furnaces of Japanese steel mills.

The B29, it was revealed today, is 98 feet long, has a wingspan of 141.2 feet, 27 feet high. Its propellor blades are 16 ft. 6 ins. long, and its four engines are each of 2,200 h.p.—Wright Cyclone 18-cyl. radials. It is officially stated to carry the greatest load farther, faster and higher than any other plane in existence.

Several weeks ago, some of these planes had a try-out over Burma and shot down two out of 12 Zeros encountered.

The King Drives to the Front

The King driving with General Sir Harold Alexander during his tour this week of the Italian battlefronts.

WHOLE NORMANDY LINE BEGINS TO CHANGE WITH NEW OFFENSIVE

SHAEF, Thurs.—General Montgomery's two-day-old offensive is altering the whole line of the Normandy front. Bit by bit he is tearing territory away from the Germans and—more important—his troops are inflicting severe casualties upon the hard-fighting enemy.

South and east of Caen villages are falling into our hands. Fauborg de Vaucelles, Louvigny, Tourffreville, Demouville, Cormelles, Giberville—these are some of them. Their capture means that Montgomery's Orne break-through is being rapidly widened.

Noyers Battles

Our troops are on the outskirts of Troarn, ten miles east of Caen, and other units are battling against strong enemy armour around Cagny, six miles south-east of Caen, and at Grentheville, south of the Caen-Vimont road.

The Germans continue to withdraw their lines in the Hottot area, south of the Caumont-Caen road, and British troops have established firm positions south of the road.

Bitter fighting is still going on inside Noyers, but one mile to the west our troops have taken Landelle.

The enemy defences which the British and Canadians have cracked are formidable. The country is "stiff" with anti-tank guns. As every village, farmstead, wood, and hill for miles is a Nazi strongpoint the defences cannot be said to be broken. But gradually they are being overcome.

On the Canadian sector all German machine-guns nests have been wiped out. No pocket of resistance remains behind our lines. The Germans admit withdrawals from 1,000 to 2,000 yards west of Caen but the town of Caumont is still in enemy hands.

Bad weather reduced air activity.

Yanks Cut Road

In the American sector, US troops have taken Remilly-sur-Lozon and three more villages to the south. They have cut the Periers-Saint Lo road south of Armigny.

One Nazi pocket is still holding out in Saint Lo itself and the Americans are busy mopping up. To the east and west of the town, however, they are gradually advancing and are within a 400-yards of the Vire north-west of the city.

1,200 BOMBERS AT LEIPZIG

LONDON, Thurs.—More than 1,200 US heavy bombers today attacked factories and oil refineries in the Leipzig area. The weather was good and bombing excellent.

Lancasters last night attacked a flying bomb depot 30 miles north-east of Paris. Mosquitos hit Bremen.

RAIN SLOWS US AGAIN IN ITALY

ROME, Thurs.—Today's Allied communiqué says that torrential rain over the battlefront has seriously interfered with our forward movement.

Following the capture of Leghorn, American troops of the Fifth Army have reached the River Arno on a front of about 25 miles and there is now only scattered enemy resistance south of the river in this sector.

Further west, troops of the Fifth have advanced three miles, having cleared Carna Certaldo, and Sandonato.

West of Arezzo, troops of the Eighth have been in heavy fighting in the area of Montevarchi and in the hills around Radda.

BIG JOB FOR LORD GORT

LONDON, Thurs.—Field Marshal Viscount Gort, VC., now Governor and C-in-C of Malta, has been appointed High Commissioner and C-in-C of Palestine and High Commissioner of the Transjordan.—Reuter.

5 MILES TO GO

ROME, Sat.—The Allied advance on Florence is meeting fierce opposition. Further progress was made during the night. Latest reports say New Zealand troops are five miles from the city.

3,000 BOMBERS ON THE JOB

LONDON, Sat.—In 24 hours ending at midday 3,000 British and American heavy bombers attacked German industrial targets.

Stuttgart was attacked last night for the third time this week, and Hamburg and Frankfort were also main targets.

We lost 62 planes, and destroyed 21.

This morning 1,100 bombers struck at a flying bomb depot, and airfields near Paris.

Several flying bombs were shot down over England today.

HEAVIEST BARRAGE YET FOR BUZZ-BOMBS

LONDON, Thurs.—Flying bombs were over Southern England today and last night.

The AA barrage was the most concentrated and heaviest yet.—Reuter.

Lord Louis Thanks The Fleet

The following message has been sent by Admiral Lord Louis Mountbatten, Supreme Allied Commander, South East Asia, to the C-in-C, Eastern Fleet, Admiral Sir James Somerville:

Heartiest congratulations on the great success of the Eastern Fleet's operations against Sabang.

This is the first time since we turned to the offensive that the Eastern Fleet guns have been in action against the Japanese shore defences and the results will hearten all forces in South East Asia.

UNION JACK

Friday, July. 21, 1944
No. 34   Two Lire

FOR THE BRITISH FIGHTING FORCES

ATTEMPT ON HITLER'S LIFE

HITLER RECEIVED LIGHT BURNS AND CONCUSSION, BUT NO INJURIES, WHEN AN ATTEMPT WAS MADE ON HIS LIFE WITH "HIGH EXPLOSIVE," THE GERMAN NEWS AGENCY ANNOUNCED YESTERDAY.

Several members of his entourage were seriously injured, said the agency, among them Lieutenant-General Schmundt, Colonel Brandt, Lieutenant-Colonel Borgmann and the Fuehrer's collaborator Berger. Slightly injured were Colonel-General Jodl, Hitler's Chief of Staff, Generals Korten, Buhle, Bodenschatz, Heusinger, Scherf, and Admirals Voss and von Puttkammer.

The agency report added that Hitler immediately resumed work " as scheduled," shortly afterwards receiving Mussolini, with whom he had a long conversation. Reichmarshal Goering went to see Hitler as soon as he heard of the attempt.

Lieutenant-General Buhle has for several years been a member of Hitler's personal military staff. General Gunther Korten is Chief of Staff of the Luftwaffe, and Admiral von Puttkammer has been Hitler's *aide-de-camp* since 1939. Bodenschatz is an air force general and is a member of Goering's personal staff.

This is the third reported attempt on Hitler's life. The more dramatic of the previous failures was the bomb explosion in the beer cellar at Munich during the annual meeting of the Brownshirts. The bomb, the Germans said, had been placed with a time fuse to explode while Hitler was speaking, but he made a very short speech and had left the beer hall before the bomb went off. The Nazis alleged that British secret agents had been concerned with the placing of the bomb.

Writing from a country house near Moscow, where he is held prisoner by the Russians, Lieutenant-General E. M. Hofmeister, former commander of the German 41st Tank Corps, has confirmed in a letter what has long been suspected to be the cause of the German disasters in the east.

The letter is in Hofmeister's handwriting. He wrote: "I have no objection to this being published," and Russian newspapers published photostatic copies of pages from the letter.

He gives a long catalogue of the events which led to tension between the level-headed older German generals and the fanatical younger ones who gave support to the grandiose military strategy of Hitler.

After listing the causes for the series of great reverses which followed Stalingrad and extended to the present rout, General Hofmeister reached the following conclusion :

" Germany will have to find an answer to the question as to which way she can create the basis for carrying out peace negotiations with other States. These States will not negotiate (TURN TO PAGE TWO.) '

Another new offensive

FIGHTING on the eastern front now extends from Pskov in the north to the foothills of the Carpathians and almost everywhere the German defences are caving in before uneasy blows.

The latest sector to boil up is that of the Third Baltic Front around Ostrov, 30 miles south of Pskov and 10 miles east of the Latvian border.

An Order of the Day announcing the offensive stated that in two days Soviet forces broke the German defences, advanced up to 24 miles, and captured 700 localities.

In Southern Latvia the Russians are now fighting well within the border. More than 100 places were liberated on Wednesday west and south-west of Opochka, including the railway station of Mirza and the town of Vetsloboda.

Another thrust from Drissa has reached the railway station of Indra, only 35 miles from Dvinsk.

The new Russian offensive in the direction of Lvov also made good progress. After encircling an enemy force consisting of five divisions in the area west of the town of Brody the Russians advanced at great speed and captured the towns of Sokal, 45 miles north of Lvov, and Mosty Velikie, 25 miles to the north. Late messages say that the Russians are nine miles from Lvov and are shelling the outskirts.

Entire Japanese cabinet resigns

GENERAL TOJO'S Cabinet resigned en masse on Tuesday, according to Japanese news agency messages. This came a day after Premier Tojo had been removed from his post of Army Chief of Staff, and shortly after he had announced in a radio talk the loss of Saipan island—the nearest point to Tokio the Allies have yet reached.

Tojo spoke in his broadcast of the "deep anxiety" that had been caused to his "Imperial Majesty," and added that Japan was faced by "the greatest crisis in her history."

Explaining the reasons for the resignation, the newsagency said "in the face of the grave situation, realising the necessity of strengthened personnel in a time of urgency for the prosecution of the war, it was decided to strengthen the Cabinet by a wider selection of personnel.

"By utilising all means available the present Cabinet was not able to achieve its objective; then the Government decided to renovate its personnel in order to continue to prosecute the war totally and having recognised the fact that it was most appropriate to carry out the total resignation of the Cabinet, Premier Tojo gathered together the resignations of each member of the Cabinet and presented them to the Emperor on July 18.

"SITUATION SERIOUS"

In his weekly radio broadcast talk yesterday, General Dittmar, German High Command spokesman, emphasised the extreme seriousness of the German military situation.

Of Normandy, he said: " Reports leave no doubt about the unparalleled concentration of the most formidable assault weapons which the German troops have to withstand."

" At this decisive time in the war, to have come to the present state is causing the Emperor much concern. The present Cabinet is filled with trepidation because of this. Acknowledging the Government's meagre power to the men on the fighting front and the people of Japan it has been decided that this Cabinet should be dissolved."

The agency added later that the reason for the resignation of General Tojo's Cabinet " to put it straightforwardly is that the individuality of the Cabinet was unable to keep up with the intensity of the burning war spirit of the people."

General Kuniaki Koiso, Governor of Korea, and Admiral Mitsumasa Tonai, former Premier, "have been chosen to form a new Cabinet."

Earlier it was stated that Emperor Hirohito had ordered Marquis Koichi Kido, who was Minister of Home Affairs, to form a new Cabinet.

The Japanese people and Japanese-occupied areas first heard the news of the resignation from American and other Allied broadcasts. The Japanese newsagency transmitted the news in morse with a "hold for release" note. The agency then ordered its clients to kill the story, indicating the uneasiness of Japanese officials concerning the effect the news would have for the peoples in the Far East. The English transmission to the United States, however, carried the news.

Rain slows advance in Italy

TORRENTIAL rain over the battlefront of Italy has seriously interfered with the Allied forward movement. Following the capture of Leghorn, American troops of the Fifth Army have reached the River Arno on a front of about 25 miles, and there is now only scattered enemy resistance south of the river in this sector.

Farther west, other Fifth Army troops have advanced between two and three miles, having cleared the towns of Varna, Certaldo and San Donato.

West of Arezzo, the Eighth Army have occupied Radda, and made further progress to the north. Heavy fighting is taking place in the Montevarchi area.

In the Tiber valley, our troops made slow progress north-west of Citta di Castello.

Polish troops found Ancona thoroughly mined and demolished. The harbour is full of sunken ships, including the King of Italy's private yacht.

Eighth Army pushed on beyond the port and cut the coast road at Torrette a Mare. Using some armour, troops moving inland established a bridgehead across the Esino River, 10 miles west of Ancona and south of Chiaravalle. By Wednesday afternoon, Eighth Army forces were along the river from the mouth to six miles or more inland.

Fifth Army elements cleared the town of Colle Salvetti, seven miles north-east of Leghorn.

OUR TANKS STRIKE DEEPLY

BRITISH and Canadian troops have driven five miles from the start line of General Montgomery's offensive at some points, and units striking towards Troarn have reached the railway half-a-mile from the town.

The five-mile penetration has been made by the armour striking east of Caen, which has reached the villages of Cagney and Grentheville. West of Caen, about half-way between the city and Tilly-sur-Seulles, another force is fighting in the area of Hottot, which is unofficially reported as captured. In between these two prongs, Germans, resisting near Caen, are being steadily driven back from the outskirts of the city.

Late reports from the battlefield yesterday say that British troops have captured the village of Landelle, a mile west of Noyers.

Other forces which had taken part in the clearing of Louvigny and Vaucelles have driven the enemy from the villages of Cormelles and Ifs, south-east of Caen.

"To the south and south-east of these villages our armour has been in action against enemy armour and anti-tank defences based on villages and farmsteads," yesterday's SHAEF communique stated.

Describing the battle, William Steen, Reuter's Special Correspondent, says that the fierce duel between British tanks and German anti-tank gunners is being fought in country full of tank obstacles. " In haystacks, hedges, barns and behind walls, the Germans lie in wait for our tanks," he says.

To the west, the German line has been pulled back between 1,000 and 2,000 yards to try to form a new front between St. Germain and Noyers.

It was announced at SHAEF yesterday that Lieut.-General Sir Richard O'Connor, who is 54, is commanding our tank formations in the plain of Caen.

American troops, having seized Rampan, three miles north-west of St. Lo, are moving south.

To the east, the US hold on the Periers-St. Lo road south of Armigny has been strengthened, and armoured counter-attacks have been held.

It is announced that prisoners captured in Normandy total more than 60,000. This brings to more than 237,000 the number of German troops who have surrendered on the east, west and south fronts since the Allied offensives from these directions started.

TURN TO PAGE 4

STOP PRESS

MARSHAL STALIN ANNOUNCED LAST NIGHT THAT TROOPS OF FIRST UKRAINIAN FRONT, ADVANCING FROM KOVEL, BROKE STRONG ENEMY DEFENCES AND PENETRATED TO A DEPTH OF 40 MILES, ENLARGING BREAKS TO A BREADTH OF 100 MILES. THEY OCCUPIED OVER 400 TOWNS AND VILLAGES, INCLUDING MALORYTA, LUBOMIL, AND OCALIN, REACHING THE WESTERN BUG.

PARADE

No. 208   Vol. 16   August 5, 1944

INVESTITURE IN ITALY

TOWN OF THE HUSH
Pages 6-9

EGYPT P.T. 2   CYRENAICA P.T. 2   CYPRUS 5 C. Prs.   ERITREA 55 Cents   IRAQ 30 Fils   IRAN 3½ Riels   ITALY 10 Lire   LEBANON 30 S. Prs.

MALTA 6d   PALESTINE 25 Mils   SICILY 10 Lire   SUDAN 20 Mils   SYRIA 30 S. Prs.   TRANSJORDAN 25 Mils   TRIPOLITANIA 12 M.A. Lire   TURKEY 10 Krs.

UNION JACK

Thursday, August 24, 1944
No 203   Two Lire

FOR THE BRITISH FIGHTING FORCES

GENERAL DE GAULLE

PARIS

City is liberated by Patriots after four-day battle in streets

PARIS is free. The city has been liberated by French Forces of the Interior.   First news of its release after more than four years of Nazi occupation was given by the B.B.C. shortly after mid-day yesterday. It was described how 50,000 of General Koenig's patriot forces, supported by several hundred thousand unarmed Frenchmen, started a general uprising in Paris and the surrounding area last Saturday morning.

FRENCH REPORT NEW LANDING

FRENCH military authorities in Hendaye, on the Franco-Spanish border, have reported a new Allied landing in the area of Bordeaux, on the west coast, in co-ordination with inland attacks by American and French columns.

An Associated Press message from Spain last night said that the landing was reported to have begun on Tuesday night, and explosions from the intense air and sea bombardments could be distinctly heard on the frontier. The report has not been officially confirmed.

Grenoble taken

IN a rapid thrust inland from the southern France bridge-head, Seventh Army troops have captured Grenoble, in the French Alps, 125 miles north of Marseilles and 350 miles south-east of Paris, liberating six other towns on the way.

Armour drives on SENS AND DEAUVILLE CAPTURED

AMERICAN forces have captured and are beyond Sens, 60 miles south-east of Paris on the direct route to Berlin, through Troyes and Nancy.

Behind this American spearhead the towns of Stampes, 20 miles south of Paris, and Pithiviers, 25 miles north-east of Orleans, have been captured.

The Falaise pocket has been finally cleaned up, the destruction of German material being described as "terrific."

Vimoutiers, 15 miles south of Lisieux, has fallen and with it all signs of resistance in the pocket ended.

Allied forces are now closing in on remnants of the German army falling back on Evreux. In a big new pincer movement American columns have struck north from the Dreux area and are threatening the enemy in Evreux.

Simultaneously Allied forces have reached Deauville, less than four miles from the Seine estuary.

The capture of Grenoble, capital of the Isere Department and only 80 miles from the Swiss frontier, puts American armoured columns only 55 miles south-east of Lyons, in the heart of the Rhone Valley industrial belt.

Farther south American forces are driving for the entrance to the Rhone Valley, and reconnaissance units were reported yesterday to be in the outskirts of Apt, on Highway 100, and 30 miles from Avignon. This places them 40 miles inland west of Marseilles.

French armoured troops have also made further substantial advances westward along Highway 8, while an American spearhead pushing on from Aix has penetrated the Ventabren area. Other columns moving along Highway 7 are nearing Saint Cannat, to the north-west. Reuter adds that Ventabren is on the main road from Aix to Etang de Berre, a great lake at the mouth of the Rhone, and is one of the biggest seaplane bases in Europe. It is only nine miles from the town of Berre.

In the fighting along the coast, Allied spearheads are reported to be within three miles of Marseilles. High ground to the north - east has been captured.

French troops have occupied Hyeres and have closed in on Toulon from the east. Here they have improved their positions in the northern and western suburbs of the port.

STOP PRESS

Special communique stated last night that Marseilles fell to French troops yesterday. The port was taken with a minimum of resistance as its encirclement was completed, and the last escape route for the German defenders severed.

"SHUTTLE" SUCCESS

The United States Military Mission in Moscow has announced that since the beginning of the shuttle bombing 119 enemy aircraft have been destroyed in operations to and from American bases in the Soviet Union.

rounding area last Saturday morning.

Four days of bitter fighting followed. The Paris police, who had been on strike, captured their own headquarters, and other forces took complete command of the "city" of Paris, on the island in the centre of the Seine, resisting all attempts to dislodge them.

By Tuesday night, the Germans were beaten. Those who were not dead and had not escaped were held prisoner, together with the Vichy representatives. All the public buildings were in patriot hands.

Paris was occupied by the Germans at seven o'clock on the morning of June 14, 1940. German motorised units moved into the French capital without a shot being fired against them. Since then, with Paris under the Nazi heel, first Bordeaux and then Vichy have been the capitals of France.

Meanwhile, German control clamped down tighter and tighter on the Parisians. There were nearly 3,000,000 at first but they dwindled to 1,000,000 as the result of the deportation of labour parties. But as life grew harder for the people of Paris so their resistance increased.   They were told by the Allies to wait until it was time to strike a decisive blow. That blow has been struck.

Joyful scenes

Frenchmen all over the world—and their Allies—celebrated the liberation of the city yesterday. Bells were ringing throughout Algeria last night, and St. Paul's Cathedral is to have a special 30-minute peal by a team of 12 ringers at noon to-day.

Throughout Tunisia and Algeria and all parts of liberated France artillery fired salutes, while all ships in French ports last night gave long success blasts on their sirens.

French flags are flying on all official buildings in the City of London, and the Lord Mayor of London has sent a telegram of congratulation to General Koenig.

Excited crowds in Algiers thronged the streets crying "Vive la France," and every tricolor and Allied flag in the city was displayed from balconies and public buildings. An impromptu parade of citizens, bearing signs inscribed "Honour and Glory to the patriots who have liberated Paris," was organised and was followed by a French Army band, greeted with cheering and paper streamers tossed from office buildings.

Frenchmen in New York received the news jubilantly. Some wept with joy, the Associated Press reported. Moscow radio carried the full text of General Koenig's communique in yesterday's mid-afternoon broadcast.

Salute to Paris from London

The Lord Mayor of London, Sir Frank Newson Smith, has sent a message to General Koenig congratulating him on the liberation of Paris, in which he said:

"We in London salute the citizens of Paris. A world without Paris is unthinkable, and we look forward to a new and more glorious epoc in the future."

WRONG PORT

It was announced from San Sebastian that a German minesweeper entered the port of Pasajos, where it was given 48 hours to leave. In case it failed to do so, it would be taken over by the Spanish authorities (Reuter).

General Koenig's message

"ON Saturday morning, August 19, the National Resistance Council and Paris Committee of Liberation, in agreement with national delegates representing the Provisional Government of the French Republic, decreed a general uprising in Paris and in the Paris area.

"French Forces of the Interior, 50,000 strong, armed, and supported by several hundred thousand patriots not armed, went into action.

"Paris police, who had previously gone on strike, took over the Prefecture of Police, and the "City" Island of Paris (the administrative part of the town) was turned into a bastion before which the German attacks broke down.

"Yesterday, August 22, after four days of fighting, the enemy was beaten everywhere. Patriots occupied all public buildings. Representatives of Vichy have been arrested or have taken to flight.

"Thus the people of Paris have taken a decisive part in the liberation of the capital."

Mystery of Petain arrest is cleared

MARSHAL PETAIN, head of the Vichy Government, has now become officially what he has in effect been for many years—a prisoner of the Germans.

A *Daily Mail* special correspondent reports that he was seized last Sunday morning and at once taken to an unknown destination, probably Germany. His guards even refused him time to shave—but allowed him to write a farewell letter.

Copies of this letter are already circulating in France although as yet its terms are not known.

Petain is said to have at first defied German efforts to remove him from Vichy. He refused their request that he should go to Belfort, close to the Swiss frontier, where Laval is trying to set up his Government offices.

The Marshal insisted that he would stay in Vichy but eventually left because the Germans said if he defied them further the town would be bombed to ruins.

The arrest of Petain virtually ends the Vichy regime. The Swiss Minister at Vichy is returning home and Swiss affairs will in future be handled through Berlin.

SEAC

THE DAILY NEWSPAPER OF
SOUTH EAST ASIA COMMAND

No. 232   One Anna
MONDAY, 28 AUGUST, 1944.
Printed by Courtesy of
THE STATESMAN in Calcutta.

RAILMEN STOLE TROOPS' FAGS

Thousands of cigarettes withdrawn from bond for shipment to troops overseas were stacked on a table as exhibits in the Bakewell, Derbyshire court when six railwaymen were sent to jail for six months for theft. Three others were fined £20 and a fourth £10 for receiving.

Piled beside the cigarettes were chocolate, soap, crockery, boots, pyjamas and sheets, other loot which the six men had taken from trucks at the Rowsley LMS sidings.

The prosecutor said the men were exposed by officers of the Special Branch of the Railway Police who went to work as porters at the sidings and gained the confidence of the thieves.

Special padlocks had been fitted to vans carrying stores in short civilian supply, in addition to the ordinary locks, but they did not foil the gang.

Losses at these sidings and elsewhere on the railways had reached staggering proportions recently—and a particularly unpleasant feature was the theft of the cigarettes destined for troops overseas.

MAQUIS 'EXECUTE' CHEVALIER

PARIS, Sun.—Maurice Chevalier, former film idol and cabaret star of London, Paris and New York, was executed by men of the Maquis on Friday, says a report reaching Paris today.

Chevalier soon after the German occupation, became notorious as a collaborator. He went to Berlin and was prominent in high Nazi society.—Reuter.

STRUCK OFF

LONDON, Sun.—The Yugoslav Government yesterday announced that "High Command" headed by General Mihailovich has ceased to exist—by an order of King Peter.—Reuter.

ALLIES NEARER GOTHIC LINE

ALLIED MEDITERRANEAN HQ, Sun.—British and Indian troops of the Eighth Army, says today's communiqué, have continued to gain ground towards the Gothic line east of Florence and in the mountains on either side of the Upper Arno and the Tiber valleys, representing in some cases advances of three miles.

Other troops of the Eighth Army have crossed the Metauro River, driving in enemy outposts, and have established on the north bank of the river a bridgehead which incorporates high ground above Monte Della Mattera just south of Mombaroccio.

On the Fifth Army front, there has been no change in our forward fixed positions.—Reuter.

EASTERN FLEET OUT AGAIN

KANDY, Sun.—A special communiqué from S. E. Asia Command Head-quarters today says:

"A carrier-borne air attack, supported by Allied units of the Eastern Fleet, under the command of Rear-Admiral Clement Moody, was carried out against the large Indaroeng cement manufacturing plant near Padang, on the west coast of Sumatra and also against Emmahaven, the port for Padang during the early hours of 24 August.

Large numbers of heavy bombs fell on the cement works, which were left in a cloud of smoke and flame rising to between 800 and a thousand feet.

In Emmahaven a merchant vessel of about 3,500 tons received four hits and a smaller merchant vessel of about 2,500 tons two hits. Both vessels were left burning fiercely.

Airfield Strafed

Wharves, warehouses, the coaling jetty and railway yards received numerous hits and were heavily damaged.

The airfield at Padang and the harbour installations at Emmahaven were strafed by fighters.

Complete surprise was achieved and our aircraft encountered only moderate anti-aircraft fire. Although a few enemy aircraft were in the air at the time of the attack, no serious attempt was made to interfere with our air striking forces.

No attempt was made by the Japanese to intercept our surface forces either during this attack or after the operation had been carried out.

In the course of this operation one of our aircraft was shot down.—API.

36 DIV. ADVANCE IN N. BURMA

KANDY, Sun.—In North Burma elements of the 36th Division are now approximately half a mile from Pinbaw, says today's SEAC communiqué. There was no change in the area south of Myitkyina.

Fourteenth Army artillery shelled enemy positions on the Tiddim road. Ahead of our main forces, raiding parties have inflicted casualties and wrecked more transport on the Jap lines of communication.

Widespread rain greatly restricted air operations.

EISENHOWER IN PARIS

PARIS, Sun.—General Eisenhower, Supreme Allied Commander, today visited Paris and called on the French Military Governor, Gen. Koenig, to pay tribute on behalf of the Allied forces to the "indomitable spirit of the people of Paris."

ATTEMPT TO KILL GEN. DE GAULLE

Battle in Notre Dame Cathedral

LONDON, Sun.—Battle broke out in the streets of Paris and in the historic Notre Dame Cathedral yesterday, when collaborationists made a dramatic and determined effort to assassinate General de Gaulle soon after his triumphal entry into the liberated capital.

Thousands of patriots, many of them armed, lined the streets as de Gaulle drove from the tomb of the Unknown Warrior to the Cathedral for a service of Thanksgiving.

As the procession was nearing the end of the Champs Elysees, dozens of shots were fired by snipers hidden in trees bordering the famous advenue.

Patriots returned the fire with Thompsons and rifles. Crowds panicked and fled, while the cars of the procession speeded up.

As the General and his encourage reached the Place de Notre Dame there was a fresh outburst of firing, and a new battle developed. Then, as they entered the cathedral, there was a hail of machine-gun fire from the galleries round the great nave. The congregation threw themselves to the floor while loyal troops and patriots crowded into the building to answer the assassins' fire.

Indignation at this murderous desecration of the city's holiest place swept through the city and primed the patriots for a new hunt for collaborationists.

No statement on the casualties suffered by the General's party has yet been released in Paris.

RAF BOMBS KOENIGSBERG

LONDON, Sun.—Koenigsberg, capital of East Prussia, which is 100 miles from the Russian front, was the target for a major RAF raid last night. Large fires were started during a concentrated attack

Koenigsberg's industries include cellulose, railway trucks, textiles, chemicals, engineering and shipbuilding. It has been bombed several times by the Russians but has received little attention from the RAF.

The Russians' Third Baltic Army advancing on Central Estonia has taken the town of

RAF Has New Fire-Weapon

The Air Ministry reveals that the attack on Koenigsberg lasted only nine and a half minutes and the defences were "quickly saturated."

Large quantities of a new flame-throwing incendiary were in the bomb load.

Tartu. Stiff fighting continues before Warsaw, and a German report says the Red Army has launched a big offensive on a 45-mile front east of the Polish capital, with 12 or 14 infantry divisions and several tank units —probably 150,000 men.

In Rumania, the Germans have suffered one of their biggest defeats of the war. In five days fighting, trapped between two Russian armies, the Nazis have lost 100,000 men killed, and 104,000 captured, says a special Soviet communiqué. A further twelve divisions are now encircled.

The Red Army is pouring into the Galatz Gap, within 100 miles of Bucharest and 80 miles from the Ploesti oilfields. If the present rate of advance is maintained

PARIS: 10,000 HUNS CAPTURED

Ten thousand enemy troops, including the German commander and his staff were taken prisoner in Paris, states yesterday's communique from Eisenhower's HQ

Within the city, except for sniping, resistance has ceased. Small German groups are still operating in the suburbs.

Paris was heavily bombed by the Germans at 23.05 hours on Saturday. Large fires were started and there were a number of victims.

British troops have stormed across the Seine at Vernon and Louviers in a double thrust which threatens to outflank the flying bomb coast and cut off Rouen, says Reuter's SHAEF correspondent. The bridgeheads are 15 miles apart

Rouen is now closely menaced. Allied troops who captured Honfleur have advanced another three miles.

As their position worsened the trapped Germans attempted to cross the Seine by daylight Allied aircraft took a tremendous toll destroying and damaging scores of tanks and motor transport.

Crossings Cease

By evening practically all German movement across the river had ceased. One air force group alone accounted for 140 transports and 10 tanks.

In the past few days 118 German fighters have been shot down by Spitfires and Thunderbolts.

Allied troops advancing eastwards towards the Upper Seine valley have reached the river in the northern outskirts of Troyes and at a point twelve miles further north, states Eisenhower's communique.

Troyes is 87 miles south-east of Paris and 130 miles from the German frontier.

Heavy fighting is in progress north of Brest, where the enemy garrison is offering stubborn resistance.

DEAD—OR PRISONER?

LONDON, Sun.—General Arthur Hauffe has been killed in action east of Lvov, says the German radio.

Eighth Army raced into the southern suburbs of Florence meeting opposition mainly from suicidal stay-behind German snipers and bridge-defending parties. In centre of the former capital the Germans proceeded to destroy and block. Recce patrol found five of six Arno bridges wrecked. Ponte Vecchio was intact.

RACE INTO FLORENCE
South African Tanks Lead The Way

Last lap in Eighth Army's drive on ancient Florence, former capital of Italy, developed into a race between South African and New Zealand forces. The Springboks won: Italian partisans were at the southern outskirts and led them into the city, fighting a pitched battle with Nazis left to hold the northern end of a wrecked bridge. A motor battalion followed; shortly after came the Guards, lending the streets a parade ground atmosphere.

Imprunetta, situated in the hills south of Florence, provided a German stronghold which delayed the liberation of Florence. It fell to Springbok armour and the Guards. Picture shows entry into the captured town.

South African tanks penetrate to the centre of Tuscan hill town of Imprunetta which had bas...

BRUSSELS FREED: BRITISH NEARING DUTCH BORDER

LONDON, Mon.—The greater part of Belgium has been liberated by Allied armoured columns which are sweeping the roads at will. Brussels is in our hands; Namur, scene of the Guards' epic fight in 1940, is captured; and a report late tonight says that Antwerp, great port near the Dutch frontier, has been entered.

The advance has brought to the fighting men the greatest of all morale-boosts—the knowledge that they have brought relief to their people in Southern England, for the great majority of Germany's flying bomb sites have been completely overrun or cut off.

Late this evening, London has been without a bomb for more than 60 hours, the longest respite since the attacks started on 15 June.

Great crowds lined the streets of the Belgian capital last evening, when the Allied tanks roared into the city. Not a shot was fired.

The advance on Brussels outpaced any move in military history—even rivalling Hitler's unopposed march on Vienna. Our armour crossed the frontier yesterday morning at the industrial town of Tournai, and, less than twelve hours later, was in the capital—50 miles further on.

120,324 Prisoners

Latest figures from SHAEF say, that the Americans have now taken a total of 120,324 prisoners since the campaign in Northern France opened 12 weeks ago.

With those taken by General Dempsey's British forces and General Crerar's Canadians, the grand total is now believed to be well over 200,000, with a lot more to come when those pocketed by our sweep parallel with the French Channel coast are mopped up.

Only reports of organised fighting by the enemy come today from Abbeville, now firmly in our hands after two-days' fighting with small enemy parties, and Le Havre, where Belgian, French and Canadian troops are closing in on the port's defences, still powerfully manned by a rearguard of SS troops.

General Eisenhower's communique today says:

Brussels has been liberated. Allied troops which crossed the Belgian frontier early yesterday morning rapidly freed Tournai and pushed on to north and east to enter the capital in the late evening.

Yanks near Nancy

Further West, other armoured forces drove North through Bethune and Lille.

In the Abbeville area, the river Somme was crossed on both sides of the town, now in our hands after some fighting. Our troops pushed on Northward from the river.

North and east of Le Havre we closed in on the main defences of the port.

Some forty miles South-west of Brussels, the Belgian frontier has been crossed by other columns advancing North-east. Elements are in the area of Charleroi.

Further South, the advance eastward has brought our troops to the vicinity of Nancy. Units following up this thrust have made another crossing of the Meuse river near Chalaines, ten miles South-east of Commercy, and our troops entered Saint Mihiel.

Enemy road and rail movements in Belgium and Pas de Calais were attacked by fighters and fighter-bombers yesterday. Considerable numbers of motor

5 SEPTEMBER, 1944.

Belgian Govt. will be Home in Week

LONDON, Mon. A Belgian Civil Mission left London today for Brussels, to provide a temporary administration pending the departure of the Government, which expects to leave at the end of the week.—Reuter.

vehicles, locomotives and railway cars were destroyed or damaged.

Giving details of the advance, General Dempsey told correspondents today that it began last Tuesday from the Seine area by six o'clock on Wednesday Amiens was taken.

An advance of 130 miles had been made in 4½ days to reach the Belgian frontier. As our troops have swept on beyond Brussels they have added more than 50 miles to that advance.

A communique from the HQ of the Belgian Forces of Resistance says that during the last month patriots carried out widespread sabotage on railways, destroying 18 bridges and derailing many trains.

LYONS IS OCCUPIED

LONDON—Mon.—A communique from General Jan Gabriel Cochetin, commander of the FFI in Southern France, reports today that his men have crossed the frontier into Italy.

The advance of the Seventh Army is now nearly twenty miles beyond Lyons, which was occupied yesterday. Lyons, centre of France's great silk industry and the third city of France, is 200 miles from the landing points.

Most of the enemy forces which for more than week have been falling back on Lyons pulled out before our men arrived—making apparently for the Jura mountains by the road which runs through Bourg.

Villefranche, fifteen miles north of Lyons, has been entered by our advanced forces, says General Wilson's communique today. Our pursuing columns met an enemy counter attack on the road north of Bourg, but this was beaten off and the enemy withdrew.

Six of our planes are missing from the bombing and strafing activity of the last 24 hours. One enemy plane was shot down. The MAAF flew 1200 sorties.—Reuter.

4 Divs. Break Up

On the Northern sector, British, Canadian and Polish troops of Montgomery's Army Group are nearing the Dutch border along most of its length. There are signs that the German defence, after two weeks of slogging fighting, is giving way.

RED AIR FORCE AIDS WARSAW

MOSCOW, Sun.—Russian troops have entered Sofia, capital of Bulgaria. Making this announcement, the Soviet communiqué also reports advances north of Praga, the Warsaw suburb captured two days ago.

Battles continue in the streets of the Warsaw suburbs on the east bank of the Vistula, says a supplement to the communiqué Repeated German counter-attacks were beaten off.

Inside the city, the forces of General Bor are still fighting strongly against heavy German shelling. The Germans are carrying out mass demolitions, blowing up barracks, factories and public utility buildings. "We are establishing closer contact with the Soviet army inside Praga,' says Bor's communiqué.

Polish patriot broadcasting station inside Warsaw claims that German planes had dropped poisoned food to patriots in an attempt to discredit the aid which Soviet planes are continuing to give.

Czechs Meet Russians

At key points along the 600-mile front from the East Prussian border to the Danube. Hitler's panzers and the Soviet Army are locked in a violent conflict.

It is the first major battle of the Soviet September offensive. Czechoslovak forces have established contact with Russians who have crossed their frontier.

The German news agency said last night that Russian spearheads reached the Jelgara Krustpils railway, which has put the Soviet troops less than 20 miles South of Riga.—Reuter.

NAZIS PULLING OUT OF CRETE?

CAIRO, Mon.—The Germans are today reported to the withdrawing some of their troops from the Aegean Islands, chiefly from Crete and the islands facing Turkey.

GREEK PATRIOTS HOLD TURK BORDER

CAIRO, Mon.—Greek partisans are reported to be in complete control of the Greek side of the frontier with Turkey.—Reuter.

BERNHARD TAKES NFI COMMAND

LONDON, Mon.—SHAEF announces that Prince Bernhard of the Netherlands has been appointed Commander of the Netherlands Forces of the Interior.—Reuter.

EIGHTH ARMY 12m INTO GOTHIC LINE

ROME, Mon.—Allied armies in Italy are pushing the Germans back on both the west and east coasts.

On the Adriatic sector United Kingdom, Canadian and Polish troops now control the Gothic Line for a distance of 20 miles. In places they have penetrated it to a depth of 12 miles.

Fifth Army troops, after crossing the Arno river, have bypassed important mountain features and now hold the land overlooking the road from Florence to the coast above Pisa.

37 ENSA PLAYERS ARE COMING OUT

SEAC Staff Reporter

Following the raising of the travel ban, 37 ENSA artists, making four parties, are ready to leave home for India and Burma.

This means that, with luck, some of them should be seen in the 14th Army area within two months. More artists are following this batch "it is promised," so there seems every chance of forward area Christmas entertainment being stepped up.

Four shows will form welcome replacements for the first ENSA parties seen here. These parties had successful tours, but there has been a serious entertainment gap—to which SEAC drew attention on 13 Sept since they left.

There is still a serious need out here for pianists and comedians, and now that travel difficulties have been smoothed away, perhaps more comedians will come out to take laughter right forward. Comedians however, especially those with "big names" are not yet congesting the boats to India.

Several new "theatres" are going up in the 14th Army area, for visiting artists and Service entertainments.

ARNHEM, LAST DAY

Guy Byam of the B.B.C. gives this eye-witness account of the last stage at Arnhem and the return across the Rhine by night

Wednesday, September 28.

The tired, weary men in the Arnhem area got up out of their foxholes and faded into the night out of the hell they had lived in for over a week. They came out because they had nothing left to fight with except their bare hands. All day, as for days before that, tanks and mortars and flamethrowers had smashed at their positions. For some time they had been fighting without food and practically with no water, fighting an enemy whose growing strength was almost in our midst, fighting with small arms against all the might of German armour. I remember thinking that Stalingrad must have been something •like this because every brick of every wall of every house was part of the battle that ebbed to and fro, a yard here and a yard there.

Those men who climbed out of their foxholes and slit-trenches were not beaten, mind you. They had to get out because of events on the other side of the river. No German soldier ever really beat them. The *panzers* could come in and they could shell us from a distance hour after hour. But when S.S. troops were sent in they got murdered and they hated every minute of it.

On the morning of the day that we came out I was asked as a non-combatant to go through the lines and contact the enemy to enable us to evacuate our wounded. As I was making my way back to the area where we were dug in, after having seen a German medical officer, I was stopped by an S.S. lieutenant who said I was his prisoner, despite the fact that I was carrying the Red Cross flag. I managed to get away and soon got back to our own lines in a jeep going to fetch some more wounded. As I came back I must admit it was with dread.

All through the afternoon it went on, the afternoon of that last day, more and more of it, shells and shells, mortars and sniping and machine-gunning. One found oneself almost wanting to stand up and scream. "Come and show yourselves. Let's get to grips with you." But they just sat, two or three miles away in the woods, somewhere in a world outside that didn't seem to matter any more, and shelled us. Yet the men found time to laugh. They did not look like men much now. Many were wounded and many were so tired that they smiled as if it hurt them to move their mouths. The afternoon wore on and attack after attack came in. The log sheet at divisional headquarters—50 yards away from the nearest point on the front line—went something like this:

3.35: enemy forming up. Such and such and such position. About one company strength, two mobile guns (and we would wireless our own artillery over the river to give us support.)

3.45: glider pilots are hard-pressed in their sector. (That was about 100 yards from divisional H.Q.) Attacks died down. Glider pilots have restored position.

The log had read something like that for four days. As night fell we wondered what the next day would bring. We had lived this far but to-morrow—well? Then the division heard that they were to be evacuated over the Rhine. They hated to go because they were not beaten, but they got ready the meagre equipment they had left. At divisional H.Q. the padre said a prayer. About ten o'clock we slowly groped our way through the woods. The whole area smelt of the dead. Farms and little houses were on fire. The sky was a red glow. Then we came out of the woods into a field and crept in long lines down to the Rhine. Mortars were bursting in what seemed like a spray of sparks almost among us now and we grovelled on the ground, pressing our faces into the wet grass. It was then that I decided to have a go at swimming the river.

What of the men? Did they panic or rush? No. They patiently waited their turn to get in a boat and if a man, floundering in the dark, got ahead of somebody else there would be a quiet "Come on, chum, take your turn." The boat loads got over the Rhine. Swept down by the current I at last managed to reach the other bank. Hell was behind us. But not all of them got across, for as it got light the last ones were still left patiently waiting their turn. Not all of them could swim and the Germans, seeing them, poured machine-gun fire into the men who huddled against the hedges and lay on the causeway. If ever men fought harder, with greater courage, more cheerfulness and with a greater spirit of sacrifice I would like to know where. I do not think any one man who was not there could possibly believe it. There is surely nothing finer in the annals of the British race.

Radioed picture shows British troopers of First Allied Airborne

Pictures from Home

Who's who and What's what

Above : What would December be without the Picture of the Girl with the Turkeys ? This year's selection is 23-year-old Vera Smith, who works on a farm near Colchester.

And the horses ? Part of the National Stud which has been brought home from Eiré to Gillingham (Dorset).

Left : She's American but she's at home in Britain. California's Corporal Ruby Newell has been voted the most beautiful W.A.C. in the E.T.O. General James Doolittle introduced her to the crowd at the U.S. Army-Navy ball game at the White City, London.

HEROIC CHAPTER

The battle of Arnhem, "a heroic chapter of military history", is explained and its results are analysed by "Strategicus"

September 29.

It is scarcely my part to emphasise the epic nature of the stand at Arnhem. History will do ample justice to that, but to understand this amazing battle it is necessary to emphasise the extent of the success and the immense risks taken in the attempt to seize the last crossings of the Rhine and turn the Siegfried defences. As I pointed out in my last article there are about 70,000, possibly 100,000 Germans in the west of Holland. When an Airborne Division was landed on September 17 at Arnhem it may have mustered some 8,000 men. Clearly it could dispose of only small arms and possibly some light artillery. It had no communications except by air. And yet it had to face attack by as many of the great German Army to the west, and greater resources to the east, as the German Command could concentrate against it.

The Germans in fact had to crush this daring challenge at almost any cost. Whatever risks they took elsewhere they had to close the door into the Westphalian plain and under Field Marshal Rundstedt they struck as skilfully as they hit hard. Up to Wednesday the Division held and controlled the bridge across the river. Up to that day in spite of constant shelling by a great concentration of artillery and mortars they prevented the Germans using the bridge to deal with the other airborne detachments to the south.

It was part of the Allied plan to advance from the Albert and Escaut canals to link up with these heroic men. If there seemed from the beginning a touch of a gamble about this operation it was at worst only a touch. Under normal circumstances the venture might have entirely succeeded.

I have frequently emphasised the effect of having one arm "shot out." The German theorists recognise this in their textbooks and it has been observed how the Germans have almost come to that position in the *Luftwaffe*. But it must be realised that what turned the scale against this gallant venture was a somewhat similar effect caused by a caprice of the weather. How often has the weather come to the assistance of the Germans!

In the neighbourhood of Arnhem, prevalent cloud and rain made a vital difference. It has been pointed out that the only communications of the Airborne Division at Arnhem were by air and they were cut by bad weather. It was not until Saturday, not until the troops had been fighting incessantly for a whole week, that the Tactical Air Force was able to assist them. There had been some reinforcements and supplies dropped by air but that intimate and full support which was necessary if the venture was to succeed fully could not be given.

This factor also fettered the advance of the Allied armour from the south. On the raised roads the armour made a good target for enemy artillery but that risk was not a great matter while the weather permitted movement. When mud stopped progress it became important. The Second British Army pressed its advance steadily and linked up with the landings at Eindhoven and Nijmegen, where it captured the two bridges. It reached Arnhem and got troops across the river, but rain made it impossible for transport and armour to secure a grip on the banks and after several attempts it was decided to withdraw all the unwounded men.

But failing of its complete effect this battle at Arnhem undoubtedly contributed to the capture of the bridges at Nijmegen and the advance to the Lower Rhine south of Arnhem. The Germans cut through the salient created by the British advance on three occasions, the last as late as Monday. But now Gen. Dempsey's Army is pressing it out both toward the east and west. It has pressed out into a loop of the Meuse toward the east and it is being strengthened at its base.

If the Germans have contrived to postpone the loss of one of the most brilliant prizes of the war they have not prevented the Allies establishing a very promising position across the broader course of the Rhine, the Waal.

But the battle of Arnhem is merely an episode in a developing campaign. It had a brilliant prologue and the heroic chapter it has contributed to military history will have its epilogue. It is this that concerns the spectator more. The end is not yet. It is not even possible to write finis to this episode. The Germans may attempt to improve the occasion by counter-attacking the Second Army salient. They may find there a very different fate. In spite of stirring developments about Riga, on the Hungarian plain and across the Rubicon the developments in southern Holland will rivet the attention.

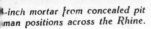

-inch mortar from concealed pit
man positions across the Rhine.

SOUTH PACIFIC ISLANDS

THE SERVICES NEWSPAPER OF SOUTH EAST ASIA COMMAND

No 271   One Anna
FRIDAY, 6 OCTOBER, 1944.
Printed by Courtesy of
THE STATESMAN in Calcutta.

ALLIES LAND IN GREECE FROM AIR & SEA

PRINCESS BEATRICE DIES AT 86

LONDON. Thurs.—Princess Beatrice youngest child of Queen Victoria, died at 05.15 today, aged 86.

She had lived quietly in the country since the outbreak of war and had been in failing health for some time.

Ex-Queen Victoria Eugenie of Spain, her only daughter, flew from Switzerland to be with her mother on Tuesday.

Princess Beatrice married Prince Henry of Battenberg in 1885 and had been a widow since his death in 1896. Her eldest and only surviving son is the Marquis of Carisbrooke. The second son, Lord Leopold Mountbatten, died in 1922. The third, Prince Maurice, was killed in the last war.—Reuter.

LONDON FLY BOMBED

LONDON. Thurs.—Two of a number of flying bombs the Germans directed against Southern England, including London, last night are known to have been destroyed by fighters. Others hit by gunfire exploded in midair—Reuter.

City Council Accused
½LB MINCE FOR 29 CHILDREN

BRADFORD Wed.—Bradford City council is in trouble with the Ministry of Health following an inspector's report on the 'Oliver Twist' scenes and conditions in the city's Bowling Park Welfare Institution.

The Ministry's inspector stated that young children at the institution looked pale and listless and were brought into meals naked from the waist down to sit on bare wooden forms.

Half a pound of mince, it was alleged, had to be divided among 29 children for dinner. The first course consisted virtually of potatoes only.

"The whole picture reminded us of feeding time at the zoo," the report added.

Members of Bradford Social Welfare Committee met in private to consider the criticisms and adjourned after a 2-hour talk. They point out that the administration was carried out under great difficulties because of overcrowding and shortage of staff, but the Ministry reply that conditions need not have got into the state disclosed.

PRIMATE DEAD

LONDON. Thurs: The Archbishop of Canterbury. Dr. William Temple, died today aged 63.

Dr. Temple, who was Archbishop of York from 1929-42, became Primate in succession to Dr. Lang. At one time he was headmaster of Repton School.

MORE SCOUTS

There are 436,871 Boy Scouts in the United Kingdom, 2,000 more than in 1938.

ALLIED HQ, Mediterranean, Thurs.—Allied forces have landed on the Greek mainland and on some of the Greek islands. They are already in contact with the enemy in some places, although at Tripolitsa, in the Peloponnese peninsula, Quisling security battalions surrendered without any fighting.

The landings were made by parachute, sea and transport aircraft. The units taking part are attached to the new formation, Land Forces of the Adriatic, which last week landed in Albania.

Troops have entered Patras in the northern Peloponnese, according to a communiqué issued by the Balkans Air Force.

The Greek Government states that British officers have arrived in Tripolitsa, presumably to make contact with patriot leaders.

The capture of Patras, near which is a valuable airfield, is believed to deprive the Germans of one of their last strongholds in the Peloponnese.

Partisans helped

Greek partisans of varied guerrilla units co-operated with the invasion forces and are still offering more valuable assistance.

Correspondents believe that the landings are designed to harrass and hasten the German withdrawal from Greece.

Very quickly the Balkans Air Force had seized an airfield from which Spitfires are now operating.

A land transport system is also working smoothly. Infantry, commandos, engineers and men of the RAF Regiment who established themselves on the mainland were given a terrific welcome by Greek guerrillas and civilians.

Before the landings heavy bombers for four successive nights smashed German airfields, road and rail systems, ports and submarine bases.

14th CUT ROAD IN JAP REAR

KANDY, Thurs.—In the Chin Hills Jap infantry and gun positions at the Chocolate Staircase on the Tiddim road have been turned by Indian troops, says today's SE Asia Command communiqué.

Four miles north of Tiddim the road has been cut in the enemy's rear. An attack on this roadblock was repulsed and large fires were seen burning in the Jap positions. Enemy outposts guarding Tiddim to the east suffered further losses in renewed attacks.

Allied aircraft of Eastern Air Command supported ground operations in the Arakan and the Chindwin Valley yesterday. Targets in the Bhamo area were also attacked.—API.

THEY GIVE UP

STOCKHOLM, Thurs.—Germans holding out in buildings in Torneo on the Finnish-Swedish frontier, have capitulated.—Reuter.

10 FREIGHTERS SUNK

ALLIED HQ, SW PACIFIC, Thurs.—Ten Jap freighters have been sunk or damaged by Allied planes over the Philippines, the Celebes and the Moluccas, it is officially announced.

JAPS LOST 14

CHUNGKING, Thurs.—Gen Stilwell's HQ announced today that combat losses for the week ending 27 Sept were 14 for the Japs against none for the Fourteenth Air Force.—Reuter.

RUSSIANS MEET 'EASIEST' NAZIS

MOSCOW, Thurs.—Red Army forces on the outskirts of Belgrade, the Yugoslav capital, are fighting their way into the city at the point of the bayonet.

Worn out by a long war of attrition with Marshal Tito's partisans, the Germans are proving easy opponents.

The advancing Russians are meeting only slight artillery action. The defenders of the capital are the "easiest" Germans the Red Army has met.

The Russians' capture of Banatsko-Kralicevo, 15 miles north-east of Belgrade was announced in last night's Soviet communiqué.

Garrisons Smashed

It also announced the capture of Vladimirovce 22 miles north-east of Belgrade, and 24 miles from Vraso, which has been captured.

German garrisons in the Yugoslav sector west of Negotin, where the Red Army and Marshal Tito's partisan troops have linked up are being smashed.

In the sector south-west of Turnu Severin, crack German Alpine troops are battling with Soviet troops.

An official Polish report of the Warsaw rising states that in six weeks' fighting 200,000 people were killed, wounded or are missing. A further 100,000 are in concentration camps.

According to a German News Agency report General Bor Komorowski, commander of the Polish forces inside Warsaw, is a prisoner with all his staff, in German hands. Reuter.

EPIC OF WARSAW

LONDON, Thurs.—Prime Minister Churchill paying tribute to Warsaw in the Commons today said its final fall at a time when Allied armies are everywhere victorious and when the final defeat of Germany is in sight, must come as a very bitter blow to all Poles.

Expressing Britain's confidence that the Poles' days of tribulation were rapidly ending, Churchill said: "When the final Allied victory is achieved the epic of Warsaw will not be forgotten."—Reuter.

COLOGNE BY DAY

LONDON, Thurs: More than 1,000 Fortresses and Liberators today attacked marshalling yards at Cologne and the Rhineland.

Last night RAF Wellingtons and RN Avengers attacked enemy shipping off the Dutch coast, hitting E-boats as well as a merchant ship. Vessels believed to be tank landing craft were also hit.

VC FOR GURKHA

LONDON, Thurs.—The King has approved the award of the Victoria Cross to Rifleman (Acting Naik) Agansing Rai, of the Fifth Royal Gurkha Rifles (Frontier Force).—Reuter.

All Burned Up

SHAEF, Thurs.—After a terrific battle between underground defenders and attacking Americans, Fort Driant, key fortress five miles south-west of Metz is reported captured tonight.

Nazis resisted strongly in casemates and underground positions. Crude oil was poured into some sections of the fort and ignited. Elsewhere Americans armed with flame throwers burned the Germans out.

Several forts, pillboxes and casemates were taken by infantry who crawled up and tossed grenades through slit windows or pushed in explosive charges with poles.—Reuter.

NEW SIEGFRIED LINE BREACH

LONDON, Thurs.—The German Newsagency reported today that Americans have made a new breach in the German lines at Palemberg seven Kilometres south of Geilenkirchen.

United States troops driving into the Siegfried line around Ubach, have broadened their salient to a width of three miles. South in the vicinity of Stolberg the Germans made counterattacks, all of which were thrown back.

Gen Eisenhower's communiqué today states; North of Antwerp the enemy is being driven from perimeter forts. Cappellen and Stabroek are in our hands. Further progress has been made north and north-east of Turnhout and we are advancing north of Popple and Baarle Nassau.

Marsh and Mines

The capture of Hilvarenbek has brought us to within five miles of Tilburg. South of Arnhem our troops have gained some ground in heavy fighting. On the east of the salient in the area of Overloon, we are moving ahead slowly, hindered by marshy terrain and enemy mines.

"Allied infantry, supported by armour, is making slow progress near Ubach, north of Aachen, against heavy opposition from small arms, mortars, antitank guns and artillery.

"Fighters and fighter-bombers supported ground forces during day and went for transportation targets in Western Germany. Night bombers attacked trains and barges in Holland and Northwestern Germany."—Reuter.

PO VALLEY DRIVE

ALLIED ADVANCED HQ, MEDITERRANEAN. Thurs.—Today's Allied communiqué says that in their drive towards the Po valley American and British troops of the Fifth Army made important gains.

Americans captured the key feature of Monte Venere, and are engaged in heavy fighting south of Loiano, an important road junction on the main Bologna-Florence road.

33 CORPS KILLED 9,746 JAPS

After six months fighting the 33rd Ind. Corps, under Lt.-Gen. Stopford, have advanced 295 miles from Dimapur to Tiddim.

The corps have killed 9,746 Japanese, taken 450 prisoners, and captured 81 guns, and 1,284 vehicles.—API.

Coming Changes in the West

● WAR REVIEW

R. CHURCHILL has deemed it wise to administer another dose of ›ld sober realism to the ore exuberant prophets at ome.

It is indeed a pity that such arnings should be necessary, r they may seem to make eir author take an unduly oomy view.

But the fact remains that hurchill's brief interpretation the battle picture is entirely ue and not at all discouraging.

Substantial gains of position ave already been made on the estern Front, and a large part Alsace has been cleared of the nemy.

Fiercest

Yet the movement in strength gainst the enemy's main defences front of the Rhine is only just eginning.

Fighting is fiercest where we ould expect it to be—at the pproaches to the two main indus- ial regions of the west, the Ruhr- hine basin and Saar.

These two the Germans will efend with everything they have, great is their economic import- nce even now, after repeated ombings.

And the Germans, be it remembered, now have the stimulus that we experienced in 1940—the life-or-death threat of invasion.

So much for the circumstances s they are Now what sort of hanges are we likely to see in the oming weeks or months?

First. a great building up of llied strength in the west: Ant- verp, "that incomparable base or the nourishment of the nor- hern group of armies," has only ust been put into full operation.

The Allies' vastly increased xpenditure of ammunition is lready being supported by in- reased output from British fac- ories, and America. too, is to edouble her efforts of production.

There has been nothing like this ain of shells and bombs in this war or the last—nothing compar- able, that is over a period of weeks.

Important changes may be xpected, too. in the part to be layed by air attack. For the first ime in six months the Luftwaffe has been drawn into action in ubstantial force with not very ncouraging results for the de- enders.

Losses

In one series of engagements last week 98 out of 400 enemy ighters were destroyed.

The Germans have been husbanding their remaining air strength in the west for months, and now it appears that the last battle over Germany is beginning.

No defending air force could long support such a rate of loss. Even if it were much better placed than the Luftwaffe is for replacement of aircraft and crews.

The enemy has no effective answer to the concentrated power of Allied air attack. (The figure of 50,000 airmen over the Reich in two days last week gives some idea of the scale of operations.) His main defence now is bad flying weather, though dense cloud alone is no longer an obstacle to accurate bombing, as is shown by the recent disclosure of the radar secret—a principle which has been in use for nearly two years.

It may be asked why such targets as Cologne and Duisburg, the great inland port at the confluence of Rhine and Ruhr, should still need attention from our bombers after all the punishment they have already taken, but the purpose of the current attacks is different; the aim now is to throw communications into chaos and the importance of that aim will increase as the battle draws nearer the Rhine.

It may well be that the timing of new strokes on land will depend on the conditions for air support, just as the weather in the Channel determined our choice of D-day.

Certainly no armies have ever had air support on such a scale.

One change of circumstances we cannot count upon, yet it may have an important influence on the battles, and that is a change in the nature of German resistance, begotten of weariness, despair, or disillusionment.

The theory has been advanced that the skilful conduct of the German defence in the West is proof that Hitler is no longer the directing power.

And that without the presence of Hitler as figurehead German morale at home and at the front cannot endure.

It is a theory which begs all sorts of questions. For one thing, Hitler's blunders as a strategist were offensive rather than defensive. And if he is no longer in supreme authority, then the power which has displaced him has a stronger, not a weaker, hold over German life—stronger, that is, in this moment of crisis.

No doubt there are many Germans who cling to the mystical ideas with which the Fuehrer sought to surround his person.

But is not the core of German resistance to be found in a much simpler idea, which has nothing to do with loyalty to Hitler or to the Nazi party—the basic aim of survival for the German way of life.

Anthony Eden got nearer to the heart of the matter when he spoke in the House of Commons on Friday about the problem of the Nazi philosophy and its roots in German history.

Those roots go deep, and the flower of this malignant growth is the individual German's subservience to the idea of the aggressive state, destined to dominate Europe.

This truth is more widely realised now than it was at the start of the war, when the issue was confused by arguments about the difference between active and passive supporters of the Nazi cause.

The simple fact is that when the war is won the Allies will have to find a way of restraining all Germans from further violence and re-educating all Germans in decent ways of living.

Just how they are going to set about that task remains to be declared. No fuller statement of Allied policy can be expected before the next meeting between Churchill, Roosevelt and Stalin.

When such a declaration is made, it will have the concurrence of France as the fourth great Power, for that is plainly part of the purpose of General de Gaulle's visit to Moscow.

The restoration of France is a vital link in Allied policy for post-war Europe, and nothing has been more encouraging in recent battle news than the success the French have already had in the drive towards the Rhine.

Lend Lease

We have been warned to keep our eyes on the immediate tasks of battle. But there are changes on foot for the period after Germany's defeat which cannot be ignored if the development of the war is to be properly understood.

Most important is the new basis for Lend-Lease which will come into force next year. It prepares the way for two great transformations—the re-direction of our war effort against Japan, and the first step towards rebuilding Britain's export trade.

The Lend-Lease figures published last week and the impressive record of Britain's industrial mobilisation show two things; Lend-Lease has been a process of giving as well as of receiving, and Britain's contribution to the war was made possible only by sacrificing the export trade on which we normally live.

Lend-Lease supplies cannot be used for normal export trade, so we are to cut down our Lend-Lease imports and pay cash for what we need in raw materials to win back our export markets.

America will continue to help us in our war production for common use against the common enemy, but exports are our own affair, in which we must depend on our own efforts.

More will be heard in the new session of Parliament about the needs of the export trades—needs ranging from modern machinery to skilled workers. Houses and home needs will have first claim on men released from the Forces after the victory over Germany.

So we may see the export trades bidding for the retention of some women workers until men are available to replace them.

● Yes, it's a mighty fine bomb and it's got a mighty fine job to do. You can read about it below. ●

Fighting Man's Platform

A Present from the Bryants

ABOUT two months ago, while on leave in Sorrento, my pal and I met an Imperial soldier, Sapper Bryant of the R.E.

His family had suffered bereavement both in this and the last war, and he was bitter in the fact that he had had no opportunity of retaliation.

When he heard we were in the S.A.A.F. he asked us to send Jerry a special bomb from the Bryants.

We promised to do this, and to show we have kept our word would it be possible to publish the enclosed snap so that he or his family may see it?—**Cpls. R. M. Robertson, P. G. Oertel, S.A.A.F.**

* * *

It is rather amazing to realise that after all these years there are people with the simple mentality of Gdsmn. May.

Perhaps he is one of those who think the S.S. is just an exclusive club for retired German business men, and the Gestapo the German version of the Boy Scouts.

How Himmler and Co. must smile when they read such blatherings, and not only smile but be full of hope that when the hideous edifice they have built finally crashes around their ears, they may escape scot free from any punishment for their crimes against humanity.—**L.-Sgt. W. J. Wilson.**

* * *

Please permit us to protest and press a pertinent point appertaining to the prevalent penchant of Peter Wilson for producing piles of painful "press-ese" in respect of "punch-pounding, leather-larruping, tonsil - tickling, canvas-crawling" pugilists performing on the "mat of massacre" at the Bellini Theatre.

Pungent prose, Mr. Wilson, very quickly becomes so pungent that it begins to smell.

May we be your best friends ? ?—Five Pint-Punchers, R.A., C.M.F.

(Cash customers' criticism cheerfully conceded.—P.W.)

* * *

Mr. Churchill's announcement of home leave is most opportune.

It has occurred to me that most of us would be willing to forego leave here if it would enable more to have home leave.

I do not suggest that fighting men be denied spells in rest camps, but I do think we would be keen to give up leave if it would improve the man-power situation.

The prospect of home leave is more satisfying than a holiday in Sunny Italy!—**Cpl. M. Goodman.**

* * *

I cannot understand why you waste the valuable space of your paper by printing letters from A. B. Bunker, R.A.F.

His letter was presumably designed to defend private enterprise in the building trade.

But he really only succeeded in demonstrating his power of abuse and his inability to express himself in simple English.

I am sure very few of your readers are interested in such questionable attributes.

The sorely - debated question of Private Enterprise versus State Control can best be settled by asking the object of each.

The real object of private enterprise is to make as much money as possible for the individual.

While the object of State control is the greatest happiness of the greatest number.

Which then is preferred by the majority?

A policy of each for himself and the devil take the hindmost, or a policy of mutual co-operation?—**Lt. J. R. Fitch.**

* * *

What utter drivel you print, occasionally, in this column.

The latest example is "the disgust" felt by Pte. Symes over the incident of the "rat poison" sent to a vicar (not, I believe, to a P.O.W. camp as your correspondent states).

It is high time the British people decided to treat the Germans for what they are: inhuman, sadistic beasts with a thin veneer of civilisation.

Shall we never, never learn?—**Pte. C. Rundle, R.A.O.C.**

Background

THE Tarquins were trying to restore their lost power and retake Rome with the help of Porsena, king of Clusium. As soon as the invading army entered the suburbs, everyone rushed into the city, behind the Tiber and the walls.

Horatius Cocles was the officer of the guard at the Sublician bridge, when he saw the hill of the Janiculum, overlooking the Tiber, suddenly taken by assault.

As the enemy rushed down on the bridge his troops deserted the post.

Horatius shouted to them to break down the bridge behind him while he challenged the Etruscan chiefs to single combat.

They were just getting the better of him when, with a crash, the bridge fell in behind him, and he leapt fully armed into the Tiber, and through a hail of missiles swam in safety to the other side.

For this heroic stand the state rewarded him by setting up his statue in the Comitium and presenting him with as much land "as he could drive the plough round in one day."

You can see the remains of Horatius's bridge to this day.

—**H. BARTY KING.**

The Two Types —by Jon

"Not sure whether he's a Colonel or our new batman."

From Bradford

Lt-Col. D. C. Melagan, secretary of the Society of Motor Manufacturers and Traders, addressing Bradford Chamber of Commerce, urged the production of a standard car after the war which would also be suitable for export. He said this would result in increased trade at home and abroad and many more than the present 1,250,000 workers would be then engaged in the industry. To do this there would have to be less restrictive legislation against motor cars, a lower tax and lower running costs.

After nine years' work Bradford Corporation Cleansing Department has completed Bradford Northern Rugby League Football Club ground at Odsal. There is now accommodation for 200,000 spectators. The ground was constructed from the city's dry refuse which was tipped at Odsal. This idea of using refuse has earned Bradford world-wide fame; some years before the war cleansing experts from Germany, Japan and the U.S.A. visited Bradford to see how it was done.

By winning the Priestley Cup and gaining promotion to Division "A" in the same season Spen Victoria has created a record for Bradford Cricket League. The recruiting of "star" players for next season has already begun and this is leading to high fees being offered the players. This is likely to lead to heated discussions at Bradford Cricket League Committee meetings between now and next season. Mr W.H. Foster, president of the League, speaking at the presentation of the Priestley Cup to Spen Victoria, appealed for moderation in the payment of wages to professionals.

Bradford, who finished third in the Football League (northern) section last season are again doing well. They have obtained a "double" at the expense of Newcastle United this season and have secured nine out of a possible ten points this season. Their new manager, Mr Fred Emery, is certainly making an impression.

Among new houses to be erected on extensive estates at Idle and Eccleshill after the war the Corporation Health Committee have been asked to include a number of one or two-roomed dwellings for single blind persons.

Special efforts are being made to increase Bradford's Lord Mayor's Comforts Fund in order to send gifts to every serving Bradford soldier in time for Christmas. One idea which has taken on is that citizens who have now been released from firewatching should contribute a shilling per week until Christmas as a "thank offering."

When a Bradford policeman was talking to a man he suspected of having broken into a house the suspect suddenly jumped a wall, ran for nearly a mile over the fields at Esholt, dived into the River Aire and succeeded in making his escape, only to be captured by the same officer three days later.

From Shrewsbury

The lifting of the blackout has given welcome relief to the townspeople generally but still the lighting of the borough is but a fraction of the glare we were accustomed to before the war.

HOME NEWS

Soldiers previously engaged in the building trade were called on to assist in repairing bomb-damaged buildings in southern England. These two are covering a roof with tarpaulin.

The mayor, Captain Harry Steward, M.C., after holding office for six successive years, has accepted an invitation to continue in it for yet another year. Shrewsbury has never had a more active mayor or one who devotes himself more to his duties. Everybody wished both him and the mayoress, Mrs Steward, another successful year of office, and deeply sympathises with their sorrow on hearing recently that their eldest son Harry, a flying officer, is missing.

News was also received in the town a few days ago of the death in France of Lt. John McLaren Rowlands, R.A.S.C. Lt. Rowlands was chairman and manager of the Shrewsbury Chronicle Ltd, and David Rowlands Ltd., proprietors of The Montgomery County Times.

Boys of Liverpool Mission, which is wholly supported by the boys of Shrewsbury's famous public school, have been again enjoying their hospitality and spending some days pleasantly in camp on the beautiful grounds of the school.

Brenda Owen, aged ten, of Roundhill Green, Cotton Hill, and Margaret Hughes, aged ten, of Coton Mount, wishing to do something for the Red Cross, started to collect gifts and did so well that they had sufficient for an auction sale. The articles were sold on the green by Mrs F.M. Ball and £10 10s. was realised.

From the South East

I have just returned from a visit to Dover, made at a time when, once more, enemy shells were falling in the area. From the mighty sentinel which is Shakespeare Cliff I saw a sight familiar to thousands in pre-war days; with visibility at its best for weeks I saw the deep fissures in the cliffs of France and then, through powerful glasses, the Town Hall clock at Calais, and the sweep of the derricks in the harbour.

For so long now Dover has been in the front line. Yet the spirit of her people is as tempered steel, and will continue to withstand any future test. It may surprise some to know that Dover's total number of alerts —that is air raid or shelling warnings— now constitutes a world's record. The figure (at the time this copy is written) is 3,100. Not even Malta can beat this, although it is true the island once held a substantial lead.

I met Inspector Alfred J. Fenn, Dover's A.R.P. Sub-Controller; tall, quite imperturbable, and a man widely known for his originality and ingenuity in Civil Defence organisation. Inspector Fenn is seconded to C.D. from the Kent Constabulary, and a better choice could not have been made. I believe I am right in saying he has not been out of Dover once since the war started and, what is more, he has no intention of moving. To quote his own words, he is "determined to see the whole show through."

In his office he has an amazing collection of souvenirs of the many missiles the enemy has hurled at Dover, not the least interesting being the base of a German shell which, complete, would weigh nearly a ton.

Then there is Vin Hoyle, north-countryman who is warden of one of the town's deep cave shelters which honeycomb the high white cliffs. Much of these were hewn out of the virgin chalk by French prisoners during the Napoleonic wars, and local historians refer to their usage as operational bases by South Coast smugglers. Vin looks after the welfare of dozens of Dover families who for more than four years have known no other night life but that of the caves; but, like Queen Victoria, these families admit no depression, for Vin sees they have plenty to occupy their evenings. Concerts, film shows, dances, and regular nightly whist drives are included in entertainments he arranges.

Among Vin Hoyle's charges is one youngster of four and a-half who has not slept a night at home since he was ten days old.

Dover has her ugly wounds and scars, but when the last "All Clear" echoes along the valley in which she nestles her people may justly raise their heads on high and say that they led the people of Britain along the hard and difficult pathway of endurance.

Before this despatch reaches you, hop-picking will be in full swing, in fact the bines will already be stripped. At the moment, though, all roads lead to the hop-picking centres and especially the south-east. Many families are trudging long, weary miles from London to such palces as Paddock Wood and Yalding, pushing their essential belongings on handcarts, and preparatory to taking up temporary residence in what are known as hoppers' huts. Thousands are crowding the special trains which are daily steaming into Kent and Sussex, and soon the Cockney voice will predominate in country lane and byway.

The hoppers hut will be made a home from home; curtains will go up at the windows and, such is progress, most hop-picking camps will have all possible amenities such as running water, and revolutionary sanitary arrangements. Saturday nights there will be singing and dancing in the camps and, above all, laughter despite the war. There will be improvised jazz bands in most villages, and Irish jigs in the roadways and girls looking slightly ridiculous but happy and attractive in home-made sun-suits.

The manager of Messrs. Whitbread's huge farm in Kent estimates that he will have to cater for 1,000 families on his premises alone. But this should be no hardship for this particular farm has long been noted for its concern for the well-being of the hop-picker and provides such amenities as rest and writing rooms, as well as information bureaux.

The hop crop, it is understood, will be light compared with last year, but for all that it is likely big money will be earned. The shortage of labour and the need for quick clearance of the bines are essential factors.

So the Battle of the Beaches has been won, and Eve is free to disport on much of the coast from the Wash to Lands End, albeit her costume is dated 1940 or Utility. But then, so far as I recollect, her bathing garb for the past ten years has left little enough to be torn by barbed wire.

Brighton's crowds are now almost as in peacetime. So delighted was Captain Balfour, M.P. for Thanet and Under-Secretary of State for Air, when he heard of the removal of the ban, that he sent a telegram to the Mayor of Ramsgate, Alderman G.W. Twigger. "The lifting of the ban" he said "is the first step toward our post-war rehabilitation."

Ramsgate lives again, to a limited degree. A mile of sands has been opened for bathing, and I am reminded of that epic occasion when the former Mayor, Alderman A.B.C. Kempe, resplendent in top hat, served tea to 30,000 holiday-makers on the seashore. Margate, too, shows signs of coming to life, while the optimists of such towns as Hastings, Eastbourne, and other South Coast resorts are beginning to believe there are more words in the dictionary than depression and moratorium.

BRITISH BOYS: They're from the Elephant and Castle, London, off for a day's outing.

GERMAN BOY: This sad-faced youngster aged 15 was among German prisoners taken by the 8th Army on the Italian front.

311   One Anna
ONESDAY, 15 NOVEMBER, 1944.

Printed by Courtesy of
THE STATESMAN in Calcutta.

NAZIS PULLING OUT OF METZ FORT RING

SHAEF, Tues.—Signs that the Germans are pulling out in the Metz area increased today after Gen Patton's troops had taken three of the southern forts and enlarged their Moselle bridgeheads south of the city. The first fort—that at Verny, five miles south of Metz—fell yesterday afternoon when the Nazis fled from the attacking troops.

The two others were taken soon after. In each case the Germans withdrew. The capture of the forts does not mean that the ring around the city has been shattered since all have interlocking fire.

But it does mean that a serious dent has been made in the southern defences. The city is under artillery fire.

Capt Sertorius, the German commentator, says Gen Patton has opened an assault against Fort Driant, the greatest structure of its kind in western Europe.

Fort Driant held off the American attacks last month; now armoured divisions are within striking distance.

North-east of Metz the Germans are blowing up dams on canals and rivers.

Forest Battle

Some American units are 3½ miles from Metz.

On the southern flank of Gen Patton's forces, troops of the American 7th Army made advances on a 10-mile front.

Gen Hodges' 1st Army is continuing its give-and-take action in the woods south-east of the Hurtgen area, one of the most important German defence pivots.

In the Netherlands activity has been restricted to patrol activity and artillery duels in bad weather.

The Koenigsmacher bridgehead has been expanded in every direction with gains up to 2½ miles. The nearest point reached to the German border is now one and a half miles.

GUNS WRECK NAZI TANKS

MOSCOW, Tuesday—What the "Red Star" today calls "heavy artillery systems"—which include the biggest guns in the Red Army—are being used to smash up at point blank range German tanks making counter-attacks in the battle on the approaches to Budapest.

The Red Star said these guns do not just knock out enemy tanks but "smash them to pieces."

The battle on the Roads to Budapest has now become considerably more open despite heavy rains which have ruined the road surfaces and made low-lying sectors almost impassable.

Marshal Malinovsky has won a big infantry battle north of Czegled, 40 miles south-east of Budapest.

REPAT: GRIGG ANSWERS WIVES

LONDON, Tues.—The Secretary for War, Sir James Grigg, has told young wives of soldiers serving in the Far East that to bring men home before their service is over would only lengthen the war.

Answering a petition signed by 1,000 wives from all over Britain, the War Minister wrote: "At one time the obstacle to repatriation was quite definitely shipping. Convoys had to go round the Cape and had to be heavily escorted. Apart from that there were heavy losses from U-boat attacks.

Drastic Cut Dangerous

"Now the Mediterranean is open and the obstacle has shifted to that of manpower. Unlike the RAF and Americans we have not got abundant reserves of trained manpower. Consequently any drastic shortening of the period of overseas service would in point of hard fact lengthen the war.

"I believe that the great generality of troops serving abroad would willingly forgo a greater reduction in their all-too-long service overseas, if it meant the hastening of the final defeat of Germany.

"Nothing would give me greater pleasure than to be able to promise definitely an improvement in the arrangements, but at present I cannot."—Reuter.

THEY NEED MORE THAN GLAMOUR

LONDON, Tues.—Glamour girls are not essential in troops stage shows, says Lt. Richard Gilbert, who commands the 56th London Division Entertainment Unit.

"Experience proves that even a pretty girl, with an attractive figure, has to act, sing or dance effectively to gain the full appreciation of the average critical Services' audience," he says.

Gilbert, a professional actor, is running a review with an all-male chorus of 16 serving soldiers.—Reuter.

PREMIER'S 100m IN BLIZZARD

VOSGES FRONT, Tues.—Prime Minister Churchill, accompanied by Gen de Gaulle and senior French generals yesterday visited troops of Gen Tassigny's First French Army who for weeks have been engaged in slow slogging fighting among the snow-clad Vosges mountains.

Thirty cars set out with the Churchill party; only ten finished the course, the others being either ditched or snowbound. Mr Churchill's car covered 100 miles in blizzard over tortuous ice and snowbound roads. One Press jeep somersaulted from the road down a 12-feet embankment into a field.

The Prime Minister's car was first to have trouble when its snow-chains snapped, causing a hold up. Gen de Gaulle and Miss Mary Churchill were with him.

Hours Late

At Valdahon, near Besancon, one of the biggest training camps in France and famous as a shooting school, Mr Churchill stood up in his open car and drove through the slight snow to inspect the troops. The rest of time he travelled in a big black saloon.

He did not reach Vosges until three hours after the scheduled time. Crowds waited anxiously in the town's square.

With the party were Gen Sir Alan Brooke and Gen Alphonse Juin, the French chief-of-staff.

Will Share Occupation

A communique issued in Paris says: "The ceremonies gave the population of Paris an opportunity to demonstrate by its enthusiasm.

8th NEAR RAVENNA

ROME, Tues.—Eighth army troops have driven to within four miles of Ravenna on the Adriatic.

Considerable progress has been made in the Apennine foothills south of Faenza, a big town on the Rimini-Bologna highway.—Reuter.

3 DIRECT HITS SINK TIRPITZ

LONDON, Tues.—The Tirpitz, last battleship of the German fleet in fighting trim, is sunk.

Tirpitz was lying in a fairly exposed position off the small Norwegian island of Eidfiordbotn, about five miles from Tromsoe.

An Air Ministry communique today announcing the sinking on Sunday, says:

"Twenty-nine Lancasters of Bomber Command, led by Wing Commander Tait and Squadron Leader A. G. Williams, attacked the German battleship 'Tirpitz' with 12,000-lb bombs.

"There were several direct hits and within a few minutes the ship capsized and sank. One of our aircraft is missing."

A later Air Ministry announcement says that after capsizing, Tirpitz settled on the bottom of Tromsoe Fjord and only her keel and some parts of the bottom of the ship can be seen above the water.

Completely Capsized

Reconnaissance after attack showed the battleship completely capsized with about 700 feet of her keel sticking out of the water.

This was the third attack on Tirpitz with 12,000-lb. bombs, but it was the first time the attackers were able to see the ship properly.

The weather was clear and there was no smokescreen. One 12,000 pounder apparently hit Tirpitz amidships, another in the bows and the third hit towards the stern.

F/Lt. B. A. Buckham, of Sydney, New South Wales, pilot of an aircraft from an Australian squadron sent to film the attack, said just beyond the ship. Agonising moment.

"Three Direct Hits"

"Then came three direct hits in quick succession, the first amidships, the next in the bows and the third towards the stern.

"Her guns had been firing like blazes when we arrived, but after the first bomb hit, her guns stopped firing.

"Smoke began to spiral up, then it spread out over the doomed ship in the shape of a mushroom. Afterwards there were several explosions. Finally, she capsized."

Though 32 Lancasters flew to the fjord only 29 took part in the actual attack. W/Cdr Tait, who led the attack, is a 28-year-old triple DSO.

Prime Minister Churchill has sent a message of "heartiest congratulations to all" to the Chief of the Bomber Command. Air Chief Marshal Sir Arthur Harris, and the Admiralty has also sent congratulations and thanks for "the good job well done."

Bad News for the Japs—See Good Morning.

WOMEN START PAY CAMPAIGN

LONDON Tues.—The opinions of women working in British factories, hospitals and official departments have helped to compile 64 pages of printed evidence to be submitted next month to the Royal Commission on Equal Pay to the Government.

This unofficial "White Paper" is to be the women's opening action.

JANE

GOODNESS!—I CAN HEAR THEM TALKING IN THE CAFE—AND THERE'S NOWHERE TO HANG YOUR CLOTHES—AND NOW WHERE'S THAT TOWEL?

-IT'S SO STEAMY I CAN'T SEE WHICH IS THE DOOR AND WHICH THAT CONFOUNDED—

—SCREEN! HELP!

ENTER THE WAAFs . . . .

We don't know the names of the girls who greet you th the portholes, but smiling lass above is Cpl Moyra Bl Enfield, London, first WAAF to step ashore.

Welcome!

THEY'RE here to help finish the Jap. These two pages show the arrival in India of 500 WAAFs who volunteered to work in S.E.A.C. alongside the RAF. They will do medical, clerical, plotting, motor transport and other jobs that will release men.

Pictures on the opposite page show RN personnel arriving in Ceylon. They form part of the huge draft now coming out to join the Eastern Fleet.

Indian dock workers (above) watch the 500 WAAFs march smartly along the dockside after disembarkation. This was the first time they had worn their khaki tropical uniform and blue forage caps.

They obviously like their first sight India—and the two " boy friends " see pleased about something, also. Le hope it won't be long before we're s smiling as broadly—and on the way o' not in !

...THE NAVY'S HERE

HEAVE HO!—Hammocks and kitbags are loaded into the lorry by POs and ratings as the draft prepares to move off to RN camps. They'll soon get them sorted out at the other end.

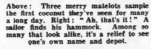

Above: Three merry matelots sample the first coconut they've seen for many a long day. Right: "Ah, that's it!" A sailor finds his hammock. Among so many that look alike, it's a relief to see one's own name and depot.

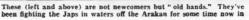
These (left and above) are not newcomers but "old hands." They've been fighting the Japs in waters off the Arakan for some time now in

• WAR REVIEW by
RALPH S. THACKERAY

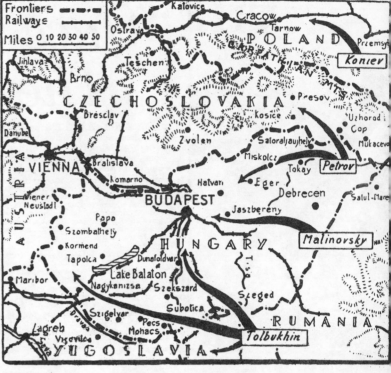

CONCERN about events in Greece has taken some attention away from the main European battlefronts in the past week.

But there has been no lack of important news in these other quarters, so let us look first at the progress of the Allied Armies in the west, in Hungary and in Italy.

The German retreat through Alsace to the Saar has left the enemy's line longer, though more defensible, than it was when the Allied onslaught began.

The hard spots in this line have been quickly found in the expected places—along the Roer in the north, and at the edge of the Saar basin in the centre.

Farther south the only possibility seems to be a thrust down the Rhine Valley rather than across it, for the mountains of the Black Forest to the east of the river are too formidable an obstacle for a direct entry in Germany by this route.

Heavy Fighting

General Patton's forces have made several crossings of the Saar into the Siegfried Line, and there has been heavy fighting all along this sector, particularly around Saarbrucken, the main industrial and railway centre of this coal and iron region.

The German defence here is just as bitter as it is in the north-east of Aachen, and for the same reasons.

Each region is of vital importance industrially, and each offers a route to the Rhine Valley.

There is a further parallel, too, in the possibility of outflanking moves on either front—by the American 7th Army in the south against the Saar, and by the British and Canadian forces at the northern end of the line.

The battle may not develop that way, but the potential threat is one which the defenders must take into account.

The northern and southern hinges are on the Roer and the Saar, but the enemy will not be told in advance which way the door is going to open.

On Germany's south-eastern front, in Hungary, the door is already opening to the Russian armies—and closing, incidentally, on what remains of the German forces in the Balkans.

A glance at the map on this page will show the Germans' danger.

Four Soviet army groups are involved, from Koniev's in Southern Poland to Tolbukhin's in Southern Hungary and Northern Yugoslavia.

Here Budapest is the hinge. By sweeping to the south of the capital, across the Danube and beyond Lake Balaton, Tolbukhin has dealt the Germans a double blow.

He is now within striking distance of the Austrian border, and he has greatly narrowed the gap through which the enemy's Balkan

December 2, 1944
RETREAT FROM THE BALKANS

forces must attempt to get away to the north, harried as they are by Tito's Partisans.

The retreat from the Balkans has been going on for more than three months, and the Germans have already had a rough time at the hands of the Greeks, the Yugoslavs, Bulgarian units under Soviet command, British detachments of Land Forces Adriatic, and, of course, the Mediterranean Allied Air Forces.

Their original 15 divisions, never strong in first-class troops, cannot be in very good shape.

They have lost all the Dalmatian coast except the naval base of

Kotor; but inland they are still a long way to the south.

It is doubtful whether many of them will see Germany again in time to be of any further use to their Fuehrer.

The drive through Southern Hungary brings substantially nearer the prospect of a continuous southern front, with the Soviet armies on one flank and the 5th and 8th Armies in Italy on the other.

The Germans at least have never

made the mistake of underestimating their commitments in Italy. They are acutely aware, as their propaganda shows, of the danger from the south—the potential danger on land, and the very real and present danger in the air.

Now that Ravenna has fallen to the 8th Army, in spite of all the Germans could do by stubborn defence and by flooding, they are again talking of this as one of the focal points of the Allied effort.

It is reported that the German Command has had to move some troops from Northern Italy to Southern Hungary in an attempt to stem the Russian advance there.

German communications here, long subject to Allied air attack, are already seriously restricted, and winter weather will not protect them.

General Eaker has promised that the greatest weight of bombardment from the south has yet to come.

Disturbances in Greece, culminating in armed clashes and the use of British troops to clear the capital, have shown the Allied world once more how difficult is the way of liberation and how unity in the face of an enemy may break down when the common danger is removed.

The case of Greece was fully discussed in Parliament on Friday, and Mr. Churchill made Britain's position clear in a speech which might be summed-up in his phrase "Democracy is not mob law."

Concern

But apart from the Greek situation there was evident concern in the House about the principles involved in Allied dealings with all the problems of liberation, and the debate did serve to illuminate a subject in which it is all too easy to over-simplify the issues.

There should be no room for feelings of resentment that such problems should arise: they have to be properly understood if they are to be reasonably solved, and they cannot be disposed of by pretending that they do not exist.

"The Economist," in a recent article about political developments in Belgium, points out that "revolutionary ferment has been the inevitable aftermath of every modern war," and says it would be wrong to exaggerate the tension which has so far shown itself in liberated Europe. (This was written before the Greek disturbances).

"What is surprising," the paper adds, "when it is seen against the background of the tremendous un-

settlement caused by this war, not that the ferment exists, but that it has been so relatively weak."

Recollection of what va changes arose after the last wa should help to balance our jud ment.

Substantial progress in Burm and the latest raids on Toky made encouraging news last wee but to offset this there was warning from General Wed meyer, C.-in-C. United State Force in China, that the situat there was serious, because Japanese progress in the south.

The Japanese aim is to repla their sea-route by a land rou to Burma and Indo-China, an at the same time to cut Chin supply life line along the easter sector of the Burma road.

Nor are China's difficultie purely military.

Co-operation between th Chungking Government and th Communist armies in the Nort regarded by foreign observers a essential to a full war effort, ha still to be achieved.

The Two Types — by Jon

"Any complaints, old man?"

"Once More Unto The Breach!"

LAURENCE OLIVIER'S production of Shakespeare's "Henry V" has been acclaimed by the critics at home as the greatest film to come out of British studios.

This is as it should be. Apart from the not-too-successful Bergner version of "As You Like It," our film people have been content to leave Shakespeare to Hollywood, which produced "Midsummer Night's Dream" (with Cagney and Rooney!) and "Romeo and Juliet." These contributed to the world of controversy if not to that of art.

Full-blooded

Olivier's "Henry V"—he plays the title role—is a full-blooded techni-colourful drama which catches the glory and spirit of our country, expresses it in the tongue that Shakespeare spoke, and makes you thrill with pride that you, too, are part of its tradition.

It is a war film, but the war is one in which chivalry and pageantry are kept alive and the stirring clash of colours that is the Battle of Agincourt is a refreshing change from the mud and brutality of modern Hollywood wars with which we have been "entertained" in the midst of the current conflict.

"Henry V" should be shown to the troops overseas as soon as possible.

It would enable not only us but also all our Allies to understand the better our historical background.

"A kingdom for a stage, princes to act."
Leslie Banks as "Chorus."

"... When the blast of war blows in our ears, Then, imitate the action of the tiger!"
Laurence Olivier as Henry V.

"We happy few, we band of brothers."

On the eve of the great battle of Agincourt, English archers prepare obstacles to thwart the charge of the French cavalry. The battle scenes have been hailed as the finest piece of filmcraft to come from British studios.

Which Way Again?

IT all started with Major Stanford imagining that flags correctly flown should be flying left to right. Now we have received another letter, from Sgt. L. K. Felpham, R.A. He writes:

I don't get it. What difference does it make whether the Union Jack on your title head is flying this way—

OR THIS WAY—

the flag looks just the same whatever way it is flying and anybody who has been anywhere near a ship would know that provided the flag is hoisted the correct way up it can do anything it likes.

As the Commander says, the way it appears to the observer depends on the wind.

But I don't agree that your artist could have based his drawing on the flag of a ship that was sailing backwards. I have never heard of a ship flying a Union Jack.

And Modern Generals

General Sir Henry Maitland Wilson receives America's Legion of Merit for outstanding services to the Allied Nations. Making the award is Lt.-Gen. J. T. McNarney.

Supreme Allied Commander, General Eisenhower, confers with Field-Marshal Montgomery at his headquarters somewhere in Belgium.

The Two Types — by Jon

"Would you care for a nice drop of Desert Port, sir?"

Fifth Army's Arrow Route front offers almost every kind of unpleasantness. The ground favours the defender. Weather makes any semi-static position a mud hole. Formations in reserve don't get much of a break from mud and water either. These Scottish troops manhandle rations across precarious bridge

APENNINE PILGRIMS' PROGRESS

"Parade" reporter PAUL CHADBURN and cameraman BELA ZOLA show how men of Fifth Army, fighting on peaks, struggling upward with supplies, or stuck in the mud to fire a gun, find terrain, weather and the Hun allied against them.

The Arrow Route in its crooked way leads the regiments of the First British Division back to England and Scotland.

They have become a strange, almost unearthly-looking (though most earthy) lot, these British infantrymen. We stood in the rain beside a precarious footbridge over a swollen mountain stream. Damp grey cloud was flopping into the valley, thin water jets spurted down the hillside; the only track, a yard broad, was foot-deep mud. Along it and upward into the mist there passed from time to time weird figures, cowled and cloaked in gas capes, bulged out with kit, gripping on to sticks cut from the hedges. One of them was a D.R., riding shanks mare, another a Scot returning to his unit after four days' leave in Florence. Then, over the plank, came a file of soldiers carrying rations for the men on the mountain peaks.

Mules were waiting to take over the loads. The mules, too, have become fantastic. They look normal enough, plugging and picking their way round the side of the hills with their Indian and Italian muleteers, but they are being trained to do strange tricks; for instance, in an emergency, to get their heads down without breaking the rum rations. It is even said that they lie down best, though unexpectedly and inconveniently, after partaking of the rum rations. Like Chesterton's donkey, they also have their hour.

It is difficult to describe this front beyond saying it has almost every kind of unpleasantness. If anything can be said for it in this season, then there is probably less disease than on the fronts further east. But a few hours' rain here makes knee-deep mud, bogs the gun emplacements wheel-deep, sticks up even bull-dozers (they winch themselves out with cables made fast about thick trees —if they find them).

Water and mud fills up the valleys, and infantrymen's dugouts on the peaks are valleys too, most concentrated valleys. The gunners are not too comfortable either. The ones we came across were lying on straw laid across the mud in their bivouac tents.

One of them had just come down from an Observation Post in the hills. He'd been relieved the previous afternoon. In the pitch darkness, he could get no further after midnight. Where and how he had spent the hours till dawn he didn't say. But he did tell, with some humour, how he had spent his last night in the O.P. The rain had come down in buckets. He was in his dugout over the crest, looking across at the Germans—or, at least, in their direction,

for it was black as pitch. All the time, as the rain fell, he had to keep baling out. But it made no difference, for, as he at last discovered, the man in the foxhole above his was doing the same thing, if anything even more energetically; and, for all he knew, so it had gone on, tier above tier, the man on the peak sitting comparatively pretty.

Infantrymen have died of exposure on the peaks. Getting the wounded down is terrible going. Rapidly-mounting streams may carry the bridge away at any time. The enemy keep on shelling the tracks. Attacks must often be made on two-men fronts over razor-edge connections between peaks. Officers leading their men are the first casualties. The Germans, on the defensive, sit back and take toll.

A story came through from one of the regiments in the division the other day. There had been an attack on an enemy hill position. The British officer leading it had been wounded, but for a long time carried on. At length he was forced to lie down for a while. But the next in command, his sergeant, was not informed. The enemy made a surprise counter-attack and scored a local success. The officer eventually recovered sufficiently to lead back his men, who still had no idea what had

happened to him. On arrival, the officer collapsed, wounded in seven places. He was dispirited about the failure of the attack. As he was being carried down the hill by an ambulance party, a stray shell came over and killed them all.

And so this battle goes on, from hill to hill, and, as the hill positions fall on either side of the historic Arrow Route, from blown bridge to blown bridge, for the sappers under shell fire there is always one more river to cross. Infantry are on the peaks; sappers and gunners (including light ack-ack gunners, who have switched over to making smoke screens, to portering and even bridge-building) are in the valleys, pushing that Arrow Route forward, come wind come weather, come whatever deviltry the boche dishes out, toward the plain, toward home.

These are indeed the pilgrims, if not unheralded, for our artillery sees to that, at least unsung.

There were some scenes on this First British Division's front that remain firm in the mind, firm as no photograph could make them. We had set out to reach the end of the road, the point where the jerky and deviating "Arrow" pointed at the heart of the German hill positions.

Continued overleaf

Movement Is A Nightmare

Transport is a continual problem. Weather, terrain, demolitions combine to offer gaping chasms at swollen streams. Jeep struggles through torrent.

Lancashire man i/c ration party loads one of the mules for the climb to his unit. He is wearing anti-gas kit as protection from the drenching rain.

Jeeps fade out early. There are places along Arrow Route where loaded mules come to a standstill. This is one. Scots soldier climbs muddy bank.

Front is D.R.'s nightmare. It would be if the route were dry and there were no demolitions. As it is, spectacle of a D.R. on foot has ceased to be strange

Beyond the next blown bridge north country infantry were holding a position. To reach it we had to skirt round the hills through a mule track. There was some shelling, most of it from our field artillery, but now and again one came the "wrong way." Over the edge a patch of full-blown cabbages. But you didn't look over the edge much—you were too occupied pulling your legs out of what felt like octopus tentacles.

The track led eventually on to the road again, beyond the blown bridge. As we branched into Arrow Track, acrid gusts from a smoke screen over the village just ahead merged with the sagging clouds. A fog driven briskly by the wind. In gaps you saw a straight stretch of road lined with bits of trees and shell craters. The officer with us pointed out the German positions. "That feature behind the near ridge —they usually shell movement on this road..."

The road was almost deserted here. Motor traffic was ruled out. The bridge was blown behind us. Only the hooded, caped figures moved along, with branches in their hands.

UNION JACK

Tuesday, December 19, 1944
No. 303   Two Lire   **FOR THE BRITISH FIGHTING FORCES**

GERMANY'S ALL IS THROWN IN

Told: 'Our last effort'

FIELD - MARSHAL VON RUNDSTEDT, Nazi commander in the West, told his troops going into the counter - attack against American positions on a 30-mile front running along the Belgian and Luxembourg frontiers, "Give your all in this one last effort."

A striking indication of the size of the effort is the fact that von Rundstedt is sending up his valuable and sorely needed Luftwaffe planes in their biggest strength since "D" Day. Yesterday 108 Nazi planes were shot down over the battle area for the loss of 33 Allied aircraft.

This all-out effort to break the back of Eisenhower's grip on the Western Front is being made in the Monschau area, southeast of Aachen. The enemy went over the Belgian and Luxembourg frontiers in a sudden push carrying the weight of hundreds of hoarded planes and masses of tanks and infantry.

While front-line reports say that the counter-attack is now at its maximum possible strength, a Reuter report from the U.S. First Army headquarters adds that the assault appears to be "fairly well under control."

The thrust has so far made appreciable gains at three points in the Monschau - Montmedy sector. At the same time, Nazi paratroops were dropped at several scattered points in both the First and Ninth Army fronts to distract attention from the main drive.

One attack was made near the Belgian town of Honsfeld, two miles west of the German border; a second penetration was made southwest of the Luxembourg border town of Vianden, while a third was made just south of Echternach, 18 miles northeast of the city of Luxembourg.

General Hodges' men have so far plugged and sealed several penetrations, but others have been opened and it is likely that the German forces will be strengthened as their advance continues.

Uncommitted reserves are already moving in the background, says one report. Roads behind the Nazi lines are jammed with columns of vehicles moving forward. They are receiving attention from Allied aircraft.

On the other sectors of the
(Turn to page four)

Without any visible means of support this railway truck has remained stuck up in the air like this since R.A.F. bombs hurled it into this position. It is just one of the many queer things that our bombs have done to the railways being used by the Nazis. This picture was taken at Vaires, France.

Dec. 19, 1941

To-day is the anniversary of a memorable event for Germany—and her Allies. On December 19, 1941, Hitler took over personal command of the German Army from General von Brauchitsch. After three years of being led by "intuition," the German Army is now fighting desperately in the defence of its own soil. Once more it is being led by military men—and Hitler is "missing."

STOP PRESS

S.H.A.E.F. reports, quoted last night by the B.B.C., said that the German counter-offensive on the Western Front had made "substantial penetrations."

MOVE BACK NEW— AND TEMPORARY

LEE CARSON, an American correspondent with the First Army on the Monschau sector, described in a dispatch last night the reaction of American troops to the German offensive. He wrote:

"The retreat, in face of Germany's smashing counter-offensive on the Luxembourg-Belgium frontier is a new experience to the battle-tested doughboys of the American First Army.

"*There are no frightened faces among the Yank troops, no frantic milling about and very little confusion. Everyone is concentrating on one thing—and that is to ram this retreat back down the Nazis' throats.*

"As this is being written, the Germans are roaring up nearby roads in their Tiger tanks, zooming down from the pink-streaked skies to shower our front-line positions with streams of hot lead, and tearing the world apart with their heavy artillery barrages.

"A first-class armoured clash, involving 29 Nazi tanks, is in progress at a crossroads only a few miles to the southeast. Some American tank destroyers are trading punches with the enemy.

"'All this is enough to make us a little excited back here behind the lines,' one major calmly told me, adding, 'But you can see there is nothing to get in a tailspin about. It's serious—yes, but it certainly isn't critical.

"'Things are pretty well in hand now, I think,' he said, then strolled out of the command post to the blood and thunder at the crossroads.

"*At his departure, the colonel came in with a report to the commanding general. The general nodded rather absently and took a sip of coffee from his canteen cup.*

EVERYTHING IS AT STAKE

Von Rundstedt told his troops in his Order of the Day that unless the present offensive succeeds everything is lost. The order continued:

"Soldiers of the Western Front, your great hour has struck. Strong attacking armies are advancing to-day against the Anglo-Americans. I do not need to say any more to you.

"Everything is at stake. You have a sacred duty to give everything to achieve the superhuman for the Fatherland and our Führer."

Hallmarks of past

THIS first big counter-attack launched by the German High Command since the attempt to cut the Allied lifeline at Avranches four months ago is not unlike that desperate Normandy attempt, writes Reuter's military commentator.

It has all the hallmarks of careful preparation. The Luftwaffe has been brought forward in an all-out attempt, while another feature is the concentration of three to four hundred mobile guns of all calibres on comparatively small targets.

Its test, however, is whether it can unbalance the Allied line sufficiently to require general reorganisation which might affect Allied plans elsewhere. That is undoubtedly the German objective.

A big attempt has been made to stop the Allied advance in the south and the consolidation of Allied positions on the Roer. This speaks of disquiet on the German side about the consequence of further Allied penetrations.

From a purely military point of view, the time for counter-attack had not yet come. If Rundstedt had any choice he would have waited. That is why the possible objectives of the German attack seem only limited.

It can spoil certain immediate Allied plans, but it is in no way comparable to the ambitious last throw of Ludendorff in 1918.

FIGHTING MAN'S PLATFORM

Forces Sweetheart?

THERE is a film knocking around Italy at the moment called "One Exciting Night," which, for me at any rate, turned out to be One Dull Evening.

The star of this British contribution to the world of entertainment is Miss Vera Lynn, whose acting is considerably worse than her voice.

And the quality of her voice is a matter for debate.

Some time ago the B.B.C. did the fighting men of Britain a disservice by boosting Miss Lynn as the "Forces Sweetheart," and I am eager to discover just how right they are.

Personally I can get along very nicely without her—but can the rest of the Army?

It seems that she has certainly clicked with the A.T.S. because you can never run into a group of them without finding one girl who can sing "just like Vera Lynn"; and that's another grudge I bear her.

One voice like that is enough for this suffering world.

Should anyone inquire why I went to this film, the answer is because I wanted to see the newsreel. And, as it as raining outside, I found it more pleasant to stay in the comparative comfort of the cinema, even with Miss Lynn, than to brave the rigours of the Italian night. — **Sgt. Murtough, A.A.C.**

* * *

Do we really want all these post-war tourists in England? The Pedestrians' Association, and Mr. E. R. L. Fitzpayne, general manager of Glasgow's Passenger Transport Board (vide Motoring Press, October issues), and Bernard Brett, and others who have recently voiced their opinions, don't appear interested.

They want to destroy pleasure motoring as we knew it before the war.

Will our tourists content themselves with trains, motor coaches and bicycles? Or walking? I hardly think so.—**Lieut. H. S. Beardmore, R.A.S.C.**

Battle in Italy

*

This is from STEVE ROBERTS, "Union Jack" reporter on the Italian front.

*

THE battle for this village has been raging for a couple of days.

During the first day infanteers of a south-country battalion who had captured the place held off a number of strong counter-attacks by the Germans but were forced to withdraw just before dusk.

The Rifles took over during the night and after sending out feelers launched a strong assault to recapture one building.

The Boche was still in the other. Both sides had parties in and out of the church.

Grenades were being tossed from window to window bullets were flying in all directions.

Out into this inferno went two British sergeants.

One sergeant was hit in the stomach, but his companion, in spite of his five-foot-nothing, carried him to the shelter of a nearby pig-sty.

They were almost at the door of the German stronghold and a German N.C.O. and stretcher-bearer came out and took them both into the house.

There were a couple of officers and about 40 Boche in the building manning Spandau and rifle posts at every hole in the wall—and there were plenty.

No proper treatment was available for the injured sergeant so his pal asked the stretcher-bearer to carry him back to the other riflemen.

Converts

While the two German officers were upstairs the remaining sergeant—he was a solicitor's clerk living at Eltham before the war—thought he'd try his persuasive powers again.

After a couple of hours parleying in soldier Italian in which he kept repeating "Per voi guerra finito" he found his listeners prepared to follow him into captivity.

Shortly afterwards the Boche, receiving reinforcements, launched a strong counter-attack.

Here the fifteen captives, prompted by the sergeant, tried to get their countrymen to join them.

It did not work, but the persuasion of concentrated small arms fire supported by mortars drove them back.

Battle in the West

*

Bill Taylor, "Union Jack" Front Line Reporter, sends this dispatch from Germany.

*

THE soil of the Fatherland is just as damp and muddy and unpleasant as any other variety.

And the small German towns so far captured by the 7th Army on the Western Front are entirely unpopulated.

It is not quite lifeless, but the only living German things remaining are odd cows and chickens.

The chickens don't live long either.

Troops joked that it would be their last chance of fraternising.

But from all appearances it does not seem that they are going to meet any civilians at all this side of the Siegfried Line.

On the French bank of the river the few remaining locals tentatively extended a timid "bon jour," and then had to revert to their usual German tongue.

There had been a fierce battle for the approach to the river in which the enemy had even brought their 20mm. ack-ack guns into action as artillery, but during the night they disappeared and, of course, blew the bridge.

But one small footbridge through a mill was forgotten and the infantry crossed at first light, the last span of the bridge being improvised by planks and a ladder.

And the ladder seemed to be a strangely appropriate way of bridging the very last lap.

Empty

Mortar and heavy shelling came in but the only Germans seen were three soldiers who promptly got on bicycles and pedalled like blazes through the woods.

Coffee was still brewing on the stoves in the doll-like houses. Empty and open rabbit hutches proclaimed the hasty evacuation. A beautiful wintry sun shone, but nothing was peaceful.

Massed artillery along the river pounded Germany, while heavy shells sounding the "plop-plop" of corks in a bottle left the Siegfried guns only 4,000 yards distant.

Artillery is gradually piling up on each side. The Germans now have the "double-bank" of their mobile guns and the heavy calibres in the main line.

That Other War

Philippines were ready when the Allies called again

BY BRUCE GRANT

NO noise could have been more welcome to the Philippine Partisans hiding in the jungles and hills of Leyte, many of whom are Moslems, than the booming waves of sound echoing over the island from the great sea and air battle.

This was the prelude to the freeing of the islands after a three-year-long occupation.

Almost since the last United States and Philippine troops were herded into the Japanese P.O.W. cages a bitter underground struggle has been going on.

Hard Core

The hard core of the resistance movement was provided by those Philippine troops who fled to the hills and a handful of American officers who went with them.

Since those far-off days the Japanese have provided thousands of recruits for the pulahanes—the Maquis of the Philippines.

In Leyte the commander, Colonel Ruperto Kangleon, nut-brown and tough as a steel spring, built up the advance guard for the American landing forces.

He saw his men tied to telegraph poles and bayoneted to death because they did not surrender quick enough.

He watched the wounded marched to concentration camps, those who dropped out were mutilated and left to die.

Typical of the men under Colonel Kangleon's control is Julio Justo, a 60-year-old farmer whose sons and wife were murdered by the Japanese.

At first he went berserk and slashed off the heads of Japanese sentinels until he was forced to hide in the hills.

The small partisan army on Leyte merged into the natural background of the farmers and fishermen who worked in the coconut groves, cornfields or along the rocky inlets.

The Philippinos fed them and gave them shelter when they were not fighting.

It was not chance that made General McArthur choose Leyte as his striking point.

Radio Manila broadcast the complaint that the "whole town and villages had been razed to the ground because the local leaders instead of fighting the real enemy . . . gave arms and help to the guerrillas."

Almost 12 months ago Allied submarines landed a handful of officers and a cargo of arms and explosives on the white, sandy beaches.

With them they brought "walky-talky" radio transmitters, which kept them in touch with distant United States battle headquarters.

From the Jap-held ports news arrived at the Partisan Headquarters with uncanny speed, whispered into the "jungle telegraph."

From a neighbouring island a 27-year-old U.S. flying officer, Lieut. Leon Tinnell, was able to flash the news of a Japanese convoy moving on the island.

Ships Sunk

Thanks to his information, 50 of the Jap ships were lost to the Allied warships and planes.

This officer, who could pass himself off as a Philippino, was given the vital task of preparing for the liberation of Leyte. He found thousands of islanders anxious to throw off the Jap control but very poorly armed.

Their chief weapon was the razor-sharp "Bolo," a long-bladed machette which was equally efficacious in chopping bamboo canes or splitting a Japanese skull.

Japanese spies warned their General Yamachita that something was afoot.

The Japanese commander contented himself with burning down a few villages and impaling the suspects on the bamboo stockades.

According to Lieut. Tinnell the Japanese were as stupid as they were brutal.

Large sections of the peasants were forced to abandon sugar crops to grow rice for the invader. This brought ruin to whole regions, and the crops were purchased with valueless pesos, printed in Tokyo.

The handful of quislings the Japanese commander was able to buy had little or no prestige.

The islanders take poorly to invaders. It took 80,000 American troops four years to pacify the Philippines when they landed in 1898.

Independent

Under American rule the people have grown up to a greater measure of independence than ever before, and they bitterly resent the arrogant Japanese.

Among the guerrilla troops the American officers found, perhaps some of the most fearless were the moros, Philippines of Dyak origin, who are still fiercely independent and devout Moslems. Almost 70,000 of them are scattered among the western islands.

It was from this strange mixture of rebellious farmers, peasants and unemployed workers from towns that the advance guard of General MacArthur's invasion force was built up. During the last two years they claim to have killed 3,000 Japs.

Bridges and railway tracks were dynamited, roads were mined. At the same time another guerrilla force launched a feint offensive on the island of Mindanao to draw off the Japanese reinforcements.

Before the bulk of the 25,000 Japanese troops garrisoning Leyte realised what had happened the American steel landing craft were spilling out men and tanks on to the sandy beaches. Waiting for them were the Philippino partisans.

Together they fought their way into the burning town of Taclo, the island's capital.

From this tree-covered island, General MacArthur will launch the final assault in the freeing of the Philippines.

This is half-way house in the steady march on Tokyo and an important step towards ending the war in the east.

Fighting Man's Platform

IT seems there is a strong tendency these days to allow the necessity for post-war planning and especially our (and our Allies) urgent need of overseas markets to obscure and even hinder our war effort.

The recent decision to reduce Lease-Lend commitments by cutting those imports down to military essentials is, I think, a case in point.

As I see it, the object of this step is to release the British Government from its obligation to America not to export those types of goods which are Lend-leased, thus allowing us to compete on equal terms for export markets.

Doesn't this mean that the same old scramble is going to start all over again, with subsidised industry laying the foundations for renewed enmity between the nations?

I think most people will agree that the Allies have pulled together pretty well in the common cause of destroying Fascism.

I'd like to see them do the same in peace, but this early resumption of industrial strife is far from encouraging.

Finally, those markets will still be there when the war is over—and if we *must* rush to get there first, let's delay the "off" until this job's finished.—**Cpl. W. E. Stephenson, R.A.F.**

THE TWO TYPES—by JON

"Considering the time of the year, old man, I think a visit to Naafi is indicated."

* * *

I sailed from England on December 3, 1941. Exactly three years later, I wrote to my wife for the 1,190th time.

The remainder of my correspondence is slight. My parents have one letter a week, and all other letters added together do not amount to a dozen a year.—F/O. G. Bibby, R.A.F.

UNION JACK

Issued free to the British Fighting Forces.

SPECIAL TWELVE-PAGE
CHRISTMAS ISSUE, 1944

Monday December 25, 1944.

TO-DAY

We drink a

toast to our Allies

INSIDE: The story of Bethlehem . . . other Army Christmases recalled . . . a year of triumph on the battlefields . . . What 1944 has meant to our fighting men . . . Christmas Eve at the local . . . Special Quiz . . . Damon Runyon . . . Messages to the folks at Home . . . Our own ghost story . . . Peter Wilson's sporting memories . . . George Maracco . . . AND, interrupting everywhere, the TWO TYPES spend Christmas with you.

1945

US landings on Luzon (Philippines)

Red Army captures Warsaw

Land route to China reopened

Yalta conference

Allied air raid on Dresden

Allied crossings of the Rhine

US landings on Okinawa

Death of Roosevelt

United Nations conference in San Francisco

Mussolini killed by partisans

Hitler commits suicide

British recapture Rangoon

German unconditional surrender ends the war in Europe

Labour victory in British general election

Atomic bombs dropped on Hiroshima and Nagasaki

Japanese unconditional surrender ends the Second World War

SEAC

THE SERVICES NEWSPAPER OF
SOUTH EAST ASIA COMMAND

No. 368   One Anna

THURSDAY, 11 JANUARY, 1945.

Printed by Courtesy of
THE STATESMAN in Calcutta.

SOLDIERS RUSH TO BUY SHOPS

LONDON, Wed.—Without waiting for the end of the fighting, many soldiers with money to spend are buying small businesses, retail and wholesale, through their wives or solicitors.

In this way some City and West End firms are having a monthly turnover running into tens of thousands of pounds.

A Board of Trade official said. "There is no official restriction on businesses changing hands, but it is essential that would-be buyers should know the licence does not necessarily go with the business.

"Before putting down any money for a shop or factory a soldier should first apply for continuation of the licence."

Demand Exceeds Supply

A West End estate agent now busy finding shops and small factories for men still in the forces, for discharged servicemen and former Civil Defence workers said: "Though some people are now advertising businesses, the need is far greater than the supply.

"Every day we get requests for shops, especially draper's newsagent's, grocery businesses and hairdresser's shops in the suburbs south and west of London.

"We are looking for snack bars on the main or arterial roads for three men still serving overseas, a jeweller's shop for a sailor, a hairdresser's shop for a Wren and a delicatessen store for a man serving in the Pioneer Corps."—Reuter.

SUPREMO THANKS WEST AFRICANS

The Supreme Allied Commander, South East Asia, Admiral Lord Louis Mountbatten, has sent a message of congratulation to all ranks of the 81 (WA) Division on their recent exploits in Burma. "Keep them rolling," he added.

The commander of the Div replied: "All ranks deeply appreciate your interest and heartening message. Rest assured we shall continue to hit them a crack. In fact, we did so in a small way this morning."

Churchill Sends Congratulations

The Prime Minister has sent this message to SEAC on its first birthday :

One year ago today I sent my best wishes for the success of the South East Asia Command newspaper. Since then SEAC has come to be highly regarded in our famous 14th Army, for which I send you my congratulations and my hope for your continued success.—(Signed) Winston S. Churchill.

FAR EAST WAAF TO GET SLOUCH HATS

Members of the W.A.A.F. will in future be issued with slouch hats before leaving for South-East Asia. These are on the Australian pattern, with a turn-up at the left.

In addition to providing first-class protection against the sun, the slouch hat is considered smarter and more comfortable than the topee.

EDEN NAMES MAJOR WAR CRIMINALS

LONDON, Wed.—Foreign Secretary Eden stated in the House of Commons today that the British Government regards Goebbels and Von Ribbentrop as major war criminals coming within the scope of the declaration on German atrocities at the Moscow Conference in 1943.—Reuter.

£4,000,000 TAX WRITTEN OFF

Nearly £4,000,000 of income tax and other duties were remitted, or written off as irrecoverable, for 1943, says the report of the Comptroller and Auditor-General.

Investigations into fraud and evasion resulted in settlements in 1,355 cases for a total of £1,906,577.

Tobacco Shop ABC

Q. What capital shall I need to start a tobacconist's shop?

A. Not less than £250. More, according to the size and the position.

Q. Why do many tobacconists combine the business with other goods, such as confectionery or newspapers?

A. Because the profit on cigarettes and tobacco is small. Most brands of cigarettes show a profit of 12½ per cent. (or 3½d. on a 2s 4d. packet of 20). Profit on pipe tobacco varies, but in many instances is even less. Most retail goods give a profit of 33⅓ per cent.

Q. Is it possible to make a living by dealing solely in tobacconist's goods?

A. To make a living, a minimum weekly turnover of £120 to £140 is necessary. From the gross profits the tobacconist will have to pay for his lease, rates, light and heat, insurances, and so on. He may also have to provide accommodation for himself and his family, because rents, if the shop is in a good position, may be too high to enable him to live on the premises.

The Right Spot

Q. What is the most important consideration in starting a tobacconist's business?

A. The position of the shop. The proximity of a bus-stop may make all the difference to the amount of trade done. Factories, places of entertainment, and other enterprises will produce customers. It should be borne in mind that a shop which is dependent on the proximity of a factory may suffer badly should the factory be closed down.

Q. What of competition?

A. The tobacconist's is probably one of the most competitive trades. Not only are the multiple shops and stores in competition with the individual tradesman, but grocers, public-houses, restaurants, cinemas, all can sell cigarettes and tobacco on the payment of 5s. 3d. for an annual licence.

Q. How do I obtain supplies?

A. Direct from the manufacturers or through a wholesale agent. Manufacturers are usually under an agreement with the existing retail shops not to supply new entrants to the business. The wholesale agent will deal in all the branded goods, and will usually charge 2½ per cent on top of the manufacturer's price.

Q. On what will my capital be spent?

A. Stock, fittings, and possibly goodwill of an existing business.

GERMANS QUIT BUDA SUBURB

LONDON. Wed.—The German news agency says Kispest, south eastern suburb of Budapest, has been evacuated in complete order and without major losses in men and material.

It said that the civilian population was evacuated to other parts of Budapest. The defenders withdrew to a second defence belt.

No fighting had yet taken place in the inner centre of the city and around Parliament House.

Messages from Moscow say the struggle on the north western approaches to Budapest is surging around the electric railway, less than 25 miles due west of the city

Over 400 German tanks and guns have been knocked out since the attempt to rescue their Budapest garrison was launched last week.

The Soviet communiqué says: In the area of Budapest our troops occupied the principal racecourse, which the Germans had converted into an aerodrome, a city park, an oil refinery, a tank plant, iron works and engineering works, and are now mopping up the city district of Kispest.

S.A. MEN WON'T BE FORCED TO GO EAST

CAPETOWN. Sat.—When the European war was over, no S. African men would be forced to go to the Far East, FM Smuts told the South African Senate yesterday. A certain number of air squadrons would be needed there, and probably small bodies of the Union's specialist units, including Engineers and Medical Services.—Reuter

BEFORE 'FRISCO

LONDON, Sat.—Viscount Cranborne, Dominions Secretary, will preside at the Empire Conference to be held in London early next month, preceding the San Francisco Conference.—Reuter.

462 JAPS KILLED IN ATTACK ON MEIKTILA

KANDY, Sat.—In a fanatical attempt to dislodge 4 Corps troops from their perimeter at Meiktila the Japanese launched an attack in two-battalion strength during the night of Thursday-Friday 22/23 March. So far, 462 Japanese dead have been counted.

At one stage during the fighting the Japanese brought a 75 mm gun to within 10 yards of the perimeter wire. The gun was captured.

SOVIET ATTACK FACING BERLIN

LONDON, Sat.—The German High Command communiqué announced last night that the Red Army has opened a new attack against the flank of Kuestrin bridgehead on the Oder front opposite Berlin and made "slight initial gains."

An American broadcast from Moscow forecast that the attack, little more than 30 miles from the German capital, would be a full scale assault against Berlin

The Red Army attacking the Baltic ports of Gdynia and Danzig won an important victory in the capture of Zoppot, a seaside resort between the two cities.

AFRICANS GET 10s A MONTH MORE

Expatriation Allowance for African ORs in SE Asia Command has been increased to 15s a month with effect from 1 Nov. 1944, it is officially announced.

The increase applies in the area in which Japanese Campaign Pay is payable to British ranks. This includes India, Burma and Ceylon.

Both East African and West African troops will get this advance, Formerly Expatriation Allowance was 5s a month.

Our armoured columns continue to strike out from Meiktila and are inflicting heavy losses on the enemy.

In one sweep towards Thazi, 14 miles to the east, 197 Japanese were killed. Further south, another column captured five guns and killed another 25 enemy.

It is now known that the Japs defending Wundwin were mainly administrative men. They numbered 200 and almost all were killed when the 20 Ind Div column swept into the town from the west.

Further north, 19 Ind Div continue to liquidate Japanese near Mandalay. One brigade killed 118 Japs in a day.

Consolidating

Today's SE Asia Command communique, after reporting the Meiktila area fighting, says:—

Our troops are consolidating their newly won positions at Myingyan, on the Irrawaddy SW of Mandalay.

Northern Combat Area Command: Troops of 36 British Div have occupied Mong Long, 21 miles SE of Mogok, and patrols have advanced further.

Chinese 50 Div troops made gains east of Hsipaw towards the junction with the road to Mongyai and Mongkung.

15 Ind Corps Front: West African troops operating in the Letmauk area captured two features. Japanese counter-attacks were repulsed.

Air: Allied fighter-bombers of Eastern Air Command successfully attacked seven bridges on the Rangoon-Prome and the Rangoon-Mandalay railways yesterday and hit rolling stock and locomotives.

REES WAS IN AT THE 'KILL'

Maj-Gen T. W. Rees, Commander of 19th Ind Div, was there when Mandalay fell. Owing to a transmission error, it was reported that he had left in a plane a few minutes before Fort Dufferin was entered, and that he returned later.

The commander who missed the "kill" by a few minutes was Lt-Gen Sir Oliver Leese, C-in-C, ALFSEA, who had been watching operations against the Fort. Gen Leese returned and was in the Fort soon after its fall.

WAVELL IN LONDON

LONDON, Sat.—The Viceroy, FM Lord Wavell, and party arrived in London last night. He was greeted by Leopold Amery, Secretary for India, and other senior officials.—Reuter.

Lord Louis Mountbatten. Supreme Allied Commander, SE Asia, sat on a gun to talk to men of the 14th Army during his recent visit to Mandalay.

QUICK POST-WAR HOMES

HERE you see examples of prefabricated homes from three countries. The two pictures at the foot of the page are from Russia and U.S.A. The others illustrate British ideas. Interior views are of the type of furniture and equipment to be used in the British Portal House and in other prefab houses claimed to be an improvement on the Portal designs. These photographs show a three-room Portal—living room, kitchen, bathroom, and the view from the living room into the kitchen. The kitchen contains a refrigerator, an enamelled steel sink, washing copper, gas cooker and cupboards. Hundreds of thousands of the quickly-constructed house will be needed in Europe and America after the war.—See 'First Sandys House' on page three.

LEFT: PORTAL HOUSE, THREE-ROOM BUNGALOW TYPE. RIGHT: SECTIONAL HOUSE AT WEDNESBURY, NEAR BIRMINGHAM, CONSTRUCTED OF BRICK-FACED CONCRETE SLAB EQUAL TO 160 BRICKS. THE SLABS CAN BE MADE BY GIRL LABOUR IN FOUR MINUTES; THE ENTIRE HOUSE CAN BE COMPLETED IN SEVEN DAYS.

Yalta, Athens, Egypt was the Prime Minister's itinerary. At Alexandria he conferred with President Roosevelt, later he met the Emperor of Ethiopia, had separate talks with King Ibn Saud, King Farouk and the President of the Syrian Republic. King Ibn Saud and Mr Churchill lunch at Fayoum.

CHURCHILL AND ROOSEVELT MEET M. E. MONARCHS

Returning to Egypt after his second visit to Athens in two months Mr Churchill met President Roosevelt at Alexandria to discuss the Far East war. Previously the President had started a unique series of East-meets-West meetings aboard a U.S. cruiser in the Bitter Lakes—whither he had gone from the aircraft which had brought him from the Crimea—and had talked with King Ibn Saud of Saudi Arabia, King Farouk of Egypt and Emperor Haile Selassie of Ethiopia. Mr Churchill continued the series in Cairo where he saw King Farouk and Emperor Haile Selassie as well as the President of the Syrian Republic. The Premier also visited King Ibn Saud at his headquarters in the country where they exchanged gifts. Mr Eden was present at all the talks except the one with President Roosevelt.

EGYPT MOURNS HER MURDERED PREMIER

Gen. Sir Bernard Paget, C.-in-C. M.E.F., and Air Marshal C.E.A. Medhurst, A.O.C.-in-C. were among senior officers at the funeral.

As flag-draped coffin, flanked by mounted Royal Bodyguard and Egyptian sailors, passes, mourners cover points of vantage. Flag on left is workmen's union tribute.

THE TROOPS' OWN PAGE
They Write To SEAC

Advice from Ike

NA 35416 Sigm J. Ike, 82 (WA) Div Sigs, S.E.A.C.

I should like to send through SEAC a message to all West African troops serving in Burma and India. Here it is:

Dear Brothers.—I thank you very much for your gallantry. Do your darndest to be good soldiers, but do not let soldiering make you forget that you are gentlemen and Christians.

It may be necessary to kill, but it is never necessary to like it. You will live in tough company and see suffering, cruelty and coarseness, with hardness of every kind; do not let it get the better of you. War is a hell but a soldier does not need to be a devil.

Let us fight on with a united heart and hand, though we can not all be heroes and make a glorious name.

Our country is going to need a lot of men with ideals, decency, and morals, when the war is over. Pray God that you may be one of those men to build up what war and crime has torn down.

Advice to Nancy

CH X108268 Mne V. Ward, Commandos, S.E.A.C.

Lady Astor says "soldiers would rather have a fried egg than a glass of beer any day" (SEAC, 15 Feb).

How does she know? Let her speak for herself. The answer in this unit is "Beer."

3126194 Cpl N. Ellis, 15 (Ind) Corps Signals, S.E.A.C.

I suggest to Nancy Astor, a non-drinker, that she does not know her subject.

Give the lads their glass of beer and make it a big 'un. If the honourable lady wants to do something for the fighting services, let her agitate for decent smokes in place of the localmade "Woodbines" we have had to contend with for the past month.

Keep 'Em In

1720123 Gnr. E. Durkin, HAA Bty, RA, S.E.A.C.

The only safeguard for world peace I can see, and it is one that seems to be escaping our peacemakers, is to impose an anti-emigration law on Germany for at least ten years. This would prevent the disciples of Nazi and Fascist creeds from traversing the earth still sowing the rotten seeds of rule by the sword.

Germany for the Germans, and no German allowed to step outside—that should be our postwar slogan.

Pocket Book

1137749 Gnr A. Elliker, LAA Bty, RA, S. E. A. C.

I have a paper-covered copy of Cronin's "The Keys of the Kingdom," a small compact book which goes easily into my blouse pocket. It is one of the many Armed Services Editions issued to American troops by a non-profit organisation to enable troops to read the best of current and past books in convenient and economical form.

Cannot a similar scheme be inaugurated for the British forces?

give young men the opportunities which, but for the war, would have been theirs, but not at the expense of the older men who have the same ambitions and greater responsibilities.

Is the majority of the nation destined to go through life labelled "Other Rank"?

Scot's Lament

T/180581 Cpl G. A. Symington, RASC, S.E.A.C.

I am Scottish, and for weeks I have longingly looked at your Home pictures for just a little of the mellow beauty and rugged grandeur of Scottish West Highland Kyles and Isles.

Is 'Home' England? I have no thought of being selfish: surely there are hundreds like me who would like a Scottish 'Home,' even if only on paper.

SEAC likes to give all parts of UK a show and keeps sending home for fresh pictures. We have printed a number of Scottish photographs—Ed.

Mandalay Home

1601987 Sgt F. A. Strange, RA, S.E.A.C.

I sympathize wholehearted with Mr P. D. Webb, of Delhi, (SEAC 10 Feb), who fears for the safety of his home during bombing, and I hope when we recapture Mandalay he will find his house intact, although he must not be downhearted if he finds otherwise.

If he stopped to think, I am sure he would sooner lose his house than us lose our pals. Bombing out the Japs is better than using the bayonet.

Have a thought for the infantrymen whom we all admire for the good job of work they have done.

Gratuities

S/13060024 L/Cpl W. B. Gallie, Adv HQ, ALFSEA.

I understood the gratuities scheme was to compensate men who had served their country during the war and enable them to purchase immediate requirements when they take up civilian life.

When the gratuities become effective we shall be civilians. A tube of tooth-paste and a bedroom suite will cost the same whether the buyer has been a commissioned officer or a footslogging infantryman.

10351099 Sgt H. A. Smith, Intelligence Corps. S.E.A.C.

The Government is perpetuating the old British tradition of giving most to those who already have most and least to those who have least. There should be no discrimination whatever; payment to be made on length of service alone.

3511458 Pte J. H. Gower, 14th Army Signals, S.E.A.C.

Team work will bring us victory. Out here and on other fronts class distinction more less goes by the board. So why should there be any difference in gratuity for privates and officers and NCOs?

Parable

1619378 Cpl J. O. Watt, RAF, India.

The gratuity rates just published reveal a continuation of the marked discrimination between the treatment of commissioned and other ranks. We have become resigned to the differences in pay; it is probably impossible to equalize it during this war, but a step in the right direction would be to arrange a flat rate of gratuity for all ranks based on length of service only. Is there any objection on the grounds of efficiency or discipline?

Here is a story. Mr Firkin and Mr Jerkin are called up together. Mr F is serving his time as a plumber; Mr J, having just left Harrow, is learning to be a bank manager. Mr F becomes Pte F; Mr J becomes 2-Lt J.

They both learn completely new jobs, both are conscientious, neither is dim, and they do their new jobs with reasonable skill.

The war ends. They are both demobbed. A grateful democratic country gives for their four years' service £28-16-0 to Cpl Firkin and £84 to Capt Jerkin. I don't "get it."

The Regular

823294 SSM E. Rogers, R.A.C., S.E.A.C.

I have read of the various emoluments to be paid at the end of this war, including the sixpence a day placed in the bank for us since 1 Jan, 1942.

I notice that the emphasis is all on immediate payment on discharge. No doubt this is gratifying for the militiaman, reservist and time-expired soldier, but what is the position of the regular soldier who has several years to serve yet? I have nine years to do to complete my 21. Have I to wait until discharge for my gratuity? I hope the scheme visualised is not to place it to our "credit", because I'd rather have it in my pocket.

Gin and Lime

7101056 Sgt A. Gray, RAMC, CCS, S.E.A.C.

I believe with VAD E. M. How (SEAC, 7 Feb) that many women come to India with high ideals, and that there are still some men who don't consider a woman "a joke" who neither drinks nor smokes.

But I submit that sometimes the environment is such that a girl who replies "Lime" when asked what she will drink is in six months replying to the same question, "Gin and lime"—and enjoying it.

1154227 Gnr W. J. Jones, Fd Regt, RA, S.E.A.C.

It was good to read of a woman "detailed" to go to an officers' party having the grit to stand by her own opinion on what is best to drink. That is more than many Servicemen would think of doing.

"We came out here to nurse and intend to carry out such work"—I feel sure those words of VAD How speak for at least 90 per cent of the whole.

It is good for morale just to see a Sister now and again. I am sorry it has been Miss How's misfortune to have met only a few sincere men, because there are many.

3771041 Pte T. W. O'Brien, York and Lancs Rgt, S.E.A.C.

Why shouldn't nurses have a good time? They deserve it. Have they to go to a basha every night and sit brooding over an oil lamp?

How do you feel, Sgt. Green, when you can't get a little enjoyment? I say "Good luck" to the folks who can go to a few parties and dances.

EASTERN ITALY EDITION

UNION JACK

Forces Daily

NO. 354 Thursday, February 15, 1945 TWO LIRE

Irrawaddy oilfield town falls

EAST AFRICAN troops of the 14th Army have captured Seikpyu, on the Irrawaddy.

Seikpyu is in the important Burma oil-field area, about 110 miles southwest of Mandalay.

The amount of equipment taken indicates that the Japanese withdrew hurriedly, but Reuter's correspondent pointed out that it was unlikely that they would let the oilfields go without a fight.

The enemy is reported to be busy on defences in the area, and the Irrawaddy affords a natural barrier which, no doubt, the Japanese will exploit.

In the Myiston area, troops of the 36th British Division were engaged in mopping-up operations. The main bridge and its by-pass on the Burma-Siam railway were wrecked in a low-level attack by heavy bombers of Eastern Air Command.

Fifteenth Indian Corps captured a hill north of Kangaw, in the northern combat area, when Chinese First Army troops consolidated their positions on the Burma Road and advanced to milestone 55.

Surprise for Nazi raiders

THE effective co-operation between our land and naval forces is well illustrated by the story of a German raiding party that landed on an island in the Aegean in search of food and supplies and was cut off.

News was received that a force of about 40 Germans from a neighbouring island had landed on the island of Nisiro, in the Dodecanese south of Cos. Their craft, a 90-foot motor-launch was found and sunk by the destroyer *Exmoor*.

Then, supported by the *Exmoor* and another destroyer, the *Ledbury*, a small party of Greek and British troops landed on Nisiro from an infantry landing craft in the afternoon.

The surprised German raiding party lost eight killed, and 30 others were taken prisoner.

Yesterday's Allied communique stated that Eighth and Fifth Army patrols had maintained contact with the enemy on the Italian front.

Brazilians on the Fifth Army front, supported by artillery, raided a hill feature about a mile east of Gaggio, in the upper Revo valley.

Strong forces of escorted heavy bombers of Strategic Air Force bombed communication targets in Austria and Yugoslavia, also harbour installations in northern Italy. At the same time forces of medium bombers and fighters of T.A.F. struck at rail targets on the Brenner line with good results.

LATE NEWS

Sixty-five thousand incendiaries were dropped on Dresden as well as 8,000-lb. bombs and hundreds of 1,000 pounders.

Orders of the Day by Marshal Stalin announce capture of Schneidemuhl, in Pomerania, and a further broadening of Koniev's front.

New Spitfire outpaces FW 190

IT was disclosed yesterday that the Spitfire, Mark 14, has a speed of about 450 miles an hour. This is the first time that any British warplane has been officially credited with anything above 400 miles an hour.

The Spitfire 14 is one of the fastest fighters flying to-day, and its ability to outpace Germany's ace fighter, the F.W.190, has been of special value to Second T.A.F. on the West Front.

A new type of F.W. fighter is being used by the Germans on the "Berlin Front" against Marshal Zhukov's army. Known as the 190A/8, it has six guns, two 13 mm. machine-guns, and two 20 mm. and two 30 mm. cannon.

Land, air target

WE POUND DRESDEN FOR KONIEV

RAF pilot over city sees Soviet gun flashes

MORE than 1,200 heavy Allied bombers from the west struck at Dresden yesterday and on Tuesday night.

They struck in direct support of Marshal Koniev's columns advancing on the city from the east, only 62 miles away.

One of the pilots, F/Sjt. Bamley, said that he could see the battle raging on the East Front.

He declared: "As we left the target I could see endless fires and explosions in the east. The Russians were laying down all kinds of stuff on the Germans."

At night 1,400 R.A.F. bombers were over Germany, 800 of which went to Dresden. Others went to Magdeburg.

They made two attacks with an interval of three-and-a-quarter hours between them. Bombing was well concentrated and soon after the first attack started clouds over the city were glowing red from the great fires below.

When the second force reached the city the sky was clear and the results of the first attack could be seen.

During daylight yesterday nearly 1,400 Liberators and Fortresses of the U.S. Eighth Air Force smashed at Dresden, Chemnitz and Magdeburg and road bridges across the Rhine River at Wesel. Six hundred went to Dresden.

They were escorted by 900 Mustangs and Thunderbolts.

Dresden is the seventh largest city in Germany. With an original population of 640,000 it is the meeting place of main railway lines to eastern and southern Germany, Berlin, Prague and Vienna and branch lines lead to Leipzig and other industrial towns.

Almost at the same time as the first attack on Dresden strong forces of bombers made a heavy attack on a synthetic oil plant at Bohlen, south of Leipzig which had an output equal to the largest plants in the Ruhr.

R.A.F. night bombers from Italy attacked rail centres in Vienna and Grauz.

The Marshal is only 62 miles away

MARSHAL KONIEV'S monster tanks, firing their massive guns of nearly five-inch calibre, are to-day shooting their way along the mud-covered roads towards Dresden.

Latest Moscow reports place them only 62 miles from the city.

This new advance by Koniev's forces was made after his tanks and infantry had battled their way across the Bober River, through an area of densely-wooded hill country to the east bank of the Quess River, a tributary of the Bober.

They have taken several places on the east bank, including Neuhammer, which is 19 miles from the great industrial town of Gorlitz, on the main Dresden road and 62 miles from Dresden itself.

Farther north, the right wing of Koniev's drive has crossed the border of Brandenburg, Berlin's province, and has now reached Somerfeld, 75 miles from Berlin, according to Berlin reports.

Col. Ernst von Hammer, Berlin commentator, said: "Koniev is advancing between the Breslau and Brandenburg border with a force of five armies—about 500,000 men—on a front of 85 miles wide, but," he added, "the German High Command has massed vast reserves ready for a gigantic counter-attack at the right moment."

Two of Koniev's spearheads are now threatening to pincer the railway town of Sagan, almost exactly 100 miles south-east of Berlin.

The Germans are digging hard again—this time along the banks of Neisse, which seems to have been earmarked as their next defence barrier guarding the roads to Dresden, 53 miles to the west.

Crerar's men slog forward

AS Welsh troops slogged ahead against steadily increasing resistance yesterday, Canadian troops were extending their 10,000 yards hold on the west bank of the Rhine and its tributary.

William Steen, Reuter's special correspondent at Shaef, reported that the Welsh infantry were closing on Goch, one of the most strongly-fortified Siegfried towns in the north.

Staggered lines of pillboxes ring this vital junction of six roads and three railways, and it is not expected to fall without a full-dress battle. Bursting out from the eastern side of the Reichswald Forest, the Welsh troops were last reported less than three miles from Goch, sister town of the already captured Cleve.

Heavy fighting was reported along the whole Canadian Army offensive front, but it is essentially an infantry battle and spectacular gains should not be expected.

The steady progress being made is regarded as highly satisfactory.

West country troops are now striking down the road which runs southeast from Cleve to Udem, while to the south other Allied forces are exploiting their bridgehead over the Niers river along which the Germans had been expected to make a stand.

According to another Reuter's correspondent, Doon Campbell, British troops south of the Reichswald Forest, which has now been cleared, have broadened their hold across the Niers river between Gennep and Hommersum into a solid bridgehead.

South of the Forest fighting is going on in the village of Viller, about three miles north-west of Goch. Other forces have captured Hasselt on the Cleve-Calcar road, and the Allies are now halfway between Cleve and Calcar.

Kellen, a mile northeast of Cleve and just over three miles south of the Rhine opposite Emmerich, has also been taken.

General Crerar's men are blowing up dykes to neutralise flood water which is spreading over wider areas. Mud, floods and rain clouds are the greatest obstacles to the Allied advance.

So far 5,300 prisoners have been taken since the opening of the new attack.

Air Marshal Sir Arthur Coningham's Tactical Air Force fighters and medium bombers destroyed or damaged 116 railway trucks, 116 vehicles and effected 14 railway cuts.

In the Echternach bridgehead sector, troops of the U.S. Third Army have penetrated the first and probably the thickest belt of the Siegfried defences. Half of the Siegfried town of Ernzen is in American hands, but fighting continues in the streets.

Third Army troops have deepened their bridgehead into Germany from Luxembourg by a quarter of a mile, following an advance beyond Ferschweiler nearly four miles north of Echternach. Liberation of the entire Duchy of Luxembourg has been completed.

Yesterday's Shaef communique stated that the Third Army bridgehead across the Sauer and Our rivers is now ten-and-a-half miles wide and two-and-a-quarter miles deep.

General Eisenhower has issued an Order of the Day congratulating the First French Army on its achievements. Latest figures from official sources indicate that since D-Day 887,000 German soldiers have surrendered.

ALLIED POWs ON THE MOVE

TWELVE German prisoner-of-war camps, which once contained about 60,000 British and Commonwealth prisoners, have either been overrun by Soviet forces or are in their direct path, declared Sir James Grigg, British War Minister, in reply to a question in Parliament yesterday.

"The men are apparently moved on foot by daily stages of between 12 and 18 miles. It is likely, however, that many have been overtaken by Soviet forces," he said.

According to official information announced in Washington, all the camps in East Prussia, Poland and East Pomerania are being moved westward. These include Stalag Luft IV, Stalag A and Stalag B.

Stalag C is being moved westward, Stalag III to the southwest. Those in northern Silesia are moving northwest and those in southern Silesia, i.e., Stalag VI B, Stalag VII and Stalag 214, are being moved southwest across Bohemia. Officers from Oflag 64 are being sent to Stalag IIIA at Luckenwalde, between Berlin and Leipzig.

Western-front bogyman

As elsewhere in the Army, improvisation is often the keynote on the Western Front, and bad weather conditions call for new ideas. His friends might not know it, but this is 1st Sjt. Pershing Wadsworth, of Rockmary, Georgia, and he is wearing a wind-mask which he has made out of a scarf.

CIGS for Berlin control body

Field-Marshal Sir Alan Brooke, Chief of the Imperial General Staff, it is understood in London, will be the British representative on the Allied Control Commission which is to sit in Berlin, according to the "Daily Mail." The paper points out that this would leave Field-Marshal Sir Harold Alexander or Field-Marshal Sir Bernard Montgomery free for other duties in the Far East.

The three British Chiefs of Staff, Admiral Sir Andrew Cunningham, Field-Marshal Sir Alan Brooke and Air Marshal Sir Charles Portal, have returned from the Big Three Crimean conference, the Ministry of Information announces.

The present whereabouts of Mr. Churchill were not disclosed.

Personnel
whose Menfolk
Serve in South
East Asia

Sgt. IVY POWELL, of Tonbridge, Kent, whose husband L/Bdr SYDNEY POWELL, is with the RA in S.E.A.C.

Pte CONNIE PARKER, of Nottingham, engaged to L/Cpl WILLIAM GRAY of the Gordon Highlanders.

" Sgt EVE DUNLOP whose husband is a corporal (cadet) in the Intelligence Corps.

Pte IRIS SILBURN, engaged to Sgt THOMAS PERRY, Indian Artillery.

Sgt BERTHA SMITH whose husband, Gunner JAMES SMITH, is with a Light AA Battery.

"THIS HALF A TIN OF BOOT POLISH PER MAN IS JUST RIDICULOUS."

Reproduced by permission of the proprietors of "Punch"

AN attempt was made on Friday night to wreck a special train in which the German Commander-in-Chief in Denmark, General Lindemann, was travelling, the Swedish radio said yesterday.

The train was en route from Thisted to Silkeborg, in Jutland, and the explosion destroyed two carriages and derailed a sleeping car.

* * *

Good progress has been made by the conference of Arab Foreign Ministers and the constitution of a proposed Arab League is expected to be ready shortly

* * *

Paris radio says that martial law has been declared in all of Rumania

"Now to make this authentic BBC. we should cancel something occasionally and play records instead"

An explosion, followed by fire, occurred at Elsinore shipyard, Denmark, on Friday All labourers and moulders had left the premises at the time, but engineers were injured.

* * *

The French Council of Ministers has accepted the US lend-lease proposals and decided to send M Jean Monnet back to Washington for the signature Monnet headed the French economic mission which went to Washington in December.

JANE

I ALREADY FEEL NERVOUS, DI!

—H'M—HAH—YES—
DO YOU EVER HAVE AN UNCONTROLLABLE DESIRE TO STRIP OFF YOUR CLOTHES AND DANCE NAKED?

NO!—(GULP!) AND I'M NOT GOING TO START NOW!

AH!—I THOUGHT AS MUCH!—YOU'VE LOST YOUR NERVE!

YOU DON'T SEEM TO HAVE LOST YOURS, DOCTOR!

COLOGNE OURS: ALLIES WIN 100m FRONT ON THE RHINE

LONDON, Wed.—The capture of Cologne, the greatest prize on the Western Front, by the American First Army was announced yesterday. A correspondent with the First Army writes: "Cologne is in surrender white today. It is estimated there are still between 80,000 and 180,000 civilians in the city, 85 per cent of which is officially stated to be in ruins.

"There seems to be almost a liberation spirit among the civilians. It is not uncommon to get a smile from refugees as they trek back to the rear areas. Air force officials say there are 65 other German cities as badly damaged as Cologne, and Dusseldorf will probably be worse.'

Later reports say American troops have fought through Cologne to reach the west bank of the Rhine.

Allied armies are along the Rhine's west bank from Niejmegen to Cologne for more than 100 miles except for a small ten mile stretch at Wesel and other unimportant pockets where the river bends.

The Wesel bridgehead is shrinking rapidly and during the past 36 hours it is believed the Germans made the best use of the bad weather and darkness to withdraw.

Now the bridgehead has no more than nuisance value. Only one of the main crossroads now remains in German hands and British troops are driving towards it.

The fanatical infantry of the First Paratroop Army manning the bridgehead have little hope of escape unless they can improvise last minute repairs to the road and rail bridges at Wesel.

Heavy Losses

Welsh troops of the First Canadian Army yesterday drove almost two miles into the centre of the Wesel bridgehead and last night were only 5,000 yards from the river itself.

Troops, armour and transport crowded in the devastated town of Wesel on the east bank of the Rhine were attacked yesterday by RAF Mosquitos escorted by Mustangs.

American First Army troops in a three-mile spurt have entered the town of Alfter, three miles west of Bonn, where the Germans are fighting to hold the evacuation point for their retreating Rhine armies.

The German Overseas News Agency military correspondent Capt Ludwing Sertorius admitted that German armies have suffered "heavy losses" in the withdrawal to and over the Rhine.

The 9th US Army has reached the Rhine along a 30-mile front.

Physical difficulties presented by the Rhine here are not such as to prevent the bridging of the river.

Lightly Held

Marshal Rundstedt's position is not easy—even though he has managed to save a great part of his armies. He is still unsure of the whereabouts of the Second British Army and when it may come out of its hiding.

The Germans are organizing their defences on the east bank of the Rhine and are getting more guns into position.

The defences, hastily-dug trench systems, ditches and machine-gun and artillery positions, are in no great depth and are manned by troops from formations which fought west of the Rhine and from units brought from northern Holland, which is drained of German troops apart from garrison forces.

'HONEYMOON' BEGAN IN CELL

After Pte. George Robinson, of Mosley-street, Leeds, with a policeman as his bestman, had been married at a Leeds register office he kissed his bride and then, with his bestman as escort, went off to spend the first night of his "honeymoon" alone in a police cell.

Shortly before his wedding Robinson, alleged to be an Army absentee, had stood in the dock at Leeds Police Court jointly accused with another man of housebreaking.

When the magistrates ordered the two prisoners to be remanded in custody the first information of Robinson's intended marriage came out.

After telling the Court of the arrangements Police Superintendent Mackereth said, "I think, however, that subject to your worship's approval we can arrange for him to be taken to be married—in custody, of course."

ENSA STARS TOO SNOBBISH

LONDON, Sat.—Basil Dean, Director of ENSA, who has returned from a 15,000 miles tour in the Far East, told a Press conference yesterday that certain popular stage personalities had demanded all sorts of special privileges and "rushed about the place like scalded cats in special aircraft, thus providing less entertainment for the men than if they were not too snobbish to accept ENSA's directions."

Three stars with parties in India made things very difficult for ENSA by their behaviour while he was there, he said.

'Some stars recently there seem to have expected that the Order of Battle should be altered to suit their convenience. It is plumb crazy for such people to come home and suggest that their services are not wanted because they cannot be accepted in the front line at a particular moment.

"There are thousands and thousands of chaps in back areas lacking the excitement of an active operation who need entertainment just as badly. Stars could stay in India for a whole year and not outstay their welcome"

Dean has submitted a long report on the present position to the C-in-C, India, and the Supreme Allied Commander, SE Asia.

SUPREMO FLIES 100,000 MILES

ADV HQ, ALFSEA, Sat.—Lord Louis Mountbatten, Supreme Allied Commander SE Asia, has flown 100,000 miles since his appointment 18 months ago—equal to four times round the world at the equator.

This figure was reached when flying 60 miles SW of Nagpur on March 12. Most distance was covered visiting his forces at the front.—API.

SOVIET TANKS MASS FOR BERLIN

MOSCOW, Wed.—Marshal Zhukov's tank forces are now massing on the Lower Oder to sweep down on Berlin.

In the Baltic battle huge German forces have been cut off and considerable Red Army units are being used to smash them but it is to the west of this vast encirclement area that the next big strategical move is coming.

The German Overseas News Agency yesterday quoted a Berlin military spokesman as saying that Marshal Zhukov's northern columns have reached the area of Kammin and the mouth of the Oder after an advance of 38 miles.

This German statement means that within two days of Zhukov and Rokossovsky reaching the Baltic shore the Red Army has spread out and now holds a 75-mile stretch of the coast eastward from the mouth of the Oder.

More than 4,000 Germans were killed in the battle for Stargard, defence outpost of the Baltic port of Stettin, says the supplement to the Soviet communiqué.

Greifenberg, 15 miles from the Baltic and 18 miles from the Oder mouth has been captured by the Red Army.

MONTY LAUNCHES RHINE ASSAULT

SHAEF, PARIS, Sat.—Allied Forces today are crossing the Rhine on a wide front north of the Ruhr. Elements of the First Allied Airborne Army have also been landed East of the Rhine. The operations are being assisted by Allied Navies and Air Forces following an intensive aerial preparation.

The announcement of the Allies crossing the Rhine came in a special communiqué issued at SHAEF shortly after 13.00 hrs. GMT. Prime Minister Churchill was at FM Montgomery's HQ when the Rhine assault was launched.

At FM Montgomery's HQ it was officially disclosed that the Rhine crossings are being made in the areas of Wesel, Rees and Xanten. Formations taking part include the 51st and 15th Scottish Divisions. The assault is described here today as "going extremely well".

The German News Agency announced: ".Powerful British formations launched the expected large scale offensive on the Lower Rhine last night on both sides of Wesel

"The offensive began with a terrific artillery barrage and with an attempt to cross the Rhine. A withering German artillery barrage was directed against the assailants. Streams of bullets from hundreds of German machineguns rained upon the British assault troops."

This news followed the announcement early in the day that Gen Patton's 3rd U S Army had made a crossing of the Rhine near Worms, and later came a despatch from Gen Simpson's 9th U.S. Army that his men too have established a bridgehead east of the Rhine.

An earlier dispatch from the Western Front said strict censorship was imposed on the British 2nd Army front yesterday.

Across 500 yards of the Rhine, British and Canadian troops watched growing clouds of smoke and dust shroud German strongpoints, villages, and concentration centres as RAF bombs and rockets found their targets.

Ammunition dumps. petrol depots, barracks, suspected HQ, signals centres and supply bases were among the objectives attacked and so dense was the smoke over the north German plain by late afternoon that the bomber programme had to be curtailed.

RAF Bomber Command, U.S. 8th and 9th Airforces and the entire strength of the British 2nd TAF were put into the attack as the great air offensive mounted.

Not A Shot

Without air or artillery preparation, troops of Gen Patton's 3rd U.S. Army crossed the Rhine on Thursday night and established a bridgehead which they have since expanded steadily. The new crossing, the second by the Americans, was announced from SHAEF, Paris, for Gen Bradley's 12th U.S. Army Group.

The Germans reported that Gen Pattons men crossed near the Oppenheim sector. Other Berlin reports said the Americans set up the crossing gear in the Worms area, 16 miles south of Oppenheim.

New York Radio today reported: "Not a shot was fired when the first wave of infantry crossed the river in assault boats. Ten minutes later, as additional waves crossed, sporadic shooting broke out. Reports say the Germans were caught by surprise. They failed to fire a single round

of artillery until two hours after the Americans had crossed.

Lack of Opposition

"Third Army troops are pouring inland against complete lack

Continued Back Page Column 1.

YANKS LAND ON OKINAWA

Admiral Nimitz's HQ, Guam Sun.—United States troops have landed on Okinawa Island. The landings were made by the 10th Army.

Tokyo Radio reports that 1,500 American troops landed on Okinawa Island, only 360 miles from the Japanese mainland, equipped with 100 tanks.

Occupation of Okinawa would bring American air forces within fighter range of the Japanese mainland.

Later, the Tokyo Radio stated that American troops are landing on Okinawa itself and in the adjacent islands in the group in the central part of the Ryukyu chain.

Yesterday Tokyo reported mine-sweepers moving into position behind a fleet bombardment to pave the way for a landing.

Fifteen battleships and other heavy warships have joined the surface craft already on the scene and a powerful armada is following close behind." the Japanese Radio declared

The bombardment lasted for nine days along a 700-miles front

British and American naval guns are raking all the Ryukyu islands between Formosa and the Japanese mainland, while Marianas-based Superfortresses have been ordered into a powerful attack against airfields on the southernmost home island of Kyushu to kill any possible Japan-based interference.

Air Attacks Fail

Plane and torpedo attacks against the four Task Force operating in against Ryukyu have been brushed off

American carrier planes sank or damaged 46 Japanese ships and destroyed 87 planes on Thursday and Friday, said Admiral Nimitz's communiqué.

73,000 TONS ON NAZIS IN MARCH

LONDON, Sun.—U.S. 8th Air Force created a record by yesterday's operations. which brought the total weight of bombs dropped on targets during March to over 73.000 tons

More than 300 heavy bombers escorted by about 850 fighters yesterday attacked a synthetic oil plan at Zeitz. railyards at Halle, and rail and industrial targets at Erunswick.

DUTCH 'DECORATE' DESERT RATS

LONDON, Sun.—So impressed were the people of a Dutch village with the exemplary conduct of British troops billeted with them that the Burgomaster insisted on presenting locally made ribbons, badges and formation signs to the Divisional Commander.

Troops were of the Seventh Armoured Division, famous Desert Rats who fought the Germans from Alamein to Tunis, through Italy, and from Normandy on the D-Day.—Reuter

NAZI TROOPS DRIVEN FROM VIENNA CENTRE

Koenigsberg Captured

MOSCOW, Tues.—Russian troops are cutting up the remnants of the Nazi garrison in Vienna after storming their way forward to take the centre of the city Faced by veteran Soviet street fighters and surrounded by a population which is largely hostile the Germans, little more than a disorganised mob, are trying to get out of the city before it is entirely occupied by the Red Army.

Main buildings captured in the centre of Vienna include the Parliament Buildings, the Town Hall, the Police HQ and the Opera House.

Koenigsberg, capital of East Prussia, has been captured, says Marshal Stalin in an order of the day. More than 27,000 prisoners were taken, including the commander of the fortress.

The German News Agency reports that fighting is going on in Franz Josef station, Vienna's main terminus in the very heart of the city.

There is little hope for the remnants of Hitler's Vienna garrison. To the north-east of the Austrian capital a big Soviet Army Group under Marshal Malinovsky is threatening the last main escape road—to Brno in Czechoslovakia.

The German news agency military correspondent Col. Ernst von Hammer, reported last night that the Russians have captured both Kalenberg and Leopoldsberg, two mountain features in the north-west dominating Vienna.

Breslau Flare-up

"Furious battles took place behind the hastily set up barricades of tram cars and other obstacles," he said.

An intensified onslaught on Breslau, has begun. The city has been holding out against fierce Soviet attacks from every side for weeks. It is one of three German "pockets" isolated far behind the main front.

Nine German transports, totalling 36,000 tons, and one destroyer were sunk by Soviet aircraft in the port of Pillau and the Gulf of Danzig on Saturday and Sunday, reports the Soviet air communique. One cruiser and one destroyer were damaged.—Reuter.

'NORWAY, DENMARK FREE VERY SOON'

WASHINGTON, Tues.—President Roosevelt said today, "The period of martyrdom of the Danish and Norwegian peoples will be ended very soon."

In a statement on the fifth anniversary of the Germans' attack on the two Scandinavian nations, the President said the peoples of the two nations had never ceased to resist.—APA.

NAZIS MAY LINK UP FOR FINAL BATTLE

LONDON, Tues.—Considerable movement of German convoys north and north-eastwards in the entire area of the central German plain including Hanover, Brunswick, Bremen and Lubeck strengthens the belief that the German High Command is merging its western and eastern armies into one for the last battles of the war.

It is believed that in this last throw of German strategy, Bremen and Hanover and possibly Brunswick and Hamburg will be totally destroyed in the role of hedgehog outposts to hold up the Allied advance by blocking great eastbound autobahns.

The first week of April cost the Wehrmacht 250,000 men killed or captured on the west front.—Reuter.

JAPS DIG IN ON OKINAWA

OKINAWA, Tues.—Marines have gained control of half the Motobu Peninsula in the north of Okinawa, after an advance of about 4,000 yards.

Increasingly heavy artillery held 25th Army Corps to small gains in the south. Gen Buckner's 10th Army has reached a Jap defence line of blockhouses and pillboxes.

Immediately north of the capital, Naha, American troops have been slowed down. What remains of the Jap garrison of 60,000 men is inside a defensive ring

Katera airstrip, one of the first Jap airfields taken on the invasion day, is ready for operation, and the large Yontan airstrip is already in operation.

SECOND ARMY HQ, Tues.— The whole of the 21st Army Group front is today on the move as Field-Marshal Montgomery throws every man, tank and gun into a 100 per cent. offensive.

Thousands of tanks, troop carriers, armoured fighting vehicles and lorries are pushing forward.

In Normandy, at Falaise and at Arnhem, the burden of battle was on two or three divisions, but now every element in the Second British Army is engaged.

5m To Bremen

While our troops tighten their grip on Bremen and Hanover against stiffening opposition, reports from the 3rd Army front indicate that Gen. Patton is packing supplies into a great 50-mile wide Huringian bulge which may lead to a breakthrough "more massive and conclusive than that in Normandy."

Ninth Army troops are within four miles of Hanover and the city is gripped from three sides. The British Seventh Armoured Division, after a rapid thrust to within five miles of the southern outskirts of Bremen, are firmly across the escape corridor for German troops further west.

The "Desert Rats," exploiting the situation, are broadening their front before moving in for the kill.

North Front Breaking

Brunswick, third big German city now threatened by the Allied advance is only 20 miles from powerful units of the 9th Army.

Further south, 3rd Army troops are just over 50 miles from the Czechoslovak border and 170 miles from the Russian forces in the easst.

Kesselring's northern front, from the Hague to Bremen, is being broken up into three isolated segments as British and Canadian troops, closing in on the North Sea and the Zuyder Zee, carry out one of the greatest enveloping movements of the war.

Hundreds of thousands of German troops face the prospect of a last-ditch stand or attempted "Dunkirk" escapes from ports on the North Sea coast.

U-BOATS ACTIVE BUT FEWER KILLS

LONDON, Tues.—In a joint statement. President Roosevelt and Premier Churchill say that during March the U-boat effort continued to increase, but there were fewer successes against shipping than in February.

Casualties inflicted on U-boats were again severe and extensive bombing and minelaying undoubtedly delayed the introduction of the new type.

The capture of Danzig helped to cut off the evil at source.—

WESTERN ITALY EDITION

UNION JACK

LATE SPECIAL

Friday, April 13, 1945 • • • No. 458 Two Lire

DEATH OF PRESIDENT ROOSEVELT

WE deeply regret to announce the death of President Roosevelt, which occurred suddenly yesterday at Warm Springs, Georgia, from cerebral hemorrhage. He was 63.

In accordance with precedent, the Vice-President, Senator Harry Truman, becomes President.

President Roosevelt has died in the first months of his fourth term of office as President of the United States. For some time he had been under constant medical care.

HIS SMILE WAS FAMOUS

An Architect Of Victory

Vice-President Harry Truman, former lawyer and farmer, comes from Missouri. He defeated Senator Henry Wallace in the vice-presidential ballot. He is 61.

Key-note of his election campaign was his message: "As we march forward to certain victory we must make plans for a lasting and just peace . . . To lay a foundation in the post-war world that will secure for all men everywhere basic human rights."

FRANKLIN DELANO ROOSEVELT made American history by being the first President to have three full terms in office, and then to be triumphantly elected for a fourth. And it was those third and fourth terms which established him as not only a great American but a great figure in world history.

He will be for ever remembered as one of the chief architects of Allied victory, and in more ways than one his greatness was the product of adversity—first the infantile paralysis which threatened to end his political career when it was only half begun, and then the tremendous strains of world war, which brought out his highest qualities in his association with the other great war leaders on the Allied side.

Roosevelt was born at Hyde Park, New York State, on January 30, 1882, a descendant of a Dutch family which had been in the States for two centuries or more. He studied law, graduated in 1907, joined the Democratic party, and was elected to the New York State Senate in 1910.

In Woodrow Wilson's first Administration in 1912 he was appointed Assistant Secretary of the Navy, and he came to Europe at the end of the last war on army inspection work and to supervise the demobilisation of the American forces.

Defeated as a candidate for the vice-presidency in 1920, Roosevelt returned to his law practice. In the following year he was stricken with infantile paralysis, as the result of an unlucky swim in an ice-cold sea, and it was years before he could even shuffle along on crutches.

A man of less vigorous spirit would have been broken, but not so Roosevelt. His personality was far more than a charming way with people—valuable though that itself was in later years; he had in fact a temperament which banished all defeatism from the minds of his associates, and erased the very word from his own vocabulary.

Sheer spirit and will-power made him able to continue his political activity.

In 1928 he was elected Governor of New York, and again in 1930. Two years later he attained the Presidency, which he was to hold for more than 12 years.

On assuming office on March 4, 1933, he at once started on the policy of bold social and economic reforms which became known as the New Deal.

It was a policy which aroused great opposition among some powerful sections of American opinion, yet in 1936 Roosevelt was re-elected to the Presidency, and again in 1940—this time with the additional difficulty of creating a precedent in taking office for a third term.

It was said of Roosevelt even as long ago as his second election that "everybody is against Roosevelt—except the electorate." That was certainly true of the great majority of the American Press. But his popularity among the mass of the people was enormous, and his own personal gaiety and resilience were inexhaustible. The famous smile of the photographs was the expression of an attitude to life, and not just a politician's pose.

Domestically, Roosevelt was a crusader for the common man. The President did not believe that one of the wealthiest countries in the world was so spiritually bankrupt that it could afford to support millions of unemployed.

Roosevelt gave new hope and courage to the little man, the under-privileged of the nation which he was to lead so brilliantly through the slough of depression into the bright days of the middle 30's across the abyss of Pearl Harbour and within hailing distance of complete victory over Germany.

He was one of the greatest internationalists as far as relations between the United States and other countries were concerned. His was the policy of the "Good Neighbour" towards the South American countries.

When Roosevelt took office great bodies of American citizens were, at best, natural isolationists, and some centres were definitely hostile to Europe and all its problems.

It was the genius of the President which gradually conveyed to the overwhelming majority of his people that just as peace is indivisible so a war in which European democracy was threatened with extinction was the business of all true and thinking Americans.

Roosevelt made so light of his physical handicap that all but his political enemies were inclined to forget it. One of these once said to his wife: "Don't you find that your husband's disability is inclined to affect his judgement?"

There was a murmur of disapproval from people who had overheard, but Mrs. Roosevelt held up her hand and answered gently:

"Why, yes. I've found that it makes him make more allowances and think more kindly of all the people who have difficulties of their own."

Roosevelt was the product of adversity in more than the physical sense. The economic tornado which struck the world in the early thirties threw up two men into power and ultimate conflict—Roosevelt in the new world and Hitler in the old. And Roosevelt was among the first to see the shadow of Nazism lengthening across the Atlantic's wide waters.

Throughout the years before

(Continued on Page Four.)

President Roosevelt has been present at twelve of the big meetings of the war. He met Mr. Churchill on eight occasions, at sea, in Washington, Casablanca and Quebec; met Mr. Churchill and Marshal Stalin at Teheran and the Crimea; Mr. Churchill and Generalissimo Chiang Kai-shek at Cairo; and Mr. Churchill and President Inonu at Cairo. The picture above was taken at the Teheran meeting in Nov-Dec., 1943.

War Fronts

WEST: Ninth Army tanks are across the Elbe on the last lap for Berlin. Field-Marshal Montgomery has begun the battle for the North Sea ports. (Page Four.)

ITALY: Eighth Army offensive goes well. Santerno river has been crossed in strength. Fifth are 14 miles from Spezia. (Page Four).

RUSSIA: With the Battle for Vienna almost over Marshal Tolbukhin's troops are already pouring west towards Linz and the Bavarian border. (Page Four).

FAR EAST: Super Forts blast Tokio in big daylight raid. 14 Army troops inflict heavy losses on enemy forces retreating East. (Page Three).

PARADE

No. 244   Vol. 19   April 14, 1945

THE LAST RACE IS ON

Page 3

EGYPT P.T. 2   CYRENAICA P.T. 2   CYPRUS 5 C. Pis.   ERITREA 55 Cents   IRAQ 30 Fils   IRAN 3½ Riels   ITALY 10 Lire   LEBANON 30 S. Pis.

EVE OF BATTLE VISIT

On the eve of what may well be the decisive battle of the Italian campaign, the Archbishop of York addressed a large gathering of troops in the front line town of Forli. The service took place in the former sports stadium and, from an improvised pulpit erected on the shell-torn grandstand, Dr Cyril Garbett told Eighth Army men of a message from home—a message full of hope for the future.

It was a quietly impressive service and, even as it progressed, new arrivals steadily filled the big arena. Dust-covered troops came in from the forward areas when they could get away. They came at the dictates of their own thoughts and, with bared heads, listened and sang. A band played for hymns.

Dr Garbett enjoys a reputation as one of Britain's most humanitarian Churchmen; he believes in the personal touch. Not so many years ago, as Bishop of Winchester, he frequently travelled his diocese on foot, relying on a knapsack to supply his personal wants. The Archbishop has given much of his time to visiting the battle fronts. The work of Padres will, he thinks, extend into the future. The man in the street will find it easier to voice his problems to the parish priest, and the clergy will benefit from war-time associations.

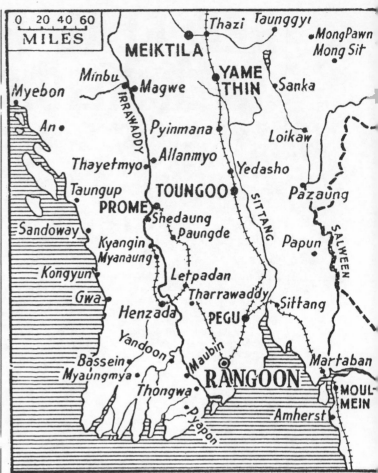

400 POWs RESCUED IN RANGOON DRIVE

KANDY, Tues.—Four hundred British, American and Indian prisoners of war, many prisoners since 1942, have been liberated by 14th Army troops in their drive south of Rangoon. The Japanese, surprised by the speed of our advance, abandoned the prisoners in a village near Pegu 51 miles NE of Rangoon.

In the present campaign since our break through into Central Burma troops of a Corps in 14th Army have killed 16,002 Japanese and have taken 239 prisoners.

Of these totals 6,352 were killed and 144 taken prisoner during the period 1—28 April. The number of guns captured or destroyed was 229.

By smashing Japanese resistance at Payagyi, 10 miles north of Pegu and 46 air miles from Rangoon, 14th Army troops have cut one of the main enemy escape routes to the east over the Sittang river.

Mown Down by Tanks

The attack on Payagyi was preceded by the most spectacular artillery concentration put down since the push south started from Meiktila. More than 90 guns shelled the town for an hour, and then the infantry went in.

Japanese attempting to escape into the open paddy were mown down by tanks waiting for them. Tanks, guns and motorised infantry rushed through the burning town towards Pegu.

Men of the Wests Yorks, Borders and Indian infantry with tank support mopped up Japanese remnants scattered in villages to the east and west of the road.

Pegu, last important town on the way to Rangoon is being cleared. The Japanese made desperate attempts to hold our troops up before Pegu with mines and suicide squads of tank hunters.

General Killed

Tanks of an Indian Cavalry Regiment with Rajput and Gurkha infantry dealt with these delaying forces.

Meanwhile, the spearhead pushed on and road blocks were laid by them further down the road. A Japanese staff car fleeing east ran into one of these blocks. Amongst the bodies was that of a Japanese major-general.

There is increased evidence of a Japanese withdrawal of heavy equipment from Rangoon

WEDNESDAY, 2 MAY, 1945.

Printed by Courtesy of
THE STATESMAN in Calcutta.

RED FLAG FLIES OVER REICHSTAG

LONDON, Tues.—As the Red Flag of Soviet Russia flew from the Reichstag—Germany's Parliament captured in the drive into Berlin—Marshal Stalin in an eve-of-May-Day Order addressed to the fighters and workers of Russia declared "The collapse of Hitlerite Germany is a matter of the nearest future."

And from Hamburg Radio Germany's last powerful transmitter—former Berlin announcer Dr Schapping said "The war will probably last only a few hours more. The end may come tomorrow."

Russians fighting in Berlin captured the Central Post Office building in the heart of the capital. The Germans still offer stiff resistance.

Battalions of women are fighting in the streets in an effort to stem Red Army tanks and infantry and an attempt was made to parachute reserves into the heart of the city, but they either fell wide or were quickly mopped up.

Stalin's May-Day Order revealed that more than 800,000 Germans have been captured and about 1,000,000 killed during the past three or four months.

Still Fighting

Latest Reuter cables show there is still stubborn resistance in some of the fragments of the Reich, particularly at the northern edge round the ports.

But in the south, Munich was captured undefended and American troops could find nobody in authority.

Between the north and south pockets of Germany the gap has widened to over 50 miles

ALLIES INVADE BORNEO

NEW YORK, Tues.—The Tokyo Radio says that Allied forces landed on the east coast of Borneo late last night It states that the landing was made in the Tarakan area and that Allied troops are in "fierce combat" with Japanese forces. The radio adds that an earlier attempted landing at noon was repulsed.

Tarakan is on the east coast of Borneo, facing the Celebes Sea, about 500 miles from the Philippine island of Mindanao.

American troops occupied several small islands between the Philippines and the North Borneo coast after the landing on Mindanao.

Borneo, one of the largest islands in the East Indies, has oil refineries indispensable to the Japanese.

Port Blair Shelled

The Japanese News Agency later said a British force of two aircraft carriers, two battleships, five cruisers and three destroyers, bombarded Car Nicobar.

The agency also said two battleships, two cruisers and four destroyers believed to be part of the same force also shelled Port Blair in the Andaman Islands.

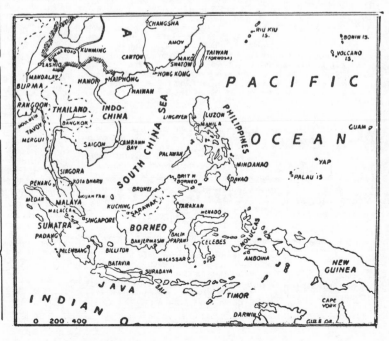

THE LAST HOURS OF MUSSOLINI

MILAN, Tues.—This is the stranger-than-fiction story of Mussolini's last hours, writes Cecil Sprigge, Reuter's correspondent.

Mussolini was at Como, north of Milan, and there he assembled a "phantom" Council of Ministers.

He was the showman to the end and issued dramatic orders by radio to Fascists south of the River Po to proceed at once to Como or Milan.

About 20,000 men rallied to Como by car from all directions augmenting the tens of thousands of other Fascist refugees who mingled with the population of the town and surrounding villages.

Mussolini still had 15,000 armed men at his disposal and the Liberation Committee was informed by the Allies that unless these left the town it would be bombed. The Como Committee, therefore, requested Mussolini to order evacuation.

Forced to Flee

The ex-Duce refused to utter a word to save the town, though Allied planes repeatedly flew over signifying that they meant business.

Mussolini spent two days and nights at Villa Meterno, nearby with his mistress Clara Petacci.

Later Fascist troops retreated against Mussolini's orders so that he was forced to flee.

He was recognised near the village of Dongo, not far from Como, by a commissar of the 52nd Communist Garibaldi Brigade, while seeking to escape.

Mussolini wore a German military greatcoat which he hoped would help him in crossing the Swiss frontier. Members of his "cabinet" were with him.

Red-Tie Partisans

The Partisans decided on summary justice—against the orders of the Liberation Committees in Rome and Milan

After a 10-minute trial at Giuliano di Mezzegra, near Como, Mussolini was sentenced to death.

It was at 16-10 hrs 28 April that a firing squad of 15 men of the Garibaldi Division, commanded by the Communist Col. Moscatelli, ended Mussolini's life.

Mussolini wore a shirt, officer's trousers and jackboots. Accompanied by Petacci, his mistress, he was led to a wall behind the villa.

Far thinner than in his heyday, but erect and unwavering, he walked to the place of execution followed by Petacci. She wore a simple dark brown silk dress. Tears came to her eyes when she saw the "death squad"—the Partisans with red neckties and tommyguns.

She quickly regained her composure. Mussolini turned and smiled to her.

GERMANS YIELD TO MONTY STILL FIGHT RUSSIANS

SHAEF, PARIS, Sat.—Field-Marshal Montgomery reported to Gen Eisenhower last night, that all the German troops in Holland, North-West Germany and Denmark, including Heligoland and the Frisian Islands, had surrendered to the 21st Army Group, effective at 08.00 hrs. today Double British Summer Time.

This battlefield surrender involved the forces facing the 21st Army Group on the Northern and Western flank and from 21st Army Group HQ it is authoritatively learned that the number of men involved in the surrender is well over 1,000,000, of whom 250,000 are naval men.

The "cease fire" order to 21st Army Group forces came into effect this morning and today Montgomery's men were busy enforcing the surrender terms.

Remnants of the German 9th and 12th armies surrendered to the US Ninth Army yesterday. The 11th Panzer Division completed its surrender to the US 90th Infantry Division.

With the surrender of all German forces in Holland, NW Germany and Denmark to FM Montgomery and the surrender of all German forces in Italy and Western Austria to FM Sir Harold Alexander, there is no longer any German army in actual fighting contact with the Western Allies.

Facing East

In theory, German land, sea and air forces in Norway might still carry on the struggle.

There are still isolated pockets in the French ports and in the Aegean.

But the only fighting German armies are now facing east—the force under FM Ferdinand Schoerner in Eastern Saxony, Western Silesia and Northern Czechoslovakia and NE Austria, and remnants of the German Balkan armies in Croatia and parts of Styria and Carinthia adjoining it to the north.

Thus the Germans have put into effect their plan to surrender in the West and fight on as long as possible in the East, whether the Allies like it or not.

Monty Says 'Thanks'

FM Montgomery in a message to Army Commanders of 21st Army Group, today said: "The German Armed Forces facing 21st Army Group have surrendered unconditionally to us

"At this historic moment, I want to express to Army Commanders and Commanders of Lines of Communication my grateful thanks for the way in which they and their men have carried out the immense task that was given them.

"I hope to express myself more adequately later, but I feel I must at once tell you all how well you have done and how proud I am to command 21st Army Group.

"Please tell your commanders and troops that I thank them from the bottom of my heart."—Reuter.

DOENITZ: WHY WE FIGHT RUSSIA

LONDON, Sat.—The German Radio today broadcast an appeal by Admiral Doenitz to soldiers of the army groups in the Centre, South and South East.

He said: "In the North, West and South, single armies have laid down their arms after an honourable struggle.

TRIBUTE, yesterday by FM von Rundstedt, former German Supreme Commander in the West, now a prisoner in Allied hands:—

"Montgomery proved he is Britain's greatest general in Libya, Tunisia, Sicily, Italy and again since D-Day."

INVASION of Britain, Rundstedt said, was planned and wanted, but never really tried. The Germans were too weak at sea to risk it.

2,500,000 LEFT TO FIGHT ON

LONDON, Sat.—Germany's last fighting force in the Central European zone is estimated to consist of some 2,500,000 men in parts of 50 divisions south of Berlin.

The last battles of the war are likely to be fought in Czechoslovakia, now almost completely encircled by Russian and American armies.

Only a 70-mile gap along the southern borders separates the two Allied armies and through it German convoys are streaming into Austria as Gen. Patton's troops are reported within three miles of Linz, in Austria.

The Last Citadel

Dresden, set in the valley of the Elbe 100 miles south of Berlin, is today the sole German city not under the control of the Allied armies, and stands a lonely citadel in the last 4,000 sq miles of the Third Reich that remains for Admiral Doenitz to administer.

Red Army troops are pushing back the Germans in the Magdeburg pocket west of Berlin towards the Allies.

This move heralds an extension of the linkup between the West Allies and Russian from the Baltic to the gates of Dresden.

In the last stages of the NW Europe fighting, 10 German ships were sunk and 61 damaged by the British Second Tactical Airforce in attacks on remnants of German shipping evacuating from the Baltic coast to Denmark and Norway.

BACK IN RANGOON

[Map of Burma/Rangoon area showing locations: Taungup, TOUNGOO, PROME, Pazaung, Shedaung, Sandoway, Kyangin, Paungde, Myanaung, Papun, Nyaunglebin, Kongyun, Letpadan, Shwegyin, Gwa, Tharrawaddy, Henzada, Sittang, Danubyu, PEGU, Bilin, Yandoon, RANGOON, Hlegu, Thaton, Bassein, Thongwa, Martaban, Myaungmya, Maubin, Syriam, Kyauktan, Thongwa, Elephant Pt., MOULMEIN, Dyapon, Amherst, SITTANG, SALWEEN rivers; scale 0 20 40 60 MILES]

LINCOLNS LED 26 DIV RANGOON ASSAULT

KANDY, Sat.—Twenty-Sixth Indian Division of Lt-Gen Sir Philip Christison's 15 Ind Corps, covered by battleships, cruisers and destroyers of the East Indies Fleet, the RIN, carrier-based planes and Eastern Air Command, made the assault landings on both banks of the Rangoon river on May 2, it is revealed today. Leading troops were from the Lincolnshire Regt and the 9 Jats.

Despite torrential rain, 26 Div men made rapid advances across paddy fields knee deep in mud and water and have already entered the city and captured the jail and Government House. South East of Rangoon they occupied Syriam.

An Indian army observer who reported the landings writes:—Apparent confusion reigned as hundreds of craft manoeuvred for position, but rapidly resolved into orderly formation and dawn saw a splendid spectacle of twin assault forces destined for the east banks of the river, complete with guns, tanks and supporting weapons, moving off on flood tide, exactly according to schedule.

Timing was all-important for the plan, which provided for our troops to move up river with a strong six-knot tide in their favour, disembark at H Hour (07-00 hrs) and allow the craft to return to their ships on the ebb tide for the next wave of the assault force.

19 Lancers There

Initial landings met with little opposition.

The first wave included Jats, Frontier Force Rifles and 8 Gurkhas on the west bank, and Lincolns Garhwalis and Punjabis on the east bank of the river. Sherman tanks of 19 Lancers supported the assault.

NAZIS WHIPPED

SHAEF, PARIS, Sat.—The Germans have been thoroughly whipped and any failure to surrender now is due only to their stupidity or stupidity of their leaders, said a proclamation by Gen. Eisenhower, last night.—Reuter.

STORMS OVER BURMA BATTLE

The break in the weather is general over the whole Burma battle areas as the monsoon draws near.

Bad weather added to the difficulty of 15 Ind Corps sea-borne assault on Rangoon and 14th Army troops pushing south from Pegu have had to swim flooded chaungs (besides having to deal with mines and booby traps) to reach Milestone 32½ from Rangoon.

TUESDAY, 8 MAY, 1945.

Printed by Courtesy of

THE STATESMAN in Calcutta.

DOENITZ GIVES 'FULL SURRENDER' ORDER

RHEIMS, Mon.—The Allies today officially announced that Germany had surrendered unconditionally.

The surrender took place at 02-41 hours (French time) today at a little red school house which is Gen Eisenhower's Headquarters. Colonel-General Gustav Jodl, the new German Army Chief of Staff, signed for Germany.

Earlier the German Flensburg radio reported that Admiral Doenitz has ordered unconditional surrender of all German fighting troops.

The radio said: "This is German Radio. We are now broadcasting an address by Reichminister von Schwerin von Krosick to the German people: German men and women— The High Command of the armed forces have today at the order of Grand Admiral Doenitz declared unconditional surrender of all fighting German troops.

"As leading Minister of the Reich Government which the Admiral of the Fleet has appointed for dealing with war tasks, I turn at this graphic moment of history to the German nation. After a heroic fight of about six years of incomparable hardness, Germany has succumbed to the overwhelming odds of her enemies.

"To continue the war would only mean senseless bloodshed and futile disintegration. The Government, which has feeling of responsibility for the future of its nation, was compelled on the collapse of all physical and material forces to demand of the enemy cessation of hostilities."

New York, radio, giving an account of the reported Rheims ceremony, says that Gen Biddell Smith, Gen Eisenhower's chief of staff, signed for the Supreme Allied Command.

Gen Susloperoff signed for Russia and Gen Francois Sevez for France.

The broadcast added that the Germans in Bohemia will continue the fight until they receive free passage out of the country.

There is still nothing official from London, although BBC listeners were told: "The moment for the Prime Minister's broadcast is very near."

'Cease Fire' to U-Boats

The Danish Radio announced this afternoon that German forces in Norway have capitulated. The radio gave no details, but after the announcement it broadcast the Norwegian national anthem.

Earlier, Flensburg Radio reported that Doenitz has ordered all U-boats to cease activity. The cease fire order to U-boat commanders was given in an order of the Day on Saturday, the radio said.

A special radio message from Doenitz ordered crews of all German ships to abstain from any act of war in waters affected by the surrender to FM Montgomery. The crews were forbidden to scuttle ships or to render them unserviceable.

Swedish sources had for the past 24 hours been issuing reports which indicated that the Germans in Norway were about to capitulate.

Norway Huns Ready

The Stockholm newspaper "Dagens Nyheter," reported that Dr. Hans Thomsen, German Minister to Stockholm, who was said to have left for Norway, had signed the capitulation in Oslo.

It is believed that Dr Thomsen immediately forwarded the documents to the Allied legations in Stockholm

The Swedish Radio reported minor German troop movements close to the Swedish frontier.

PRAGUE FIGHTS RADIO BATTLE

LONDON, Mon.—Rival radio stations inside Prague—one controlled by the Germans and the other by the patriots—are giving the world conflicting reports of the battle for the ancient capital of Czechoslovakia.

The German Radio said: "German reinforcements, including all arms, are standing by at the fringe of the city."

Prague "Free" Radio, however, broadcast that "Cease fire" had been ordered.

Reports reaching London last evening said that some German troops continued fighting, others were giving up and being disarmed.

In a broadcast from London the Czech Government warned the Germans that Czech patriots were to be considered as soldiers in accordance with international law.

Gen Patton's forces, racing to the aid of the patriots, are more than 23 miles inside Czech territory.—Reuter.

6,000 U.S. TROOPS WILL BE HOME SOON

HQ, U.S. INDIA-BURMA, Mon. —The first of about 6,000 soldiers to be immediately returned to the US, under the India-Burma Theatre temporary plan initiating War Department re-adjustment regulations, left New Delhi today by plane.

IRRAWADDY JAPS TRAPPED

HQ, S.E.A.C., Mon.—Enemy forces east and west of the Irrawaddy are facing defeat in detail, cut off by twin drives southward, one down the axis of the Irrawaddy and the other down the main Mandalay-Rangoon railway.

Even if they escape our troops near the Irrawaddy and move eastward, these Japs have still to cross the Pegu Yomas, a malarial country with poor communications. Beyond that they enemy would have to get through our men on the railway axis.

North of our bridgehead over the Pegu river, retreating enemy have been having difficulty crossing the river in opposite direction. Some of these forces have been wiped out.

Continued progress is being made by our troops down the Irrawaddy axis beyond Prome, and on both sides of the river.

Today's S.E. Asia Command communique says:

82 (West African) Division Front: Our troops advancing eastwards from Taungup along the Prome road have encountered road blocks ten miles from Taungup.

Fourteenth Army Front: Mopping-up operations in Rangoon continue satisfactorily. Our troops advancing south on Rangoon are being hampered by heavy rain.

MONTY'S MAP FORCED NAZI SURRENDER

LONDON, Sat (delayed).—The German mission which surrendered more than 1,000,000 soldiers to Field Marshal Montgomery tried at first to surrender three German armies withdrawing in front of the Russians, it is revealed.

Montgomery declined "These German armies are fighting the Russians," he said. "Therefore if they surrender to anyone it must be to the forces of the Soviet Union. Go and surrender to the Soviet commanders."

When Montgomery asked, "Are you prepared to surrender German forces on my northern and western flank—those forces between Luebeck and Holland and forces supporting them such as those in Denmark?" the Germans said "No."

Commanders Shocked

Then the British Field Marshal took the offensive. "I wonder," he said, "whether you know the battle situation on the Western Front."

And he produced his operational map. This map was the final straw—one factor which precipitated the surrender of a million Germans. The German commanders were shocked and astounded by the progress of the Allies in the East and West.

After the Germans had consulted further montgomery told them: "You must understand three things. Firstly, you must surrender to me unconditionally all German forces in Holland, Friesland and the Frisian Islands and in Heligoland and all other islands and Schleswig Holstein and in Denmark.

'I'll Fight On'

"Secondly, when you have done that I am prepared to discuss with you the implications of your surrender—how we will dispose of those surrendered troops, how we will occupy the surrendered territory, how we will deal with civilians and so forth.

"And my third point—if you do not agree to point one, the surrender, then I will go on with the war

---

ALLIED POWs WERE PUNISHED AFTER RANGOON RAIDS

FROM REG FOSTER

RANGOON, Sat. (delayed).— The greatest day in their lives came out of the blue for more than 400 British and American prisoners of war in Rangoon prison when they were released by our occupation of the port.

The first man to enter the jail was a little Edinburgh sailor wearing a tin hat and carrying a rifle nearly as big as himself. He and others with him were given a terrific welcome by the men, who were ragged, pale and thin from their imprisonment.

Most of the men have been in this jail for three years—one who had been kept in solitary confinement for more than 18 months was one of the first to be removed to the ship which took the men to hospital.

Men had been compelled to dig gun pits in the broiling sun; they were given the scantiest of food and beaten and flogged for breaches of discipline. After air raids the Japs found extra punishments for RAF prisoners.

WESTERN ITALY EDITION

UNION JACK

SPECIAL EDITION

Thursday, May 3, 1945 • • • No. 478 Two Lire

A Million Of The Enemy Lay Down Arms

FULL SURRENDER OF NAZIS IN ITALY

ALTHOUGH fighting continues in other parts of Europe, the entire enemy forces in Italy have surrendered unconditionally to the Allies under Field-Marshal Alexander. This triumphant end to the campaign was announced last evening.

Hostilities ceased at 14.00 Italian time yesterday, when nearly a million of the enemy laid down their arms in the surrender area, which includes part of Austria,

The Italian campaign, which began with Montgomery's landing at the base of the peninsula in September 1943, has thus resulted in the first mass surrender of a complete German front.

The grand climax came after the great break-through to the Po Valley by the Fifth and Eighth Armies, aided in their sweeping advance by Italian Partisans. In three weeks the German defending forces were torn to pieces. The last act is described in this special communique from AFHQ:

Enemy land, sea and air forces commanded by Col.-Gen. Heinrich von Vietinghoff-Scheel, German C-in-C S W and C-in-C Army Group "C," have surrendered unconditionally to Field-Marshal Sir Harold Alexander, Supreme Allied Commander, Mediterranean Theatre of operations.

The terms of surrender provided for the cessation of hostilities at 12 noon GMT Wednesday, May 2, 1945.

The instrument of surrender was signed on Sunday afternoon, April 29, at AFHQ Caserta, by two German plenipotentiaries and by Lt.-Gen. W. D. Morgan, Chief of Staff, AFHQ.

One German representative signed on behalf of Gen. Von Vietinghoff and the other on behalf of Ober-grupenfuehrer Karl Wolff, Supreme Commander of SS and Police and German General Plenipotentiary of the Wehrmacht in Italy.

After signing the document of unconditional surrender the two German plenipotentiaries returned by secret route to Gen. Von Vietinghoff's HQ in the High Alps to arrange surrender of the German and Italian Fascist land, air and naval forces.

Territory under Gen. -Von Vietinghoff's South - Western Command includes all Northern Italy to the Isonzo River in the north-east, and the Austrian provinces of Vorarlberg, Tyrol, Salzburg and portions of Carinthia and Styria.

The enemy's total forces, including combat and rear echelon troops surrendered to the Allies, are estimated to number nearly 1,000,000 men. The fighting troops include the remnants of

22 German and six Italian Fascist Divisions.

The instrument of surrender consists of six short paragraphs. Three appendices giving details appertaining to land, sea and air forces were attached to the instrument. The following terms are imposed:

1. Unconditional surrender by the German C.-in-C. South-West of all forces under his command or control on land, on sea, or in the air, to the Supreme Allied Commander Mediterranean Theatre of Operations.

2. Cessation of all hostilities on land, on sea or in the air by enemy forces at 1200 hrs. GMT, May 2, 1945.

3. The immediate immobilisation and disarmament of enemy ground, sea and air forces.

4. Obligation on the part of the German C.-in-C. South-West to carry out any further orders issued by the Supreme Allied Commander Mediterranean Theatre.

5. Disobedience of orders or failure to comply with them to be dealt with in accordance with the accepted laws and usages of war.

The instrument of surrender stipulates that it is independent of, without prejudice to, and will be superseded by any general instrument of surrender imposed by or on behalf of the United Nations and applicable to Germany and the German Armed Forces as a whole.

The instrument of surrender and appendices were written in English and German. The English version is the authentic text. The decision of the Supreme Allied Commander Mediterranean Theatre will be final if any doubt or dispute arises as to the meaning or interpretation of the surrender terms.

The signing took place in

(Continued on Page Four)

Special Orders Of The Day

Special Orders of the Day were issued by the Allied commanders in Italy to mark the surrender.

From Field-Marshal Sir Harold ALEXANDER, Supreme Allied Commander, Mediterranean Theatre:

SOLDIERS, sailors and airmen of the Allied Forces in the Mediterranean Theatre :

After nearly two years of hard and arduous fighting, which started in Sicily in the summer of 1943, you stand today as the victors of the Italian campaign

You have won a victory which has ended in the complete and utter rout of the German armed forces in the Mediterranean. By clearing Italy of the last Nazi aggressor you have liberated a country of over 40,000,000 people. Today the remnants of a once proud army have laid down their arms to you—close on a million men, with all their arms, equipment and impediments.

You may well be proud of this great and victorious campaign which will long live in history as one of the greatest and most successful ever waged. No praise is too high for you soldiers, sailors, airmen and workers of the United Forces in Italy for your magnificent triumph.

My gratitude to you and my admiration is unbounded, and only equalled by the pride which is mine in being your Commande -in-Chief.

From Gen. Joseph T. McNARNEY, Deputy Supreme Allied Commander, Mediterranean Theatre:

THE enemy in Italy has surrendered unconditionally.

Your magnificent victories in the spring offensive left him only two alternatives, to surrender or to die.

This hour is the glorious climax to one of the greatest triumphs in the long, hard-fought war in Africa and in Europe. Your triumph will live always in the hearts and minds of our people. The attack against the enemy's so-called inner fortress began in the Mediterranean. You have come from Alamein and from Casablanca to the Alps. After the successes in North Africa you smashed the enemy in Tunisia. You drove him from Sicily. You invaded Italy, and despite ferocious resistance and incredibly difficult terrain and weather you drove him back, always back. You have destroyed the best troops he possessed. At this moment of surrender he is against the Alps, helpless under your blows to defend himself.

The victory is yours—you of the ground, sea and air forces of many nationalities who have fought hard as a single combat team The surrender today is to you.

Now, with final and complete victory in sight, let us go forward until the last foe. Japan, is crushed. Then, and not till then, will freedom-loving men and women be able to enjoy lasting peace

From Gen. Mark W. CLARK, Commanding General, 15 Army Group:

TO the soldiers of the 15 Army Group : With a full and grateful heart I hail and congratulate you in this hour of complete victory over the German enemy and join with you in thanks to Almighty God.

Yours has been a long hard fight—the longest in the war of any Allied troops fighting on the continent of Europe. You men of the Fifth and Eighth Armies have brought that fight to a successful conclusion by your recent brilliant offensive operations,

(Continued on Page Three)

FALL OF BERLIN

Great news also came from Germany itself last night. Marshal Stalin announced the capture of Berlin and vast numbers of prisoners in a complete rout of the garrison. (See Page 4.)

SEAC

THE SERVICES NEWSPAPER OF SOUTH EAST ASIA COMMAND

No. 481   One Anna.

FRIDAY, 4 MAY, 1945.

Printed by Courtesy of
THE STATESMAN in Calcutta.

BERLIN FALLS: HITLER COMMITTED SUICIDE

FLASH FLASH FLASH FLASH

\\ MOSCOW 2/5:--- BERLIN IS COMPLETELY /
CAPTURED, MARSHAL STALIN ANNOUNCED.
REUTER 3/5 BBS/SUSIL 2-54 AM

How the tape machine recorded the end in Berlin

MOSCOW, Thurs.—The fall of Berlin, capture of more than 70,000 prisoners and the news that Hitler and Goebbels committed suicide in Berlin are announced in an Order of the Day issued by Marshal Stalin yesterday.

The Order addressed to troops of the Red Army and the Red Navy said : "Troops of the First White Russian Front, commanded by Marshal Zhukov, in co-operation with troops of the First Ukrainian Front, commanded by Marshal Koniev, today, after stubborn street battle, completed the route of the Berlin garrison and captured the city of Berlin.

"The garrison of Berlin defending the city, headed by the Officer in Command of the Defence of Berlin and General of the Artillery Webling and his staff, today at 15.00 hours ceased resistance and laid down their arms and surrendered.

"On 2 May, by 21.00 hours, our troops in Berlin took more than 70,000 prisoners."

The Order adds that Red Army troops completed the destruction of the German grouping, surrounded SE of Berlin and between 24 April and 2 May killed 60,000 Germans and took more than 120,000 prisoners.

Goebbels Dead, Too

The Soviet communique last night says prisoners captured included Goebbels's propaganda deputy Hans Fritsche.

Fritsche declared that Hitler, Goebbels and the newly-appointed Chief of General Staff, Gen. Krebs committed suicide.

A message from SHAEF, Paris says Gen. Eisenhower yesterday authorised a statement saying that the report of Hitler's death at his post "is in direct contradiction with the facts given by Himmler and Gen. Schillenburg."

Eisenhower's statement says Count Bernadotte met Himmler and Gen Schillenburg at Lubeck at 0100 hours on 24 April.

"At this meeting Himmler admitted that Germany was finished. He told Count Bernadotte that Hitler was so ill that he might be already dead."

CIVVIES FREED

LONDON, Fri.—Many Dominion civilians have been liberated from four civil internment camps overrun in Allied advances in the West the Foreign Office reports.

PEACE COUNT DENIES ALL

LONDON, Wed.—In Stockholm yesterday Count Bernadotte so-called German "surrender envoy" stated at a press conference "I have not seen Himmler during my last visit to Germany and Denmark. I have not forwarded any message from Himmler or other authoritative German to the Allies."

Prime Minister Churchill told the House of Commons yesterday that he will broadcast the news of victory on the Western Front, and will inform the House. The King will broadcast to the world in the evening of V-Day.

(See Back Page.)

RAF DROP WATER TO PARATROOPS

HQ, EASTERN AIR COMMAND, Fri.—RAF supply-dropping aircraft of EAC's 850 Combat Cargo Task Force flew 850 miles to Rangoon and back today through pre-monsoon storms to parachute tons of water and ammunition to Paratroops on the banks of the Rangoon River.

This was the longest operation ever undertaken by RAF transports in this theatre and lasted seven hours.

"British here." This was the welcome sign, worked out in huge letters on roof top spotted by the crew of a RAF heavy bomber flying over Rangoon yesterday to drop medical supplies and food to Allied POWs in Rangoon Central Jail.

OUR MEN ENTER RANGOON

KANDY, Thurs.—Troops of the Allied Land Forces entered Rangoon this morning says a special SE Asia Command communiqué.

An APA message says that Allied prisoners released from internment camps on the way to Rangoon say that the Japanese began evacuating Rangoon three weeks ago, by sea and land.

Airmen flying low over the city saw a sign on one Burma building saying: "Japs gone." The sign was framed out of strips of cloth.

Other airmen report seeing about 1,000 men whom they believed to be Allied prisoners, They were in a camp on the west bank of the river opposite Rangoon. They were dressed in khaki-coloured clothes and waved white flags with red strips.

No AA Fire

The past two days have indicated that only pockets of fighting Japanese are left. Airmen have reported no A-A fire over Rangoon for several days.

There is little news yet of the operations at the mouth of the Rangoon estuary, where paratroopers and amphibious forces were landed. Airmen say the gun positions on both banks of the estuary appear largely deserted.

A Press Note says that rocket and cannon-firing Hurr.-strafers of Eastern Air Command are taking a big toll of Japanese transport and materials as the enemy tries to remove accumulated stocks from Rangoon.

Pegu Captured

Never in 221 Group's support of the 14th Army in its drive on Rangoon, has enemy transport been seen in such quantity, but the swift advance had compelled the Japanese to move vehicles and supplies by daylight. Without air cover, and in country ideal for low-level strafing, the enemy has had to rely for protection on small-arms fire, which has done little to interfere with low-level dawn-to-dusk attacks.

An earlier communique reported the capture of Pegu and the entry of 14th Army troops into Prome, 178 road miles NNW of Rangoon. They have advanced to the railway station. Pyawbwe, to the west of the Irrawaddy, 19 miles SW of Minbu, has also been captured.

Following the capture of Pegu, and the repair of one of the bridges across the Pegu River, our armour has been pouring across it on the road towards Rangoon.

In the operations to mop up Pegu, 283 Japs were killed. Only the clearing of small parties to the west of Pegu River remains.

50 Cars in Booty

Between Pegu and Rangoon there is no natural obstacle or obvious defence line for the Japs, although efforts had been made to hamper our advance by mining the road and blowing bridges.

Ten miles to the north of Pegu, 100 tons of MT stores, and 150 vehicles, including 50 saloon cars have been taken.

Enemy artillery and mortars have been active near Toungoo, 124 miles north of Pegu.

NAZIS REPORT HITLER DEAD

LONDON, Wed.—The German Radio reported that Hitler died yesterday afternoon, and that the former C-in-C of the German Navy Admiral Doenitz, is his successor.

Admiral Doenitz, speaking over the radio later, said: "German men and women, soldiers of the German Wehrmacht: our Fuehrer, Adolf Hitler, has fallen.

"German people, bow in deepest mourning and veneration.

"Adolf Hitler recognised beforehand the terrible danger of Bolshevism and devoted his life to fighting it. At the end of this his battle, and of his unswerving straight path of life, stands his death as a hero in the capital of the Reich.

Supreme Command

"The Fuehrer has appointed me as his successor as Head of the State and Supreme Commander of the Wehrmacht.

"I am assuming supreme command of all branches of all services of the German Armed Forces

"Against the British and the Americans I shall have to pursue the fight so far and so long as they hamper my struggle against the Bolsheviks."

The announcement of Hitler's death was preceded by the playing of solemn Wagnerian music, including "The Twilight of the Gods."

U-Boat Boss

Doenitz is 53, and was born of a family of landowners and ship-owners in Mecklenburg, on the Baltic.

Grand Admiral Karl Doenitz was the organiser and inspiration of the U-boat attacks on Allied shipping during this war, for which he began to prepare many years in advance.

Doenitz was inspired by a hatred for Britain and a conviction that in any battle he could beat British sailors. He was determined to be revenged for 1917 when he was taken prisoner by a British sloop after it had sunk his U-boat in the Mediterranean.

He was then kept in a Manchester lunatic asylum as out of his mind, but was one of the first German war prisoners to be repatriated.—Reuter.

YANKS LIBERATE 110,000 POWs

3rd US ARMY HQ, Wed.—The US 14th Armoured Div. has liberated 110,000 British, Dominion and American POWs at Moosburg.

At Wievertinke, 8,000 Allied prisoners were liberated by British troops.

8,000 LANDED OFF BORNEO—Japs

LONDON, Wed.—The Japanese News Agency today reports that the Allied force which they say landed yesterday on Tarakan Island, off the east coast of Borneo, is engaged in heavy fighting to expand its bridgehead.

"About 8,000 troops, equipped with seven tanks, effected the landing under cover of naval bombardment, and supported by three cruisers and 13 destroyers, which have repeatedly shelled the island since last Friday," the agency added.—Reuter.

DOLE SURPLUS MAY AID EMIGRANTS

LONDON, Wed.—Britain has untouched the "nest egg" of £295,000,000 in the Unemployment Insurance Fund, and it is still accumulating.

In schoolhouse at Rheims, headquarters of Gen. Eisenhower, Supreme Commander-in-Chief Allied Expeditionary Force, early on morning of May 7, Germans prepare to sign unconditional surrender. In centre is Col-Gen. Jodl, on left Maj-Gen. Oxenius, and on right General Admiral von Friedeburg.

SURRENDER AT RHEIMS

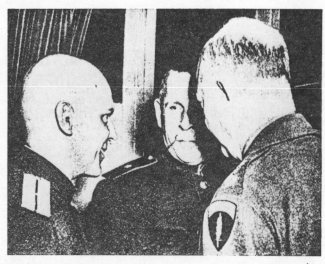

General Dwight D. Eisenhower makes his V.E.-Day speech after the surrender. On his left is his deputy, Air Chief Marshal Sir Arthur Tedder.

Russian Gen. Ivan A. Suslapatov, centre, and Gen. Eisenhower converse through an interpreter after surrender which ended Hitler's Third Reich.

PARADE

No. 248   Vol. 20   May 12, 1945

SURRENDER SIGNED

EGYPT P.T. 2   CYRENAICA P.T. 2   CYPRUS 5 C. Pis.   ERITREA 55 Cents   IRAQ 30 Fils   IRAN 3½ Rials   ITALY 10 Lire   LEBANON 30

MALTA 6d   PALESTINE 25 Mils   SICILY 10 Lire   SUDAN 20 Mills   SYRIA 30 5 Pis   TRANSJORDAN 25 Mil   TRIPOLITANIA

1945

PARADE

EUROPEAN VICTORY NUMBER

PT 3
PM/LS 35
PLS 40

THE VICTORY OF THE COMMON MAN

"...London and our big cities have had to stand their pounding.
They remind me of the British squares at Waterloo.
They are not squares of soldiers, they do not wear scarlet coats:
they are just ordinary English, Scottish and Welsh folk,
men, women and children standing steadfastly together.
But their spirit is the same, their glory is the same,
and in the end their victory will be greater than famous Waterloo."

Winston Churchill, *1941*

Churchill on Victory in Europe

General Dwight (Ike) Eisenhower, who has led the Western Allies to victory. He was Supreme Commander in North Africa and afterwards held the Supreme Command in Western Europe.

The war in Europe officially ended at one minute past midnight this morning. Announcing this in his broadcast to the British peoples last night, Prime Minister Churchill said that any Germans who continued to resist after this time would deprive themselves of the protection of the laws of war and would be attacked from all sides by the Allies.

Both Mr Churchill and the King, who broadcast later, warned the people that they still had to deal with the Japanese. "We will do so with the utmost resolve and with all our resources," said the King

Mr Churchill, in his broadcast, said:

Yesterday at 2-31 a.m. at Gen Eisenhower's HQ, Gen Jodl, representative of the German High Command, and of Grand Admiral Doenitz, the designated head of the German State, signed an act of unconditional surrender on behalf of the German land, sea and air forces in Europe to the Allied Expeditionary Forces, and simultaneously to the Soviet High Command.

Gen Biddell Smith, Chief of Staff of the US Army, and Gen Francois Sevez signed the document on behalf of the Supreme Commander of the Allied Expeditionary Forces, and Gen Susloperov signed on behalf of the Russian Command.

Cease Fire Sounds

Today this agreement will be ratified and confirmed at Berlin, where Air Chief Marshal Tedder, Deputy Supreme Commander of the Allied Expeditionary Forces, and Gen Tassigny will sign on behalf of Gen Eisenhower. Gen Zhukov will sign on behalf of the Soviet High Command.

The German representatives will be Field Marshal Keitel, Chief of High Command, and Commanders-in-Chief of the German Army, Navy and Air Forces.

Hostilities will end officially at one minute after midnight tonight, Tuesday, 8 May, but, in the interests of saving lives, the "Cease Fire" began yesterday to be sounded all along the fronts, and our dear Channel Islands are also to be freed today.

The Germans are still in places resisting Russian troops, but should they continue to do so after midnight they will, of course, deprive themselves of the protection of the laws of war and will be attacked from all quarters by the Allied troops.

Enemy Disorder

It is not surprising, with such long fronts, and in the existing disorder of the enemy, that the commands of the German High Command should not in every case be obeyed immediately. This does not in our opinion, with the best military advice at our disposal, constitute any reason for withholding from the nations the facts communicated by Gen Eisenhower of the unconditional surrender already signed at Rheims, nor should it prevent us from celebrating today and tomorrow (Wednesday) at Victory in Europe Days.

The German war is at an end. After years of intense preparation Germany hurled herself on Poland at the beginning of Sept 1939, and in pursuance of our guarantee to Poland, and in common with the French Republic, Great Britain and the Empire declared war upon this foul aggression.

Japs Unsubdued

After gallant France had been struck down, we from this island and from our united Empire maintained the struggle single-handed for a whole year until we were joined by the military might of Soviet Russia and later by the overwhelming power and resources of the United States.

PICCADILLY CROWDS GO WILD WITH JOY

LONDON, Tues.—The European War was over for London last night. Though spirits had been momentarily damped by the announcement that Prime Minister Churchill would not speak until today, London made up her mind that last night was the night and at nine o'clock in Piccadilly Circus scenes were fantastic.

It seemed as though there were tens of thousands of people—civilians and servicefolk. It was the Coronation, the Jubilee, the liberation of Rome, Brussels and Paris all rolled into one.

Soon after 9 o'clock, traffic in Piccadilly came to a standstill when a sailor climbed aboard the bonnet of a bus to the tumult of wild cheering and clambered up still higher.

With the bus still moving inch by inch the sailor, with arms upraised, stood on the roof of the bus and yelled to a crowd almost hysterical with joy.

Within a few minutes the bonnet was alive with moving servicemen all trying to clamber to the roof.

A mass of people jammed the streets between Piccadilly Circus and Leicester Square.

The hundreds of specially-drafted police trying to control the jam were helpless.

Servicemen Rejoice

British Servicemen and tens of thousands of civilians took complete control. Sailors climbed to the tops of Piccadilly's tall lampposts, cheering wildly, trying to head the throng in victory songs. Military policemen were the butt of all sorts of good natured chaff. Servicemen took liberties that would have put them in the guard room in ordinary days.

All over the world the report of the German surrender was celebrated today.

This is an account, city by city, of how the news was received, as told in Reuter cables.—

STOCKHOLM: Streams of confetti floated through the sunny air of Drottningaten, Stockholm's main shopping thoroughfare, as typists tore up paper and threw it through windows with cries of joy.

Swedish, Danish and Norwegian flags with a sprinkling of British, American and Russian were hoisted everywhere.

Danish and Norwegian refugees rushed through streets with rosettes of national colours in their buttonholes shouting "the war is over."

Liners and tugs in Hudson River sounded their sirens and planes roared overhead to add to ceaseless honking of motor horns and yelling of crowds.

SAN FRANCISCO: The conference city celebrated, but it was officially stated the work of the Conference would go on uninterrupted.

PARIS: Crowds cheered wildly outside the big newspaper office in Paris as loudspeakers announced the capitulation.

Evening papers gave the surrender news in six-inch headlines.

Paris'ans are waiting for the signal from sirens and bells before letting themselves go.

ROME: Sirens sounded in the city while church bells, including those of St Peter's, rang merrily. British and American troops have started to "make whooppee."

FOURTEENTH ARMY: Forward formations of the 14th Army heard the news phlegmatically. The troops knew their own release would be hastened by the victory, but they are anxious to "keep cracking" against the Japs.

NIEMOELLER, BLUM FREED FROM NAZIS

ALLIED HQ, MEDITERRANEAN, Tues.—The former French Prime Minister Leon Blum, opponent of the Nazis, Pastor Niemoeller, and the former German C-in-C in Belgium and Northern France, Gen. Falkenhausen, who was reported to have fallen into disgrace, were among the prisoners freed from a German prison camp near Obiacco.

Others freed were Kurt von Schuschnigg, former Austrian Chancellor, and his wife, Nicholas de Kallay the former Hungarian Prime Minister and Madame Blum.—Reuter.

10,000,000 IN BIGGEST SURRENDER

LONDON, Tues.—News that Germany had capitulated absolutely and unconditionally to the Allies was expected yesterday, but it was not until five hours after the first German broadcast that Germany had capitulated, that the British Ministry of Information announced that Prime Minister Churchill would broadcast today, and that today would be treated as "Victory in Europe Day."

Reason for the delay was that the official statement announcing the end of the war in Europe had to be co-ordinated with a statement from Washington and Moscow.

First news of the German surrender was given by Count Schwerin von Krosigk, Foreign Minister appointed by Admiral Doenitz.

'Blow' To Norway Huns

The Oslo Radio last night broadcast an Order of the Day from Gen Boehme, German C-in-C in Norway, stating "Soldiers in Norway, Count von Krosigk has announced unconditional surrender of all the Forces.

"I know that this message is a hard blow to us. And yet we, too, shall have to bow to the dictates of our enemy for the benefit of the whole of the German cause."

Declaring that German forces in Norway stood undefeated, Gen Boehme called on them to bear themselves "in an exemplary manner which even the grimmest enemy cannot but in all fairness appreciate."

The Allied controlled Netherlands Radio reported last night that British troops entered the Dutch city of Utrecht and arrested the chief Dutch Nazi Anton Mussert, so-called "Fuehrer of Holland."

Prague Accepts

Prague Radio this morning stated: "Germans in Prague and the whole of Bohemia have accepted the terms of the unconditional surrender."

Lt-Gen Majewlski, General Commanding the German Garrison of Pilsen, committed suicide after surrendering with his staff to American forces which entered the city yesterday.

"The Six Years' War" in Europe has ended with the greatest surrender in history, cables Reuter's Military correspondent.

It is estimated that about 10,000,000 Germans will now become prisoners. The Western Allies will hold more than they have troops in the field.

HAW HAW: I AM A GERMAN

LONDON, Tues.—When the Crown case against William Joyce (Lord Haw-Haw), who is charged with high treason, was opened at Bow-street yesterday it was stated that Joyce claimed that he had adopted German nationality in 1940.

The charge against Joyce is that "being a person owing allegiance to His Majesty the King, he adhered to the King's enemies."

Joyce was formally remanded until Thursday, when he will be committed for trial to the July sessions at the Central Criminal Court.

Impressed by Hitler

A long statement alleged to have been made by Joyce after he was captured in Germany was read. It contained the following passages: "I was greatly impressed by the constructive work which Hitler had done for Germany. I thought that in Britain there must come a reform on the lines of National Socialism, but I did not consider that every aspect of National Socialism would be acceptable to the British people.

"I thought that war between Britain and Germany would be a tragedy which the British Empire would not survive."

The Iron Cross

Among the documents read in court was one announcing the award of the Iron Cross to Joyce by Hitler, and another saying that he was a member of the German Volksturm.

Evidence heard included that of a police inspector who said that he had recognised Joyce's voice on the German Radio.

'HITLER ALIVE IN ARGENTINE'

Karl Germer, anti-Nazi editor of Das Volk, official organ of the German Social-Democrat Party, says Hitler is not dead but escaped to the Argentine in a special U-boat.

"Arrangements for Hitler's getaway to the Argentine were made by Ernst Wilhelm Bohle, chief of the Nazi 'Germans Abroad' organisation. Our spy service received the information that the U-boat was ready to take him away if things went wrong," Germer told Globe.

"Bohle himself went to the Argentine to choose Hitler's hide-out. I don't think for a minute Hitler is dead."

JAP HOMELAND POUNDED AGAIN

WASHINGTON, Tues.—A very great force of Superfortresses—the term usually means 450 or more—struck early today against multiple important military and industrial targets in the areas of Nagoya, Osaka, Akashi and Gifu on the Japanese mainland.

All the targets are on Honshu, main island of the Japanese homeland, and each is a site of industries vital to her war effort; about 375 miles South of Mindanao.

The Japanese garrison was resisting fiercely.

The same agency announced that the Japanese "Home Guard" have orders never to surrender alive. "The people's volunteer corps should not leave their duty, however intense the fighting. They should not be taken prisoner alive or die a dishonourable death," the orders say.

POWs FLY TO UK

LONDON, Mon.—RAF Lancasters yesterday brought back to England more than 1,800 freed POWs. Their nationalities were not disclosed.—Reuter.

Six-year-old Angela and grandfather make sign of Bobby Bear Club. Angela was member.

Evacuee In Hollywood

Grand-daughter of George Lansbury—Bow's "Uncle George"—Angela Lansbury went to America in 1940 as an evacuee, but she may be a Hollywood film star before long. Angela, who was born a couple of years before her grandfather took office as Minister of Works, was an ordinary London schoolgirl when she left England. Today she has a contract with M.G.M. and is considered one of the most interesting young actresses in Hollywood. Already she has had important parts in four films—Gaslight, the Grand National story, National Velvet, Oscar Wilde's The Portrait of Dorian Grey and a Technicolour musical, The Harvey Girls. Much of her talent is no doubt inherited from her actress mother, Moya MacGill.

Among the first R.A.F. to leave the Service is this officer who selects a civilian hat from rows of different colours and styles.

In their tent, soldiers who decided to vote direct by post instead of by proxy study candidates' addresses which they have received with ballot papers.

This is the first opportunity many Service men and women have ever had to vote and N.A.A.F.I. girls discuss how they can use votes to best advantage.

POLLING BY THE PYRAMIDS

For the first time in history voting in a British General Election took place in the Egyptian deserts as well as in the towns and villages at home

Above, before he makes up his mind how he will vote, this corporal reads several newspapers from home giving the different party views. Below left, at the Royal Artillery Base Depot, near Cairo, as at other Middle East bases, tents serve as polling booths and (below right) gunners queue up to vote.

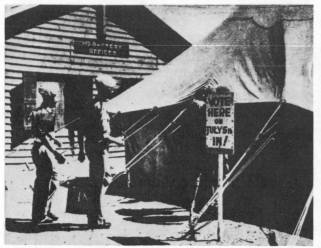

LONDON VOTES

Millions of British people went to the polls on July 5 to vote in the General Election. "Parade" photographer MARY MOLLO saw Londoners go to churches, schools and offices which became polling stations for the day

A few people, like this woman, were lucky enough to find taxis to take them to polling stations to record votes.

City of Westminster's mobile canteen, staffed by W.V.S. provides tea and cakes for the polling officials.

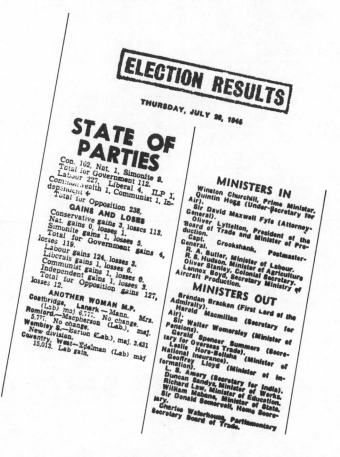

Woman failed to put ballot paper in the box and is followed out by an official who says she may not take it away

ELECTION RESULTS

THURSDAY, JULY 26, 1945

STATE OF PARTIES

Con. 102, Nat. 1, Simonite 8.
Total for Government 112.
Labour 227, Liberal 4, ILP 1,
Commonwealth 1, Communist 1, Independent 4.
Total for Opposition 238.

GAINS AND LOSES

Conservative gains 3, losses 113.
Nat. gains 0, losses 1.
Simonite gains 1, losses 5.
Total for Government gains 4, losses 119.
Labour gains 124, losses 3.
Liberals gains 1, losses 6.
Communist gains 1, losses 0.
Independent gains 1, losses 3.
Total for Opposition gains 127, losses 12.

ANOTHER WOMAN M.P.

Coatbridge, Lanark — Mann, Mrs. (Lab.) maj 6,777. No change.
Romford—Macpherson (Lab.), maj. 5,777. No change.
Wembley S.—Barton (Lab.), maj. 3,431. New division.
Coventry, West—Edelman (Lab) maj 15,013. Lab gain.

MINISTERS IN

Winston Churchill, Prime Minister.
Quintin Hogg (Under-Secretary for Air).
Sir David Maxwell Fyfe (Attorney-General).
Oliver Lyttelton, President of the Board of Trade and Minister of Production.
Capt. Crookshank, Postmaster-General.
R. A. Butler, Minister of Labour.
R. S. Hudson, Minister of Agriculture
Oliver Stanley, Colonial Secretary.
Lennox Boyd, Secretary Ministry of Aircraft Production.

MINISTERS OUT

Brendan Bracken (First Lord of the Admiralty).
Harold Macmillan (Secretary for Air).
Sir Walter Womersley (Minister of Pensions).
Gerald Spencer Summers (Secretary for Overseas Trade).
Leslie Hore-Belisha (Minister of National Insurance).
Geoffrey Lloyd (Minister of Information)
L. S. Amery (Secretary for India).
Duncan Sandys, Minister of Works.
Richard Law, Minister of Education.
William Mabane, Minister of State.
Sir Donald Somervell, Home Secretary.
Charles Waterhouse, Parliamentary Secretary Board of Trade.

WE MADE THE FIRST FLY BOMB

UNTIL existence of the 'Larynx' pilotless aircraft was made known recently, it was generally supposed that the Germans were the originators of the flying bomb. The British version, however, was perfected nearly twenty years ago.

Air Staff requirements for a mechanically-controlled, pilotless aircraft were formulated in 1925, and experimental work on the project was initiated at once.

A committee, set up in 1927 to direct further work on the subject, defined the object of research as: A mechanically-controlled aeroplane which would fly on a pre-arranged course for a pre-arranged time and distance, and then either release its bombs or dive to earth and explode.

250lb Bomb Load

The minimum requirements, as laid down by the Chief of Air Staff, were: Bomb load, 100 lb.; range, 200 miles; level speed, 180 m.p.h. It must be a weapon which would not be destroyed by enemy fighters or A.A. fire, and would have an adequate explosive effect.

The design of the original weapon, known by the code name 'Larynx,' was based on these requirements, and the performance of the 'Larynx' actually produced was as follows: Maximum air speed, 200 m.p.h.; bomb load, 250 lb.; range, 200 miles.

It was designed to be mass-produced at a cost of £200.

Work Suspended

As a result of many tests, investigations were continued to produce similar weapons with improved performance, but in 1935 the Committee for the Scientific Study of Air Defence pointed out that the weapon might be so much more effective against London than against corresponding areas of possible enemy country, and that the wisdom of developing its use in the absence of information that such possible enemies were using it required serious consideration.

By 1936 technical developments had so modified the relationships between piloted bomber aircraft and pilotless aircraft of the 'Larynx' type that the latter no longer offered the same advantages as an offensive weapon, and the Air Staff therefore recommended that development work on the 'Larynx' should be suspended.—*London Calling.*

EXILE.

Seek not in mine eyes; seek not
   in my face—
For what if in my heart remains
   unseen.
Of my scattered thoughts and
   cares—not a trace,
Nor yet a gesture, showing what
   I mean—
Thoughts that are crystal clear
   and thoughts obscene
That turn, and toil and then
   themselves efface,
Panorama of an ever changing
   scene,
Fleeting steeds of a never ending
   race;
The future, present and all that
   has been.
In vain seek those things to
   which I aspire;
In vain seek to know that which
   I desire.
It is on my thoughts for comfort I lean.
When relief from anguish is dire,
Though ever my soul roasts on a
   martyr's pyre.
               Anglo

Dark-haired, dimpled actress Winifred Shotter, of Aldwych farce and West End fame, has just arrived in Calcutta. She will star in the ENSA production of " Normandy Story " which is to tour India and S.E.A.C.

Eee By Goom, Gracie's Coming Here

GRACIE Fields is coming to sing to South East Asia Command. The news comes from ENSA's Calcutta HQ. "We have just received a cable from Gracie in Australia," they say. "She sends her love to the boys in India and S.E.A.C. and hopes to be with them soon."

Gracie will arrive sometime towards the end of September from Australia where she is entertaining Aussie troops. Her husband, Monty Banks, is travelling with her.

'Gaslight' Coming

At the beginning of the war Gracie came in for a good deal of adverse criticism. Many accused her of "not doing her bit." Since then she has toured the UK, North Africa and Sicily.

Fate joined forces with ENSA to re-open the Calcutta Garrison Theatre a week early.

The GI Theatre Guild had a production ready but no theatre. ENSA had a re-decorated theatre but no suitable show. So the US Army Special Service stepped in: "We can give you a show if you can lend us theatre, props and setting."

For a fortnight, eleven GI's and two American Red Cross girls are playing John Cecil Holms' and George Abbott's "Three Men on A Horse" to enthusiastic Allied audiences.

Says show director, S/Sgt. Daniel Chugerman, who used to direct Hollywood pictures: "Thanks to ENSA we have at last been able to put the show on. It's been difficult getting the GI cast detached for the job but now we are hoping that your ENSA will be able to fix our Burma tour."

Pfc Dan Tobin was worried that his American articulation might not "register" with British audiences. But it was just that forthright machine-gun speech which linked the audience with an actor they had seen in the American film "Woman of the Year." That was Pfc Dan Tobin, too. He played the West End with the late Dame Marie Tempest in "Mary Goes to Sea."

An empty theatre and a waiting audience threw the GIs and ENSA together. Judging from the British reception S.E.A.C. men could do with more shows like this.

Leave men who will be in Calcutta for the week beginning 13 Aug. are booking for ENSA's production of the Victorian thriller.

SHOW NOTES
By
ED. BISHOP

"Gaslight." Managing the show, D. J. Marsh, pre-war manager at the Savile, tells me his chief worry is the movement of props. "Until recently" he said "I was in charge of salvage and repair at Vickers Weybridge factory. Now I'm in charge of a silver tea set, Victorian whiskers, high cravats and all the junk that goes to make a Victorian atmosphere." Taking bustles to Burma,' he says, is no joke.

Acclimatizing themselves after a speedy air lift from UK, stage and screen stars Winifred Shotter and Lawrence O'Madden, who have arrived in Calcutta (SEAC 30 July) hope that ENSA will send them as far forward as transport and operational considerations permit.

The fashionable clubs, once used as a dance hall by the Japanese. Lighting expert LAC Fred Needham, of 207 Glodwick-road, Oldham, who installed colour systems and spots, has 60 stage lights to control—all provided with the latest stage equipment by RAF Welfare.

Travelling Light

More RAF entertainment news comes from F/Lt. Leon Cassel-Gerard who has converted the hill depot at Shillong into a "show" camp. His revue "In the Springtime" with George Boyd and the RAF Theatre Orchestra casts Margaret Clow, daughter of Sir Andrew Clow, Governor of Assam, in several sketches.

Cpl. C. Hailes, of "It's in the Air," writes: "Four five-piece dance bands from RAF Central Band, Uxbridge, have arrived in India. Each band is touring India and S.E.A.C. as a complete stage show."

Touring Burma: ENSA artists Evelyn Kiff and Bill Harding travel light so that they can visit camps and hospitals in forward areas They aim to take light entertainment to isolated spots where it would be impossible to transport a full-sized party. Pretty, brunette Evelyn, who describes herself as "just a singer," is sufficiently versatile to do pot-pourri opera and old time ballads with musical comedy and can hold her own at the jammiest of jam sessions

RAF's Rangoon Theatre

O'Madden, who was in "Lisbon Story" at the London Hippodrome before touring the BLA,

Says
IAN BEVIN,
News Chronicle
Special Correspondent

BERLIN.

A NIGHT out in Berlin—why not? Any policeman will direct you to a cafe with girls and music. If he knows his job there will be food and wine as well.

The gayest and most elaborate all-night cafe is the Cafe Femina in Nurnberger Strasse. You drive through miles of ruins, along deserted roads, past scenes of utter desolation to the doors of the Femina, where a uniformed commissionaire greets you with elaborate politeness in perfect English.

Now the scene changes You go through glass swing doors, up stairs lined with flower boxes filled with hydrangeas into a richly carpeted foyer. Here a pretty blonde in a diaphanous black dress takes your hat and another blonde charges you 2 marks 50 pfennig (1s. 3d. sterling) for your entrance ticket.

Up more stairs, through heavy velvet curtains—and you are in a cabaret which might be in any city in the world. Well .. not "any city." Stalin's portrait hangs over the bandstand facing a table crowded with Russian officers and their very pretty partners.

HIS BARK LED JAPS TO DEATH

Bhalu is a handsome Naga dog, and a battalion mascot. Though his bark is worse than his bite, it leads to death— for the Japs.

He was presented by patriotic Nagas during last year's Kohima fighting and has played the part of a soldier throughout the Burma campaign.

Trained by his former hillsman owners to smell out Japs, he has led patrols and given warning of ambushes. Once he unearthed a party of Japs hidden in foliage with the result that 28 were killed without a single Jap shot fired.

Swallowed Snake

Bhalu saved the life of a British sergeant. A snake was about to strike the sergeant, who was asleep, when the dog jumped and swallowed it whole. The battalion M.O. worked hard for two weeks to get the dog fit again.

JAPS LINE UP FOR CORRIDOR BREAKOUT

PEGU, Mon.—There is a feeling of imminent battle along the flooded west bank of the lower Sittang river, writes Doon Campbell, API war correspondent. A staff officer said to me: "The Japanese now seem to be lined up for a big crossing of the Rangoon-Mandalay Corridor."

If the fight starts, it will be a breakthrough battle, an effort by the Japanese to join their 10,000 trapped men, cut off west of the Rangoon-Mandalay Corridor.

A British officer told me: "We know that the Japanese in the foothills of the Pegu mountain ranges must make a break or perish where they stand from disease and starvation.

Todays S.E. Asia Command communique from Kandy says aggressive patrol activity by our troops continued, particularly in the area of the Sittang River bend.

The Japanese were known to be established, with an 81-mm calibre mortar, one mile SW of Myitkyo, 29 miles NE of Pegu.

The Japs Fled

Following an artillery concentration our troops attacked, but found that the main body of enemy had withdrawn, leaving a covering screen who fled as the attack went in. Our troops followed up, but were unable to regain contact.

Five villages in the area 16 miles SE of Pegu have been reported clear of enemy.

Air: Making a round flight of about 2,500 miles, Liberators of Air Command yesterday bombed warehouses at the southern Siamese port of Singora on the South China Sea.

They also hit a 100-foot freighter towing a 60-foot barge.

Spitfires and Thunderbolts on 14 July bombed and strafed enemy troop concentrations and positions in the Sittang bend.—API.

86deg IN LONDON

LONDON, Mon.—London recorded its highest temperature of the year—86 degrees Fahrenheit—during the weekend, in the wake of a severe electrical storm.

Temperature in Calcutta yesterday afternoon: 90 deg.

WHEN ONLY 17 SECONDS SAVED ST. PAULS

LONDON, Tues.—By a few seconds and at risk of his life, Lieut (now Lt-Comdr), Ronald James Smith, RNVR, saved St Paul's Cathedral from being blown up during the London blitz, it is now disclosed.

An unexploded mine had fallen in the churchyard about three yards from the Cathedral wall.

Smith, a mine disposal expert who lives at Edgware, Middlesex, was sent to make the mine safe. He found it completely covered by its parachute, which could not be removed.

So Smith crawled on all fours inside the parachute. He started to unscrew the disc from the bomb fuse, which he had to do before he could fit a safety gag.

Just then a fire engine passed and vibration started the clockwork mechanism of the fuse. Smith knew he had only about seventeen seconds in which to insert the safety gag to stop the mine exploding.

He began a race against time and won with a second or two to spare.

For courage and devotion to duty he was awarded the George Medal in 1942.

FAIR TRIAL FOR WAR CRIMINALS

LONDON, Thurs.—Men whose deeds have caused devastation of half of Europe and whose inhumanities have made their names bywords of ill-fame will soon stand their trial in Nuremberg.

With the signature of the Four-Power Agreement setting up an international military tribunal for the trial of major war criminals, it is thought that only a short period will elapse before the first trial will begin.

The agreement makes clear that it does not prejudice the Moscow declaration of October, 1943 to the effect that Germans responsible for or consenting to take part in crimes and atrocities will be sent back to the countries in which they committed them for trial there.

The agreement is supplemented by a charter, setting out the constitution of the tribunal and the principles governing its operations.

The charter lays down elaborate rules to ensure fair trial for defendants who will have the right to conduct their own defence or be assisted by a counsel.

CONSOLATION PRIZE

LONDON, Tues.—The Japanese News Agency has reported that the Japanese War Ministry has promoted Lt.-Gen. Heitaro Kimura Commander-in-Chief

CHILDREN BACK

LONDON, Thurs.—The Health Minister has authorised the return home of 500,000 London evacuees. He sent a telegram to 1,500 local authorities, "Operate London return plans."

Mr TRUMAN PLAYS PIANO AT POTSDAM

POTSDAM, Sat.—The news black out on subjects being discussed at the Big Three talks shows no sign of being lifted. President Truman entertained his guests with a piano recital at a state banquet he gave in honour of Prime Minister Churchill and Generalissimo Stalin.

After the American pianist Sgt Eugene List had regaled the Big Three with Tschaikowsky, Chopin, Shostakovitch, and Russian and American folk music, President Truman, whose mother was a music teacher, played Beethoven's Minuet in G.

This led Marshal Stalin and President Truman to discuss animatedly the folk music of their two countries, while Mr Churchill called for "Missouri Waltz."

WEDNESDAY, 8 AUGUST, 1945

Printed by Courtesy of
THE STATESMAN in Calcutta.

ATOM BOMB HITS JAPS 20,000 TON BLOW

LONDON, Tues.—An "atomic bomb"—releasing an explosive blast equal to more than 20,000 tons of TNT or 2,000 of the RAF's 10-ton bombs—was dropped on Hiroshima, fortified port and army base on West Honshu Island—on which Tokyo stands—on Monday.

The destructive power of the Allies' most terrible secret weapon of the war was revealed in simultaneous statements from No. 10, Downing Street and from the White House, Washington. President Truman declared that "this awful bomb" is the answer to Japan's failure to heed the Potsdam demand to surrender or be destroyed.

President Truman's announcement threatening Japan with ruin from the air is being broadcast repeatedly from medium-wave transmitters in the Marianas as well as from short-wave transmitters along the U.S. Western seaboard.

Dramatised in leaflet form, details of the Atom Bomb will soon be scattered over the Japanese home islands.

Washington reports that complete plans for an all-out Atom Bomb assault against Japan are ready for immediate implementation.

Complete reconnaissance reports on the effect of the first raid are still awaited.

The bomb is the product of a £500,000,000 research and production venture inaugurated by President Roosevelt and Mr. Churchill.

More Powerful

U.S. War Secretary Henry L. Stimson predicted in Washington that it will "prove of tremendous aid" in shortening the war. He added that scientists were confident of developing even more powerful atomic bombs.

The statement issued from Downing Street by Prime Minister Attlee was prepared by Mr. Churchill before the change of the British Government.

Mr. Churchill gave details of the work on the Atomic Bomb since 1939 and said the British Government had carried on research in spite of many competing claims on scientific manpower.

A committee of leading scientists was presided over by Sir George Thomson, the Nobel Prize Winner.

Ideas were fully interchanged between scientists in the U.K. and in the U.S.

Before End of War

Such progress was made by the summer of 1941 and that Sir George Thomson's Committee reported that there was a reasonable chance that the Atomic Bomb could be produced before the end of the war.

A special Research Division was set up to direct work and Mr. W. A. Akers was released by Imperial Chemical Industries, to preside over the technical committee originally composed of Professor Sir James Chadwick and Drs. Halban, Simon and Slade.

Later it was joined by Sir Charles Darwin and Professors Cockcroft, Oliphant, and Feather.

In Oct 1941, British and American efforts were co-ordinated and a number of British scientists went to the U.S.

Great Britain was fully extended in war production within easy range of German bombers, and the risk of raiders from sea or air could not be ignored.

Good Morning...

This is it or pretty near it. This points to the end of the story. Japan is done.

After the first news of the hellish bomb that will blast every house and human in Japan, or in Japan's mainland Empire comes the Soviet declaration of war. If it is necessary to occupy the graveyard the Russian Far Eastern Army have a million troops to do it.

Will the war continue? Perhaps, and for a time. But it has ceased to be a war, and has become massacre. There may still be resolute or ignorant enemy garrisons who will fight on. But it will be as bandits, not as the organised and equipped armies of a great Power.

Japan can quit, or she can die. Eighty million people can die, as ants when petrol is poured and lighted on their anthill.

*

It won't be necessary to kill 80 millions. If it were, the power to perform the deed is in our hands.

Yesterday the man who said "we should exterminate the whole damned lot" talked like a fool: because there were not enough butchers in the world to do it, even if we called in the Germans.

Today, it can be done by a handful of pilots, flying on a milk-run routine.

*

Years ago, as a schoolboy after the last world war, this writer speculated to his old science master "Will it ever be possible for one madman, by pressing a button, to blow up the world?"

He was told severely "young man, don't mix your political speculations with your science, which isn't too sound anyway judging by your last exam result. Incidentally, your idea is nonsense".

We seem to be getting round to it however. And we had best speculate pretty rapidly about the politics of it.

*

Mr. Churchill, who was one of the architects of this terrifying weapon and who is also a humane and just man, warns of the consequences which may flow from it.

This revelation of the secrets of nature, so long mercifully withheld from man" he says "should arouse the most solemn reflection in the minds and conscience of every human being capable of comprehension".

And to jog the brain of the veriest blockhead Churchill reveals that the Germans were almost on top of the same discovery when their armies folded up.

BURMA JAPS HANG ON

HQ, SEAC, Tues.—Determined resistance was encountered by our troops operating in the flooded area between Myitkyo and the old Sittang River channel, says today's SE Asia Command communique.

In the Abya area enemy positions astride the Pegu-Martaban railway, behind our forward troops, were cleared.

An enemy attack on a village on the South bank of the Sittang channel, 20 miles East of Pegu, was repulsed.

British troops who crossed the Sittang in the Shwegyin area, 12 miles East of Nyaunglebin met opposition on the North bank of the Shwegyin chaung. On the Toungoo-Nawchi road our troops advanced to Milestone 30—1 without opposition.

Screaming Japs

Air: On 5 August Spitfires and Thunderbolts of Air Command bombed and strafed Japanese positions and machine gun posts from Pyu to Kyaikto (SE of Mokpalin), hitting an enemy HQ and destroying many jungle huts.

Reports from our ground troops confirm that Spitfires, attacking the Shwegyin chaung last Friday, killed many Japanese, says a Press note.

The enemy panicked and tried to cross the creek. They were screaming as they struggled across. On the other bank guerillas were waiting and killed 70 of the enemy.

BRITISH PLANES RAID JAPAN

LONDON, Tues.—The Japanese News Agency stated today that Mustangs attacked the South Western section of Keihin district, Honshu, for about an hour this morning, bombing towns and military installations.

"Several British planes of unspecified category joined in the raid," said the Agency.

KILLED BY FIRST ATOM BOMB

LONDON, Tues.—Tokyo Radio reported today that the Governor General of Western Japan and the Lord Mayor of Hiroshima were both killed in the Atomic bomb raid on the town last week.—Reuter.

ATTACKING JAPS SHELLED

ADV HQ, S.E.A.C., Thurs.—In the lower Sittang area, the enemy continued harassing tactics against our forward positions which were again shelled, says today's SE Asia Command communique.

East of Abya, on the Pegu-Martaban railway, 22 miles NE of Pegu, our patrols probed enemy defensive screens astride the road and railway West of the Sittang River.

Eight miles North of Nyaunglebin, a force of more than a hundred enemy was engaged by our troops who inflicted a large number of casualties. Our troops operating on the Toungoo-Mawchi road continued their advance without opposition.

Jap Planes Hit

The attack by Air Command Liberators on Benkoelen airfield on the SW coast of Sumatra on 7 August, is believed to have destroyed damaged eight or ten single-engined enemy aircraft on the ground the bombers were intercepted by two enemy fighters, one of which was probably destroyed and the other damaged.

In the harbour, the Liberators left one 180-foot coaster on fire from end to end and damaged one 120-foot coaster by strafing.

Other Liberators destroyed a bridge on the Bangkok-Singapore railway and hit the rail bridge at Peanburi several times.

50 CHIP PRIZE

The Museum Leave Centre, Calcutta, is offering a prize of Rs. 50 for the best essay (about 250 words) on "My Stay at the Museum leave Centre" to be published in the Museum's monthly bulletin.

BUFFALO BEEF IN JAP MESSES

The export of Australian buffaloes on the hoof to the Philippines may result from a recent survey in northern Australia.

It is hoped by this means to replace many of the 100,000 water buffaloes killed for food in the Philippines by the Japanese, says Globe

STILL AT WAR WITH SIAM

Siam, Japan's only satellite ally has not associated itself with Japan's reported surrender and the United Nations appear to have framed no armistice conditions yet for that country, says Reuter.

Siam contributed very little to Far Eastern fighting beyond a few clashes with Chinese units in the Shan hills in the early days of the war. The notorious PoW camps in Siam are understood to have been under complete control of Japanese military authorities.

Siam's hostilities are a highly complicated business: not long after Pearl Harbour, she declared war on Britain and the U.S. Now Britain, China, Australia, New Zealand, South Africa and France are at war with her.

JAPAN QUITS—
Mountbatten Flies Back From U.K.

WEDNESDAY, 15 AUGUST, 1945.

Printed by Courtesy of
THE STATESMAN in Calcutta.

At 18.30 yesterday, the Swiss Radio announced that Japan has accepted the terms laid down for her by the Allies last Saturday and agrees to order her armed forces to cease resistance.

This announcement came after a day of tension which began with a premature announcement by the United States' Government agency, USOWI.

Their radio monitoring service picked up a message from the Japanese which suggested that the surrender would be forthcoming.

OWI construed this as official acceptance. Then came deflation. Reuter said that nothing official had been received. For hours listeners could hear code messages flashing between Japan and Switzerland, whose Foreign Minister had been acting as intermediary.

Acceptance of last Saturday's terms means that the Mikado agrees to exercise his prerogatives only under the direction of General of the Army Douglas MacArthur, the Supreme Allied Commander in the Pacific.

At South East Asia Command HQ last evening, it was stated that Admiral Mountbatten, the Supreme Commander S.E. Asia, returned yesterday from London.

Separate Pact

A spokesman said that a separate surrender agreement would have formally to be concluded with the Japanese Commanders in this theatre.

Recently it was reported that the key enemy command in this theatre, at Singapore, is held by General Itagaki, a former War Minister in the Japanese Government, a man with a black record as a firebrand.

According to Associated Press, the first forces to occupy Japan will be Americans, but later, British, Russian and Chinese troops will take over zones, probably something on the lines followed in Germany.

The Swiss Radio announcement was worded as follows:—

"Japan has accepted the capitulation offer.

"The Japanese Information Office this morning announced on the basis of a report from the Japanese Ministry of War the acceptance of the Allied capitulation formula.

MOLOTOV BREAKS
NEWS TO JAPS
PEACE BID
By MIKADO

LONDON, Thurs.—First news of Russia's declaration of war came when Moscow radio interrupted its programme last night to make this curt announcement:—

"The Soviet Commissar for Foreign Affairs, M Molotov has seen the Japanese Ambassador Naotaoke Sato He informed him that Russia will be at war with Japan as from midnight. He added that the decision to declare war was taken at the request of Britain and the United States".

At a Press conference after he had handed Russia's "bombshell" to the Japanese Ambassador, M. Molotov stated that, in the view of the Soviet Government, its decision "is the only method capable of hastening peace to free peoples from further suffering and give the Japanese people a chance of avoiding the dangers and destruction which Germany experienced after her refusal of unconditional surrender."

The Soviet Union was acting "true to its obligations as an ally."

Turned Down Cold

M. Molotov revealed that in the middle of July, the Soviet Union was approached by the Japanese with a request that it should mediate between Japan and the Allies. The appeal was turned down cold, but other Allied leaders were fully informed at Potsdam, M. Molotov said.

According to later reports from Moscow it was the Mikado himself who made the appeal through his Ambassador in Moscow.

The full declaration, as given by the Moscow radio, reads:—

M Molotov, the Soviet Foreign Commissar, today received the Japanese Ambassador and made the following declaration: Taking into consideration Japan's refusal to capitulate, the Allies addressed to the Soviet Government an invitation to join in the war against Japanese aggression thereby shortening the duration of the war, reducing the number of victims and assisting in the speediest restoration of general peace.

Peace Nearer

"True to its duty to the Allies the Soviet Government accepted the offer of the Allies and has associated itself to the Allied declaration of 26 July this year.

"The Soviet Government considers that such a policy on its part is the only means capable of bringing peace nearer, freeing people from further sacrifices and sufferings

PARLIAMENT OPENS TODAY

LONDON, Tues.—The world tomorrow will hear from the King in Parliament the programme of the first Labour Government with a widespread Socialist policy and the power to enforce it.

The Address from the Throne, which is the constitutional means by which successive British Governments announce the details of their policy, will indicate what the Labour Government hopes to accomplish in the first session and will give a broad outline of its plan for Parliament's expected five-year span of life.

Housing Priority

Measures to relieve the acute housing shortage are expected to receive high priority in the speech together with proposals to nationalise the Bank of England, to establish a national investment and development board, and to Nationalise the coal mining industry.

High in the list is a measure to which all parties to the Coalition Government were equally committed—the enactment of a great scheme of social insurance for rich and poor, from the cradle to the grave.

YANKS ATOM-BOMB SECOND JAP PORT

GUAM, Thurs.—Nagasaki, big Japanese port on the southernmost Jap homeland island of Kyushu, was attacked with an atomic bomb at noon (Japanese time), today. This is the second atomic bomb, most devastating weapon of the war, to be dropped on the Japs inside four days.

A message received in New York says the bomber crew reported excellent results, according to a special communiqué issued by Gen Carl Spaatz.

Nagasaki which stands on one of the most beautiful bays in the world is an important coaling station and its exports include tea, cement, coal, rice, lacquer wares and porcelain.

By waiting until today for this second devastating atomic bomb attack, the Allies are following the declared policy of an official American announcement that the Japanese would be given time to investigate the ravaging effect of the attack on Hiroshima "before the U.S. reluctantly looses the second bomb."

Burned To Death

Two days after the first atomic bomb had been dropped—on the fortress city of Hiroshima, population 318,000—Tokyo Radio gave the world the first detailed report of its terrible effect.

LAST DAY BOMBING?

GUAM, Tues.—Japan paid a heavy price for every hour's delay in surrendering with Allied land, sea and air blows on all fronts.

Today, Superfortresses made their first raid since the Jap surrender offer on Friday.

They attacked Marifu railroad yards and ships off the Japanese coast South of Kure.

Gen. Karl Spaatz, stated in a communique that the raids were still under way.

What is believed to be the full power of the British and US carrier task forces attacked the Jap mainland yesterday.

A swarm of 1,200 to 1,500 carrier based bombers, fighters and torpedo planes took part.

A single Japanese plane scored a hit on a major US warship anchored in Buckner Bay, Okinawa.

Red Army Tear On

After Monday's fighting, Soviet troops tearing into Manchuria from three directions, are over the Khingan mountains from the North and threaten Tsitsihar (Lungkiang), one of the chief industrial cities.

Other advancing from Outer Mongolia are reported by the Jap News Agency, to be in the vicinity of Linsi, which is in the Japanese-occupied China province of Jehol.

Linsi is 250 miles NE of Peiping and this report indicates that the Red Army has cut right through Meng Chiang, the Japanese puppet state.

While one Red Army force followed up its landings of the Korean mainland by pushing down the coastal highway, two big army groups led by Marshals Malinovsky and Meretskov, began to battle for the great Manchurian plain leading to Harbin.

To the West of Harbin Malinovsky's tanks, armoured cars and cavalry hurled the Japanese back on to the plain.

Japs Surrender

Meanwhile Malinovsky's Southern wing developed a new threat to the Japanese: a drive parallel to the one coming Eastward across the Chinese Far Eastern railway.

This push threatened to break out towards Mokden and reach numerous Japanese POW camps.

A New York radio report states that Jap troops of Bougainville have surrendered.

Bougainville, the largest island in the Solomons, is about 130 miles long and 900 miles NE from the Northern tip of Australia.

The first Allied landings were made on 1 November, 1943, and fresh landings in March and June this year.—Reuter and APA.

SOLDIERS KILLED IN LEAVE TRAIN

Twenty-seven Allied soldiers, including some British, are believed to have been killed and 32 injured in a railway collision at Goch, near Cleve, Germany, says Reuter.

A train travelling from Brussels to Munster collided head on with a short-leave train.

The injured included British, Belgians and Poles. An officer said most of the casualties were British.

(Continued on Back Page, Col. 1.)

THE BEACHCOMBER

INCORPORATING SALERNO TIMES

NEWSPAPER OF 35 BRICK		C/O 35 BRICK SALERNO

2164   August 12th 1944

To:-
The Librarian,
 Imperial War Museum,
  LONDON.

Dear Sir,

I have today learnt that you are making a collection of army newspapers for the Imperial War Museum. In view of this I am inclosing some copies of THE BEACHCOMBER, a Unit Newspaper which I founded and edited for some time.

Copy Number 1 of our first edition was dated September 12th. It was produced on the Salerno beaches, three days after landing. It was hammered out on a typewriter in a very damp orange grove close to the shore. We ran off a maximum of twenty copies daily, contain primarily the news of the local fighting which naturally concerned us very closely during those first few days.

On the 24th of September we had more breathing space and produced a second edition of THE BEACHCOMBER printed on both sides of a sheet. A copy of No 9 is attached. The Staff during this time consisted of Cpl F.D.SHAW of the D.L.I. and myself. There were many handicaps as can be realised; mud, no cover from rain, machine gunning and continuous shelling of the beaches which made excellent targets during the first fortnight.

The Beach Brick moved into Salerno Town in the second week of October. With the capture of Naples there was much less work to be done so on October 11th I took over an Italian Printing Works and Editorial Offices. Here, with the help of Cpl Shaw, I started the final and third edition of the paper Working under our direction were a staff of fifteen Italians. The biggest handicap here was that neither Shaw nor myself could speak Italian with the result that the proofs often came up six or more times. With a small wireless set for the monitored news, and blocks from PWD, we managed to get much needed information of world happenings to the troops in the Salerno Area.

The paper was supplemented with a daily Editorial, Articles and Italian blocks of young women and pictures of local interest found in dusty corners of the building. Every so often, when time was freeze on our hands, we produced a four-page edition. Also, as the Italian population were starved of news, an Italian column was inserted every Wednesday and Saturday.

Eventually twenty-nine issues were produced before the official Army Newspaper, THE UNION JACK, arrived in Italy and started to print in Naples.

Our largest daily sale was just over seven thousand copies. We charged 1 Lira per copy and after paying all expenses managed to give £40 Stirling to the 96 Area Welfare Fund.

I was posted away from the Beach Brick before the last issue and left the editing to Col RALSTON, the OC, and to Cpl Shaw. I corresponded with Cpl Shaw regularly.

For sentimentalities sake I am writing to you on a sheet of our old notepaper. For interest, neither Shaw nor myself have ever had any experience in editing a paper before. Shaw was a reporter on one of the provincial papers before the war and I was in the Tobacco Trade in Africa.

I am,
    Yours faithfully,

(D.G.JEFFREYS)
    Capt.

516·87

K58106

207831 Lieut.J.Batson,
13(EA)Field Information Platoon,
CEYLON COMMAND.
29 Dec 43.

The Director,
Imperial War Museum,
LONDON.

2085

Dear Sir:

I have been told by a former editor of the "Morning Pioneer", a newspaper produced for British troops in Madagascar, that you have asked for copies of field newspapers to be despatched to you for your museum records. Here are the first issues of "Rhino", produced for the East African troops in Ceylon.

The poor quality of production is accounted for partly by the fact that these issues were produced under field conditions of the most exacting kind——the editorial "office" roof was a truck tarpaulin and the table was a crate——and also the fact that the heat was so intense that even duplicating ink specially manufactured for the Tropics melted to the consistency almost of water. Ants did their best to ruin the paper stocks.

The actual printing was done by native Africans, who quickly became expert with a hand duplicating outfit. Distribution was by despatch riders.

Material was provided by B.B.C.News Bulletins taken down in the not-very-expert shorthand of the editor, a former "Daily Mail"(London) reporter. Biggest trouble in this respect was the spelling of Russian place-names. When the first wax stencil had been cut, a carbon copy of the news in English was given to an African, who translated it into Swahili and typed a column——"Habari Ya Swahili" means "The News in Swahili"—— for the benefit of the African askaris. The Africans followed General Montgomery's battles with the keenest interest. It is also interesting to note that when they wish to describe anything or anyone as "cheap","shoddy" or "not worthwhile", they say "japoni"(Japanese).

An editorial crisis occurred one morning when the editor, up very early to listen-in to London, discovered that a stencil page of "Rhino" which he had"put to Bed" the previous night,had been eaten by jackals. His remarks led one to believe that all these animals were vermin-ridden and none of their mothers had been virtuous.

It is planned that "Rhino" will function as a "national newspaper", a weekly or a magazine as the occasion demands. Copies herewith feature "Rhino" in its "national newspaper" guise because the troops were far away from the lay Press and radios were few.

If you wish to have more details, they will be sent to you, Security Regulations permitting.

J. Batson
Lieut.

899710 S/Sgt S.H.HOLMES
HQ RA 1 Brit Armd Div
C.M.F.

23 Jul 44

The Collector,
The British War Imperial Museum,
LONDON.

Dear Sir,

In answer to a recent request which appeared in the Union Jack, we are sending you herewith the first two editions of our weekly unit magazine, The DART. Also enclosed, by way of interest, is an appreciation of it which the Union Jack made in their edition of July 14th.

The history of the magazine might bear recording.

The idea of producing it was originally thought of by No.907440 Bombardier William Lyall and No.3191021 Gunner John Currie, owing to the fact that they considered there was not enough reading matter available for the troops - the Union Jack being issued on a restricted scale of one copy per about 20 men, and they always seemed to be about the twenty-first and twenty-second!

They asked me about it, and if I would help them. After much discussion it was decided that the three of us would carry through the project, and so The DART came to be.

Only our spare time is devoted to it, usually after nine o'clock at night, as we have our normal routine work to contend with. The 'press room' is the back of our 3-ton lorry, where the typing, printing and binding is carried out.

We are not certain whether you are only concerned with making a collection of just one issue of each unit newspaper produced, or a series of each. If the latter is the case, we shall be very glad to oblige, and a few words from you will do 'the trick'.

Yours faithfully,

Sidney Holmes..

Subject:- REME Bullutin.   43ME/676
                                                  3 Nov '44.

Secretary,   1693
Imperial War Museum,
Whitehall,
LONDON.S.W.1.
----

1.   Herewith enclosed are two copies of a REME
Bulletin which has been produced since we landed on D +
16, by two men in my 129 Inf Bde Wksp:

                Craftsmen B.Webster.
                Craftsman C.D.Bates.

        in their spare time.

2.   These two numbers are of special interest since
during operations this wksp was billetted and worked in the
Technical School of the Sacred Heart, TESSENDERLOO, BELGIUM.

3.   The Monks who run the school, offered to print
a copy of the daily bulletin, this was done and completed
in 6 hours on Tuesday 6 Sep 44.   During one of the
 craftsman's recent rest periods he visited the Monks, and
the second issue was the result.

4.   I thought that the two Bulletins might in years
to come be of historical interest, firstly being typical
of news sheets produced by units in the B.L.A. and secondly
on account of the somewhat unusual manner in which these two
numbers were produced.

                                                  Lt-Col.
B.L.A.   C.R.E.M.E.43rd Division.

        Copy to:- 129 Inf Bde Wksp.

RESTRICTED
INSTRUCTIONS TO EDITORS OF ARMY NEWSPAPERS AND FORMATION BROADSHEETS
PURPOSE OF ARMY NEWSPAPERS AND NEWS BROADSHEETS

1. The purpose of Army Newspapers and News Broadsheets is to give to all ranks accurate and speedy news of world and home events.

EDITORIAL POLICY

2. Army Newspapers and News Broadsheets are official publications. While allowing for various difficulties which will frequently limit facilities for checking the reliability of the news available for publication, Editors must regard accuracy as the chief objective.

It follows that on all controversial issues every effort must be made to present fairly and fully both sides of the question and to leave judgment to the decision of the reader rather than to try to lead opinion by a partial presentation of the facts. In particular, Editors must not express a view of their own which is contrary to Government policy. The following rules are presented for the guidance of Editors.

GENERAL RULES

3. (a) On controversial matters the object of an Editor will be to improve knowledge rather than to form opinion.

   (b) Any Editorial opinion contained in Army Newspapers or Formation Broadsheets will be confined to the Editorial Column. The Editorials will reflect the policies of the Commander and will be directed to the interest, understanding and morale of the troops. News articles, headlines or picture captions will not contain expressions of opinion.

   (c) Army Newspapers and Formations Broadsheets will not contain political editorials nor will they include comment, criticism, analysis or interpretation of news of a political nature.

   (d) Editors must not criticise Government policy, seeing that it is the policy of the authority invested by the nation with the control of its affairs. An Army Newspaper or Formation Broadsheet is the organ of a disciplined body of men. It is given exceptional facilities to speak to large numbers of them and it is contrary not only to sound discipline but also to every principle of reason and commonsense that it should contribute to shake confidence in His Majesty's Government or in any other authority whose decisions it is the duty of the Armed Forces to implement.

ARTICLES DEALING WITH MILITARY MATTERS

4. When preparing articles on military matters, Editors will ensure that:-

   (a) There will be no criticism expressed or implied of the War Office, Command, Staff or any particular Unit, Service or official organisation e.g., NAAFI.

   (b) Before publication, the article will be referred to the Staff of the Command in which the paper is published, in order to ensure its accuracy and suitability from a security point of view.

   (c) The article will not make recommendations for improving military organisations, training etc. Any such proposals will be submitted officially through the usual channels to the Headquarters concerned and only on the authority of that Headquarters may a statement be made that "the following proposal is under consideration."

   (d) Comments on such matters as morale, training organisation and equipment should be restrained and in general terms only.

   (e) Reproduction from classified Service publications, such as the Army List (restricted) is not permitted.

5. Much information, especially information pertaining to Orders of Battle may be disclosed to an enemy by:-

   (a) Extra Regimental Employment List showing locations of Officers in Formations the existence or locations of which which may not have been made public. The following rules govern the publication of these items. To assist Editors, examples of the correct and incorrect methods are given.

   (i) Any Unit location should be limited to the Command in which it is situated, unless such information has already been released for publication by the daily Press.

   Examples:-

INCORRECT	CORRECT
15 Bde. Workshops, R.E.M.E. HANOVER	15 Bde. Workshops, R.E.M.E
	or
R.E.M.E.	B.A.O.P.
1 BLANKSHIRES TRIPOLI	1 BLANKSHIRES M.E.L.F.

   (ii) No indication should be given of the location (even by Commands) of formation Headquarters.

   Examples:-

INCORRECT	CORRECT
Brigade Major, H.Q. 55 Inf. Bde. FARELF	Brigade Major, Inf. Bde. FARELF
	or
	Brigade Major, 55 Inf. Bde.
O.C., 66 Inf. Bde. Workshops MELF	O.C. 66 Inf. Bde. Workshops
	or
	O.C., Inf. Bde. Workshops MELF

INCORRECT	CORRECT
G.S.O.2., R.A. 17 Inf. Div., HONG KONG	G.S.O.2. R.A., H.Q. 17 Inf. Div.,
	or
	G.S.O.2., R.A. HONG KONG

   (iii) No indication should be given of the formation to which a unit belongs.

   Example

   1 WESSEX Regt. 90 Inf. Bde. M.E.L.F. is WRONG

   The correct notification is 1 WESSEX Regt. M.E.L.F.

   (b) Sports news giving details of formations involved. Examples giving the correct and incorrect ways of publishing this news are given below.

   NOT PERMISSIBLE

   "At the 17th Armoured Division sports meeting held last week at BREMEN we narrowly missed winning the trophy when we were just beaten by 54 Armoured Brigade Workshops with the 2nd Loamshires a close third.

   Our team put up a grand fight in the relay race but were beaten on the post by 100 Infantry Brigade Signals Regiment who displayed the same form with which they won the same event in their recent Brigade championships from the 2nd Wessex Regiment and the 1st Mercian Regiment".

   ACCEPTABLE FORM

   "At the sports meeting held last week in this part of the world we narrowly missed winning the trophy when we were just beaten by Brigade Workshops with the 2nd Loamshires a close third.

Our team put up a grand fight in the relay race but were beaten on the post by the Brigade Signals Regiment who displayed the same form with which they won the same event in their recent Brigade championships from the Infantry Battalions".

CORRESPONDENCE COLUMNS

6.   Correspondence columns offer an opportunity for the expression of critical views, but they present considerable problems to the Editor. Care should be taken in the selection of letters to ensure the presentation of both sides of a question. Those letters published should have a case to argue, and should argue it reasonably, however little it may be in argreement with the policy of the Newspapers.

7.   Avoid allowing correspondence columns to degenerate into a collection of grievances. Letters should not be published in which statements are made which are known to be contrary to fact. As much care should be taken to verify statements in letters as will be taken for a similar statement in an article. Use can be made of Editorial information to correct mis-statements or bias.

8.   Care should be taken that Security is not prejudiced by such correspondence and in cases of doubt reference should be made to Headquarters concerned.

QUESTIONS OF TASTE

9.   While editors will wish to avoid a "highbrow" treatment of subjects which would repel the readers for whom Army Newspapers and News Broadsheets are intended, they must avoid anything likely to provoke reasonable criticism from the troops on the grounds that it offends against the canons of taste or religious tolerence. Editors must remember that any statement or feature published in an Army Newspaper or Formation Broadsheet may be called in question in Parliament.

LIBEL AND COPYWRIGHT

10.   Editors of Army Publications have no inherent immunity against action under the Libel and Copyright Laws and must realise that they are responsible legally for everything they publish.

GOVERNMENT STATEMENTS AND PARLIAMENTARY DEBATES

11.   Frequently questions of general interest to Service personnel arise from Parliamentary Debates and Government pronouncements and it is highly desirable that this information should be given to the troops without delay.

  (a)   In the case of important Government pronouncements affecting the Armed Forces, the War Office (British Army News Service) will issue a statement by the fastest means available with instructions that it is to be printed verbatim. Such messages will also be addressed to the Headquarters concerned.

  (b) In the case of less important pronouncements and Parliamentary Debates the War Office (British Army News Service) will issue a summary by the fastest means available which can be published or used as a background for explanatory articles.

ADVERTISING

12.   No commercial advertising will be allowed in Formation Broadsheets.

INFORMATION TO BE SHOWN ON THE HEADING

13.   Each Army Newspaper and Formation Broadsheet will include the following information in a heading:-

  (a)   Name of the Newspaper or Broadsheet;
  (b)   The day, month and year of publication;
  (c)   The volume and number of the publication.

INFORMATION TO BE SHOWN AT THE BOTTOM OF THE BACK PAGE

14.   (a)   Published by;   for Commander   Command.
  (b)   The Post Office address or A.P.O.

EDITORIAL RESPONSIBILITIES

15.   Although in practice, due to the time factor and to the technical nature of Editorial work, it will be necessary to delegate considerable responsibilities to Editors, the responsibility for the publication of, or emphasis given to, any particular item rests with the G.O.C.-in-C. of the Command in which the Newspaper is published. An exception to this rule will be important Government pronouncements sent by the War Office for printing verbatim.

DISTRIBUTION

16.   Two copies of each issue of any Army Newspaper or Formation Broadsheet will be sent on publication date to the War Office (AE4).

Printed in the United Kingdom for
Her Majesty's Stationery Office
Dd 290155 C 100 9/89